Descartes and Augustine

This book is the first systematic study of Descartes' relation to Augustine. It offers a complete re-evaluation of Descartes' philosophy, and of the philosophical ideas in Augustine that were Descartes' starting point. *Descartes and Augustine* will engage the attention of historians of medieval, neo-Platonic, and early modern philosophy.

That Descartes was indebted to Augustine is not in itself a fresh discovery. What distinguishes Stephen Menn's book is his detailed demonstration that the key to the *Meditations* is Descartes' use of Augustine's method for establishing a knowledge of God and the soul independent of any theory of the physical world. This method gives Descartes an independent starting point for reconstructing the system of the sciences. Where the scholastics had tried to show that Augustine's metaphysics of God and the soul is compatible with an Aristotelian physics of matter and form, Descartes argues that they are *not* compatible, and that Augustinian metaphysics provides the foundation for an anti-Aristotelian mechanistic physics. Menn gives a detailed analysis of the *Meditations*, showing how the novel form of Descartes' argument arises from the challenge of presenting Augustine's metaphysics in a way that makes it suitable for its new foundational task.

Descartes and Augustine includes a complete reading of the *Meditations*, a historical and philosophical introduction to Augustine's thought and to Plotinian neo-Platonism, and a discussion of the contemporary context of Descartes' earlier and later philosophical projects.

Descartes
and Augustine

STEPHEN MENN

McGill University

PUBLISHED BY THE PRESS SYNDICATE OF THE UNIVERSITY OF CAMBRIDGE
The Pitt Building, Trumpington Street, Cambridge CB2 1RP, United Kingdom

CAMBRIDGE UNIVERSITY PRESS
The Edinburgh Building, Cambridge CB2 2RU, United Kingdom
40 West 20th Street, New York, NY 10011-4211, USA
10 Stamford Road, Oakleigh, Melbourne 3166, Australia

© Cambridge University Press 1998

First published 1998

Printed in the United States of America

Typeset in Imprint

Library of Congress Cataloging-in-Publication Data
Menn, Stephen Philip, 1964–
Descartes and Augustine / Stephen Menn.
p. cm.
Revised version of the author's thesis (Ph.D.) – University
of Chicago, 1989.
Includes bibliographical references and index.
ISBN 0-521-41702-3 (hard)
1. Descartes, René, 1596–1650. 2. Augustine, Saint, Bishop of
Hippo – Influence. 3. Descartes, René, 1596–1650. Meditationes de
prima philosophia. I. Title.
B1875.M38 1997
194 – dc21   97-7878
                                                            CIP

*A catalog record for this book is available from
the British Library.*

ISBN 0 521 41702 3 hardback

For Alison

Contents

CONTENTS

Preface

The question of Descartes and Augustine is an old one, but it has never been answered satisfactorily, and it seems not to have been studied seriously for more than half a century. My work picks up from studies of Gilson and Gouhier dating mostly from the 1920s; and while I disagree with many of their conclusions, I do so with deep respect for their pioneering work, and I will be happy if this book has the effect of directing scholars' attention back to a line of inquiry that was too soon abandoned.

It may help to explain two things that this book is not. First, although I have already seen my title misstated in print as "Descartes and Augustinianism," the book is not a study of Descartes and seventeenth-century Augustinians, or an attempt to relate Descartes to the Augustinian tradition. I am not sure there was an Augustinian tradition: this phrase suggests a series of thinkers reading Augustine through their predecessors, and distinguished by some common doctrine from thinkers outside the school. There was, in that sense, an Aristotelian tradition. But the history of Augustinianism is the history of the many revivals of Augustine by different thinkers, who have each discovered some new aspect of Augustine's thought, and seen in it a way to answer the philosophical or theological challenges of their own times. In Descartes' time there were many such Augustinianisms, and there was a hope of constructing out of Augustine a new philosophy to replace that of Aristotle. I propose to read Descartes as trying to fulfill that hope.

To understand how Descartes did this, it is more crucial to understand Augustine than to understand (say) Bérulle or Jansen. Now, while we know that Descartes read Augustine, we do not know that his reading was extensive or deep, or that it was early enough to explain the Augustinian features of his philosophy, which go back to 1628–30. I, like most other scholars, think it was; but my project does not depend on that assumption. My first aim has been to understand what attracted Descartes in Augustinianism, that is, to understand what Descartes had been trying to do in his philosophical work, and then how Augustinianism helped him do it. To understand this, we have to understand Augustinianism, and so we have to understand Augustine: it would be impossible to understand Bérulle or Jansen without understanding Augustine first, and understanding Augustine is already a major task. And what Descartes found in Augustine is different from what Bérulle or Jansen found there. So my approach has been, after sketching Descartes' philosophical goals and the expectations

ix

of his contemporaries (including Bérulle and Arnauld), to study first Augustine's thought, and then the use Descartes made of that thought. Had I chosen to write a longer book, I would not have looked harder for "intermediaries" between Augustine and Descartes, since my judgment is that he simply read Augustine; but I would have gone deeper than I did into the philosophical expectations of Descartes' contemporaries, and especially of his Oratorian friends, which must have influenced *how* he read Augustine. I would be delighted to see this research carried forward.

On the other hand, this book is also not a *comparison* between Descartes and Augustine, let us say on the *cogito*, or on the nature of the mind, or on the relation between faith and reason. I think the idea of such a comparison is unhistorical. As I wrote in an early section of this book (written before 1989!), a seventeenth-century French thinker could not simply *resemble* Augustine, any more than a twentieth-century Russian thinker could *resemble* Marx. Augustine was part of the background against which Descartes and his contemporaries defined themselves (even those who chose to disagree with him, or to ignore him, or pretended insincerely to be following him). So the task is to understand how Descartes *used* Augustine's thought in his own philosophical project. And this is best done, not by looking at Descartes and Augustine on particular issues, but by looking at Augustine's project as a whole, and at Descartes' project as a whole. For the core of what Descartes took from Augustine was not any particular doctrine, but a hope and a discipline of drawing the mind away from the senses, through a special kind of contemplation of itself, to a special kind of contemplation of God. I will try to explain this in the following chapters.

My aim has been, not simply to settle a historical question of influence, but to use Augustine as a key to understanding Descartes, and especially the rich and puzzling text of the *Meditations*. I had read the *Confessions* and the *De Libero Arbitrio* before reading the *Meditations*: and, after all, so did Arnauld and Malebranche, and (I think) Descartes. So it has been natural for me to take from Augustine a set of questions to ask of the *Meditations*, to the reverse of the many scholars who have begun with Descartes and have looked back to Augustine for "anticipations." Readers who are used to this approach will need some patience, since I am asking them to spend a long time with Augustine (and some time with Plotinus, and some time with Cicero) before I try to give an account of the *Meditations*. If I am right, it will be worth it.

This book began, as a term paper, in the spring of 1984, in an attempt to convince Dan Garber of something that seemed obvious to me but not to him, that Descartes was in some sense an Augustinian. I had no idea how complex the question of Descartes' relation to Augustine would turn out to be. The work has assumed other forms since: it became a Ph.D. dissertation, it generated a number of articles, and, as a book, it has been for some years an object of rumor, expectation, and doubt. (But I console myself with the fact that Descartes himself did not publish until he was forty.) The work has profited, in all its forms, from the comments of my teachers, colleagues, and students. I would like to thank especially, for their comments at different stages, Heather Blair, Eyjólfur Emilsson, Dan Garber, Rachana Kamtekar, Alison Laywine, Ian Mueller, Calvin Normore, Eileen O'Neill, and Howard Stein, as well as Terry Moore and Jane van Tassel at Cambridge University Press and two anonymous referees.

While most of this book bears no close relation to anything I have published elsewhere, there are several individual sections whose material overlaps, in different ways, with articles I have published. The closest relation is between Chapter 7 of this book and my "Descartes, Augustine, and the Status of Faith" (in *Studies in Seventeenth-Century European Philosophy*, ed. M. A. Stewart, Oxford: Oxford University Press, forthcoming): that article is essentially an abridgment of Chapter 7, and the somewhat fuller version I give here supersedes what I said there. There is also a close relation between Chapter 8, Section D, and my "Descartes and Some Predecessors on the Divine Conservation of Motion" (*Synthese*, 83, May 1990): in this case the article is not superseded, since it goes further into some issues, from a history-of-science perspective, than the corresponding section of the book. There is a much looser relationship between some material in Chapter 8, Sections B and C, and my "The Greatest Stumbling Block: Descartes' Denial of Real Qualities" (in *Descartes and His Contemporaries: Meditations, Objections and Replies*, ed. Roger Ariew and Marjorie Grene, Chicago: University of Chicago Press, 1995), which treats some of the same questions from a rather different perspective: readers interested in the details of Descartes' confrontation with the scholastics, on the problem of sensible qualities and more generally on the ontological composition of bodies, should look at that article as well as at what I say here. Chapter 2, Section A, represents a drastically abridged version of what I did in "The Intellectual Setting of Seventeenth Century Philosophy" (in *The Cambridge History of Seventeenth Century Philosophy*, Cambridge: Cambridge University Press, forthcoming): readers interested in the broader contemporary context of Descartes' work may wish to look there. Finally, my "The Problem of the Third Meditation" (*American Catholic Philosophical Quarterly*, vol. 67, Autumn 1993) is a popular introduction to some broad themes of the book, with some overlap with Chapter 5.

My language has sometimes been a compromise between English and the language of my authors. I have used the generic "he" more than I would like to, and certainly I have spoken of the collective singular "man" more often than I find natural. More substantially, I have had to borrow several terms from Greek or Latin. Let me here flag some of this terminology, which might risk confusing the reader.

The most important technical term is "Nous," which I write as an English proper noun (i.e. in normal roman type, and with a capital N).

This is intended to represent the Greek word *"nous,"* as used by philosophers including Plato, Aristotle, and Plotinus, but only in *one* of the senses of that equivocal Greek term, a sense which I discuss in Chapter 3, Section B, and which, according to Plotinus, is the strict sense of the term. "Reason," with a capital R, is a first approximation. The conventional English translation, "intellect," is misleading, because "intellect" suggests a rational soul (or rational part or faculty of a soul), whereas Nous is supposed to be something existing independently of souls, such that souls have rational perceptions by participating in it or being acted on by it. Those Christian writers (including Augustine) who take up the Platonist concept of Nous usually identify it with God; whereas, for most pagan Platonists, it is only one of several divine principles, and even for Christians, it is not simply synonymous with "God," but picks out one particular way of conceiving God. Augustine's usual equivalent for *"nous"* in this sense is *"veritas"* (naturally rendered as "Truth" with a capital T), though sometimes he uses *"sapientia"* (Wisdom) or other terms. Some of the ideas I discuss under the head of "the concept of God as Nous" (in the Platonists, in Augustine, and in Descartes) are discussed by Gilson under the head of "the illumination theory of knowledge": but I am chiefly interested in these ideas, not as a way of understanding human knowledge, but as a way of understanding God.

I have also borrowed the Latin noun *cognitio* (plural *cognitiones*), which I italicize as still a foreign word. This does not mean anything special: it is simply the most general Latin word for "knowledge," including conceptions or apprehensions of all kinds, whether clear or obscure, whether of an object or of a proposition (*scientia* is knowledge in a stricter sense, either of an object or of a proposition, but scientifically certain). As long as this is understood, "knowledge" would be a perfectly good English equivalent for *"cognitio,"* except that "knowledge" is not a count noun, and I often need to speak of one *cognitio*, two *cognitiones*. So, while I will sometimes render the Latin *"cognitio"* as "knowledge," I will sometimes leave it as *"cognitio"*; I will also sometimes render the French *"connaissance"* as *"cognitio,"* and I will use *"cognitio"* freely in English paraphrases of Descartes' thought.

I have tried to distinguish between "Platonic" and "Platonist." The Platonists are members of the Platonic school, the school that tried to extract a systematic philosophy from Plato's dialogues, which flourished especially from the first through sixth centuries AD; their philosophy is Platonism, and Platonist doctrines are their doctrines, while a Platonic doctrine is a doctrine found in Plato's dialogues. It is customary to use "middle Platonist" for the Platonists before Plotinus, and "neo-Platonist" for the Platonists of Plotinus' time and after (most of whom were not in any strong sense followers of Plotinus); I have avoided these terms. Since writers from Augustine's time through Descartes', whether or not they read Plato directly, always interpreted him either through late ancient Platonism or through the doxographical reports in Cicero or Aristotle, I am more interested in Platonism than in Plato, though naturally any under-standing of Platonism starts with Plato. To speak of a writer's being in-fluenced by neo-Platonism (rather than by Platonism) is misleading, inasmuch as it suggests that there was a new philosophy invented by Plo-tinus (rather than an ongoing ancient attempt to make systematic and de-fensible sense of Plato), and inasmuch as it suggests that there was some other variety of Platonism available before the eighteenth century.

References

References to the works of Descartes (and to the Objections to his *Meditations*) are to *Oeuvres de Descartes*, ed. Charles Adam and Paul Tannery, nouvelle présentation (Paris: Vrin, 1974–83). This will be cited as "AT," followed by volume and page numbers, e.g. "AT VII,3." "AT IX2,20" means page 20 of Part 2 of Volume IX. Sometimes I cite only the page number if the rest of the information is obvious from the context.

Exception: the *Rules for the Direction of the Mind* will sometimes be cited by Rule number, and the *Principles of Philosophy* by Part and paragraph numbers, in the forms "Rule 6," "*Principles* II:8" (with a colon rather than a comma, to avoid confusion with AT references).

Adrien Baillet's *Vie de Monsieur Descartes* (Paris, 1691) will be cited by volume and page numbers, in the form "Baillet I,324."

References to the works of Augustine are to the classic edition of the Benedictines of St. Maur, originally published in 1680 and reprinted many times since. Works will be cited by the title of the work, followed by the book, chapter, and paragraph numbers of the Benedictine edition, or however many of these exist: e.g. "*De Libero Arbitrio* II,iii,7," "*De Quantitate Animae* xiii,22." These chapter and paragraph numbers are given in most modern editions. I will cite only one passage, *De Beata Vita* 4, where there is a serious difference in meaning between the reading of the Benedictine edition and modern scholarly opinion, and in this case the problem of the proper reading will be discussed in the text. I accept a minority view on the correct reading of *De Libero Arbitrio* II,xi,32; again, references will be given in the text, though no great issue hangs on this. I often abbreviate the title "*De Libero Arbitrio*" as "DLA." The best modern editions of Augustine are generally those of the *Corpus Scriptorum Ecclesiasticorum Latinorum* and the *Corpus Christianorum* where available. I have used W. M. Green's *Corpus Christianorum* edition of the *De Libero Arbitrio* (*Corpus Christianorum, Series Latina*, vol. 29, Turnholt: Brepols, 1970), and Martin Skutella's Teubner edition of the *Confessions* (revised by H. Juergens and W. Schaub, Stuttgart: Teubner, 1981).

Plotinus will be cited from A. H. Armstrong's Loeb edition (essentially reproducing the text of Henry and Schwyzer), by Ennead and treatise number, chapter number, and line number; sometimes I also give the title of the treatise: thus "Plotinus *On Nous, Ideas, and Being* (V,9,3,14–15)."

Owing to a complex transmission history, there is a special situation in the treatise IV,7, *On Immortality of Soul*: between Chapters 8 and 9 are five chapters numbered 8.1 through 8.5, and there may thus be citations of the form "IV,7,8.3,10."

Porphyry's *Life of Plotinus*, printed with editions of Plotinus, will be cited as "VP" (= *Vita Plotini*), followed by the chapter number.

Plato, Aristotle, and Plutarch will be cited by the numbers and letters of their classic pagination, reprinted in modern editions of their works; when necessary, the line number will also be given. Alternatively, I will cite the works of Aristotle, by title, book number, and chapter number, in the form "*De Anima* III,5." Cicero, Sextus Empiricus, and Diogenes Laertius (abbreviated "DL") are cited in the same form as Augustine. The fragments of the Stoics are cited from the edition of Hans von Arnim, *Stoicorum Veterum Fragmenta* (Leipzig: Teubner, 1903–5); this will be cited as "SVF," followed by volume and fragment number. The works of Thomas Aquinas and other scholastic authors will be cited by the traditional divisions (book and chapter, question and article, etc., as appropriate).

Translations are mine unless otherwise noted. For the authors who are most closely discussed, Descartes, Augustine, and Plotinus, I have preferred to translate very literally, and to clarify any resulting difficulties through my explication of the text. It is thus rare that I reproduce the text of any existing translation: but I have looked at translations, and I have not tried to avoid being influenced by them. I would therefore like to extend general credits to the following translations:

A. H. Armstrong, Plotinus (Cambridge, MA, and London: Loeb Classical Library, 1967–88)

Anna S. Benjamin and L. H. Hackstaff, Saint Augustine, *On Free Choice of the Will* (Indianapolis: Bobbs-Merrill, 1964)

John Cottingham, Robert Stoothoff, Dugald Murdoch, and Anthony Kenny, *The Philosophical Writings of Descartes*, 3 vols. (Cambridge: Cambridge University Press, 1984–91)

Donald Cress, Descartes, *Discourse on Method and Meditations on First Philosophy* (Indianapolis: Hackett, 1980; the third edition, 1993, incorporates some of my suggestions)

Valentine Rodger Miller and Reese P. Miller, Descartes, *Principles of Philosophy* (Dordrecht: Reidel, 1983)

Introduction

I

Descartes and the history of philosophy

Descartes stands at a turning-point in the history of philosophy. The old philosophy of Aristotle had lost its credibility, and the new philosophies of the Renaissance, planned to replace it, turned out to be dead ends. It was Descartes, with such contemporaries as Hobbes and Gassendi, who staked out the road leading, past many further twists and forks, to the philosophy and science of today.

In these circumstances it is natural for modern philosophers to turn back to look at Descartes. Much good interpretive work has been done, and often it has been concerned to compare Descartes' philosophy with the philosophies of his contemporaries and predecessors. Especially in France, which has devoted itself most intensely to the study of its national hero, scholars have investigated the continuity or discontinuity of Descartes' thought with earlier philosophy, particularly in the scholastic and Augustinian traditions. By setting Descartes' thought in relation to these earlier traditions, these scholars have tried to clarify the origin and nature of modern philosophy as such, and of its complicated relations to science and to religion. Both because of his historical importance and because of his intrinsic merit, Descartes is an ideal case study for anyone who wishes to assess the extent of constancy and change, of harmony and disharmony in the history of philosophy; for anyone who wishes to see how far an old philosophy can survive and how much it can contribute in a new scientific or religious setting; and for anyone who wishes to draw a moral for the present and future of traditional philosophy. In this study I will attempt to interpret Descartes' philosophy by understanding its relations to Augustine and the Augustinian tradition. I will try to show what Descartes' goals were and what expectations he was trying to meet in constructing his new philosophy; what intellectual materials the Augustinian tradition provided him for achieving these goals; how Descartes was able to make these old concepts and doctrines useful for his new purposes; and to what extent he preserved them or transformed them in the process.

If we exclude the mathematical disciplines and look strictly at philosophy, then the most important influences on Descartes' thought were Augustinianism and Aristotelian scholasticism. Although the history of Augustinianism and the history of scholasticism interconnect and overlap, Descartes' relation to Augustinianism is very different from his relation to scholasticism, and we can study one without studying the other.

Descartes' attitude toward scholasticism is clearly hostile. Especially in

3

its physics, his philosophy runs directly counter to the philosophy of Aristotle, which he hopes to replace in the schools. Certainly, in trying to elaborate a complete philosophy, he borrows many technical details from his scholastic opponents, and a comparative study of Descartes and late scholasticism can throw interesting sidelights on his philosophy. But there is no continuity between the fundamental projects of scholastic and Cartesian philosophy.

It seems much more promising to try to interpret Descartes through his relations with the Augustinian tradition. Augustine was an important authority for the scholastics, more or less harmonized with Aristotle by different thinkers; the Augustinianisms of Bonaventure or of Bradwardine are attempts within scholasticism to remain as faithful as possible to the model of Augustine's thought as these thinkers understand it. But Augustinianism is also much wider than scholasticism; and especially in the sixteenth and seventeenth centuries Augustine was the chief human authority and model for many thinkers throughout Latin Christendom who were indifferent or hostile to the thought of Aristotle. Was Descartes one of these thinkers?

On the face of it, Descartes' philosophy bears many resemblances to the thought of Augustine. Indeed, we know of several people who within Descartes' lifetime were sufficiently struck by these resemblances to call them to Descartes' attention.[1] Prominent among these was Antoine Arnauld, the intellectual leader of the Jansenist movement: throughout his long life (1612–94) an upholder of the doctrine of Augustine on all questions, he was also, from his first reception of the manuscript of the *Meditations* in 1640, to be strongly attracted to the philosophy of Descartes because of the connections he saw between this and Augustine. In the *Fourth Set of Objections* which Arnauld sent to Descartes, he finds the relation to Augustine to be the most remarkable thing about the *Meditations*:

Here it first occurs [to me] to marvel [*mirari*], that the most eminent man [Descartes] has established as the first principle of his philosophy the same thing that was established by the divine Augustine, a man of the most acute intellect and entirely admirable [*mirandus*], not only in theological but also in philosophical matters. For in the second book of his *De Libero Arbitrio*, chapter 3, Alipius says, in arguing with Evodius and preparing to prove that God exists, "First, in order that we may begin with the things which are most manifest, I ask you whether you yourself exist. Are you afraid that you will be deceived in this questioning, seeing that you certainly cannot be deceived if you do not exist?" Like these are the words of our author [Descartes]: "But there is I know not what deceiver, supremely powerful and clever, who always intentionally deceives me; doubtless then I too exist, if he deceives me." (AT VII,197–8)[2]

---

[1] For a full list of references, see below, Chapter 2, Section D; and Henri Gouhier, *Cartésianisme et augustinisme au XVIIe siècle* (Paris: Vrin, 1978).

[2] Arnauld's reference is to Augustine *De Libero Arbitrio* II,iii,7, and the textual citation is correct; the speaker, however, is not Augustine's friend Alypius, but Augustine himself.

Descartes in his reply (AT VII,219) briefly thanks Arnauld for the citation from Augustine, and moves on to other business. But Arnauld's comment marks the beginning of a long history of philosophers upholding Cartesianism as Augustinianism "in philosophical matters." Probably the comparison most frequently drawn is the one Arnauld mentions here, on the so-called "*cogito*" argument which Descartes shares with Augustine. But this is only one of a great many points of contact, and often the "*cogito*" is cited as a kind of abbreviation for a more general sympathy of metaphysical sentiments between Descartes and Augustine. Even in the passage I have cited, Arnauld says not merely that Descartes shares a certain view or argument with Augustine, but that he anchors his whole philosophy where Augustine does, proceeding to draw the consequences of what Augustine too regarded as the starting-point of our knowledge of God and the world. And indeed the metaphysics that Descartes proceeds to construct upon this base closely resembles the metaphysics of Augustine. Speaking very generally and crudely to establish a framework for discussion, we may note a number of points of contact.

Descartes, like Augustine, believes that metaphysical knowledge, being purely intellectual, is independent of the testimony of the senses, and even somehow opposed to what the senses habitually conceive: thus it cannot be based on inferences from physics, as Aristotle and many other thinkers believe. It will be concerned primarily with God and with the human soul, and not with God and the soul as they may be inferred from sensible objects. The human soul will be known primarily as a thing that thinks: not as an act of an organic body, but as something only extrinsically related to a body. God will be known primarily as the highest object of our thought, not as the governor of the physical world, although he becomes that too when he creates the world. Beyond this, the detailed working-out of Descartes' conceptions of the soul and God, in themselves and in their relation to body, will have many points of contact with Augustine's conceptions: most obviously, both Descartes and Augustine develop strongly voluntarist accounts of both divine and human action. Thus God freely decrees the laws of nature, rather than recognizing them as intellectual necessities to which he must conform; and the human mind too, made in God's image, has a freedom that makes it superior to the law-governed natural order, even while it is limited by the constraints of its natural environment.

If we take metaphysics in the strict sense, as the science of immaterial things or of God and the soul, and distinguish it from loosely "metaphysical" doctrines belonging either to Christian faith or to natural philosophy, then the agreements I have broadly outlined will cover the entirety of Augustinian metaphysics. No one supposes that these are

---

Arnauld was probably using an edition that referred to the speaker only by the initial "A." Arnauld knew the texts of Augustine very well, but tended, as we shall see again, to cite them in a rather casual manner.

merely accidental resemblances between the doctrines of Descartes and Augustine; nor are they simply the product of two similar minds in similar situations. A seventeenth-century French thinker could not simply "resemble" Augustine, any more than a twentieth-century Russian thinker could "resemble" Marx. In Protestant Germany, Luther, for whom Augustine was the chief authority after the scriptures, might have come to eclipse his master; in Spain, to a lesser degree, St. Thomas might have done the same; but in France there was no rival to Augustine's prestige. He was an ineffaceable part of the intellectual background against which thinkers of the seventeenth century defined themselves. They might draw on him or pretend to draw on him, they might choose to ignore or even to disagree with him, but they could not "agree" with him on equal terms.

Precisely because Augustine's authority was so universal, however, it is doubtful what significance we should attribute to Descartes' Augustinianism. Descartes is certainly an Augustinian in the sense that he agrees with Augustine's central metaphysical theses; but in this sense it would have been more surprising, and more illuminating for Descartes' thought, had he turned out *not* to be an Augustinian. We must do more to clarify the phenomenon of Augustinianism in the seventeenth century before we can use it to locate Descartes. We might begin, crudely, by distinguishing between a wide, *doctrinal* Augustinianism and a narrow, *conceptual* Augustinianism. Most French thinkers in the seventeenth century would be able to assent to Augustine's doctrinal formulae; but many of these thinkers would interpret the *terms* of these formulae through conceptions drawn from Aristotelian or other non-Augustinian sources. So already, in making a *prima facie* case for Descartes' Augustinianism, I have tried to indicate not merely doctrinal but conceptual and structural parallels between Cartesian and Augustinian metaphysics. But the question can still be posed whether Descartes is drawing in an essential way on the Augustinian conceptual scheme, or whether he is using the old Augustinian vocabulary with a new dictionary of his own.

Indeed, for half a century the reigning view has been that there is a fundamental break between Descartes and the earlier Augustinian tradition, and that Augustinianism cannot yield the key for interpreting Descartes' philosophy. Such was the conclusion in the 1920s of Etienne Gilson and Henri Gouhier, and later, from a different point of view, of Martial Gueroult; and while their conclusion has been doubted, nobody has mounted a systematic effort to reassess Descartes' relation to Augustine. In attempting such a reassessment in the present study, and in using an understanding of Augustinianism to interpret Descartes' philosophy, I will to this extent be challenging the views of the scholars I have named. But there are positive lessons to be learned from their reasons for discounting the apparent connections between Descartes and Augustine. Some reflections on these scholars' work will indicate how deeply their interpretations, both of Descartes and of Augustine, have been informed by their own philosophical concerns; and while this should lead us to be

6

cautious about accepting their conclusions, it should also lead us to reflect more critically on what it might mean to say that Descartes is an Augustinian. To understand what Augustinianism was, or the variety of things it could have been, we must in the first instance know what Augustine himself thought, but we must also understand the range of stances that seventeenth-century thinkers could take up in relation to Augustine; and we must reflect critically on what we mean in speaking of an Augustinian "influence" on Descartes, who claims to construct a new philosophy using only his own reason, without any appeal to authority.

At the beginning of the twentieth century a number of scholars were drawing connections between Descartes and Augustine or Augustinianism. Even Gilson, in his doctoral dissertation *La liberté chez Descartes et la théologie* (published 1913), had allowed himself to say that the spirit of Descartes' metaphysics was that "of a neo-Platonic theology, itself renewed by the Fathers and above all by St. Augustine."[3] But Gilson was later to lead a massive reaction against this view, a reaction whose first published statement was the doctoral dissertation of Gilson's student Gouhier, *La pensée religieuse de Descartes* (originally published 1924).[4]

We know that Descartes, in the years around 1630, had been in contact with Augustinian theologians belonging to the French congregation of the Oratory, and with the founder of that congregation, Cardinal Pierre de Bérulle. There is biographical evidence, including a report of a meeting between Descartes and Bérulle, which has suggested to many scholars that the thought of the Oratory was a formative influence on Descartes' metaphysics (see below, Chapter 2, Section C). But Gouhier denies this: "Augustinianism and Cartesianism met up with each other, just as Bérulle and Descartes found themselves one day in the same salon; the essential problem of French philosophy in the seventeenth century is perhaps in this paradox of two radically different inspirations producing fruits with so strange a resemblance."[5]

In asserting that Cartesianism and Augustinianism proceed from radically different inspirations, Gouhier and the mature Gilson require an interpretation not only of Descartes but also of Augustinianism. These two scholars speak in similar ways about Augustinianism, and draw similar consequences for locating Descartes. "Augustinianism, let us not forget, is less a system than a spirit; when it blows, speculations are seen to

---

[3] Etienne Gilson, *La liberté chez Descartes et la théologie* (Paris: Alcan, 1913), p. 160.

[4] Henri Gouhier, *La pensée religieuse de Descartes*, 2nd ed. (Paris: Vrin, 1972).

[5] Ibid. p. 262. This would be (in the words of Lautréamont, describing his hero Maldoror) "as beautiful as the chance encounter, on a dissecting table, between a sewing machine and an umbrella." If Gouhier seriously means that the resemblances he notices between Descartes' and Augustine's philosophies are historical coincidences, then he is the only scholar I know who has ever maintained this. Gilson, in his extremely sympathetic review of Gouhier's book, rightly points out the historical implausibility of such a conclusion (*Etudes sur le rôle de la pensée médiévale dans la formation du système cartésien* (Paris: Vrin, 1930), pp. 289–94), while agreeing with Gouhier's main thesis of an opposition between the Cartesian and Augustinian spirits.

arise where philosophy and religion are not separated, where faith and reason are fused together"; thus "to recognize this spirit in a system, it is sufficient to explicate the doctrine of faith and reason."[6] But Descartes does not fuse faith and reason; on the contrary, he keeps them rigorously separate, following the Thomist rather than the Augustinian model. Therefore, say Gouhier and Gilson, Descartes does not share the Augustinian spirit, nor the Augustinian conception of philosophy itself. Thus, as Gouhier puts it:

It matters little that the matter is the same in the two systems; it matters little that the *cogito* is found in the one and in the other; it matters little that the two apologetics have recourse to the same procedures; it matters little that the two dialectics work themselves out beyond the bounds of the sensible world. Should their proceedings be rigorously parallel, should their expressions be identical, above all this there is a *soul* which these resemblances do not touch, and it is to this soul that a study like ours should lead. Understanding the relations between faith and reason in the philosophy of Descartes is not piecing concepts together to reconstruct a fragment of a system; it is placing oneself at the moment where, before every concept, thought engages itself, or is engaged, on a way that closes every other way to it; it is, perhaps, coming up against that portion of individuality which resists analysis and cannot be further defined. The path Descartes followed is not the path that the bishop of Hippo had opened up for Christian thought; all the comparisons of texts that can be made weigh nothing against this fact.[7]

Gilson agrees with Gouhier that the relations between faith and reason are decisive on the question of Descartes' Augustinianism: in developing a philosophy unconnected with faith, Descartes is "pursuing radically anti-Augustinian ends."[8] Gilson continues to insist that the systematic expression of Descartes' thought, although not its animating spirit, is influenced by Augustine, and by the Augustinianism of Descartes' Oratorian friends: he thinks that Descartes made use of the Oratorians' Augustinian metaphysics, but that he transformed it radically in using it for his own ends. Gilson regards Descartes as essentially a mathematical physicist who, wishing to apply his "mathematical method" to the natural world, must pass "idealistically" from thoughts to objects. To execute this pas-

---

[6] Gouhier, *Pensée religieuse*, p. 258. So too Gilson: "let us add that the Augustinian filiation of the *cogito*, once admitted, would not authorize us to speak without qualification [*sans plus*] of an *augustinisme de Descartes*; for Descartes remains opposed to St. Augustine on the most essential point of Augustinianism: the relations between reason and faith, and, in general, his idea of philosophy itself. Thus Descartes incorporates into his teaching a whole series of Augustinian theses, although it is not St. Augustine's spirit that animates him . . . and this explains why, despite everything, the partisans of his philosophy were pleased to underline its agreement with the principles of St. Augustine" (René Descartes, *Discours de la méthode: texte et commentaire par Etienne Gilson* (Paris: Vrin, 1925 [hereafter cited as "Gilson, *Discours*"]), p. 298). Gilson's insistence here on Descartes' opposition to true Augustinianism comes in concessive clauses and without argument ("despite everything" – despite what?); he refers to Gouhier's work for discussion.

[7] Gouhier, *Pensée religieuse*, p. 258.

[8] Gilson, *Etudes*, pp. 290–1.

sage, Descartes requires a metaphysics; and "surrounded by Augustinians, Descartes needed no more than a short conversation to see opening before him the path of a metaphysics along which his method might proceed."[9] But when Descartes subjects this metaphysics to the constraints of his scientific method, excluding the fusion of faith with reason, he destroys the spirit of Augustinian metaphysics, and can only scavenge particular Augustinian assertions.

The conclusion of Gilson and Gouhier, that Descartes' thought is radically anti-Augustinian, follows directly from their interpretation of Augustinianism as a certain "spirit," as Christian devotion expressing itself through reason. But this interpretation of Augustinianism is not forced on us by the historical facts, and Gilson and others, in adopting it, have been influenced by the philosophical controversies of their own times. Gilson is especially open about his motives. In his essay "The Future of Augustinian Metaphysics," he is explicitly aiming to preserve Augustinianism as a still-living tendency in Christian philosophy from "the two most dangerous temptations imperiling the integrity of its essence . . . Cartesian idealism and modern ontologism."[10] When Gilson speaks of "Cartesian idealism" as a still present philosophical option, or speaks of Descartes' "mathematical method," he is thinking of the secular philosophers of the Third Republic, notably Léon Brunschvicg, who claimed Descartes as their forerunner. By contrast with the Cartesian corruption of Augustinianism, Gilson praises as true Augustinians the Catholic philosophers of his own time who tried to show that reason could not form an autonomous system of thought apart from grace: "to deny the sufficiency of reason is as essential a function of Augustinianism as to deny the sufficiency of nature, and the possibility of a philosophy developing itself validly without worrying about the data of revelation is the radical negation of St. Augustine's *De Utilitate Credendi*, of his whole doctrine, indeed of his whole experience."[11] Gilson's point is not that a Christian philosophy can never develop itself as a complete scientific system, for he thinks that Thomism is a (true) system of this kind. But Thomism is the *only* complete or scientific Christian philosophy; Augustinianism is essentially incomplete, and its value is not in any scientific contributions but precisely in reminding us of the incompleteness of human reason. Augustinian philosophy is valuable for its "spirit," as a discipline of intellectual devotion, but when (as in its Cartesian versions) it leaves aside this "spirit" and sets itself up as a precise scientific system, and thus as a rival to Thomism, Gilson is quick to denounce it as a corruption.

Gilson is led, in part by his position in the twentieth-century French debate on philosophy and religion, to give historical interpretations of

---

[9] Ibid. p. 200.
[10] "The Future of Augustinian Metaphysics," in *A Gilson Reader: Selected Writings of Etienne Gilson* (New York: Image Books, 1957), p. 85.
[11] Gilson, *Etudes*, p. 290.

Augustinianism, scholasticism, and Cartesianism that deny Descartes any but a superficial appropriation of the earlier traditions. Gueroult comes to the same conclusion from an apparently very different starting-point. Gueroult protests against what seems to him the arbitrariness of previous interpretations of Descartes, and pursues instead a method of investigation that he claims to derive from Descartes' own maxims on the interpretation of his philosophy, and that does not depart from the Cartesian texts to consider broad currents in the history of philosophy. But Gueroult, just as much as Gilson, is influenced by the contemporary situation: standing on the secularist side of the debate, he wishes to claim Descartes as the founder of modern critical idealism, from Kant and Fichte to Husserl and Brunschvicg.

> The statement of this principle ["that nothing can be known before intelligence, for it is from intelligence that things can be known, but not conversely"] ushers in the era of modern idealism and reverses the Scholastic point of view. Together with the rejection of all that is not certain in the eyes of intelligence, it shows incontestably, despite quibbles of detail, that as early as the *Rules* Descartes was aware of the need for methodological doubt, of the Cogito, and of the unity of knowledge.[12]

This unity of knowledge, the result of a reason that has recognized its own autonomy, determines the form of Descartes' system as a "unified and monolithic block of certainty . . . established, like mathematics, by a rigorous chain of propositions according to the order of reasons."[13] The philosophy that results from this order of reasons has cut its links with earlier philosophy, and can no longer be described in terms of Augustinianism or scholasticism, or any other previous figures or movements. We must interpret Descartes' philosophy as Descartes himself constructed it, as "a pure geometry," without reference to anything outside the system.

While it is clear enough that Gueroult is interpreting Descartes through the perspective of the mathematical idealism of the early twentieth century, this does not settle whether Gueroult is right or wrong, because it does not decide how far this modern idealism is genuinely Cartesian. Certainly Descartes presents his teaching as a "new philosophy," and certainly he disdains to appeal to authority: especially in the *Meditations* he offers the fundamental principles of his philosophy as the results of a solitary reason meditating with itself, which any rational being should be able to reproduce. Gueroult is right that Descartes wants his philosophy to be both historically new and rationally autonomous, and any interpretation that misses these concerns has missed the point. But what precisely Descartes' concerns entail, and how far he puts them into practice, are themselves matters for historical interpretation, which we must not allow Gueroult's idealism to preempt. By examining first Gueroult's statement

[12] Martial Gueroult, *Descartes' Philosophy Interpreted According to the Order of Reasons*, tr. Roger Ariew (Minneapolis: University of Minnesota Press, 1984), 1, p. 3.
[13] Gueroult, 1, p. 5.

of his method, and then the texts of Descartes that he cites in support of it, we may see how far these texts justify Gueroult's "analysis of structures," and his disregard for history.

Gueroult undertakes, in his book *Descartes selon l'ordre des raisons*, to explain the text of the *Meditations*. There are, he says, two techniques for explaining a philosophical text, "textual criticism itself and the analysis of structures."[14] Textual criticism, which Gueroult takes in an extremely broad sense to include "problems of sources, variations, evolutions, etc.," has already been handled by Gilson, Gouhier, and Laporte; but this is only preliminary to understanding a philosophy, and it is time to get on to the analysis of structures. The structure of the *Meditations*, in particular, is given by a strict "order of reasons," in which each "thesis enunciated before another is a condition of that other."[15] We can understand Descartes' meaning only by analyzing the complex structure relating each sentence of the *Meditations* to each earlier and later sentence, since the meaning of each assertion is determined by the whole system to which it belongs.[16] Conversely, nothing outside this order of reasons can contribute to determining the meaning of anything inside it; and so "we can draw the conclusion, which is no longer entirely Gilson's, that everything in Descartes' philosophy is new, even what appears to be old."[17] But in fact Gueroult has arrived at much the same conclusion as Gilson's, that "even when the two philosophies [of Descartes and Augustine] employ the same

---

[14] Gueroult, 1, p. xviii.

[15] Gueroult, 1, p. 6. Gueroult is apparently basing himself on a text of the second Replies (which Gueroult cites earlier on the same page), where Descartes says that the proper order for demonstration "consists only in that the things which are put forward first ought to be known without any help from the things that follow, and then that all the rest should be arranged in such a way that they are demonstrated only from the things that precede them" (AT VII,155). But this is just a description of the logical order that would normally be followed in, say, a geometry text (the model that Descartes cites in context). Descartes is not saying what Gueroult apparently takes him to mean, that the proof (or interpetation) of a proposition depends on *every* proposition that precedes it, but merely that it does not depend on any proposition that comes after it.

[16] "[N]o single truth of the system can be correctly interpreted without reference to the place it occupies in the order" (Gueroult, 1, p. 6); "thus philosophy is developed as a pure geometry, which owes all its certainty to the internal linkage of its reasons, without any reference to external reality" (p. 7). In speaking of a "pure geometry" (as opposed to an applied or physical geometry), and in saying that the meanings of the terms in such a theory are determined by the logical structure of the theory, rather than by reference to something given in experience independently of the theory, Gueroult is apparently alluding to David Hilbert's philosophy of geometry, and suggesting that Descartes' metaphysics has the same autonomous status as Hilbert's geometry. For Hilbert, the axioms of a geometry are not propositions that we perceive to be true once we understand the meanings of the terms; on the contrary, the axioms are free stipulations of reason, and the meanings of the terms are determined by the axioms rather than vice versa. A term is "defined" only by the whole theory derived from the axioms; "every axiom contributes something to the definition, and hence every new axiom changes the concept" (letter from Hilbert to Gottlob Frege, p. 40 in Frege's *Philosophical and Mathematical Correspondence* (Chicago: University of Chicago Press, 1980)).

[17] Gueroult, 1, p. 284.

concepts and arrange them in the same order, they do not mean the same things."[18]

When Gueroult explains the text of the *Meditations*, he ignores the historical background completely. In a book longer than the present study, he mentions St. Thomas four times, Aristotle five times, and Augustine eight times, mostly in passing. But he refers to Husserl eight, to Fichte fifteen, and to Kant twenty-seven times, often at some length: not, of course, as sources for Descartes, but as points of comparison to elucidate the structure of Descartes' idealism.

How far is Gueroult justified in claiming that Descartes' own declarations endorse this method of interpretation? Gueroult's most important text is from the preface to the *Meditations*, where Descartes insists that his work be judged as a whole, and not split apart into isolated assertions:

As to those who, not bothering to comprehend the order and connection of my reasons, will apply themselves to finding fault with the conclusions one at a time, as is the habit of many, they will not derive much fruit from reading this book; and although perhaps they will find many occasions for quibbling, they will not easily make any objection that is pressing or worthy of a response. (AT VII,9–10)

This passage brings out Descartes' belief that it is the "order and connection of his reasons," and not the individual doctrines, that gives value to his work. All the doctrines could already be found scattered piecemeal among the works of the different philosophical schools, in their perennial controversies with each other; Descartes will not have accomplished much if he has simply chosen a bouquet of doctrines and presented them, without proof of their correctness, as "his" philosophy. Descartes has tried to show how one thing follows from another, and his work stands or falls with such connections of reasons. It is thus misguided for a hostile critic of the *Meditations* to attack each doctrine with the usual weapons of philosophical polemic, ignoring Descartes' demonstrations; and, as Gueroult rightly insists, it would be equally misguided for a historian of philosophy to separate Descartes' philosophy into its component doctrines, and to think Descartes has been accounted for when each doctrine is traced back to its historical source.

Descartes was himself aware, not only of critics who would deny that his doctrines were true, but also of those who would deny that they were original to him. Descartes' reply to these critics is worth bearing in mind when we try to describe his dependence on Augustine or on anyone else: we may hear it and then ask how far it justifies Gueroult's anti-historical conclusions on the method of interpreting Descartes.

As we can write no words in which there are letters other than those of the alphabet, nor complete a sentence unless it consists of the words that are in the dictionary, so neither [can we compose] a book except out of the sentences [or opinions, *sententiae*] that are found in others. But if the things I say are so coherent

---

[18] Gilson, "The Future of Augustinian Metaphysics," pp. 92–3.

among themselves and so connected that they follow from each other, then it will not follow from this argument that I have borrowed my opinions [*sententiae*] from others any more than I have taken the words themselves from the dictionary. (AT X,204 = Baillet II,545)

This passage shows that Descartes is aware that the *elements* of his philosophy are *sententiae* in common circulation, but that he hopes to have put them together in such a way as to constitute a new philosophy, which will achieve some purpose that the scattered *sententiae* do not.[19] Gueroult is quite right that we cannot understand the meaning of Descartes' philosophy without observing the order and connection of his doctrinal affirmations: just as, at a more obvious level, we cannot understand the meaning of a sentence without observing the order of its words, or of a word without observing the order of its letters. But it does not follow that we need not be able to recognize the individual letters of the alphabet, or that we may discard the dictionary and divine the meanings of words from their place in the syntax of the sentence. Speakers of a language do not *invent* their words, but choose them from a preexisting range of possibilities, confident that the words will call up given ideas and expectations in the minds of their hearers; if we do not know their language sufficiently from our daily commerce, then we have recourse to a dictionary or to previous uses that can clarify the meaning of their terms. Similarly, the traditional concepts, affirmations, and arguments, which Descartes lays out in a new order in his writings, each call up definite expectations in the minds of Descartes' intended readers, which we cannot now divine without historical study. Descartes intends his philosophy to say something new, to fulfill some hope that had not been previously fulfilled: but in order to understand what he said, or to assess what he accomplished by saying it, we need to consider both the old intellectual materials that he uses, and the new goals and expectations that he hopes to use them to satisfy. Only when we bear both of these factors in mind can we understand how Descartes uses the traditional materials for his purposes, and to what extent he preserves them or transforms them in so using them. This is the only way we can answer the question whether Descartes is an Augustinian, or whether he belongs to any other earlier tradition; the answer will not be simply yes or no, but it will illuminate Descartes' philosophy far more than a simple yes or no could do.

It is worth being explicit here about some methodological assumptions of my approach to Descartes. Gilson and Gouhier and Gueroult will concede that Descartes takes over intellectual materials of various kinds (concepts, doctrines, arguments, etc.) from Augustine and from other earlier thinkers, but they all think that Descartes' philosophy is in its essence independent of these influences, whether because it expresses a personal

---

[19] Compare AT I,479, where Descartes says that his treatment of curves in Book II of his *Geometry* is "as much beyond ordinary geometry as Cicero's rhetoric is beyond the children's ABC."

"spirit," or because of the "order and connection of reasons" within the system. I agree, of course, that Descartes' philosophy cannot be explained simply as the sum of various historical "influences," and that in understanding Descartes' philosophy we must understand *what he did* with the intellectual materials he took over, how he made them serve new intellectual purposes, or constructed a new order of reasons among them. I have provisionally accepted the metaphor (Schleiermacher's) of a conceptual "language," and I have used it in arguing against Gueroult's antihistorical approach to the *Meditations*. Since the *Meditations* are written in Latin, to understand them we must first master Latin vocabulary and syntax, though what we are aiming to understand is not the Latin language but a particular text expressing something new within an old language; so, likewise, the *Meditations* are written in a particular conceptual "vocabulary" and "syntax," which we can understand only by learning the "language" of Descartes' contemporaries and predecessors, though what we are aiming to understand is not this language but a particular text using this language to express something new. However, this metaphor is dangerous, because it suggests that the language is extrinsic to what we are seeking to understand, so that, just as the *Meditations* could be translated from Latin into French, a philosophical interpretation of the *Meditations* would "translate" the text into the conceptual "language" of our own day, freeing it from the terms in which, as a matter of historical accident, Descartes' message was expressed. The absurdity of this approach is shown up if we apply it to the history of science: Newton's *Principia* takes up Kepler's laws of planetary motion and Descartes' law of the persistence of uniform rectilinear motion, and builds something new and important out of them, but this does not mean that Newton is using the "language" of Kepler and Descartes to express some fundamental message that could equally have been expressed in the "language" of Ptolemaic astronomy and Aristotelian physics. For this reason, I prefer to speak of the "intellectual materials" out of which something is constructed, rather than the "conceptual language" in which something is expressed.

There is another, closely connected, danger in the "language" metaphor. One point of this metaphor, and one point in urging people to read Descartes' contemporaries and predecessors if they want to understand Descartes, is that it is important to distinguish what is new and peculiar to Descartes (the "message" his text expresses) from what is common to the whole intellectual discourse of his time (the "language" in which his text is written). The essence of a thinker's philosophy, and what interpretation seeks to capture, is what is new and peculiar to him; and the "language" metaphor tends to suggest that this is something "prelinguistic," something perhaps very simple but deeply personal to the author,[20]

---

[20] So Gouhier says that the historical study of a past thinker should aim at uncovering the "spirit" or "soul" of his philosophy, at finding "the moment where, before every concept, thought engages itself, or is engaged, on a way that closes every other way to it . . . that

which the author's texts then "translate" into the "language" of his time. Instead of speaking of a "message" or a "spirit" expressed in a language, I speak of a "goal" that the author tries to achieve by a new use of given materials. This does not come to the same thing. The goal is not the essence of the philosophy, it is not independent of the historical context, it need not be personal to the author, and it need not be anything especially fascinating in itself. Perhaps the goal of the *Principia* was, roughly, to use Kepler's laws and other observations of planetary motions, together with the persistence of uniform rectilinear motion, to discover the laws of the forces acting on the bodies of the solar system. That short sentence does not capture the essence of the *Principia*. Newton is important, not because he conceived that goal, but because he was able to achieve it, and the task of understanding is to explain *how* he achieved it. Likewise, in interpreting Descartes, while I will begin by determining the goals of his philosophical work (roughly, to construct a complete scientific system, including a mechanical physics and ending in the practical disciplines, on the basis of an Augustinian metaphysics), I will not end there, but will go on to examine what Augustinian metaphysics was and how Descartes was able to use its intellectual resources to achieve his philosophical goals, to the limited extent to which he did indeed achieve them. It is important to understand that Augustinian metaphysics figures in Descartes' philosophical goals, not because this answers the question about the essence of his philosophy, but because it shows us what questions to ask when we read the *Meditations*.

One consequence of these reflections is that, when we say that Descartes was trying to achieve new goals, we should not mean that his conception of his project breaks with the philosophical expectations of his time. Descartes regards his philosophical goals as new in the sense that nobody has previously achieved them, not in the sense that nobody has wished or tried to achieve them. The hope of establishing a new philosophy, both more scientific and more practically useful, was a commonplace of Descartes' time. Nor does Descartes' ideal of demonstrative certainty mark a break with the past: Descartes shares this ideal with his scholastic opponents, who bear witness that an insistence on proof is compatible with wholesale borrowing, and that arguments may be borrowed as easily as opinions. Descartes' ideal of a new philosophy is itself one of the starting-points that Descartes takes over from other philosophers, and must be subject to historical investigation: seeing what his contemporaries expected of a new philosophy will help us understand Descartes' goals in constructing his philosophy, both because he was trying to meet his contemporaries' expectations, and because he shared these expectations himself.

Descartes was genuinely concerned to make his metaphysics self-justifying and independent of any doctrine of the physical world; this was

portion of individuality which resists analysis and cannot be further defined" (*Pensée religieuse*, p. 258).

15

necessary if the metaphysics was to be strong enough to support a complete philosophy, and in particular a physics, without the risk of circularity. It is nonetheless clear that Descartes took the central concepts of his metaphysics from Augustine or Augustinians; if he altered, or even mutilated, this metaphysics in the process, this was because of the constraints imposed by his project of making it the foundation of a mechanical physics. This project may strike us as bizarre and incongruous, if we take our notions of Augustinianism and of the new physics from twentieth-century versions of Augustinianism and Cartesianism. We might be led to conclude (like Gueroult) that because Descartes is a modern rational philosopher he cannot really be building on Augustine; or (like Gilson) that if Descartes *is* building on Augustine, he must not be using what in Augustine is really essential. In the next chapter I will put Descartes' project in context by examining both the seventeenth-century expectations of a new philosophy and Descartes' strategy for answering these expectations: besides arguing that Descartes did intend to build his new philosophy (including his physics) on the old Augustinian metaphysics, I will try to show why he might think it reasonable to try to accomplish the goals of a new philosophy by using the Augustinian metaphysics as a foundation for a new science.

Once we have established what Descartes is trying to do, we can go on to examine how he does it. In Part One, through a study of Augustine, I will survey the intellectual materials that Descartes had available to him; then, in Part Two, I will study the use Descartes made of this old material for his new purposes, and the degree to which he preserves or modifies the Augustinian metaphysics in the process. As the entire metaphysics of the *Meditations* is the result of this process of adaptation of Augustinian metaphysics, I will in fact be giving a full exposition of Cartesian metaphysics.

If my interpretation of Descartes' metaphysics succeeds, I will have answered the challenges presented by Gilson and Gouhier and Gueroult. Gueroult challenges us to follow out Descartes' order of reasons in all its rigor, to display what Descartes has done that is new and valuable and rational on its own terms. I will try to show that we can do this better by considering the historical background than by bracketing it. Gilson and Gouhier challenge us to explain what Descartes could have found valuable in Augustine, if he rejects the Augustinian understanding of the relations of faith and reason. By a broader study of Augustine, I will set Augustine's doctrine of faith and reason in its proper perspective, showing that it does not have the priority in Augustine's thought that Gilson supposes, and that it does not dictate a fusion between faith and reason. By exploring other equally important aspects of Augustine's thought, his method in his metaphysical project, his conceptions of God and the soul, and his doctrine of the origin of evil, we will be able to see what Descartes found so fruitful for the foundations of a new philosophy. And in examining Descartes' new presentation of the Augustinian metaphysics, and in showing how he transformed it to make it serve as a foundation for physics, we will see that he does not distort Augustine in the way that Gilson supposes – and, *inter alia*, that he does not abandon Augustine's understanding of the relation between faith and reason. Thus I hope to show how Arnauld and Malebranche and other seventeenth-century Augustinians could embrace Descartes' philosophy as a novel but promising development of Augustine's thought "in philosophical matters" (to use Arnauld's phrase, AT VII,197); so that, as Mersenne told the hostile Voetius, "the more learned someone becomes in the teaching of Augustine, the more willingly he will embrace the Cartesian philosophy" (AT III,603).

2

Descartes' project for a new philosophy

A. The expectation of a new philosophy

To understand what Descartes hoped to accomplish through his philosophical work, we should first orient ourselves against the intellectual background of this work. It is not enough to know the condition in which Descartes hoped to leave philosophy; we must also understand the condition in which he found it, if we are to appreciate what features he wished to alter, and what expectations he hoped to fulfill. In what follows I will try to indicate this background condition, briefly and in the broadest of strokes.[1]

Descartes is widely regarded, alone or with such associates as Bacon or Hobbes, as the founder of modern philosophy. Already in Descartes' lifetime, people were speaking of the "new philosophy," meaning either Descartes' philosophy or more generally the approach to nature shared by Descartes with other "moderns." Now, to speak of a "new" or "modern" philosophy beginning in the early to mid seventeenth century implies a contrast with a previous situation, in which there was only an "old" or "ancient" philosophy. Thus David Hume, writing one hundred years after Descartes, draws sceptical conclusions from a contrast of two opposing philosophies, the "ancient" and the "modern." Hume does not use the word "medieval," which is a fairly recent invention; but neither does he have a simple dichotomy of ancient and modern times, so that the period before (say) 1500 or 1600 would all be "ancient." Rather, for him as for us, the word "ancient" has a strong connection with Greek and Roman antiquity. The philosophers living before Descartes, and those of his own time who refused to accept the new philosophy, were "ancients" not in the sense that they themselves lived in ancient times, but only in the sense that they favored an ancient philosophy, a philosophy derived chiefly from Aristotle, and elaborated into a system of academic instruction. This ancient philosophy was the doctrine taught in the schools and universities

---

[1] For a more detailed picture of this background, see my article "The Intellectual Setting of Seventeenth Century Philosophy," in *The Cambridge History of Seventeenth Century Philosophy* (Cambridge: Cambridge University Press, forthcoming). The present section is essentially an abridgment of that article, presenting only those parts of the picture which are most directly relevant to interpreting Descartes.

of Descartes' time; the modern philosophy developed outside the universities, and won its place in them only through protracted struggle.

In seeking to interpret the modern philosophy, it is helpful to contrast it, not to "medieval philosophy" as the philosophy of the preceding period, but to "the ancient philosophy" or "the philosophy of the schools," as the philosophy that followed the ancient model. The new philosophy did not develop out of the old philosophy, and it did not primarily address itself to the professors of the old philosophy. It made its appeal rather to those who had no faith in the old philosophy, and who might hope for a new philosophy, but had not yet found one.

Disillusionment with the scholastic philosophy, and with the allied scholastic theology, was widespread among the intellectual elites of the sixteenth and seventeenth centuries. The grounds for dissatisfaction were many, and are recited with varying emphases by the different writers of the period. The philosophy of Aristotle, it is said, gives no genuine knowledge: the schools are enmeshed in debates over words, and their formulae tell us nothing about reality. Their philosophical instruction will teach you to memorize authorities and to dispute, but it cannot achieve the goal of philosophy, which is to teach wisdom. A philosophy could teach wisdom only by teaching sound morality and sound religion, but Aristotle does not do that: he stands accused of denying God's creation and providence and the immortality of the individual soul, and of teaching an ethics of human pride and self-satisfaction. If we aspire to wisdom, we will have to find some other discipline to lead us there.

Some critics of Aristotle had attempted to give a new philosophy to replace the old, which would succeed in teaching wisdom: such a philosophy would not dispute about words, but give genuine knowledge of the essences of things; it would give a demonstrative basis for knowledge of God and the soul. Typical of the many "new philosophies" of the sixteenth and seventeenth centuries is Francesco Patrizi's *Nova de Universis Philosophia*:[2] but, despite the grand title, little in Patrizi's teaching is new. He, and many of his competitors, are taking up ancient sources (in Patrizi's case the late ancient Platonists and the forgeries attributed to Zoroaster and Hermes Trismegistus), and attempting to systematize them to the point where they could become serious competitors with scholastic Aristotelianism in the educational institutions.[3]

[2] Ferrara, 1591; reprinted, with Croatian translation, as *Nova sveopća filozofija* (Zagreb: Liber, 1979). For fuller discussion, see my article cited in the preceding note.
[3] In "The Intellectual Setting of Seventeenth Century Philosophy" I survey a cross-section of "new philosophies" from the time of Ficino down to the early seventeenth century: most have in common with Patrizi's that they are, or claim to be, revivals of something ancient. Besides Patrizi and other Platonists, there were revivals and systematizations and Christianizations of Stoicism (especially by Justus Lipsius), of Epicureanism, and of different versions of scepticism, as well as more specifically Christian efforts, including the various "Mosaic philosophies" that tried to extract a physics out of the book of Genesis.

Unconvinced by these new philosophies were such humanist thinkers as Erasmus at the beginning of the sixteenth century, and Montaigne and Charron, writing in French for a wider audience at the end of the century. These thinkers, too, had aspirations to moral and religious wisdom that could not be satisfied by what they saw as the stultified doctrine of the philosophical and theological schools and the corrupt practice of the institutional church; and they sought to return to the pattern of an earlier time before thought and practice were corrupted. Thus they turned to ancient texts, uncovering those that had been neglected, and correcting the interpretation of those that had been misappropriated in the past. But (unlike Patrizi) they were not looking for a new system of philosophy or theology to replace the doctrine of the schools. Philosophy should concern itself with moral virtue, and Christianity with a simple faith; they decay when they are elaborated into technical systems, and argument over doctrinal details becomes more important than a firm conviction of the main point, and a corresponding conduct of life. Thus the humanists are led to break the connection between *science* [*scientia*] and *wisdom* [*sapientia*]. The benefits of virtue might ideally be demonstrated from a scientific understanding of the nature of man in both mind and body, and of his relation to God and the world; but all attempts to carry out this project have stalled in a mass of disputed details. It is better to renounce the hope of a scientific argument for virtue, and settle for a rhetorical praise of virtue which, if not scientifically demonstrative, will be more effective than science in presenting a model for human life and in inspiring those of the present day to imitate it. The ancient writers who interest the humanists will not be the dogmatic philosophers, but more popular philosophers and philosophical orators, Cicero, Seneca, Plutarch; these writers can provide the starting-point for reflection on human nature and for deliberation on how to live.

Many humanist writers of the sixteenth and seventeenth centuries followed Cicero, in particular, in their interest in ancient scepticism. Cicero was essentially an orator rather than a philosopher: his interest in philosophy was not to acquire (still less to teach) a systematic knowledge of the world, but to "imitate" Greek philosophy (considered as a literary form) into Latin, and to make philosophical commonplaces available for the orator. It was difficult for the humanists, and it remains difficult, to determine Cicero's own philosophical views, since he is ready to imitate sources

---

The cumulative effect of these new philosophies was not to usher in a "new attitude toward the world" – for the different "new philosophies" had nothing in common except their opposition to scholasticism – but rather to foster the *expectation* of a new and better philosophy to replace Aristotle's, together with a sense of the frustration of all past efforts. These Renaissance philosophers, to whom I cannot do justice here, are important for understanding, not only Descartes, but also Gassendi and Hobbes, proponents of rival versions of what ultimately became the successful "new philosophy," corpuscularianism: Gassendi would never have thought of presenting a Christian Epicureanism as a systematic alternative to scholasticism if Lipsius had not already done the same for Stoicism.

from different Greek philosophical schools, often without making clear his own judgment; but Cicero seems to be attracted to the Stoic position in ethics (while inclined, following the "Old Academy" of Antiochus of Ascalon, to moderate the Stoics' severe judgment on the value of ordinary goods and pursuits), and to the sceptical position in physics and logic. The Stoic ethics is valuable in presenting the ideal of the wise man, but the physics and logic on which it is based have no such attraction. Cicero is merely selecting available philosophical arguments to imitate; and, as a professional orator, he is just as ready to argue on both sides of a question as on one. Where matters of conduct are not concerned, he inclines naturally toward scepticism, which offers the fullest scope for rhetorical skill in arguing both sides of a question, and which confirms the view that philosophy is an adjunct to oratory and not an alternative to it: the ability to argue philosophically is useful for the orator and statesman, and a fitting crown for a liberal education, but there is no further advantage in wisdom that the professional philosopher could enjoy over the gentleman amateur.

The "scepticism" of the humanists is largely Ciceronian: it is not a worked-out philosophical position, but a rhetorical weapon directed against the claims of dogmatic philosophy, especially scholastic Aristotelian philosophy, to teach wisdom. The humanists do not seriously doubt that the philosophers have achieved knowledge of many things; but they think that the philosophers' knowledge, to the extent that it is genuine, is concerned with morally uninteresting trivialities, and makes no contribution toward wisdom. As we will see, it is this sceptically tinged humanism, rather than any serious philosophical scepticism, against which Descartes sought to measure his philosophical achievement.

The history of philosophy in the sixteenth and seventeenth centuries is intimately bound up with the history of Christianity. The protests of the humanists were directed at least as much against religious as against philosophical corruption: Aristotelian philosophy was objectionable largely because it provided the framework for scholastic theology. Erasmus published editions of ancient pagan authors, but also of the New Testament and of the Fathers of the Church, seen as living before the period of corruption. The Fathers, to be sure, were often involved in theological controversy; but at least they preached the faith without trying to make it conform to the criteria of an Aristotelian science, and without allowing ecclesiastical authority to replace the Christian virtues in providing the means of salvation. Thus, in the early sixteenth century and beyond, Christian reformers of all stripes appealed to the Fathers over the scholastics as offering a model for Christian thought and practice.

The reforming movement, of course, produced the Protestant Reformation, and thus divided western Christendom into two opposing camps; but even in countries that remained Catholic, as France did for the most part, the agitation for reform continued, and the hierarchy gave it institutional form at the Council of Trent, as it had to if Catholicism was to compete effectively with Protestantism for the loyalties of Europe. The

Catholic Reformation or Counter-Reformation was an exceedingly complex phenomenon; here I want to bring out only the aspects that are of most importance in understanding Descartes.

The Catholic reformers (including reforming bishops and popes, the reformers of old religious orders, and the founders of the new orders that proliferated in the sixteenth century) were concerned to *broaden* and *deepen* the base of Christian commitment within the Catholic camp; both Protestant and Catholic reformations were attempts to re-Christianize, or, as it has recently been put, to Christianize for the first time a society that had been only superficially converted in the past. An educated Christian elite had for too long been talking to itself; the new orders of the sixteenth and seventeenth centuries made it their business to educate the children of the wider population, and to give a proper training to the parish priests outside the religious orders (the "secular" as opposed to "regular" clergy), who through their sermons and other religious offices might be a means of Christianization for the whole society. The situation of the church in the sixteenth century was, of course, very different from its situation in the first or second: Christianity had enormous advantages of prestige and social power, and (except for the Jews, isolated and sometimes persecuted) had no serious rivals in western Europe. Despite much agitation against the "deists, atheists and libertines," the real opponent was (in the lower classes) ignorance, or (in the upper classes) indifference to religion among nominal Christians. Propaganda against this enemy would be carried out not by works of controversial theology aimed against heresy (although the age was saturated with such works, across and within confessional lines), but rather by works of *spirituality*, by meditations or spiritual exercises designed to concentrate the mind on the central truths of Christianity, and thus to sanctify daily life. Untold numbers of such popular handbooks of devotion were printed throughout the seventeenth century, for the benefit of the secular clergy and of the laity.

It is natural that many of the Catholic reformers should wish to dispense with Aristotle. The alliance with Aristotle had detracted from the central concerns of Christian thought, and damaged the credibility of the church; thus a large part of the Catholic Reformation (like Erasmus before) sought to bypass the scholastics, and to draw their theology directly from the Fathers of the church. Above all, they turned to Augustine.

From very early on, Augustine had become the chief authority, second only to scripture, for western Christian theology. Already in the sixth century, popes and Councils had designated Augustine as the chief authority on the controversial issue of grace.[4] But Augustine's deeper and more subtle contributions were not on matters of controversial theology. He had attempted to think through the Christian faith, to pass from faith to understanding, and thus to extract the intellectual content of the faith.

---

[4] See Henricus Denzinger, *Enchiridion Symbolorum, Definitionum et Declarationum de Rebus Fidei et Morum* (Freiburg: Herder, 1937), article 173a, and following through article 200b.

The body of philosophical doctrine that later thinkers will take to be axioms of all Christian philosophy is in fact (at least for the Latin West) the work of Augustine. To take one key example, Augustine and his teacher Ambrose are the first Latin Christian writers to maintain that the human soul is incorporeal; by the thirteenth century, the scholastics simply assume that this is in the Bible (because they assume that "spirit" means "incorporeal substance"). So, although scholastic philosophy takes its conceptual framework from Aristotle, it is heavily influenced by Augustine in doctrine. Thomas Aquinas distinguishes his Aristotelianism from that of the Averroists by harmonizing Aristotle with Christianity, which means, in effect, with Augustine: what Thomas regards as universal Christian doctrine, the Averroists describe as merely "the opinion of Augustine" on disputed questions.[5] Thomas' successors take the Christian and Augustinian modification of Aristotelian philosophy even further. In 1277, three years after Thomas' death, a series of Aristotelian and Averroist theses were condemned as contrary to Christian doctrine, often because, by claiming that Aristotelian doctrines were logically necessary, they denied the power of God to falsify them. Thus the schools that develop after 1277, while they continue the main lines of the Thomist reconciliation between Aristotle and Christianity, are more critical of Aristotle; they continue to regard Aristotle as the authoritative exponent of unaided human reason, but they take pleasure in making "advances" over Aristotle on many questions that might seem purely philosophical, by invoking arguments depending on the extraordinary power of God. Thus even within scholastic Aristotelianism, there develops an odd resentment of Aristotle as a pagan philosopher to whom Christian philosophers should not be subservient. Further, alongside the main philosophical schools of Christianized Aristotelianism, the Averroist tradition survived and indeed grew in the fifteenth and sixteenth centuries, providing a continued target for those who attacked Aristotelianism as such as contrary to the Christian (and thus largely the Augustinian) understanding of God and the soul.

The prestige of Augustine gained an added boost from the Reformation. The Protestant reformers had taken Augustine as their chief authority (after the scriptures) for their theology of grace; the Catholics, at Trent, sought to reclaim him, and so, individually, did each of the different tendencies of the Catholic Reformation. Augustine was the authority whom each sought to interpret on the controversial issue of grace; Augustine was the model whom each sought to emulate in Christian spiritual reflection; perhaps he could also become the source for a new philosophy, through which Christians could develop their reasonings without becoming captive to a discredited pagan philosophy. The bishop Cornelius Jansen, in his controversial work on the doctrine of grace entitled simply *Augustinus*, had held up Augustine as the sole authority in Christian theology, specif-

---

[5] See Fernand van Steenberghen, *Thomas Aquinas and Radical Aristotelianism* (Washington: Catholic University of America Press, 1980).

ically awarding to him each of the traditional titles of honor that had been given to the great scholastic Doctors; among the Jansenist propositions condemned at Rome was that "where anyone finds a doctrine clearly founded in Augustine, he is absolutely permitted to hold it and to teach it, irrespective of any papal bull."[6] We have seen that Jansen's defender Antoine Arnauld (whose sister Mère Angélique Arnauld had reformed the Cistercian convent of Port-Royal) wrote to Descartes of "the divine Augustine" as "a man of the most acute intellect, and entirely admirable not only in theological but also in philosophical matters." Later in the century, Nicolas Malebranche (a member of the Oratory of Jesus and Mary, founded in 1613 by Pierre de Bérulle as a mutual improvement society for the secular clergy) will speak of his astonishment that "Christian philosophers, who should prefer the spirit of God to the spirit of man, Moses to Aristotle, St. Augustine to some miserable commentator on a pagan philosopher," should follow Aristotle in linking the soul more closely with the body than with God.[7] A whole range of religious sentiment in Catholic France thus joined with more secular concerns in seeking a new philosophy to replace that of Aristotle.

Was such a philosophy to be found? Father Marin Mersenne, the apologist for Christianity, researcher and supporter of research into nature, the intellectual patron of Descartes, Gassendi, and Hobbes, also defended Aristotle against many of the "new philosophies." It would not be enough to criticize Aristotle; it was necessary to surpass him, and his achievement was vast. If some new philosophy were to replace Aristotle's, it would have to be at least as systematic and scientific, at least as compatible with Christianity, at least as practically productive for empirical research and for morality. Mersenne judged the available "new philosophies" by these standards, and not unreasonably found them wanting; he chose to remain with Aristotle for the time being, while continuing to encourage those who might turn out to be the new Christian Aristotle for the modern age. There were exciting new discoveries in "mechanics" or technology and in the mathematical sciences; Galileo had created a new astronomy with the telescope and was attempting to construct a mathematical science of sublunar motions. But these discoveries were not yet a coherent program: someone was wanted to produce a satisfactory new philosophy that would embrace them. Descartes was one of those who tried; so were Gassendi, Hobbes, and many lesser figures. In trying to understand Descartes (or any of these others), it is reasonable to begin by asking how he worked

---

[6] Denzinger, article 1320. Jansen's *Augustinus* (3 vols. in 1, Louvain, 1640) has been reprinted: Frankfurt am Main: Minerva, 1964.

[7] Malebranche, *De la recherche de la vérité*, in his *Oeuvres*, ed. Geneviève Rodis-Lewis (Paris: Gallimard, 1979), 1, pp. 3–4; "some miserable commentator" refers specifically to Averroes, "the commentator" *par excellence*. Malebranche is, of course, influenced by Descartes; but the sentiment he is expressing here is independent of his Cartesianism, and indeed helps to explain why he, like Arnauld, was attracted to Descartes' philosophy.

out his own conception of what he could accomplish, in relation to this whole network of expectations for a new philosophy.

B. Descartes: science and wisdom

Descartes speaks most clearly about what he hopes to accomplish in the prefaces to his various publications: the preface serves to set out the contents of the following text, and to persuade readers that the book will be worth their time and money. There is however a difficulty in taking these works as our sources for Descartes' view of his project. Descartes did not publish until 1637, when he was already forty years old: we have only fragments and drafts of writings from before that time. But, by his own account, there were two decisive turning-points in his conception of his work, the first in 1619 and the second in or around 1628: it is therefore unsafe to assume that Descartes, before 1628, already held the views that are expressed in his mature, published writings. Our chief interest will be in Descartes' mature work, both because of its intrinsic merit and because it is only here that he makes use of Augustine; but we will be interested in his early thought to the extent that it reveals the motivations that led him to his mature project. From 1619 on, Descartes was trying to fulfill the general hope for a new philosophy; but only after 1628 does he appear to take up the more specific project of a systematic philosophy based on Augustine. Descartes tells us that he took up this project because someone suggested to him that he do so; and this is hardly surprising in the spiritual atmosphere of the time. But Descartes would not have taken the suggestion when he did if he had not seen in Augustine's thought a means of achieving the goals that he had already set for his philosophy. Thus in order to understand how and why Descartes hoped to use Augustinian elements in his philosophy, it will help to discuss first the general goals that Descartes had set for himself in 1619, and retained throughout his life, before we go on (in Section C below) to describe the specific project that he adopts after 1628. We may try to isolate the original stratum of Descartes' thought by following his autobiographical remarks in his published works, and by comparing these with surviving fragments of his early writings.

In 1637 Descartes published what he called his "essays," the *Geometry*, the *Dioptrics*, and the *Meteors*: these are studies on specialized scientific topics, culled from his larger work as advertisements for what he could accomplish in the sciences. To these he prefaced an autobiographical *Discourse on the Method of Rightly Conducting His Reason and Searching for Truth in the Sciences*, setting out "the considerations and maxims out of which I have formed a method by which I think I have a means of increasing my knowledge by degrees, and raising it bit by bit to the highest point that the mediocrity of my mind and the short duration of my life could permit me to attain" (AT VI,3). It is this method for cultivating his reason that has produced the fruits exhibited in the *Essays*; Descartes will not *teach* this method as a new organon of science to replace the Aristotelian logic, but will simply advertise the method by recounting his discovery "like a history, or, if you prefer, like a fable" (p. 4), offering his own life as an example for his readers to imitate or avoid as they see fit. Descartes divides the *Discourse* into six parts: "in the first, one will find various considerations regarding the sciences" (p. 1), that is, a critical review of the condition of the existing disciplines; "in the second, the principal rules of the method that the author has sought out" (ibid.), Descartes' own project, as he formulated it in 1619, for a transformation of the sciences.

Part One of the *Discourse* presents, in highly stylized form, a humanist critique of the existing disciplines.

I have been nourished on letters since my childhood, and because I was persuaded that by their means one could acquire a clear and assured knowledge of everything useful for life, I had an extreme desire to learn them. But as soon as I had completed the whole course of studies at the end of which one is commonly received into the ranks of the learned, I entirely changed my opinion: for I found myself embarrassed with so many doubts and errors that it seemed to me that I had made no other profit in trying to educate myself than to have discovered more and more my ignorance. (P. 4)

Descartes enumerates the scholastic disciplines, or "exercises" as he calls them, more or less ironically praising the utility of each; he then goes on to show, again by enumeration, that none of these disciplines fulfills the promise of a knowledge both certain in itself and usable as a guide for practical conduct. The best of the existing disciplines can satisfy only *half* of the promise. Descartes praises the existing disciplines of mathematics and morals, and by a formal comparison reveals the weaknesses of each. "Mathematics possesses very subtle inventions, which can be very useful, as much to content the curious as to facilitate all the arts and to relieve human labor"; while "the writings that treat of morals contain many teachings and many exhortations to virtue which are very useful" (p. 6). This praise already has a hollow ring, and Descartes reveals its emptiness in the comparison:

I was pleased above all with mathematics, on account of the certitude and evidence of its reasons; but I had not yet noticed its true use, and, thinking that it was useful only for the mechanical arts, I was astonished that, its foundations being so firm and solid, nothing more elevated had been built upon them. *As, on the contrary*, I compared the writings of the ancient pagans that treat of morals to very proud and magnificent palaces, that are built on nothing but sand and mud. They elevate the virtues very high, and make them appear estimable above everything in the world; but they do not sufficiently teach us to know them, and often what they call by so fine a name [sc. "virtue"] is only insensibility, pride, despair, or parricide. (Pp. 7–8; my emphasis)

"Morals" here are not Aristotelian ethics but Stoic exhortations to virtue, as elaborated by Roman popular philosophy and its modern imitators.[8] Descartes regards these as essentially rhetorical rather than scientific: they lack logical foundations, and, like the house of the parable, may be over-turned in a storm. Only mathematics is firmly enough established to be called a science: but if its only use is to satisfy idle curiosity or to perform mechanical functions, it cannot be the desired wisdom. Descartes requires a discipline as well-grounded as mathematics, and as high-reaching as Stoic ethics.

The scholastic philosophy, with the higher disciplines that rely on it, might pretend to meet these opposed criteria, but Descartes is not im-pressed: the most he can say in their praise is that "philosophy gives the means of speaking with probability on all things, and of making oneself admired by the less learned," and that "jurisprudence, medicine, and the other sciences bring honors and wealth to those who cultivate them" (p. 6). Descartes' judgment on the existing philosophy is Ciceronian: "seeing that [philosophy] has been cultivated by the most excellent minds who have lived for many centuries, and that nonetheless there is still nothing in it that is not disputed, and consequently nothing that is not doubtful, I did not have so much presumption as to hope to meet with better success in it than others; and considering how many different opinions there may be concerning one and the same subject, that are maintained by learned people, while there can never be more than one that is true," Descartes decides to "regard everything that was only probable almost as if it were false" (p. 8), and thus to pay no heed to philosophical doctrines.[9]

Descartes accepts the *negative* component of the humanist message. He rejects philosophy for humanist reasons; but he finds the alternative hu-manistic (or Christian) disciplines equally insufficient to teach wisdom. Poetry and eloquence are "spiritual gifts," matters of inspiration, as is the Christian faith; the teachings of *ars poetica* and rhetoric, or of Christian theology, contribute nothing to the end. Following instead the amateur side of humanism, and Montaigne in particular, "I entirely abandoned the study of letters; and resolving to seek no other knowledge [*science*] than what could be found in myself, or else in the great book of the world, I spent the rest of my youth in traveling" (p. 9), to educate his judgment

---

[8] Insensibility, pride, and despair are uncharitable ways of referring to the Stoic *apatheia* and indifference to fortune, which Descartes will turn around and praise in Part Three of the *Discourse*, AT VI,26–7. "Parricide" is even harsher, and may mean something like "unnatural lack of feeling"; or there may be an allusion to Marcus Brutus' participation in the assassination of his rumored father Julius Caesar. See Gilson, *Discours*, pp. 131–2, for discussion.

[9] Further down, on p. 16, Descartes notes that he had learned in school that "one could not imagine anything so strange or so incredible that it has not been said by one of the phi-losophers," which is a direct citation of Cicero (*De Divinatione* II,lviii,119). Descartes intends this citation as a tribute to his humanist education, not as a criticism of his teachers.

through reflection on experience. We are no more likely to find a positive knowledge abroad than at home, but at least we will observe the variability of customs and beliefs, and thus learn to avoid excessive confidence in our own judgments.

Descartes, more intellectually ambitious than Montaigne, was not long satisfied with this merely negative wisdom. As he puts it in the *Discourse*, he turned from studying the book of the world to "studying also in myself, and employing all the forces of my mind in choosing the paths which I should follow" (p. 9). He will take whatever road might lead him to wisdom; but what roads remain to try? Descartes represents his discovery, in the *Discourse* and elsewhere, as a sudden conversion, the work of a single day. There is no reason to doubt that his reflections came to a climactic resolution on the day he mentions, November 10, 1619; but they had long been in preparation. Throughout 1618 and 1619 Descartes had not merely been seeing the world and developing his judgment: he had also been working on mathematical problems. In trying to overcome the separation between science and wisdom, we can only begin from the side of science: Descartes therefore casts himself not as a moralist, still less as a philosopher (except in the etymological sense), but as a mathematician. Mathematics alone is a true science, which might yet be transformed into a scientific wisdom, if we could abstract from it more universal principles applicable not merely to the mechanical arts, but to all the concerns of human wisdom. Thus already in March of 1619 Descartes is writing to his friend Isaac Beeckman that he wishes to propound "an entirely new science, by which in general all questions can be solved that can be proposed in any genus of quantity, continuous as well as discrete" (AT X,156–7). This would be what is called a *mathesis universalis*, a universal mathematics containing the principles common to arithmetic and geometry, such as Viète and others had been trying to develop. This development is internal to mathematics, and would not seem to have any revolutionary impact on the general state of the disciplines; but it is clear from parallel passages that Descartes thought that it would produce a genuinely universal science of wisdom, and that Beeckman was right to summarize Descartes' proposal simply as "a general art for solving all questions" (from Beeckman's marginalia on the letter, AT X,156, note d).

On November 10, 1619, Descartes satisfied himself that he had discovered at least the principles of this art. He describes this discovery in various ways in the fragments of his *Olympica* preserved in Baillet, in the early parts of his half-finished *Rules for the Direction of the Mind*, and in the second part of the *Discourse*. I will not discuss these texts in full detail, but will extract their common elements that describe Descartes' general strategy, as of 1619, for unifying science and wisdom.

The *Olympica* is most dramatic. "On the tenth of November, 1619 . . . I was full of enthusiasm, and had begun to discover the foundations of a marvelous science" (Baillet I,51 = AT X,179). That night, Descartes tells us, he had three dreams, which he was convinced had been divinely sent, and which were accompanied by equally authoritative interpretations. The third of these dreams in particular, with its very elaborate interpretation, serves remarkably well as an emblem for the whole Cartesian project for the sciences as conceived in 1619 and executed in various forms over the next thirty years. As it is not easy to abridge a dream, I translate the relevant pages of Baillet in full.

A moment later he had a third dream, which had nothing terrible in it like the first two. In this last he found a book on his table, without knowing who had put it there. He opened it, and seeing that it was a *Dictionary*, he was much taken with it, in the hope that it could be very useful to him. In the same instant he discovered another book under his hand, which was not new to him, not knowing whence it had come to him. He found that it was an anthology [*recueil*] of Poems of different Authors, entitled *Corpus Poetarum* etc. He was curious to read something there: and upon opening the book he came upon the verse *Quod vitae sectabor iter?* etc. At the same moment he perceived a man whom he did not know, but who presented him with a piece of Verse, beginning with *Est et Non*, and praised it to him as an excellent piece. M. Descartes told him that he knew what it was, and that this piece was among the Idylls of Ausonius which were in the fat Anthology of Poets that was on his table. He wanted to show it himself to this man: and he set himself to leafing through the book, whose order and economy he was confident of knowing perfectly. While he was looking for the passage, the man asked him where he had gotten this book, and M. Descartes answered that he could not tell him how he had come by it: but that a moment earlier he had handled yet another which had just disappeared, without knowing who had brought it to him, or who had taken it away. He had not finished speaking, when he saw the book reappear at the other end of the table. But he found that this *Dictionary* was no longer whole as he had seen it the first time. Meanwhile he came upon the Poems of Ausonius in the Anthology of Poets that he was leafing through: and not being able to find the piece beginning *Est et Non*, he said to the man that he knew another of the same Poet still more beautiful than that one, and that it began with *Quod vitae sectabor iter?* The person begged him to show it to him, and M. Descartes set himself to look for it, when he came on several little portraits engraved in copperplate: which made him say that the book was very beautiful, but that it was not the same edition as the one he knew. There he was, when the books and the man disappeared, and erased themselves from his imagination, without however awakening him. What is singular to remark is that, doubting whether what he had just seen was a dream or a vision, not only did he decide while sleeping that it was a dream, he even made an interpretation of it before sleep left him. He judged that the *Dictionary* meant nothing other than all the Sciences gathered together: and that the Anthology of Poets entitled *Corpus Poetarum* indicated in particular and in a more distinct manner Philosophy and Wisdom joined together. For he did not believe that one should be so astonished to see that the Poets, even those who do nothing but jest, were full of graver, better sensed, and better expressed opinions than those that are found in the writings of the Philosophers. He attributed this marvel to the divinity of Enthusiasm, and to the force of Imagination, which makes the seeds of wisdom (which are found in all men's minds like sparks of fire in stones) come out with much more ease and even with much more brilliance than Reason can in the Philosophers. M. Descartes, continuing to interpret his dream in his sleep, judged that the piece of

Verse on the uncertainty of the way of life that one must choose, which begins *Quod vitae sectabor iter?*, indicated the good advice of a wise person, or even Moral Theology. Thereupon, doubting whether he was dreaming or meditating, he awoke without emotion: and continued with open eyes the interpretation of his dream on the same idea. By the Poets gathered together in the Anthology he understood Revelation and Enthusiasm, with which he did not despair of seeing himself favored. By the piece of verse *Est et Non*, which is the Yes and No of Pythagoras, he understood Truth and Falsehood in human knowledge and the profane sciences. Seeing that the application of all these things would succeed so well on his behalf, he was bold enough to persuade himself that it was the Spirit of Truth who had wished to open the treasures [or treasuries] of all the sciences to him by this dream. And as there remained nothing to explain but the little copperplate portraits that he had found in the second book, he looked for no further explanation after the visit that an Italian Painter paid him the following day. (Baillet I,82–4 = AT X,182–5)[10]

How did Descartes take this dream as revealing, or declaring an intent to reveal, the treasures of all the sciences? We will not find any particular scientific discoveries mystically veiled behind the symbolism of the dream; but, by carefully interpreting Descartes' interpretation, and puttting it alongside texts of the *Discourse* and the *Rules*, we can begin to understand Descartes' vision of the *form* his project for the sciences was to take.

Descartes is to discover the treasures of *all* the sciences. The Dictionary symbolizes "all the Sciences gathered together," and it is because of its completeness that it had so ravished Descartes with "the hope that it could be very useful to him." He had first seen this work on his table, and then seen it vanish and reappear incomplete; Descartes' mission will be to restore this Dictionary, or rather to produce it in reality as he had seen it in the vision. In all the texts deriving from the vocational experience of 1619 – the second part of the *Discourse*, the earliest *Rules*, and the fragments – Descartes takes up this theme of the *unity* of science to be achieved in his projected system of all the sciences. Thus Rule 1 complains that the professors of the existing disciplines have divided the labor of the sciences, making a false analogy with the division of labor in the manual arts: so "distinguishing [the sciences] from one another according to the diversity of their objects, they judged that each of them should be sought by itself, with all the others left out" (AT X,360). But this, says Descartes, is a mistake: for unlike the arts, which demand a particular practice and condition of the body, the sciences consist exclusively in the soul's knowledge [*cognitio*], so that "all the sciences are nothing other than human wisdom, always remaining one and the same, however much it is applied to different subjects, not being any more distinguished on account of these than the sun's light is by the variety of things it illumines" (ibid.). From this Descartes concludes that "there is no need to restrain the mind with

---

[10] Baillet generally admires Descartes, but is critical of the excesses of enthusiasm, and the remark about the Italian painter is editorial ironizing, whether it refers to a real incident or not.

any limits, for neither does the knowledge [*cognitio*] of one truth, like the practice of one art, distract from the discovery of another, but rather it assists" (ibid.). For this reason, a person who seriously wishes to investigate the truth of things is advised not to pursue one particular discipline among others, but rather to cultivate good sense or universal wisdom, which will lead him to achieve greater things in the particular sciences than those who study them in the conventional way can hope for (ibid.).

Science will be unitary because good sense is unitary. This good sense, according to the first sentence of the *Discourse*, is "the best-shared thing in the world," with which everyone is equally endowed, but which not everyone applies equally well.[11] When Descartes identifies good sense with the universal wisdom that is applied to particular subjects to produce the particular sciences, he is thinking not of wisdom in the strict sense, which could be achieved only by the successful completion of the scientific project, but of the "seeds of wisdom" he had envisioned in his dream, pre-existing in each human mind like sparks of fire in stones, and waiting to be educed into actual wisdom. These seeds of wisdom (or of truth or virtue) are a Stoic commonplace to which Descartes helps himself freely in explaining the contrast between the poets and the philosophers: there are "grave sentences in the writings of the poets more than in those of the philosophers," because "the poets wrote through enthusiasm and the power of imagination: there are in us seeds of knowledge, as in a flint, which are educed through reason by the philosophers, [but] are shaken out through imagination by the poets, and shine more brightly."[12] But the poets, being wise at random, are unable to plan their wisdom before or to explain it after; so that it becomes the task of the philosopher to extract methodically from the innate powers of the human mind what the poets extract unmethodically and as the inspiration seizes them. If the philosopher has really completed this task, he will be able, not merely to discover the truths of the particular scientific disciplines, but also to produce moral apophthegmata with all the ease and brilliance of the poets, but generated and justified according to a rational method. This conjunction of the two ideals, "Philosophy and Wisdom joined together," is symbolized in the *Corpus Poetarum* of the dream. In the notes called *Cogitationes Privatae* written about this time, Descartes declares that "the sayings of the sages can be reduced to some few general rules" (AT X,217): once we master the rules for working out the seeds of wisdom, the Stoic praise of virtue will appear no longer as a paradoxical higher wisdom, but as the straightforward application of our natural knowledge to the conduct of our life.

Descartes devotes the second part of the *Discourse* to describing his

---

[11] This is a commonplace, although Descartes is putting it to a new use; see Gilson, *Discours*, pp. 81–4, and below, Chapter 7, Section A. Gilson has useful comments on the histories of the French phrase "*bon sens*" and of the Latin phrase "*bona mens*."

[12] I am quoting here from Descartes' *Cogitationes Privatae*, AT X,217; Baillet seems to have interpolated this passage from the *Cogitationes Privatae* into the *Olympica* to help in explicating Descartes' interpretation of the dream.

31

meditations, on a day that must have been November 10, 1619, on "choosing what roads I should follow" (AT VI,10), and also on the right method for developing our inborn seeds of wisdom. Descartes here presents his thoughts as a fresh start, uninfluenced by anything he had read or seen: he does not mention the dreams or the poem of Ausonius whose phrase "what road of life shall I follow?" he is echoing; nor does he mention what was certainly the crucial text for his thoughts that day on the errors of received opinion and the problem of extracting the seeds of wisdom. It is from Cicero's *Tusculan Disputations* III,i,2:

If nature had brought us forth such that we could contemplate and observe her, and complete the course of life with herself as the best of guides, then surely it would hardly have come about that anyone should need argument and instruction. But as it is, she has given us [only] little sparks, which, depraved by bad habits and opinions, we rapidly extinguish so that the light of nature is nowhere visible. For there are seeds of the virtues inborn in our mind, and if they were permitted to mature, nature herself would lead us through to the happy life; now, however, as soon as we are brought forth into the light and have been picked up, immediately we are plunged in all depravity and in the highest perversity of opinions, so that we seem to have sucked up error almost with our nurse's milk. But when we are returned to our parents, and then handed over to teachers, then we are steeped in such various errors that truth gives place to vanity, and nature herself to confirmed opinion.

Reflecting on this text, Descartes considers that "often there is not as much perfection in works composed of many pieces, and made by the hand of several masters, than in those on which only one has labored" (VI,11). The "work of many pieces" that Descartes is thinking of is the body of our received opinions, and specifically the received system of the sciences. Descartes begins by giving some innocent practical examples from architecture and legislation, but the value of these examples is as analogies to support Descartes' analysis of what is wrong with the present condition of the sciences.

Descartes first observes that "buildings that a single architect has undertaken and completed are generally more beautiful and better ordered than those that several architects have tried to patch up, making use of old walls that had been built for other purposes. Thus those ancient cities which, having been at the beginning only little towns, became great cities in the course of time, are ordinarily very badly laid out, compared to those well-ordered towns that an engineer lays out on a plain according to his fancy" (p. 11). There is no want of skill on the part of the architects who have labored over the ancient cities; the faults arise because these architects are constrained to place their work within the plan constructed by their predecessors, trying to extend for new purposes a work that was adequate only for uses on a smaller scale. Because of this diversity of purpose between the older and the newer builders, the city as a whole will lack rational order, and its streets will become "crooked and uneven," so as to appear the result of chance rather than of "the will of men using their reason." Realizing that the greatest skill and the best intentions have been able to do no better than this, "one will well understand that it is not easy, while laboring only on the works of others, to make things fully accomplished" (p. 12). Descartes draws similar inferences from legislation: it is better for the laws of a city to be decreed by a single legislator, like those of Sparta according to legend, than to evolve over the centuries like the common laws of England, new rules and institutions being created piecemeal to resolve new disputes. Only the former are genuinely the work of reason, while the latter arise chiefly from the obduracy and quarrelsomeness that generate fresh disputes. Here too a framework for human activity can be effective only if it is created by some one person with a rational master plan, and not simply through an accretion of reactions to circumstances, without a rethinking of principles.

But the sciences, and our opinions generally, are just such accretions:

And thus I thought that the sciences of the books, at least those whose reasons are merely probable, and which have no demonstrations, having been put together and enlarged bit by bit by the opinions of many different people, do not approach the truth so well as the simple reasonings that a man of good sense can naturally make concerning the things that present themselves to him. And thus again I thought that, because we have all been children before being men, and had for a long time to be governed by our appetites and by our teachers [*précepteurs*], which were often contrary to one another, and neither of which perhaps always counseled us best, it is almost impossible for our judgments to be as pure or as solid as they would have been if we had had the full use of our reason from the point of our birth and if we had never been led except by it. (Pp. 12–13)

The reflections on our childhood and on our teachers come directly from the Cicero text: if we had been able from birth to develop the seeds of wisdom that are within us, then all of us would have discovered wisdom on our own, and would be able to lead our lives in accordance with this wisdom. But as it is, we are born into a condition of dependency, so that we are forced by practical necessity to follow the inclinations of our bodily nature and the judgments of those in authority over us. However, our teachers are in no better condition than ourselves: they too have begun by accepting the conclusions of their appetites and of their teachers, and have developed their mature views by a process of modifications and additions to this base. In this way a whole series of teachers may generate a traditional body of doctrine, which will not be a true science developed from the seeds of wisdom, but merely an elaboration of childish prejudice. What is ultimately wrong with the scholastic teachers is not just that they corrupt the children and smother their natural light, but that they have not outgrown childhood themselves, having merely systematized their childish beliefs without rethinking them from the beginning.[13]

---

[13] Although Descartes is drawing his account of our childish condition from Cicero's Stoicizing description, he is reading Cicero through the Platonist and Christian filters imposed

If the traditional sciences are as bad as that, it will be very difficult to construct genuine scientific knowledge "while laboring only on the works of others." The alternative would be to begin again, like an engineer constructing a city on a plain. "It is true that we do not see people knocking down all the houses of a city, with the sole purpose of remaking them in another fashion, and so making the streets more beautiful; but one does see that many people pull down their own houses in order to rebuild them, and that sometimes they are compelled to do so, when they are in danger of falling of themselves, and their foundations are unsound" (p. 13). Thus while Descartes sincerely disclaims the intention of reforming the state, and is willing at least to defer any attempt to "reform the body of the sciences or the order established in the schools for teaching them," he decides that

for all the opinions that I had accepted up till then into my belief, I could not do better than to banish them once for all, in order that later I might establish either others in their place, or even the same ones again, once I had corrected them by the rule of reason [les ajustées au niveau de la raison];[14] and I firmly believed that by this means I would succeed in conducting my life much better than if I had built only on old foundations, and if I had relied only on principles of which I had allowed myself to be persuaded in my youth, without ever having examined whether they were true. (Pp. 13–14)

In order to achieve the wisdom that he had missed the first time around, Descartes will undo what he has learned in his childhood, and repeat this process of learning again, learning as he would have learned had he been born self-sufficient, by developing his innate rational powers. In the terms of the architectural metaphor, Descartes finds it necessary to clear a space if he will rebuild, to rid himself of his old opinions so that they will not be in the way when he constructs new opinions on the same subjects. Besides knocking down the old house, he will have to "provide for materials and architects or practice in architecture himself, and furthermore to carefully lay out the floor plan," and also to "provide himself with some other [home], where he can be comfortably lodged while he is working [on the house]" (p. 22), that is, to prescribe for himself a set of practical rules, preserving his religious and moral and pragmatic opinions as a guide to action, while the rest of his opinions are being destroyed. In this way he will guarantee for himself the safety and independence he had not had as a child, so that he can develop his thoughts in peace, without worrying about practical necessities. In accepting this provisional code of morals without scientific knowledge that it is right, Descartes is in agreement with the humanists, and indeed he follows Montaigne and others in some details of his code; but for Descartes this is to be only a temporary

by Augustine. I will discuss Descartes' description of childhood at more length in Chapter 7, Section A, and again briefly in Chapter 8, Section C.

14 See Gilson, *Discours*, p. 172, for a discussion of Descartes' meaning.

34

shelter, until he is able to construct a practical wisdom on a scientific basis.[15]

Descartes gives in the *Rules for the Direction of the Mind* (or rather of the *ingenium*, the innate power, equivalent to good sense or to the seeds of wisdom), and again briefly in Part Two of the *Discourse*, his rules for systematically extracting the seeds of truth. Considered as a system of formal logic, these rules are simple and almost banal; what is important is the way they are applied. As Descartes says, "the multitude of the laws often provides excuses for the vices, so that a state is better ordered when, having very few laws, these are very strictly observed" (p. 18); thus he will take a few simple rules, not as an ideal of a perfected science, but as a charter for actually reconstructing the sciences from the ground up. Descartes proposes to accept into his science only those things that he clearly perceives to be true, omitting anything that he could ever have occasion to doubt. All questions of any practical interest are, in themselves, subject to doubt; so that if we wish to gain scientific knowledge of these things, we must begin by reducing them analytically to the simpler questions that they presuppose. Once we have collected the fundamental intuitions of all the simplest objects, bringing out the primitive seeds of truth implanted in human nature, we can proceed to derive synthetically, step by step, a knowledge of more complex things, until finally we arrive at matters of practical interest. These rules are empty in themselves: the concrete meaning of the method depends on which fundamental intuitions we select as the basis for constructing the scientific system. Indeed, Descartes changes his mind about this: where in 1619 and in the earlier *Rules* he took as his fundamental science a universal mathematics based on the intuition of quantity, he substitutes in later works the fundamental intuitions of psychology and metaphysics. But in all stages of Descartes' thought, the process of construction begins with simple and obvious truths of no practical interest, and proceeds from these to the questions that are the subject matter of wisdom. Descartes' problem in advertising his method will therefore be to persuade people to take an interest in obvious truths.

In the second Rule, after setting out the program of trusting only in perfect and indubitable *cognitiones*,[16] Descartes criticizes the learned people, the *litterati*, who despise obvious truths:

Although perhaps the men of letters will convince themselves that very few such *cognitiones* exist, evidently because, by a common failing of the human race, they

---

[15] See below, Chapter 7, Section B, for a discussion of the significance of the provisional morals for Descartes' project.

[16] The Latin word "*cognitio*" is close in meaning to the English "knowledge," but unlike "knowledge" it has a plural; I will therefore keep the word in the original, and I will use it, from time to time, as a technical term. I will also sometimes use *cognitio*, in an English context, to render the French "*connaissance*."

have neglected to reflect on such *cognitiones*, as too easy and obvious to everyone; however, I advise them that there are far more than they think, and that these suffice for demonstrating with certainty innumerable propositions that they have hitherto been able to discuss only with probability. And because they thought it unworthy for a man of letters to confess that he does not know something, they have so accustomed themselves to prepare their fictitious reasons, that afterwards they gradually persuaded themselves, and thus advertised them as true [or in place of the true ones]. (AT X,362–3)

Again, in Rule 1, he warns against the various interests that might distract us from the cultivation of universal wisdom: he emphasizes that he is speaking not of interests that are "perverse and blameworthy," but "even of ones that are honorable and praiseworthy, for by these we are deceived more subtly: as if we should seek those sciences that are useful for the good things of life, or for the pleasure that is found in the contemplation of the truth, which is almost the only happiness that remains whole and untroubled by sadness in this life" (p. 361). Descartes agrees that "we can expect these things as legitimate fruits of the sciences; but if we think about them in our studies, they often bring it about that we leave out many things that are necessary for the knowledge of other things, because at first sight these appear either of little use or of little interest" (ibid.). This is a direct attack upon the humanists, who would have us ignore such disciplines as arithmetic and geometry on the grounds that they contribute nothing toward a happy and virtuous life. If Descartes is to persuade such people to follow him on his way to wisdom, he must show them that obvious truths are more interesting than they think, that the sciences they have dismissed contain the grounds for the wisdom they are seeking. Descartes is ready to agree that the sciences in their present state contain little genuine knowledge beyond obvious truths with no practical use; but he wants to argue that this *need* not be the case, that if we attentively consider the obvious truths that we now have, we will be able to derive a further knowledge that will be non-trivial and useful, and thus achieve a wisdom supported on something better than the probable syllogisms of the scholastics and the rhetorical exhortations of the humanists.

To support his project of deriving an interesting knowledge from obvious truths, Descartes appeals to the geometers as a counter-model to the humanists and scholastics. Descartes' interest is not in geometry as such, at least not to the extent that geometry relies upon sensible representations of quantities; but he takes the geometers as his standard in demonstrations, respecting not merely their rigor, but also their economy in the use of premises, their ability to extract the full wealth of consequences from truths that are evident of themselves or have become evident in the course of demonstration.[17] This quality of the geometers is something Baillet

---

[17] "These long chains of reasons, very simple and easy, which the geometers commonly make use of to arrive at their most difficult demonstrations, gave me occasion to imagine that all the things that can fall under human knowledge might follow one another in the same

praises most highly in Descartes himself: "never did a man show to a higher degree than M. Descartes what we call the *geometric spirit* and *justness of spirit*, so as not to confuse the principles among themselves, to penetrate all the consequences that it was possible to draw from them, and never to reason falsely on known principles" (Baillet II,476–7). Even after Descartes has decided that the fundamental science is not a science of quantity at all, he still considers his own practice in mathematics to be the best training for philosophical work, and he urges his readers to follow him: they should learn the logic that "teaches how to conduct one's reason rightly for discovering the truths of which one is ignorant," not by reading scholastic textbooks of logic, but chiefly by "exercising oneself for a long time in practicing its rules concerning easy and simple questions like those of mathematics" (preface to the French translation of the *Principles of Philosophy*, AT IX2,13–14, following Descartes' account of his own practice in Part Two of the *Discourse*). He publishes his own *Geometry* in order "to demonstrate that I had found many things that had previously been unknown, and thus to give occasion to believe that one might yet discover many more, in order by this means to encourage all men to the search for truth" (AT IX2,15–16). If Descartes can introduce this geometric spirit into philosophy, collecting the first principles of knowledge and methodically extracting the consequences, resisting the temptation to jump ahead to matters not yet understood, then perhaps he, or others following him, might succeed in extending scientific philosophy until it becomes a true wisdom, completing the encyclopedia of the sciences so that without losing its order and reliability it becomes a new and rationalized *Corpus Poetarum*. As Descartes prophesies in the *Cogitationes Privatae*: "the sciences now are under masks; when the masks are taken away, they will appear most beautiful. To someone who discerns the chain of the sciences, they will seem no more difficult to hold in the mind than the series of numbers" (AT X,215).

If we look ahead to Descartes' mature, published writings, we can see that he is still very much concerned to present his program of exploiting first principles as an alternative means to the humanist goal of practical wisdom. Indeed this is one of his main reasons for publishing. In the sixth part of the *Discourse on the Method* Descartes says that he would not have published simply to share his discoveries about problems of the speculative sciences (he means mathematics), or his provisional code of morals; but he has also made discoveries in physics, which he thinks could lead "to *cognitiones* that would be very useful for life, and in place of the *speculative* philosophy that is taught in the schools . . . [to] a *practical* philosophy," which would enable us to comprehend and to control the forces

---

way, and that, provided only that one abstains from accepting any of them as true which is not, and that one keeps always to the order that is necessary for deducing some of them from others, then there can be none so remote that one cannot finally arrive at them, or so hidden that one cannot uncover them" (*Discourse on the Method*, Part Two, AT VI,19).

of nature, not merely in order to devise machines through which "one would enjoy without any trouble the fruits of the earth and all the good things that are in it," but "also and principally for the conservation of health, which is without doubt the primary good and the foundation of all other goods of this life" (AT VI,61–2). Descartes decides to publish because, "intending to spend my whole life in the search for so necessary a science, and having found a path [that should lead] infallibly to finding it," and unsure that he will have the time and resources himself to pursue this path to its end, he wishes to appeal to the *"bons esprits"* to take up and complete his work (p. 63). Descartes feels that he has a difficult case to make, that the jury will be prejudiced against him; he attempts, through the apologetic autobiography of the *Discourse*, and through the *Essays* as samples of his achievement, to overcome this prejudice and win them to his cause.

Descartes gives the fullest apology for his philosophy in the *Letter to the Translator* which serves as a preface to the French translation of the *Principles of Philosophy*.[18] Here, as in the *Discourse*, Descartes is appealing to the *bons esprits* of his time; and he is concerned that "most of the best minds [*la pluspart des meilleurs esprits*] have conceived such a bad opinion of all philosophy, because of the faults they have noticed in the philosophy that has been current up till now, that they will be unable to apply themselves to searching for a better one" (AT IX2,20). He therefore hopes to show them "the difference . . . between these principles [i.e. those of Descartes' philosophy] and all those of others, and the great series of truths that can be deduced from them" (ibid.). The whole book *Principles of Philosophy* is an attempt to display the advantages of Descartes' principles, and so to win the humanists back to philosophy as he understands it; the preface sets out Descartes' claims in outline.

Descartes begins by declaring the subject of the book, which is philosophy and its principles. Philosophy is not wisdom itself, but the love or the study of wisdom; by considering the criteria that this wisdom must satisfy, we can understand how to pursue it. "By 'wisdom' is understood not only prudence in one's affairs, but a perfect knowledge of all the things man can know, for the conduct of his life as well as for the preservation of his health and the discovery of all the arts" (AT IX2,2): that is, the sciences of mechanics and medicine envisaged in Part Six of the *Discourse*, and the scientific morals that Descartes has long desired. But for this wisdom to be a perfect knowledge, and not a mere ungrounded supposition, it must proceed from first causes; it therefore follows that the first step philosophy can take in the direction of wisdom is the "search for these first causes, that is, for principles" (ibid.). These principles or first causes of things are equally the principles of philosophy, since at every stage of the project our conclusions will be derived from them; and since

---

[18] I will refer to this *Letter to the Translator* for short as the *Letter to Picot*, since Abbé Claude Picot was the translator in question.

the purpose of the book is simply to set these forth, it is reasonably entitled *Principles of Philosophy*.

But how is the reader to know that Descartes' assertions, rather than those of other philosophers, are genuinely principles of this nature? "These principles must have two conditions: one, that they are so clear and so evident that the human mind cannot doubt of their truth when it applies its attention to consider them; the other, that it is on them that the knowledge of other things depends, so that they may be known without the other things, but not conversely" (ibid.). So in order to show that "the true principles by which one can arrive at that highest degree of wisdom, in which the sovereign good of human life consists, are the ones I have put in this book" (p. 9), Descartes must prove two things, both that the principles are supremely clear (and, therefore, true), and also that they are sources of the knowledge of other things. Descartes finds it much easier to prove the first of these claims, and that in two ways. In the first place, the principles have been selected as those beliefs which can survive the rejection of anything I have the least occasion to doubt: they are the ideas I cannot but assent to when I consider them attentively, and are thus as clear as any I could hope to know. Descartes also feels free to appeal to the *consensus gentium*: the clarity, as well as the truth, of his principles is shown by the fact that "they have been known for all time, and indeed accepted as true and indubitable by all men, excepting only the existence of God, which some have put in doubt, because they have attributed too much to sense perception, and because God cannot be seen or touched" (p. 10). But Descartes is so untroubled by these few doubters that he assumes his readers will grant, not only that his principles are true, but also that they are entirely clear. What Descartes has to tell his readers that they do not already know, and that it will be difficult to convince them of, is not that his principles are true, but that they are principles of other truths: "although all the truths that I put among my principles have always been known to everyone, there has nevertheless been no one up to now, as far as I know, who has recognized them as principles of philosophy, that is to say, as such that one can deduce from them the knowledge of all the other things that are in the world" (pp. 10–11). And Descartes undertakes to show just this, that is, to exhibit the principles as principles, by deriving from them in the body of the book consequences bearing on as wide a range of questions as he can.

These passages make very clear the nature of Descartes' conflict with the sceptical humanism of his time. He is not especially concerned to establish our knowledge of the basic truths of philosophy against the few sceptics or atheists who might deny them;[19] he is concerned rather to

---

[19] Descartes speaks dismissively of scepticism at AT IX2,7, commenting that "the error of those who inclined too much to the side of doubt was not followed for long"; there are more dangerous and more seductive errors which it is more urgent to refute. For a fuller discussion of Descartes' attitude toward scepticism, see below, Chapter 5; in a note to

show, against humanist suspicions, the fecundity of this knowledge for the derivation of practical consequences. Descartes' principles are generally agreed, and are as clear as any principles could hope to be; he does not stop to consider the sceptical critique of the idea of self-evidence (as seen in the "five tropes" and "two tropes" of Sextus Empiricus, *Outlines of Pyrrhonism*, I,xv–xvi) or the thesis of Sanchez *quod nihil scitur*. Descartes' concern is rather to advertise his brand of wisdom, to show its superiority to the humanist alternative as displayed in Charron's *De la sagesse*, and to overcome the prejudice that the humanists had stirred up against the scientific path to wisdom.

The *Principles* in their French translation are (among other things) Descartes' answer to the *De la sagesse*. Charron too had begun by clarifying in his preface the sense in which he intended to treat of "wisdom":

Now from the beginning we advertise that we do not here take this word subtly, in the lofty and elevated sense of the theologians and philosophers (who take pleasure in describing and picturing things that have never yet been seen and heightening them to a perfection of which human nature does not find itself capable except in imagination) for a perfect knowledge of things divine and human, or even of the first and highest causes and principles of all things.[20]

Such a wisdom, says Charron, is almost impossible to attain; and even after it has been attained it is useless, inactive, and private unless supplemented by other virtues. The wisdom we should seek will be neither an abstract knowledge, nor a mere prudence in one's external conduct, but right practical thought together with the right action that proceeds from it. Wisdom therefore "consists in two things: to know oneself well, and constantly to be well ruled and moderated in all things by all things,"[21] and Charron proceeds to deal in turn with each of the departments of self-knowledge and then of self-rule. Since Charron, unlike Descartes, does not consider the knowledge of the series of the causes of things to be an essential constituent of wisdom, he has no need to follow an order of reasons in his approach to wisdom. Descartes begins his progress toward a perfect ethics in the *Principles* by discussing the principles of human knowledge and of material things, the visible universe and the earth; but Charron does not expect to make science serviceable to wisdom, and so he dispenses with these preliminaries. He proceeds instead according to the order of matters, subdividing each topic in turn, and assigning to each heading a well-formulated maxim, supported not by argument but by rhetorical expansion, with historical illustrations and quotes from the classical

---

Chapter 5, Section B, I discuss the particular question of whether the sceptics are extinct (as Descartes affirms at AT IX2,7, and denies at AT VII,548–50).

[20] Pierre Charron, *De la sagesse* (Paris: Fayard, 1986), pp. 25–6. This is the text of the first edition of 1601; in the revised edition, published posthumously in 1604, Charron – or his editors – takes a more moderate tone, and speaks less sarcastically about the higher species of wisdom. But Charron meant what he said in the first edition.

[21] Charron, p. 28.

authorities on moral subjects. Indeed, as Charron describes his own method, "I have searched here and there, and drawn the greater part of the materials of this work from the best authors who have treated this moral and political matter, true knowledge of man, the ancient – especially Seneca and Plutarch, great teachers in this – as well as the modern. It is the assemblage [*recueil*] of a portion of my studies; the form and the order are mine";[22] and again, "I have strewn about some Latin *sententiae*, but short, strong, and poetic, drawn from very good sources."[23]

Charron's *Sagesse* is thus a *recueil* much like the *Corpus Poetarum* of Descartes' dream, before Descartes appeared to reconstruct it on rational principles. Charron's poetic maxims are far from encouraging the development of the sciences. Indeed, he examines science only once in the *Sagesse*, in discussing the duty of parents to educate their children; and this becomes the occasion for an extended rhetorical comparison between science and wisdom, entirely to the benefit of the latter and the embarrassment of the former. Charron begins by discussing the aim of education, which is to form the mind; and he distinguishes the various components within the mind, of which judgment is the chief. The formation of judgment ought consequently to be the chief goal of education; but instead, thinks Charron, the education that most parents procure for their children, namely education in the arts and the sciences, develops the memory instead. Charron takes it for granted that science is concerned with memory, and wisdom with judgment; he argues only about which is to be preferred.

But "what more egregious madness [is there] in the world than to admire science, what is acquired, memory, more than wisdom and what is natural?"

Now, all do not commit this fault in the same spirit: some simply led by custom, thinking that wisdom and science are not very different things, or at least that they always go together, that it is necessary to have one to have the other; these deserve to be corrected and taught; the others do it out of malice, and know well what comes of it: but they want art and science at any price, for it is a means in western Europe now of acquiring fame, reputation, wealth. These people make of science a trade and a merchandise, a mercenary, pedantic, sordid, and mechanic science: they buy science to sell it back later. Let us leave these salesmen as incurable.[24]

To convince the others, Charron must show two things:

one, that science and wisdom are very different things, and that wisdom is worth more than all the science in the world, as heaven is worth more than all the earth, and gold than iron; the other, that not only are they different, but that they almost never go together, that they exclude each other ordinarily: who is very learned [*savant*] is hardly wise, and who is wise is not learned. Indeed there are some

---

[22] Charron, pp. 33–4.
[23] Charron, p. 36.
[24] Charron, p. 686.

exceptions to this, but they are quite rare. These are great, rich, fortunate souls. There were some in antiquity, but they are hardly to be found today.[25]

Charron goes on to prove this point at considerable length. He gives definitions, or rather contrasting characterizations, of science and wisdom; he lists with great thoroughness all the unsavory accompaniments of science; he separates the temperament of science from that of wisdom. The most logical strand of Charron's objection to science may be extracted from his maxim that "science is a small and sterile good at the expense of wisdom."[26] The first thing wrong with science is that it is useless: it makes life neither pleasanter nor morally better, as is shown from historical examples. Science is still a good, and not an evil in itself; but it is not acquired without great pains, or without the devotion of energies that could have been spent in the pursuit of wisdom. From this a second objection arises. The acquisition of science detracts from the development of wisdom. They require different temperaments, or, in modern jargon, different values. The devotees of science are memorizers, compilers; this renders them dependent on other people's accomplishments instead of on their own good qualities, making them both servile and proud, when they should be self-sufficient and modest. Thus science, though not itself bad, tends to make its followers bad; except under extraordinary conditions, and for an extraordinary soul, it is incompatible with wisdom.

Descartes, appealing to Charron's audience, finds himself described as a salesman of science, who for self-interested motives misrepresents his product as a means to wisdom. Descartes agrees with Charron that most existing sciences are matters of memory, dulling the natural light; this makes his own position all the more difficult in presenting his yet-to-be-achieved new science as the genuine wisdom. Here in the *Letter to Picot* Descartes makes many of the same points that he had made in the *Rules* and *Discourse* to justify beginning the study of wisdom with obvious common notions; but he is forced to make his appeal in more vivid terms. This is the meaning of Descartes' famous image of the tree of the sciences: "all philosophy is like a tree; of which the roots are metaphysics, the trunk is physics, and the branches that come out of this trunk are all the other sciences, which reduce to three principal ones, namely, medicine, mechanics, and morals, I mean the highest and most perfect morals which, presupposing a complete knowledge of the other sciences, is the last degree of wisdom" (AT IX2,14). The point of the simile is that "as it is not from the roots or the trunk of trees that one gathers the fruits, but only from the extremities of their branches, so the principal utility of philosophy depends on those of its parts which can only be learned last" (p. 15); so we must begin with the roots, and methodically work our way upward, not impatiently demanding the fruits before we have reached the highest branches. After completing the preliminary training in logic described in

[25] Charron, p. 687.
[26] Charron, p. 687.

the second part of the *Discourse*, and forming a provisional code of morals as in the third part of the *Discourse*, the student of wisdom should begin to "apply himself to true philosophy" (p. 14). He will begin at the roots, with "metaphysics, which contains the principles of knowledge, among which is the explication of the principal attributes of God, of the immortality of our souls, and of all the clear and simple notions that are in us" (ibid.). Earlier in the *Letter to Picot* Descartes had listed his metaphysical principles, in order to show by exhaustive enumeration that he had made use of only the simplest and best-known truths: these are the existence of the thinking soul, and the existence of "a God who is the author of everything that exists in the world, and who, being the source of all truth, has not created our understanding of such a nature that it could be deceived in the judgment it makes of things of which it has a very clear and very distinct perception" (p. 10). From these roots of the tree we ascend to the trunk, to physics, and firstly to "finding the true principles of physical things" (p. 14), which are merely "that there are bodies extended in length, breadth, and depth, having various figures and moved in various ways" (p. 10). This principle Descartes derives from his metaphysical principles, and "behold, in sum, all the principles from which I have deduced the truth of other things" (p. 10)! From these few principles of metaphysics and physics we may go on to "examine in general how the whole universe is composed, then in particular what is the nature of this earth and of all the bodies that are found most commonly around it, like air, water and fire, and of the magnet and other minerals" (p. 14). This much Descartes undertakes to do in the *Principles*. After that, if we are to ascend from these purely theoretical disciplines to the useful sciences of medicine, mechanics, and morals, we will need also to "examine in particular the nature of plants, that of animals, and above all that of man" (p. 14), using only the principles of general physics. Descartes cannot do this himself, for he has been unable to raise the funds to "perform all the experiments that I would need in order to support and justify my reasonings" (p. 17). But he will give, in the *Principles of Philosophy*, a demonstration of the unsuspected fertility of the clearest and most universally recognized principles concerning physical and metaphysical things; and he hopes that his successors, bolstered by his positive results, will be able to overcome the widespread suspicion of scientific philosophy (and thus to secure the necessary patronage) and carry his project through to completion.

C. Descartes: Augustine against Aristotle

The *Letter to Picot* gives a programmatic statement of two different aspects of Descartes' philosophical project. It restates Descartes' vision, constant since 1619, of a fundamental science developed into a scientific wisdom; but it also declares that the fundamental science will be a knowledge of God and the soul, and that God and the soul are the most

43

knowable of all things. This is not how Descartes had envisaged the fundamental science in 1619, but only since the second great turning-point of his thought, in 1628.[27] The vocational texts of 1619 are silent about what our fundamental intuitions of simples will be intuitions *of*, and thus about what the fundamental science will be; but we know that Descartes had first intended it to be universal mathematics (a general science of quantity), and that he had tried out other possibilities before turning in 1628 to metaphysics.[28] The principles of metaphysics, as Descartes states them in the preface to the *Principles*, are that God is the creator of all beings and the source of all truth, and that the human soul is immortal and separable from the body. These principles, Descartes declares, are both evident in themselves and witnessed by universal consensus; what is new and surprising is that they have implications for general physics and for the particular sciences.

The principles concerning God and the soul are *metaphysical* principles because they concern "immaterial or metaphysical things" (AT IX2,10); and the scholastic Aristotelian tradition, which had invented the word "metaphysics," does admit this as one way (though not the most usual) of defining the scope of metaphysics. But Descartes' principles do not have their origin in scholastic metaphysics: they are rather the Augustinian doctrines of God and soul, which had become accepted as axioms of Christian philosophy, and which the major Christian Aristotelian schools had therefore grafted into Aristotle's metaphysics. The principles of Aristotle's metaphysics are obscure; their meaning is contested by those within the school, and their truth by those outside it; nothing stable could be built upon them. Descartes represents Augustine's doctrines of God and soul, by contrast, as matters of universal agreement, and suitable first principles for philosophy.

It is not, as Descartes assumes, a matter of universal consensus that God created the world, or that the human soul is immortal. But from Descartes' perspective, at the height of the French Counter-Reformation, the oversimplification seemed innocent enough. Everyone in view, except the shadowy background figures of the libertines, is committed to believing these truths. They are as widely known as the axioms of universal mathematics, and as little regarded. In this latest as in the earliest form of his project, Descartes must persuade his readers to reflect on these matters of common knowledge, and to take them seriously as principles of philosophy.

Descartes' attempt to satisfy the humanist aspiration for wisdom here intersects the Counter-Reformation expectation of a Christian philosophy, based integrally on Augustine and without appeal to Aristotle. When Descartes chose metaphysics as his fundamental science, he was answering the call of the Catholic reformers to take up Augustine's method of reflection

---

[27] Compare the beginning of Section B above.
[28] I offer a rough reconstruction of this development in Chapter 5, Section A, below.

on soul and God, and to make it the basis for thought; when Descartes claims to derive from this reflection a new system of philosophy to replace that of Aristotle, he is putting himself forward as the philosopher of the Catholic Reformation.

At the end of the second part of the *Discourse on Method*, after recounting his programmatic reflections of 1619, Descartes describes his policy in the following period: feeling himself too young at twenty-three to establish anything certain in philosophy, he devoted himself instead "to preparing myself, by rooting out of my mind all the bad opinions that I had accepted before that time, as well as by making a collection of many experiences [or experiments] that might afterwards be the matter of my reasonings, and by exercising myself constantly in the method I had prescribed for myself, in order to strengthen myself in it more and more" (AT VI,22). In the third part of the *Discourse*, after setting out his rules for practical conduct, he tells us that he had spent nine years as he had resolved, traveling and observing the "comedies" of the world, discovering and eliminating the roots of error, gathering experience, exercising himself in the method, spending several hours a day applying the method "in difficulties of mathematics, or in some others that I could assimilate to those of mathematics by detaching them from the principles of the other sciences, which I did not find sufficiently firm" (p. 29). Thus "these nine years passed before I had yet taken any position concerning the difficulties that are customarily disputed among the learned, or begun to search for the foundations of any philosophy more certain than the usual one" (p. 30). What then made Descartes decide to construct a philosophy for himself?

Descartes gives an explanation at the end of Part Three of the *Discourse*, but this explanation, though not false, is not revealing: it is indeed a standard rhetorical explanation for why one has undertaken a seemingly arrogant project. Descartes tells us that he might not have ventured where so many "excellent minds" had failed, had he not heard a rumor that he had already succeeded, whereupon, "having a good enough heart that I did not want to be taken for something other than what I was, I thought that I should try by all means to make myself worthy of the reputation that I had been given" (pp. 30–1). For this reason, says Descartes, he has retired to Holland, where, removed from all private and public demands, he has been able to enjoy a solitary life for eight years at the time of writing, and to devote himself to the construction of a new philosophy.

Other sources confirm that around 1628 there was such a turning-point in Descartes' life; and they give us some better information on the events that led up to it. In the dedicatory letter to the *Meditations on First Philosophy* of 1641, which contain his first full exposition of his science of God and the soul, Descartes explains the motives that have led him to undertake the work. He begins by showing the utility to the Christian religion of sound demonstrations for the existence of God and the separability of the soul, which leads him to judge that "nothing could be more

45

useful in philosophy than if the best of all [such demonstrations] were once carefully sought out, and so clearly and accurately set out that it would thenceforth be publicly established that they are demonstrations" (AT VII,3). He then adds a special reason why he personally feels called to take up this task:

Since some persons [*nonnulli*] to whom it was known that I had cultivated a certain method for resolving any difficulties in the sciences – not a new [method], for nothing is older than the truth, but one they had often seen me use with some success in other matters – demanded this of me in the strongest terms [*hoc a me summopere flagitarunt*; the French has merely *ont desiré cela de moi*, but Descartes' language is very strong: *flagitare* suggests measures to collect a debt, or a legal subpoena], I therefore thought that it was my duty to attempt something in this matter. (Ibid.)

While this too might look like a mere rhetorical flourish, by sheer good fortune we know that it refers to a definite historical incident.

Baillet preserves the story of Descartes, Chandoux, and Bérulle. Toward the end of 1628, Descartes was in Paris.[29] There he attended

an assembly of learned and inquiring persons at the residence of the Papal Nuncio, who had wished to gather listeners of importance for le sieur de Chandoux, who was supposed to deliver some new opinions on philosophy. Chandoux was a man of spirit, who made a profession of medicine, and practiced chemistry in particular. He was one of those free spirits who appeared in great numbers in the time of Cardinal Richelieu, and who undertook to shake off the yoke of scholasticism. He had no less aversion to the philosophy of Aristotle or of the Peripatetics than did a Bacon, a Mersenne, a Gassendi, a Hobbes. The others might have more capacity, more force, more breadth of mind: but he had no less courage and resolution than they for clearing a new path, and doing without a guide in the search for the principles of a new philosophy. He had predisposed in his favor the minds of many persons of respect: and the talent he had for explaining himself with much boldness and much grace had gained him great access among the great, whom he was accustomed to dazzle by the pompous appearance of his reasonings. (Baillet I,160)

Chandoux had for some time been promising to reveal the principles of a new philosophy, which he claimed to have established on unshakable foundations; before this notable assembly, comprising not only such "learned men and fine minds" as Descartes and Mersenne, but also "many persons of quality, among whom was noted Cardinal de Bérulle" (Baillet I,161), he was at last to show his hand. From Baillet's description, it appears that Bérulle, or Bérulle and a few other "persons of quality," were the principal audience whom Chandoux wished to impress. Bérulle was the spiritual leader of the Catholic Reformation in France, and had been the chief of the "devout party" at court; by 1628 he had lost out to the absolutist cause, and was in some disgrace at court; but the Papal Nuncio

---

[29] According to Baillet, the events took place in November of 1628, but modern scholars have cast doubt on Baillet's chronology; see Gilson, *Discours*, p. 278, for discussion.

would very naturally have wanted his philosophical protégé Chandoux to appeal to Bérulle. Descartes and Mersenne and the others appear rather as expert referees on whom the persons of quality can rely to help them judge the technical merits of Chandoux' philosophy.

Chandoux therefore "spoke in the assembly like a man perfectly prepared. He produced a long discourse to refute the manner of teaching philosophy which is ordinary in the School. Indeed, he put forward a worked-out system of philosophy which he claimed to establish, and which he wished to pass for new" (ibid.). All present were much impressed, and praised the speaker, except only Descartes; whereupon Bérulle, noticing Descartes' silence, asked him to state his sentiments on the discourse that the company had thought so fine. When Descartes coyly declined to add anything to "the approbations of so many learned men whom he judged more capable than himself of judging the discourse they had just heard," Bérulle and then also "the other most notable persons of the assembly" (p. 162) all pressed him to speak his mind. Descartes began by praising highly Chandoux' rhetorical talents, and went on to commend "this noble freedom [généreuse liberté] that le sieur de Chandoux had displayed in trying to deliver philosophy from the vexation of the scholastics and the Peripatetics, who seemed to wish to reign over all the other sects" (ibid.). But Descartes also took occasion to remark "the force of probability [vrai-semblance] which occupies the place of truth, and which appeared in this encounter to have triumphed over the judgment of so many grave and judicious persons." In order to demonstrate the ease with which an accomplished speaker could make the false appear the true to "people obliging enough to be willing to content themselves with probability, as had just been done by the illustrious company before whom he had the honor of speaking," Descartes proceeded to give a rhetorical display in the best tradition of Gorgias and his Renaissance disciples. Soliciting from the audience an evident truth and an evident falsehood, Descartes exhibited a dozen arguments, "each more probable than the others," to show that their truth was false, and another dozen to reveal their falsehood as a plausible truth. The audience, much sobered by Descartes' demonstration of the perils of probability, begged of him "some infallible means for escaping sophisms" (p. 163); to which Descartes obliged, informing the company "that he knew of none more infallible than the one he himself was accustomed to use . . . which he had drawn from the depths of mathematics, and that he did not believe that there was a truth that he could not clearly demonstrate by this means according to its own principles." This was his "universal rule" or "natural method," by which he was able to examine any proposed problem, to determine with mathematical certainty whether or not the problem was capable of solution, and then infallibly to provide the solution if possible.

Baillet at this point tries to defend Descartes' behavior, stressing Descartes' sincere resolve to discover for himself some doctrine genuinely superior to the teaching of the schools, and his refusal to settle for any merely rhetorically effective alternative. Here Baillet is apparently drawing on Descartes' own explanation to Chandoux' audience, as recorded in a manuscript of Clerselier. Descartes agreed that Chandoux' philosophy as it had been presented "was much more probable than what was delivered according to the scholastic method" (p. 164), but that ultimately it was no better, being indeed "almost the same thing as [the philosophy] of the School, disguised in other terms." This new philosophy had the same fault as the scholastic philosophy which it deplored: its principles satisfied neither of the criteria that Descartes would lay down in the preface to his *Principles*, being neither clear in themselves nor productive for the clarification of other things. After showing in some detail the defects of Chandoux' principles, Descartes allowed himself to remark "that he did not believe that it was impossible to establish in philosophy principles more clear and more certain, by which it would be easier to give an account of all the effects of nature."

Given this story, it is difficult to be too sympathetic with Descartes' embarrassment, as he describes it in the *Discourse*, on hearing the rumor that he had already discovered the principles of philosophy. It is natural enough that, as the Chandoux story suggests, the encounter with someone else's attempt at a "new philosophy" should have provoked Descartes into trying to do better himself. But we can go further than this. We can now interpret, and appreciate the importance of, Descartes' comment in the dedicatory letter of the *Meditations* that some people had demanded that he apply his method to natural theology. Baillet tells us that several of those who had been prepared to follow the new philosophy of Chandoux instead decided to wait for Descartes to establish a philosophy on his own principles. But

Cardinal de Bérulle above all the others appreciated marvelously everything he had heard of it, and asked M. Descartes to hear him again in private on the same subject. M. Descartes, sensible of the honor that he received from so obliging an invitation, paid a visit to him a few days later, and told him of the first thoughts that had come to him on philosophy, after he had perceived the inadequacy of the means commonly used to treat it. (P. 165)

Descartes stressed, as usual, the practical utility these philosophical thoughts would have if they could be applied to medicine and mechanics. Bérulle, on hearing this proposal,

had no difficulty in perceiving the importance of the plan: and judging [Descartes] most appropriate to execute it, he made use of the authority he had over his [Descartes'] spirit to induce him to undertake this great work. Indeed he made it an obligation of conscience for him, in that having received from God a force and penetration of spirit, with insights [*lumières*] into things that he [God] had not given to others, he [Descartes] would have to give an exact accounting of the use of his talents, and would be responsible before the sovereign Judge of men for the wrong he would have done the human race in withholding from it the fruit of his meditations. He went so far as to assure him that with intentions as pure and a capacity of spirit as vast as he [Bérulle] recognized in him [Descartes], God would not fail to bless his [Descartes'] labor and to supply all the success that he could hope for. (Ibid.)

Baillet follows his sources in representing "the exhortations of this pious cardinal" as a turning-point in Descartes' life, and he is right to do so; but Baillet also notes that Descartes had long been awaiting just such an external stimulus to call him to the task of philosophical construction. Baillet rightly refers here to the passage of the *Discourse* where Descartes describes his resolution, after nine years of travels and preliminary exercises, to retire to Holland and to begin the search for the principles of a new philosophy. But there is more to be said than this. In the dedicatory letter of the *Meditations* Descartes says not simply that some persons had told him to start working on philosophy, but that they had demanded in the strongest terms that he apply his method to natural theology, by proving the existence of God and the immortality of the soul. Descartes' "*summopere flagitarunt*" (AT VII,3) corresponds to Baillet's "made it an obligation of conscience," and the subject must again be Bérulle; "*nonnulli*" is merely a literary plural.[30] Thus when Bérulle told Descartes to construct a new philosophy, he also told him to begin with metaphysics, and with metaphysics as conceived in Augustinian terms, as a discipline of reflection on God and the soul.

From this time on Descartes takes such a metaphysics as the fundamental discipline, from which the principles of philosophy must be drawn. Thus at the beginning of the fourth part of the *Discourse*, immediately after describing his retirement to Holland, Descartes expresses some reluctance to describe "the first meditations I made there; for they are so metaphysical and so uncommon that perhaps they will not be to everyone's taste" (AT VI,31). Descartes agrees to discuss them nonetheless, because these are the foundations he has chosen, and his readers must be able to judge whether his foundations are sufficiently firm; and the meditations he goes on to describe are reflections in the Augustinian style on the soul and God.

We can confirm this same transformation in Descartes' thought from documents closer to the events. In the spring of 1630 Descartes writes to Mersenne from Holland that he has spent his first nine months in that country studying metaphysics, and in learning how to demonstrate metaphysical truths with more than geometrical certainty. He tells Mersenne that he has studied this matter more than any other, and that "it is here that I have tried to begin my studies" (AT I,144); this is obviously false if we take "studies" broadly, and must mean instead that Descartes began with metaphysics in his *constructive* studies, in his post-1628 attempt to build up a new philosophy. Descartes explains in two different ways why it was important for him to study metaphysics. In the first place, "I judge

---

[30] Such a literary plural is not an uncommon device in Latin; we will encounter it again in Augustine, who uses "*libri Platonicorum*" and "*libri Plotini*" to refer to the same books.

that all those to whom God has given the use of this [sc. human] reason are obliged to employ it principally in trying to know him and to know themselves"; here Descartes is surely echoing Bérulle's "obligation of conscience." But Descartes then adds, in what seems to be a bit of confidential advice for Mersenne, that "I would not have been able to discover the foundations of physics if I had not searched for them along this path [that of the knowledge of God and the soul]." The suggestion is that Descartes had taken up the metaphysics of soul and God because of the intrinsic value of the subject, and had then discovered that the truths of natural theology were also the desired principles of philosophy, from which a science of nature could be derived.[31]

This is a real change in Descartes' thought, and Descartes presents it as one. Descartes, from his mature standpoint, regards this change as a transition from preparatory mathematical exercises to the main work of philosophical construction; but he is making retroactive sense of his development. Descartes was exploring mathematics in the 1620s in the hope of discovering a universal science. He says that he had not proceeded to a systematic physics, or any other part of philosophy, because he did not yet feel himself sufficiently mature; but the deeper reason is that he had no candidate for a foundational science outside of mathematics, and mathematics by itself was not sufficient to give him the principles of physical things. Around 1628, Descartes becomes acquainted with the Augustinian ideal of attentiveness to soul and God, and the Augustinian discipline of metaphysical reflection, associated with Bérulle and with his Congregation of the Oratory; Descartes finds this ideal and this discipline well-suited to his goal of developing simple truths into a scientific wisdom, and from this time on he integrates the Augustinian program into his own.[32] According to what biographical evidence we have, Descartes came into contact with this Augustinian program through Bérulle and then through other Oratorians who number among his correspondents; but nothing depends upon a psychological reconstruction. We know *that* Descartes integrates the Augustinian program into his own; the important question that remains is not *why* he decided to do this, but *how* he made an old discipline serve new functions.

Descartes spent his first nine months in Holland studying metaphysics, and he mastered it to his satisfaction. From this time on, he makes it his task to exhibit the Augustinian understandings of soul and God as principles of physics, and thus of the rest of philosophy. In the same letter in

---

[31] It is curious to see Descartes lecturing the reverend father Mersenne, the author of one large volume in defense of reason and two in defense of Christianity, on the advantages to be gained from studying God and the soul, tacitly implying that Mersenne has not yet got around to such a study.

[32] On the internal difficulties of Descartes' project during the 1620s, and on why he might see Augustinian metaphysics as solving these difficulties, see below, Chapter 5, Section A. We cannot say anything very informative about this prior to the detailed study of Augustine given in Chapters 3 and 4.

which he tells Mersenne of his metaphysical studies, Descartes states his intention to publish, in three years' time, a short but systematic treatise on physics, which will begin by stipulating some metaphysical conclusions about the nature of God; he will commit his metaphysics to writing only after he sees how his physics is received. This *Physics* is what Descartes later entitled *The World* (comprehending both the *Treatise on Light* and the *Treatise on Man*), and he completed it on schedule in 1633. In that same year, however, the Roman Inquisition condemned Galileo's *Dialogue concerning the Two Chief World Systems* for defending the Copernican hypothesis, which Descartes' treatise had also maintained; and Descartes, unwilling either to defy the Roman authorities by publishing the condemned doctrine, or to publish his treatise in mutilated form without it, instead suppressed the treatise. The *Essays in the Method* are Descartes' substitute for this physics: being unwilling to offer the public his full physical system, he shows them instead in the *Dioptrics* and the *Meteors* a selection of the fruits that might be obtained if it were possible to pursue the philosophical project to its end. The *Discourse*, in setting out the method by which Descartes achieved these results, gives an outline of the metaphysics in Part Four and an outline of the physics (including human physiology) in Part Five; but these outlines merely *describe* Descartes' principles, with omissions, and do not pretend to demonstrate them. Indeed, at the time of the *Discourse* it seems that Descartes will do no more: since he will not "speak of many questions that are in controversy among the learned, with whom I do not wish to quarrel" (AT VI,40), or violate the prohibition of the Roman authorities, "persons to whom I defer, and whose authority has hardly less power over my actions than does my own reason over my thoughts" (p. 60), he resolves not merely to suppress his treatise on physics, but "to publish no other, in my lifetime, that was so general, nor one from which the foundations of my physics could be understood" (p. 74).

By the end of 1639, however, Descartes is telling Mersenne of his work on a treatise on metaphysics, which will expand and clarify what he has said on the subject in the *Discourse*; and by the end of 1640 he is thinking of this *Metaphysics* as the first step toward publishing a complete course of philosophy including a *Physics*.[33] Descartes decides to retitle this *Metaphysics* as *Meditations on First Philosophy*, because, suitably to its Augustinian method, it is cast as a series of meditations, and because it treats not only God and the soul, "immaterial or metaphysical things" as Descartes calls them in the *Letter to Picot* (AT IX2,10), but "all the first things one can know in philosophizing," including the first principles of

---

[33] Descartes describes his plans for publication at AT III,233, and at other places in his letters to Mersenne. It is hard to know whether to take "Metaphysics," "Physics," and so on as projected titles or simply as descriptions of projected works; there are no typographical conventions which would allow us to decide, and the distinction between titles of books and descriptions of their subject matter was not as sharp then as it is now.

physics.[34] Thus these *Meditations*, published in 1641, contain the first full publication, and the first full extant treatment, of the metaphysics Descartes had thought out in 1628–9.

From the first mention of his *Metaphysics* on, it is integral to Descartes' plan to circulate the work among the theologians, not only to receive criticisms and improvements on the text, but also to win the endorsement of individual doctors of theology and, if possible, the institutional endorsement of the theological faculty of the University of Paris. Descartes' motivation is in part defensive: he tells Mersenne that if he can gain the approval of a few of the doctors, he will dedicate the work to "Messieurs de la Sorbonne in general,"[35] begging them to be his protectors in the cause of God, since the malicious attacks that have been made on his work "have made me resolve to fortify myself henceforth, as best I can, with the authority of others, since truth by itself is so little valued" (AT III,184). Descartes cites this motive in other places, even to the doctors themselves in his dedication, and it is clearly important to him: if learned and pious men, St. Augustine or the theologians of Descartes' own day, agree with Descartes' doctrines, this shows at least that the doctrines are neither absurd nor heretical in themselves, as will be alleged by "those who mix up Aristotle with the Bible . . . I mean those who had Galileo condemned" (AT III,349–50).[36] But Descartes' interest in the theologians' support goes deeper than this. When Descartes asks Mersenne to secure the approval of those theologians whom Mersenne regards as "the most capable, the least prejudiced by the errors of the School, and the least interested in maintaining them, and men of good will, for whom truth and the glory of God weigh more than envy and jealousy" (III,127), he is attempting to establish an alliance based on shared concerns. Reforming theologians wish to free the faith from its embarrassing alliance with Aristotelian philosophy, but wish to retain some philosophy to prove the existence of God and the immortality of the soul; Descartes offers them a new approach to philosophy, which begins with the doctrines of God and the soul, and detaches them from the Aristotelian context in which they had become embedded. Descartes

---

[34] So Descartes tells Mersenne at AT III,235; but Descartes allows the French translation to be called *Méditations métaphysiques*, and he does not maintain consistently his distinction between a narrower metaphysics and a wider first philosophy. It is difficult, after 350 years, to pronounce the title of this work correctly, but the reader should perform the exercise at least once: "Meditations on *First* Philosophy," with the emphasis on "first."

[35] The *Meditations* are in fact dedicated "to the Dean and Doctors of the Faculty of Sacred Theology at Paris" (AT VII,1). Descartes must be using "Sorbonne" to refer to the Paris faculty of theology. Strictly speaking this is incorrect: the Sorbonne was a college of theologians, but it was only one of several colleges in the university, and there were many theologians outside the Sorbonne; as Jean-Robert Armogathe suggests in correspondence, Descartes' use of "Sorbonne" is best taken as *pars pro toto* for the whole faculty. I will follow Descartes' usage.

[36] See Gouhier's *Cartésianisme et augustinisme au XVIIe siècle* for discussion of this strategy of theological protection, as practiced by Descartes and later Cartesians.

stresses in his dedicatory letter that his work belongs to "human philos-ophy" (AT VII,5), but the dedication is addressed not to philosophers but to theologians: the new philosophy will bypass the established philos-ophers, and appeal over their heads to the theologians. Descartes offers his work to the theologians as the true philosophy of the Catholic Ref-ormation: he will carry into the hostile territory of philosophy the re-formers' struggle to restore the pristine simplicity of truth and to eliminate scholastic corruptions.

Descartes' aim in the *Meditations* is to exhibit the Augustinian meta-physics as the fundamental discipline from which the principles of all other knowledge must be drawn. He does not wish to discuss physics as a science, that is, as *systematic* knowledge of the physical world; but he will show that whatever knowledge we have of body must proceed from knowledge of God and the soul. To say that God and the soul are prin-ciples of physical things is to assert, contrary to common opinion, that they are better known than bodies; and indeed Descartes says that he has "taken as his aim [*scopus*: this is the standard term for the proper subject matter of a work] in these Meditations the proof of this one thing," that even the reasons that prove "that there really is a world, that men have bodies, and the like, which no one of sound mind has ever seriously doubted," are "neither as firm nor as clear as those by which we come to a knowledge of our mind and God, so that these things [the mind and God] are the most certain and evident of all the things the human mind can know" (AT VII,16). This claim is in the grand Counter-Reformation tradition of spiritual hyperbole, which Descartes shares with the doctors of the Sorbonne. Thus Descartes begins his letter of dedication by saying that he has always judged "two questions, about God and about the soul, to be chief among those that should be demonstrated with the aid of phi-losophy rather than of theology," and by arguing that purely rational proofs of these two truths are necessary for Christian apologetics.

And indeed I have observed not only that you and all the other theologians affirm that the existence of God can be proved by natural reason, but also that it is inferred from holy scripture that the knowledge of him is easier than the knowl-edge we have of many created things, and is indeed so easy that those who do not have it are culpable. For this is clear in the Book of Wisdom from these words: "nor should they be forgiven: for if they were able to know so much that they could pass judgment on this world, how did they not discover its Lord more easily?" (Wisdom 13:8–9). And in the letter to the Romans, they are said to be "without excuse" (Romans 1:20). And in the same place too we seem to be ad-monished through these words, "what is known of God is manifest in them" (Romans 1:19), that all those things that can be known of God can be shown from reasons sought nowhere but in our mind itself. Therefore I have not thought it improper for me to inquire how this comes about, and in what way God is known more easily and more certainly than the things of this world. (AT VII,2)

Thus Descartes regards it as the duty of a Christian philosopher to apply his reason, not simply to knowing God, but to knowing him better than

and prior to all physical things; that is, to take him as a principle of philosophy.

Likewise for the soul,

although many have judged that its nature cannot easily be investigated, and some
[*nonnulli*] have even dared to say that human reasonings would persuade us that
it perishes with the body, and that the contrary is held by faith alone; yet because
the [Fifth] Lateran Council held under Leo X [1512–17] condemned these people,
and expressly commissioned Christian philosophers to refute their arguments and
to prove the truth to the best of their ability, I have not hesitated to undertake
this as well. (Pp. 2–3)

Now, Aristotle had said at the beginning of his book on the soul that
"to acquire any confidence about it is altogether and in every way one of
the most difficult things" (*De Anima* I,1 402a10–11); and his followers in
Christian Europe agreed. Christian philosophers had felt bound to maintain the doctrine of the separability of the human soul, which Augustine
(following the Platonists and the Greek Fathers) had made normative for
Latin Christianity; and Thomas Aquinas had managed to interpret Aristotelian philosophy in accordance with this doctrine, following Avicenna
and the older tradition of Platonist commentary on Aristotle. But many
later scholastics, even within the school of Thomas, felt unable to prove
that the soul was separable from the body. The question of the soul, they
thought, was too difficult for reason to decide: reason could only submit
both possibilities to the judgment of faith, and faith, on their interpretation, would decide for separability. The doctrine condemned by the Fifth
Lateran Council was an extreme development of this position, asserting
that human reason would lead us to conclude (either demonstratively or
probably) that the soul is inseparable and perishes with the body. Descartes does not say who it was that held the condemned position, but he
must know that the Council was condemning a thoroughgoing Aristotelianism, and he cannot be sorry to remind the theologians that it is the
philosophy of Aristotle that has led this heresy. Aristotelian philosophy
began with sensible things, and encountered the soul only at the end of
its journey, as the last and most obscure question of physics: it is not
surprising that the answers it gave were not always in accord with Christian faith. Descartes undertakes to reverse the journey of Aristotelian philosophy: beginning, with Augustine, by reflecting on the human soul, he
will show that it can be known better than and prior to bodies, and that
it can subsist apart from them. Descartes thus offers a philosophy which,
unlike that of Aristotle, will satisfy the Christian expectation of a knowledge of the things essential for religion and morality.

When Descartes describes his work to the theologians, he naturally
emphasizes the summons he has received from the Catholic reforming
movement in general, and from Bérulle in particular. In answering this
summons, he says, he has carefully sought out the best of all proofs for
the existence of God and the incorporeality of the mind, in order to set

54

them out according to his method "so clearly and accurately that it would thenceforth be publicly established that they are demonstrations" (AT VII,3). Descartes is not trying to discover *new* proofs of these doctrines, nor does he believe that the old proofs are inadequate: on the contrary, he says, "I hold that almost all the reasons that great men have brought to bear on these questions have the force of demonstration when they are sufficiently understood, and I am persuaded that hardly any [reasons] could be given that have not already been discovered by others" (ibid.); he hopes nonetheless to make an important contribution by setting out the best of these reasons according to his method. This is because method is concerned with the *order* of the propositions we entertain in our reasonings: to consider the questions of God and the soul according to method is to consider them in their proper order, without introducing considerations from sensible things into the study of the things that are known first and most clearly of all. If I take physical things as the principles of metaphysical things, and attempt to derive knowledge of God and the soul from physical premises, then my judgments about God and the soul can be no more certain, and my concepts of God and the soul no clearer, than the judgments and concepts I have accepted concerning physical things. Descartes will take the traditional body of proofs, inherited from Augustine, Anselm, Thomas, Scotus, and others, and by presenting it in methodical order he will eliminate everything that depends on physical conceptions and judgments, above all everything that depends on the philosophy of Aristotle: he will thus present a purified natural theology, an Augustinian metaphysics disentangled from Aristotelian physics, which will make God and the soul better known than physical things.

We recall from the preface to the *Principles of Philosophy* that principles must not only be very clear and very evident in themselves, but also such that "the knowledge of other things depends on them, so that they may be known without the other things, but not conversely" (AT IX2,2). It is not always clear in the preface to the *Principles* how many distinct criteria for principles Descartes intends to enumerate; but we may distinguish three theses, all of which Descartes must demonstrate in order to exhibit metaphysical things as principles of physical things: he must show that we can know God and the soul without knowing bodies, that we *cannot* know bodies without first knowing God and the soul, and that we *can* know bodies once God and the soul have first been known. The "Synopsis of the Six Following Meditations" which Descartes circulated with the Meditations, and published after the dedicatory letter (and after a short "preface to the reader") but before the text of the Meditations themselves, shows what contribution each of the six Meditations makes toward establishing these three theses, and thus toward achieving the goals of the work. The first Meditation will prove the negative thesis that we cannot know bodies unless we first know God and the soul; the second and third Meditations show that we can know the soul and God independently of bodies, and the fourth through sixth Meditations show that we can proceed from this knowledge of God and the soul at least as far as the first principles of physical things.

The first Meditation, says Descartes, sets out "the causes . . . on account of which we are able to doubt about all things, especially material things: so long, that is, as we do not have other foundations for the sciences than those we have had hitherto" (AT VII,12). This Meditation exercises the mind in doubting material things, and it shows that we will always have occasion for doubt unless we know that our soul is the creature of a God who is the source of truth to it: it thus proves that the "other foundations for the sciences" that might give them certainty could only consist in such a knowledge of God and soul. Descartes demonstrates this negative thesis before the positive thesis that God and the soul can themselves be known, because doubt about bodies will help to purify our knowledge of God and the soul: if we can prove the existence of God and the soul while continuing to doubt all material things, we will have established a metaphysical knowledge free from sensible unclarities and uncertainties. Thus Descartes advises the reader that "even if the utility of so great a doubt does not appear at first sight, still [this utility] is very great, in that it delivers us from all prejudices, and clears a most easy way for leading the mind away from the senses; and finally it brings it about that we shall not be able to doubt further about the things that we shall afterwards discover to be true" (ibid.).

The second Meditation, on the human mind, and the third Meditation, on God, give Descartes' version of the Augustinian discipline of spiritual contemplation. In both, Descartes is at pains to maintain the separation from the senses, and from all physical theories, which he has achieved in the first Meditation; as he points out in the Synopsis, this gives rise to some difficulties of exposition. He adjoins to the original title of the second Meditation, "of the human mind," the subtitle "that it is better known than the body,"[37] since this is what he proves by establishing an intuition of the soul independently of body; he cannot yet prove any attributes of the soul that would depend on a knowledge of body, not even the assertion that the soul is not the body or that it is separable from the body. Similarly, in the third Meditation, "because, in order to lead the minds of the readers as much as possible away from the senses, I have not wished to use any likenesses drawn from corporeal things, many obscurities may perhaps have remained" (AT VII,14). Descartes finds it necessary to use a proof for the existence of God less immediately plausible than the usual causal proofs, not only because the corporeal references in these proofs render the conclusion less certain, but also and more importantly because they yield an insufficiently clear conception of God. Thus if we prove that there is a first cause of motion, or even a first cause of the

[37] In a letter to Mersenne, AT III,297; the word "nature" which appears in the printed title seems not to be Descartes'.

existence of contingent things, we will know in a general way that something like God exists, but not that there is a God who is the source of
truth to the human soul; and this is what Descartes needs to know.

After Descartes has shown in the second and third Meditations that
God is the source of truth to human souls, he proceeds in the fourth
through sixth Meditations to apply this knowledge to constructing a
knowledge of bodies. He first shows that the geometrical properties that
we clearly perceive to follow from spatial extension must belong to the
essence of bodies, whether or not the bodies actually exist; then, in the
sixth Meditation, he discusses the relation between mind and body, and
then finally adduces "all the reasons from which the existence of material
things can be concluded":

not that I thought that they were very useful for proving what they prove, namely
that there really is a world, that men have bodies, and the like, which no one of
sound mind has ever seriously doubted; but because, by considering [these rea-
sons], it may be recognized that they are neither as firm nor as clear as those by
which we come to a knowledge of our mind and God, so that these [the mind and
God] are the most certain and evident of all the things the human mind can know.
(AT VII,16)

And Descartes adds the remark I have already cited, that he has "taken
the proof of this one thing as my aim [scopus] in these Meditations"; for
which reason, in composing this Synopsis, he "omits the various other
questions I have also had occasion to treat in these [Meditations]" (ibid.).

This last expression resonates with what Descartes tells Mersenne in
the letter where he fixes the full titles of the various Meditations. The
subjects that he indicates in the titles, he says, are

the things I would like people to pay the most attention to; but I think that I have
put there many other things, and I will tell you, between ourselves, that these six
Meditations contain all the foundations of my Physics. But please do not say so,
for those who favor Aristotle might make more difficulties about approving them;
and I hope that those who read them will become insensibly accustomed to my
principles, and recognize their truth, before perceiving that they destroy those of
Aristotle. (AT III,297–8)

The aim of the *Meditations* is to show that God and the soul are better
known than bodies; but this demonstration has not only the religious and
moral utility that Descartes stresses to the doctors of the Sorbonne, but
also a scientific utility. If a doctrine of body can be truly scientific only
when it is derived from knowledge of God and the soul, then the Aristotelian physics of the schools is not a true science; this is clearly implied
in Descartes' assertion that we can doubt about all material things as long
as we do not have other foundations for the sciences than those we have
had hitherto. Now that Descartes has set out a knowledge of God and the
soul that is prior to any knowledge of bodies and a suitable foundation for
such knowledge, Descartes himself or some follower of his might be able

57

to construct a doctrine of body which, for the first time in the history of physics, might be truly scientific.

Already in the fifth and sixth Meditations, Descartes had used his metaphysics to derive certain basic truths about the essence and existence of material things. These are truths that no one of sound mind has ever seriously doubted, and they do not directly contradict anything in Aristotle; but by setting out the reasons that demonstrate these truths, and by showing how far these reasons can and cannot take us, Descartes had sketched the outlines of a systematic science of bodies. This science would be *new*, in that no one before Descartes would ever have derived its conclusions from its principles. Perhaps, in the end, the new science would ratify all the opinions that the schools had taught before a true science of bodies was discovered; but this would be a most unlikely coincidence. As the letter to Mersenne shows, Descartes was quite convinced by the time he wrote the *Meditations* that this would not be the result.

Because Descartes wants as many theologians as possible to give their approval to the *Meditations*, he keeps silent about the anti-Aristotelian scientific utility of his work. This does not mean that Descartes is insincere about the religious and moral utility, merely that he perceives that there are two different expectations current for a new philosophy, the scientific and the religious, both of which he hopes to satisfy, and both of which he has sincerely appropriated as his own philosophical goals. Descartes confides to Mersenne that there is a scientific utility to his work, and asks Mersenne not to tell the theologians of the Sorbonne; but this is not because a metaphysics with a scientific function could not also have a religious function. If it were so, Descartes would hardly have confided the scientific function of the *Meditations* to the man who had defended Christianity against the impiety of the deists, atheists, and libertines. Descartes keeps silent, not because the scientific function of his work would offend the theologians as such, but because theologians as such are not concerned with science, and because *some* theologians, those committed to the scholastic program, would resent an attack on Aristotle, their one proven philosophical support; and Descartes wants *all* the theologians to approve. Descartes' tactical silence here is characteristic: it is a matter of prudence not to say things that will limit the reception of his work, and a matter of honor not to say anything he does not believe. Thus when Regius insinuates his doubts about Descartes' sincerity in the *Meditations*, Descartes tells him that

those who suspect me of having written something other than what I thought about any matter do me a very great wrong, and if I knew who they were, I could not do otherwise than to regard them as enemies. Indeed, to be silent for a time, and to be unwilling to make public everything we think, is [the work] of a prudent man; but I think that to write, under no compulsion, something foreign to one's own opinion, and to try to persuade one's readers of it, is [the work] of a contemptible and wicked man. (AT IV,256)

Descartes' policy here may be contrasted with that of such other "new philosophers" as Patrizi and Gassendi. Gassendi had composed his first published work, the *Exercitationes Paradoxicae contra Aristoteleos*,[38] by compiling all the arguments against Aristotle's opinion on any given topic; this was an essentially rhetorical procedure which did not lead to any coherent philosophical alternative to Aristotle. Mersenne had persuaded Gassendi that a more constructive approach was needed; and Descartes too agreed. Instead of launching a rhetorical attack against Aristotle, Descartes will peacefully establish foundations for a better scientific system, and hope to persuade potential opponents to join him. Thus in the passage we have seen from the letter to Mersenne, Descartes hopes that his readers, even those initially inclined to favor Aristotle, will by insensible degrees accustom themselves to Descartes' principles, and will recognize the truth of these principles; when they later see that these principles contradict their habitual belief in Aristotelian physics, Descartes expects that they will give up their old system of physics and adopt his new one. In the long run, everyone should be pleased that Descartes has derived a new physics from his metaphysics; it is merely for the time being that Descartes prefers not to raise their alarms.

Descartes' plan is to give his readers a few years to accustom themselves to his *Meditations*, and then to show them the consequences for systematic philosophy. In an earlier letter to Mersenne, written in November of 1640, Descartes describes his plan to "write in order a whole Course of my Philosophy in the form of theses" (AT III,233), including an explicit statement of his differences from the usual philosophy of the schools. Here too Descartes asks Mersenne not to alarm the Aristotelians, and especially not before the *Meditations* could be published. Thus even as Descartes was readying the *Meditations* for publication, he was beginning work on what was to become the *Principles of Philosophy*.

In the *Principles* itself, or in the preface to the French edition, Descartes admits this way of proceeding: "finally, when it seemed to me that the preceding treatises had sufficiently prepared the minds of my readers to receive the *Principles of Philosophy*, I published these as well" (AT IX2,16). The first part of the *Principles* is, as Descartes notes, largely a recapitulation of the *Meditations*, converted into scholastic format and augmented by discussions of some basic scholastic topics. But in the second part, on general physics or the "principles of material things," corresponding to Aristotle's *Physics*, Descartes presents an account of the nature of bodies which differs radically and unmistakably from the Aristotelian account accepted in the schools; and in the third and fourth parts he derives particular accounts of celestial and sublunar bodies which di-

---

[38] Originally published in 1624; there is a modern edition, with French translation, *Dissertations en forme de paradoxes contres les aristotéliciens*, ed. Bernard Rochot (Paris: Vrin, 1959).

verge further and further from the Aristotelian systems. To put the difference in the terms in which Descartes himself conceives it, Descartes is abstaining from the unclear principles that Aristotle had used in explaining physical things; he will construct a system of natural philosophy using only the clear and evident principles of the geometers.

We recall that in the preface to the French translation, Descartes had sought to prove by exhaustive induction that the principles of his philosophy were the most clear and evident of any the human mind could know. In metaphysics, Descartes' only principles are the universally accepted truths of "Christian philosophy" concerning God and the soul; from these Descartes derives his only principle of physical or corporeal things, "that there are bodies extended in length, breadth, and depth, which have various figures and are moved in various ways" (AT IX2,10). Extension, figure, and motion are clearly understood; but all the other principles that have been used in natural philosophy are obscure. Thus after Descartes has reviewed the history of philosophy, and declared that none of the schools has the desired knowledge from first principles, he supports his claim with "a proof . . . which I do not believe that any of [the philosophers] would disavow: that they have all supposed as a principle something they did not know perfectly" (AT IX2,7–8). His chief example is the quality of gravity or heaviness, which the Peripatetics had posited to explain the descent of heavy bodies; Descartes makes the usual complaint that this is a verbal cheat, since "although experience shows us clearly enough that the bodies that are called heavy descend toward the center of the earth, we do not therefore know the nature of what is called heaviness, that is to say, the cause or principle that makes them descend in this way, and we must learn this from some other source" (p. 8). To show that he is not favoring the modern innovators over Aristotle, Descartes adds that "one can say the same of the void and atoms, of the hot and the cold, of the dry and the moist, of salt, sulphur, and mercury, and of all such things which some have supposed as their principles" (ibid.). Descartes, by contrast, will not assume that there is anything in bodies beyond the clear geometrical principles, extension and figure and motion; indeed, he will assert that the essence of body consists in extension alone.

Aristotle had maintained that the true substance of any given body is not its matter, but the form that constitutes that matter as the particular thing (a stone, a mouse, etc.) that it is; this form is the nature from which all the activities of the body derive. The scholastic tradition had systematized and generalized this conception, and distinguished between substantial and accidental forms: a substantial form is "a certain partial substance that can be united to matter in such a way that together with [the matter] it composes a substance that is complete and one *per se*,"[39]

---

[39] Francisco Suárez, *Disputationes Metaphysicae*, in his *Opera Omnia* (Paris: Vives, 1856–78), vols. 25–6 (these volumes 1866; both reprinted Hildesheim: Olms, 1965). I will cite

whereas an accidental form is merely an accident that comes to qualify the already constituted substance. The scholastics take pride in substantial forms: for without these, they insist, there can be no real plurality of bodily substances, and bodies would be distinguished merely by the different accidents that exist at different times and places. But the scholastics are aware that substantial forms are controversial, and that there are difficulties in particular about how substantial forms could be generated. Suárez, writing fifty years before Descartes' *Principles*, considers these difficulties, and remarks that

on account of this difficulty the ancient [i.e. pre-Socratic] philosophers denied substantial forms, and considered that all things came to be through a change of accidents alone. But their opinion has already been disproved through the demonstration of substantial form, and of generation and corruption; but we add now that they have not solved the difficulty by denying substantial forms, unless they deny even accidental [forms], which come to be really and truly *de novo*, and consequently say that there is no change in things, except perhaps in place; but that things only *seem* to change, in that things that will be manifest are now hidden, and things that will be hidden are now manifest; and it is clear how absurd this is.[40]

This is precisely Descartes' challenge. By identifying the substance of body with extended matter, and refusing to posit substantial forms or even accidental forms (or "real qualities"), Descartes commits himself to the conclusion that there is no change except change in place; he is therefore challenged to explain the appearances of change without the Aristotelian principles.

Descartes has in fact two difficulties. If bodies contain nothing beyond extension, it is unclear how bodies can be sensed at all; again, if they contain nothing beyond extension, they possess no active power that could impel them to pass from one sensible appearance to another. Descartes attempts to solve both difficulties by relying on his understanding of God and the soul. God, for Descartes, is the source of motion to bodies, and impresses on bodies the laws of the communication of motions. God, again, conjoins the human mind with its body, and institutes laws of communication between mind and body: thus a particular configuration of an external body gives rise to a particular configuration within the human body, which gives rise in turn to a particular sensation in the human mind. The principles of Descartes' physics are body, motion, and God as the source of motion, from whom the laws of motion are derived; from these principles Descartes must proceed to the complex particular configurations of moving bodies that result from the consistent application of the basic laws. The third part of the *Principles* derives the gross structure of

this work by Disputation, section, and paragraph numbers; the present citation is from Disputation 15, section 1, paragraph 6.

[40] Suárez, Disputation 15, section 2, paragraph 2.

the visible world of the heavens, and the fourth part descends to explain sublunar phenomena; in the projected but unwritten fifth and sixth parts, Descartes would have derived the phenomena of plants and animals and of the human body, culminating in an account of the union of mind and body that would finally explain the origin of sensible qualities.

By taking extension and motion as the principles of his physics, Descartes gives a new importance to the mathematical discipline of mechanics: so much so that he is able to tell a correspondent that "my whole physics is nothing other than mechanics" (AT II,542). He does not mean mechanics here in the narrow sense as one of the practical branches of philosophy, the science of useful machines, whose fundamental problem is to move a given weight by means of a given force; he means mechanics in the broader sense, as the science of the local motions of bodies, which develops the principles required for the theory of machines. The physics that Descartes derives from his doctrines of God and the soul is, in this sense, a mechanics; and Descartes' philosophy is a "mechanical philosophy" in that it chooses the principles of mechanics as the principles from which the desired practical wisdom will be derived. Since mechanics was both a mathematically secure and a practically applicable discipline, and since the mechanics of the moderns was clearly superior to that of the ancients, it was plausible to expect that mechanics might support a new philosophy; Descartes and, somewhat later, Hobbes and Gassendi, construct their new philosophies to meet this expectation. To construct a *whole* physics that is nothing other than mechanics, however, is a very great task: it requires the philosopher to banish all real qualities and active powers from bodies, to explain all natural phenomena and especially the physiology of sensation in purely mechanical terms, and then finally to use the mechanics of human and non-human bodies to derive the practical disciplines, morals and medicine and mechanics in the stricter sense. Descartes and Gassendi and Hobbes did not, of course, succeed in this grand project, although they might have limited success with particular components of the scheme; but they succeeded in establishing the mechanical conception of bodies, and the mechanistic *project* for wisdom, so firmly that in the end "the new philosophy" became a mere synonym for "the mechanical philosophy."

D. Outline of research

Having seen the main lines of Descartes' mature project as he presents it in the *Meditations* and the *Principles*, we can formulate more concretely the goals Descartes has set for himself. We have already seen that Descartes had been trying since 1619 to satisfy the expectation of a union of science and wisdom, and since 1628 to satisfy the expectation of a new Christian philosophy derived from St. Augustine. More concretely, Descartes proposes to satisfy these expectations by establishing a particular sequence of demonstrations, which we can describe as follows.

Descartes will first present the Augustinian metaphysics of God and the soul. Although everyone believes the metaphysical *doctrines* that Augustine had derived from his intellectual intuitions of God and the soul, not everyone possesses the original intuitions. Descartes undertakes to reproduce the Augustinian intuitions of God and the soul in the minds of his readers, so that they will have an *understanding* of metaphysical things, and not merely true beliefs about them. Descartes will then argue that this metaphysics, once understood, implies a mechanistic physics. Where St. Thomas had argued that Augustinian metaphysics and Aristotelian physics were compatible, Descartes will argue that they are *not* compatible, that the Augustinian metaphysics in fact implies a physics contrary to that of Aristotle. Thus Descartes' first task, after setting out his understandings of God and the soul, will be to derive the further knowledge that only extended matter pertains to the essence of bodies, and that forms and active powers do not. Then, from his intuitions of God and soul and body, he must go on to derive a science of the apparent qualities of bodies, and a science of the laws that govern the motion of bodies, explaining what the Aristotelians would explain through forms and active powers. Descartes' ultimate goal is to derive, from this metaphysics and from this mechanistic physics, the practical sciences of mechanics and medicine and morals.

I will follow Descartes' argument only as far as his derivation of the principles of physics. In a sense, perhaps, this is as far as Descartes himself got: Descartes' derivations of the details of physics and of the physiology of sensation are fragmentary and hypothetical, and he does not pretend to have finished the derivation of the practical sciences. And, notoriously, the detailed derivations Descartes does give are often clear failures by his own standards. But the fact that Descartes' applied physics is mostly wrong is not a good reason for ignoring it; nor am I suggesting that his metaphysics and fundamental physics are mostly right. But my goal is to understand both the meaning of the metaphysics as Descartes presents it, and the use to which he puts that metaphysics; and we cannot understand either the use or the meaning unless we observe how Descartes derives the foundations of his physics. By contrast, Descartes' derivation of celestial or terrestrial mechanics from his fundamental physics will not make much further use of the metaphysics, nor shed much light on what the metaphysics means.[41] It is important to know that Descartes does try to derive particular physical doctrines, because it is important to know that

---

[41] A possible exception would be the *Passions of the Soul*: Descartes' attempt at a partial anticipation of a perfect ethics draws not only on his physics and human physiology, but also directly on his metaphysics, and might shed more light on the meaning of the metaphysics. But I will not make much use of this work here.

Descartes' final goal was not merely a fundamental physics, but a universal science united to practical wisdom. The fact that Descartes chose a goal that was (to our eyes) obviously unattainable is relevant; the precise way that he falls short of this goal is not.

To understand how Descartes uses and transforms the Augustinian metaphysics, we must first understand the intellectual material that Descartes is working to appropriate; so, in Part One, I will examine Augustine in himself, without referring ahead to Descartes. This study of Augustine is especially urgent because, as we saw in Chapter 1, Gilson and Gouhier interpret Augustinianism in such a way as to make an *augustinisme de Descartes* impossible. These scholars identify the essence of Augustinianism with its "spirit," which dictates the fusion of faith and reason; since Descartes' philosophy does not share this "spirit," they conclude that it can resemble Augustine's only superficially and accidentally. But they give no real reason for taking this "spirit" as the essence of Augustinianism: so we must reconsider afresh what Augustinianism was, or risk allowing an arbitrary interpretation to blind us to a real Cartesian use of Augustinian material. Still, Gilson and Gouhier have raised a real issue. It is beyond doubt that Descartes takes major elements of his accounts of soul and God directly or indirectly from Augustine; but it remains possible that Descartes, in removing these elements from their context in Augustine's project for wisdom, has lost or altered much of their original meaning. To understand whether and how we can speak of Descartes' Augustinianism, it is not enough to trace certain elements of Descartes' philosophy back to a source in Augustine: we must understand what they meant and how they functioned for Augustine, so that we can understand why Descartes chose them as useful for his own philosophical goals, how he was able to use them, and whether or to what extent he transformed their meaning in the process.

It is not enough to say that Descartes took over Augustine's *doctrines* of soul and God: he did, but so did everyone else. I will argue that Descartes took over something more, Augustine's *concepts* or *intuitions* of soul and God. But we can identify the content of these intuitions only by locating them within the discipline of spiritual contemplation that is designed to bring the meditator to these intuitions. To the extent that Descartes genuinely appropriates Augustine's intuitions, he can do so only by appropriating Augustine's discipline of contemplation. So, in discussing Descartes in Part Two below, I will center my discussion on Descartes' use and transformation of Augustine's discipline of contemplation; but first we must discuss this discipline as Augustine originally presented it. And just as the content of the intuitions is determined by the discipline of contemplation, so, ultimately, the practice of the discipline is determined by the *goal* this discipline is designed to achieve. Both Augustine and Descartes are trying to carry through their disciplines of contemplation, and to achieve intellectual intuitions of soul and God, because they aspire to wisdom: but they do not have the same expectations of what wisdom should be. So in studying Augustine we must study his ideal of wisdom and his program for achieving this ideal; and in studying Descartes we will observe how Descartes brings Augustine's ideal of wisdom into relation with the seventeenth-century expectations of wisdom that he is trying to satisfy. The study of Augustine's ideal of wisdom is the proper context for taking up the question of the relationship between philosophy and Christianity in Augustine's thought: for, as we will see, Augustine values *both* philosophy *and* Christianity only instrumentally, as complementary means for achieving wisdom. By setting the problem of faith and reason in this context, we can go beyond Gilson's and Gouhier's crude characterization of the Augustinian "spirit," while addressing their concern about how far Descartes preserved or abandoned the ultimate intentions of Augustine's philosophy.

For these reasons, Part One will be organized around Augustine's program for achieving wisdom, examining Augustine's intellectual goals, the intellectual materials available to him, and his use and transformation of these materials. Augustine had, by his own account, struggled vainly on his own to find some discipline for understanding himself and God, until he discovered such a discipline in "the books of the Platonists," works chiefly of Plotinus: so first, in Chapter 3, I will examine the content of these books. Then, in Chapter 4, I will show how Augustine appropriated and transformed the Plotinian discipline of contemplation, and how he used it to derive intuitions of soul and God and a solution to the problem of the origin of evil; this is also the place to see what Augustine considers to be the *limits* of Platonic philosophy as a means to wisdom, and the ways in which Christianity must supplement or correct it. Chapter 3's apparent detour into Plotinus, besides being absolutely necessary for understanding Augustine, will also give us the original core of the method Descartes applies, in the second and especially the third Meditations, for turning the reader's mind away from bodies and toward the mind itself, then through the mind to God. Certainly Plotinus in the raw, untransformed by Augustine, would have been worse than useless for Descartes' scientific project; nonetheless, the same discipline for achieving metaphysical knowledge (and the same conceptions of the soul and God, resulting from this discipline) that Plotinus had developed within the context of a vitalist physics was successfully detached from that physics by Augustine, and used by Descartes to provide the foundations of a radically different physics.

In Part Two I take up the central task of showing how Descartes uses this Plotinian and Augustinian discipline of contemplating the soul and God to give the foundation for a science that (he hopes) will satisfy seventeenth-century expectations of wisdom. In Chapter 5, beginning from the impasses of Descartes' pre-1628 project, I show why he would find Augustinian metaphysics an attractive candidate for a foundational science, as offering a solution to the difficulties confronting his earlier candidates, mathematics and psychology; and I show how the design of the

Meditations, framed by the sceptical arguments of the first Meditation, emerges from Descartes' attempt to resolve these difficulties of his early project and to make Augustinian metaphysics an adequate foundational discipline. In Chapter 6, the core chapter of the book, I examine the arguments of the second and (especially) the third Meditations, showing how these texts apply the basic argumentative and meditative strategy that Descartes had taken from Augustine, but also showing in detail how Descartes' novel and elaborate way of presenting this sequence of thoughts emerges from the requirements of the foundational project. In Chapter 7 I show how Descartes, in the fourth Meditation, uses Augustine's solution to the problem of evil to justify his method for reconstructing the sciences; and I address the question of Gilson and Gouhier, whether Descartes' attempt to put Augustine's metaphysics to scientific use undermines Augustine's original religious purpose. Finally, in Chapter 8, I examine how Descartes actually uses the content of these intuitions of soul and God, in the fifth and sixth Meditations and the second part of the *Principles of Philosophy*, to derive the principles of his mechanistic physics.

This study has its difficulties, and some cautions are in order. The available evidence does not permit a study of Descartes' *literary* dependence on Augustine or on other Augustinians. We have direct evidence from Descartes' correspondence that Descartes did read Augustine, but we cannot say when or how much; certainly we cannot "prove" by this type of evidence that Descartes drew on Augustine in composing the *Meditations*, the metaphysics of the *Discourse*, or the lost metaphysics of his first months in Holland. Gouhier, in the first two chapters of his *Cartésianisme et augustinisme au XVIIe siècle*, has reviewed the explicit references to Augustine in Descartes' correspondence (including Arnauld's objections to the *Meditations* and Descartes' reply); this material allows Gouhier to draw interesting conclusions about attitudes toward Cartesianism and Augustinianism among Descartes' contemporaries, but it yields no knowledge, positive or negative, about Augustinian influences on Descartes himself.[42]

---

[42] There are three letters to Mersenne (AT I,376, II,435, and III,261) and one to Colvius (AT III,247–8) where Descartes responds to his correspondents' urging him to look at a passage of Augustine, apparently in each case the same passage (*De Civitate Dei* XI,26), a not very interesting instance of the standard Augustinian argument that my conviction of my own existence cannot be deceptive, since, if I am deceived, I exist; Descartes tells Colvius that he has looked up the passage in Augustine, without expressing much interest in it. There are three more letters to Mersenne (AT III,248–9, III,283–4, and III,543–4) responding to other passages of Augustine that Mersenne had cited either as supporting or as creating a difficulty for something Descartes had said: the most important of these is the last, where Mersenne had apparently warned Descartes that he was in danger of falling into (or of being accused of falling into) Pelagianism; Descartes' reply shows that he has very little understanding of what the anti-Pelagian excitement was about. At AT III,386–7 (in June 1641) Descartes tells Mersenne that he has not yet seen Jansen's *Augustinus*, but would like to find a copy of it. Descartes writes to Mesland (AT IV,113), "I am much obliged to you for letting me know of the passages of St. Augustine that can

It should not, in fact, be surprising that Descartes leaves few clues in his letters, and none in his published works, about his reading of Augustine. It is important for Descartes' presentation of his project that he should discover the truths of philosophy, and lead his readers to discover them also, as if for the first time, with no appeal to authority; indeed, as we will see, this is a distinctively Augustinian aspect of Descartes' project. Authority is needed to guide the conduct of life, and it may also be useful in warning us against false conclusions reached through a misuse of reason, and in setting targets for reason to aim at (as when the Fifth Lateran Council urged Christian philosophers to demonstrate the existence of God and the immortality of the soul, or when Bérulle told Descartes to do so); but reason can succeed in producing understanding only if it carries out

serve to give authority to [*authoriser*] my opinions; some of my other friends had already done the same, and it gives me great satisfaction that my thoughts agree with those of such a holy and excellent person. For I do not at all share the temperament [*humeur*] of those who want their opinions to appear new; on the contrary, I accommodate mine to those of others, so far as the truth permits me." Further on in the same letter (AT IV,119) Descartes makes an interesting use of a passage of Augustine (*Confessions* XIII,xxxviii,53, apparently supplied by Mesland) to support his doctrine of the creation of the eternal truths; I will discuss these texts in Chapter 8, Section A, below. Finally, in the fourth Objections, Arnauld cites Augustine five times: besides the citation of *De Libero Arbitrio* II,iii,7 on the certainty of our own existence (already discussed in Chapter 1 above), Arnauld at AT VII,205 cites texts of *De Quantitate Animae* xv,25 and *Soliloquies* I,iv,9 on the superior certainty of intellection to sensation, at AT VII,211 gives a general reference to Augustine on the timeless eternity of God, and at AT VII,216–17 cites *De Utilitate Credendi* xi,25 on the threefold distinction between understanding, believing, and opining; I will return to this last passage in Chapter 4, Section D, and Chapter 7, Section B, below. Descartes' reply to the fourth Objections thanks Arnauld for the citation of Augustine (AT VII,219), as usual without expressing much interest; at AT III,358–9 Descartes mentions to Mersenne the bibliographical data of Arnauld's citations of Augustine in the fourth Objections, apparently to complain that Arnauld had not originally given the source for the *De Utilitate Credendi* passage. In a later letter (AT V,186, from 1648) Arnauld calls Descartes' attention to another passage of Augustine (*De Trinitate* X,x, more interesting than *De Libero Arbitrio* II,iii,7, and much more interesting than *De Civitate Dei* XI,26) on the mind's certainty of its own existence: in this passage Augustine tries to use this certainty to reach a knowledge of the *nature* of the mind, and in particular to distinguish it from bodies; Arnauld says, with some justification, that Augustine had argued here "almost the same things" as the second Meditation (on which see Chapter 6, Section A, below); unfortunately Arnauld only refers to the passage, without citing it at length, and Descartes gives no response. No issue of any philosophical interest is raised in any of these texts, except for Descartes' use of the *Confessions* passage in the letter to Mesland, and Arnauld's citations from the *De Utilitate Credendi* and *De Trinitate* (which Descartes does not discuss in his replies). These texts show that Descartes had read at least some of Augustine, at least at other people's urging, by the fall of 1640, after he had already written the *Meditations*; they do nothing to show a literary dependence on Augustine. They do show (what we knew already) that several of Descartes' contemporaries were struck by resemblances between his arguments and Augustine's; and they help to show Descartes' attitude toward the use of authoritative writers of the past to support his conclusions – namely, that authority is useful for defense against charges of innovation or heresy, or to help win a hearing for Descartes' work, but that it must never be allowed to obscure Descartes' chains of reasoning, which have their validity independently of all authority.

its arguments autonomously, assenting only to what it has come to perceive clearly, without ever relying on authority. Descartes is perfectly willing to make an external, defensive use of authority, to show that, since his opinions agree with those of respected Christian authorities, they cannot be absurd or heretical, and deserve a hearing on their own terms: this is why Descartes tells Mesland that he is happy to find passages of Augustine "that can serve to give authority to my opinions" (AT IV,113, cited in the preceding footnote), and why he tells Colvius that, though it is "so simple and so natural to infer that one exists from the fact that one doubts, that it might have fallen from anyone's pen," nonetheless "I am happy to meet up with Saint Augustine, be it only to stop up the mouth of the petty minds who have tried to find fault with [*regabeler sur*] this principle" (AT IV,248).[43] Augustine can therefore serve the same purpose as the doctors of the Sorbonne, whom Descartes will "beg to be my protectors in the cause of God," as he tells Mersenne, since "Father Bourdin's cavils have made me resolve to fortify myself henceforth, as best I can, with the authority of others, since truth by itself is so little valued" (AT III,184).[44] Descartes' remarks on Augustine are absolutely neutral on the question of whether he took something intellectually important from Augustine's arguments or intellectual methods (without, of course, taking it on Augustine's *authority*); but Descartes' attitude toward authority in general helps to explain why he tries to present his philosophy as a new departure, and to suppress all mention of its sources.

Descartes tells us in the *Discourse* that when he was old enough to leave school, "I abandoned entirely the study of letters" (AT VI,9), and he gives the impression that this abandonment was permanent. Baillet tells stories (often repeated since) about Descartes' total renunciation of book learning; but Baillet knew better than to believe such stories.

To tell no lies, his renunciation was never entire, and indeed it puts him under suspicion of dissimulation. And those who have been well versed in his works have not been able to take for a true disdain this indifference he sometimes unreasonably affected to show for books. They have remarked, on the contrary, that he made much greater use of books than he would have it believed. (Baillet II,468)

Indeed, we have already seen that in Part Two of the *Discourse* Descartes suppresses mention of the texts of Ausonius and Cicero that he had been reflecting on in November 1619; and we will see several more clear cases where Descartes neglects to mention a source that would have helped to shed light on his thought. But we can forgive Descartes this concealment of his literary sources, if, while making our scholarly work more difficult,

---

[43] For the bizarre phrase *regabeler sur*, cf. Gouhier, *Cartésianisme et augustinisme au XVIIe siècle*, p. 187: "*regabeler*: chercher des difficultés comme les gens de la gabelle, impôt sur le sel."

[44] On Descartes and the doctors of the Sorbonne, see above, Section C. See Gouhier, passim, for a discussion of the defensive use of Augustine's authority by Descartes and by the Cartesians.

it keeps us from forgetting the important questions. Since Descartes was not simply a writer, but a philosopher, our primary concern must be not with his reception and transmission of texts, but with his use and transformation of thoughts, of the broad range of intellectual materials that I have labeled intuitions, disciplines, ideals of wisdom. It is these intellectual materials, rather than particular passages of text, that we want first to locate in Augustine, and then to pursue in Descartes.

Obviously we must take these materials from the texts: but we are not forced to take them from any particular text, of Augustine or of some intermediate figure, that we can "prove" Descartes to have read. Augustinianism as a collection of intellectual materials was undeniably available to Descartes, and it is clear that he used it to some extent;[45] in trying to get clear how he used it, the first demand is to discover, by any means possible, what it was. I propose to do this by studying texts of Augustine, above all the *Confessions* and the *De Libero Arbitrio*, which contain Augustine's fullest statements of his claims of knowledge, his discipline for achieving this knowledge, and his ideals of wisdom; these texts have always been widely read, whether or not Descartes read them. It is possible that we might learn more by studying other Augustinian writers who might serve as "intermediaries" between Augustine and Descartes. I will not try to do this here, and I do not know whether it would be a fruitful endeavor. It seems to me probable that Descartes read in Augustine himself everything that he needed to know about Augustinianism: I have considered a number of historically plausible intermediaries, and in each case Descartes seems to follow Augustine more closely than the supposed intermediary does. But this, I think, is what we should expect. The history of Augustinianism is a history of plural Augustinianisms, of individual revivals of Augustine by individuals who had been attracted to the texts of Augustine by his fame and "authority," and who had discovered there some new aspect of Augustine's thought which seemed to offer a way out of the impasses of their contemporaries, and to suggest a new philosophical or theological project. This is by sharp contrast with the history of Aristotelianism, which was above all a teaching and commentary tradition, in which each master perceived Aristotle through the framework of questions disputed by the schools, and it was all but impossible to return to the text for a fresh discovery of what Aristotle's own agenda had been. In

---

[45] Recall that Gilson agrees with this conclusion, even while thinking that Descartes' peculiar way of using Augustinianism destroyed the essential Augustinian "spirit." Gilson (rightly) takes it as obvious that Augustinian intellectual materials were available to Descartes on all sides, while judging that this very omnipresence of Augustinianism makes it impossible to trace Descartes' precise sources. "To know how, by what channels, Descartes entered into contact with St. Augustine, seems to us to be beyond the power of history in the present state of our knowledge"; but ultimately "it is not of much importance whether or not we know whether he read Augustine and what he read of him. Surrounded by Augustinians, Descartes needed no more than a short conversation to see opening before him the path of a metaphysics along which his method might proceed" (Gilson, *Etudes*, pp. 199–200).

Descartes' time there were certainly a plurality of Augustinianisms, relying on different aspects of Augustine's thought, and in some cases on texts from different periods of Augustine's life. Descartes' was a *De Libero Arbitrio* Augustinianism, though it was only one of many possible *De Libero Arbitrio* Augustinianisms; it is very different from anti-Pelagian Augustinianisms such as that of Jansen, although Arnauld tried his best to reconcile the two.[46] In studying Descartes' Augustinianism, if we wish to broaden the scope beyond simply studying the texts of Descartes and of Augustine, the right direction of research is not to look for writers who might have been strictly "intermediaries" between Augustine and Descartes, but rather to explore further the range of attitudes to Augustine and varieties of Augustinianism available in the seventeenth century, so that we can understand better the forces that influenced the way Descartes assimilated the texts of Augustine (or of other Augustinians) that he read. I have said just enough to indicate why many seventeenth-century thinkers might want to derive a new philosophy from Augustine's thought, in the distinctive Renaissance and post-Renaissance sense of "new philosophy"; and this is already a distinctive way of reading and of using Augustine. Much more might be said, about Bérulle and Augustine, about Gibieuf and Augustine, about Mersenne and Augustine, that might further illuminate Descartes' philosophy. But a study of Descartes himself and Augustine himself is surely the place to begin.

[46] Perhaps Arnauld gave up in the end. Note his expression of shock on seeing Clerselier's edition of Descartes' correspondence, after Descartes' death: "I find it strange that this good monk [Desgabets] takes M. Descartes for a very enlightened man in matters of religion; whereas his letters are full of Pelagianism, and apart from the points of which he was persuaded by his philosophy, such as the existence of God and the immortality of the soul, the best that can be said of him is that he seems always to have submitted to the church" (Arnauld *Oeuvres* I,671). But Arnauld is distinguishing between Descartes the man (whom he must now disown), and the good force that kept tugging Descartes upwards against himself, namely his philosophy – that is, although Arnauld does not say so explicitly, the influence of Augustine.

Part One
Augustinian Wisdom

3

Plotinus

A. Augustine and the Platonists

To understand Augustinianism, we must read Augustine's written work as the product of a search for wisdom. The desire for wisdom is constant throughout Augustine's life; he tries different means, and in the end he thinks he has succeeded in part, but only in part. Augustine will transmit to later thinkers both the ideal of wisdom and the means that he has discovered or adapted from earlier sources, whether Christian authorities or Platonic philosophers, for achieving this end. We can best understand Augustinian wisdom by focussing both on his *Confessions*, describing his search for wisdom, and on those texts, especially the early dialogues culminating in the *De Libero Arbitrio*, in which he tries to communicate the wisdom that he discovered, both in the Platonists and in Christianity, in the *annus mirabilis* 386. The *Confessions* and these early dialogues give consistent and mutually illuminating accounts of Augustine's discovery; undeniably, though, Augustine's thought develops after 386 (both before and after the writing of the *Confessions* around 397), and we will discuss later changes where they are relevant to the Augustinianisms of later thinkers, including Descartes.[1]

---

[1] I will come back in Chapter 4, Section D, to some issues, mainly about the relation of Christianity to philosophy, on which Augustine's position seems to have changed after 386; also, in Chapter 4, Section B, I note some Plotinian theses that Augustine endorses or experiments with in early work, but abstains from or suspends judgment about later. But the main thread of my exposition of Augustine is not affected by any of Augustine's post-386 reconsiderations. There is no doubt about the basic historicity of the *Confessions'* retrospective account of the events of 386, which is confirmed by texts Augustine wrote in 386 and soon after. Prosper Alfaric, in his *Evolution intellectuelle de saint Augustin* (Paris: Nourry, 1918), accused Augustine of systematically falsifying his intellectual autobiography, and said that "it was to neo-Platonism, rather than to the Gospel, that he was converted" in 386, his Christian conversion having come much later (p. 399). Pierre Courcelle's *Recherches sur les Confessions de saint Augustin* (Paris: De Boccard, 1950) decisively refuted Alfaric, and this is now a dead issue. This does not mean that the autobiographical narrative of the *Confessions* is accurate on every point, or that Augustine is not simplifying and making retrospective sense of some aspects of his development. There is some recent discussion of these issues in the introduction to James J. O'Donnell, ed. and comm., Augustine, *Confessions*, 3 vols. (Oxford: Oxford University Press, 1992); for Augustine's life in general and its social context, see Peter Brown, *Augustine of Hippo* (Berkeley and Los Angeles: University of California Press, 1967). Against Alfaric, it is clear that Augustine was converted in 386 *both* to Platonism *and* to Christianity. Augustine thought that both

The *Confessions* is about wisdom. It is misleading to think of the book as describing Augustine's conversion to Christianity: *conversio* is indeed a central theme, but for Augustine this word means, not a change of religious allegiance, but a turning toward God and away from other things. From the beginning, Augustine identifies his desire for wisdom with a desire to "fly from earthly things to you" – that is, to God, the addressee of the *Confessions* – "for with you is wisdom" (*Confessions* III,iv,8). Christianity (that is, the authority of the scriptures and the discipline of the Catholic church) is only a means for achieving this flight to God: Augustine comes to think that it is an indispensable means, but he never thinks that it excludes other means to wisdom, or that it is sufficient in itself. A look at the history of Augustine's *conversio ad deum*, as he recounts it in the *Confessions*, will show the complementarity of Christianity with other means to wisdom; it will bring out, in particular, the importance of Platonic philosophy both in effecting Augustine's conversion, and in determining the content of the wisdom he was to grasp. Indeed, Augustine's dependence on Platonism is such that the only reasonable way into understanding Augustinian wisdom is through studying Platonic philosophy; at the same time, if we keep in mind the particular use that Augustine will make of this philosophy, this will give us a guiding thread to follow in studying the Platonists.

Although Augustine was born to a Christian mother and registered from infancy as a catechumen or candidate for baptism, he was not baptized in childhood, and grew up with only a sentimental attachment to Christianity, and very little direct knowledge about it. He studied rhetoric as a young man, and in the course of his studies discovered Cicero's *Hortensius*, an exhortation to philosophy as a fitting accomplishment for an orator. It was this book that first "inflamed" Augustine with the desire for wisdom, or for flight to God (*Confessions* III,iv,8). This desire initially led Augustine to become an auditor in the sect of the Manichees, who promised the wisdom he desired.

The Manichees were an eclectic Gnostic sect, who sometimes claimed to represent the true Christianity, though rejecting the Old Testament; this was important for Augustine, who would not entrust himself to any sect that was "without the saving name of Christ" (V,xiv,25). The Manichees, as Gnostics, based their religion on a sacred cosmology revealed to their founder Mani. The world, which they represented as entirely corporeal, was composed of two interpenetrating masses, a good mass composed of light and identified with God, and an evil mass opposed to God, from whose entanglement the good mass was struggling to free itself.

Platonism and Christianity were true; what needs to be discussed is what he thought their content was, and how he thought they functioned together to yield wisdom. Only if we prejudge the questions of what Platonism was, and of what Christianity was, and conclude that Augustine cannot have followed both at the same time, will we be led to conclusions like Alfaric's.

Although this struggle was primarily represented in cosmological terms, the Manichean elect were able, by performing the appropriate acts, to help the side of God. The human soul, or its central part, is good, and is thus a fragment of the divine light; through gnosis and appropriate acts it can shake off the body that surrounds it, and be reunited with the great mass of light.

Augustine could not be satisfied for long with such "wisdom." He recognized the contradiction between the Manichean cosmology and the science of astronomy; he decided that the astronomers were right, and that the Manichean revelation was therefore spurious. His desire for wisdom remained, and he continued to search for it among the different sects, although driven toward scepticism by the collapse of his Manichean understanding of reality. Augustine was attracted to the Catholic church by the preaching of St. Ambrose, which, like Cicero's *Hortensius* before, initially engaged his professional interest by its rhetorical technique, and then brought him around to listening to its content. According to Augustine's later report, he had been sympathetic to Catholic teaching for a long time, but was unwilling for several reasons to submit to baptism and Christian discipline. Augustine had thought, owing in part to misunderstandings and to Manichean polemics, that the Catholic doctrine of God was irrationally anthropomorphic; in addition, he was unable to understand where evil could come from if, as orthodox Christianity insists, the good God is the omnipotent creator of the world. Augustine's first difficulty was resolved by Ambrose's allegorical exposition of the scriptures, but the second difficulty remained. Augustine tells us that "the greatest and almost the only cause of my inevitable error" was that "I did not know how to conceive anything except corporeal masses, for whatever was not such [sc. corporeal] did not seem to me to be anything at all" (*Confessions* V,x,19). From the point of view of the *Confessions*, the Manichees' chief error was not (as is often hastily assumed) their dualism: beyond the falsity of their claims to cosmological knowledge, their deepest error is their corporealism, and Augustine says that this error made it inevitable, even when he had renounced the Manichean "fables," that he would continue to conceive of the soul as a portion of God, and of evil as a nature independent of God. *Why* Augustine thinks this follows, we will see later; but the intellectual struggle that Augustine depicts in the *Confessions*, culminating in Book VII, is primarily a struggle to conceive God as something real yet incorporeal: Augustine thinks that this was a necessary and almost a sufficient condition for coming to understand how the Catholic doctrine of creation could be true.

Augustine could not succeed on his own resources; the turning-point came when someone brought him "certain books of the Platonists, translated from the Greek language into Latin" (*Confessions* VII,ix,13). From these books he learned to "seek an incorporeal truth" as God; and, seeking in the way these books taught him, he did in fact succeed (by his own never-retracted judgment) in perceiving God, and in understanding God as the incorporeal being he truly is (VII,xx,26). This understanding of God allowed Augustine to solve to his satisfaction the problems about the relation between God and the soul and about the origin of evil; but it did not succeed in giving him the wisdom he was seeking. As Augustine puts it, he could "see the country of peace from a hill in the forest" (VII,xxi,27), but he could not find a path through the dangerous territory between his present position and his goal, and he could not sustain the vision amid the cares of the world. In Augustine's mature judgment, then, Platonism gives a true vision of the goal of wisdom, and specifically of God, while only Christianity gives a rule of life that allows us to attain the goal. For a Catholic bishop (as Augustine was already when he wrote the *Confessions*), this is giving remarkable credit to pagan philosophy. It is not obvious from what we have seen – and for a long time it was not obvious to Augustine himself – that Christianity will contribute any in-tellectual content at all to wisdom, over and above the content that it shares with Platonism. Ultimately Augustine does decide that Christian-ity, besides giving authorities to be obeyed and a practical rule of life, also gives some positive intellectual content, not only going beyond Platonism but actually contradicting some Platonic tenets (although not affecting the validity of the vision of God, or its consequences for the God–soul relation and for the origin of evil). I will discuss the question of specifically Chris-tian doctrines in Chapter 4, Section D; until then, I will be asking what was in the books of the Platonists, and what Augustine got from them to answer his own concerns.

After Augustine had acquired the true understanding of God, he was able (*how*, we will see in Chapter 4, Section C) to discover an origin for evil without having to posit a primitive cause outside God's control; and this resolved his remaining intellectual objection against orthodox Chris-tianity, although it did not prove that Christianity was true. But since he feels that Platonism has not given him the needed path to wisdom (but only the vision of the goal), and since he has expected all along that the successful "treatment of the illness of my soul" would come with the authority of "the saving name of Christ" (V,xiv,25), Augustine was now naturally inclined to accept Catholic Christianity. It took him some fur-ther internal struggle to decide that it was reasonable to commit himself to Christianity in the absence of proof, and then actually to do it; but he did make this commitment, under the circumstances described in *Confes-sions* VIII, and was baptized in 387, only a year after reading the books of the Platonists. Augustine gave up his profession of teaching rhetoric (which for reasons both Christian and Platonist he regarded as dishonest), and engaged himself in religious teaching and writing, working to bring his readers and hearers to the same understanding of God that he had achieved, showing how the scriptures (including the contested passages of the Old Testament) could be understood in accordance with reason, and arguing against Manichees and other heretics and pagans, either that the doctrines of the Catholic church were true, or that it was reasonable to believe them in the absence of proof. The vast body of Augustine's work that has been preserved, including the *Confessions*, emerges from his pursuit of these goals.

This sketch serves to bring out the enormous importance of the "books of the Platonists" in forming Augustine's conception of wisdom. As we will ultimately see, the discipline of intellectual contemplation that Augustine took from the Platonists, the resulting conceptions of the soul and of God, and the resulting explanation of evil, are central not only to Augustine's project of wisdom but also to Descartes'. By studying the books of the Platonists, and studying them in the proper way, we can grasp the core of what Augustine took from the Platonists and of what Descartes then took from Augustine, transformed at each stage but with the central conceptions remarkably preserved: thus the study of the Platonists, absolutely necessary for understanding Augustine, will also turn out to give direct insight into the argument of the *Meditations on First Philosophy*.

In the *Confessions* Augustine fails to cite either the titles or the authors of the "books of the Platonists"; but it is possible (as the result of much past scholarly labor) to say some things with confidence about what books Augustine read.

Augustine gives us some information on who the authors might have been when he speaks of "Platonists" in other places. In the *De Civitate Dei* he explains that "the most noble recent philosophers, who were pleased to follow Plato, did not wish to be called Peripatetics or Academics, but Platonists," and that "among these the Greeks Plotinus, Iamblichus, and Porphyry are very eminent, and the African Apuleius was an eminent Platonist in both languages, i.e. in both Greek and Latin" (VIII,xii). Augustine agrees with modern scholars in considering Plotinus as the chief of these thinkers: further on in the *De Civitate Dei* he calls him "this great Platonist" (X,ii), and in the early dialogue *Contra Academicos*, written only months after his conversion, he had praised Plotinus, as the reviver of Platonic philosophy, in florid terms:

The voice of Plato, which is the most purified and lucid in philosophy, has shone out from the parted clouds of error most of all in Plotinus, who has been judged to be a Platonic philosopher so like to him that one would think that they had lived together, or rather, since there is so much time between them, that he [Plato] had lived again in him [Plotinus]. (*Contra Academicos* III,xviii,41)

In the *De Civitate Dei* Augustine cites works of three Platonists, Plotinus, Porphyry, and Apuleius, and of these he takes a favorable attitude only toward Plotinus: the others are cited only on questions of worship and salvation, to attack their support of the worship of demons.[2] And in the early dialogue *De Beata Vita*, written about the same time as the *Contra*

---

[2] Apuleius was not a thinker of the stature of Plotinus and Porphyry; Augustine discusses him because he wrote on demons and because he was, like Augustine, an African who wrote in Latin. There is no reason to suppose that Augustine knew anything of Iamblichus but the name.

Academicos, when he refers to his recent reading of Platonist works (pre-sumably the same as those mentioned in the *Confessions*), he seems to identify them as works of Plotinus. He writes,

> Having read a very few books of *****, to whom I have heard that you [Manlius Theodorus] are most devoted, and having compared them as much as I could with the authority of those who have treated of the divine mysteries, I was so inflamed that I would have cut loose all those anchors [aspirations to marriage and honor], if the judgment of men had not influenced me. (*De Beata Vita* 4)

The missing name here is in some manuscripts *Platonis*, and in others *Plotini*; the Benedictine editors print *Platonis*, but since a correction from *Plotini* to *Platonis* is far more plausible than a correction from *Platonis* to *Plotini*, most modern scholars have assumed that *Plotini* was the orig-inal reading, and Paul Henry succeeded in establishing this beyond rea-sonable doubt, through a close inspection of the manuscript tradition.[3]

Assuming that it was Plotinus (or perhaps Plotinus and Porphyry) that Augustine had read in 386, a series of scholars have tried to discover sources for Augustine's "Platonist" conceptions in the extant Plotinian texts. The crucial work in this project was Henry's *Plotin et l'Occident*, which laid down canons for reconstructing Augustine's reading of Ploti-nus, against the dogmatic excesses of many earlier writers (who uncriti-cally traced to Plotinus ideas that Augustine could have taken from many other sources), and against the sceptical excesses of Willy Theiler (who denied that Augustine had ever read Plotinus, and asserted that all Au-gustine's apparently Plotinian ideas, and all his references to Plotinus, were taken from Porphyry).[4] As Henry says, there are three kinds of pas-sages in Augustine's writings that can give evidence for his indebtedness to Neoplatonic philosophers: in the first rank are "Augustine's own tes-timonies on the writings of the philosophers which he has read, on the circumstances in which he read them, on the intellectual or moral profit which he drew from them, and on the impressions with which they left him"; then, in the second rank, are "the [unattributed] textual citations of Neoplatonic philosophers embedded in Augustine's works," and in last place "the doctrinal passages where Augustine proposes an idea as his own, but where modern criticism, by a comparative study, detects traces of Platonism."[5] The early students of Platonist influences in Augustine, by focussing on evidence of the third and weakest kind, were each able to decompose Augustine into his sources, each in a different arbitrary fash-ion. Henry, by contrast, restricts his attention to testimony of the first type where it is available and otherwise to close textual parallels of the second type: he thinks that textual parallels, unlike doctrinal parallels, are objectively recognizable and provide a small but solid basis for passing

---

[3] Henry, *Plotin et l'Occident* (Louvain: Spicilegium Sacrum Lovaniense, 1934), pp. 82–9.
[4] Theiler, *Porphyrios und Augustin* (Halle: Niemeyer, 1933).
[5] Henry, p. 65: I have rearranged the order in which Henry lists these three types of passages to make it conform to the order in which he ranks them as evidence.

judgment on the relations between Augustine and Plotinus. Henry succeeded in collecting many close verbal parallels between texts of Augustine, mostly from the *Confessions* and the *De Civitate Dei*, and passages from several of the treatises of Plotinus' *Enneads*. More recent scholars have discovered further textual parallels, and have therefore extended Henry's list of the Plotinian treatises that Augustine could be asserted to have read; they have also given evidence of some indirect transmission of Plotinian ideas to Augustine through Porphyry and Ambrose.[6]

Such scholarship, while useful, is insufficient. Once we know that Augustine read the texts of Plotinus, we must ask what he found there, and how he could use it to help him on toward wisdom or toward the apprehension of God, and to resolve his difficulties with Christianity. Henry and his successors have avoided dealing directly with these questions, perhaps because they think they can be addressed only by the old and inadequate method of doctrinal comparisons between Augustine and Plotinus.[7]

[6] On all this, see Courcelle's *Les lettres grecques en Occident* (Paris: De Boccard, 1943), Courcelle's later *Recherches sur les Confessions*, and the introduction to Robert J. O'Connell, *St. Augustine's Early Theory of Man* (Cambridge: Belknap Press of Harvard University Press, 1968). It probably makes very little difference whether Augustine was influenced by treatises of Porphyry or not; there is no reason to think he took anything from Porphyry that would be significantly different in content from what he could equally have read in Plotinus. The question of Porphyrian influence seems to excite some (mostly Catholic) writers because of the air of scandal that apparently still attaches to Porphyry as the author of the *Against the Christians*. Thus when Augustine, at *Confessions* VII,ix,15, defends his use of pagan philosophy by saying that, while he took what was good (and hence belonged rightly to God) from the pagans, he did not accept the idolatry that he found mixed in with the true doctrine, O'Connell argues that Augustine must be thinking only of Plotinus' "idolatrously" exalted conception of the soul, and not of "Porphyry's theurgic tendencies" (p. 110). But – apart from the fact that Augustine never criticizes Plotinus' doctrine of the soul – the difference between Plotinus and Porphyry is beside the point: Plotinus was just as much a pagan as Porphyry was, and there is no reason to think he would have been any better disposed toward the Christians than Porphyry was, if he had known as much about them.

[7] Within the line of scholarship founded by Henry, the most ambitious attempt to explore Augustine's use of Plotinus has been O'Connell's *St. Augustine's Early Theory of Man*, which tries to understand the development of Augustine's view of the soul as a creative reaction to descriptions of the soul taken from Plotinus (O'Connell has pursued the same line of thought further into Augustine's works in *St. Augustine's Confessions: The Odyssey of Soul* (Cambridge: Belknap Press of Harvard University Press, 1969), and more recently *The Origin of the Soul in St. Augustine's Later Works* (New York: Fordham University Press, 1987)). O'Connell is concerned with cases where Augustine internalizes and consciously or unconsciously modifies Plotinus' words, rather than repeating them verbatim. While O'Connell recognizes that he cannot produce the strict certainties Henry demands, he tries to achieve as much certainty as possible by looking for "parallel patterns" or parallel sequences of thought illustrated by similar images (but not necessarily extended *verbal* parallels). O'Connell draws on a number of these parallel patterns to show Augustine at work constructing his understanding of the faith, using Plotinian materials where they are available and appropriate, but progressively separating himself from elements of Plotinus' thought that he recognizes as incompatible with Christianity.

A great advantage of O'Connell's work is that he takes Augustine seriously as a thinker, and that he shows Augustine thinking, not just helping himself to bits of other people's

But there is better evidence than this, namely, as Henry himself says, "Augustine's own testimonies on the writings of the philosophers which he has read, on the circumstances in which he read them, on the intellectual or moral profit which he drew from them, and on the impressions with which they left him." Henry does not fully exploit this class of evidence: he addresses himself chiefly to the question of what treatises Augustine read, and not to the subtler question of what profit he took from them. But Augustine gives us, above all in *Confessions* VII, a valuable and powerful report on just this question. This report is compressed, allusive, and obscure; but it is perfectly sufficient, when it is used intelligently, and with a parallel use of Augustine's dialogues and with an understanding of Plotinus, to show what insights Augustine found in the books of the Platonists and what he did with them in his own books. There is no question here of doctrinal comparisons between arbitrarily selected passages of Augustine and equally arbitrary passages of Plotinus: we are starting from what Augustine himself says about his own reading and thinking, and using this to interpret Augustine's writings.

Previous attempts to interpret Augustine through Plotinus have been deficient largely because they have not seriously tried to grasp Plotinus' thought in itself, and so have not been able to say what he gave to Augustine, beyond some isolated assertions or images. In the remainder of this chapter our goal will be to understand Plotinus' thought, naturally with a view to what Augustine took from it. We will not try to isolate the particular passages in which Augustine found that thought (given the number of repetitions in Plotinus, this will often be impossible), but will use whatever combination of texts brings out the thought most clearly. We are looking not so much for a set of doctrines as for a strategy of

thoughts. But his method remains a liberalized version of Henry's: he turns to texts of Plotinus only to illuminate difficulties in Augustine, and so presents Plotinus merely as a none-too-consistent collection of passages displaying a variety of themes and images. O'Connell is not able to specify what the intellectual content was in these books of the Platonists that could set Augustine's mind afire in the way Augustine describes. To do this, it is not sufficient to take Augustine seriously as a thinker: we must take Plotinus seriously as well. By stating clearly *what Plotinus said* that addressed the problems Augustine was concerned with, we will be in a better position to see how it was able so fundamentally to take hold of Augustine, to reorient him away from Manicheism and toward Catholicism, and to direct his understanding of his new faith.

O'Connell's work has not been especially well received among Augustine scholars, and certainly his readings of some particular texts are eccentric. But on the basic issue, there seems to be a general feeling that O'Connell has exaggerated Plotinus' influence on Augustine. I think this feeling is wrong, and often it seems to come from a protective attitude toward a Christian saint, and from no great understanding of Plotinus' philosophy. What is truer is that O'Connell does not capture accurately what Plotinus' influence was: he puts an exaggerated stress on the preexistence and fall of the soul, and more generally the soul's "divinity," as what Augustine took from Plotinus. But Augustine found much more in Plotinus than this (a discipline of intellectual contemplation, understandings of soul and Nous and of the origin of evil); and, as we will see, one crucial insight Augustine took from Plotinus was the essential *difference* between the soul and God (= Nous), whose natures the Manichees had assimilated.

thought, which is the essence of what Augustine took over from Plotinus, and which led Augustine to the understanding he needed.

Augustine describes his reading of the books of the Platonists in *Confessions* VII,ix–xvii. In Chapter ix he says how he discovered these books, and retrospectively compares them with the Christian scriptures, showing how much of Christian truth the Platonists had, how much of it they omitted, and how much they contradicted. In Chapters x–xvii he presents the understanding he received from his reading, framed in Chapters x and xvii by a general and a more precise account of the vision of God that formed the core of this understanding. The initial account of Chapter x can give us an epigraph for our study of Plotinus, since it sets the question we must answer: what is Plotinus doing that could be described in the terms Augustine uses, and how could that solve Augustine's problems?

Augustine writes:

> And being admonished thence [by the books of the Platonists] to return to myself, I entered under your [God's] leadership into my innermost parts, and I was able to do so because you had become my helper. I entered, and by some kind of eye of my soul I saw above that same eye of my soul, above my mind, an immutable light, not the [light] that is common and apparent to all flesh, nor as if it were something greater of the same kind, as if that [light] had become much brighter and occupied the whole [world] with its magnitude. This was not that [light], but a different [light], very different from all these things. Nor was it above my mind as oil is above water or as heaven is above earth, but it was above because it had made me, and I was below because I had been made by it. (*Confessions* VII,x,16)

Augustine identifies this light with "truth," while reminding the reader of Biblical descriptions of God as truth, and he says that knowing this truth is our way to know the eternal and immutable: "who knows truth, knows [this light], and who knows [this light] knows eternity." Augustine says that God lifted him up to look at this light, but that he was unable to bear the sight: he could not see God, but heard the word of God from above, promising a transformation by which he would be assimilated to God and become able to look on him. Augustine recognizes his inability to face God as a punishment for his sins; he then says to himself,

> "Is truth nothing because it is spread out neither over finite nor over infinite extensions of places?" And you [God] called out from afar: "I am who am." And I heard as it is heard in the heart, and straightway there was no ground for doubting it, and I would more easily have doubted that I was alive than that that truth existed which is perceived when it is understood through the things that are made. (Ibid.)

Thus in a sense he was able to see this divine light, but not to look at it or to see it distinctly; but he came away convinced that this light existed without corporeal extension, and that it was possible to see it. In the next six chapters Augustine recounts the thoughts or visions, concerning the things below God in their relation to God, that he derived from his original vision of divine truth; then in Chapter xvii he retraces the path of the original vision of Chapter x, explaining how he searched for God as something immutable, and how he came for an instant to see him.

It is above all the vision of Chapter x, or its explication in Chapter xvii, that we must understand; the rest will follow automatically for us, as it did for Augustine. Augustine says that his vision came through the help of God; but his reading of Plotinus gave the stimulus. Nor did the texts merely "admonish" him to take the first step of returning into himself: they gave the plan for the whole series of intellectual operations that Augustine describes, and so they shaped the content of the resulting visions.

It is not immediately obvious what Augustine is claiming to have learned. But he had learned something with a definite intellectual content, which he would develop at great length in his later work: we cannot allow the ecstatic tone of his description, or his emphasis on the moment of vision, to persuade us that this was a "mystical experience" without content. Understanding Augustine and Augustinianism depends on understanding that content, and turning to Plotinus will allow us to understand it. We must understand what the series of intellectual operations was that Plotinus taught and that Augustine learned; how this process was used to undermine corporealism; what understanding of the soul and God resulted; and how this understanding yielded a solution to the problem of the origin of evil. Once we understand how Plotinus did all these things, it will be easy to see how he gave Augustine what he needed to develop an understanding of the Christian scriptures against the Manichees.

B. Platonism, anti-Stoicism, and the method of ascent

B.1. What was Platonism?

The conflicts between the Greek philosophical schools give the essential context for Plotinus' intellectual discipline of turning inward to the soul and upward to God. If we grasp this context, we can explicate both the content of the intuition of God which Plotinus provided to Augustine, and the anti-corporealist polemical consequences of that intuition, which Plotinus intended against the Stoics and which Augustine applied against the Manichees.

Any understanding of Plotinus' work depends on understanding his relation to the Platonic school. When Augustine praises Plotinus, it is always as an eminent Platonist; as we have seen from the *Contra Academicos*, he thinks of Plotinus as a reviver of Platonism (so that Plato can be said to have "lived again" in Plotinus), and not as an innovator. What attracts Augustine in Plotinus is the Platonic philosophy; Plotinus' particular way of presenting that philosophy is important to him, but only as the path, not as the goal.

To understand in what sense Plotinus' work was a revival of Platonism, we must know what Platonism was: many commentators have gone wrong here, and have proceeded to misconstrue Plotinus' whole philosophy. Plotinus is sometimes considered as an essentially independent thinker, a mystic, a man with his own experiences who wished to construct a picture of the universe as he had experienced it. For this purpose, so it is said, Plotinus found the way of thought of the Platonic dialogues congenial, and helped himself to whatever conceptions in Plato he found useful, transforming them by his own interpretations in the process; but this did not imply a monogamous attachment to Plato, and Plotinus borrowed equally freely from the thought of such later thinkers as the Stoics, whenever they might say anything useful to articulating his own experience of the universe. On this understanding, Plotinus' Platonism would consist, not in affiliation to an established school, but simply in a personal appreciation of Plato.

This interpretation is found to varying degrees in a great many writers, but it is entirely false. Plotinus was a Platonist, and to be a Platonist in the third century AD meant something definite: it meant to be a member of a certain school or *hairesis*.[8] When in the year AD 176 the emperor Marcus Aurelius established four chairs of philosophy in Athens, he assigned one to the Epicureans, one to the Stoics, one to the Peripatetics, and one to the Platonists; and from this time onwards there was a Platonic philosopher in Athens claiming the title of "successor of Plato" and thus the headship of the Platonic school. Plotinus studied in Alexandria and taught in Rome, and was not the recognized head of the school in his day; but it is everywhere clear from Porphyry's *Life of Plotinus* that he regarded himself as a member of the school, and that he used the texts of Plato together with the accreted commentaries of the later Platonic tradition as the basis for instruction. When Porphyry describes Plotinus' teaching, he says that "at the meetings he would have [the students] read the commentaries, whether it was of Severus, or of Cronius or Numenius or Gaius or Atticus, and among the Peripatetics those of Aspasius and Alexander and Adrastus, and of those that we chanced to find" (VP 14). Porphyry goes on to say that "he did not say anything out of these [books] once and for all, but he had his own distinctive mode of consideration, and he brought Ammonius' thought to bear in examining the questions" (ibid.). This means that Plotinus did not feel himself bound to what any particular earlier commentator had said in interpreting Plato, but that he used the commentary tradition as a basis for discussion, and would use his own insights or those of his teacher Ammonius to stake out a particular position within the hermeneutical debates. That the debates were debates within the Platonic tradition would be clear, even if we did not have the evidence of Plotinus' writings, from the way Porphyry lists the authors that were read: he lists the Platonists first without explicitly calling them Platonists, taking it as obvious that the Platonists would be the primary authors discussed, but he regards it as noteworthy that Plotinus also had his students

---

[8] On the notion of *hairesis*, and on Platonism as a *hairesis*, see John Glucker, *Antiochus and the Late Academy* (Göttingen: Vandenhoeck und Ruprecht, 1978), pp. 159–225.

read the works of the Peripatetics, members of a distinct though allied sect. No authors are listed from the Stoics or the other philosophical schools; Plotinus was well aware of these authors, but he did not *teach* them; they represent the alternate philosophy that he had to respond to, not the positive doctrine that he taught.

Porphyry does say that "concealed [*lanthanonta*] Stoic and Peripatetic doctrines are mixed in among his treatises" (ibid.), and this is true in an important sense. But we must be very careful in determining the sense in which they are "concealed" or implicitly present in Plotinus' work. They are *not* present *explicitly*, *not* stated as the Stoics or Peripatetics would have stated them; they have been transformed in the debate between the Platonists and the other schools. The Stoics, in particular, were enemies of the Platonists, and there was a long tradition of Platonic polemic against them. If we understand what Platonism was and how it came into conflict with Stoicism, and then assess Plotinus against the background of this controversy, we will see that it was precisely in the course of Plotinus' peculiar strategy for defending Platonism against the Stoics that he presented a version of Platonism with "concealed" Stoic doctrines, and that there is no *positive* Stoic influence in his work. This will be important for understanding Augustine, since it was precisely this peculiar strategy for defending Platonism against the Stoics which Augustine took over from Plotinus to defend Christianity against the Manichees.

What, then, was Platonism? What was the distinctive teaching of the school?

The Platonists are distinguished from the other recognized philosophical schools of antiquity by the fact that, following Plato, they "believe that there are two worlds, an intelligible world in which truth itself resides, and this sensible world which it is plain that we perceive by sight and touch; so that the former is true, and the latter is like the true [*veri similis*] and made in its image," as Augustine rightly says when he describes the doctrines of Plato at the beginning of his history of the Academy (*Contra Academicos* III,xvii,37). This doctrine is enough to distinguish the Platonists from the other schools, and especially from their chief rivals, the Stoics, who believed, as Augustine goes on to say with regard to Zeno, that "there is nothing beyond this sensible world, and that nothing is done in it except by some body" (III,xvii,38). But Platonism did not consist merely in this doctrine; as Augustine says, Plato "is said to have put together a complete discipline of philosophy, which there is now no time to discuss" (III,xvii,37). Augustine wisely cites the lack of time to avoid discussing in detail the philosophy that Plato is said to have put together: for it is very difficult to determine to what extent Plato did indeed himself construct the comprehensive philosophy that was later ascribed to him. But at a minimum it is true that Plato's followers were able to elaborate the doctrine of the intelligible and sensible worlds into a comprehensive philosophy by following out hints in the Platonic dialogues. The tasks of Platonic philosophy which were not resolved simply by the

84

positing of an intelligible world largely concerned the problematic status of the sensible world as an imperfect likeness of the truth. What kind of subsistence does a world have if it is not "real" or "true"? How does it come to exist in such a way that it imitates intelligible order in some respects, while falling short of it in others? After first recalling how Plato himself tried to approach these questions, I will sketch the systematic philosophy which later Platonists put together out of these Platonic suggestions, and which Plotinus and Augustine accept as Plato's authentic teaching.[9]

Plato first puts forward the hypothesis of a separate intelligible world in the dialogues of his middle period. In the *Phaedo* he distinguishes the ordinary objects which we perceive by the senses from certain eternally existing things which are named by such expressions as "the beautiful itself" or "the equal itself." Plato asserts that we must have intellectual knowledge of the X itself before we come to sense particular objects which are X, and that we judge the sensible objects by reference to the intelligible standard: we say that a sensible object is X when it participates in the X itself, but it will still somehow fall short of the X itself, and be less than perfectly X. Plato does not explore the ontology of these intelligible objects in the *Phaedo*, beyond asserting that there are such things; but in the *Republic* he goes on to assert that *only* the intelligibles are real beings, and that the objects of sensation are not. Plato says that the sensibles "participate in both being and not-being, and would not rightly be said to be purely either" (478e1–3), and again that "these things are ambiguous, and none of them can be firmly thought either to be, or not to be, or both, or neither"; the best we can do, he concludes, is to "place them in between being and not being" (479c6–7). But this is not a precise account of the status of these sensible semi-beings; Plato seems to feel that their nature excludes precision.

Further on in the *Republic* Plato offers an analogy to explain how such a sensible object can be related to an intelligible being: the sensibles are images or imitations of the intelligibles, so that a sensible object which participates in the intelligible X would *resemble* X without really *being* it, just as a reflection or a painting of a body resembles that body without being it. But this account raises more questions than it answers. It does not answer for the case of the sensibles any of the questions we would immediately want to ask about images: how are they produced and in what medium, and how faithfully do they reproduce the thing they represent?

In the middle dialogues Plato does not explain the properties of a sensible object in any other way than by saying that it participates in some intelligible form. Thus he can give no account of the properties of sensibles *qua* sensibles: any attempt to explain by participation why there *is* a

---

[9] I give a much fuller treatment of these themes of Plato's later philosophy in my book *Plato on God as Nous* (Carbondale: Southern Illinois University Press for the *Journal of the History of Philosophy* Monograph Series, 1995).

sensible world in addition to the intelligibles, or how and to what extent the different parts of that world come to participate in the different intelligible forms, could only result in tautology. In the later dialogues, therefore, he tries to give a different kind of account of the sensible world, one that would explain its particular mode of being and how it comes to mirror the intelligible world to the extent that it does. The different later dialogues are not all saying the same thing, but they are frequently trying in different contexts to address the same problems, and the solutions that Plato proposes share the same central themes, however they may differ in detail. Here I will take the *Timaeus* as my main point of reference for the philosophy of the later dialogues, since all branches of the Academy took this dialogue as Plato's authoritative statement on the problems of the sensible world.

What distinguishes sensible objects from intelligible forms is that they exist in matter. This matter, the "receptacle and nurse of all becoming," as Plato calls it (*Timaeus* 49a5–6), is entirely without qualities in itself, and is neither an intelligible form nor a sensible body, but "provides a location to all things as have becoming" (52b1), in that it can "receive the likenesses of all intelligible and eternal things" (51a1–3).[10] Thus sensible objects come to be when some piece of the receptacle receives the likeness of an intelligible form, like wax receiving the impression of a seal. This is still no more than a remote analogy; but at least it gives some coherence to the notion of a sensible world having its own (inferior) form of existence, and it offers an explanation for why sensible things do not participate perfectly in the intelligibles. If a sensible object that resembles some intelligible form still falls short of it, Plato will not attribute this to a further intelligible form of imperfection, but rather to the inherent unruliness of the matter, which cannot receive likenesses of perfect and eternally stable things without weakening and distorting them. Thus perfection and order in the sensible world proceed from an intelligible cause, but imperfection and disorder come from the material substrate underlying bodies.

This hypothesis still does not explain why pieces of matter should reflect the intelligibles to any degree at all, or why they should do so in an orderly way, so that, for example, the planets should follow regular orbits. On Plato's account there is order in the separate intelligibles, and these are

---

[10] At *Timaeus* 51a1 I accept Cook Wilson's *pantôn noêtôn aei te ontôn* instead of the *pantôn aei te ontôn* printed in the OCT; the change in the sense is not philosophically significant. Plato himself uses no Greek word that would correctly be translated as "matter," although later Platonists use the word *hulê*, coined as a philosophical term perhaps by Aristotle, perhaps by some other Old Academic (the word occurs in a fragment of Speusippus, but one whose authenticity is disputed). But I think, in agreement with all the ancient Platonists, that it is legitimate to describe the "receptacle" of the *Timaeus* as matter; although the phrases I quote here might perhaps be applied to mere empty space, many of the comparisons that Plato uses to describe the receptacle imply that he is conceiving of it as a material substrate.

the proper objects of science; but he has not yet explained how even an imperfect order might come to exist in the sensible world, or how there can be even an approximate science of bodies. The metaphor of impressions from a seal is insufficient to explain this: the intelligibles are absolutely constant, and cannot have a tendency to impress themselves on a piece of matter at one particular time rather than another. Plato must assign some other cause for the form's impressing itself upon matter, other than the form itself.

Plato solves this problem by taking up a traditional theme of pre-Socratic philosophy: the world is governed by an intrinsically rational divine power, and this power is the source of rational order to the things it governs. A science of the world is possible because both the objective rationality of the world order and the subjective rationality of the human mind proceed from the same divine source. Heraclitus calls this source of rationality *logos*; Plato follows Anaxagoras in calling it *nous*. As Plato says in the *Philebus* (28c6–8), "all the wise agree that *nous* is king of heaven and earth," producing order throughout the world, and especially in the regular circuits of the heavenly bodies. Plato builds the physics of the *Timaeus* on this hypothesis, and the divine "demiurge" of that dialogue is identical with the world-governing *nous* that Plato invokes in the *Philebus* and also in passages of the *Laws*.

It is very important, not only for understanding Plato, but for understanding the whole current of thought that passes through Plotinus to Augustine and Descartes, to understand what Plato means when he says that *nous* is king of heaven and earth. Rather than trying to translate the word "*nous*," I will generally transcribe it in English as "Nous," with a capital N, reserving this usage for one special sense of the equivocal Greek word "*nous*," the sense Plato is using at *Philebus* 28c6–8 and parallel theological passages.[11] Since I have devoted a whole book, *Plato on God as Nous*, chiefly to interpreting these passages of Plato, I will here simply summarize my main conclusions about the meaning of "*nous*." The conventional rendering of "*nous*" by "intellect" is misleading, because it suggests that *nous* is the mind or rational soul, the substance or faculty within us which is capable of intellection. While "*nous*" can mean the rational soul (and can also mean the act of intellectual perception), Plato is using the word, in theological contexts of the *Philebus* and *Laws*, to mean a separately existing *virtue* of rationality. At *Philebus* 30c6ff., clearly referring to the same Nous that was earlier called "king of heaven and earth," Plato calls it "*sophia kai nous*," wisdom and Nous: context and sentence structure require that the "and" be epexegetic, connecting two names for the same entity rather than two entities. Wisdom is a virtue, a virtue which, for Plato, exists eternally by itself, separate from the souls which become wise by participating in it; and this is Nous. We might render the word, a bit archaically, by "Reason" with a capital R. The Nous that is

---

11 See the Preface for this technical usage.

the universal source of order to the sensible world is not the rationality immanent in human souls (or even in the world-soul), nor is it the objective rationality exhibited especially by the heavenly bodies, but the separate Reason that souls (and, in a different way, bodies) must participate in, in order to become wise and rational and orderly. Since we see that the heavenly bodies are moved in a rational and orderly way, we conclude that they are governed, directly or indirectly, by Reason-itself. Because Nous is Wisdom-itself, it is eternally and essentially wise, having (indeed *being*) knowledge of all the intelligible objects; because it is Reason, and because the nature of reason is to impose order on an intrinsically unordered multiplicity, Nous is able to order the world, causing different portions of matter to participate in different intelligible forms at different times, according to a single all-encompassing rational pattern.

Plato thinks that the causality of Nous, that is, rational causality, is characterized by a striving to make something the best possible. He represents this dramatically in the *Timaeus* by showing the demiurge deliberating (30a2ff) how to introduce order into the world, and make it as perfect as the conditions of its matter allow: "for it neither was nor is fit for him who is the best to produce anything except the most beautiful." "Thus he found, after reasoning, that of the things which are visible by nature, no work that is irrational [*anoêton*] will ever be more beautiful as a whole than one that possesses reason [*nous*]." The best order in matter will be the most rational order, the one that comes closest to the rationality the demiurge himself possesses; but how is he to introduce this rationality into matter? The demiurge finds that "it is impossible for *nous* to come to be in something without soul," and therefore he makes the world as a *zôon empsuchon ennoun*, an animal possessing soul in its body and *nous* in its soul, making it in the likeness of the intelligible animal-itself.

The theory of the soul of the world is Plato's solution to the problem of how rational order can be transmitted from the intelligible to the sensible world. The divine Nous does not impose order on bodies by martial law, by personally intervening and moving them where it is rational for them to go; instead it forms the world-soul as an instrument of government. Plato does not say precisely why this arrangement is preferable: but presumably he feels that non-living bodies could be ordered only by an external physical compulsion which would contradict the rational and incorporeal nature he ascribes to his divinity. Soul, on the other hand, can be made to perceive the truths of reason, and thus can be made rational without violence. The demiurge therefore creates a soul for the world and makes it rational and harmonious (whether or not, as Plutarch thinks, there is a previous irrational state of soul). Once this rational soul has been completed and "interwoven" with the body of the world, and "makes a divine beginning of unceasing and intelligent life" (36e2–5), then, according to Plato's conception of soul in the later dialogues, it will naturally communicate its rational order to the body it animates. Plato says in the *Phaedrus* that "the essence and definition of soul is to be self-moved," and that "every body, if it is moved from without, is soulless, but if it is self-moved from within it is ensouled, because this is the nature of soul" (245e3–6). Souls with their connate motion are the "source and principle of motion to such other things as are moved" (245c9), so that if the motion of a soul is made rational, the motion it communicates to the bodies it governs will also be rational, and a rational order will be imposed on bodies, not by external compulsion, but by the soul or principle of life and motion which dwells within them. It is this process, according to Plato, which accounts for order in nature, and above all for the regular motions of the heavenly bodies.

According to this account, the soul is the medium through which rationality is transmitted from the intelligible to the sensible world. This raises the question: what is the nature of soul itself, if it is not part either of the intelligible or of the sensible world? It seems that it must somehow be intermediate, and Plato seems to be trying to explain how this can be when he describes how the demiurge forms the world-soul. At one stage in the preparations, "he blended together, from the undivided and always constant substance, and from that which becomes divided about bodies, a third intermediate form of substance from the two of them" (35a1–4), and then composes the soul from this blend and from similar intermediate realities. Plato gives no clear picture of how the two kinds of substance could be "blended," and the obscurity of the text has led to a wide variety of interpretation among both ancient and modern commentators. But it seems most natural, rather than asserting that Plato had one particular interpretation in mind, to suppose that he simply wanted to describe the soul as some kind of intermediate reality in contact with both the sensible and the intelligible worlds, and that he chose the description of "blending" to indicate how this might be conceived, without being able to fill in the details. A systematic Platonic philosophy will have much work to do in explaining the relations between body, soul, and Nous, as also between the sensible and intelligible worlds.

B.2. From Stoicism to Platonism

Platonism, as a systematic school-doctrine, emerges only after Stoicism and in reaction to Stoicism. This is paradoxical and important. Plato's first successors in the Academy seem to have tried to elaborate a systematically teachable Platonism, but little of their work has survived, and it does not seem to have had much impact on the Platonism of late antiquity. Zeno of Citium, the founder of the Stoic school, was a student of Polemon, Plato's third successor as head of the Academy; and for two hundred years or more after this time it was the Stoics who pursued the constructive problems of Platonic philosophy, while the Academy took up a sceptical position. But although Stoic physics unmistakably arises out of reflection on the *Timaeus*, and although the Stoics at least sometimes claimed Plato as an authority, they diverged sharply from Plato's real doctrine in holding (as Augustine puts it) that "there is nothing beyond this sensible world, and that nothing is done in it except by some body." Stoic physics thus rewrites the *Timaeus* in corporealist terms. Diogenes Laertius quotes the Stoic Antipater of Tyre as saying that "the whole world is an ensouled and rational animal [*zôon empsuchon kai logikon*]," much as Plato had called it a *zôon empsuchon ennoun*; but Antipater then adds that "it has aether as its ruling principle [*hêgemonikon*]" (DL VII,i,139). "The world is governed according to *nous* and providence [*pronoia*]," say Chrysippus and Posidonius, "*nous* pervading every part of it, as the soul does in us" (ibid.); but there is no suggestion that Nous or soul also exist *outside* the corporeal world, or that they have been introduced into bodies by the will of an incorporeal God. Instead, the world-soul, the *nous* in the world, and the divine demiurge must all be identified with each other, and with the active principle in bodies: "for they think that there are two principles of all things, the active and the passive. The passive is unqualified substance, or matter, while the active is the *logos* which is in it, or God: for he, being eternal, produces [*dêmiourgein*] each thing throughout all of it" (DL VII,i,134). Furthermore, this active principle is not in matter merely as a Platonic or Aristotelian quality or immanent form, but is itself a subtle body, a *pneuma*, blended with matter as wine is blended with water (cf. texts at SVF II,1028–48). Thus the Stoics will explain how Nous pervades all parts of the world according to the peculiarly Stoic doctrine of total blending: "blending happens throughout the whole [*di' holou*], according to what Chrysippus says in the third book of the *Physics*, and not [merely] by circumscription or juxtaposition [of microscopic parts of the substances]: for even a bit of wine which has been thrown into the sea will be coextended with its whole breadth, and then will be combined with it" (DL VII,i,151; cf. texts collected in SVF II,463–81). If the divine Nous is blended with matter in this way, even an arbitrarily small piece of matter will contain some portion of this active principle, and so can be governed by it. Different bodies will receive different kinds of order, as the active principle is present in them in different forms: "some are governed by *hexis* [cohesion], some by nature, some by irrational soul, and some by a soul having reason and thought" (SVF II,460), but all of these are portions of the same active principle coextended with matter: in particular, "our soul is a fragment" of the soul of the world (DL VII,i,143).

From the time of Zeno until about the first century BC, this was the closest approach in organized philosophical teaching to the cosmology of the *Timaeus*. When Platonism reemerges (sometime in the first century BC or AD) as a particular school of dogmatic philosophy in competition with the others, it emerges out of Stoicism and in opposition to Stoicism, as an attempt to defend the strict doctrine of Plato, and above all of the *Timaeus*, with its incorporeal soul, incorporeal Nous, and incorporeal world model, against Stoic corporealism. The first issue, for any would-be Platonic philosopher, is to decide whether Plato was a dogmatist or a sceptic: Antiochus of Ascalon in the early first century BC (still calling himself, not a Platonist, but an Academic like his predecessors) seems to have won the day for the dogmatic interpretation; but Antiochus was largely following the lead of the Stoic Posidonius, and Antiochus' Plato is essentially a Stoic in physics, who denies incorporeal substances. Platonism proper, as it emerges in the century after Antiochus, takes it for granted that Plato is a dogmatist, and it is therefore free to turn its energies against the Stoicizing interpretation of Plato that Antiochus had represented. The first philosophical business of the new Platonic school was to vindicate against the Stoics the incorporeality of the principles of physical things, both as the true interpretation of the *Timaeus* and as the philosophical truth.[12] We may fairly say that the school was constituted, not so much by any particular set of theses, as by a progressive process of de-Stoicization and decorporealization, and that the new characteristic theses of the school (e.g. the incorporeality of qualities) were merely the precipitates of this process. To place Plotinus in the context of the Platonic school is to locate his work within this process of de-Stoicization, recognizing what conclusions and arguments and strategies of thought he took over from earlier Platonists, but also seeing what Plotinus added, and how he was able to deepen and radicalize their work – and, in so doing, gave Augustine what he needed to overcome Manicheism.

Although we possess vast amounts of writing from two first-century-AD Platonists, Plutarch of Chaeroneia and Philo of Alexandria, neither of these men was a professional teacher of philosophy, and the value of their works as evidence for the school is complicated by Philo's Judaism and by the literary character of Plutarch's work. But we have a good picture of typical Platonic school teaching in the second-century *Didaskalikos* of Albinus.[13] This is not primarily a polemical work but an expository hand-

---

[12] For a survey, both of what is known of Antiochus' philosophy, and of the subsequent development of Platonism in the first and second centuries AD, see John Dillon, *The Middle Platonists* (London: Duckworth, 1977).

[13] Both the title of this treatise and the name of its author are disputed. The treatise survives in two manuscripts, one of which calls it *Didaskalikos tôn Platônos dogmatôn* ("[book] for teaching Plato's doctrines"), the other *Epitomê tôn Platônos dogmatôn* ("summary of Plato's doctrines"). Both manuscripts attribute the book to "Alcinoos" (otherwise unknown), but the correction to "Albinus" (a known second-century Platonist) has been widely accepted, although it has recently been challenged by John Whittaker, and the majority of scholars at present favor "Alcinoos." I favor "Albinus," but it will make very little difference (although the mid-second-century date is more secure if the book is really by Albinus, and we know that Albinus was a student of Gaius, one of the Platonist authors whom Porphyry says that Plotinus discussed with his students). I will cite the text by chapter, page, and line numbers, following the edition of John Whittaker and Pierre Louis, Alcinoos, *Enseignement des doctrines de Platon* (Paris: Belles Lettres, 1990). Albinus' exposition is generally parallel to that of the *De Platone et Eius Dogmate* of Apuleius (ed. Paulus Thomas, *Apulei Madaurensis Opera Quae Supersunt*, vol. 3, *De Philosophia Libri* (Leipzig: Teubner, 1938)), probably not because of any direct connection between these two men, or even because they both studied with the same teacher, but simply because they both represent the standard Platonist teaching of the time. For a discussion of Albinus and Apuleius and their place in second-century Platonism, see Dillon, *The Middle Platonists*.

book of philosophy from the Platonist position, going through all the standard topics of logic and physics and ethics. But the (relative) novelty and the stress of the *Didaskalikos* are on the physics, or as Albinus prefers to say, the "theoretic" (first at iii,153,28–30); and, within this, on anti-Stoic theses asserting the incorporeality of various principles of physical things. Indeed, Albinus' reason for preferring Aristotle's term "*theôrêtikê* [*philosophia*]" to the customary and Stoic "*phusikê*" is precisely that physics is the science of bodies, and that theoretical philosophy must include not only physics but also a science of incorporeal things. Following Aristotle's *Metaphysics* VI,1, Albinus divides the theoretical sciences into physics, mathematics, and theology (iii,153,43–154,5 and vii,160,43–161,9): theology is about "the first and highest and most principal causes" (vii,161,1–3), and Albinus insists, with Aristotle and against the Stoics, that the divine first causes are incorporeal, and therefore that the Stoics are wrong to treat theology as a part of physics. The three highest principles are matter, the Ideas, and "the god who is the father and cause of all things" (ix,163,11–14), and Albinus devotes a chapter of his theology to each of these principles. It seems paradoxical to treat matter under theology, but Albinus insists that matter too, although not properly incorporeal, is also not corporeal, but only potentially corporeal (viii,163,4–10), against the Stoics, who had identified matter with the passive body. Albinus gives several arguments that "the first god" (or "the first *nous*") must be incorporeal (x,165,42–166,14), and the Ideas too (which are the *noêmata* and *noêseis* of this *nous*) must be eternal substances apart from sensible things (Chapter ix). As an afterthought, Albinus adds Chapter xi, proving that even the qualities of bodies and the active principles [*ta poiounta*] in bodies are incorporeal, against the Stoics, who had identified these things (like God and souls) with *pneumata*.

As we see from Albinus, the task of Platonic "theoretic" is simultaneously constructive and polemical; but the negative aspect of the work tends to be better developed. This is natural especially because the central Platonist thesis is that the principles of physical things are incorporeal, and this is a *negative* thesis, since "incorporeal" is a negative term: it is much easier to refute the Stoic claim that soul and Nous (and so on) are bodies than to give a distinct positive conception of what these things are and of how (being incorporeal) they act upon bodies. Certainly the Stoics, in working out a consistently corporealist version of "Platonism," had committed themselves to many uncommonsensical conclusions about bodies, and laid themselves open to easy attack. This negative side of Platonism is compatible with an underlying scepticism about human abilities to grasp or to communicate positive metaphysical knowledge; and our fullest compendium of Platonist anti-Stoicism comes in two works of Plutarch (a Platonist with some real sympathy for the sceptical New Academy), his *On Stoic Contradictions* and his *On Common Notions against the Stoics*. In the former work, Plutarch "does not undertake to examine anything wrong they may say, but only those things where they differ from themselves" (1049b), and in the latter "I set aside many of their absurdities, sticking with those that go against the [common] notion" (1083a): that is, he will show that the Stoics fail to meet their own standards of consistency and fidelity to intuition, but he will not confront their philosophy with an alternate system. This applies in particular to Plutarch's criticism of the doctrine of corporeal principles. The Stoics, to maintain their corporealism, must regard gods and souls (and even passions of souls, 1084a–b) and qualities as kinds of body; this is not immediately absurd, but Plutarch and the other defenders of incorporeal principles try to derive absurdities from this premiss.

The most basic violation of common notions that Plutarch and the other philosophers discover in the Stoic theory of principles is the doctrine of the total blending of bodies. The Stoics are forced to this doctrine, if the color (say) or the soul which is present everywhere within a body is also itself a body; and "they make a doctrine out of the refutation, as they do in many other cases, accepting hypotheses which conflict with the [common] notions" (1077f). But, say Plutarch and the others, "it is against the [common] notion for a body to be a place for a body, and for a body to pass through a body which contains no void, but where one full thing enters into another full thing and receives the admixture of something which, on account of its continuity, contains no interval or space" (1077e). If this is so, the Stoic theory of principles is built on an absurdity, and this one criticism is enough to overturn the whole edifice. For this reason, Platonic and also Aristotelian philosophers show great enthusiasm for this line of attack: the Peripatetic Alexander of Aphrodisias (ca. AD 200) devotes a whole treatise, *On Blending and Growth*, to refuting the Stoic doctrine of blending. Albinus, too, makes this the final point in his series of arguments that qualities are incorporeal: "if qualities too are bodies, then two or three bodies will be in the same place, which is most absurd [literally 'out of place']; and if qualities are incorporeal, what produces [*to dêmiourgikon*] them is also incorporeal" (xi,166,25–8).

Such negative arguments are unable to give us any positive knowledge of what the different incorporeal realities (qualities, soul, Nous, etc.) are, or of what causality these beings exercise on bodies: certainly such arguments cannot bring us to the traditional goal of Platonic philosophy, an intellectual "vision" of the highest objects of knowledge. If Augustine had read a treatise like Plutarch's *On Common Notions against the Stoics*, then Plutarch's refutation of Stoic corporealism might have helped to free Augustine from his Manichean corporealism, but it could not have led him to wisdom: Augustine might have been brought as far as scepticism, but he would still be unable to see God or to know what God is, and he would still be unhappy and alienated from God. To acquire his positive knowledge of God, Augustine needed a different kind of Platonist anti-Stoicism, one that would teach how to conceive the incorporeal divine principles, as well as exposing the confusion at the heart of the Stoic doctrine of a corporeal God. This is what Augustine found in Plotinus, and probably no earlier author could have given Augustine what he needed. Still, Plotinus' way of philosophizing is not something radically new, but a natural step in the ongoing Platonist struggle against Stoicism and Stoicizing interpretations of Plato. As we can see from Albinus, the Platonists of the second century AD did at least officially keep the higher goals of Platonism in mind, and they offer some arguments (or some strategies of thought) to lead us to a more positive conception of God, free from Stoic corporealism. We can find some of these ideas in Albinus' Chapter x, on God, although they are not marshaled there into a coherent program for attaining knowledge: but they show the resources that the Platonic tradition provided for achieving a "vision" of God. Most strikingly, they show how the Platonists, in trying to clarify the Platonic conceptions of divine things against Stoic corporealism, were forced to rely on Aristotle.

Albinus begins Chapter x by mentioning the difficulty (for human beings, immersed in the senses) of knowing God, then gives an account of God anyway; only then does he discuss the ways that we can know God, and then he goes back to arguing that God is incorporeal and free from bodily conditions. To see what is interesting in this rather disorderly material, it is best to start with the ways of knowing God: Albinus distinguishes three. The first conception [*noêsis*] of God is by stripping away the attributes that do not belong to him, but the second and third are positive conceptions, through "analogy" and through "superiority in honor [*en tô(i) timiô(i)*]": to use the standard terms, these are the ways of negation, of analogy, and of eminence. Albinus refers the ways of analogy and eminence back to Platonic sources, and his explanation of the passages from Plato shows how he intends us to conceive of God.

Plato takes us to God by the way of analogy in the Sun simile of the *Republic*, and by the way of eminence in the ascent to beauty of the *Symposium*. Albinus mimics the wording of these passages (without explicitly naming them), but he goes beyond what Plato says to assimilate these texts both to each other and to the concept of Nous. Someone who has completed the ascent of the *Symposium*, says Albinus, "intellectually perceives [*noei*] the good-itself and the object of love and of desire, like a light appearing to and illuminating the soul that ascends in this way" (x,165,30–3). But this is not quite what Plato says: the *Symposium* speaks of a vision of the beautiful [*kalon*], not of the good [*agathon*], and does not compare it to a light. While Albinus is not really doing violence to the text, he is clearly assimilating it to the passage in the *Republic* (508–9) where Plato does speak of the good, and where he does compare it to a source of light. More significant is what Albinus does with the *Republic* passage itself. He says:

as the sun is to vision and to the visibles, not being itself sight but providing seeing to the former and being-seen to the latter, so the first *nous* is to the intellection [*noêsis*] in the soul and to the intelligibles [*ta nooumena*]: for, not being the same as intellection, it provides thinking [*to noein*] to it and being-thought [*to noeisthai*] to the intelligibles, illuminating the truth about them. (x,165,21–6)

Everything here is Platonic except the key phrase, "the first *nous*": Plato says these things not about Nous but about the Good.

Albinus is not being entirely unreasonable in identifying Nous and the Good. In the *Phaedo* and *Timaeus* Plato associates the (efficient) causality of Nous with the (final) causality of "the best." In the *Timaeus* and *Philebus* the transcendent Nous, the source of intelligible order in the world, is also the source of intelligence in souls; and it is tempting to connect this with the Good of the *Republic*, which is "the cause both of knowledge and of truth as what is known" (508e3–4), as the sun is the cause both of vision and of what is seen. Plato does not say here that the Good is *nous*, but only that it is the cause of the *nous* or *noêsis* in the soul; but Albinus cannot see what else the separate Good would be, and how else it would cause *noêsis* in the soul, unless it is the Nous-itself that the soul participates in to become rational. In identifying the Good with this Nous, Albinus is identifying the Good of the *Republic*, not only with the demiurge of the *Timaeus*, but also with the divine *nous* of Aristotle's *Metaphysics* XII,7 and XII,9, and with the *nous* that "produces all things" in *De Anima* III,5. Whether or not Albinus is interpreting these passages of Aristotle correctly, it is clear that he is using them to fill out what is described only cryptically and indirectly in Plato.[14]

In *De Anima* III,5 Aristotle passes from discussing the part of the soul that can be called *nous*, the part that is capable of intellection, to speak of the *cause* that produces *noêsis* in the soul: as in every other genus there is a matter "which is potentially all these things," and also an art or something analogous to an art, the efficient cause that makes or produces [*poiei*] all these things, "necessarily these differences must exist also in the case of soul [*en têi) psuchêi)*]" (430a13–14).[15] In the case of the power of

---

[14] I discuss the Platonic issues (on which I think Albinus is wrong) in *Plato on God as Nous*; I discuss the Aristotelian texts and their relation to Plato in "Aristotle and Plato on God as Nous and as the Good," *Review of Metaphysics*, 45 (1992), pp. 543–73. As I point out there, Aristotle says that his God is not only *nous*-itself (or *noêsis*-itself) but also the good existing "separated and itself-by-itself" (*Metaphysics* XII,10 1075a12–13); he denies that the good-itself is the *idea* of the good, because he thinks that (if there were such an idea) this would be simply one more good, differing from other goods only by being eternal, and none the better for that (cf. *Eudemian Ethics* I,8, esp. 1218a11–14; cp. *Nicomachean Ethics* I,6 1096b3–5). Aristotle is arguing, against Plato, that Nous is already the good-itself, and it is unnecessary and unintelligible to posit a good even higher than this. Albinus, however, interprets Plato in such a way as to make him agree with Aristotle, by identifying the idea of the good with Nous.

[15] I will use the traditional phrase "*nous poiêtikos*" (conventionally translated "agent intellect") for the principle that is *to aition kai poiêtikon, tô(i) poiein panta* (430a12) in the case of soul; "*nous poiêtikos*" is not Aristotle's own phrase. Readers who think that this *nous poiêtikos* is something internal to the soul often translate "*en tê(i) psuchê(i)*" (430a13) as "within the soul." While the words can mean this, they can also mean merely "in the case of the soul"; and in the analogous case that Aristotle has just cited, the efficient cause

---

intellection, "the former is *nous* by becoming everything, and the latter [is *nous*] by producing everything, being a state like light: for light somehow makes the things that are potentially colors actually colors [i.e. actually seen as colors]" (*De Anima* III,5 430a14–17). Aristotle's description of the action of this *nous poiêtikos* echoes the *Republic*'s description of the Good: but what kind of being is the *nous poiêtikos*? Some late ancient commentators on the *De Anima* take it to be a special part within the rational soul itself. But Albinus, like his younger Peripatetic contemporary Alexander of Aphrodisias, takes it to be Aristotle's version of the Platonic Nous-itself, identical with the unmoved mover of the outermost heaven described in *Metaphysics* XII. I think Albinus and Alexander are interpreting Aristotle correctly, but I cannot and need not argue that here; it is enough to point to the passages in Aristotle that Albinus is using, rightly or wrongly, and to show how he uses them to clarify the Platonic concept of Nous.

In *De Anima* III,5, immediately after introducing the *nous poiêtikos*, Aristotle says that it is more noble [*timiôteron*] than the potential *nous*, being "separate and impassible and unmixed, since it is actuality by its essence" (430a17–18). Since this *nous* is not potentially anything beyond what it actually and essentially is, it cannot undergo change: "it does not *sometimes* intellectually perceive, and *sometimes* not perceive [*ouch hote men noei, hote d' ou noeî*]" (430a22), but rather, by its essence, it always actually *noei* whatever is *noêton* for it. Aristotle says that "when this has been separated out, it is only what it [essentially] is, and this alone is immortal and eternal" (430a22–3).[16] This is close to what *Metaphysics* XII says about the divine substance that moves the outermost heaven. Aristotle there rejects any description of this god that would imply that "its essence is not *noêsis* but [merely] a potentiality [for *noêsis*]," since in that case "it would not be the best substance, since the noble [*timion*] belongs to it through *noein*" (1074b19–21), and the external cause that actualizes its potentiality for *noêsis* would be more *timion* than it, contrary to Aristotle's postulate that this god is most *timion* of all. Aristotle concludes that the god's essence is actual *noêsis*, so that it never ceases intellectually perceiving, never shifts its perception from one object to another, and is unchanging and eternal and immortal. (He also concludes that the objects of its

(the art) is something external to the matter or the thing formed out of the matter. It is thus at least possible that the efficient cause in the case of soul is also external to the soul.
[16] This text helps explain why Platonist commentators on the *De Anima*, eager to harmonize Plato and Aristotle, took the *nous poiêtikos* as something internal to the human rational soul: if only the *nous poiêtikos* is immortal, and if this is not part of the human soul, then the human soul is entirely mortal, contradicting a basic Platonic commitment. (The commentators take it for granted that Aristotle believes that the soul participates in a separate Nous-itself, but they insist that he *also* believes in an immortal active part of the human soul, and that this is the *nous* he is referring to here.) Albinus and Plotinus, unlike the later Platonist commentators, do not have to make Aristotle agree with the Platonic thesis of the immortality of the rational soul, since they are merely using ideas from Aristotle to clarify Plato, without claiming to produce a systematic harmony of the two authors.

noêsis cannot be other than itself, since otherwise it would have *noêsis* not through itself but from something else, which would be more *timion* than it.) In short, Aristotle is saying that the divine Nous that moves the heaven cannot be a potential *nous*, but must have all the attributes that *De Anima* III,5 assigns to the *nous poiêtikos*: this is true whether (as Albinus apparently thinks) the Nous presiding over my soul is numerically identical with the Nous above the soul of the heaven, or whether they are merely the same *kind* of being.

Albinus is using these Aristotelian descriptions of Nous already in his initial account of God:

Since better than soul is *nous*, and better than the potential *nous* is one that always *actually* perceives [*noôn*] all things at once, and more beautiful than this is its cause and whatever exists above these, this will be the first god, being the cause of eternal activity to the *nous* of the whole heaven [or world, *ouranos*]. And it acts without being moved, being to this [the *nous* of the heaven] as the sun is to vision when [the vision] looks toward it, and as the object of desire moves desire but remains itself unmoved: in this way this *nous* too will move the *nous* of the whole heaven. (x,164,18–27)

Albinus' reasoning here corresponds to his own description of ascending through "superiority in honor [*en tô(i) timiô(i)*]" (x,165,33–4); and although Albinus there cites the ascent of the *Symposium* as his model, here he clearly draws his details from Aristotle, both from *De Anima* III,5 and from *Metaphysics* XII, and uses these to clarify what God is. Even the Stoics agree that God is *nous* (interpreted as a special kind or state of soul); but Albinus, using Aristotle's analysis of potentiality and actuality, gives the description of God as *nous* enough content to entail that God is above all souls. The rational soul can be called *nous* in a sense, but since its essence does not entail actual *noêsis*, it is only *potential nous*: even if (like the soul of the heaven) it always actually perceives all the intelligibles, it still does not have this actuality by its essence, but requires a cause to actualize its *noêsis*. This argument gives us a positive knowledge of what God is: as the cause actualizing the soul's *noêsis*, God must be an essentially actual Nous, and thus essentially superior to souls.[17] The *Republic* and *Timaeus* give names and images that can be applied analogically to God, but these are unclear and could be interpreted in the Stoic fashion, assimilating Nous to souls and souls to bodies; the Aristotelian distinction between potentiality and actuality allows us to rule out Stoicizing inter-

---

[17] John Dillon (pp. 282–4) gives a different account of Albinus on *nous* and soul: I think he introduces serious confusions by insisting on translating "*nous*" consistently as "mind." "*Nous*" sometimes means the kind of soul that is capable of intellectual perception; sometimes means the act of intellectual perception; sometimes means a soul that is actually intellectually perceiving; and sometimes means Nous-itself, which makes a potentially intellectually perceiving soul actually intellectually perceive. Once we grasp the concept of Nous-itself, and learn not to imagine it as a magnified "mind" or rational soul, Albinus' theology is straightforward enough. God is Nous-itself, and eternally causes the world-soul to intellectually perceive; no further hierarchy or distinctions are involved.

pretations, and gives a clearer positive conception of what God is and of how God acts on the sensible world, while being pure actuality and therefore remaining unmoved.

Although Aristotle thought that in *Metaphysics* XII he was criticizing the *Timaeus'* account of Nous as the creator of the world, Albinus takes him merely to be offering an appropriately non-corporealist interpretation of the *Timaeus'* descriptions:

[God] is a *father* [cf. *Timaeus* 28c3–5] by being the cause of all things and by ordering the heavenly *nous* and the soul of the world toward himself and toward his thoughts [*noêseis*]. For by his will he has filled all things with himself, awakening the soul of the world and turning it toward himself, being the cause of its *nous*: and when this has been ordered by its father it orders the whole nature in this world. (x,164,40–165,4)

Aristotle had said that, since Nous is unmoved, it can move only as an object of desire; Albinus accepts this as a description of how Nous creates, and why it must do so through the soul of the *ouranos* – whether this is simply an Aristotelian celestial soul or the Platonic world-soul. Aristotle had said that Nous would think only perfect things, and would therefore think only itself, and not direct itself toward the physical world; Albinus turns this argument in a Platonic direction to explain the nature of the Ideas which are the model for creation: "since the first *nous* is most beautiful, it must also take the most beautiful as its *noêton*, and nothing is more beautiful than itself: thus it will think [*nooiê*] itself *and its own thoughts* [*noêmata*], and this act of its is an Idea" (x,164,27–31; my emphasis). The agent Nous can function as a demiurge by perceiving not only itself, but also the different thoughts or Ideas that are in it: it "awakens" the celestial or cosmic soul by actualizing its potential *nous*, so that this soul too comes to perceive the Ideas, and is moved to form the sensible world in their image. Against his own intention, Aristotle has given the means, not only for forming a "pure" or "high" concept of God, free of Stoic corporealism, but also for reading the *Timaeus* as an adequate description of God and his activity.

B.3. Plotinus' strategy of ascent

Albinus' theology illustrates the directions in which the Platonists were forced to turn when they tried to give an adequate positive account of divine incorporeal realities; especially in his use of the Aristotelian potentiality–actuality distinction, and of Aristotle's descriptions of the *nous poiêtikos*, he is marking the path that Plotinus and later Platonists were to follow. For a reader like Augustine, eager to learn how to conceive an incorporeal God, Albinus' presentation would be much more useful than the negative anti-Stoic arguments of a Plutarch. But Albinus' theology remains inadequate. Albinus takes over from Aristotle some slogans about what God is, and cryptic shorthands for some arguments, but not the arguments themselves that could lead us to knowledge; Albinus could hardly expect his followers to achieve an intellectual intuition of God after reading the few lines he devotes to describing God's nature, and though he does also describe the means of our knowing God, he does this only as an afterthought, and as a summary of the different descriptions of God in Plato. Although Albinus speaks (in passing) of an ascent of the soul, his own theology in the *Didaskalikos* is not designed to give the soul the kind of intellectual discipline through which it could achieve a knowledge of God. Plotinus, by contrast, consciously works out his philosophy as a program of ascent, modeled on the ascent of the *Symposium*, taking the student from contemplating bodies, through contemplating souls, to contemplate Nous and what is beyond: by this kind of training, the would-be philosopher will learn to overcome the popular and Stoic habit of thinking through corporeal images, and he will reach not simply a correct verbal formulation of what God is, but a direct knowledge-by-acquaintance of the incorporeal principles. This is what Augustine, in particular, will need.

Plotinus' philosophical doctrine differs from the teaching of Albinus and other second-century Platonists chiefly on two points, in his doctrine of the first God and in his doctrine of soul. Plotinus, like Albinus, identifies the first God with the Good of the *Republic*; unlike Albinus, he refuses to identify this Good with the first Nous, but places it instead above the first Nous and its *noêta*. In this Plotinus is following tendencies in other branches of second-century Platonism to place the supreme God above the demiurge, as well as obscure indications in the Platonic texts themselves. Plotinus' doctrine that the souls present in bodies all originally come from a single transcendent Soul, and never fully lose their identity with it, is more of a departure from traditional Platonic teaching; but here too he is offering a solution to the problems of the earlier tradition, by reinterpreting (against Stoicizing interpretations) difficult passages of the *Timaeus* and *Philebus* about the formation of individual and cosmic souls. In neither of these cases is he making a radical departure from earlier Platonism, and in neither case is his modification of earlier doctrine what principally recommends him to Augustine.[18]

---

[18] Since Plotinus' doctrinal innovations (as opposed to his philosophical method in presenting Platonism) are not important for what Augustine took from Plotinus, I will not try to discuss them here in any serious way. I briefly discuss Plotinus' claims about the unity and multiplicity of souls in Sections C and D below (without claiming to make fully consistent sense of his position). In Chapter 4, Section B, I have some discussion of Augustine's tentative experiments with the Plotinian theses of a unity of souls and of a first God superior to Nous. For the Platonic passages bearing on the origin of individual and cosmic souls, see Section D below. In recognizing a god superior to the demiurgic Nous, Plotinus is following the second-century Platonists Moderatus and Numenius, on whom see Dillon; also, encouraged by Aristotle's testimony on Plato's doctrines, Plotinus identifies the Good of the *Republic* with the simple One of the first hypothesis of the *Parmenides*. Plotinus' identification of the first God with a One above Nous is important (for my purposes in this book) chiefly because it allows him to admit a plurality of forms

Plotinus' version of Platonism is characterized, not so much by a particular doctrine, as by a personal *seriousness* in his approach to philosophy, which clearly distinguishes him from such philosophers as Albinus and Apuleius, at least as they appear in their surviving works, and which leads him to develop the discipline of intellectual contemplation that Augustine will take over from him. Porphyry in his *Life of Plotinus* praises Plotinus' eagerness in the search for wisdom as well as his success in finding it, and in addition to his own recollections he calls many witnesses, culminating in the response of the oracle of Apollo to the question "where the soul of Plotinus had gone." Porphyry gives the long and rather pompous oracle in Chapter 22, and goes on in Chapter 23 to explain what Apollo meant. Porphyry describes the oracle as saying of Plotinus, among other things, "that he was vigilant and kept his soul pure, and always hastened towards the divine, which he loved with his whole soul, and that he did everything to be delivered, to 'escape the bitter swell of the life that feeds on blood' here-below" (where the quote is from the oracle). And Porphyry adds his own comment on Plotinus' diligence and its reward: "thus especially to this daemonic man, who many times led himself on in his thoughts to the first and transcendent [*epekeina*] God according to the ways indicated by Plato in the *Symposium*, that God appeared who possesses neither shape nor form [*morphên . . . idean*], established above Nous and above all the intelligible [*noêton*]"; Porphyry adds that this happened four times to Plotinus in Porphyry's presence, and that it has happened once to Porphyry himself.

It is hard to know how to respond when one man says he can vouch for the fact that another has seen God at least four times. Fortunately, we need not try to determine what was actually happening at those four moments in Plotinus' life; it is enough to know that Plotinus and those around him believed that it was possible, with the appropriate moral and intellectual discipline, to come to "see" God with the mind, and that this was the proper goal of a philosopher. Plotinus and his school therefore directed their philosophical activity, not simply toward stating and defending a doctrine, but toward an intellectual vision of the objects of that doctrine, the first God and the other incorporeal principles of corporeal things. And the ways to this vision had been indicated by Plato in the *Symposium*: the task of the philosopher was to follow them.

As we have seen, Albinus believes this too, as one item of Platonic doctrine; but he does not take it seriously enough to organize his writing around it, following instead the prescribed order of topics needed for a general education. Dillon attempts to explain Albinus' apparent "dryness," in comparison with other second-century Platonists, "simply from

in Nous without admitting a plurality in the first principle. I will return to this issue especially in discussing Descartes' doctrine of the creation of the eternal truths in Chapter 8, Section A.

the fact that he is engaged in writing an elementary handbook,"[19] but one must also explain why Albinus wrote an elementary handbook and Plotinus did not. This will become clear enough, from Plotinus' side, when we look at both the theory and the practice of philosophical education in the *Enneads*.

Plotinus discusses the theory of education in several places, notably in the short treatise *On Dialectic* (I,3) and in the introductory chapters of *On the Three Principal Hypostases* (V,1) and *On Nous, Ideas, and Being* (V,9); in all of these the question is "what art or discipline or practice leads us up to where we ought to go?" (I,3, from the beginning). "That where we ought to go is to the Good, and the first principle may be taken as agreed and as proved in many ways" (ibid.), and the only question is how to get there; Plotinus always answers by paraphrasing and harmonizing the Platonic accounts of the soul's ascent in contemplation from the *Symposium*, the *Republic*, and the *Phaedrus*, and laying out the stages of the ascent. From the *Phaedrus* in particular, and perhaps from the allegory of the cave in the *Republic*, we learn that our soul is in a fallen state when it is in the body; it has seen the intelligible forms in the supercelestial place before falling, but it has forgotten them upon immersion in the senses and passions of the body. It therefore needs to be reminded of the higher world it once inhabited. Our souls, says Plotinus at the beginning of *On the Three Principal Hypostases*, "have forgotten their father God, and though they are portions from the intelligible world [*ekeithen*],[20] and are entirely of it [*ekeinou*], are ignorant both of themselves and of it [*ekeinon*]." Having deserted the intelligible world, "they were ignorant even that they came from there [*ekeithen*], as children who have been immediately torn away from their fathers and grow up for a long time far away are ignorant both of themselves and of their fathers," in that, being ignorant of their parentage, they do not really know who they themselves are. For this reason, says Plotinus, they do not give proper honor to themselves, and prefer body to soul. "Therefore one must give a double account [*logos*] to those who are thus disposed, if indeed one is to turn them toward the opposite things and toward the first principles [*ta prôta*], and would lead them up to the highest and the one and the first [*tou prôtou*]." The first account "shows the worthlessness [*atimia*] of the things now honored [*timômena*] by the soul," a task Plotinus defers; the second "teaches and reminds the soul of its race [*genos*; both 'ancestry' and 'nature'] and of its value." Plotinus regards this as the primary task, and accordingly organizes the remainder of the treatise around the stages of the education of soul in

---

[19] Dillon, p. 285; cf. also p. 268.
[20] Plotinus frequently uses forms of *ekei* ("there") and *ekeinos* ("that") to refer to the intelligible world, and *entautha* ("here") and *hode* ("this") to refer to the sensible world. A translation must read in either too little or too much. I will try to indicate this dilemma where it occurs.

coming to recognize first its own value and then that of the things prior to it: thus in Chapter 2 he leads us from the contemplation of body to the contemplation of soul, and in subsequent chapters he leads us beyond that, first to soul's "father" Nous, and then finally to the Good as the "father" of Nous.

Thus Plotinus, unlike Albinus, explicitly organizes his work in accordance with his theory of philosophical education. Soul is to be led out of its immersion in the body to an awareness of increasingly better realities: first itself, then Nous, then the Good itself. In each case, the transition is to be accomplished by the method of the *Symposium*: we ascend from contemplating the beautiful object X to contemplate the higher and more beautiful object Y which is the source of X's beauty. In the treatise *On Dialectic*, this was Plotinus' primary answer to the question of how to get to the Good and first principle: perhaps a few "naturally philosophical" people have never fallen into admiration of bodies, and can proceed directly to contemplation of the incorporeals, but most even of the people who are potentially philosophers have been willing to settle for corporeal beauty, and must therefore be led up to its incorporeal source. This will have to be done by stages, and the aspirant will dwell for a while with the beauties on the level of soul which are mentioned in the *Symposium*, beauties of practices and laws and then of arts and sciences and virtues. But at least the higher kinds of beauty in soul are intellectual, and from these we can proceed to their source in Intellect: "from virtues already [one can] go up to Nous, to being; and there [*ekei*] one must go the upper way" (I,3,2,13–15). What Plotinus describes in *On Dialectic* he does in such treatises as *On the Three Principal Hypostases* and *On Nous, Ideas, and Being*, and this method largely determines his accounts of soul, of Nous, and of the Good. We may note in particular that Plotinus, like Albinus, takes over the Aristotelian ascent from potential to productive Nous and uses it to interpret one of the stages of the ascent of the *Symposium*; thus Plotinus, like Albinus, will give a positive explication of the Platonic concept of Nous that is largely derived from Aristotle, although unlike Albinus he will not identify this Nous with the Good.

Plotinus' determination to model his practice after his theory of philosophical education affects not only his positive teaching, but also his polemic against the Stoics. Indeed, the two can hardly be separated: since most of us have sunk to the contemplation of bodies, Plotinus' work will mostly be to lift us up again; and to the extent that we have formulated a "philosophy" to defend and explicate our contemplation, Plotinus' work in lifting us out of this will be a polemic against this fake philosophy. In practice, Plotinus identifies this with a polemic against Stoicism, or less often against Epicureanism. From the introductory chapters of *On Nous, Ideas, and Being* we can see how he conceives these different schools of philosophy in terms of his general theory of philosophical education, and how this leads him to formulate a polemical strategy which is significantly different from the strategy of earlier Platonists and Aristotelians; then, by

turning to the central parts of *On Nous, Ideas, and Being* and other treatises, we will see how Plotinus carries out his strategies of polemic and
positive philosophy.

I quote in full the first chapter of *On Nous, Ideas, and Being*:

All men, as soon as they are born, use sensation before intellection, and necessarily
attend to the sensibles first; some spend their life remaining here [*entauthoi*], judging that these things are the first and the last, and taking the painful and pleasant
in them for evil and good they judge that this is sufficient, and go through life
pursuing the one and warding off the other. And those of them who have pretensions to reason [*logos*] take this as wisdom, like heavy birds who are weighed down
by the many things they have taken from the earth, and are unable to fly up,
although nature has given them wings. Others have risen up a little, the better
part of the soul moving them away from the lower things, from the pleasant to
what is more beautiful; but having been unable to see what is above, because they
do not have anywhere else to remain, they are borne down, with the name of
virtue, to 'practical actions' and 'selections' of the things below, from which they
had originally intended to arise. But a third kind of divine men, by a better power
and by the sharpness of their eyes, have seen the upper light as by sharp-
sightedness, and have risen there [*ekei*] as if above the clouds and mist here below
[*entautha*], and have remained there, looking down on all things here and enjoying
the true place which is their own, like a man arriving from much wandering at
his well-ordered fatherland.

This chapter is interesting because it gives Plotinus' diagnosis of the
spiritual condition of his philosophical opponents, and his way of classi-
fying them within the Platonist framework. He refers to specific opponents
only by allusion (as is his practice generally), but it is still perfectly clear
who he means. There may be many people who never arise from the fall
into childish dependence on the senses, but "those of them who have
pretensions to reason" and formulate their concern for sensible things into
a version of wisdom are clearly the Epicureans, the only major school of
Greek philosophy to identify pleasure and pain with good and evil.

Similarly, the second group, those who have incompletely risen and
have been unable to extricate themselves from the demands of life in the
body, are represented in philosophy by the Stoics. These people have
taken the first step in the ascent to beauty by rising to admire the beauty
of soul, which is virtue; but not being able to grasp the true origin of
virtue in Nous, they have taken virtue to be essentially practical rather
than contemplative, and have consequently pursued the beauty to be
found in right human action in the world. Plotinus applies to this class
the terms of mild disparagement traditionally reserved for those who practice only the political and not the philosophical virtues. The mention of
the philosophers as a "third kind of divine men [*triton genos theiôn an-
thrôpôn*]" suggests that he is taking the threefold division of humanity
from a passage of the *Phaedo* describing the fate of different types of soul:
the lovers of pleasure will be reincarnated as lower animals, "those who
have practiced the popular and political virtue, which they call temperance

and justice, which comes to be by habit and exercise without philosophy or *nous*" will be reincarnated as social animals or again as human beings, but only "those who have been philosophers and are entirely pure" will arrive after death at the "kind of the gods [*theôn genos*]" (82a11–c1). But what is noteworthy is that Plotinus, in keeping with his treatment of philosophy as a process of both moral and intellectual ascent, uses this classification of ways of life to classify schools of philosophy as well; thus each type of person, practicing a characteristic way of life and admiring a characteristic type of beauty, will also possess at least implicitly a characteristic interpretation of reality, which if he is a professional philosopher he can make explicit.[21] Plotinus emphasizes the connection between political virtue and Stoic philosophy by speaking of the "selections" of bodily things (using the Stoic technical term *eklogê*) which the middle kind of men fall down to and justify with the name of virtue: the Stoics say that bodily things are indifferent, and only virtue is good; but then since they cannot identify the good of the virtuous life with the contemplation of a metaphysical Good-itself above the soul, they are driven to locate it instead in rational selection among the "indifferent" bodily things.[22] On Plotinus' diagnosis, this means that the Stoics are driven back "with the name of virtue" to the same things they had attempted to escape, and that they work out their philosophy to justify this relapse, and the life "selecting" bodily things and looking no higher; in modern jargon, Stoicism is the "ideology" supporting the life of practical virtue.

The Stoics, and most people, fail to reach a resting-place above this world; only the "divine men" have been able to lead their soul back up to the place from which it fell. Platonism, as a doctrine, expresses the vision associated with this life, as Stoicism expresses the vision associated with political virtue; but the enunciation of the doctrine is not of itself enough to produce the vision. Most people are naturally inclined to Stoicism or worse, and need assistance to rise to "the true place which is their own"; this Plotinus tries to provide, according to the plan he lays out in Chapter 2, which follows the *Symposium* and leads us up from corporeal beauty to its source in psychic beauty, from psychic beauty to its source

---

[21] In correlating moral conditions of the soul with standpoints in theoretical philosophy, Plotinus seems to be developing Plato's claim, shortly after the *Phaedo* passage cited above, that the person who takes the pleasures and pains of the body for the chief goods and evils will also take bodily things as the most real beings (*Phaedo* 83c5–d5), whereas the true philosopher will have a higher understanding both of the good and of reality.

[22] The Stoic doctrine that Plotinus is criticizing is stated most explicitly by Diogenes of Babylon (SVF III Diogenes 44–6) and Antipater of Tarsus (SVF III Antipater 57–9), but is common to the whole school. It was a common criticism, from both sceptical and Platonic opponents of Stoicism (and from the "common sense" dogmatism of Antiochus), that the Stoics, in making the good life consist in an activity of selecting the things according to nature, must in fact be thinking of external things as good, and hypocritically pretending to regard them as indifferent; for if they are not good, why would it be good to select them? For the Stoic answer to this criticism, see my "Physics as a Virtue," *Proceedings of the Boston Area Colloquium in Ancient Philosophy*, vol. 11.

in intellectual beauty, and from intellectual beauty to its source in the Beautiful itself.

By taking his understanding of Stoicism from the theory of the fall and return of the soul, Plotinus is able to develop a new strategy for philosophical polemic. Plotinus, like Plutarch and Alexander, considers the Stoics his serious adversaries; unlike Plutarch and Alexander, he has a sympathetic understanding of the Stoic mentality. The attitude expressed in the polemical writings of these earlier philosophers – no doubt exaggerated for rhetorical purposes – was that the Stoics were philosophical wild men, wilfully contradicting what the rest of society knows to be true; to cite the title of a (mostly lost) treatise of Plutarch, "that the Stoics speak more paradoxically than the poets." There are indeed places where Stoic theory diverges widely from common sense, in its view of the passions, in its fatalism, and (at least according to some interpretations of common sense) in its theology and the doctrine of total blending. The strategy of the second-century Platonists and Aristotelians was to exploit these Stoic divergences from common sense, and discredit all of Stoic doctrine by showing its dependence on these paradoxes. Thus both Plutarch and Alexander present themselves as the champions of aggrieved common sense against the Stoics. Plotinus, while he makes use of some of the same techniques, takes an essentially different position: the Stoics are not too far removed from common sense, but rather too close to it. They are altering common opinions not in the wrong direction but in the right direction; unfortunately, they have been unable to complete the process. Stoicism is useful to the extent that it gives us a glimpse of the truth, and moves us away from Epicurean sensualism and hedonism to an intermediate point along the path to wisdom; it becomes damaging when it digs in its heels at that point, and by setting up its own corporealist physics and activist ethics rejects the fuller enlightenment which Platonism has to offer.

The way to deal with the Stoics, then, is to urge them on from contemplating the beauty of soul to contemplating the higher beauty of Nous, and thus to bring them to recognize that there are such incorporeal realities as the Platonists describe. Plotinus will start by conceding to the Stoics that there are such realities as they describe, that there is, for instance, a soul which pervades the physical universe, and a soul which is the locus of choice and of praise or blame in each human individual; starting from an agreed point of departure, Plotinus will try to lead the Stoics up to what their conception presupposes, and to argue that, when it is properly understood, it presupposes the Platonist series of incorporeal principles. Thus Plotinus will argue, on the one hand, that such souls as both Stoics and Platonists describe cannot exist or acquire their perfections unless there first exists a Nous which is separate from souls and *a fortiori* from bodies; at the same time, he will also argue that if soul is all that both Stoics and Platonists affirm it to be, it must itself be incorporeal. Both by arguing about what must be prior to soul and by arguing about what soul itself must be, Plotinus is trying to display and differentiate the whole series of incorporeal principles of corporeal things which the Stoics had collapsed into identity with each other and with corporeal elements. His goal in this is no different from the goals of Plutarch or Albinus, and, given the rigor with which he distinguishes the different levels of being, his final position is even further from Stoicism than theirs had been. It is simply his method of bringing others up to that position that can make it appear as if he were accepting the Stoic account of the soul or other active principles, and of the manner of their presence to the world of bodies.

This is the sense in which there are "concealed" or implicit Stoic doctrines in Plotinus. The Stoic doctrine of (for example) the omnipresence of the world-soul to bodies is in Plotinus, in the sense that both Plotinus and the Stoics believe that the world-soul is omnipresent to bodies, and that Plotinus does not mind pointing out this agreement; but he notes the agreement merely so that he can argue from Stoic premises to the anti-Stoic conclusion that if the world-soul is truly omnipresent, so that *all* of it is present to every part of body, it must be incorporeal and present to corporeal things in an incorporeal way. Plotinus and Porphyry think that Stoicism is (as it were) "eminently" but not "formally" contained in Platonism: everything that is said truly in Stoicism is also in Platonism, but understood there in a higher way which eliminates the falsehoods of Stoic doctrine. Porphyry asserts the presence of concealed Stoic doctrines in Plotinus to praise Plotinus and Platonism, not to praise the Stoics; he, like Augustine and every other pre-modern writer, correctly regards Plotinus' relation to the Stoics as the relation of cat to mouse.

Plotinus' method for vindicating Platonism against the Stoics, and for bringing us to understand incorporeal principles for ourselves, is the core of what he gave to Augustine: from this method Augustine drew his vindication of Christianity against the Manichees, and his understanding of the soul and God. But we can understand how Augustine reached these results only if we understand the content of the metaphysics that Plotinus used his method to present. What is most important for Augustine in this metaphysics is the doctrine of Nous, and of soul as related to Nous; so I will concentrate on how Plotinus works out an anti-Stoic understanding of these realities, passing quickly over his doctrines of nature, qualities, matter, the Good, the substance of the soul, and the life of the intelligible world. Following Plotinus, I will begin with soul and then ascend to Nous, showing how Plotinus' "high" conceptions of these realities differ from the "low" Stoic conceptions; then I will examine how such a soul and such a Nous would relate to the physical world, and then turn to Augustine.

C. Soul and Nous

The first step in philosophical education, according to Plotinus, is to turn from the contemplation of body to the contemplation of soul. Only when we have perceived soul, and perceived it rightly, will we be able to ascend to the contemplation of Nous and the intelligible world. The Stoics, as Plotinus describes them in *On Nous, Ideas, and Being*, have caught a glimpse of the beauty of soul, and aspire to be guided in their lives by soul instead of body; but they are unable to conceive soul properly, and, far from being able to ascend beyond soul to Nous, cannot even remain at the level of soul, and fall back to conceiving the nature and perfections of soul in bodily terms. Plotinus will try first to show us the true concept of soul that the Stoics have missed, and then to lead us from this understanding of soul to an understanding of Nous.

We must first understand the difference between the Plotinian and the Stoic conceptions of soul; we can then see also how Plotinus' understanding of soul prepares for a further ascent to Nous. Plotinus is most explicit about what he finds wrong with the Stoic conception of soul in the treatise *On Immortality of Soul* (IV,7), much of which is occupied with a polemic against the Stoic doctrine that soul is a *pneuma*. Without analyzing this treatise in detail, we may draw from it the principal contrasts that Plotinus sees between himself and the Stoics.

Plotinus argues, against various corporealist positions, that living bodies do not have their life of themselves, but from some prior ordering and animating principle; and he further argues that this principle or soul cannot be merely some other body, but must be "outside and beyond all bodily nature" (IV,7,3,17–18). As for the Stoics, "they too, led by the truth, bear witness that there must be some form of soul prior to bodies and better than them" (IV,7,4,1–3). The Stoics wish to represent the soul that animates the world and its living parts as being itself a subtle body, a *pneuma* diffused throughout the grosser bodies; but since "not every *pneuma* is a soul, for there are thousands of soulless *pneumata*, they say that it is a *pneuma* somehow disposed [*pôs echon*]" (IV,7,4,11–13). The Stoic admission that the soul is not simply a *pneuma* comes from their glimpse of something higher; but since they cannot conceive the soul as an incorporeal substance, they refer it back to bodily terms by describing it as a disposition [*pôs echon*] of body, or rather as the body disposed in this way.

Plotinus is here reflecting (in an unfriendly way) on Stoic discussions of the *pôs echon* as one of the four categories of being: he calls this Stoic category *poluthrullêton* ["much-talked-of," with a sarcastic tone] and complains that "they flee to it for refuge when they are constrained to posit some other active nature besides bodies" (IV,7,4,10–12).[23] To say that X

---

[23] For Stoic uses of the category of the *pôs echon*, and its place in their ontology, see my "The Stoic Theory of Categories" (unpublished). As I point out there, Plotinus' account of the Stoic theory is geared to his polemical concerns, and is unfair at several points. For my present purposes, however, I need only discuss the Stoic position as Plotinus saw it. One particular caveat, however, seems appropriate. Plotinus suggests that because the Stoics regard *nous* (or the *hêgemonikon*) as soul somehow disposed, the soul as *phusis* somehow disposed, and *phusis* as *pneuma* somehow disposed, where *pneuma* is active body (fire or air or a mixture), the Stoics must be regarding *nous* and the other higher principles as

pôs echon is Y is to say that, while X only becomes Y under some circumstances, Y is nothing over and above X: in particular, there is no need
for a further entity, a quality or form of Y-ness, to inhere in X and make
it Y. So, in the present case, although not every *pneuma* is a soul, the
Stoics also insist that there is no further quality of "soulness" present in
some *pneumata* and turning them into souls: if this "soulness" were a
body, then the soul should initially have been identified with this body
(rather than with the *pneuma* it is present in), and if the "soulness" were
incorporeal, it would contradict the Stoic doctrine that incorporeals cannot
act on bodies. This is Plotinus' point in saying that the Stoics "flee for
refuge" to the *pôs echon* to avoid positing "some other active nature besides bodies." Presumably the Stoics would try to flesh out the indefinite
"*pôs echon*" by explaining just *how* a *pneuma* must be disposed to be a
soul, by the particular way its parts are configured and moved, without
any further entity present in them.

Plotinus reacts so sharply against the Stoic theory of the *pôs echon* because he thinks it is their way of evading Platonist arguments for incorporeal principles, and, at a deeper level, because he thinks they use it to
reverse the true order of dependence among things, and so to reverse what
things are principles and what things need to be derived from the principles. As Plotinus says (in IV,7,4 and again in IV,7,8.3), the Stoics "generate" superior things such as soul and *nous* out of inferior things, or
"establish" [*hidruein*] the superior things in inferior things, and ultimately
in bodies, by asserting that, at each link of the chain, the superior thing
is the inferior thing *pôs echon*. This assumes that "without fire and *pneuma*
the superior portion could not stay in existence, and that it needs a place
to be established in; whereas they ought to be seeking somewhere to establish bodies in, since in fact these are established in the powers of the
soul" (IV,7,4,5–8). For Plotinus, the Stoics in positing the inferior things
first, and seeking to ground the existence of the superior things in them,
are proceeding in exactly the wrong direction. Plotinus asserts, following
Aristotle, that what is perfect and actual is prior to what is imperfect and
potential, and that the imperfect can be perfected only through the agency
of something already possessing the perfection; if so, the attempt to "reduce" the superior to the inferior is misdirected and self-defeating. For
Plotinus, the *pôs echon* is a way of evading the issue whether the principles
acting on bodies are real things existing beyond the bodies: certainly a
living being contains some *pneuma*, and certainly this *pneuma* will be disposed differently from a non-living *pneuma*, but the real question is about
the *cause* of this special disposition. If "the *pôs echon* is [just] a name,"

---

posterior to *pneuma*. This is misleading, since the Stoics too accord a causal priority to
what is most divine: in the *ekpurôsis* there is only Zeus, who is pure *hêgemonikon*, and it
is he who produces out of himself the active powers (*pneumata* variously disposed) of the
diakosmêsis. Plotinus might still insist that since Zeus himself is active body somehow
disposed, the Stoics must grant a *logical* priority to the bodily element.

and the living *pneuma* is simply a body without any other agent present to it, "it will follow that they will not be saying that anything is different from matter, even soul and god; all these will be names, and matter alone will exist," whereas, by the Stoics' own admission, matter is passive and cannot produce anything, much less a living and rationally ordered world. If, on the other hand, the disposition (or what causes it) is a being other than the matter, then what is really active in the body would be this immaterial disposition in the matter, "and this would be a *logos*, not a body, and a different nature," prior to and presupposed by the bodies it produces (IV,7,4,15–21).

Plotinus believes that the special disposition of a living *pneuma* could proceed only from a real incorporeal principle. Indeed he believes, with the whole Platonist school, that *all* active principles in bodies are incorporeal, and that bodies can produce no effects in themselves. But there is a particular issue in the case of soul:

> If, seeing the actions of bodies heating and cooling and pushing and weighing down, they rank the soul here [with bodies] as if [they were thereby] establishing it among active beings, then they are ignorant, first, that bodies too perform these things by the incorporeal powers which are in them, and, further, that we do not judge *these* powers to belong to soul, but thinking, sensing, reasoning, desiring, administering intelligently and well, all of which require a different substance. (IV,7,8.1,1–9)

The effects we attribute to soul are rational thought and the rational government of bodies, effects which require one single principle coordinating diverse operations, and which therefore cannot be produced even by the incorporeal powers dispersed in bodies, much less by the bodies themselves.[24] Even if we condone the Stoics' confusion between bodies and their incorporeal qualities, their conception of soul remains inadequate: in order to conceive soul as a body somehow disposed, they have degraded it to the level of an irrational power, since this is all that bodies (or more properly their qualities) could be imagined to produce.

To understand soul in a way that is suitable to it, not reducing it to a modification of bodies, we must conceive it as an incorporeal substance which, without subsisting in the separate parts of a body like the irrational powers, is able to control the parts of the body and their powers, and to subordinate them to a single rational order. It is not obvious that we *can*

---

[24] Compare IV,1 *On the Essence of Soul*, where Plotinus interprets *Timaeus* 35a1–b3 (saying, among other things, that the soul is intermediate between "the undivided and always constant substance" and the substance that "comes to be divided about the bodies") as meaning that the soul, while inferior to the purely undivided Nous, is superior not only to bodies themselves, but also to what "comes to be divided about the bodies," namely heat and other powers and qualities in bodies. Plotinus argues in this treatise that the *sumpatheia* of ensouled things shows that soul, unlike qualities, is not divided by the different parts of the body it is coextended with: when the soul in one part of the body is affected, the soul in the whole body responds, whereas a change in the whiteness in one part of a body does not affect the whiteness elsewhere.

conceive such a thing; as we have seen, the Stoics could not, and therefore reduced the soul to a specially disposed body. Certainly, if we form our concepts of possible powers by contemplating bodies and imagining how they might act, we will never arrive at such a conception. But Plotinus believes that it is in our power, with the appropriate discipline, to understand such an incorporeal rational power, because we *are* such an incorporeal rational power.

This is a basic theme of the opening chapters of the treatise *On the Three Principal Hypostases*, which we touched on in describing Plotinus' conception of the task of philosophical education. Human souls, having fallen away from the intelligible world, have forgotten their origin and their nature; they therefore turn away from the intelligible, and away from themselves, to the contemplation of bodies, and "honor other things, and admire everything rather than themselves" (V,1,1,12–13). Human souls in this condition have their gaze directed outwards to their physical surroundings; the philosopher's aim is to "turn them around" so that they are looking inwards at themselves, and ultimately so that they can look back through themselves to their intelligible origin, and be rejoined to it. I cited this passage before for its process of ascent from body to soul to Nous; here we note that the turning to soul is a turning *to oneself*, an act whereby the soul turns back from the bodies it perceives and attends instead to itself as what perceives and administers them. This, for Plotinus, is the key to understanding the incorporeal principles of corporeal things. If we try to conceive them by looking outside us we will end up, like the Stoics, with nothing but body; only by modeling our conceptions of these things on our knowledge of our own rational activity can we come to perceive the intelligible reality of the world-soul and, beyond it, of the demiurgic Nous.

An individual human soul, turning away from bodies to contemplate itself, will not thereby perceive the soul of the world, if the world-soul is something different from the individual human soul. But Plotinus claims that it is not, at root, something different. He takes it as generally agreed that we cannot come to know the world-soul unless we are somehow akin to it (V,1,1,30–5); and both Stoics and Platonists assert that there is some kinship. But the conceptions of the relationship are different: for the Stoics, who regard the soul as distributed through the parts of the living body, souls of individual animals are parts, and indeed organs, of the world-soul;[25] our souls come into accord with the purposes of Zeus, that is, of the world-soul, when they properly perform their subordinate role in its management of the world-body. For Plotinus, however, soul does not have

---

[25] For the human soul as a part of the world-soul, see SVF I,495 and II,774. SVF II,633 calls the human soul a fragment [*apospasma*] of the world-soul, as if it had been *detached* from the world-soul, and at SVF II,776 St. Jerome cites the Stoics as thinking that the soul has come (or, perhaps, that it has "fallen") from "the substance of God himself"; both of these are very close to the views of the Manichees as Augustine reports them.

its being in the extended parts of the body it governs, and a soul that administers a more extensive body need not contain, or be superior to, the souls that govern the parts. The world-soul has the same task in governing its body that our souls have in their bodies, namely, to think rationally, and to impose its internal rationality on its body as far as possible. If the world-soul is better than ours, this is because it thinks more rationally or masters its body more completely, not because it is a superior being with a superior function. The world-soul cannot be entirely identical to ours, since it administers a different body; but this applies only to the soul once it has descended into the body. In the intelligible world, souls are the same not only in essence but also in activity, being purely rational and not yet related to any particular body: Plotinus says that souls in the intelligible world are in some way all one, but also in some way many, since they are capable of descending separately into bodies.[26] A human soul thus discovers its relation to the world-soul, not by going through the world, but by returning into itself and discovering the intelligible origin that it and the world-soul share.

Each individual soul, reflecting on itself, can recognize that "*it* made all living things, breathing life into them," that "*it* [made] this great heaven, and *it* ordered it," that it is a nature different and superior to "what it orders and what it moves and what it makes to live" (V,1,2,1–2 and 4–6). All this Plotinus encourages it to do in the second chapter of *On the Three Principal Hypostases*, in a passage of remarkable rhetorical power. The rhetoric is a device to induce the soul to reflect on itself, to recognize that *it* is the source of all the beauty it admires in bodies. In a particularly heightened passage Plotinus asks us to imagine the world devoid of soul: it will be dark and motionless, "a dead body, earth and water, or rather the darkness of matter and not-being and what the gods abhor" (lines 26–7). When soul enters into it, "it gives it life, gives it immortality, and wakes what lies there" (lines 22–3); under the administration of soul, the world gains the perfections described in the *Timaeus* and in the whole subsequent tradition of Greek cosmic piety. The point of the exercise is that the perfections of body are perfections of rational order, which body

[26] For Plotinus on the unity and multiplicity of souls, see his treatise IV,9, *Are All Souls One?*; I come back, briefly, to this difficult topic in Section D below. Plotinus' basic theses are that all souls present in the sensible world have the same status, and that each soul in the sensible world is not an *image* of a soul-itself in the intelligible world, but is *identical* with a soul-itself in the intelligible world, which has descended so that it is present in the sensible world as well (I discuss Plotinus' arguments for this second thesis in an unpublished paper, "Plotinus on the Identity of Knowledge with Its Object"). Plotinus takes it as obvious that souls in the sensible world are many, and that soul-itself in the intelligible world must be one; since he argues that the many souls down here are not many *images* of a soul up there, but are *identical* with souls up there, he concludes that soul up there must be somehow many (as well as one), and that souls down here must be somehow one (as well as many). How intelligible and coherent he is able to make these paradoxes, and what kind of unity he is and is not claiming, I am not entirely sure. Plotinus' doctrine of the unity of souls had almost no impact on the later Platonist tradition, or on Augustine.

cannot grant itself; the only thing that can grant this order is a soul, separate from body, unitary and rational in its essence, and yet capable of applying itself to an extended body and managing its irrational powers. This is what, upon reflection, we recognize ourselves to be.

It is crucial that for Plotinus, unlike the Stoics, soul is essentially *rational* soul. All soul is originally rational, and becomes irrational, to the extent that it does, only on its descent into the body. Plotinus is apparently the earliest philosopher to make rationality essential to soul, and therefore to conceive soul through the "first-person" reflection which will be most prominently found, divorced from Platonist vitalism, in Augustine and Descartes.[27] For Plotinus, as for Augustine under his influence and Descartes under his, soul's reflection on itself is the necessary point of departure for coming to a "high" or purely intellectual understanding of the realities underlying sensible phenomena. For Plotinus (as for Augustine and Descartes) the "high" conception of soul as rational leads us directly to a "high" understanding of God as a separate Nous. The Stoics (as, for Augustine, the Manichees, or, for Descartes, the Aristotelians) cannot understand God because they have not properly understood the soul.

Plotinus leads our thoughts up from soul to Nous using the same strategy that was implicit in Albinus: once we understand soul as potential *nous*, we can use Aristotle's reasoning in *De Anima* III,5 to perceive the *nous poiêtikos* which actualizes the potential *nous*; and this higher productive Nous will be the demiurge. Plotinus carries out this project most explicitly in the treatise *On Nous, Ideas, and Being*. I have already cited the first chapter of this treatise, which analyzes the condition of the human soul, fallen into dependence on the senses and trying to philosophize its way back into the intelligible world. The soul can do this if, following the guidelines of the *Symposium*, it considers sensible beauty and traces it back to its intelligible source. The first stage in the process is to trace the beauty in bodies back to its immediate source in soul: this is the same mental operation that Plotinus asks us to perform in the second chapter of *On the Three Principal Hypostases*. All form or beauty in bodies, Plotinus asserts in both treatises, is implanted in them by some soul which molds them either by nature or by art. This soul possesses the form before the body

---

[27] Perhaps Plato already thinks that the "true nature" of the soul is purely rational: this seems to be the point of the comparison of the soul to the sea-god Glaucus at *Republic* X 611–12; and in the *Timaeus*, the human soul as originally produced by the demiurge is purely rational, before the "young gods" attach the irrational parts, and the motions of the infant body disrupt its rational motions. But Plotinus believes that soul is essentially rational in the very strong sense that all souls (and even "nature," according to III,8, *On Nature, Contemplation, and the One*) are "images" of rational souls in bodies, and (as III,8 maintains) all psychic activities including vegetation are the result of desire for contemplation. Plato suggests in the Glaucus passage that the original "core" of the human soul is purely rational, and that it is difficult for us to discern this core in our present condition; Plotinus is the pioneer of the method of "first-person" reflection that enables us to discern this core, and both Augustine and (later, independently) Avicenna seem to have taken the method up from him.

does, and in a different and less contingent way: it is therefore more beautiful. Plotinus runs through this argument quickly, because his real concern is with the further question: is there something prior to soul, which is the source of soul's beauty?

Soul, for Plotinus, is essentially potential intellect, striving to imitate the cognitive perfection of the Nous whose offspring and image it is. The incarnate soul has the task of introducing order into bodies, but this is accidental to it: what is essential to it is rationality, and only by rationality can it succeed in introducing order into bodies.[28] Soul is beautiful, and can provide beauty to bodies, to the extent that it exercises reason; to seek a source for a soul's beauty is to seek a source for its rationality. "What then? Is soul beautiful of itself? No, it is not: for one would not be wise and beautiful, and another unwise and base. For beauty is in the soul through wisdom. And what is the giver of wisdom to the soul? Necessarily Nous: not a *nous* which is sometimes *nous* and sometimes lacking *nous* [*nous . . . ou pote men nous, pote de anous*], but the true Nous. For this is beautiful of itself" (V,9,2,19–23).

The picture of Nous that Plotinus is presenting is originally Aristotelian, modified (as in Albinus) to support the cosmology of the *Timaeus* and the educational theory of the *Symposium*. The description of the true or separate intellect is taken directly from *De Anima* III,5: where Aristotle says that it "*ouch hote men noei hote d' ou noei*" (430a22), Plotinus says that it is "*ou pote men nous, pote de anous.*" But when such a Nous is presiding over the world-soul, it becomes the source, not simply of the soul's wisdom, but of the soul's activity in applying its wisdom to body, and of the forms that the soul introduces into matter. As Plotinus sketches the process in Chapter 3 of *On Nous, Ideas, and Being*, the forms of all things have their original home and their truest existence in Nous; then Nous communicates these forms to the world-soul, and to the souls of human artisans according to their capacities; then these divine and human souls can in turn impose likenesses of the original forms on matter, to the extent that the soul is capable of communicating the form and the matter of receiving it.[29]

This picture is already in Albinus, and must have been a commonplace of the Platonic school. What is not apparent in Albinus is Plotinus' concern to lead the soul, through the intuition of itself, to an intuition of its divine father. Albinus poses the questions about soul and Nous in a cosmological context; the soul involved is the soul of the heaven or of the

---

[28] On the connection between the soul's rationality (arising from its relation to Nous) and its ability to introduce order into bodies, see further Section D below.

[29] Plotinus, like all Platonists, agrees with Aristotle that there are forms of sensible things, immanent in matter and inseparable from it; the question is whether there are *also* separate forms of (at least some kinds of) sensible things existing in the intelligible world. Plotinus is trying to solve this problem by asking what forms in bodies proceed from forms in soul, and what forms in soul proceed from forms in Nous. Since the intelligibles are not outside Nous, what exists in the intelligible world is precisely what exists in Nous itself.

world, not our soul. Nor is it clear that Albinus hopes, by discussing the world-soul and the demiurgic Nous, to induce an intellectual intuition of this Nous. As we have seen, Albinus uses Aristotelian slogans about the *nous poiêtikos* without really repeating Aristotle's arguments that such a Nous exists: he seems to feel that detailed argument is out of place in an expository handbook. But however it is with Albinus, Plotinus' intentions are clear: once we have properly understood soul by perceiving *ourselves* as rational souls, we will perceive that the soul that governs the physical world is of the same essence as our own, that it masters the world by the same rationality by which we master our own bodies. Then Plotinus' task is to turn us from contemplating soul as *potential* intellect (in ourselves or the world), to perceiving the single *nous poiêtikos* that presides over both cosmic and individual souls, which makes these souls *actually* rational and makes them govern their bodies in accord with reason. As Plotinus tells us in the first chapter of *On the Three Principal Hypostases*, human souls have their paternity in the divine Nous, but, having forgotten their relation to it, have forgotten their own nature as well; once they have rediscovered what they are, their next step is to rediscover their relation to their divine father, and thus to achieve their perfection as rational souls by "returning" to the source of rationality.

"Why then must we go up beyond soul, and not posit that it is the first?" (V,9,4,1–2). This is to ask why we must posit a Nous prior to souls. "It is ridiculous enough to ask whether there is a Nous among beings: although there may be those who would doubt even this. But [we should ask] rather whether it is as we say, and if it is something separate, and if it *is* the beings, and the nature of the forms is there; and what we will now say concerns this" (V,9,3,5–9). The Stoics, though they admit the obvious truth that there is an intellect in the world, identify it with soul somehow disposed; so they deny the thesis of the Platonists that it is something separate from soul, and even the weaker thesis that it is separate from body. Plotinus chooses to confront the Stoic opponents of the Platonist doctrine of separate Nous, and to work through the Aristotelian arguments against them, because he is not content simply to state the Platonist thesis in a plausible way: he wants to induce actual knowledge of the separate Nous, and he takes the Aristotelian form of argument as the best means to this end. Once he has used the Aristotelian argument to show *that there is* a separate Nous, he will also have provided a clear concept of *what it is*; he can then use this concept to demonstrate, as a corollary to the proof that a separate Nous exists, the answer to the second disputed question about Nous: "that it *is* the beings, and the nature of the forms is there."

The Aristotelian argument for the separate existence of a *nous poiêtikos* is essentially an argument about potentiality and actuality. Aristotle states as a general principle that the potential comes to actuality only through something already actual, and, therefore, that the actual is prior to the potential; he proves the existence of a separate Nous by applying this principle to the process by which the soul acquires actual knowledge. Plotinus accepts this principle, and the whole theory of potentiality and actuality, as a legitimate explication of Platonism, and he sets up a direct confrontation between this principle and Stoic explanations through the *pôs echon*. But he reinterprets the Aristotelian principle in a Platonic sense. In *On Immortality of Soul* he criticizes the Stoics for "making the inferior first" (IV,7,8.3,7), and says that it happens by nature that "the inferior should always be later" (IV,7,8.3,11); it is plain from context that he intends this to be equivalent to the Aristotelian principle of the priority of actuality to potentiality. If the potential were first, he says, it would never come to actuality: "for what would lead it [to actuality] if there is nothing different and prior to it? Even if it leads itself to actuality, which is absurd, it will lead looking toward something, which will not be in potency but in actuality" (IV,7,8.3,15–18). Anything that is actualized is actualized to conform to some standard (what the agent "looks toward"), which must already exist in actuality: so the prior actual being that this argument establishes will be an *eternally* actual standard, the model for changeable things: "what is prior is what is superior and what has a different nature from body and what is eternally in actuality" (IV,7,8.3,21–2). This is not what Aristotle intended: although Aristotle uses the principle of the priority of actuality to prove the existence of something *eternally* actual in *De Anima* III and in *Metaphysics* XII, these are special cases. An animal comes to actuality, for Aristotle, through the prior actuality of its father, and the father does not have this actuality eternally, but received it from more remote ancestors; and Aristotle puts this account forward precisely as an *alternative* to saying that the animal receives its actuality or its form from an eternal model.[30] Plotinus, however, uses the Aristotelian form of argument to argue, against the Stoics, that the generation of higher things from body presupposes the existence of eternal incorporeal principles.

Plotinus makes this argument generally in *On Immortality of Soul*, but his main interest there is in applying the argument to show the priority

---

[30] "It is clear that there need not, for this reason at least [to account for the generation of individual sensible things] be ideas: for a man is generated by a man, an individual by an individual [sc. and not by the Platonic idea of man]" (Aristotle *Metaphysics* XII,3 1070a26–8); Aristotle develops the argument at more length in *Metaphysics* VII,7–8, concluding that "the generator is sufficient to produce and to be the cause of the form in the matter" (1034a4–5), and therefore that the coming-to-be of sensible things does not require separate forms. But there is an interesting qualification: in *Metaphysics* XII,3 Aristotle says the forms of artifacts do not exist separately *ei mê hê technê*, "unless the art does" or "except as the art" (1070a14–15). The form of house exists separately from individual houses, in the art of housebuilding in the soul of the artisan; but Aristotle thinks that this art cannot exist separately from souls, or even in souls separated from matter. Plotinus accepts the terms of the debate from *Metaphysics* XII,3, but argues that at least some of the arts that are in the soul exist already in the separate Nous: so in V,9,11 Plotinus approaches the question "are there forms of artifacts in the intelligible world?" by asking "do the *arts* exist in Nous?" For Plotinus this approach covers the forms of natural things as well, since for the Platonists and Stoics (but not Aristotle) the products of nature *are* artifacts, produced according to an art existing in the world-soul.

of soul to bodies or to material forms. But in Chapter 4 of *On Nous, Ideas, and Being* he applies it specifically to prove the priority of Nous over soul. "Nous is other and better than soul; but the better is first by nature" (V,9,4,2–4). The argument is the same as in the earlier treatise, with the same Aristotelian origin and anti-Stoic direction. "Nor, as they [the Stoics] think, does soul, when it has been perfected, generate Nous; for whence will the potential be actual, if there is no cause leading it to actuality? For if it is by chance, it is possible that it would not come to actuality" (V,9,4,4–7). The conclusion is the Platonic thesis, illustrated by the Aristotelian example of paternity. "We must posit that the first things are in actuality and unwanting and perfect; and that the imperfect are later than these, and are perfected by the same things that had generated them, like fathers who perfect what they had originally generated imperfect; and that they are matter toward their first maker, which then is informed and perfected" (V,9,4,7–13). Thus things that are imperfect, or not entirely actual, receive their actuality from something completely actual: that is, first they are generated in an imperfect state, receiving their existence or first actuality from their perfect generators, and then they are nourished and brought to maturity, receiving their perfection or second actuality from the same generators. Plotinus here speaks the language of paternity (the verb for "generate" is *"gennan,"* to beget), but the generation of animals is only an illustration: Plotinus' real interest is in the procession of things from the "father and maker of all things," as the demiurge is called at *Timaeus* 28c3–4. A biological father, changeable and imperfect, cannot be a sufficient explanation for its offspring's perfection: even if there is an infinite regress of biological generators, there must also be a cause outside the series to explain how the process keeps going, how the perfection of the species is transmitted to the offspring (a Platonist would naturally expect that, if in each generation the form of the offspring is "copied" from its father, the copies would become progressively less and less perfect). Aristotle thinks that the constant rotation of the heavens is enough to keep the cycle of generation going, and that this rotation in turn depends on Nous as an eternally constant cause, although not an eternal paradigm of the particular sublunar species. However, to explain how the offspring is shaped (in the womb, for viviparous animals) into the pattern of the species, Aristotle must invoke a mysterious art-like shaping power in the seed, which is of course not a conscious being and cannot truly possess an art: Plotinus (following the Stoics) infers that this power is an art in the world-soul for forming members of the particular species, and then infers that the world-soul must work "looking toward" an eternal paradigm of the species (namely, the species-forming art contained in Nous) and not simply toward the father. The crucial point is that explanation through a temporal generator is insufficient, and that an eternal "generator" is needed to bring it about that the generation of temporal things is necessary and regular, not random and irrational.

In *On Nous, Ideas, and Being*, Plotinus applies these general principles to the relation between soul and Nous. The Stoics think that soul arises from inferior things, and becomes or generates Nous when it is complete; but the reverse must be the case. Soul can arise only from Nous, not from the soul's own intellect [*ho tês psuchês nous*] but from a *nous* that is perfect, eternally actual, and prior to soul. Soul, as the offspring of intellect, has a likeness of intellect, and so may itself be called intellect, but of itself it is a merely potential intellect; it can become actual intellect only by returning to the original intellect from which it proceeds, receiving the perfections of that Nous and becoming conformed to that Nous.

To say that a soul is a potential intellect is to say that it potentially knows or understands. If it knows, it knows the intelligible forms. The Nous prior to soul, which is always an actual *nous*, always actually knows all the intelligibles. Soul, by contrast, acquires this knowledge only to the extent that it receives it from Nous. By participating in Nous, and receiving knowledge of the forms, a soul is perfected, and is able to apply its knowledge to the bodies it controls, transmitting to them the forms or *logoi* that it has received from Nous. This description holds for the world-soul just as it does for the souls of human artisans: "soul gives to the four [simple bodies] the shape of the cosmos, but it is Nous that has supplied it with the *logoi*, just as in the souls of artisans the *logoi* for activity are from the arts" (V,9,3,29–32). Here Nous is compared not to an artisan but to his *art*, and Plotinus intends the comparison to be exact: Nous is itself an art (and a virtue) existing separately from souls, and Nous comprehends within itself all the arts, to the extent that they can exist separately from souls and from the conditions of matter (and Plotinus thinks that all the arts are separable to the extent that they are theoretical or scientific, and in particular to the extent that they are mathematical: cf. V,9,7,1–6). So when a soul participates in Nous, it is participating (to a greater or lesser degree) in the arts, or in the apprehensions of the different forms, which it can then impose on matter. If we start with a body that has beauty by possessing a form F, and then at each stage we investigate the efficient cause that produces the beauty or the form by making the potentially-F actually F, we will ascend, first to the soul (human or not) that has the art of F-making, and then to *the art itself*, existing in Nous, which perfects the soul and makes it actually knowing-F, and thus also capable of producing F in matter. Since this cause of knowledge to the soul is just the separate art of F-making (or rather the separable core of the art, the separate science of F), this separate cause will itself know F, not just potentially or by participation, but by its own essence, and thus in eternal actuality. Since Nous is a universal separately existing science, containing within itself all the "theorems" of the theoretical sciences (V,9,8,3–7), it is essentially omniscient, not in the sense that it knows material things (since these are unknowable in themselves), but in the sense that it knows everything whose nature it is to be intelligible, that is, all the forms.

By going up to the first cause of actual intellection in the soul, Plotinus is confident that he can discover a Nous that is essentially omniscient in this way; if not, there would be (absurdly, Plotinus thinks) an infinite regress of agent intellects, each needing to be actualized by a prior agent intellect. "We must take Nous, if we are to be true to the name, to be not what is potential [*nous*], or that which has come from foolishness to intellection [*ex aphrosunês eis noun*] – otherwise we will again seek another [*nous*] before it – but that which is actually and always *nous*" (V,9,5,1–4). By isolating the Nous that is *nous* in this special and primary sense, Plotinus can resolve the disputed question "whether it *is* the beings, and the nature of the forms is there" (V,9,3,7–8).

If it does not have its wisdom [*to phronein*] as something borrowed, then if it thinks [*noei*] something, it thinks it of itself, and if it has something, it has it of itself. And if it thinks of itself and from itself, it is itself the things it thinks: for if its substance [or essence, *ousia*] were one thing, and the things it thinks were different from it, then its substance itself would be unintelligent [*anoêtos*], and potential rather than actual: so we must not separate either [Nous or its *nooumenon*] from the other. (V,9,5,4–10)

Here Plotinus is taking over (within a Platonic context) Aristotle's argument that what Nous thinks cannot be outside Nous itself. In *Metaphysics* XII,9, Aristotle had connected the question whether Nous has its actual *noêsis* from itself with the question whether it *noei* itself or something else: Aristotle says that "if it *noei* [something], and something else is master over it (for its substance [or essence, *ousia*] is not *noêsis* but potentiality), it will not be the best substance: for the *timion* belongs to it through [the act of] *noein*" (1074b18–21); then, a few lines further down, Aristotle says, "first, if it is not *noêsis* but potentiality, the continuity of its *noêsis* would probably be laborious; next, it is clear that something else would be more *timion* than *nous*, namely the *nooumenon*" (1074b28–30). Aristotle does not make the logical connection between these two questions entirely clear, but Plotinus does: if what *noei* is *A*, and the *nooumenon* is some *B* external to *A*, then *A* is not knowing-*B* *just by its own nature as A*: the actuality of knowledge depends on its becoming related to something outside itself, and it will have to reach outside itself and "come into contact" with *B*.[31] So if we abstract the substance *A* from its external conditions, we can say that the *ousia* of *A* is unintelligent, or at best potentially intelligent: if, to the contrary, we have discovered *A* as a *nous* that has its *noêsis* from itself, what it *noei* cannot be other than itself. So Plotinus concludes, "therefore it *is* the [intelligible] beings: for it will think them either in something else

---

[31] Cp. a parallel passage in Plotinus: "since Nous knows, and knows the intelligibles, if it knows them as being other than it, how would it meet up [*suntuchoi*] with them? For it would be possible that it would not, so that it would be possible for it not to know except when it has met up with them, and it will not have its knowledge eternally" (V,5,1,19–24). For Aristotle, see above, Section B.2. Albinus apparently does not use this Aristotelian argument that *nous* is identical with its object: he uses the argument (also Aristotelian, but much less deep, and not depending on the precise conception of Nous) that because Nous thinks what is best, and because it is itself the best, it must think itself.

[*heterothi*], or in itself, as *being* itself. In something else is impossible: where would it be? So [it knows] itself, and in itself" (V,9,5,14–15). Aristotle had used this conclusion to argue that, since Nous knows only itself, there cannot be a plurality of Platonic forms for it to know; but Plotinus says instead that "it is itself *the things* it thinks," identifying a singular with a plural.[32] Plotinus thus denies the Aristotelian thesis that Nous is *simple*: if the one Nous is the many forms, then the forms are somehow *parts* of Nous, although eternally and essentially inseparable parts, so that they must (as Plotinus says) somehow exist in each other as well as in the whole. This sounds mysterious, but Plotinus can give us a way to understand it, if the different intelligible forms are just the different theoretical sciences of themselves, and if the different sciences, or the different "theorems" within the all-comprehensive science, are inseparable and mutually implying, so that each theorem can be derived by reflection on the others, and each single theorem virtually contains the whole science.

Following this line of reasoning, in essential dependence on Aristotle's strategy for ascending from soul to Nous, Plotinus can hope to lead his reader to an intellectual "vision" of Nous, and thereby also to resolve disputed questions about its nature. In particular, he can vindicate against the Stoics the Platonic doctrine of separate intelligible forms, albeit a peculiarly Aristotelian version of that doctrine (as we have seen also in Albinus). A Nous must exist to actualize intellection in souls; forms in bodies come from forms in soul which come from forms in Nous; and the forms in Nous are the intelligible beings, which most properly *are*, and are the sources and standards of everything else that can be said to be. Bodily things, which the Stoics regard as primary and most real, are merely the result of soul's passing on to matter what it has received from Nous; everything real or perfect in them comes from an archetype in Nous, and only their defects must be explained in a different way. It remains, then, to examine Plotinus' understanding of the presence and action of soul in the sensible world, and in particular of the production of perfect and im-

---

[32] The question of whether Nous can know many things reduces to the question of whether Nous can *be* many things. Aristotle argues in *Metaphysics* XII,9, not only that Nous cannot know anything outside itself, but also that it cannot be knowledge of a plurality of contents, since it could not be simultaneously *actual* knowledge of all of them, but would have to include different *potentialities* for knowing different things. This rests on Aristotle's general claim that something can be a whole of parts only when, though actually one, it is *potentially* many (because, if the parts were not potentially separable, they would be identical with one another, and not really parts of a whole): Aristotle concludes that no eternal being can have a part–whole structure. Plotinus rejects the basic thesis about wholes and parts, and has no reason to accept the conclusion about Nous. Plotinus does agree with another Aristotelian consideration, namely that the first principle must be simple (since otherwise it would require another principle prior to it, and it would not be truly the first principle); but for Plotinus this does not imply that Nous is simple, since he thinks that the first principle, the One, is something prior to Nous. I will return to these issues, as they arise for some scholastic thinkers and for Descartes, in Chapter 8, Section A.

perfect things through soul's action in bodies. This is a corollary to Plotinus' understanding of the relation of soul to Nous, but a very important corollary: if we understand how this corollary follows, we can understand how the discipline by which Augustine learned to contemplate himself and God as incorporeal beings also gave him a solution to the problem of the origin of evil.

D. Soul in bodies

Both Platonists and Stoics picture the world as a totality of body interpenetrated and governed by soul and Nous. For the Stoics (as Plotinus portrays them) the problem is to understand how the superior principles arise as modifications of the inferior, how the active principles in bodies are organized to order the totality of body into a rational whole. For Plotinus, by contrast, the problem is to explain, given the existence of Nous and soul apart from bodies, how they come to be *in* bodies, how they come to bestow life and reason, to the extent that they do, on the extended mass which of itself is "the darkness of matter and not-being and what the gods abhor" (V,1,2,26–7).

"Nor, as they think, does soul, when it has been perfected, generate Nous"; on the contrary, "Nous, since it is a perfect Nous, generates soul" (V,1,7,37). "For, being perfect, it had to generate, and not be without offspring, when it is so great a power" (ibid.), according to the general principle that "whatever comes to perfection . . . generates, and does not bear to remain by itself, but makes another" (V,4,1,27–8). This principle represents Plotinus' interpretation of the Aristotelian, and anti-Stoic, thesis that the imperfect is generated, and then perfected, only by the perfect. The soul that is generated from Nous is "a lesser image of it" (V,1,7,40), potential and indeterminate of itself but becoming determinate through its relation to Nous. Soul as it proceeds from Nous will naturally think, but it will not naturally animate bodies. It will naturally reside in the intelligible world, and will not naturally reside in extended bodies. As the product of a single act of a single and undivided substance, it will naturally be one; and although Plotinus thinks that its unity is weaker than the unity of Nous, so that soul is somehow multiple (as well as being one) even within the intelligible world, it will not naturally be divided into the souls of different organisms.

If we are not naturally Platonists, we may have trouble understanding how such a soul, purely intellectual, separate from body, and unique, could come to be the souls we ordinarily conceive as inhabiting the many living bodies large and small, and as governing the extended parts of these bodies, sometimes rationally but sometimes irrationally. The Stoics find this "downward" transition unintelligible, and they posit instead that the souls of living things arise from the active elements mixed in with the grosser parts of bodies. If soul arises in this way, it will be naturally divided among the different extended parts of the cosmos, and so naturally able to operate throughout the different bodies where it is present; thus soul in the universe, or even in an individual animal, will be "one" only as a whole of parts. Plotinus rejects this Stoic conception of soul, saying that (so far from enabling souls to govern their bodies) the Stoics in fact prevent souls from exercising their function: soul (considered as essentially divided by bodily extension, like the irrational powers of heating and cooling) will lack the unity that would enable the animal as a whole to perceive and respond to the affections of its different members, and it will lack the rationality that would enable it to coordinate the activities of the whole body according to an intelligent plan. Plotinus' soul has just the opposite difficulties: it is naturally related to Nous, but how does it come to be related to bodies? After explaining in *On the Three Principal Hypostases* how soul comes to be generated by Nous, he notes its status as an intermediary connecting Nous and body: what Nous generates is "on one side connected to it [sc. Nous] and thus filled with it and enjoying it and participating in it and thinking [*nooun*], and on the other side in contact with the things that are after it; or rather it in turn generates, and the things it generates are necessarily inferior to soul" (V,1,7,44–8). Thus soul, having come to perfection through Nous, in turn generates its image, the living body: soul does not begrudge a share of its life to the "darkness of matter and not-being" which lies beneath it, but "soul seeing it, since it was lying there, shaped it" (IV,3,9,26) into a living body.

When soul produces a living body, the soul in one sense "descends" to become present in matter, but in another sense it does *not* descend: the living body, "having come-to-be like some beautiful and intricate house, is not cut off from its maker, nor did he share himself with it" (IV,3,9,29–31). Rather, the soul cares for the living body it has made without building itself into its work, "for [the soul] governs while remaining above; it is ensouled in this way, having a soul not *of* it but *to* it, [the body] being ruled not ruling, possessed not possessing" (IV,3,9,34–6). Although we commonly say that soul is in body, Plotinus thinks this expression is not correct, since what is *in* body or contained by body depends on body to sustain it; Plotinus prefers (with *Timaeus* 34b, correcting *Timaeus* 30b) to say that body is in soul, and that what is contained in a living body is not properly soul but only an image of soul, that is, the irrational psychic powers that operate through the body. Soul constructs and animates not only the body of the world but also many smaller bodies, and each one equally receives a "soul" or image of soul: these many souls come to be out of one intelligible soul, and in a sense they still are one soul. "One and the same soul is present in many bodies, and before this one-in-many there is another not-in-many: the one-in-many [derives] from this, as if it were an image coming to many places from the one-in-one, as if many pieces of wax were stamped by one ring and bore the same impression" (IV,9,4,15–20); but the souls are one not just *qualitatively*, as likenesses of the same thing, but *substantially*, as growths from the same root (IV,9,4,22–5,7). Even in the intelligible world, souls were potentially distinct, but now they realize their separation as different bodies receive the impression of different facets of soul. Thus my soul, which in a sense is and in a sense is not the same as your soul or as the world-soul, finds a special appropriateness to the matter which will become my body, shapes it into a living body, and sends a projection of itself down to govern it. Once this lower soul arrives in my body, it is as omnipresent within that circumscribed domain as the world-soul is in the world; remaining united to itself, to the undescended soul, and to Nous, it is able to govern the various parts of my body according to a rational order.[33]

Even if we grant to Plotinus (very generously) that this is an intelligible account of how the one soul comes to be many souls and to rule the many bodies, it could only explain how it comes to rule them *well*; yet we observe that some souls rule their bodies well, and others badly. If souls arose out of something corporeal and imperfect, we might understand how they might fail to act perfectly rationally; but Plotinus has argued that, if they are to be rational at all, they must proceed from an absolutely rational first principle. He has therefore acquired the task of explaining how, from a good first cause, a mixture of good and bad actions could arise.

Plotinus manages to turn this apparent disadvantage against the Stoics. Plato himself, in the *Timaeus* and other dialogues, had had to confront the problem of the origin of evil actions in souls, and he had given at least the sketch of a solution, which was accepted and elaborated by both Platonists and Stoics. Plotinus endorses the Platonic solution as the only possible one, and although the Stoics too wish to uphold it, he argues that their corporealist conceptions of soul and Nous are insufficient to support Plato's account, and that they have inadvertently destroyed the only possible account of the origin of moral evil in a world ordered by a good and rational divinity. If we recall Plato's solution to the problem, we can see how Plotinus thinks the Stoics have destroyed this solution, and how he himself intends to rescue it.

Plato believes that the physical world, and the souls in it, are the products of a divine craftsman; this god "is good, and in the good no envy ever arises about anything," and therefore "the god desired that all things should be good and nothing bad as far as possible," since "it is not right for the best [*aristos*] to do anything but the finest [*kalliston*]" (*Timaeus* 29e1–3, 30a1–3, a6–9). Plato must therefore explain how this world is the best, and how its creator does nothing but the finest in producing it, despite the evils which do exist in it. Plato's answer is complex, and involves a number of different kinds of explanation of evil; I will note only the

---

[33] On Plotinus' notoriously difficult doctrine of the unity of soul, compare the brief account in Section C above. I discuss the related doctrine of the undescended soul in "Plotinus on the Identity of Knowledge with Its Object." Since these Plotinian doctrines made almost no impact on later thinkers, we do not need to explore them more deeply here. Augustine toys with the Plotinian doctrine of the unity of soul in one passage (see Chapter 4, Section B), but he does not commit himself to it and makes no use of it.

principal heads of his discussion. To begin with, the demiurge cannot make the world absolutely as he wishes, but is limited by the intrinsically disorderly matter that he is given (*Timaeus* 30a3–6). The demiurge chooses to work on this matter because it is there, and because it is better to make it as orderly as possible than to abandon it to anarchy; some evils can therefore be ascribed to the conditions of matter. Secondly, the way to make the world as good as possible is to make it complete, containing images of all the different types of beings, especially all the types of *living* beings, that exist in its intelligible model (*Timaeus* 30c3–31a1). So the world must contain both perfect and immortal living beings, the heavenly bodies, maintaining their regularity within matter, and also imperfect living beings, mortal because liable to the vicissitudes of sublunar matter (*Timaeus* 41b7–c2). The world is better containing both perfect and imperfect living things than if it had only perfect inhabitants; such evils as death, and the human liability to natural evil in general, can therefore be ascribed to the need for perfection in the universe as a whole. But the types of explanation so far mentioned refer only to *natural* evil; they cannot account for moral evil in the human soul, or, if virtue is sufficient for happiness, even for unhappiness.

Plato therefore gives a different kind of account for the origin of human vice. The details of the explanation vary from dialogue to dialogue, but the basic concerns remain constant. Plato is concerned above all to absolve the gods of responsibility for human wrongdoing, and to show that they have not created the human soul defective. Thus he asserts that the soul is originally created in sound condition, and becomes evil and unhappy only through its own action. It is not clear exactly how this condition of self-induced evil is related to the soul's being in a body (and, more specifically, being in a corruptible sublunar body). Sometimes Plato seems to regard incarnation as an evil for the soul, and therefore (since, if it is an evil, it must result from the soul's own action) as a punishment or a natural consequence of wrongdoing in a previous life or outside the body;[34] but in the *Timaeus* he regards at least the original incarnation of the human soul as a positive part of the demiurge's plan for a complete universe. The soul is first "sown into" a heavenly body and given the knowledge of the universe to prepare it for its mission (*Timaeus* 42d2–e4), then put into its body. The chaotic motions of sublunar matter, unlike the regular celestial motions, disturb the soul's knowledge and confront it with irrational sensations and passions (43a4–c7). These are the *conditions* of vice (and thus of misery), but they do not yet *constitute* vice. If the soul's intrinsic rational motion dominates and is not disrupted by the irrational motions from bodies, then the soul retains its rationality and virtue (and although this never happens in infancy, it may in maturity – Plato does not make

---

[34] For this view, see especially *Phaedrus* 248a1–e3; Plotinus complains at IV,8,1,23–50 about Plato's apparent variations on the question.

it clear how far the outcome is in the soul's own power); but if the soul's motion is dominated by the bodily passions, the soul becomes irrational and vicious (43c7–44c4).

Plato's theodicy, then, absolves the gods of responsibility for evil by attributing it to the conditions of matter, to the need for imperfect parts of the world alongside the perfect, and to the actions of the soul under conditions of ignorance and physical dependency. While he does not systematically work out how much each of these causes can explain, he does at least provide an outline and a series of illustrations for a project of reconciling the existence of evil with the rule of a good and rational God. This project becomes part of the substance of Greek philosophy; no doubt it was taken up by Plato's successors in the Academy, and it was taken up by the Stoics and by the revivers of Platonism after them.

The Stoics have no wish to contradict Plato's theodicy, nor indeed to contradict the whole cosmology of the *Timaeus* as they understand it; but consciously or unconsciously they modify this cosmology when they deny the causality of incorporeal things, and identify both soul and the demiurgic Nous with a corporeal element. Plotinus argues that by so modifying Plato's cosmology, they have made it impossible to reconcile God and evil using Plato's explanations.

The Stoic doctrine that soul is corporeal brings with it the corollary that individual souls are parts of the world-soul. Plotinus rejects this corollary, and indeed he often seems more concerned to attack it than to attack the basic doctrine that soul is corporeal; perhaps this is because the assertion that soul is a whole of parts is less clearly un-Platonic than the assertion that it is a body, and so might be entertained more seriously by Plotinus' intended audience. Thus he devotes the first eight chapters of the great treatise *On Problems of Soul* (IV,3–5) entirely to refuting "those who say that our souls too are from the soul of the universe" (IV,3,1,17–18) and to showing that their arguments (including exegetical arguments from Plato) do not succeed in excluding Plotinus' preferred view that both individual and cosmic souls proceed equally from a transcendent soul.[35] Plotinus objects so strenuously to the Stoic doctrine because it subordinates the human soul to the world-soul, and so threatens the direct relation of the human soul as potential *nous* to Nous absolutely. On the Stoic view, my soul or your soul is a part of the world-soul "as someone might say that within one animal the soul in a finger is a part of the whole [soul] which is in the whole animal" (IV,3,3,1–3). It would seem to follow that a human soul does not think or act, except as the soul in a finger "thinks" and "acts" when the finger is used as an organ of sensation or locomotion; and the best and most "rational" life for a human being (as for a finger) would be to be used rationally by the whole of which it is a part, for the

---

[35] Plato texts that might support the position that "our souls too are from the soul of the universe" are *Philebus* 30a3–8 and perhaps the *Timaeus* passage on the mixing-bowl, *Timaeus* 41d4–7.

good of the whole and not of the part. Plotinus' whole purpose, by contrast, has been to show that the human soul can perceive the intelligibles, and can act rationally and virtuously in accord with this perception, just as much as the world-soul can; so he wants to establish that an individual human soul and the soul of the world have the same origin and the same ontological status, even though one soul inhabits a much larger body than the other.[36]

If a human soul cannot act except in the action of the world-soul, then, Plotinus argues, it follows that it cannot act contrary to the action of the world-soul. Since there are imperfect souls, which have fallen into the body and acted there in a manner contrary to reason, individual souls must have a capacity for acting separately from the perfectly rational world-soul; as Plotinus says in *On Problems of Soul*, the individual soul "is shown to be other" than the world-soul "especially in its resistance" to it (IV,3,7,28). But (Plotinus argues) the Stoics, having eliminated the independent ontological status of the human soul, will be forced to deny that there can be such resistance, or that human actions can be evil while the actions of the world-soul remain consistently good. This is Plotinus' central point in the treatise *On Fate* (III,1). Here he attempts to determine what things are subject to fate by analyzing what things have what kinds of causes. He cites the opinions of a number of schools about the causes, and especially the first causes, of things, and shows what views of fate these schools are led to; he then criticizes these views and sets out his own doctrine of the causal principles of things and of the scope of fate. His criticism of the Stoic doctrine, in particular, turns on the question of the relation between individual and cosmic souls, and the consequences for theodicy.

The Stoic doctrine of the first cause, as Plotinus represents it in Chapter 4 of *On Fate*, is that "some one soul, pervading the universe, accomplishes everything, each thing being moved as a part, in the way that the whole directs" (III,1,4,1–3). He then derives their doctrine of fate, that "since the causes proceed in sequence from it [the world-soul], their connectedness and interweaving must be fate" (III,1,4,3–5);[37] Plotinus compares

---

[36] In fact the Stoics agree with Plotinus that the human soul has the same status, and indeed is capable of the same perfection, as the world-soul; Chrysippus made the extreme statements that "Zeus does not exceed Dion in virtue . . . if they are both sages" (SVF III,246) and that "all the good" are "in no way surpassed by Zeus" (SVF III,526). Either Plotinus does not know of this Stoic thesis, or he simply thinks that it is inconsistent with the Stoic claim that human souls are parts of the world-soul and that their proper function is the function of parts serving the ends of the whole.

[37] The Stoics describe fate as the *logos* (the "rational plan," but also the *logos spermatikos*) of the whole cosmos, or of the things in the cosmos governed by providence (SVF II,913), and so they are willing to identify it, as a substance, with God or Zeus or the world-soul, which they have also described as the *logos spermatikos* of the cosmos, distributed throughout the cosmos and acting immediately everywhere to execute its providential plan (SVF II,580). But the Stoics also describe fate as a "chain" or connected series of causes, originally set in motion by the will of Zeus when he first produced the ordered universe (cf.

this to the government of all the parts of a plant by its vital principle, conceived as residing in the root. Plotinus objects that so strong a universal causality would undermine the activity, perhaps even the subsistence, of everything other than the first cause: "if in the universe what does and suffers everything is one, and not one thing [acted on] by another by causes that always lead up to something else, then it is not true that all things come-to-be from causes; rather, all things will be one" (III,1,4,17–20). Such monism would undermine any independent human action or independent human rationality: "thus neither will we be ourselves, nor will any act be ours; nor will we ourselves reason, but our intentions are the reasonings of another; nor will we ourselves act, as our feet do not kick, but we do through the parts of ourselves [sc. and so the world will act through us]" (III,1,4,20–4). Plotinus rejects this conclusion, especially because it undermines the possibility of theodicy: "each individual must be that individual, and actions and thoughts must be ours, and both the good and the evil actions of each individual must be from that individual: the doing of evils, at any rate, must not be ascribed to the universe" (III,1,4,24–8).

If God is the soul of the world, and if the human soul is a part of the soul of the whole, then when the actions that take place in human souls are evil, God is doing evil. If the explanation of moral evil is to be saved, then a different account of the principles is needed.

We must, says Plotinus, posit some first cause, so that things do not happen at random; but we cannot make it the sole locus of all activity. "We must add soul, which is another principle, to beings: not only the soul of the universe, but also that of the individual, which is not a small principle, to weave all things together; it does not, like other things, come to be from seeds, but is a primarily active cause" (III,1,8,4–9). In Chapter 7 Plotinus had considered a more liberal formulation of the Stoic doctrine, which attributes a secondary causality to the active principles, the *spermatikoi logoi*, distributed through bodies. This allows the human soul to have some activity (III,1,7,4–8), but it would not (Plotinus argues) be the activity of a free rational agent. The argument here derives ultimately from the *Timaeus* and the *Laws*: the powers present in corporeal elements, unlike the rational soul, act only when and as they are acted upon. If the soul were of this description, it would act only by blindly transmitting physical impulses. Such a soul would not be free: "the up-to-us," the human freedom which the Stoics hope to preserve at least in the act of

---

SVF II,914–21): so Cicero, following a Stoic source, defines fate as "*ordo seriesque causarum, cum causa causae nexa rem ex se gignat*" (*De Divinatione* I,lv,125; Descartes is thinking of this Ciceronian formula or something like it when he speaks in the first Meditation of those who say that I have been produced "*fato* [Stoics] *seu casu* [Epicureans] *seu continuata rerum serie* [Stoics again]" [AT VII,21]). The Stoic descriptions of fate as identical with the world-soul and as a chain of dependent causes are different expressions of the same doctrine, though Plotinus treats them as competing doctrines in *On Fate* chapters 4 and 7.

submitting to necessity, "will be only a word" (III,1,7,15); "it will be for us as it is for the other animals and for infants, proceeding according to blind impulses, and for madmen (for these too have impulses) – so too, by Zeus, even the impulses of fire and of all things which are slaves to their constitution and are moved according to it" (III,1,7,17–21). Since all these causes operate only when they are themselves impelled by some prior cause, the whole series must be set in motion by a previous cause outside it. This principle must be a self-moved mover, that is, a soul (as Plato argues in *Laws* X); and only such a principle can be a bearer of reason.[38]

Although souls are originally rational, and originally acted on only by Nous, they can come to be causally affected by bodies, and then (like the originally irrational powers) they can undergo and transmit the irrational motions that bodies would impose on them: their rationality and their freedom to initiate a causal chain are alike imperiled. "When [soul] is without body it is most master of itself, and free and outside of worldly causality; but when it has been introduced into body it is no longer entirely master, being rather coordinate with other things" (III,1,8,9–11). The things that surround the descended soul are governed more by chance than by reason, and the soul must struggle with them, "so that it does some things on account of these, but it masters others and leads them where it wills" (III,1,8,13–14). Fate, in the sense in which Plotinus chooses to accept the term, is the result of the concatenation of mere physical causes; against the Stoics, Plotinus asserts that this is the expression not of the rational will of God but of the irrationality of matter. To the extent that a soul submits to fate, it is not rational but irrational; but the soul has the power, when it does not abandon its original rationality, to resist the influence of fate and direct itself according to Nous. "The soul which yields anything to the temperament of the body is compelled to desire or be angry, mean in poverty or vain in wealth or a tyrant in power; but the soul which withstands in these same conditions, the soul which is naturally good, alters them rather than being altered, so that it makes some of them different and yields to others without vice" (III,1,8,15–21).[39]

---

[38] Plotinus, following Plato, takes it as obvious that a non-self-moving cause (or a plurality of such causes) could not be sufficient to impose rational order on the world. As I have written elsewhere, Plato at least implicitly argues "that things that move only when they are moved by other things cannot be rational causes because they will move not when it is best for them but only when circumstances external to them dictate. At best, an externally moved mover could move according to the rationality that *something else* possesses by *transmitting* a rational pattern of motion from an initial rational mover; but Plato expects that a vortex full of bodies jostling each other would rapidly degrade an originally rational motion into a chaotic motion unless they are governed continuously by something that is not moved from without" (Menn, *Plato on God as Nous*, p. 41).

[39] There is a crucial contrast here: for Plotinus (and many of his Platonist contemporaries) being governed by fate is being governed *irrationally*, whereas for the Stoics, fate is "the rational plan of the things in the cosmos governed by providence" (SVF II,913), and we live rationally by following it. Plotinus' thought is not that fate is a radically anti-rational

The doctrine that the individual human soul, just as much as the world-soul, proceeds directly from the source of rationality, and may bypass the order of bodies to govern itself according to this rationality, allows Plotinus to save the Platonic theodicy that Stoic corporealism had endangered. The divine creator does not become responsible for producing evil: for the demiurge is not soul but Nous, which is not involved in producing the bad actions of souls, and which produces souls in a purely rational condition. Soul as it is constituted by Nous does not do evil; our souls, unlike the celestial souls, spontaneously descend into sublunar bodies and become subject to the conditions of chaotic matter, and only thus can they become vicious. Even in this case, our deviation from rationality is up to us, and we can still return to follow Nous and our original nature.

Given the distinction between the divine Nous and the souls which are free to depart from it or to follow it, Plotinus thinks he can account for the evils of the sensible world by the combined tactics of explanation through matter, explanation through the good of the whole, and explanation through the voluntary action of soul. Matter is evil, but matter is neither a principle independent of God, nor something that proceeds from God *per se*; rather, matter is a privation, existing in something to the extent that it falls short of God. Since it is better that there should be imperfect things as well as perfect things, it is hypothetically necessary that matter too should exist.[40] Given that matter exists, it is better that

power, but rather that the influence of fate is the resultant of many particular influences, which may each be rational, but do not add up to a rational plan. The motions of each heavenly body are rational, being produced by a soul participating fully in reason; but the motions of sublunar bodies governed by the heavenly motions are not themselves rational. Something like this was Plato's point in having the "young gods" (the heavenly bodies) produce mortal bodies and the irrational parts of the human soul, while the demiurge directly produces only the heavenly bodies and rational souls: while Plato *says* only that the works of the demiurge (but not the works of his works) are immortal, he may *mean* that what is produced directly by Nous is also *rational* and lawlike. Likewise, for Aristotle, eternally unmoved beings produce the eternally constant (and rational and mathematizable) motions of the heavenly bodies, which in turn, as a consequence of their different positions in the sky, produce the changing motions of corruptible sublunar bodies, which are not orderly enough to be the objects of a precise mathematical science. Thus while the Stoics identify fate and providence, and take astrology as a reassuring sign of divine control, the Platonists sharply distinguish fate (often astrologically conceived) from providence, and think of fate as posing a threat which the soul must escape by coming into direct contact with Nous: the human rational soul, unlike other things in the sublunar world, can bypass the chain of derivative causes, and be ruled directly by Nous, that is, rationally. These worries about fate are also present in the *Corpus Hermeticum*, and in the Jewish and Christian literature of the time. We will see a modern analogy to these ideas in Descartes (see especially Chapter 5, Section C, below): bodies are governed not by the heavens but by the laws of motion, which are themselves rational and proceed directly from God, but may not produce rational effects in a particular complex body, or in a soul that allows itself to be swayed by the influence of its bodily environment; the soul must therefore free itself from external bodily influences, and rely only on what it receives directly from God as Nous, to achieve rationality in its judgments.

[40] Here I am following what I take to be Plotinus' argument in IV,8,6 and II,9,3; though the question of the origin of matter in Plotinus is obscure, and it is not entirely out of the

the things that proceed from God should give themselves to matter to produce in it as much order and perfection as it is capable of receiving, rather than keeping their perfection to themselves and refusing to produce less perfect things. So souls "descend" to produce the corporeal world within matter. This descent proceeds from something good, and it takes place for good: "although [the soul] is the last god, it comes to be here by a spontaneous inclination and on account of its power and for the ordering of the things after it" (IV,8,5,25–7). "If it escapes quickly enough, it has suffered no harm" (ibid. 27–8), for this "descent" does not of itself damage the soul: soul produces order in the world not by irrationality but by rationality, not by looking to the bodies beneath it but by looking to the Nous above it; thus, in a sense, the soul does not itself descend when it produces the living body.[41] But the soul, or the lower soul which governs the body, although it has done nothing irrational, has acquired the occasion for temptation, and for a "descent" that will be truly harmful for the soul. Sublunar bodies "need more care," and

as the pilots of storm-tossed ships give themselves more to the care of the ships, and unwittingly become careless of themselves, so that they are often in danger of being dragged down too in the wreck of their ships, so these too [the souls of sublunar living things] have inclined more to what is theirs. (IV,3,17,21–6)

The perfect order of things, which includes the perfect's giving itself to the imperfect, necessarily includes the possibility and even the temptation of this evil for the soul, but it does not include this evil as such. Nous does not force the souls which proceed from it to turn away from it; and once they have done so, although it is hard for them to break from their immersion in the irrational passions of the body, they retain their capacity for doing so, since they retain the image of their "father," the divine Nous. It remains possible for them to return to a pure contemplation of Nous and separation from the evils of the body, if they can recollect their true nature and that of Nous above them. Plotinus' aim in his philosophy is just to bring them to that recollection.

question that he regards matter as an independent principle. For matter as privation, see especially II,4 *On the Two Kinds of Matter*, and for matter as evil, see especially I,8 *What Are and Whence Come Evils?*

[41] Plotinus stresses, especially in III,8 *On Nature, Contemplation, and the One*, and II,9 *Against the Gnostics*, that soul introduces rational order into bodies, not by looking "down" to bodies, but by rationally contemplating eternal things: soul "gave to all body to possess however much it [body] can receive from it [soul], but it [soul] remains unbusied, not governing by deliberation [*dianoia*] nor correcting anything, but ordering by a marvelous power through the contemplation of what is before it" (II,9,2,13–16). The question of whether the soul "descends" in governing bodies is complicated, in part, by an ambiguity in "descend": we can distinguish (i) the undescended soul, remaining in the intelligible world; (ii) the soul present here, but still looking up to the intelligibles; (iii) the soul present here and looking down to the body. Plotinus can refer either to the transition from (i) to (ii) or to the transition from (ii) to (iii) as the soul's "descent," but the first does not necessarily lead to the second.

4

Augustine

A. True and false wisdom

We now have a reasonable reconstruction of what Augustine found in the "books of the Platonists"; this is the right way into interpreting Augustine's understanding of God and the soul, since (as Augustine tells us in *Confessions* VII) he reached this understanding by reading and meditating on the books of the Platonists. Turning now from the Platonists to Augustine himself, we can see how he uses the intellectual material of Platonism to work out an understanding of God and other things, compatible with Christianity and explicating the intellectual content of the Christian scriptures. Following Henry's rules of method, our primary evidence must be "Augustine's own testimonies on the writings of the philosophers which he has read, on the circumstances in which he read them, on the intellectual or moral profit which he drew from them, and on the impressions with which they left him."[1] Augustine testifies explicitly and systematically to his reading of the books of the Platonists in *Confessions* VII, and only there; so this book, with some supporting material, will provide our point of departure. Once we have learned from Augustine himself what intellectual profit he drew from Platonism, and how he applied it to his Christian intellectual project, we can turn to the treatises and dialogues where he tries to carry out this project, and observe how he actually does what, in the *Confessions*, he says he is doing.

When Augustine wrote the *Confessions*, he was already a bishop. He narrates the final outcome of his search for wisdom, not in the descriptions of the vision of God in Book VII, but in his account of his decision to accept Christian discipline in Book VIII. But the visions of God, reached by exercises in the Plotinian discipline of contemplation, are nonetheless a crucial part of the wisdom Augustine finally settles on. It is a delicate problem, and will require a detailed study of the texts, to describe precisely the role of Platonic philosophy in Augustine's final Christian version of wisdom. But some things are clear at the outset. At a minimum, Platonic philosophy served a crucial *negative* function in making Christianity possible for Augustine, by helping (together with Ambrose's preaching) to remove the intellectual obstacles that had seemed to make it impossible to look for wisdom within the Catholic church. Augustine shows us what

[1] See above, Chapter 3, Section A.

these obstacles were, to begin with, when he describes in *Confessions* III–V his association with the Manichees. Since Augustine had accepted the Manichees' claim to possess the truth about "you [God, the addressee of the *Confessions*] and the Lord Jesus Christ and the Paraclete, our comforter, the Holy Spirit" (III,vi,10), he had also accepted their attacks on the Catholic church. The Manichees, as Gnostics, saw the Christianity of the Catholics as adulterated by the irrationality and barbarism of the Jewish Old Testament, and by Judaizing corruptions of the text of the New Testament (cf. V,xi,21). They posed questions against the Catholics that depended on a literal interpretation of certain texts of the Old Testament (III,vii,12) – especially the assertion that human beings are made in the image of God – questions that seemed unanswerable to Augustine until he came to learn the technique of spiritual interpretation from St. Ambrose (V,xiv,24). Similarly, they asked him "whence evil is" (III,vii,12), if the book of Genesis is right that the good God is an omnipotent creator, and Mani wrong that God is in continual struggle with evil – a question likewise unanswerable for Augustine until he found the solution in the books of the Platonists (VII,xi,17–xvi,22). The Manichees ridiculed the Catholic demand for faith, and offered instead a supposedly scientific system of theology and cosmology, which, as Augustine says from his later perspective, he and they had believed without proof (VI,v,7). But by the period described in Book VI, "I was no longer a Manichee, though neither was I a Catholic Christian" (VI,i,1), for he had read books of the philosophers and astronomers, and realized the falsity of the Manichean system. But he had still to resolve the Manichees' objections against Catholicism. In Book VI (and the last chapter of Book V) he shows how the preaching of Ambrose removed many of the objections, but the great question "whence evil" remained until his discovery, recounted in Book VII, of the books of the Platonists. Thus the Platonists removed the last intellectual obstacle to Augustine's accepting Catholic Christianity; the crisis of Book VIII remained, but it was not an *intellectual* difficulty, but Augustine's *moral* struggle to renounce his sexual passions and his ambitions for wealth and honor.

But we can go further: Platonism did not merely remove obstacles; it gave Augustine a positive intellectual contribution toward the desired wisdom. The obstacles were not simply Manichean objections to Catholicism (or to the Book of Genesis) as such, but difficulties blocking Augustine from any adequate conception of God: difficulties blocking, in particular, any conception of God as omnipotent, as immutable, or as incorporeal. What allowed Augustine to resolve the question "whence evil" was an intellectual "vision" purporting to manifest God's true nature; and, although Augustine later decided that this vision was not sufficient to give him the desired wisdom, he never doubted that it was a genuine vision of God. Although this vision might not be sufficient for wisdom, it was certainly a positive step toward wisdom, and it gave Augustine a description (which he was never to renounce) of what the intellectual content of the desired wisdom would have to be. It is reasonable to describe Augustine's reading of the Platonists, and his consequent vision of God, as a stage in Augustine's conversion; but (as noted above, Chapter 3, Section A) "conversion" for Augustine is not the passage from one religious allegiance to another, but the soul's *conversio* or turning to God. The constant theme of the *Confessions* is the soul's turning away from God and its turning back toward him: as Augustine is capable of writing, "our good always lives with you [God], and because we have turned away [*aversi sumus*], we have turned astray [*perversi sumus*]; let us now return [*revertamur*], Lord, and not be overturned [*evertamur*], for our good, which you yourself are, lives with you without any failure" (IV,xvi,31).[2] Before his reading of the books of the Platonists, Augustine had been turned away from God, when he was a Manichee and before he was a Manichee and after he was a Manichee: "I had my back to the light . . . so my face was not illuminated" (IV,xvi,30), even while that light enabled him to see the things in front of him. Platonic philosophy reoriented him, so that "with some eye of my soul I saw an immutable light above this eye of my soul, above my mind" (VII,x,16). In Augustine's mature, Christian, judgment, this vision of God, though genuine, was not sufficient: "it is one thing to see the country [*patria*] of peace from a hill in the forest and to find no path to it . . . and another to follow the way that leads there [*illuc*]" (VII,xxi,27).[3] Platonism gave him only the vision of God, while Christianity gave him the path; but the vision was what inspired him to seek the path. Platonism made Christianity possible for Augustine not simply by answering Manichean objections, but by grasping his soul and turning it around to look toward God, overcoming the essential *aversio* and ignorance of God of which Manicheism was only an expression.

Augustine represents his efforts to "turn back" toward God as a single continuous search for wisdom. When he first read Cicero's *Hortensius*, with its "exhortation to philosophy" – which, as Augustine says, Cicero meant in its etymological sense as the love of wisdom – "suddenly every vain hope seemed worthless to me, and I desired the immortality of wisdom with an incredible burning in my heart, and I began to raise myself

[2] Augustine's description of the soul's "turning away" from God and "returning" to him does not entail that, at the time of the *Confessions*, he believed that each individual soul has fallen from a prior condition of union with God (against O'Connell, *St. Augustine's Confessions: The Odyssey of Soul*). At *De Libero Arbitrio* III,xx–xxi, earlier than the *Confessions* (discussed in Section C below), Augustine expresses agnosticism on whether the individual soul existed before being united to the body (and, if it did, on what its prior condition was); but he feels equally free to use the language of fall and return, however the question of preexistence turns out.
[3] Augustine's use of *patria* here exactly corresponds to Plotinus' use of *patris* in the first chapter of V,9 *On Nous, Ideas, and Being*, discussed in Chapter 3, Section B, above; in Section D of this chapter we will look at similarities and differences between Plotinus and Augustine on the soul's return to its fatherland. Augustine's use of *illuc* corresponds to Plotinus' use of *ekei* (there, in the intelligible world); Augustine will also contrast *illa*, the things there (Plotinus' *ekeina*), with *ista*, the things here (Plotinus' *tade*).

up to return to you" (III,iv,7). So from the beginning the desire for "the immortality of wisdom" presented itself, however obscurely, as a desire for God and for flight from the world: "I burned to fly back from earthly things to you, [though] I knew not what you would do with me: for 'with you is wisdom' " (III,iv,8). Cicero gave no prescription for wisdom, and praised no particular sect, but only "wisdom itself, whatever it might be"; but it would be some kind of knowledge of God, in whom all sects located wisdom or truth. Augustine set out to discover this wisdom from among the sects. He recounts in the *Confessions* his involvements, through reading or personal contact, with the Manichees, with unnamed "philosophers" who helped to show him the absurdity of the Manichean cosmology, with the Academics, with the Platonists, and with the Catholic Christians of the circle of Ambrose; all these are included in his narration because they are parts of his search for wisdom or for knowledge of God.

Almost immediately after describing his reading of the *Hortensius*, Augustine describes his "falling in" with the Manichees (III,vi,10). His Christian background and his classical culture were such that he could not be satisfied either with pagan philosophy (III,iv,8) or with the "undignified" Christian scriptures (III,v,9). The Manichees claimed to provide the advantages of both: they had the true doctrine of Christ and St. Paul without the barbaric Jewish corruptions, and they could set it out in eloquent language and explain it by a general cosmic theology, revealed by the Holy Spirit and full of oriental wisdom, but also scientific and influenced by Greek philosophy. Augustine treats the Manichees throughout the *Confessions* as the paradigmatic representatives of the human *aversio* from God, both deceived and deceiving, sinning through lust and pride and expiating their sins through superstitious acts (so, at length, IV,i,1). He treats the wisdom they offered as entirely false, both as philosophy and as Christianity; far from allowing him to fly from earthly things to God, it drew him down into the depths of hell (III,vi,11); by providing a false and flattering imitation, it dissuaded him from seeking a true wisdom or a truly virtuous way of life. Augustine's condemnation of the Manichees is extremely harsh, and powerfully repeated throughout the *Confessions*, but it is also very subtle: Augustine makes it his business in the *Confessions* not merely to narrate and to distribute praise or blame, but also to analyze, and if we follow carefully his analysis of the Manichees' false wisdom we will be able to understand what Platonism and Christianity had to overcome in leading him to true wisdom, and how they were able to do so.

To begin with, the Manichees are ignorant of God, and therefore are not wise. But what is worse is that they *pretend* to knowledge, both about God and about the lower things with which they confuse him:

Who asked this Mani to write about the things here [*ista*], since piety might be learned even without any expertise in these things? For you have said to man, "behold, piety is wisdom." He [Mani] might have been ignorant of *that* [the true wisdom], even if he knew these things [*ista*] perfectly; but since, without knowing these, he impudently dared to teach them, it is obvious that he could not have known *that* [*illam*] (V,v,8),

since people who know God and thus become wise do not pretend to know things of which they are ignorant. But the Manichees are dominated by pride, and, "not wanting to be thought little of" (ibid.), invent a sacred doctrine to conceal their ignorance. They speak of the things of this world because, not knowing the true God, they suppose him to be among these things. When Augustine desired truth, and truth understood as God, the Manichees spoke over and over again of truth, "with the voice alone and with many vast books; and these were the platters on which, when I was hungering for you, they brought me the sun and the moon, your beautiful works, but still your works and not you" (III,vi,10). In confusing the creature with the creator and giving a theological interpretation of the physical world, the Manichees departed from the truth about creatures: they gave him, not even the real sun and the real moon, but "corporeal phantasms, false bodies" (ibid.). The Manichean doctrines are worse than the fables of the poets, whose role in education Augustine had deplored in good Platonic fashion in Book I, because people are not really expected to believe the poets, "but these, alas, I believed" (III,vi,11).

It was easier for Augustine to recognize the falsity of the Manichean fables than to overcome the condition of ignorance of God that made him receptive to those fables; even when he had "escaped from falsehood," he had not thereby "attained to truth" (VI,i,1). In *Confessions* V Augustine describes his reading of "many [books] of the philosophers" (V,iii,3), which contradicted the Manichean doctrines: using the light that God gave them, these men had investigated the corporeal creation, and were able to give accurate predictions, many years in advance, of the eclipses of the sun and moon. These philosophers did not know God any more than the Manichees did, and like the Manichees inclined to pride in their knowledge of the things here; but at least their knowledge, unlike that of the Manichees, was genuine.[4] Augustine resolved to bring the contradic-

---

[4] Augustine does not say who these philosophers are; but they are *not* the Platonists. They might be simply astronomers, or astrologers, since Augustine was interested in astrology at this time (*Confessions* IV,iii,4); but then it is odd that he should call them philosophers (he usually calls the astrologers *mathematici*). It is more likely that Augustine is referring to Stoic philosophers who made use of astronomical or astrological results, perhaps to support a conception of fate or providence. At *De Civitate Dei* V,ii Augustine cites Posidonius, *magnus astrologus idemque philosophus* (so *De Civitate Dei* V,v), as giving an astrological explanation for similarities in the fates of twins, and (apparently) also an astrological excuse when things turn out differently. The argument of *De Civitate Dei* V against the astrologers' attempts to explain away differences in the fates of twins, or of babies born at the same moment to different parents, is parallel to the argument of *Confessions* VII,vi against the astrologers of *Confessions* IV,iii,4; this makes it likely that Posidonius, the target in *De Civitate Dei* V, is also the astronomically or astrologically inclined philosopher of *Confessions* V,iii,3. It is clear from the way Augustine cites Posidonius at *De Civitate Dei* V,ii that his information about Posidonius is entirely derivative from Cicero; so the *multa*

tions between the Manichean fables and genuine scientific astronomy before the Manichean bishop Faustus, reputed the wisest man of the sect; when he did so, and Faustus could make no response, Augustine gave up all hope of finding wisdom in the teachings of the sect (V,vii,12–13). But he had no clue where else to find it; his "philosophers" might know truths about the creation, but they did not pretend to know the creator, and "were without the saving name of Christ" (V,xiv,25), so that they held no promise of wisdom in the sense in which Augustine desired it. Thus Augustine "did not at first entirely separate myself from them [the Manichees], but as I did not find anything better than that into which I had already somehow stumbled, I decided to be content with it for the time being, unless perchance something more worthy of choice should become apparent" (V,vii,13). Without any real hope in Manicheism, and mindful of the astronomical arguments against it, Augustine naturally began to "hold it more loosely and indifferently" (V,x,19), and eventually to separate himself entirely (V,xiv,25); and thus also "there came to me the thought, that those philosophers who are called Academics were more prudent than the others, because they judged that everything should be doubted, and decided that nothing true could be comprehended by man" (V,x,19).

The Academics might be comparatively "more prudent," but, as Augustine argues in the *Contra Academicos*, someone who knows nothing cannot be called wise. Augustine remained in his condition of ignorance of God. Lacking any conception of God better than that of the Manichees, he was unable to escape the same philosophical presuppositions that underlay their revealed doctrine; it was these presuppositions of Manicheism, rather than Manicheism itself, which he had to overcome in order to find true wisdom.

Augustine was trying to conceive God rightly. He needed to do this in order to understand the Catholic doctrines that the Manichees had challenged, the image of God in man and the origin of evil under a good creator; but beyond this, he sought to comprehend God in order to become wise, whether wisdom lay with the Catholics or elsewhere. But he could not: "since, when I wished to think of my God, I did not know how to think anything except corporeal masses – for whatever was not such did not seem to me to *be* – this was the greatest and almost the only cause of my inevitable error" (V,x,19). From his mature standpoint Augustine analyzes his inability to think the incorporeal God: he had turned away from God and toward the body, and had formed the habit of thinking only through the senses of the body; he had thus become unable to extricate himself from the images of bodies and conceive what is incorporeal and therefore unimaginable. God had created him, says Augustine (VII,vii,11), inferior to God but superior to "the things here [*ista*]," to

philosophorum that Augustine had read at *Confessions* V,iii,3 would be Cicero's accounts of Posidonius and other Greek philosophers.

"the things that are contained in places"; God set him over these things, "to remain in your image, and, serving you, to dominate the body." But when, in his pride, he turned against God, he lost the position he had above these lesser things: "these lowest things came to be above me and pressed me down." Here and in many parallel passages the language is of submersion and suffocation: "and there was never respite or breath." The means of escape would be through thought, through thought of the things that are not contained in places: but "these things pressed up on all sides before my sight, thronged and massed together; and when I thought, these images of bodies blocked my return, as if saying 'where are you going, unworthy and vile?' " Until some help could liberate Augustine from this condition, he could not escape from images and think the true, incorporeal God: however much he might come to despise the Manichean fables, he would remain trapped within the conditions of thought that generated them, constrained, if he thought about God at all, to repeat the main lines of the Manichean doctrine, unable to progress toward the desired wisdom.

In *Confessions* VII Augustine describes his struggle, long unsuccessful, to free himself from his immersion in the senses and to think God. This is the context in which he describes his reading of the books of the Platonists: only they, and the grace of God operating through them, were able to lead him out of his captivity and give him a way to conceive God without the senses. If we first pause to understand what the main lines were of his earlier thought, and why he was trying to escape them, and then turn to his description of how the books of the Platonists gave him the means of escape, we can easily grasp the essence of what he took from Platonism.

Before he read the Platonists, he could not conceive of God except as a body. "Yet I was trying to think you, the supreme and the only and the true God, and I believed with all my heart that you were incorruptible and inviolable and immutable" (VII,i,1), because his piety would not allow him to attribute to God the opposite defects. But it is not easy – from his mature perspective, Augustine will say that it is impossible – to discover a body that is incorruptible and inviolable and immutable. The Manichees described God as a "luminous and immense body" (IV,xvi,31),[5] and this would have to do. As Augustine thought in independence of the Manichees, he extended the ambiguous "immense" to the clearer "infinite," and perhaps withdrew the visual image of luminosity;[6] but the essence of the conception remains the same.

---

[5] Augustine is here describing what he himself had thought, but at a period when he was still firmly a Manichee.

[6] Augustine uses "infinite" in V,x,20, again in VII,i,2, and very clearly in VII,v,7; in VII,xiv,20 he *seems* to be describing this as a post-Manichean development in his views. I have no positive evidence that Augustine abandoned the description of divine luminosity, but light is mentioned in Book VII only in an apparently metaphorical sense, VII,i,2.

Thus I thought that you . . . were great through infinite spaces, everywhere penetrating the whole mass of the world and extended beyond it through immense [spaces] without limit, so that the earth and the heaven and all things would have you [as a limit] and be contained in you, but you in nothing. For as the body of the air, of this air which is above the earth, does not obstruct the light of the sun from passing through it, penetrating it not by breaking it apart or dividing it, but by filling it entirely, so I thought that the body not only of the heaven and the air and the sea but also of the earth could be permeated and penetrated in all its greatest and smallest parts to encompass your presence, which by a hidden inspiration inwardly and outwardly administered all the things that you have created. (VII,i,2)

This, says Augustine, was the best he could conceive, a God physically blended with his creation, able to administer the whole because a part of him was present in every part; as Augustine comments from his mature position, "the body of an elephant would encompass more of you than the body of a sparrow" (ibid.).

The human soul, according to the Manichees, was a portion of this omnipresent divine body; indeed, Augustine takes this doctrine to sum up the vanity of all his early study of wisdom: "what did this profit me when I thought that you, Lord God, the Truth, were a luminous and immense body, and that I was a fragment of that body?" (IV,xvi,31). For the Manichees, this doctrine was essential to their sacred cosmology: the soul was "a portion and a member of you or an offspring of your very substance, mixed with opposing powers and natures not created by you and so much corrupted by them and changed for the worse, that it had turned from happiness into misery, and needed a helper [the word of God] by which it might be rescued and purged" (VII,ii,3). For Augustine, the philosophical implication was that, since the soul was a portion of God's substance, "I was naturally what you [God] are" (IV,xv,26). But if so, it would not be possible for the human soul to sin or err without God's sinning or erring in and with it; but sin and error do exist, so that if moral evil is not to be ascribed to God, then "it is not we who sin, but I-know-not-what other nature sins in us" (V,x,18), namely the opposing powers with which we have become intermixed. Augustine, looking back, considers this doctrine the product of a sinful pride, a flattery and excuse of himself. The result was to confirm him in his sins: he could not confess and seek to return to God until he admitted that he had departed from God.

How then is evil to be conceived, if it is not in the acts of the soul? Even when Augustine was no longer a Manichee, he could not escape the Manichean conception: evil "seemed to my ignorance to be not merely a substance but a corporeal substance" (V,x,20). Because he could not conceive anything except as corporeal, "I believed that there was a substance of evil that was of this kind [i.e. corporeal], and that it had its own hideous and ill-formed mass, whether dense, which they call earth, or rare and subtle, like the body of air, which they imagine as a malign mind diffused throughout that earth" (ibid.). God would not have created such a thing: Augustine felt himself forced to conclude that the existence of evil was independent of God and against his will, and that in this sense it imposed a limit on God. Augustine was unhappy with this conclusion, since by subjecting God to some extent to evil, it seemed to contradict his axiom that God was "incorruptible and inviolable and immutable." In particular, if the Manichees were right that the soul was a fragment of God that had become mixed with and corrupted by the opposing powers, it would follow that God himself was corruptible and could suffer evil. Augustine rejected this consequence, he tells us, as a "horrible sacrilege of heart and tongue" (VII,ii,3), but he had no alternative by which to explain how God could be forced to tolerate the existence of evil in the universe. Even if the soul is not a part of God, but a creature of God according to the Catholic doctrine, the creature of a good God should be good; but we see that there is something evil and contrary to God contaminating God's creature, and we must not ascribe the origin of this evil to God. Seeking to analyze the "root" and "seed" of the evil in creatures, Augustine could only conclude that "that from which he made them was some evil matter, and he formed and ordered it, but there remained in it something that he did not convert to good" (VII,v,7). Thus evil would ultimately reside in something resembling the evil mass of the Manichees, and it would be able to resist God, to prevent him from destroying it or converting it to good – a conclusion Augustine could neither accept nor evade.

These were Augustine's dilemmas in trying to think of God as incorruptible and inviolable and immutable, while unable to think of him as incorporeal. "Not knowing whence and how, nonetheless I saw and was certain" (VII,i,1) that the immutable is better than the mutable; and nothing better than God can be conceived (VII,iv,6). "My heart protested violently against all my phantasms, and by this one blow [*hoc uno ictu*; a violent straining in the direction of the incorruptible seen to be superior] I tried to drive away the surrounding crowd of impurity from the eye of my mind: and scarcely had they been parted when in the twinkling of an eye [*in ictu oculi*] they were there again massed together, and they rushed in upon my sight and clouded it" (VII,i,1), so that he could not conceive an immutable being that was not extended in space.

So it remained until God in his providence "procured for me, through a man swollen with the most monstrous pride, certain books of the Platonists translated from the Greek language into Latin" (VII,ix,13).[7] This is the climax of Book VII: after all Augustine's own efforts had failed to bring him to knowledge of God, he received the aid of the Platonists, genuine wise men, and of God, the source of all wisdom; and these succeeded in rescuing him from the sea of bodily images in which he had

---

[7] See Courcelle's *Recherches sur les Confessions* for a discussion of this statement; Courcelle identifies the pride-swollen individual, very plausibly, as Manlius Theodorus, the addressee of the *De Beata Vita*.

been submerged, clearing his vision, and enabling him to perceive the true, incorporeal God. "And admonished thence [by the books of the Platonists] to return to myself, I entered into my own innermost parts [*in intima mea*], with you [God] as my leader; and I was able, because 'you had become my helper' " (VII,x,16). In VII,x, and again in VII,xvii, Augustine describes the discipline of contemplation by which he was led away from bodies and up to God. "I entered and I saw, with some eye of my soul, above that eye of my soul, above my mind, an immutable light" (ibid.), not the corporeal light of the Manichees but an incorporeal light, which is the true God. The account in VII,xvii is more elaborate, but in both chapters Augustine begins with a knowledge of his own rational soul or mind, and then comes to perceive God as related to his mind, as the truth superior to his mind. In perceiving this truth he has succeeded in discovering the immutable; and he has been enabled to think it without sensible images, so that he can recognize its existence without having to regard it as corporeal. "And I said, 'is truth then nothing, because it is diffused neither through a finite nor through an infinite spatial extension?' " (ibid.),[8] and he could not doubt that this truth existed. Augustine knows that the immutable is superior to the immutable, but recognizes that he cannot find the immutable either in bodies or in his own mind as it passes judgment upon them; he turns instead to examine the the light by means of which he passed this judgment. He describes in VII,xvii how, following this procedure, he was able, if only momentarily, to reverse the condition he had described in VII,i: his mind

raised itself up to its own understanding, and withdrew my thought from its habit, removing itself from the contrary crowds of phantasms,[9] that it might discover what light shone upon it when it proclaimed without any doubt that the immutable was preferable to the mutable, a light by which [*unde*] it knew the immutable itself

---

[8] "Spatial extension" translates *spatia locorum*; "spatial" corresponds to *locorum*, not to *spatia*. *Spatia* in Augustine may be either spatial extension, *spatia locorum*, or temporal extension, *spatia temporum*.

[9] Augustine, characteristically, expresses his Platonic discovery in a Ciceronian phrase, since it was Cicero who first moved him to "fly from earthly things to God," and since he remains convinced that Cicero was at heart a Platonist (cf. the bizarre reference at *Contra Academicos* III,xviii,41 to Cicero's refuting corporealism to prepare the way for Plotinus): the phrase "withdrew my thought from its habit" [*abduxit cogitationem a consuetudine*] comes from Cicero, *Tusculan Disputations* I,xvi,38: "*magni autem est ingenii sevocare mentem a sensibus et cogitationem ab consuetudine abducere*" (Augustine quotes this phrase in full, clearly marking it as a quotation, in *Letter* 137). In context, Cicero is describing our natural tendency to imagine a human soul *post mortem* as if it still had a quasi-human body: a special effort of thought, discarding sensory images, is necessary if we are to avoid such inappropriate conceptions. Descartes also refers to this same passage of Cicero in describing what he claims to accomplish in the first and second Meditations (AT VII,12 and VII,131); see below, Chapter 5, Section B, and Chapter 6, Section A. Both Augustine and Descartes, in taking up Cicero's challenge, are doing something much more serious than what Cicero was thinking of; he is alluding to a Platonic commonplace without taking his Platonism very seriously, whereas Augustine (directly) and Descartes (indirectly) are drawing on the discipline of intellectual contemplation that is at the core of Plotinian Platonism.

– for if it had not somehow known this, it could not have preferred it for certain to the mutable – and in the twinkling of an eye [*in ictu trepidantis aspectus*, heightening the *in ictu oculi* of VII,i,1] it arrived at that which is [*id quod est*]. (VII,xvii,23)

In this way Augustine was able to come to the vision of God he had been striving for, and to escape the condition of ignorance he had shared with the Manichees.[10] Given the true conception of God, he was able to understand how God could be immutable and evils nonetheless exist; he devotes VII,xi–xvi, between the initial and the final descriptions of the vision of God, to this consequence of his vision. What he gives is simply the standard theodicy; but this had not been available to him while he was a captive of the Manichees' way of thought. By escaping from submersion in the senses and conceiving, first his own mind, then God as the truth above the mind, he was able to understand the relation between God and his mind in such a way that his mind could depart from God, and thus do and suffer evil without God's doing and suffering evil along with it. "Errors and false opinions contaminate life, if the rational mind itself is vicious. So it was in me, when I was ignorant that it needed to be illumined by another light in order to participate in truth, because it is not the nature of truth itself" (IV,xv,25). When he believed that God was corporeal, he could not conceive him as a nature different from the mind, except as the whole is different from the part; now he has perceived God as incorporeal by conceiving him as the immutable standard by which the mutable mind judges and is judged. The relation between God and the mind remains intimate, but it is a relation of a type found in incorporeal things, not the relation of whole to part. With this understanding, all the resources of the traditional Platonic theodicy become available to Augustine to solve the problem of the origin of evil.

Thus Augustine, "having read a few books of Plotinus," is using them as Plotinus intended, to raise himself up out of a false wisdom that claims

[10] Augustine, like Plotinus, describes this ascent through soul to Nous in many parallel passages, some briefer and others more extended, but with no essential difference in content. I will not try to collect all these passages, but will discuss the most useful and explicit texts (from *Confessions* VII and *De Libero Arbitrio* II) in detail in Section B below. With Augustine, as with Plotinus, there is no hope, and no point, of deciding the biographical questions of how many times he "experienced" such an ascent, and of whether the experience varied from one time to the next. There is no chronological development among the different ascent passages in Augustine, all of which describe the same sequence of thoughts, adapted as appropriate to the literary context of each passage. It is a serious mistake to treat the ascents of *Confessions* VII, as some commentators do, as reporting attempts (especially "failed attempts") at a "mystical experience." It is also hopeless to look for development between these ascents and the "vision of Ostia" (*Confessions* IX,x). In the latter passage, where Augustine is recounting his last conversation with his mother, Monica, he describes their talk about what the joys of eternal life with God might be like, and inserts a description of the ascent to Nous ("wisdom"), using terms general enough (and scriptural enough) to make it seem plausible that his pious but poorly educated mother could have gone through the same sequence of thoughts that he did; the writing is beautiful and moving, but there is no new content.

to know God and the soul but conceives them, and every other reality, as sensible and corporeal. His method is Plotinus' method: first the soul withdraws from the contemplation of bodies and enters into itself, so that it can perceive itself in the proper manner, from within, as a rational soul; then it ascends to contemplate God as the perfect standard of the truth of its thoughts, and the source of its intellectual light – that is to say, as Nous.[11] In this way it rises above the clouds of error, and is able to see the incorporeal reality that is its true *patria*.[12] Once the soul has been enabled to conceive incorporeal things, and to understand its own nature and that of Nous, it will see how it is the product and the image of Nous without being of the same nature as Nous. This vision will make theodicy possible. The soul will understand that it has the power to turn away from Nous and to return to Nous, that it becomes liable to evil by its turning away. There is no evil in God; the world is better for having inferior as well as superior parts, and for having soul present in these inferior parts; having come to be in these inferior parts, the soul turns away from God of its own free choice, and retains the ability to return if it can rise above the senses and the passions of the body.

Having come to the true wisdom, the true vision of himself and God, Augustine is naturally eager to bring others to a similar condition. Having come to wisdom out of deception, originating in his own passions and dependence on the senses, but confirmed and systematized by purveyors

---

[11] On Augustine's choice of the word "truth" [*veritas*] to render "Nous," and on what he took the word "truth" to mean, see Section B below.

[12] Augustine's language, in describing his ascent, aided by the books of the Platonists, to view the incorporeal Truth, often recalls Plotinus' language in the first chapter of Plotinus V,9, *On Nous, Ideas, and Being*, cited and discussed in Chapter 3, Section B. I have already noted some passages where Augustine speaks of the "fatherland," in close parallel to Plotinus; and Augustine also frequently speaks of clouds or mists obscuring the sight, which must be parted to allow a glimpse of the divine realities. Furthermore, in the long rhetorical introduction to the *De Beata Vita*, Augustine not only speaks of the fatherland, of our exile from it and return to it, and of fogs and other ill weather obstructing our vision of it, but also makes use of the Platonist allegorical interpretation of the travels of Odysseus, which Plotinus also uses in the first chapter of V,9 and elsewhere. This opening passage of the *De Beata Vita* is also the place where Augustine speaks explicitly of having read "a very few books of Plotinus"; and he is writing to Manlius Theodorus, who (as Augustine says) is a devotee of Plotinus, and who is probably (as noted above) the man who had given Augustine the books of Plotinus in the first place. Thus the use of descriptions taken from the introduction to one of Plotinus' most important and accessible treatises may be a deliberate allusion, a literary compliment both to Plotinus and to Theodorus. Similarly, in *Contra Academicos* III,xviii,41 (cited in Chapter 3, Section A), Augustine says that "the voice of Plato, which is the most purified and lucid in philosophy, has shone out from the parted clouds of error especially in Plotinus"; this too may be a literary allusion to Plotinus' description in *On Nous, Ideas, and Being* of the Platonists, "divine men" who "by a better power and by the sharpness of their eyes, have seen the upper light as by sharp-sightedness, and have risen there as if above the clouds and mist here below, and have remained there, looking down on all things here and enjoying the true place which is their own, like a man arriving from much wandering at his well-ordered fatherland."

of wisdom both deceiving and deceived, he is naturally eager to help break for others the spell of this deception and this false wisdom; and he has the rich stores of his own experience and of his own mature understanding to draw on in analyzing this false wisdom and admonishing against it. To a rather disconcerting extent, he takes his analysis of Manicheism from Plotinus, who does not mention the Manichees as such;[13] but Plotinus was an expert on wisdom, on how to rescue souls for wisdom, and on what they had to be rescued from. Augustine had personal proof that Plotinus' strategy for inducing wisdom worked; he accepted the intellectual framework that was established by this strategy and that gave it its justification; he therefore accepted Plotinus' analysis both of the origin and of the content of the false wisdom that he had overcome. Augustine is interested in the *Confessions*, not so much in Manicheism, as in the condition of error that Manicheism symbolizes. He says very little about the specific content of the Manichean fables. He speaks instead about the psychological conditions of Manichean belief, using Plotinus to interpret his own experience; and he elaborates the philosophical foundations of the Manichean cosmology, as he sees them by contrast with his own mature views. The philosophical foundations of the Manichean cosmology, seen from this perspective, are precisely the peculiar doctrines of Stoicism as Plotinus presents them: that everything is corporeal, especially God and the soul; that the soul is a fragment of God; that God is totally mixed with matter in every part of the world, and capable of acting everywhere in it for this reason. When Augustine learned wisdom from reading Plotinus he also learned that these were the essential errors of the false wisdom, and that the teaching of true wisdom was to be conducted as a polemic and a rescue mission against this false wisdom.[14]

Despite the dependence of Augustine's analysis of Manicheism on Plotinus' analysis of Stoicism, it remains that Augustine is much more bitter toward the Manichees than Plotinus is toward the Stoics. In part, this is due to personal reasons: Plotinus is describing a general condition of the

---

[13] Plotinus was aware of Gnosticism as a general movement (VP 16), and wrote the treatise II,9 against it; but although there are interesting similarities between this treatise and some things Augustine says against the Manichees, this treatise does not seem to have served Augustine as an overall model, and I am not certain that he had read it. While Plotinus attacks a number of theses that Augustine also is concerned to refute (notably, that the sensible world was produced, and human souls came to be in it, because the world-soul fell or was defeated by matter), Plotinus connects these Gnostic theses with other theses that Augustine accepts (notably that the sensible world was produced in time and does not follow necessarily from the existence of God).

[14] It is not clear to me how far Augustine's dependence on Plotinus' descriptions of Stoicism might render Augustine's descriptions of Manicheism inaccurate. It is also not clear to me how far Augustine himself is conscious that he is taking over Plotinus' descriptions of Stoicism and applying them to a new polemical situation. Indeed, since Plotinus never actually uses the words *Stoa* or *Stôikos* (whether from etiquette or because he wishes Stoic doctrines to symbolize a more general way of thought), Augustine might never have fully realized that it was the Stoics that Plotinus was attacking.

lower ranks of humanity, while Augustine is describing his own past, from which, but for the grace of God, he might never have been rescued. But there are also purely intellectual reasons for the difference. Plotinus agrees that the Stoics have some things right, while Augustine regards the Manichean revelation as purely fraudulent; and it is of course true that Stoicism was closer to Platonism in its teaching than Manicheism was, and that it did not claim to have been revealed by the Holy Spirit.[15] But, beyond this, both Plotinus and Augustine attach *moral* significance to the different intellectual positions. According to Plotinus' scheme in the first chapter of *On Nous, Ideas, and Being*, the Stoics have made some progress beyond Epicurean sensualism and hedonism, in coming to admire the beauty of soul, which is virtue; unfortunately, they have not been able to conceive it rightly, and have fallen back to corporealism and the political virtues. The Manichees would seem to deserve a similar ranking, since they too speak of wisdom and of the soul's relationship to God, though they too are unable to conceive incorporeal substances; but Augustine's judgment on their moral state is much more severe than Plotinus' judgment of the Stoics. This flows from a difference in their moral conceptions, and in the philosophical doctrines on which these were based. The Stoics admired the beauty of virtue, that is, of virtuous action; virtue is the soul's calling in the world order, and its means to happiness. The Manichees, like other Gnostics, expected to be saved through esoteric knowledge and through a cosmic drama having little to do with moral action. The Stoics considered that vice was a corruption of the soul, which destroyed its happiness and damaged its cosmic function; they therefore elaborated a theodicy, Platonic in origin, to show that the soul had its good and evil in its own power, and that God had put it in its situation for the best. The Manichees seem to have thought that vice was simply a condition of the soul's captivity within the domain of the hostile powers; God did not will the soul to be here, and once it is here, virtue is not within its power; its only hope is in the cosmic battle which may rescue it from the hostile powers. The moral result of the Stoic theodicy is to encourage us to virtue; the result of the Manichean lack of theodicy, according to Augustine, is to make us complacent in our vice. Plotinus argues that the Stoics, given their cosmology, have no right to their theodicy, but the Stoics remained happily ignorant of the fact. The Man-

---

[15] Certainly part of Augustine's bitterness toward the Manichees derives from their claims to inspiration and to absolute certainty, and from their derision of Catholic credulity. Augustine, who had been taken in, bears a grudge against people who claim to know what they do not in fact clearly perceive; he seems not to feel that one might be honestly mistaken about such matters. We might compare Plotinus' ferocity in II,9 against the arrogance of the Gnostics. At VP 16 Porphyry describes these Gnostic sectarians, who scorn Plato and instead "put forward revelations of Zoroaster and Zostrianus and Nicotheus and Allogenes and Messus and the like," as "deceiving many and themselves deceived"; this is close to Augustine's description of himself and his companions during his Manichean period, "*seducebamur et seducebamus falsi et fallentes*" (*Confessions* IV,i,1).

ichees, with a similar cosmology, drew the right consequence.[16] Rightly
perceiving the consequences of his corporealism, Augustine was unable to
solve the problem of the origin of evil; thus the books of the Platonists
were able both to give him the metaphysics that was the peculiar property
of the Platonic school, and simultaneously to free him to accept the theodicy that was common to Platonists and Stoics.

Augustine's description of the false wisdom represented by the Manichees, and of the obstacles he had to overcome in order to reach the true
wisdom, will guide us in describing how Augustine adapted the Plotinian
discipline of contemplation to overcome these obstacles, and in elucidating
what the content of the resulting wisdom was supposed to be. We will
start by examining Augustine's procedure for coming to perceive the soul
and God, and the consequent content of these perceptions (Section B),
and then turn (Section C) to the answer to the question "whence evil"
that is supposed to follow from these perceptions. In each case we will
begin from Augustine's brief statement in *Confessions* VII of what he
learned and how, but we will fill in the content by turning to other writings, especially the dialogue *De Libero Arbitrio*; in each case we will be
able to see how Augustine uses and develops the Plotinian intellectual
strategies discussed in Chapter 3. Then finally, stepping back from Augustine's use of Plotinus, we will examine his final judgment on the relations between Christianity and philosophy (Section D), asking to what
extent Augustine allows Platonic philosophy to determine the content of
wisdom, and what additions and alterations the special dogmatic content
of Christianity leads him to make in traditional Platonist doctrine.

B. The soul and God

Augustine learned from reading Plotinus the discipline for achieving intellectual perceptions of himself and God. Does it follow that the concepts
of soul and God that Augustine acquires by this discipline, and the doctrines of soul and God that he derives from these concepts, are the same
as Plotinus' concepts and doctrines?

To a great extent it does. But the set of intellectual problems that Augustine is trying to solve through discipline are not quite the same as the
problems that had originally led Plotinus to work out the discipline. Plotinus developed the strategy of ascent in order to explicate Platonism and
defend it against Stoic corporealism. But Augustine was not a Platonist.
The Platonists are the best of the philosophers, "great men and almost
divine" (*De Ordine* II,x,28), but Augustine does not claim to be a philosopher himself: he is a philosopher in the etymological sense, a seeker of
wisdom, but he seeks his wisdom from two complementary sources, the
reasonings of the philosophers and the authority of the Christian scrip-

[16] Compare Plotinus on the moral consequences of Gnosticism in II,9,15; but his criticism
is nowhere near as extended, or as deep, as Augustine's criticism of the Manichees.

tures. When he first read the books of the Platonists, he had not yet decisively committed himself to Christianity; but Ambrose had already persuaded him that the Catholic doctrine was not contrary to reason, and that the weight of its authority could reasonably command belief even in the absence of proof (*Confessions* VI,v,7). Augustine's thought on the relation between reason and authority is complex, and it continues to change between his reading of the Platonists and his baptism, and even after his baptism: I will return to this problem in Section D. But by all our evidence, Augustine "entirely refused to commit the treatment of the illness of my soul to the philosophers, who were without the saving name of Christ" (V,xiv,25); throughout his struggles to reach a clear perception of God, "there still remained fixed in my heart" (VII,v,7) an unformed faith in Christ. Augustine did not at this time have any clear view about Christ or about Christian doctrine; but he hoped and expected that wisdom (whatever it turned out to be) would be consistent with the authority of Christ, as interpreted by Ambrose and by the Catholic church. In order for Augustine to reach a wisdom consistent with the Catholic claim that the good God is an omnipotent creator, and that evil arises only from the free choices of God's creatures, he had to acquire a new understanding of God, the soul, and the origin of evil: and this is what the Platonists allowed him to do. He says in a work written after his final Christian conversion, but before his baptism:

No one doubts that we are impelled to learning by the twofold weight of authority and reason. I am therefore certain that I should nowhere depart from the authority of Christ: for I do not find any stronger. But as to what is to be pursued by subtle reasoning – for I am so disposed that I impatiently desire to apprehend what is true not only by believing but also by understanding – I am meanwhile confident that I will find with the Platonists what will not be contrary to our religion [*sacris nostris*]. (*Contra Academicos* III,xx,43)

As was natural, Augustine accepted, together with the Platonist methods for perceiving the soul and God, much associated intellectual baggage, which in later life, secure in his ecclesiastical commitment, he would jettison as superfluous or even contrary to Christianity. But his intention had never been to learn Platonism as a systematic school-philosophy (it apparently never occurred to him to seek out the Platonist schools of his own day), but to learn from the Platonists a way of understanding the particular questions, obscure and disputed between Catholics and Manichees, of God, the soul, and evil.

We can see both similarities and differences between the theses that Augustine on the one hand, and the Platonists on the other, are concerned to defend and to explicate through the discipline of contemplation. Both Augustine and the Platonists believe, of course, in divine creation and providence and in the freedom and immortality of the human rational soul. Both Augustine against the Manichees, and the Platonists against the Stoics, are concerned above all to show that God (Nous, for the Platonists) is incorporeal; they are also concerned to show that the human soul is incorporeal, and that the human soul is an *image* of God and that God is essentially superior to it (for the Platonists, that Nous is prior to soul and is not simply soul *pôs echon*, or the soul of the universe). But Augustine was never concerned to defend the Platonist doctrine of soul in general. For the Platonists, soul is a cosmological principle, present in man, in lower animals, in the heavenly bodies, and in the world as a whole; for Plotinus, though not for most other Platonists, soul is somehow one in all these things, proceeding to all of them from a unitary Soul-itself in the intelligible world. Augustine, by contrast, was interested in soul because he was interested in his own soul, in understanding what it was and how it was related to God so that it could turn from God to evil and still be able to return to God. Plotinus teaches us to enter into our own souls so that we may discover our identity with the soul that formed the world; in consequence, we learn that every soul has an immediate relation to the divine Nous, and we can correct the error of the Stoics, who identified the world-soul with God and subordinated us to it as parts to a whole. Augustine follows Plotinus' path in order to learn the superiority of his rational soul to the bodily senses, and to discover that it has a direct re- lation to God, as thing measured to measure and not as part to whole. This path of contemplation leads him away from the senses, brings him to knowledge of himself and God, and allows him to understand the soul's freedom to depart from God and to return. But once he has learned that he is not a part of a God conceived as a world-soul, he has no further interest in the question of the world-soul as such. It is essential to Pla- tonism, and indeed to the shared tradition of Platonism and Stoicism, to attribute a soul to the world; and it is Plotinus' favorite doctrine that the divine Soul that is first generated from Nous somehow *is* both the world's soul and our own. Does Augustine share this commitment?

In writings soon after his conversion Augustine does refer to a world- soul, and he speaks of "fall" and "recollection" and "return" in ways that suggest that our soul has fallen into the body from a previous unembodied existence. What is more surprising is that, though these early writings are heavily dependent on the Platonists, and though their discussions of the indivisibility and immortality of the soul are little more than compilations of the standard Platonist arguments, Augustine nevertheless (as far as I have been able to discover) refers to a soul of the world only three times (*De Immortalitate Animae* xv,24, *De Ordine* II,xi,30, and *De Musica* VI,xiv,44), and to the unity of soul only once (*De Quantitate Animae* xxxii,69), and apparently never unequivocally asserts the soul's preexist- ence. All of these references are made in passing, and none contribute to the arguments in which they are embedded. The reference in the *De Or- dine* is a throwaway, mentioning "the soul that is everywhere" along with ours merely as a matter of completeness. The passage in the *De Quantitate Animae* is a curious digression about the number of souls: Augustine says that he cannot say either that there is one or that there are many, finds himself compelled to assert the apparently absurd proposition that soul is "one and many at once," begs not to be questioned on so difficult a matter, and changes the subject. Evidently, while Augustine is attracted to the Plotinian doctrine of the unity of soul, he finds it deep and esoteric, and is satisfied to do without it in his ordinary reflections; he never mentions it again. The passages in the *De Immortalitate Animae* and the *De Musica* seem to show a more serious commitment to a Platonist conception of soul: in both texts Augustine says that bodies receive from souls their beauty or the form that gives them being; where souls, being superior to bodies but inferior to God, receive form from the eternal *rationes* in God, and transmit it to bodies. Thus "the body subsists through the soul, and exists insofar as it is animated, whether universally, as the world, or particularly, as each single animal within the world" (*De Immortalitate Animae* xv,24). But the contexts do not use the claim that bodies in general are ordered by souls, but only that the human soul is superior to bodies, and that both are dependent on the truth that exists in God. Augustine is happy to support these claims with the Plotinian reminder that body receives its form only through soul; but he does this only in these few texts, elsewhere using less problematic means to get the conclusions he needs.

Augustine's later attitude toward these early declarations is instructive. Reviewing his earlier work in the *Retractations*, he is troubled by various expressions, borrowed from the Platonists, that now seem to him to be unnecessary to Christianity and in some cases to suggest doctrines incompatible with it. He now withdraws or qualifies these statements, saying usually that they were too hastily asserted or that they might be misinterpreted, rather than that they were false. In particular, he interprets the "return" of the soul so that it will be compatible with his mature agnosticism about preexistence (*Retractations* I,i,3). When he comes to the *De Musica* passage saying that bodies receive their beauty through soul, he suggests that it might be saved by restricting it to terrestrial animal bodies, then notes that if taken generally it would imply that the world too is an animal:

But that this world is an animal, as Plato and many other philosophers have thought, I have not been able to investigate by certain reason, nor do I recognize that I can be persuaded of it by the authority of the divine scriptures. Whence I have noted that something of this sort that I said in the book *De Immortalitate Animae*, which might also be taken in this way, was said rashly, not because I affirm that it is false, but because I do not comprehend that it is true, that the world is an animal. (*Retractations* I,xi,4)

What is important, says Augustine here, is that whether the world is ensouled or not, it is not God but a creature; and doubtless God has angels to help him administer it, so that it is largely a question of linguistic propriety whether these ought to be called souls. Similarly in the *De Civitate Dei*, reviewing the Platonists' religious opinions, and arguing that these should lead us to worship only the highest God, he argues that the question of the existence of a world-soul is indifferent, so long as it is not confused with God: "Plotinus, explaining Plato's meaning, asserts over and over that even that soul, which they believe the whole [world] has, is not blessed from any other source [*aliunde*] than is our own, and that [its source of blessing] is a light which it *is* not, but *by which* it is created and by whose intelligible illumination it intelligibly shines" (X,ii). Plotinus' abiding lesson was not that the world has a soul, but that God is a Nous separate from every body and every soul, and that each human soul is immediately subordinated to that divine Nous. Augustine's attempts to show that he never conceived of soul as a cosmic principle mediating between God and bodies are half-hearted and unconvincing; but what is noteworthy is how easily he can prune away the few references to such a conception, while keeping most of his early work as a statement of his mature Christian understanding of God and the human soul. Plotinus, by developing the method of introspection and ascent, showed how to interpret the mediating nature of cosmic soul by understanding our own; Augustine, taking up Plotinus' approach to understanding our own soul and Nous, first accepted the cosmic soul as a subplot to the story, then abandoned it as an irrelevant distraction from God's governance of the world; as we will see, Descartes will use the same conception of the human soul and God to eliminate vitalism altogether in favor of a world ruled directly by God according to mathematical laws.

In *Confessions* VII Augustine describes how the intellectual discipline he learned from the Platonists enabled him to perceive himself and God, and thus to solve the problem of the origin of evil. *Confessions* VII,x and VII,xvii describe ascents through the soul to God; the intervening chapters work out the consequences for theodicy. I will discuss the ascent to the soul and God in the present section, then turn to theodicy in Section C.

The description of the ascent in *Confessions* VII,x is compressed and cryptic; in VII,xvii Augustine reviews more explicitly the sequence of his perceptions of body, of various levels within the soul, and of God, and indicates the train of thought that led him from each perception to the next. But even in this chapter, Augustine does not describe his ascent in enough detail to allow the reader to reproduce it for himself: he says enough about each stage of the ascent that we can locate it within Plotinus' system of the levels of being, if we already know that system; but Augustine's descriptions of his perceptions would baffle any reader who did not already know what was there to be perceived. But Augustine describes this same sequence of perceptions more fully in his earlier writings, frequently dialogues between himself and a friendly inquirer, where he tries to bring his interlocutor (and also his reader) to a true knowledge of the soul and God. The basic content is the same: but the more explicit treatment makes these earlier texts better sources than the *Confessions* for Augustine's conceptions of the soul and God. We find the fullest description of an ascent from soul to God in the dialogue *De Libero Arbitrio* – in some manuscripts the title is *Unde Malum?* – in which Augustine tries to bring his friend Evodius to apprehend, not only by believing but also by understanding, how "all things that are are from one God, and yet God is not the author of sins" (I,ii,4); "for it disturbs the mind, if sins are from these souls that God created, and those souls are from God, how sins are not referred at a small remove to God" (ibid.). Evodius can understand this only if he first understands the soul and God: so the *De Libero Arbitrio* lays out first the ascent through the soul to God that Augustine narrates in *Confessions* VII,x and VII,xvii, and then the description of things other than God, and of the place of evil among them, that he gives in *Confessions* VII,xi–xvi. The *De Libero Arbitrio* is the culmination of the writings of Augustine's early period: like earlier writings, it aims to elucidate Christian beliefs by Platonist means, and to defend the Catholic doctrine of God, soul, and evil against the Manichees; unlike some earlier texts, it holds to Augustine's mature agnosticism on the origin and cosmological functions of soul. Together with Augustine's later and more strictly theological writings, it was the main source from which later thinkers (including, apparently, Descartes) learned their Augustinianism. In trying to understand Augustine's conceptions of God and the soul (and then, in Section C, his account of the origin of evil), we can first orient ourselves by *Confessions* VII, then turn to the *De Libero Arbitrio* for a fuller explanation of his thought.

Augustine always begins by describing the soul's path to knowledge of itself, then next describes how this leads to knowledge of God. Both in the *Confessions* and in the *De Libero Arbitrio*, Augustine's account of soul concentrates on the human rational soul; knowledge of *this* soul is the starting-point for our knowledge of God, and *this* soul's relation to God makes possible our fall and our salvation. The ascent begins with body, and there are intermediate stages between body and rational soul; but Augustine disposes of these quickly, in order to arrive at the rational soul, and so to pose the problem of the further ascent to God as Nous. In *Confessions* VII,x he does not explicitly distinguish levels in the soul; he speaks only of the "mind," or "eye of the soul," which is what is immediately subordinated to God, and is also what perceives this relationship. But *Confessions* VII,xvii distinguishes three levels within the soul:

And thus [I proceeded] step by step from bodies to the soul which senses through the body, and thence to its internal power, to which the senses of the body announce external things (and this is how much beasts are capable of); and thence back to the reasoning power, to which what is received from the senses of the body is referred for judgment. (VII,xvii,23)

Augustine considers only our *cognitive* powers, the faculties of outer sense, inner sense, and reason, and he ascends to reason through the hierarchy among these powers: each faculty passes judgment on the things beneath it, and submits its report for judgment by a higher authority. The reasoning power, as the ultimate judge within the soul, stands directly under

God, and gives the only point of departure for attaining knowledge of God.

Augustine systematizes this method of ascent in the *De Libero Arbitrio*, when he undertakes to prove to Evodius that God exists (II,iii,7ff.). "That we might begin with what is most manifest," he questions Evodius about what is closest at hand, the human soul: once he elicits from Evodius a clear perception of the things within the soul, he is prepared to take him beyond the soul to God. Evodius cannot doubt that he himself exists, lives, and understands, and he accepts Augustine's suggestion that being, life, and understanding form an ascending series of perfections.[17] Through our body we merely exist, though our senses we also live, and through our reason we also understand: Evodius agrees that the later terms in this series are superior to the earlier terms, but Augustine wants to understand *why* they are superior, since the same principle that allows us to recognize this superiority will also allow us to recognize something superior to human bodies and souls, and this superior thing will be God.

Augustine starts by distinguishing the different cognitive faculties. The five bodily senses each have their own proper objects, and they also share some objects in common; but none of these senses can perceive itself, or compare its objects with the objects of the other senses. Since we do somehow perceive that we have these five senses and that their objects are sometimes different and sometimes the same, we must perceive this through some faculty other than the five bodily senses. In fact, there are *two* other faculties involved: besides reason, which human beings alone possess, there is also "a certain inner sense to which everything is referred by these five most obvious senses" (II,iii,8), which beasts too must possess, since they must somehow integrate and respond to the data of the five bodily senses. This inner sense "senses not only those things which it receives from the five senses of the body, but also those senses themselves" (II,iv,10), and it also has some awareness of itself. But inner sense is not enough to give us knowledge [*scientia*] properly so called, even about the senses and their objects: thus beasts "do not know that light is not sensed by the ears or sound by the eyes, since we do not discern these things except by rational reflection and thought" (II,iii,9). Reason brings us beyond sensing [*sentire*] to knowing [*scire*]; it passes judgment on "the things that are brought to it for examination" (ibid.) by the outer and inner senses, and so it comes to know bodies, the outer senses, the inner sense, and itself.

Granted that the later terms in this series are superior to the earlier terms, Augustine asks for the principle explaining *why* they are superior. Why, in particular, is inner sense superior to outer sense, when both belong at the level of "life," above bare existence but below understanding?

---

[17] For the sources of this list of three perfections, see Pierre Hadot, "Etre, vie et pensée chez Plotin et avant Plotin," in *Les sources de Plotin* (Vandoeuvres-Geneva: Fondation Hardt, 1960).

It is not simply that the inner sense *senses* the outer sense: there cannot be a general rule that "everything that senses is better than what is sensed by it," since "man understands wisdom and is not better than wisdom itself" (II,v,12). Evodius answers that the inner sense is a "governor and judge" of the outer senses, directing their activity and judging whether they are adequately performing their function; and while not everything that senses is better than what it senses, "no one doubts that what judges [*is qui iudicat*] is better than what it judges [*id de quo iudicat*]" (ibid.). Evodius' rule explains the hierarchy of our cognitive powers, since reason judges the inner sense, as "the inner sense judges the senses of the body, approving their soundness and demanding what is due from them, just as these bodily senses judge bodies, accepting what is pleasing to the touch and rejecting the contrary." Since there is no further faculty in the soul to pass judgment on reason, we recognize that reason is the best and highest element in our nature (II,v,12–vi,13).

Augustine uses Evodius' concept of judgment, in the *De Libero Arbitrio* and also in the *Confessions*, to gain understanding both of the rational soul and of God. Evodius' rule that the judge is superior to what it judges helps us to understand why the rational soul is superior to bodies and to the sensory powers; it also gives us a starting point for understanding why God is superior to the rational soul, although Augustine will say, not that God is the *judge* of souls and other things, but that God is the *standard* by which souls and other things are judged. It is crucial that "judgment" here is not simply judging how things are, but judging whether they are as they *ought* to be, *passing judgment* on them in conformity with some standard.[18] This is, of course, a Platonist conception of judgment: Plotinus had described the soul as passing judgment on the beauty of bodies, "applying the form that is in it, and using this for judgment as a ruler [for judging] straightness" (*On Beauty*, I,6,3,3–5). Turning inward to examine the "eye of the soul" as what passes judgment on bodies, Augustine is able to conceive the soul without imagining it as extended in space; more importantly, he is able to conceive God, and the soul's relation to God, in a new way. For Plotinus, our soul can pass rational judgments on the perfections and imperfections of bodies only by measuring them against an immutable standard, the form existing in Nous, which the mutable things imitate more or less correctly; and the soul can judge the perfections and imperfections of its own judgments only by measuring them against Nous as the immutable standard of rationality. This shows Augustine the way to solve his problem about how to conceive God. From the beginning of *Confessions* VII, in particular, Augustine had set himself the task of

---

[18] "We often say not only that they *are* this way and not that way, but also that they *ought to be* this way and not that way" (*De Libero Arbitrio* II,xii,34); so too *Confessions* VII,xvii,23 speaks of seeking the standard by which I judged "when I judged rightly about mutable things and said, 'this *ought to be* so, that *ought not to be* so'" (I go on to discuss this passage below).

discovering an *immutable* God, since (as Augustine insists in *Confessions* VII,i,1) the immutable is always better than the mutable. Since bodies are essentially mutable, Augustine could not understand how God could be immutable, as long as he was forced to imagine God as a body. The soul too is mutable, since it passes between knowledge and error; indeed, Augustine's particular problem had been that, since the soul can obviously suffer evil, God too would be susceptible to evil unless he is of a different nature than the soul. But once we recognize that the mind, "since it is not itself the nature of truth, needs to be illuminated by something else in order to participate in truth" and in order to judge rightly (*Confessions* IV,xv,25), then we can understand God, with Plotinus, as the *source* of our judgments; this source contains (or in some way *is*) the standards by which we judge, and it must therefore be immutable.

For seeking *whence* I approved the beauty of heavenly or earthly bodies, and *what was present* to me when I judged rightly about mutable things and said, "this ought to be so, that ought not to be so" – thus seeking that *whence* I judged when I so judged, I discovered the immutable and true eternity of truth above my mutable mind. (*Confessions* VII,xvii,23)

Augustine then narrates this discovery, beginning with the description (cited above) of the ascent by steps *within* the soul to the reasoning power or mind. This ascent does not yet bring him to knowledge of anything immutable; but the reasoning power,

recognizing that it too in me was mutable, raised itself up to its own understanding, and withdrew my thought from its habit, removing itself from the contrary crowds of phantasms, that it might discover what light shone upon it when it proclaimed without any doubt that the immutable was preferable to the mutable, [a light] *whence* it knew the immutable itself – for if it had not somehow known this, it could not have preferred it for certain to the mutable – and in the twinkling of an eye it arrived at *that which is*. (Ibid.)

Now, although this chapter of the *Confessions* implicitly contains an argument (indeed, it implicitly contains the argument of Descartes' third Meditation), all that it explicitly does is to report an act of vision, without trying to induce the same knowledge in the reader. Augustine gives a much more elaborate account of the same process of ascent in the *De Libero Arbitrio*, trying to bring Evodius along. A closer look at this account will show in detail how Augustine appropriates Plotinus' conception of the soul–Nous relation, but it will also show his significant differences from Plotinus on the status of soul as a cosmic principle and its relation to body.

In the *De Libero Arbitrio*, after Augustine and Evodius have established the superiority of reason to the other elements in human nature, Augustine asks whether we can also discover something outside ourselves and superior to the rational soul. Not only body and the sensitive soul, but also "reason itself, since sometimes it strives to attain to truth and sometimes it does not strive, and sometimes it attains it and sometimes it does not attain it, is surely proved to be mutable" (*De Libero Arbitrio* II,vi,14); is there also something immutable, which might be superior to the rational soul? Augustine proposes to Evodius that if reason, perceiving through reason itself and not through the sensitive faculties, "discerns something eternal and immutable, it should confess both that it itself is inferior and that this is its God" (ibid.).

This suggestion is not quite right, for two reasons. In the first place, it is not obvious that everything immutable will be superior to the rational soul: Augustine repeatedly says that the immutable is better than the mutable, but even if immutability is preferable to mutability, it does not follow that *everything* that is immutable is superior to *everything* that is mutable.[19] Secondly, as Evodius rightly objects, "I do not see fit to call God that to which my reason is inferior, but that to which nothing is superior" (ibid.); after all, Plotinus accepts not only Nous but also the One as superior to all souls, and even if this is right Evodius will not admit more Gods than one. But neither of these objections damages Augustine's argument: the particular *kind* of immutable being that his argument establishes will be clearly superior to the human mind, and it will not matter (for the purposes of the *De Libero Arbitrio*) whether this being is itself God – Evodius "will either confess that this is God, or, if there is something above it, will concede that *that* is God" (ibid.). In either case, if there is a single immutable being to which all human minds are subordinated, then (barring an infinite regress of such beings) there is also a God, immutable and different in nature from the human mind; and, from the particular way that Augustine argues for an immutable being, he thinks it will also follow that the perfections of mutable bodies and minds derive from God, and that their imperfections are deviations from an immutable divine standard.

Augustine uses the word "truth" to describe the immutable being that he and Evodius recognize as existing above human minds. Although Augustine spends much effort arguing in *De Libero Arbitrio* II that there is a single (and unchanging) truth for all minds, he never defines the word "truth," and in the *De Trinitate* he pointedly refuses to define it, asking us to remain instead with our unanalyzed first impression of its meaning.[20] But the way Augustine argues about truth in the *De Libero Arbitrio* helps

---

[19] Plotinus, in particular, would reject this general thesis, since he thinks that prime matter is immutable (this is a crucial claim of III,6, *On the Impassivity of the Incorporeal*), and he thinks that prime matter is evil.

[20] "See, if you can: God is truth. For it is written: 'God is light,' not [the light that] these eyes see, but [the light that] the heart sees when it hears 'he is truth.' Do not ask, 'what is truth?': for immediately the dark mists of bodily images and the clouds of phantasms will rise up before you and disturb the serenity that shone upon you at the first moment when I said 'truth.' See that flash of light that reached you at the first moment when you heard 'truth' – keep looking at it if you can. But you will not be able. You will fall back to these accustomed earthly things" (*De Trinitate* VIII,ii,3).

to show what he must mean by it. The argument that truth is superior to bodies and souls turns on the premiss that it is the standard by which they are judged. Sometimes Augustine seems to be arguing that any immutable standard by which the soul judges bodies must be superior to the soul that judges, as well as to the bodies judged; but there is no general reason why this inference should be valid, and Augustine's real basis for claiming that truth is superior to the mind is that the mind itself is among the things judged by this standard. So we can say, provisionally, that "truth" must be a standard that the mind looks to in judging other things, such that the mind itself is judged by its conforming or failing to conform to this standard. "Truth" in this sense cannot be simply a property of judgments or propositions, since it is something that we *look to* in judging, and serves as a standard of comparison for our judgments. Of course, in making judgments about bodies, we look to the bodies themselves; but Augustine's "truth" cannot be simply a name for the things we make judgments about, because it is a standard for *normative* and not merely factual judgments about them, and also because it is a standard for what the mind itself ought to be like. So Truth is neither the things we judge nor the true propositions about them, but a Wisdom, an art or science that gives the standard for how we should judge a thing's beauty, and for how we should ourselves produce the thing if we had the power, so both "the law of all arts" and itself "the art of the omnipotent Artisan" (*De Vera Religione* xxxi,57).

Augustine obviously intends his "Truth," as a separately existing Wisdom above the soul, to be equivalent to Plotinus' "Nous." Augustine's terminology is partly explained by the equations he wants to make between the Platonist principles and the Biblical divine persons. He is willing to grant that the Platonists had the orthodox doctrine of the Trinity, and, in particular, that they had a true understanding of the second person of the Trinity, the pre-incarnate Word: they are merely ignorant of the incarnation.[21] When Augustine speaks of a Truth above the soul (and claims to have achieved an immediate intuition of this Truth), he does not identify Truth with God as such, but with this second person of the Trinity (so that "God" is truly predicated of it).[22] Augustine's intention here

---

[21] See Section D below for discussion of Augustine's views on what parts of Christianity the Platonists did and did not have, and on the importance of the parts they were missing.

[22] Most often, rather than discussing the identification of Truth or Wisdom with specifically the *second* divine person, Augustine simply allows the identification to be inferred, by giving three descriptions of God in sequence and allowing his readers to correlate them with the three persons, or by describing Truth or Wisdom through Biblical phrases which (either in their real original context, or in the standard Christian interpretation) are descriptions of Christ. He is sometimes more explicit, as at *De Libero Arbitrio* I,ii,5, where he lists what we must believe, including that God "generated out of himself something that would be equal to himself, which we [sc. when we are following authority] call the only son of God, but which, when we are trying to explain more clearly, we call the power [or virtue, *virtus*] of God and the wisdom of God [1 Cor. 1:24]." When, at *De Libero Arbitrio* II,xv,39, Augustine and Evodius arrive at the contemplation of this Truth or

is to appropriate Biblical language about the second divine person, and to interpret this language through Platonist philosophy. "Truth" has New Testament authority as a name for Christ (John 14:6), and Christian tradition identifies the pre-incarnate Word of John 1 with the divine Wisdom of the (apocryphal) Old Testament Wisdom of Solomon – a Wisdom through which God has "arranged all things in measure, number, and weight" (Wisdom 11:20), and which "being one, can do all things, and, remaining in itself, renews all things" (Wisdom 7:27). Since Nous for the Platonists is precisely a separate virtue of Wisdom, Augustine uses what they say about Nous to interpret scriptural descriptions of God's Wisdom or of his pre-incarnate Word. So in *Confessions* VII,ix,13–14, describing the books of the Platonists and recounting what they did and did not have of Christian doctrine, he says that the Platonists maintained

that before all times and above all times your only-begotten son, coeternal with you, remains immutably; and that souls receive of his fullness [John 1:16] in order to be happy; and that they are renewed, in order to be wise, by participation in Wisdom remaining in itself. (VII,ix,14)

Here "renewed" and "remaining in itself" are from Wisdom 7:27; but when Augustine inserts the Platonic term "participation," he is interpreting the verse to mean that souls become wise only by participating in a Wisdom-itself, existing separately from its participants and remaining unchanged when they become wise or foolish. This, Augustine says, he read in the books of the Platonists, that is, in Plotinus' accounts of Nous; and when he adds that he has read there "that the Word, being God, is born not from flesh or blood, nor from the will of man or of the flesh, but from God" (ibid.; John 1:13), he identifies the eternal generation of the Son from the Father with the eternal procession of Nous from the One. Indeed, Augustine recites the whole prologue of John, and concludes that

Wisdom, Augustine concludes that either Truth or something superior to it is God. Augustine in fact believes (though he does not try to prove it here) that Truth itself is God; and in a rather cryptic aside he tries to show that this is consistent with what we believe on authority. Evodius might make an objection based on Christ's teaching "that there is a Father of Wisdom," and thus that Wisdom is not the first divine principle; "but remember that we have also accepted on faith [sc. the teaching of the councils of Nicaea and Constantinople] that equal to the eternal Father is the Wisdom which is born of him"; the conclusion, although Augustine does not make it explicit, is that since the second person is *equal* to the first, it too may be called God, as indeed it is in the Niceno-Constantinopolitan Creed. In later works, however, Augustine is more cautious about referring different descriptions of God to one person exclusively; presumably this arises at least in part from a recognition that Plotinus had made the One more distinct from Nous numerically, and more different (and superior) in what can be predicated of it, than orthodox Christianity allows. Augustine discusses these questions in *De Trinitate* V–VII, and concludes that all *non-relative* predicates that apply to any of the divine persons apply to all of them, and so in particular that "the Father and the Son are together one essence and one greatness and one truth and one wisdom" (VII,ii,3), although the Biblical writers have homiletic reasons for reminding us especially often that the Son is wisdom, rather than that the Father is (VII,iii,4–5).

the Platonists knew all of it, except that "the Word became flesh and dwelt among us" (John 1:14), and that, in this incarnate form, it offers us a way to salvation. In his earliest surviving work, the *Contra Academicos*, in explaining why something more than Platonic philosophy is necessary, Augustine says fallen souls are able to return to their fatherland only because "the highest God has . . . sent down the authority of the divine intellect even to the very body of man" (III,xix,42). We will come back to this passage in Section D to discuss what the Platonists were missing; for now, the point is that Augustine describes the incarnation of the Word as an incarnation of the "divine intellect." "Word," "Wisdom," and "Truth" have Biblical authority, but "intellect" must be the word Victorinus had used to translate "Nous"; it can have no other justification. After this early experiment Augustine stops using "intellect" to name the second person of the Trinity: he substitutes the Johannine "Truth," but we must still read this as a gloss on Plotinus' word "Nous."[23]

Augustine's account in *Confessions* VII,ix,13–14 makes clear that the main *doctrinal* lesson of the books of the Platonists (as opposed to the *discipline* of contemplation that he learned from them) was that there is such a wisdom superior to souls, in which souls must participate to become wise: this is the same as the claim of *Confessions* IV,xv,25 that the mind, "since it is not itself the nature of truth, needs to be illuminated by something else in order to participate in truth." In both texts, the claim that there is something superior to the soul is the complement of the recognition that the soul is not essentially or immutably rational: the soul becomes disordered when (as with the Manichees) it identifies itself with what is essentially rational, and to be cured it must distinguish its own nature as rational-by-participation from the essentially rational nature above it.[24] In a flourish of allegorical exegesis, Augustine describes the

---

[23] Augustine also uses *intellectus* for "Nous" in a passage of his third surviving work, the *De Ordine*: reason, guided by authority, will learn *quid sit ipsa ratio* (the rational soul), then *quid intellectus, in quo universa sunt, vel ipse potius universa* (Nous, in which are all the real [i.e. intelligible] beings, or rather, which is itself these beings), then finally *quid praeter universa universorum principium* (the One – see a note below) (*De Ordine* II,ix,26). The Johannine "Truth" as a name for the second person of the Trinity also has Plotinian authority: the last lines of the first chapter of V,5, *That the Intelligibles Are Not outside Nous*, say that "if truth is not in Nous, this kind of Nous will neither be truth, nor truly Nous, nor will there [it?] be Nous at all; and truth will not exist anywhere else either."

[24] In context, when Augustine says at *Confessions* IV,xv,25 that the mind "is not itself the nature of truth," he is reviewing and rejecting a view he had put forward in his (lost, preconversion) *De Pulchro et Apto*, where he had used some ideas of Platonist origin to explicate his still fundamentally Manichean view of the soul as a fragment of God: the view was that the rational part of the soul was essentially and immutably good (and "unity" and "truth," IV,xv,24), and that the two Platonic irrational parts (the reference is clear: "a dyad, anger in violent acts and lust in shameful acts," ibid.) formed a contrary evil substance (Augustine is here taking up neo-Pythagorean doctrines of unity and "the dyad" as good and evil principles). As Augustine now says, it is not only excessive and distorted motions of the irrational soul that are evil, but also "errors and false opinions contaminate life if the rational mind itself is vicious; which it was in me, when I did not

Platonists as knowing what the prologue of John recounts of John the Baptist: for the Baptist is just "the soul of man, which, though it bears witness to the light, is not itself the light; but the word of God is the true light that lights every man coming into this world" (*Confessions* VII,ix,13; John 1:8–9).[25] As the Baptist's task was to bear witness to the Word, so the soul's task is to bear witness to the Nous above it. Although Augustine assumes that there is also a higher God above Nous, this is not essential to his project of wisdom: just once, in the *De Beata Vita* (his second surviving work), he tries to describe an ascent beyond Nous to a higher principle.[26] But (even apart from the threat to orthodoxy in making the Father essentially superior to the Son), what Augustine needed from Plotinus, in order to achieve knowledge of an immutable God, and to explain the soul's relation to God and the origin of evil, was only the ascent to Nous. The doctrine of a One beyond Nous, like the doctrines of the world-soul and of the unity of soul, is an interesting esoteric speculation, which Augustine can experiment with in early writings, and take his distance from later, without changing his fundamental strategy for understanding God as Truth.

In *Confessions* VII,x and VII,xvii Augustine simply narrates his vision of the Truth above our minds that the Platonists and the Biblical writers had described; but in the *De Libero Arbitrio* he is trying, without appeal to his own or others' authority, to bring Evodius to recognize this Truth for himself. The problem, as Augustine sets it up, is to discover whether there is an objective truth, "something that all reasoners see in common,

know that it needs to be illuminated by something else in order to participate in truth, since it is not itself the nature of truth" (*Confessions* IV,xv,25).

[25] Augustine cites John 1:9 in the form *[erat] lumen verum, quod inluminat omnem hominem venientem in hunc mundum*; the Vulgate is essentially the same, except that it translates *phôs* by *lux* instead of *lumen*. Both the Vulgate and the version Augustine cites are wrong: *erchomenon eis ton kosmon* should be taken as neuter nominative, not masculine accusative – "the true light that lights every man was coming into the world." Augustine gives the Light a metaphysical function in the production of each soul, which the correct translation does not.

[26] "Truth, in order to exist, comes about by a supreme measure [*modus*], from which it proceeds and to which it returns when it is perfected. No other measure is imposed on this supreme measure: for if the supreme measure is measure through the supreme measure, it is measure through itself. But even the supreme measure must be a true measure. Therefore as truth is generated by measure, so measure is known by truth. Therefore there has never been either truth without measure or measure without truth. Who is the son of God? It has been said: truth. Who is it that has no father, who other than the supreme measure? Therefore whoever has come to the supreme measure through truth is blessed" (*De Beata Vita* 34). There is also a parallel, not fully developed, in the *De Ordine* (the third surviving work, still before Augustine's baptism): Augustine speaks of reason, guided by authority, as learning what the *intellectus* is *in quo universa sunt*, or rather which is itself *universa*, then speaks of learning what is *praeter universa universorum principium* (II,ix,26, cited in a previous note). Obviously, he means the One prior to the forms which are in Nous, or (rather) which *are* Nous. But in the *De Ordine* Augustine does not actually say what this principle is, or give an argument that could lead us to know it: he merely says that it can be known.

each by his own reason and mind" (II,viii,20). By the particular argument he uses to establish that there is a unitary truth present for all minds to perceive, whether or not any mind perceives it at any given time, Augustine will also (he thinks) have implicitly established that this truth is superior to minds, and that it is the source of all goods (and no evils) to minds and bodies; he will then go back to make these conclusions explicit.

Augustine sets up the problem by distinguishing two kinds of cognitive faculties. Each of us has his own bodily senses, his own inner sense, and his own reason or mind; this is shown by the fact that one person can sense or understand something which, at the same time, another person does not sense or understand. But we cannot say "that we each have individual suns which we see, or moons or morning stars or other things of this sort, although each person sees these things by his own personal sense" (II,vii,16). Thus in each of these cases a single numerically identical object is the object of sensation for many different human sensory faculties, specifically identical but numerically distinct. But, on a deeper analysis, this is not the case for every variety of sensation. Two people can smell the same air or taste the same honey, but here each person is perceiving a different part of the object; whereas with sight or hearing, Augustine suggests, each person can perceive the same *whole* object. This is because the senses operate in two different ways: "it is plain that those things which we do not alter [*quae non commutamus*] and which we yet sense by the senses of the body, do not pertain to the nature of our senses and are therefore common to [all of] us, because they are not converted and altered [*vertuntur atque mutantur*] into what is proper, and as it were private, to [each of] us" (II,vii,19). The objects of taste, to take the most obvious example, are altered in the interaction of subject and object through which they are perceived, and therefore do not remain as numerically identical objects sensed by all perceivers in common; the objects of sight, on Augustine's theory, are not altered by being illuminated, and therefore remain "common and as it were public, sensed by all sentients without any corruption or alteration [*corruptio, commutatio*] in itself" (ibid.).

The question, then, is whether reason is like sight or like taste. Is there a common object of reason which "is present to all," and "remains uncorrupted and entire, whether they see it or do not see it"; or is the object of reason somehow digested in being understood, somehow "altered into the benefit [*commutetur . . . in usum*] of those to whom it is present" (II,viii,20)? Augustine means to show that reason has an object that remains unaltered whether reason perceives it or not; this will be a common object, equally available in its entirety to all who perceive it.[27] By showing

---

[27] For what may be the source of Augustine's inspiration in putting the question this way, see Plotinus *On Omnipresence* VI,4,12 and especially VI,5,10 (the latter passage is discussed by O'Connell, *St. Augustine's Early Theory of Man*, pp. 52–8). But Plotinus does not seriously discuss the suggestion that truth might turn out to be divided between its

that this object is above all *commutatio*, he will also help to show that it meets the conditions for a genuine conception of God, as described in *Confessions* VII.

Augustine proposes to discover an immutable object of reason by two different considerations, through truths of number and through the "rules of wisdom"; both paths, he claims, lead us up to a common source of number and wisdom in a single divine Truth. Number is, of course, "conjoined with wisdom in the holy books" (II,viii,24), as at Wisdom 11:20. Augustine is particularly interested in number because, although we deal with it on an ordinary basis both in the conduct of life and in the liberal arts which Augustine had once studied and taught, it is properly grasped by reason alone and can lead us up from mutable bodies to an immutable truth. Since number is present in all things, we usually take it for granted; but Augustine argues that it is of divine origin, so that everything that depends on number also depends on God.

Do not wonder that men have thought numbers base and wisdom dear, since they can count more easily than they can be wise: for you see that they hold gold more dear than the light of a lamp, in comparison with which gold is ridiculous. But what is far inferior is more highly honored, because even a beggar lights a lamp for himself, while few have gold (II,xi,32)

– although (Augustine adds) number is not superior to wisdom, but ultimately identical with it. To show this unsuspected dignity in number, Augustine wrote, as part of a planned series of books to lead the practitioners of each liberal art "through corporeal things to incorporeal things as by certain steps" (*Retractations* I,vi), six books *De Musica*, showing "how from corporeal and spiritual-but-mutable numbers we arrive at immutable numbers, which are already in immutable Truth itself, so that 'the invisible things of God are seen through the things that have been made' " (ibid. I,xi,1; Romans 1:20). He retraces the same path more quickly in the *De Libero Arbitrio*.

Under Augustine's questioning, Evodius readily agrees that the truth of number is immutable: human minds try to grasp it and succeed or fail, but the truth remains true in itself: it does not vanish when it is not understood, nor is it transformed in the intellectual digestion when we do understand it. Augustine warns, though, that the immutability of number will be challenged by those who say that "these numbers are not impressed on our mind from some nature of their own, but from these things we are in contact with by the senses of the body, like images of visible things" (*De Libero Arbitrio* II,viii,21). Evodius answers that, even if the numbers themselves were perceived by the bodily senses, the truths about the relations between numbers would remain immutably true. Augustine agrees,

perceivers, let alone digested by them. Perhaps Augustine is simply elaborating this logical option in order to exclude it, even though no one had ever believed it; or perhaps he is somehow indirectly aware of the position ascribed to Protagoras and Heraclitus in the *Theaetetus*.

but he also argues that the numbers themselves must be immutable objects perceived by reason apart from the senses: for numbers are collections of ones, and "wherever I have come to know a one, certainly I do not know it through bodily sense, since by bodily sense I know only body, which, we argue, is not truly and purely one" (II,viii,22).[28] So numbers and their laws cannot come to the mind from bodies; nor do they come to bodies from minds, except in the special case of the numerical forms imposed on artifacts; rather, they must come both to minds and to bodies from a Truth independent of both.

The discussion of number is intended to show that even the order the mind discerns in things inferior to itself has its original location in a Truth superior to the mind. This would be enough to give us some knowledge of God; but Augustine also wants to understand the relation between the mind and God that allows the mind to perceive and possess God or to turn away from him. So he supplements the discussion of number, which takes us from bodies to God, with a discussion of wisdom, which begins from the human soul. The same question is posed for wisdom as for the truths of number: "Do you think that individual men have individual wisdoms, or is there one present to all in common, and each person is wiser as he participates more in it?" (II,ix,25). Wisdom, here, is a kind of truth, like the truth of number, but it is specifically "the truth in which the highest good is perceived and contained" (II,ix,26); Augustine thinks that the possession of such a wisdom is necessary and sufficient for true happiness. Evodius doubts whether there is one single wisdom, since different groups of people, all claiming to be wise, pursue different goods; perhaps only one of these is truly the highest good, so that there is only one true wisdom, but this is not obvious. Instead of showing that there is a single true good, Augustine argues that there is a single truth in which we might perceive a plurality of goods, just as we perceive a plurality of visible things in the one light of the sun. Augustine produces a series of true propositions, and gets Evodius to admit, first that they are true, and then that they are "immutable and present in common to all minds capable of contemplating" them (II,x,28). These propositions are all "rules and lights of the virtues" (II,x,29), concerning the things that are good and that it is wise for a human being to choose: they are all formulated as simple maxims, asserting that X is better than Y, and that X should be pursued rather than Y. Indeed, Augustine's examples all reduce to a single proposition, that the incorruptible is better than the corruptible; someone who truly knows this, and directs his life in accordance with it, will have wisdom. This is just the knowledge that Augustine had considered in *Confessions* VII: it was by seeking the source of his knowledge that the immutable was better than the mutable that he came to perceive "the

---

[28] This argument comes ultimately from *Republic* VII,524–6. Augustine also argues that, even if the senses gave us knowledge of numbers themselves, finitely many sensory observations could not give knowledge of theorems about *all* numbers, DLA II,viii,23.

immutable and true eternity of truth above my mutable mind" (*Confessions* VII,xvii,23). So also in the *De Libero Arbitrio* he traces this judgment, and this perception of the immutable, to its source in the immutable divine truth. In this way, the wisdom or intelligence that should govern human life is shown to have the same divine source as the numerical order or intelligibility that governs the physical world.

Beginning from texts of the Wisdom of Solomon, Augustine tries to explain how number and wisdom are related, and in what sense they are "one and the same thing" (*De Libero Arbitrio* II,xi,30). To-be-numbered and to-be-wise are different effects, in bodies and souls, of the same eternal cause: they are different ways of participating in the same divine Truth, although this Truth is more properly described as "Wisdom" than as "Number," because what it gives to souls is more intimately related to its essence than what it gives to bodies. Thus this Wisdom

gave numbers to all things, even those that are lowest and placed at the end of things (for even bodies, although they are the last of things, all have their numbers), but it did not give wisdom [*sapere*, being-wise],[29] to bodies or even to all souls, but only to rational [souls], as if it had placed a seat for itself in them, from which it could dispose all those things, even the least, to which it gave numbers. (II,xi,31)

Since Nous is immediately superior to rational souls, and rational souls are superior in turn to irrational souls and to bodies, it is the rational souls that are closest to Nous, and Nous affects them in the way that something affects the things immediately adjacent to it. Augustine draws on two different Platonist metaphors to describe the ways that Nous affects minds and bodies: the Platonists illustrate the procession of things from incorporeal principles, sometimes by the procession of light from its source, and sometimes by the diffusion of heat from a fire. Augustine now combines both these metaphors to suggest Nous' different relations to minds and to bodies:

As in a single fire brightness and heat are perceived to be (as it were) consubstantial, and cannot be separated from each other, and yet heat reaches [only] to the things that have been brought near to the fire, while brightness is spread further and more widely, so the things that are closer to wisdom (as are rational souls) are heated by the power of intelligence, while the things that are further away (as are bodies) it does not touch with the heat of wisdom, but floods them with the light of numbers. (DLA II,xi,32)[30]

---

[29] Augustine here uses the infinitive "*sapere*," and below the gerund "*sapiendi*," for the being-wise which the divine Wisdom communicates to rational souls; apparently he prefers to reserve the substantive "*sapientia*" for the divine Wisdom itself.

[30] I read "*intellegentiae potentia, quae sunt sapientiae propinquiora*" (the reading of Green's manuscript family γ; see his apparatus in the *Corpus Christianorum*) instead of the usual "*intellegentiae potentia, quae inest sapientiae, propinquiora*." The difference in meaning is not great, but the grammar and sense are much clearer this way.

Augustine admits that the comparison may be obscure, and that no comparison drawn from visible things can be entirely accurate; he is willing to suspend judgment on the precise relation between number and wisdom, since "it is certainly plain that both are true, and immutably true" (ibid.). Still, Augustine's comparison will be useful in understanding how he conceives the relation of Nous to bodies and souls.

The immediate conclusion is that "there is an immutable truth, containing all things that are immutably true, which you cannot say to be yours or mine or any man's" (II,xii,33); it is a single light in which all knowers perceive the things that are immutably true. The examples of numbers and of the rules of wisdom show that all who can count, or all who are wise, perceive the same truth in which these numbers and rules subsist, so that this truth is like the objects of sight rather than the objects of taste: being common to all individual minds, it must be distinct from them all, subsisting in itself and offering itself to be perceived by them.

Having established at length that there is a common object of reason, Augustine draws the further conclusion that it is "more excellent than our mind" (II,xii,34). Truth cannot be either inferior or equal to the mind, because the mind passes judgment on things inferior or equal to it (that is, bodies and itself or other souls) "according to those inner rules of truth that we perceive in common" when it judges, not merely that these things *are* as they are, but that they *ought to* conform to mathematical or moral standards.

But nobody judges these [rules of truth] themselves in any way. For when somebody says that eternal things are better [*potior*] than temporal things, or that seven and three are ten, nobody says that they *ought to be*, but recognizing simply that they *are* so, he does not correct them as an examiner, but simply rejoices as a discoverer. (Ibid.)

These rules of truth, subsisting in truth itself, by their very essence cannot be other than they ought to be; they are themselves the standard to which other things ought to conform, and there is no standard beyond them that determines what they ought to be. We may say that they are themselves the standards to which they ought to conform, or we may say, as Augustine does, that the word "ought" does not apply to them, and that they simply "are." The mind can know these rules of truth to a greater or lesser degree, but this is a *commutatio* only in the mind, not in truth: we can properly say only that the mind ought to know the truth, not that the truth ought to be known by the mind. "Whole and uncorrupted, it both gladdens those who turn to it [*conversos*] with light and punishes those who turn away from it [*aversos*] with blindness" (ibid.), not because it is disposed differently toward the mind, but because the mind is disposed differently toward it. Thus truth, which the mind recognizes as the source of its judgment that mutable things (including the mind itself) ought to be in conformity with immutable standards, is itself shown to be something immutable, unjudgeable and superior to the mind. In this way Augustine ascends from the things that the mind judges, through the mind's power of judging, to the Nous containing the immutable standards according to which the mind judges. Plotinus' account of the relations between soul and Nous, and between Nous and the intelligible standards, are thus built into the resulting understanding of God.

For Augustine, as for Plotinus, all form or beauty or order, whether in bodies or in souls, has its source in Nous; we ascend to Nous by tracing back to their source the perfections we admire in bodies and souls, along the lines of the ascent to beauty in the *Symposium*. Augustine is implicitly reasoning in this way in the passages we have just discussed, in which he brings Evodius to recognize the existence of Truth as the source of wisdom (the perfection of soul) and numerical form (the perfection of body). But now, having completed the proof of the existence of God, he makes it explicit that God has been recognized as the source of all the goods or beauties that we encounter among bodies and souls (II,xvi–xvii). The purpose of these sections is to demonstrate one of the central theses of the *De Libero Arbitrio*, that all good things come from God, but they do this by reflecting on the proof of God's existence. Having shown that wisdom and number ultimately reside in the divine truth, Augustine turns back to understand how they have come to appear in souls and bodies, and to trace the beauties of souls and bodies explicitly back to their source. This is useful, because it is not enough for us simply to know that there is a divine wisdom. Divine wisdom is primarily good and beautiful, and if we are satisfied with it, we will lead the happy life; but we are continually tempted to admire the apparently more accessible beauties of lower things. We therefore need a spiritual exercise to call us back from these temptations by reminding us of the divine beauty which is the source of every beauty we might admire. Augustine justifies this procedure out of the Wisdom of Solomon, and then gives us his version of the *Symposium* ascent, as interpreted through Plotinus and through Augustine's descriptions of wisdom and number. Augustine says, in a programmatic passage:

Wherever you turn, [Wisdom] speaks to you by certain traces that it has imprinted on its work, and, when you have fallen back to outward things, calls you back within by the very forms of outward things, so that, whatever delights you in body and lures you through the corporeal senses, you will see that it is numerical; and you will ask whence it is, and return into yourself, and understand that you could not approve or disapprove what you reach through the senses of the body unless you had in you certain laws of beauty to which you refer whatever beautiful things you sense outside. (II,xvi,41)

In this passage, and in the detailed explication that follows it, the points of departure for the ascent to God are number in bodies and wisdom in souls. Bodies have the form that gives them their beauty, and even their existence, only from number; if they are artificial bodies, they derive their numbers immediately from the soul of a human artisan who moves his limbs according to number, but the artisan can direct his activity in time according to number only by contemplating eternal numbers: "go therefore beyond even the mind of the artisan, that you may see eternal numbers: now wisdom will shine to you from its inner seat and from the very sanctuary of truth" (II,xvi,42). Both bodies and souls are mutable things, which have their being only as they receive form and number; they cannot supply these to themselves, but can only receive them from an immutable form or number, which must exist in the divine Truth (II,xvi–xvii).

Although this version of the *Symposium* ascent has obvious similarities with some ascents in Plotinus, it is as a whole distinctively Augustinian, and helps reveal some un-Plotinian aspects of Augustine's way of conceiving Nous and its relations to lower things. The transition from artificial bodies to the artisan's soul is very frequent in Plotinus, as is the further ascent from the artisan's soul to Nous. The selection of *number* as the principle of corporeal form and of the arts, although it has Platonist sources, gains emphasis from Augustine's professional interest in the liberal arts and from his attempt (as in the *De Musica*) to use the numerical principles of the quadrivium to lead us up to God.[31] But for Augustine, unlike Plotinus, the ascent from body to Nous passes through the intermediate stage of soul only when it begins from *artificial* bodies. Natural bodies, too, have form because they have number, and they have their numbers from Nous; also, no doubt, the faculty that recognizes the beauty of natural bodies by considering their numbers is akin to the artisan's faculty of discerning numerical patterns – but the faculty that merely *recognizes* beauty is not the *source* of that beauty. Plotinus recognizes the possibility of ascending from bodies to their intelligible patterns, but he does not think this leads to a clear enough knowledge of intelligible things. "What is it that has made a body beautiful? In one way the presence of beauty, in another way soul, which molded it and put in it such a shape" (V,9,2,17–18), and it is the second ascent, through soul to Nous and the Good, that Plotinus follows through. Augustine refuses to take this path. He too is interested chiefly in the ascent from soul to Nous, but he refuses to attribute to all body "a soul which molded it and put in it such a shape"; he considers only the human soul, as it passes judgment on bodies and perhaps tries to form them in accordance with its judgments. In the case of natural bodies, the only cause we can safely assign for their form is in the Wisdom of God.

Augustine's metaphors of fire, light, and heat help to illustrate his transformation of the Plotinian picture of the relations between Nous, soul,

---

[31] As a source for Augustine's program in the *De Musica*, note the following passage from Plotinus *On Nous, Ideas, and Being* V,9,11, where he is investigating whether the arts are present in the intelligible world: "all of [the art of] music which has its *noêmata* about rhythm and harmony [is there], as is that which has [its *noêmata*] about intelligible number."

and body. Nous is like a fire; it communicates the heat of wisdom to the rational souls which are adjacent to it, and spreads the light of number even to the bodies which are far from it. Augustine certainly thinks that the action of Nous on souls indicates a closer relationship, but he does not suggest that the action of Nous on bodies is *mediated* through soul; rather, the transmission of light and the transmission of heat are two distinct actions that both spring immediately from the same source. It is true that in the same section Augustine had said that the divine Wisdom gave being-wise "not to bodies or even to all souls, but only to rational [souls], as if it had placed a seat for itself in them, from which it could dispose all those things, even the least, to which it gave numbers" (II,xi,31, cited above). This suggests that rational souls are somehow instruments of Nous in the rationalization of the physical world. But in the *De Libero Arbitrio*, as in the *Retractations* (I,xi,4, discussed and partly cited above), Augustine attributes this function to the angels who assist God in adorning and governing the world. These angels may be called rational souls (though in the *Retractations* Augustine is not sure that this is appropriate without scriptural precedent), but they are not a world-soul. The decisive difference between Augustine's mature conception of the angels and the Platonist concept of the world-soul is brought out in the discussion of cosmic order in the theodicy of *De Libero Arbitrio* III.

God has created, to complete his creation, "souls that occupy the very pinnacle of order in the whole creation" (III,xi,32), which must not sin, because their functions in maintaining cosmic order are such that their sin (unlike ours) would damage the order of the whole.[32] These are "the best and holy and sublime creatures of celestial or supercelestial powers" (ibid.); they are nonetheless not superior to us in nature, and they have a free will by which they could sin and fail to perform their function. "It does not remain in the good will because it has received this office; rather, it received the office because he who gave it foresaw that it would remain" (III,xi,33). This arrangement yields the best order of things, where "the angelic power is supereminent in the arrangement of the universe through excellence of nature and goodness of will" (III,xii,35). So far this is not so different from Plotinus' account of the world-soul: but Augustine adds a decisive qualification which seems to have no parallels in the Platonic tradition.

However, if it sinned – but it has not sinned, for God foreknew that it would not sin – but if it too sinned, God's power of ineffable might would suffice to rule this universe, so that giving to all things what was suitable and just, he would permit nothing base or unbecoming in his whole empire; for even if he could rule through none of the powers established for this, if every angelic nature departed through sin from his instructions, he would rule all things most properly and well through his majesty. (Ibid.)

[32] On the complementary roles of angels and human beings in Augustine's theodicy, see further discussion in Section C below.

Augustine's God, unlike Plotinus' Nous, has the power to break an angelic strike, or to declare martial law and rule without consulting the constituted authorities. He does not need to; what is best is for each thing to fulfill its proper function, and God has the power and foresight to arrange for this to happen. But the possibility Augustine envisages here reveals a non- and anti-Platonic conception of God and the soul.

The Platonic demiurge wished to make the world rational, because this was best, and he *could not* make it rational except by giving it soul; and this seems to mean, not merely that the world could not think without a soul, but also that it could not receive order without one. Nous does not impose order on bodies without the mediation of soul; if the demiurge of the *Timaeus* seems to intervene directly at times, all later Platonists allegorize this or ignore it. Nous *cannot* impose order on bodies directly, because it is simply not the type of entity (any more than the number two is) that can be said to act on bodies. Nous has its being, its activity, and its perfection purely in eternity, and it cannot and does not want to direct its action to temporal things. Lower things proceed from it without action or awareness on its part. Soul, although eternal in its being, is temporal in its actions, and so can act on bodies; being potentially rational, it can contemplate Nous and so act *rationally* on bodies. Without the mediation of soul, any causality of Nous on bodies, thus any rationality in bodies, would be inconceivable.

Augustine can break from this tradition, even while being heavily indebted to it, because he did not draw his initial concepts of God and the soul from Platonism. He went to the Platonists to learn a method for understanding God and the soul, and he accepts a great deal of the doctrine that comes from this way of understanding them, but he knew from the beginning *what it was that he wanted to understand*: it was the God and the human souls described in the Christian scriptures. Augustine's initial strategy was to adopt the Platonist language and the Platonist conceptual apparatus, and to try to understand Christian doctrine purely in terms of it; but the fit is rough in places, and no Platonist could be pleased to read in the *Contra Academicos* that the highest God had "sent down the authority of the divine intellect to the very body of man" (III,xix,42, cited above). In his later writings, Augustine is readier to modify the Platonist doctrines where they seem to him contradictory or superfluous to Christianity, while preserving everything he found useful in the Platonists. He is able to do this because the Christian assumption of God's omnipotence has taken deeper root in him than the Platonist assumption of God's absolute eternity, so that he does not see it as violating the very concept of God to deny what the Platonists assert of him. I will discuss in Section D how and to what extent Augustine's Christianity modified his concepts of God and the soul; the point here is simply that he is using Plotinus' method of ascent to clarify and justify Christian concepts of God as creator and redeemer and the human soul as his creature fallen or redeemed – not Platonist concepts of Nous and soul as cosmological principles. He certainly accepts much of the Platonist cosmology, but he is selective, and increasingly so with time. Neither his concept of God nor his concept of soul forces him to believe that the physical universe derives its order from God by means of soul, rather than directly. Augustine experiments with such a picture; but fundamentally he conceives the God–soul relationship and the God–body relationship as two different and irreducible things. This non-Platonic element of Augustine's thought determines the particular way he describes God's relations to lower things, and the particular path he takes to ascend to God.

C. Whence evil?

Augustine had been driven to search for a new conception of God largely because his old conception of God was inadequate to account for evil; so once he discovers his new conception of God, he immediately applies it to his problems about the nature and origin of evil. Augustine describes how he came to perceive the true God in *Confessions* VII,x, and he returns to the same theme in VII,xvii. In the six intermediate chapters he describes how he "inspected the other things that are beneath you [God]" (VII,xi,17), considering their mode of being in relation to his new understanding of God; the main result is an understanding of what good and evil are in mutable things, and an account of the origin of evil that ascribes no evil to God. Augustine thinks that the corporealism he had taken from the Manichees had made it impossible to understand how evildoing could exist in the human soul unless God either *does* evil (if it is God who produces this evil in the soul) or *suffers* evil (if God must allow some contrary principle to harm a portion of himself). But when he acquires his new conception of God as incorporeal, he also acquires a new conception of the relation between God and the soul: God is no longer an extended totality of which the soul is a part, but the immutable standard by which the soul's intellectual or moral variations are judged. This conception frees Augustine to understand how the soul can bring evil on itself by departing from God in its actions, without God's being himself affected by evil.

Augustine accepts the traditional philosophical theodicy developed by Plato, by the Stoics, and by the revived Platonic school; the account of evil that Augustine presents, in *Confessions* VII,xi–xvi[33] and in parallel discussions, is a reasoned repetition, from Augustine's own intellectual standpoint, of the argument of this traditional theodicy. Augustine's chief difficulty in assimilating this theodicy had been in finding a way to understand God's relation to inferior things so that God would not be subject to the evil that exists in them; only the Platonist conception of God as

---

[33] Often I will refer to these chapters, which will be analyzed here in detail, simply by their chapter number, since (for all chapters of *Confessions* VII beginning with Chapter x) there is precisely one section per chapter: the section number is the chapter number plus six.

Nous had allowed him to overcome this difficulty. For this reason, Augustine's presentation of theodicy puts great stress on what is, for him, its chief point, the understanding of God's relation to creatures, which gives him access to all the subsidiary arguments in defense of God's management of the world. To answer the question "whence comes evil?," as Augustine does in outline in Chapters xiii and xvi, we must first resolve the prior question "what is evil?," as Augustine does in Chapter xii. Even before this, Augustine tries to circumscribe the range of things in which evil can be said to exist. Evil does not exist in God, nor is it created by him; but neither is it something that can exist on its own, independent of God and his creative activity: rather, it occurs only as a byproduct of God's creative activity, as a circumstance, not itself created, of things that God has created. So before explicitly addressing the question of evil, Augustine gives in Chapter xi a brief account of the mode of being of things inferior to God, which will allow him in Chapter xii to explain how evil can exist in them. This understanding of the mode of being of inferior things depends in turn on the understanding of God as Nous, and as what truly is, which had been described in Chapter x. It is only after establishing this understanding of God, his creatures, and good and evil in them, that Augustine proceeds (both in the *Confessions* and in the *De Libero Arbitrio* parallel) to the standard themes of theodicy: thus he defends God's creation of a world containing evil by pointing to the freedom of God's creatures and the advantage to the totality of superior and inferior parts, and draws the moral consequence that God has given the human soul the ability to liberate itself from moral (and thus from natural) evil. We will follow through the main lines of Augustine's theodicy, noting how he bases the theodicy on the understanding of God as Nous; as before, we will first use the account in the *Confessions* for orientation, then turn to the *De Libero Arbitrio* (and other works where necessary) to fill in the details of the conceptions indicated in the *Confessions*.

At the beginning of *Confessions* VII,xi, Augustine turns from his unsteady vision of God to inspect the things that are beneath God. He has said in the previous chapter that "I would more easily doubt that I was alive than that Truth existed"; it is the inferior things whose status is now in question. "I saw that they neither wholly *are*, nor wholly *are not*: that they are, since they are from you [*abs te*, God], and that they are not, since they are not what you are. For that truly *is* which remains immutably." Augustine adds nothing to clarify this in the *Confessions*, beyond a few scriptural citations, none of them *obviously* bearing on the ontology of things other than God. But the key is Augustine's citation from his favorite passage of the Wisdom of Solomon (7:27): the divine wisdom or, as Augustine says here, God himself, "remaining in himself, renews all things." In the Wisdom of Solomon, at least as Augustine interprets it, this follows from an understanding of God as Wisdom or Nous. From parallel discussions in Augustine's other writings, specifically the *De Lib-*

ero Arbitrio and the *De Natura Boni*, we can see how this understanding of God, and therefore of God's "renewal" of inferior things, leads Augustine to the ontology of inferior things that is suggested in this chapter of the *Confessions*, and that provides the context for his understanding of evil.

In the *De Libero Arbitrio*, after establishing the existence of God as the Truth manifested in number and in the rules of wisdom, Augustine argues that all good things come from God. The only things besides God that we can conceive to exist are bodies and souls; both of these are mutable, and therefore must be "formable" or capable of being informed (*De Libero Arbitrio* II,xvii,45), for a mutable thing deprived of its form would "fall back into nothing" (II,xvi,44). "Nothing can inform itself, for nothing can give what it does not have, and a thing is informed just so that it may have form" (II,xvii,45); thus mutable bodies and mutable souls must "be informed by some immutable and always remaining form" (ibid.), namely the divine Truth from which they receive number and wisdom. And Augustine cites a scriptural witness for this information of mutable things: "of this form it is also said that 'remaining in itself, it renews all things' " (ibid.). So what it means for God to "renew" mutable bodies and mutable souls is that he continually supplies them with the form, preexisting eminently in himself, that makes them what they are and preserves them from slipping back into nothingness. Augustine says that inferior things *are* because they are from God. St. Thomas might say the same; but Thomas would mean that God makes creatures actually exist by communicating the act of existence to essences that do not have existence of themselves. For Augustine, by contrast, what proceeds from God, and gives being to the other things, is primarily the *form* or essence through which things attain some definite nature. At the beginning of the *Soliloquies* (I,i,2), Augustine directs a prayer to "God, through whom all things, that through themselves would not be, attain being; God, who does not permit to perish even what destroys itself"; this has a personal sound, but it is directly derived from Plotinus' "Nous, which sustains by its marvelous nature the things that would fall of themselves" (Plotinus V,9,5,47–8).

Only what abides immutably truly *is*. All things other than God are mutable: it is because we see that they change that we recognize that they are not what God is, and that to some extent they *are not*. Neither the *Confessions* nor the *De Libero Arbitrio* sheds much light on this element of non-being in mutable things; Augustine is more helpful in the treatise *De Natura Boni*. Here he is arguing, against the Manichees, that every nature (a word Augustine uses synonymously with "substance," as he tells us at *De Libero Arbitrio* III,xiii,36) is from God. He thinks that he can convince the Manichees of this, if they are willing to listen, because "they confess that every good cannot exist except from the highest and true God" (*De Natura Boni* ii). So if Augustine can prove that every nature is good, and that evil is not a nature but a corruption of a nature, he will be able to establish, on premises the Manichees must accept, the desired conclusion that every nature is from God.

Since all goods are from God, it follows in particular that all measure, all form, and all order [*modus, species, ordo*], being goods and indeed the universal conditions of goodness, must be from God (*De Natura Boni* iii). But, Augustine argues, measure, form, and order are the conditions of natures, as well as of goodness:

Where these three things are great, there are great goods; where they are small, there are small goods; where they are not at all, there is no good at all. Again, where these three things are great, there are great natures; where they are small, there are small natures; where they are not at all, there is no nature at all. (Ibid.)

"Therefore every nature is good" (ibid.), and therefore every nature is from God. Measure, form, and order are names for what proceeds to bodies and souls from God as Nous; but bodies and souls are constituted only by receiving these things, and therefore, inasmuch as they exist, are from God. This does not imply that evil does not exist, but it does imply that we should be critical about the sense in which we speak of it as existing: "therefore when it is asked *whence* evil is, it should first be asked *what* evil is" (*De Natura Boni* iv). Evil cannot be a nature, since it does not *qua* evil possess any measure, form, or order: it can be "nothing other than a corruption of natural measure or form or order" (ibid.), which diminishes the goodness of the nature proceeding from God – although it can only diminish and not entirely destroy this goodness, for "if corruption removed all measure, all form and all order from corruptible things, no nature would remain" (*De Natura Boni* vi).

But if all natures are from God, why can they be corrupted at all? This was the problem that had led the Manichees to suppose, besides God, some other source of natures. Augustine draws a distinction: "all other goods are *from* [*ab*] him alone, but not *of* [*de*] him. For what is of him is what he himself is; but the things that are made by [*ab*] him are not what he himself is" (*De Natura Boni* i). Natures other than God are made *by* God, but they are not made *out of* God, with the exception of the divine Word; on the contrary, they are made out of nothing. If God has made nature *X* out of nothing, it will certainly be mutable: if it can be transformed from nothingness into existence, and returned to nothingness at God's will, it will hardly be immune to lesser changes. Thus the original nothingness out of which all things other than God are drawn is the condition of the mutability and corruptibility of the measure, form, and order that they receive from God.

Therefore all corruptible natures would not be natures at all, if they were not from God; nor would they be corruptible if they were *of* him, for they would be what he himself is. Therefore that they are of any measure, any form, any order, is because it is God *by whom* they have been made; but that they are not immutable is because it is nothing *from which* they have been made. (*De Natura Boni* x)

This is what Augustine means by asserting in *Confessions* VII,xi that mutable things, not being what God is, do not entirely have being, but have an element of non-being in their constitution.

Confessions VII,xi does not explicitly set out this ontology of the transmission of form, from its origin in God, into mutable things. Nor does Chapter x set out the concept of God as Nous and true being in terms that anyone not already familiar with Plotinus' philosophy and Augustine's adaptation of it would understand. But the parallel texts of the *De Libero Arbitrio* and the *De Natura Boni* make it clear that this understanding of God and inferior beings is what Augustine is trying to describe, using the language of narration and prayer in which the *Confessions* are composed. And it is only by interpreting the visions narrated in the *Confessions* through these other works that we can understand the logic behind the sequence of intuitions.

Chapter xi discusses being and non-being. Chapter xii makes the transition to good and evil. The sections I have cited from the *De Natura Boni* make the logic plain. All natures or substances, to the degree that they have being, are good; this holds even of corruptible natures. "Every nature that cannot be corrupted is a highest good, as God is. But every nature that can be corrupted is also some good; for corruption could not harm it except by taking away and diminishing what is good" (*De Natura Boni* vi) – namely, by corrupting the measure, form, and order that the nature has received from God. And this is just what Augustine is discovering in *Confessions* VII,xii:

and it was made plain to me that the things that are corrupted are good; they could not be corrupted if they were highest goods, but neither could they be corrupted if they were not good: for, if they were highest goods, they would be incorruptible, but if they were not good at all, there would be nothing in them that could be corrupted.

There is no mention here of forms proceeding from God, nor is there any explicit reference to the ontology of Chapter xi; Augustine is simply explaining the grounds of his recognition that all things derive from the good God, without involving the reader too deeply in technical philosophy. He does require one ontological assumption for the argument of Chapter xii, namely that no nature can be so corrupted as to be deprived of all good, while still remaining in existence; to avoid mentioning the theory of form which is the real basis of this judgment, he offers the bizarre alternative argument that if something has been entirely deprived of goodness, it has become incorruptible, and is therefore a highest good, so that, absurdly, the process of corruption has made it better. Using either the argument from measure, form, and order, or the argument from the absurdity of corrupting something so that it becomes incorruptible, Augustine infers that "whatever things *are*, are good" (*Confessions* VII,xii) – which does not mean that "whatever is, is right," since Augustine is speaking only of things that *are* in the sense of *substance*. This inference allows Augustine to understand *what* evil is, and thus to pose correctly the question *whence* it is: "that evil, of which I asked *whence* it is, is not a substance, for if it were a substance, it would be good" (ibid.). Once Augustine has reformulated the problem of the origin of evil by recognizing that evil is not a substance but an action or some other accident of a substance, he has no difficulty in accepting that all substances proceed from God. Indeed, he must necessarily accept it, since, like the Manichees he is attacking in the *De Natura Boni*, he had never doubted that all good things were from God: "thus I saw and it was made plain to me that you have made everything good, and that there are no substances at all that you have not made" (*Confessions* VII,xii). The problem of the origin of evil remains, but it is a problem that can be dealt with by the usual philosophical techniques: it is no longer a radical challenge to the intelligibility of the Catholic doctrine that all things proceed from the good God.

Augustine turns to address the problem in *Confessions* VII,xiii. He follows the *Timaeus* and the whole subsequent tradition by placing the perfection of the totality in its comprehensiveness: "there is no evil for you, and not only for you but also for the whole of your creation: for there is nothing outside to break in and destroy the order that you have imposed on it" (VII,xiii). Evil does not have its existence as something supervening on the totality, which is perfect; nor is it a part of the totality, for both the superior parts and the inferior parts are good; rather, evil supervenes on the inferior parts when they are judged by the standard of the superior parts. "And since you have not made all things equal, therefore there are *all* things" – that is, there are both superior and inferior things – "for individually they are good, and all things together are very good, since our God has made 'all things very good' " (VII,xii). Thus it contributes to making the whole perfect – or, in the Biblical language as Augustine interprets it, "very good" – if it includes some parts which, although individually good, are not individually "very good." Augustine could not perceive this while he still thought like the Manichees, and so he had judged it unworthy that the inferior things, which are bound up with evil, should proceed from the good God. "But now I no longer desired better things, because I was thinking of *all* things; and I determined, by a sounder judgment, that the superior things were indeed better than the inferior things, but that *all* things were better than the superior things alone" (VII,xiii). Some of the inferior things are thought to be evil because they are *inconvenientia*, unsuited or inappropriate, in relation to some other inferior things; nonetheless they are good in themselves, and the existence of these conflicting things in the inferior part of creation is appropriate in relation to the totality of superior and inferior things.

Augustine could not perceive this when he was a Manichee, because he had a false conception of God and of God's relationship to other things. He had been, he tells us in *Confessions* VII,xiv, unreasonably displeased with many of God's creatures; not wishing to be displeased with God, he had supposed that these things were not of God [*tuum*], but proceeded from some contrary principle. He can now perceive that these things do come from God, because he can recognize how evil can exist within the good things that come from God, without having to posit an evil substance of separate origin. This depends on his new understanding of the relation of finite things to God, and thus on his understanding of God as Nous. This becomes clear in VII,xv:

> I looked back at the other things and I saw that they owe their being to you, and that they are all contained [*finita*] in you, but differently: not as in a place, but because you hold all things in the hand of truth [*tu es omnitenens manu veritate*], and all things are true inasmuch as they *are*, and there is no falsehood except when what *is not* is thought to *be*.

Augustine had earlier supposed that God held or possessed [*haberet*] other things, and that they were contained [*finirentur*] in God, because God's infinite body was coextended with the whole finite body of the world, as well as extending beyond it in all directions (VII,i,2). Each thing would then be contained in God as in a place, and it would contain, besides something of God (as a *portion* of God) something else that was not of God: the portion of God and whatever is not of God in a thing (in particular, whatever is evil in it) would both be equally real positive natures. Now, however, Augustine can say that things are contained in God because God is the Truth comprehending the forms of the things. The things exist only because they receive form, thus only because they are "contained" in God, without being a part of God or having a part of him in them; and the things fall short of God, not because there is a piece of him outside them, and not because they contain a piece of another nature that is not "of God," but because they do not perfectly exemplify the forms that they must imitate in order to exist. A non-corporealist understanding of the way that things belong to God and are *in* God thus allows Augustine to understand how a diversity of more and less perfect things can belong to God, and how evil can exist in these things without arising from a different nature.[34]

Augustine is, of course, particularly concerned with the origin of *moral* evil in the human soul. It was particularly the human soul that the Manichees declared to be a fragment of God, and therefore incapable of doing evil; Augustine's intellectual struggle had been particularly to conceive the true relationship between his own soul and God, and he had finally gained his vision of God by beginning with his own soul and looking up to per-

---

[34] The problem of how all things are "contained" by God, or of how God is "present" in all things without being divided up among them, has been a persistent theme of the *Confessions*, first announced in *Confessions* I,ii,2–iii,3. Augustine is implicitly promising in Book I that we will be able to understand this mystery (among others) by means of the wisdom that Augustine discovers in the course of the *Confessions*. Earlier in Book VII he had stressed the inadequacy of his earlier corporealist attempts (when he was a Manichee, and after leaving the Manichees) to understand how all things could be contained in God (like a finite sphere immersed in an infinite body, perhaps of light?, VII,i,2) and how God could be present in all things (by Stoic total mixture?, ibid.): see Section A above.

ceive God as the intellectual Light above it. He turns to the question of moral evil or "wickedness" in *Confessions* VII,xvi: what he says here is only an application, although it is the crucial application, of the general theory of evil that we have already seen. The only kinds of evil that *obviously* exist in the universe are human suffering and human sin; and Augustine always seems to feel that the can reduce the problem of suffering to the problem of sin. He feels sure that only the wicked suffer, and that their suffering is the inevitable result of the intersection of their wickedness with the divine justice. Justice is unpleasant for the wicked, just as light is unpleasant for diseased eyes, but this says no more against justice than it does against light: although the suffering that results is, considered in itself, an evil, it is simply one of the *inconvenientiae* that necessarily attend the lower part of creation. The problem, then, is to discover how a human soul can be vitiated by moral evil so that it becomes liable to natural evil, and suffers from the things that are good for healthy souls.

"And I asked," says Augustine (VII,xvi), "what wickedness was; and I found, not a substance, but the perversion [*perversitas*] of a will that has turned away [*detortae*] from the highest substance, you, God, toward the lowest things, forsaking its own inmost parts [*intima sua*] and rushing after things that are outside it." Augustine conceives of evil in the soul as he conceives of evil in general. It is not, as the Manichees said, a substance; rather, it consists in the fact that a substance fails to maintain the measure, form, and order with which its nature is endowed by God. As bodies receive numerical form from the divine Truth, and are corrupted to the extent that they depart from this numerical form, so rational souls receive the rules of wisdom from the same divine Truth, and so they too are corrupted when they depart from these rules of wisdom. God is Wisdom itself and immutable form, but the human soul is merely a mutable thing informed by the divine wisdom, capable of turning from wisdom to foolishness, and thus giving rise to moral evil.

Augustine follows Plotinus in describing the kind of corruption peculiar to the rational soul as a *turning away*: this metaphor is constantly repeated, and indeed it is contained several times in the passage I have just cited. The fallen soul is *perversa* and *detorta* away from God: when it is turned toward God, it beholds him, and thus possesses wisdom, but it loses this wisdom when it turns away from him. When it turns away from God, it turns toward the "lowest things," namely bodies. In so doing, says Augustine, it has rejected its own *intima*: these are the same "*intima mea*" into which Augustine entered at the beginning of VII,x, namely the mind, which is what most truly belongs to the soul when it is conceived by itself without reference to the body. The soul that has turned away from God, for Augustine as for Plotinus, has also abandoned its true self: it admires the beauty of external things, and directs its desires to them rather than to itself.

Wickedness is the perversion of a *will* that has turned away from God. The immediate answer to the question whence evil (in the sense of moral evil) arises, is that it arises from the will. But whence, then, is the will? Before he discovered the books of the Platonists, Augustine had been greatly troubled by this question: if he has been made by God, "whence have willing evil and not-willing good come to me, so that I might justly suffer punishment? Who placed this in me, and sowed in me the seed of bitterness, when I have been made entirely by my God, who is most sweet?" (*Confessions* VII,iii,5). But the metaphor of a "seed" is not apt: evil-willing is not some evil nature concealed within a human being, but a *state* of the human soul. More particularly, it is an *act* of that soul: it derives neither from God nor from some diabolical power, but precisely from the soul that wills it. Certainly the will [*voluntas*], conceived as the *power* of willing, belongs to the nature of the human soul, and proceeds to it from God; but the exercise of that power for good or evil originates within the soul itself.

This brings us back to the main problem of the *De Libero Arbitrio*, how we are to understand that God is not the author of moral evil: "for it disturbs the mind, if sins are from these souls that God created, and those souls are from God, how sins are not referred at a small remove to God" (*De Libero Arbitrio* I,ii,4). At the end of Book I, Evodius reformulates the question more precisely in terms of the will: we have shown that we do evil

from the free choice of the will [*ex libero voluntatis arbitrio*]. But I ask whether this free choice [*liberum arbitrium*], by which we are shown to have the power of sinning [*facultas peccandi*], should have been given to us by him who made us. For it seems that we would not have sinned if we lacked this; and it is to be feared that God might be held in this way to be the author even of our ill-deeds. (I,xvi,35)

This question is taken up in Book II: why did God give man free will? But, as Augustine immediately points out, the question is not yet well-posed: we know that we have free will, but we do not yet know that we have it from God. Instead of assuming that God gave free will, and asking whether it was a good gift or not, we must begin by asking whether free will is good: if it is good, then we may conclude both that God gave it and that he was right to give it; but if it is evil, we must conclude that it is *not* from God, and hence that he is not to blame for it. That he and Evodius might truly *know* whether God gave free will, and whether he gave it rightly, Augustine proposes that they investigate three questions in order: "first how it is manifest that God exists; then, whether all things are from him inasmuch as they are good; finally, whether free will [*voluntas libera*] is to be numbered among the goods" (II,iii,7); for "when these things are understood it will be sufficiently apparent, I think, whether it was rightly given to man" (ibid.). Augustine promptly launches into the lengthy ascent to God that we have considered above; and having thus found that God exists, he shows as a corollary that God, whom we have come to know as the source of wisdom and numerical form, is the source of all good to all things beneath him. The remaining problem, then, is to locate free will within the ontology that has been established, and so to determine whether it is a good, and thus from God.

Free will must be a good, says Augustine, because it is impossible to live rightly without it. This proves, not merely that it is a good, but also that it is a greater good than others that we are accustomed to value very highly, such as the possession of our eyes and hands: for even if we lacked eyes or hands, it would still be possible for us to live rightly, so long as we retained our power of free choice. It is true that free will can be used badly, as can eyes and hands: as Augustine says, we use these other things for good or ill through free will (or we may say less properly, "free will uses these other things"), and we also use free will for good or ill through itself. This does not imply that we should not have been given free will, any more than it implies that we should not have been given hands and eyes; what it does show is that free will cannot be of the *highest rank* of goods that can exist within the human soul. Such are "all the virtues of the mind, in which right and noble living consists" (II,xviii,50), such as justice and right reason; since their presence *constitutes* right living, they cannot be used badly. So the will, since it is a necessary but not a sufficient condition for right living, is an "intermediate good." Goods of all three ranks are good, and they all proceed from God; it is unreasonable to say that God has given us something evil in giving us the lower ranks of goods, simply because they are not the highest goods.

Then whence evil? The nature of man, as it is constituted by God, does not contain any evil element. But it is not supremely good. All natures beneath the supreme good are mutable; so they can suffer the corruption of their measure, form, and order, and thus give rise to evil. The particular mutable natures that are endowed with free will can freely *act* so as to forfeit their good, and thus give rise to *moral* evil. Evil is never a substance, always a state of a substance; moral evil, in particular, is always an *act* of a substance.

Therefore the will that adheres to a common and immutable good obtains the great and primary goods of man, although [the will] itself is an intermediate good. But the will that has turned away [*aversa*] from the immutable and common good and has turned toward [*conversa*] a good peculiar to it [*ad proprium bonum*, as opposed to *bonum commune*], or to something external, or to something inferior, sins. (II,xix,53)

All the natures involved here are good, but the act that results from them is evil: "neither the goods that sinners pursue nor the [power of] will itself are in any way evil . . . but what is evil is [the will's] *aversio* from the immutable good and *conversio* to mutable goods" (ibid.).

"But perhaps you are about to ask, since the will is moved when it turns [*avertit*] itself from the immutable to a mutable good, whence [*unde*] this motion has its existence" (II,xx,54). Certainly it is not from God; whence then is it? "If, when you ask this, I answer that I do not know, you might be disappointed, but I will be speaking the truth. For what is nothing cannot be known" (ibid.). As we have seen from the *De Natura Boni*, created natures are corruptible "because it is nothing from which they have been made" (*De Natura Boni* x); this nothingness is therefore the condition, and in some sense the source, of the corruption that may subsequently befall the nature. Augustine reminds Evodius that every nature has its being through measure, number, and order, and must therefore always be good. "Thus when every good is entirely taken away, there will remain not a something [*nonnihil*], but nothing at all. But every good is from God; therefore there is no nature that is not from God" (*De Libero Arbitrio* II,xx,54). If something is evil, it is not a nature, not a *nonnihil*, but rather a *nihil*, a privation, or, as Augustine calls it here, a defect. Such defects do not accrue to creatures from God's activity in creating them from nothing and endowing them with form, but rather remain from the original nothingness and lack of all form out of which they were created: "every defect is from nothing [*ex nihilo*]" (ibid.), not incidentally, by being a *nonnihil* that God has created from nothing, but essentially, as being itself a *nihil*. The misordering of mutable and immutable goods is such a defect, and therefore proceeds from nothing: "that motion of *aversio*, which we confess to be sin, since it is a defective motion, and every defect is from nothing – see to what it pertains, and do not doubt that it does not pertain to God" (ibid.).

But the more important question is not *whence* moral evil is produced, but *by what* or *by whom*, as efficient cause, it is produced. "Why must we ask whence this motion, by which the will turns away from the immutable good to a mutable good, has its existence, since we confess that it must be of the mind and voluntary, and therefore culpable . . . ?" (III,i,2). So moral evil must have as its efficient cause the will itself. Augustine repeatedly insists that if sin were not a voluntary action, but a motion like the fall of a stone, necessarily determined by the nature of the thing, or following from the action of some other nature, then it would not be truly sin, and could not be justly censured, or justly punished. But the *aversio* from God to mutable goods is censured by all human opinion, and it is punished by God with loss and unhappiness; and we must believe that God's punishments are just. Augustine tries to turn this belief into understanding, arguing that "the mind cannot become the slave of lust by anything other than its own will; for it cannot be compelled to this dishonor either by something superior or equal to it (for this would be unjust), or by something inferior (for it could not)" (III,i,1). If God justly punishes the soul for sin (against the Manichean view that God, and the soul as a portion of God, are simply defeated by an external evil power), then the soul must be capable of producing good and evil in itself, by turning spontaneously to a greater or a lesser good. In understanding how God can be the author of everything, and at the same time not the author of evil, Augustine and Evodius learn both the soul's nature (as an intermediate being, placed between God as supreme good and bodies as inferior goods) and also its freedom. This freedom is the moral lesson of the analysis of sin as a defect: "this defect, since it is voluntary, is placed within our power. Thus if you fear it, you ought not to will it; and if you do not will it, it will not exist. What then is safer than to be in that life where nothing can happen to you that you do not will?" (II,xx,54).

Having shown that moral evil does not proceed from God, but is only a byproduct of his having created natures endowed with free will, Augustine devotes the remainder of the *De Libero Arbitrio* – the bulk of Book III – to the question of *Confessions* VII,xiii: why did God create inferior natures that would be liable to evil, and in particular to moral evil? His answer is the usual Platonist answer: it is better that there should be both superior and inferior natures than that there should be the superior natures alone. In *Confessions* VII,xiii Augustine brings this thesis forward to explain the origin of evil in general; in *De Libero Arbitrio* III he is applying it to moral evil in particular. Taking the general argument about evil for granted, we can examine more closely how Augustine fits moral evil into the general framework.

When God created the world, he foreknew everything that would happen in it for good or evil. In particular, he foreknew the sins of all those free natures which would fall into sin: by Augustine's reckoning, all human beings and some of the angels as well. Augustine is at pains to show that God's foreknowledge of an event does not *necessitate* that event, any more than does our memory of that event; God is therefore not morally responsible for the sins he foreknows; but we may still ask why he included in his design for the world natures that he foreknew would sin. This challenge will, of course, "not easily disturb the rule of piety, which we should remember, that we owe thanksgiving to our creator, whose most generous goodness would indeed be most justly praised even if he had established us in some inferior degree of creation" (*De Libero Arbitrio* III,v,12). All natures, inasmuch as they exist, are good, and God is to be praised for creating all of them; it is better to exist as a human being than to exist as a horse or a stone, and better to exist as a stone than not to exist at all. Sin can corrupt a rational nature only within the limits of that nature: although a sinful nature has fallen below the level of perfection for which God intended it, it remains more perfect than every irrational nature. "I would praise wine that was good after its kind, though I would blame the man who got drunk on that wine; and yet I would place the drunken man whom I have blamed above the wine on which he got drunk, which I have praised" (III,v,15). Augustine stresses that even the most corrupted soul is a greater good than the purest body, namely light, which was the summit of perfection in the universe as the Manichees imagined it. Thus it is a generosity in God, beyond what the Manichees could have imagined, to create, beyond corporeal natures and even beyond irrational souls, such rational natures as we ourselves are, even if we are in sin. We therefore cannot wish that God should have emended his creation by deleting such sinful natures as ourselves.

But we might wish, not that the natures that have fallen into sin should

178

not have been created, but that they should have been created *differently*, so that they should not fall into sin. A nature that is *incapable* of sin is unfree, and so inferior to all natures capable of sin; but God might have endowed our natures with the power of free choice, and yet still have foreseen that we would never use this power for evil.[35] We have a natural tendency to wish that God had made us in this way, but Augustine thinks that it arises, not from objective reasoning, but from our habit of referring all things to their utility to ourselves.

Reason judges in one way, custom in another. Reason judges by the light of truth, that by right judgment it might subordinate lesser to greater things; but custom inclines generally to the habit of utility, so that it judges great things that truth has shown to be small. For although reason prefers heavenly bodies to terrestrial bodies by a great interval, who among carnal men would not prefer that many stars were lacking from the heavens than one bush from his own field or one cow from his own herd? (III,v,7)

We farmers or landowners may think we are complaining about the order of the universe, but really we are complaining only about our own places in that order: we are concerned, not that God has not created great enough or numerous enough goods (for we care very little about the heavenly bodies, the best things within the bodily world), but that these goods do not belong to us. We would have an objectively valid complaint only if the greater goods that we desire did not exist *anywhere* in the universe. Augustine believes that they do, in the heavens; he does not consider the possible complaint that there are not enough stars, because nobody has in fact made such a complaint. If the greater goods do exist elsewhere, and in sufficient quantity, then to wish that the lesser goods that you possess were transmuted into the greater goods is objectively the same as to wish that your lesser goods had been omitted from the world order: the significant difference between the wishes occurs only in how you imagine *your* position within the improved world order, not in how you imagine that world order itself.

But it is not true reason, but envious weakness, when you think that something ought to have been made better, to wish that nothing else inferior should be made, as if, having observed the heaven, you wished that the earth had not been made; this would be quite wrong. For you would rightly pass censure if you saw that the earth had been made and the heaven had been left out, since you would say that it [the earth] ought to have been made as you are capable of thinking the heaven. Therefore, since you see that that has been made in whose kind you wished to remake the earth, but that this is called not earth but heaven, I believe that, since you have not been defrauded of the better thing in order that there should also be something inferior and that the earth should exist, you ought not to be envious in any way. (III,v,13)

---

[35] Augustine accepts that there are free natures (namely, the good angels) such that, at the moment of creating them, God foresees that they will never sin; foresight does not take away freedom any more than memory does.

What is in question is "fraud" only in an extended sense. God cannot (strictly speaking) have defrauded us, since he begins by owing us nothing, and gives us only what is better than nothing, not what is worse than nothing. The present challenge is not to God's justice to us, but to his *generosity* to his whole creation; Augustine asks us to rise above our own interests and judge from an objective standpoint, counting ourselves "not defrauded" of goods that we perceive to exist anywhere in the universe, even if they are not available for our use.

Augustine intends this form of reasoning to resolve the objection against God's creating natures that he foreknew would sin. These natures are analogous to terrestrial bodies; it would be right to criticize God for making them only if he had not also made superior natures, analogous to the heavenly bodies. But, according to Augustine, God has made such natures, namely the good angels: they, like we, are rational natures endowed with free will and thus capable of sin, but God foresaw that they would not choose to sin, and so he assigned them the highest place in the government and adornment of his creation. Even if we had no other evidence, we would still know *a priori*, by considering God's goodness, that he must have created such natures, and in sufficient numbers. The angels are a more important part of God's plan for the world than human beings are; but, having assured himself that there would be sufficiently many free natures that would not fall into sin, God chose to complete the world by bringing into existence also the natures that he foreknew would sin and would thus fall short of their highest possible good.

Augustine believes that the existence of the souls that will fall into sin and misery contributes to the perfection of the universe. It is important to recognize that he does *not* believe that the existence of sin and misery contributes to the perfection of the universe. Augustine considers a possible objection:

> If even our misery completes the perfection of the universe, then something would be lacking to this perfection if we were always happy. Further, if the soul does not achieve misery except by sinning, our sins too will be necessary to the perfection of the universe that God established. How, then, would he punish justly sins without whose presence his creation would not be full and perfect? (III,ix,26)

Augustine replies that "it is not the sins themselves or the misery itself that is necessary for the perfection of the universe, but souls inasmuch as they are souls; these sin if they so will, and they become miserable if they sin" (ibid.). The right ordering of the universe requires that, if any nature sins, it be punished; but what is required is only the conditional, not the antecedent and not the consequent. Sin is not required for the perfection of the universe, but is merely a byproduct of the creation of the inferior rational natures, which are required for the perfection of the universe: "since these souls are not lacking, on which either misery follows if they sin or happiness if they do rightly, the universe is always perfect and full of all natures" (ibid.).

The angelic souls occupy "the very summit of the order in the whole creation" (III,xi,32), and God in establishing this order made them responsible for administering things beneath them: "if they willed to sin, the universe would be weakened and undermined" (ibid.).[36] Human souls, by contrast, have no responsibility for maintaining cosmic order: Augustine does not say that we are inferior in essence to the angels, but merely that we have an inferior "office" to perform within the totality of creation. "The nature of the more sublime office is that it would diminish the order of the universe not only if it did not exist, but also if it sinned; the nature of the inferior office is that the universe would have something less only if it did not exist, but not if it [merely] sinned" (III,xi,33). God foresaw that certain souls would not sin, and he therefore gave them the higher office; he also foresaw that certain other souls, such as ours, would sin, and he therefore gave these the lower office, where their disobedience would do less damage. This is why we have been placed in corruptible terrestrial bodies, toward the bottom of the chain of physical causality, while the angels have been given charge over the incorruptible celestial bodies which preserve the order of the physical universe.

It seems that God has subjected us to the vicissitudes of a corruptible body, and that this is the source of our trouble: when we are born into a mortal nature, we enter into a twofold condition of *ignorance* and *difficulty*, "to approve false things as true, so as to err unwilling, and to be unable to refrain from lustful works because of the resisting and tormenting pain of the carnal bond" (III,xviii,52). Under these conditions, "it is no wonder either that, through ignorance, a man should not have free choice of the will to choose what he should rightly do, or that, through the resistance of carnal habit . . . he should see and will what is rightly to be done, but be unable to carry it out" (ibid.).[37] This seems to imply that sin or moral evil could take its origin in us from a condition we did not ourselves choose. But Augustine strenuously resists this conclusion: if we fail to do right because of a condition independent of our will, we cannot be blamed, any more than a child is blamed for failing to observe the rules of grammar when he is ignorant of them or is unable to put them into practice. If an act is genuinely sin, it can arise only from the free choice of the will; if it is genuinely sin, and if it arises from a condition of ignorance or difficulty, then this ignorance or difficulty must itself have arisen from our free choice, either because we chose this very condition or because it is the punishment for a previous sinful choice.

Augustine does not decide whether the condition of ignorance and difficulty into which we are born is indeed the result of some previous sin. This is tied to the question of the origin of the soul, on which Augustine

---

[36] See Section B, above, on God's reliance on the angels' obedience.

[37] "Difficulty" [*difficultas*] is Augustine's chosen equivalent here for the Greek technical term *akrasia* (more usually rendered *incontinentia*). For more on *akrasia* as an aspect of our fallen condition, and on what can be done about it, see Section D.2 below.

rigorously suspends judgment in the *De Libero Arbitrio*: "of the four opinions about the soul – whether it comes to be from the seed, or whether new souls come to be in each of those who are born, or whether souls that already exist somewhere are either divinely sent, or fall of their own will, into the bodies of those who are born – none should be rashly affirmed" (III,xxi,59).[38] All four of these answers are compatible with the faith, and it will not damage our spiritual condition if we fail to discover which of them is true: as Augustine says, it is more important to know our present and our future than our past. If the soul of an individual human being existed before his birth (either in a separate state or as a potentially separable element in the souls of his ancestors – Augustine does not consider reincarnation), and if its birth into a mortal body is somehow dependent on its own choice, then it may be held responsible for the condition of ignorance and difficulty into which it is born; only in this case can those failures to do right which the soul cannot escape once it is in the mortal body be considered sinful. Augustine accepts the Biblical story of the fall of Adam as a historical account of the origin of human mortality and sinfulness, and attempts to integrate it with the Platonist account of the fallen condition of the soul. The scriptures, says Augustine, do not make it sufficiently clear which of the four accounts of the origin of the soul is correct; but however the soul may have come to be in its body, the mortal condition of this body is the result of the sin of Adam.[39] "It most justly pleased God, the highest governor of things, that we should be born of that first couple into ignorance and difficulty and mortality, since they, when they sinned, were precipitated into error and hardship and death" (III,xx,55), not necessarily because we ourselves deserve this as a punishment, but "both so that the justice of him who punishes should appear at

---

[38] These theories of the soul, all held by different early Christian writers, are standardly called traducianism, creationism, and (two versions of the theory of) preexistence respectively; in Wolfson's more colorful terms, the theories of second-hand, newly made, and ready-made souls (see Harry Austryn Wolfson, *Religious Philosophy: A Group of Essays* (Cambridge: Harvard University Press, 1961), p. 86).

[39] This condition of ignorance and difficulty in which we are born, as a result of Adam's sin, is what Augustine later calls "original sin," i.e. the kind of condition of moral evil that we fall into, not by performing a particular bad act, but simply by the manner of our *origin* in the world, our birth as descendants of Adam. "Original sin" is *not* a name for Adam's sin, but for our condition which (Augustine thinks) is historically a result of Adam's sin. (On *originale peccatum* or *originale delictum*, see Augustine *De Peccatorum Meritis et Remissione* I,ix,9–xiii,16; it is clear that a sin is called *originale* if it is one "in which we are born" (I,xi,14) or which comes to be ours "by propagation" (I,ix,9). The mistaken notion that "original sin" is the name of the sin of the first man may have arisen from a grammatical misunderstanding of *"originale peccatum"* as meaning "the first sin" – although, as Augustine is at pains to point out in this passage, the first sin was not Adam's or Eve's but the devil's.) Thus the doctrine of original sin is not specifically Christian; there would be no harm in using Augustine's terminology and speaking of Plotinus' theory of original sin (i.e. of the fallen condition of souls incarnate in sublunar mortal bodies), although Plotinus does not believe the story about the first human being and what he did in the garden of Eden.

the beginning of the birth of man, and so that the mercy of him who liberates should appear further along" (ibid.). That we should exist at all is a sign of God's mercy to Adam, that even after he had fallen into mortality he could still achieve the carnal immortality of generating his own kind, who would naturally be no better than what he himself had become. If, as is possible, our soul has not sinned (and perhaps has not existed) before our birth, then our birth into the mortal condition is not a punishment for the soul, but a mercy to the body, "so that the soul, by well administering (that is, by disciplining through the virtues, and subjecting to a most orderly and legitimate servitude) the body which is born of the penalty of sin (that is, of the mortality of the first man), obtain even for it, in a suitable time and order, the place of celestial incorruptibility" (III,xx,57); if the soul *has* sinned (whether on its own, or within the soul of Adam), and is born into a mortal body for this reason, then its incarnation is *both* a punishment for the soul *and* simultaneously a mercy for the body.

Augustine has learned from Plotinus that God, in placing the soul in a mortal body, is dispensing goodness even to the lowest part of creation, allowing the corruptible body to receive perfection through a soul that is capable of following divine order; what he has learned from scripture is the historical sequence, beginning with Adam and Eve and ending with the general resurrection, in which the body first falls into, and then is delivered from, its corruptibility. Augustine has also learned from Plotinus that it is a very delicate question whether this arrangement is something evil for the soul. *Perhaps*, say Plotinus and Augustine, incarnation in a mortal body is an evil for the soul, and must therefore be the result of some prior sin; perhaps it is not an evil, being not a punishment but an honorable task, but it still involves the soul in mortal danger, like the pilot of the storm-tossed ship in Plotinus (Plotinus IV,3,17, cited at the end of Chapter 3 above). If it is true that our souls previously enjoyed a life free of trouble, then "when they enter into this life, and submit to bearing the mortal members, they also necessarily submit to forgetfulness of the earlier life and the labor of the present" (III,xx,57); from the souls' entry into the present life, whatever their previous condition, "there follow that ignorance and difficulty which in the first man were the penalty of mortality to complete the misery of the soul, but which in them are the conditions of the task of restoring the incorruptibility of the body" (ibid.). The good God would not have assigned us an impossible task: he has given us "both the power of working well in laborious tasks, and the road of faith in the blindness of forgetfulness; and above all that *judgment* by which every soul admits that it should seek that of which it is harmfully ignorant, and that it should strive with perseverance in laborious tasks in order to overcome the difficulty of doing right, and that it should implore the aid of its creator, that he might help it in its struggle" (ibid.); thus "although it is born in ignorance and difficulty, no necessity constrains it to remain in that [condition] in which it was born" (III,xx,56). But the soul is *tempted* (though not invincibly) into erroneous beliefs and lustful works, through which it might abandon its divinely given task of imposing discipline on the disorder of the mortal body; it is only in this way, when those "captured by love of this life" (III,xx,57) refuse to make use of the gifts that God has given them for overcoming their congenital ignorance and difficulty, that these (loosely speaking) "sinful" conditions can give rise to actual sin.

Augustine's conclusions about the origins of moral evil thus follow the Platonists.[40] Moral evil is not a nature created by God, nor an attribute that God bestows on a nature. Rather, it is a defective motion of a nature away from God, whose origin can only be sought in the free will of that nature. The "principle of plenitude" requires that rational natures should have the freedom that enables them to sin, but it does not require that they should use this freedom to sin in actuality. Those rational natures whose task in the world order is to govern corruptible bodies are naturally placed in a condition of ignorance and difficulty which *inclines* them to sin, but they are capable with the help of God of escaping unharmed from this condition. Ignorance and difficulty may enter into the explanation of sin as a *condition* under which it is likely to occur, but not as a *cause* of sin. Sin, in its essence, is the soul's turning away from God and toward itself, as Plotinus had described it in the first chapter of *On the Three Principal Hypostases*. A soul may live in the conditions of mortality and yet avoid sin by turning to God, or be exempt from mortality and yet commit sin by turning from God to itself: prior to any sin within the conditions of mortality, such must have been the fall of Adam, and before him of the devil. "When the mind contemplates the highest wisdom – which is not the soul, for it is immutable – it also contemplates its mutable self, and somehow becomes aware of itself" (III,xxv,76); contemplating itself as the recipient of truth and God as the source of truth, it can choose either to love God over itself, or "to imitate God in a perverse way, as wishing to enjoy its own power; thus it becomes as much lesser as it wishes to be greater" (ibid.).[41] Augustine has taken up the Plotinian understand-

---

[40] As far as I know, Augustine never comments on Plotinus' opinion – idiosyncratic within the Platonic school, and not mentioned in most of Plotinus' treatises – that matter is evil and the origin of all evil (including moral evil). If Augustine was aware of this Plotinian doctrine (and he does apparently cite a phrase from Plotinus I,8 *What Are and Whence Come Evils?* at *Confessions* VII,x,16), then he would reject it as inconsistent with the fundamental lesson he had learned from Plotinus, and as Gnostic or Manichean rather than Platonist (it is close to the popularized quasi-Platonism that Augustine had put forward in the *De Pulchro et Apto*, which the books of the Platonists had taught him to reject; see *Confessions* IV,xv,24–5). As elsewhere, Augustine is attracted by Plotinus' philosophical method in presenting Platonism, but not by his doctrinal peculiarities within the Platonic school.

[41] Compare Plotinus *On the Three Principal Hypostases*, V,1,1: the origin of the fall of the souls, which leads them ultimately to consider themselves inferior even to bodies, is their audacity, *tolma*, and their "desiring to be of themselves"; they "enjoy their own power," and use it to disastrous results.

ing of soul and God, and of evil as departure from God; he has thus been led to see that moral evil in the soul cannot derive from God, but only from the soul's own will which leads it away from God. The theodicy that he has taken from Plotinus, and set into the Christian historical scheme, leads him to understand human sin as causally related to the conditions of mortality, but also to maintain, unlike the Manichees, that it is not inescapable even in these conditions; the premiss that God is not responsible for evil, fully thought through, leads him to the conclusion that God must have provided a way by which the soul, if it so wills, can return to God, escaping sin, and in the end escaping from the evils of mortality.

D. Christianity and philosophy

D.1. Faith and understanding

We examined, in Section B, the understanding of God and the soul that Augustine took from his reading of the books of the Platonists, and, in Section C, the consequences that he derived about the nature and origin of evil in the universe, and particularly of *moral* evil in the human soul. When Augustine had come to understand that evil is not a nature opposed to God but a defect supervening upon the lower part of God's creation, he was able to resolve his chief intellectual objection against Catholic Christianity; more than this, when he had come to understand God as the Truth above the soul containing the standards by which all things are judged, he was able to attain the intuitive perception of God that he had been seeking since the *Hortensius* had first inflamed him with the desire for wisdom. What, beyond this, did Augustine require to satisfy himself that he had acquired wisdom?

To give a full account of Augustinian "wisdom," we need to consider Augustine's judgment of the relation between philosophy and Christianity. As we have seen, Augustine does not consider himself to be a philosopher, and he does not think that the philosophers can offer him the way to wisdom. When Cicero had inspired him to seek among the different sects for wisdom, he had been attracted to the Manichees, because they, unlike Cicero and the other philosophers, spoke of Christ. And even when his reading of the philosophers had persuaded him that the Manichean cosmology was in contradiction with sound astronomy, and that the Manichean claim to revelation was therefore fraudulent, this did not lead him to "commit the treatment of the illness of my soul to the philosophers, who were without the saving name of Christ" (*Confessions* V,xiv,25); he turned instead to Ambrose and other Catholics. Augustine was unable to derive any satisfactory wisdom from Christianity until he had read Plotinus and come to his vision of God; but even after reading Plotinus, he continued to look to Christianity as a necessary source of wisdom. We must therefore attempt to understand what it was in Christianity that Augustine expected to contribute to his search for wisdom.

The Catholics "required that one should *believe* what had not been *proved*" (VI,v,7), namely the truth of the scriptures of the Old and New Testaments. This distinguished them, not only from the philosophers, who attempted to bring their disciples to an intuitive knowledge of first principles and a demonstrative knowledge of their consequences, but also from the Manichees, who "ridiculed credulity with a rash promise of knowledge [*scientia*], and then demanded that so many most absurd and fabulous things should be *believed*, because they could not prove them" (ibid.). After the philosophers had convinced Augustine that the Manichees did not know what they claimed to know, their system lost all its attraction; but the result was not that Augustine abandoned one system of doctrines for another, but rather that he "doubted all things, and wavered back and forth among them, as the Academics are thought to do [*Academicorum more sicut existimantur*]" (V,xiv,25).[42] For some time Augustine despaired of ever coming to know the truth that he was seeking; but his mind was too restless to remain in such a state of despair, and began before long to explore other ways to wisdom. With the collapse of the Manichees' claim to knowledge, and thus to superiority over Catholic credulity, Augustine turned to reexamine the claims of the Christian scriptures to belief.

When Cicero had first inspired him to seek for wisdom, Augustine had begun by inspecting the canonical scriptures of the Catholic church. He had rejected them, then, as "unworthy in comparison with the dignity of Cicero" (III,v,9), and the Manichees had confirmed his cultural prejudices by attacking the barbarities of the Old Testament, seen both in its allegedly anthropomorphic conception of God and in the lives of its heroes, who "had many wives at once and killed people and sacrificed animals" (III,vii,12). It was not until he came to hear Ambrose's preaching that

it began to appear to me that these things too [the Catholic doctrines as presented by Ambrose] could be defended, and I now judged that the Catholic faith, on whose behalf I had thought that nothing could be said against its Manichean opponents, might be maintained without disgrace, above all when I had heard one mystery after another resolved from out of the old writings [*ex veteribus scriptis*, i.e. out of the scriptures of the Old Testament] (V,xiv,24),

through spiritual interpretation of passages objectionable in their literal sense. Ambrose had shown that the Old Testament writers did not literally

---

[42] Augustine adds the odd qualification "*sicut existimantur*" because he has come to accept the view (also reported at Sextus Empiricus *Outlines of Pyrrhonism* I,234) that the New Academics held a secret, Platonist, doctrine, and maintained a façade of universal doubt only as a strategic measure against Stoic dogmatism. For Augustine's views on Academic esotericism, see the *Contra Academicos*, especially III,xvii,38 and III,xx,43. It is not clear what Augustine's source is: he ascribes this view to Cicero at *Contra Academicos* III,xx,43, but I doubt that this ascription is correct. Perhaps Augustine has some Platonist source; or perhaps he has taken some more innocuous passage of Cicero and turned it in a Platonist direction.

suppose that humans were created in the image of God, and that God therefore had two arms and two legs; he had also performed rather more remarkable feats of allegorical exegesis, and revealed profound mysteries hidden under the letter of the Old Testament text. He had thus persuaded Augustine that the barbarities which the Manichees had taught him to despise were not truly representative of Catholic doctrine, and that orthodox Christianity, rightly understood, was as likely as any other doctrine to contain the true wisdom.

Ambrose had persuaded him that the Catholic doctrines might possibly be true, and that a reasonable man might believe them; he had not persuaded him that they were actually true, or induced him to actually commit himself to them. Indeed, his experience with the Manichees inclined him to suspicion: "as it frequently happens that someone who has had experience of a bad doctor is afraid to commit himself even to a good one, so was the condition of my soul, which could not be cured except by believing, but which, because it was afraid of believing false things, refused to be treated" (VI,iv,6). In this condition, "as the Catholic faith did not seem to me to have been defeated, neither did it yet appear victorious" (V,xiv,24); "I did not think that one should maintain the Catholic way, [merely] because it too could have its learned adherents, who could rebut objections at length and not implausibly" (ibid.). Nor would the Catholic way emerge as the clear victor after further debate, for the Catholics, unlike the Manichees, did not claim to be able to produce demonstrative arguments for their doctrine. Augustine thus poses the question of Catholicism in terms of the question of *faith*: was it reasonable for the seeker of wisdom to begin by *believing* in scriptures whose doctrines he could not demonstrate? For Augustine to move from scepticism to seeking his wisdom among the Catholics, he had first to be convinced that such belief was a reasonable beginning on the search for wisdom, and then to carry out this search, using the doctrines of the scriptures as a means to attain the desired knowledge and enjoyment of God.

Augustine describes in *Confessions* VI,v the line of reasoning that led him to adopt the Catholic position that it was reasonable to believe, on the authority of the scriptures, assertions that had not yet been demonstrated; he gives a longer parallel presentation of the same reasoning in his treatise *De Utilitate Credendi*, "On the Usefulness of Believing," written to persuade a Manichee friend to abandon the sect and pursue the Catholic path to wisdom.

Augustine asserts, looking backwards, that belief was the only possible cure for the condition of his soul; and it seems that, from the beginning, he sought to evaluate the claims of belief by considering it as a spiritual cure. His underlying spiritual illness (as he now diagnoses it) was an *aversio* from God and *conversio* toward inferior things, which had led him to ignorance and false belief about God, and to a desire for inferior things instead of God. Augustine speaks in a particular and personal way of desires for "honor, wealth, and marriage" (*Confessions* VI,vi,9): he "suffered the most bitter difficulties in these desires" (ibid.), and would not have been satisfied even if he had attained them. Thus his *conversio* to inferior things had brought him to a condition of misery that he could escape only by turning back from these inferior things to God, or, as he says equally, from foolishness to wisdom. Since the Manichees were themselves turned away from the true God and toward corporeal phantasms, they could not bring Augustine to wisdom. Neither could the philosophers: for he had not yet read the Platonists, but only Cicero and the unnamed Hellenistic philosophers who had shown him the error of the Manichean cosmology. These could not give him the saving wisdom, since they spoke only of "the body of this world, and every nature that carnal sense perceives" (V,xiv,25), and not of God in the desired sense; nor could they give him certainty even about the physical world, but only doubt or at most probability. Augustine wanted to pass from ignorance of God to knowledge of God, and knowledge is acquired only by reason; but those who promised to lead him to God by reason were unable to deliver him from his ignorance. In these circumstances, he began to think that he could pass from ignorance to knowledge only by passing through an intermediate stage of *belief*.

The wise man *knows* the truth concerning the chief good; he does not need to believe it on authority. "But we are now concerned *that we might be able to be wise*" (*De Utilitate Credendi* xvi,34); we are asking what we must do in order to become wise, not what we will be able to do when we are already wise. To be wise is "to adhere to the truth; which, certainly, an impure mind cannot do," and a soul that has turned away from God to inferior things is impure, for "the impurity of the soul . . . is the love of anything besides the soul and God" (ibid.). The soul that has turned away from God, and has therefore become morally impure, cannot simply purify itself by turning to look at God: rather,

the more someone is purified from this impurity, the more easily he perceives the truth. Therefore, to wish to see the truth in order that you might purify your soul – when it is purified precisely in order that you might see – is all backwards and perverse. (Ibid.)

This seems to be a vicious circle: how are we to be morally purified, if we cannot yet perceive the truth about how we ought to live? The circle can be broken, according to Augustine, only if we begin by *believing* the truth on the authority of those who already perceive it: "to a man who is not capable of perceiving the truth, *authority* is available, in order that he may become fit for this, and that he may allow himself to be purified" (ibid.). Indeed, this is the only way that a foolish person can avoid sin, "for everything that is not done rightly is a sin, nor can anything be done rightly except what proceeds from right reason" (xii,27). And if we are not wise, our actions can proceed from right reason only if they proceed from right reason in someone else, someone who is wise and whose authority we obey. The foolish person can become wise, then, only by obeying the precepts of some wise person, and through the habit of right action gradually loosening the hold of desires for inferior things, thus purifying the eye of his mind so that it may eventually be able to perceive the truth without the interference of corporeal phantasms.[43]

Even when we have recognized that we are ignorant about our own chief good, our inclination is to explore for ourselves until we know it; it seems an unreasonable demand that we should abandon our own judgments and instead believe and obey the precepts of another, when we do not know that they are right. Augustine tells us that he dropped his resistance to this demand when he recognized that, wherever practical necessity requires it, we do unquestioningly accept the authority of others.

I considered how innumerably many things I believed, which I did not see, nor had I been present when they happened, so many things in the history of the nations, so many things about places and cities I had not seen, so many things from friends, so many from doctors, so many from yet other people; if we did not believe these things we should accomplish [*ageremus*] nothing at all in this life. And finally [I considered] how unshakenly firm I held by faith who my parents were, which I could not have known if I had not believed it from hearing it. (*Confessions* VI,v,7)

In all of these cases, we must *believe* things that we do not know, if we are to be able to act rightly in securing temporal goods or in fulfilling our moral obligations. In all of these cases, we are willing to follow authority: we would judge that someone was acting unreasonably, not if he believed that the people who claimed to be his parents were really his parents, and afforded them the obedience due to parents, but if he doubted that they were his parents, and acted accordingly. We *believe* things on authority in everyday matters because we do not know them for ourselves, and because our chance to acquire some good depends on our adopting some belief to guide our action. But in matters of religion, where we are concerned with God and the soul, our knowledge is much weaker, and the good we stand to acquire is much greater: thus Augustine concludes that the willingness to believe on authority instead of waiting for certain knowledge is all the more reasonable in these matters.

Augustine carefully distinguishes such *belief* on authority from *opinion*.

---

[43] This is Platonic, with ultimate sources in the *Meno*, *Phaedo*, and *Republic*: an ignorant and vicious person cannot immediately attain true virtue, based on knowledge, but must make progress toward true virtue through a "virtue" based on true opinion (typically by following the authority of someone who knows, or of laws laid down by a wise legislator): this will preserve him from debilitating wrong actions, and help him to search for knowledge, and to recognize it when he sees it. But (as noted below) Augustine rejects the word *opinio* [= *doxa*] for the state in between ignorance and knowledge, and speaks instead of *fides* or *credere*. While Augustine is of course chiefly interested in *Christian* faith, and cites St. Paul on faith in this sense, he takes this as an instance of a broader concept (thus at *De Libero Arbitrio* I,iii,6, in seeking *intellectus* of why adultery is wrong, we begin from *fides* in Roman law). See further below for Augustine on Meno's dilemma of how an ignorant person is to recognize knowledge.

"Opinion" had become a term of abuse, for Stoics and sceptics alike; as Augustine understands the term, someone opines something if he thinks that he knows it when he does not. Opining, in this sense, cannot be a step on the road to wisdom; on the contrary, opinionated persons can be brought to wisdom only if they are first disabused of their opinions and shown their own ignorance. But believing [*credere*], or faith [*fides*], does not involve believing that one knows; indeed, the terms are most properly used of those who confess their own ignorance. It is this kind of faith of which St. Paul is speaking when he says that "we [Christians] walk now by faith, not by sight" (2 Cor. 5:7); and Paul is confident that if we now believe in what God has revealed through Christ, and live in accordance with that belief, we will eventually (if only on the day of resurrection) be able to enjoy full knowledge of God. Augustine is led by his reflections on the difficulty of coming to wisdom to accept the Catholic position that faith is the way to wisdom; and he is naturally eager to justify this position in philosophical terms to his companions in the search for wisdom, philosophers or Manichees (like Honoratus, the addressee of the *De Utilitate Credendi*), and to convince them that he has not abandoned his desire for wisdom in exchange for an unintellectual dogmatism.

Augustine repeatedly makes the distinction between belief and opinion, in clarifying his justification of belief. It will help to cite here an extended passage from the *De Utilitate Credendi* (xi,25), because it makes the distinctions very clear, and because it became the *locus classicus* on the subject:[44]

Three things which are as it were adjacent in the minds of men are most worthy of distinction: to understand, to believe, and to opine. If these are considered in themselves, the first is always without fault [*vitium*], the second sometimes with fault, the third never without fault. For to understand great and honorable, or even divine, things is most blessed; but to understand superfluous things is not harmful, although perhaps learning them was harmful, if they took time away from necessary things. It is not wretched even to know harmful things, but only to do them or to suffer them. For if someone understands how an enemy can be killed without danger to himself, he is not guilty by this understanding itself of the desire; if this is absent, what can be said to be more innocent? But to believe is blameworthy when something unworthy is believed of God, or is believed [too] readily of man. But in other things if someone believes something, if he understands that he does not know it, there is no blame. Thus I believe that the most wicked [Catilinarian] conspirators were once put to death by the virtue of Cicero; but not only do I not know it, I know for certain that I could not know it in any way. But to opine is most shameful for two reasons: both because he who has persuaded himself that he already knows cannot learn, if it is now possible to learn

---

[44] We will see this passage again in Chapter 6, when Arnauld quotes it to Descartes in his comments on the *Meditations*. Gilson had cited the *De Utilitate Credendi*, of which this passage is the intellectual core, to exemplify the Augustinian spirit which (Gilson thinks) Descartes lacks. I will argue in Chapter 7, Section B, that Descartes in fact *presupposes* the understanding of faith set out in this passage of the *De Utilitate Credendi*.

the thing, and because in itself this rashness is a sign of a soul not well disposed. For even if someone thinks that he knows what I have said about Cicero, although nothing is preventing him from learning, because the thing itself cannot be held by any knowledge, still, because he does not understand that there is a great difference whether something is seen by the mind's certain reason, which we call understanding, or whether something is profitably [*utiliter*] commended to reputation or writing to be believed by posterity, he is certainly in error, and no error is without shame. Therefore we owe what we understand to reason, what we believe to authority, and what we opine to error. But everyone who understands also believes, and also everyone who opines believes; but not everyone who believes understands, and no one who opines understands.

In context, Augustine is putting forward these distinctions in order to show, among those who do not know the truth in religion, who those are that seek it in the right way, so that they may end by finding it. Those who seek the truth rightly, says Augustine, are not the opinionated, those who (like the Manichees) think they know when they do not; nor are they those who (like the Academics) "seek the truth in despair of finding it" (ibid.) and refuse to believe anything; they are those who (like the Catholics) believe now, not to content themselves with a substitute for knowledge, but to make progress toward a genuine knowledge:

These things have been said, that we might understand that we may be acquitted of the rashness of the opinionated, while retaining our faith even in those things which we do not yet comprehend. For those who say that we should believe nothing except what we know fear this one name of opinion, which must be called shameful and most wretched; but if they diligently consider that there is a great difference whether someone thinks that he knows, or whether he understands that he does not know, but is moved by some authority to believe, then certainly they will avoid both error and the crime of inhumanity and pride. (Ibid.)

The only problem with all this is that it does not tell us which authority to believe in. In an autobiographical chapter of the *De Utilitate Credendi* Augustine recalls the mental struggles of the time when he had abandoned the Manichees and was tempted by Academic despair of truth. He could not rest with the Academic position:

I did not think that truth was hidden except in so far as the means of searching for it was hidden, and [I thought that] this means should be taken from some divine authority. It remained to seek what this authority was, since amidst so many dissensions each person promised that he could hand it on. Thus there sprang up about me a forest from which I could not escape, and which I much regretted that I had entered; and my mind was tossed among these things without any rest by the desire of finding the truth. (viii,20)

Augustine is confronted here with the dilemma of the *Meno*: how, if we do not know the truth, can we come to recognize it when we find it? "Here a most difficult question arises: for by what means will we fools be able to recognize a wise man?" (xiii,28). Wisdom is not like gold or silver, which we may see without *having* them, for "what is grasped by the intellect is internal to the soul, and *having* it is nothing other than seeing it" (ibid.); therefore, since the fool does not have wisdom, he does not know it, and cannot recognize it when he encounters it in the wise man. Therefore, Augustine observes, "no one, as long as he is a fool, can by any certain knowledge find a wise man by obeying whom he might be delivered from the great evil of foolishness" (ibid.).

Augustine concludes that only God's help can break this circle for us. He tells us in the *Confessions* that throughout his philosophical tossings he had continued to believe "both that you [God] existed and that you take care for us" (VI,v,8). Augustine is referring, implicitly here and more explicitly in the *De Utilitate Credendi*, to the precondition for the search for God set by the Letter to the Hebrews (11:6): "whoever would draw near to God must believe that he exists and that he rewards those who seek him," for otherwise we would have no reason to search. But if we begin by believing in the existence and providence of God, then "we should not despair of [finding] some authority established by that same God, by which, as leaning on a sure support, we might go up to God" (*De Utilitate Credendi* xvi,34). Beginning from this general faith, Augustine turns to look for the signs of such an authority established by God within the history of the humanity under his rule; and he finds that the strongest authority is that of the canonical scriptures recognized by the Catholic church, the faith of Augustine's parents and of the Roman state and of most of the known peoples.[45]

Therefore, since we are incapable of finding the truth by pure reason, and thus require the authority of holy writings, I now began to believe that you [God] would not have allotted to that scripture so outstanding an authority, now in every land, unless you had wished that we should believe in you and seek you through it (*Confessions* VI,v,8)

– for if God had allowed a spurious revelation to usurp such universal authority, he would have prevented a humanity fallen into error from discovering the genuine path back to wisdom. Considering the question in this way, Augustine came to regard the authority of the Christian scriptures as analogous to the authority of his parents: just as we do not doubt that the people who claim to be our parents and who habitually exercise the authority of parents over us are truly our parents, so "I should blame not those who believed in your [God's] books, which you have established with such authority in almost all nations, but those who did not believe them; and I should not listen to those who might ask me, 'whence do you know that these books have been given to the human race by the spirit of the one true and most truthful God?' " (VI,v,7). God initially established this authority, says Augustine (*De Utilitate Credendi* xvi,34), by means of miracles, and thus succeeded in gathering in an initial mass of believers;

---

[45] The barbarians of western Europe were mostly Arians, but these too recognized the same scriptures; so this does not damage the point.

once he has done this, then miracles are no longer necessary, for the great number of the believers, and their evident progress in virtue and wisdom since accepting the authority of Christ, suffice to make this the obvious authority for us to follow in choosing a path to wisdom. For these reasons Augustine decided to remain a catechumen in the Catholic church, to accept its faith in Christ as handed down in the scriptures, and to attempt to transform his belief in its assertions about God into a knowledge worthy of the name of wisdom.

This does not mean that the Catholics are wise; Augustine remains convinced that the wise are a small minority. Christ exhorts us to believe, in order that we may receive the gift of salvation; but the gift itself is not belief but knowledge. "Then to those who already believed he [Christ] said, 'seek and you shall find,' for neither can what is believed but unknown be said to have been found [already], nor is anyone fit to find God unless he has previously believed what he is afterwards to know" (*De Libero Arbitrio* II,ii,6). In this exposition, and in many parallel passages, Augustine follows the inspired Septuagint mistranslation of Isaiah 7:9: "unless you have believed, you will not understand." Thus we must begin by believing what we read in scripture, and then press on to understand it. This means, most obviously, to know or understand *that it is true*; but for Augustine, much of the difficulty lies in the preliminary task of understanding *what it means*. Before he had heard Ambrose, he had misunderstood the meaning of the scriptural assertion that man is created in the image of God, and had therefore refused to believe it; but even after he had heard Ambrose, and learned that "man being made by you [God] in your image was not understood by your spiritual children, whom you have regenerated through grace from our Catholic mother, in such a way that they believed and thought that you were limited by the form of a human body" (*Confessions* VI,iii,4), still "I did not conceive, not even through a glass darkly, how a spiritual substance could be constituted [*se haberet*]" (ibid.). Thus he could understand only what the image of God in man *was not*, not what it was. Once he had learned to understand himself as potential nous and God as essentially actual Nous, he could understand what was meant by the image of God, and simultaneously he could understand that it was true that man was created in that image. It seems from this example that the wise among the Catholics are those who (like Ambrose) are able to conceive the spiritual things allegorically indicated in scripture, and can therefore also understand the truth of the doctrines that follow from these conceptions.

Augustine illustrates the value of beginning from faith, and proceeding to understanding, in his account of his difficulty in understanding how God could be the author only of goods and not of evils, and yet could also (against the Manichees) be the creator of all things. As we have seen, Augustine thinks that this problem was insoluble for him as long as he could not form a conception of God as a spiritual substance. While Augustine suffered from this intellectual limitation, the easiest path for him was to reject one of the two apparently incompatible assertions about God; and he felt constrained by piety to reject the Catholic doctrine of creation rather than to doubt God's pure beneficence. But once Augustine accepts on faith the truth of the Old Testament scriptures, he is committed to believing both of the assertions about God; this does not immediately give him understanding of how they can both be true together, but it forces him to *persevere* in struggling toward such an understanding, and to trust in God to reward his struggle.[46] Augustine thinks that this perseverance and trust were a precondition for his achieving his understanding of God, but that they were not sufficient without God's help. So in *Confessions* VII, describing a purely intellectual struggle, Augustine can write that

you [God] were driving me with inward goads, that I should not rest until I had fixed upon you with my inner vision. And my swelling subsided through the hidden hand of your cure, and the disturbed and darkened vision of my mind was being healed from day to day by the salve of healthful pains. (VII,viii,12)

Nonetheless, no actual understanding of God resulted from this purifying process until "you [God] procured for me," through a human intermediary, the books of the Platonists (VII,ix,13). "Admonished by them to return to myself, I entered into my own inmost parts with you as my leader, and I was able, because you had become my helper" (VII,x,16); this means, not simply that God as Nous is the source of illumination, but that, were it not for the preparatory discipline of believing on the authority of Christ and of struggling to understand that authority, Augustine would have been psychically unable to perceive the light.

D.2. The doctrinal content of Christianity

It is important to recognize that none of this implies that Christianity has any peculiar intellectual content distinguishing it from pagan Platonist philosophy. Certainly Augustine thinks that Christianity is something

---

[46] Augustine retrospectively describes this struggle, and offers it to Evodius as a model, at *De Libero Arbitrio* I,ii, 4-5. If rather than giving up our belief in one of the two apparently conflicting propositions (that God is the author only of goods, and that God is the creator of all things), we persevere in trying to understand how they can both be true together, then "God will assist us, and will make us understand what we have believed. For we confess that it is best for us to hold to the course prescribed by the prophet [i.e. Isaiah], who says, 'unless you have believed, you will not understand.' For we believe that all things that are are from one God, and yet that God is not the author of sins; but it disturbs the mind, if sins are from these souls that God created, and those souls are from God, how sins are not referred at a small remove to God" (I,ii,4). It is the fact that we do (on the authority of the church) believe these two apparently conflicting propositions that, as Evodius says, "torments me when I think and has forced me and dragged me to this questioning" (I,ii,5). Augustine assures him that this is the best possible starting-point for coming to understand: "be of stout heart and believe what you believe; for nothing is believed more finely than this, even if the reason why it is so remains hidden. For to think the best of God is the truest beginning of piety" (ibid.), and this requires believing not only that he is entirely good but also that he is omnipotent and thus the sole creator.

other than Platonism, in that it possesses the authority of the inspired teachers, culminating in Jesus Christ, whose teachings are recorded in the scriptures; it therefore requires, what Platonism does not, obedience to the concrete precepts of these teachers as a practical path toward acquiring wisdom. But it does not immediately follow that the intellectual content that Christians will perceive as the fruit of their obedience is something other than the content of the books of the Platonists. Christians who have become wise will perceive the things that are spoken of in scripture; but they, unlike the masses of believers, will have discerned the allegorical sense of scripture, especially of the scriptures of the Old Testament. And once they have understood the Christian scriptures through an allegorical interpretation, it is not obvious that anything specifically Christian will remain. If the inner meaning of each scriptural assertion is a doctrine also put forward by the Platonists, then the scriptures will have no surplus of intellectual content: what is only in the scriptures and not in the Platonists will be merely the literal or historical meaning of the assertions, and even if this is not false (as in the assertion that God made man in his own image), nonetheless (like the chronological fact that Isaiah saw God in the year King Uzziah died) it will contribute no intellectual content toward the desired wisdom. If this is what Augustine intends, then the Christian scriptures would be like a ladder by which we may climb to philosophical understanding, but which we may kick out from under us once we have reached the top.

It is a very delicate question how far Augustine believes that Christianity exceeds Platonism in intellectual content; and we must be cautious about attempts to answer it by quoting some decisive passage in one or the other direction. There have certainly been people (like the philosophers of Islam) who have believed in the scriptures of some revealed religion, and who have thought they could extract from these scriptures an intellectual system identical with the results of pagan philosophy; there have been others (like the theologians [*mutakallimûn*] of Islam) who thought they could extract from the same scriptures an intellectual system directly contradicting pagan philosophy. And there is a whole spectrum of possible positions between these two extremes. Not every thinker who affirms the truth of the scriptures and their superiority to pagan philosophy is therefore a "theologian," and not every thinker who allegorizes the scriptures where their literal meaning seems contrary to reason is therefore a "philosopher." All we can do is to try to understand each individual thinker's motives in turning to the scriptures and in interpreting them in a particular fashion, and then to follow him in working out his individual position on the relations between scriptural authority and human reason. Here I will merely indicate some of the main motives that incline Augustine in the philosophical or the theological direction, without trying to determine what precise balance he strikes between them.

There are certainly passages, especially in Augustine's earlier writings, which seem to present Platonist philosophy as the legitimate interpretation of the intellectual content of the Christian scriptures. We have seen already perhaps the most striking of these:

it is not doubtful to anyone that we are impelled to learning by the twofold weight of authority and reason. It is therefore certain to me that at no point at all should I depart from the authority of Christ: for I do not find any stronger. But as to what is to be pursued by subtle reasoning – for I am so disposed that I impatiently desire to apprehend what is true not only by believing but also by understanding – I am meanwhile confident that I will find with the Platonists what will not be contrary to our religion [*sacris nostris*]. (*Contra Academicos* III,xx,43)

Similarly, at *De Beata Vita* 4, Augustine says that he was inspired to break his chains and flee to philosophy when he had "read some few books of Plotinus . . . and also compared with them, as far as I could, the authority of those who have handed down the divine mysteries." It seems, from these passages of Augustine's earliest Christian works, that as we have found in Christ (and in those who have transmitted his teaching) the authority that brings us to *believe*, so we will find in the books of the Platonists the reason that will bring us to *understand*. When we come to perfect wisdom, we will have coordinated the two sources of truth in such a way that the "mysteries" of the Christian faith – its sacred words and sacred actions – will have been rationally elucidated by the Platonic teaching. There is no suggestion here of an irreducible Christian intellectual content unknown to pagan philosophy.

But this is not the only aspect of Augustine's thought on Christianity and Platonism. In the *Retractations* (I,i,4), reviewing the *Contra Academicos*, he finds that "I have been rightly displeased by the praise with which I exalted Plato or the Platonic or Academic philosophers more than is fitting for impious men, especially those against whose great errors Christian doctrine must be defended." Plato and the Platonists are "impious" because they participated in pagan worship of beings inferior to God, and because such Platonists as Apuleius and Porphyry (discussed in the *De Civitate Dei*) gave a theoretical justification for the practice. Certainly Augustine had never been interested in taking advice from the Platonists *in sacris*, in matters of religious practice; but there is a marked progression in his writings from the statement of 386 that what is in the books of the Platonists "*sacris nostris non repugnet*" to the statement of 426 that Christian doctrine must be defended against their great errors. This is because Augustine gradually forms a more distinct conception of the Christian doctrine that is bound up with the Christian *sacra*, and concludes that a purely Platonist understanding of these *sacra* cannot preserve what distinguishes them from pagan disciplines as our only possible path for returning to God. By following Augustine's analysis of the intellectual presuppositions of the saving efficacy of the Christian *sacra*, we can understand his motives in moving some distance toward the theological end of the spectrum of positions on scripture and reason.

Augustine gives us in the *Confessions*, in portions of Book VII that we have not yet examined and in Book VIII, an account of how he moved away from a purely Platonist interpretation of Christianity. Augustine is writing around 400, describing events of 386, and it is possible that he is reading back some of his later conceptions into an earlier period of his life.[47] This is a delicate question, but we need not pass judgment on it here, since we are trying only to understand the reasons moving Augustine in the theological direction, not to determine how far they had moved him at a given time in his life. We may begin by returning to *Confessions* VII, and examining how Augustine's vision of God, achieved by meditating through the books of the Platonists, fits into the process of his appropriation of Christianity.

When Augustine came to his vision of God, he was already thinking of himself as a Christian. He had accepted the Catholic justification for believing on the authority of the scriptures. He believed, on this authority, that the good God was the creator of all things, and he had purified his mental vision by holding fast to this belief and struggling to overcome his habits of thought in order to understand. Throughout this struggle "a faith in the Catholic church of your [God's] Christ, our Lord and savior, remained steadily in my heart; though it was still unformed in many things and wavered from the rule of doctrine, my mind did not let it go, but drank it in more and more from day to day" (*Confessions* VII,v,7). But this unformed faith was chiefly based on his general impressions of the Catholic church and his old memories of its scriptures, and on the sermons of Ambrose allegorically expounding the mysteries of the Old Testament; he had not made any serious study of the scriptures for himself. Toward the end of Book VII, after describing the fruits of his reading of the Platonists, he sees providential order in the fact that he had "discovered them before I had considered your [God's] scriptures" (VII,xx,26); only afterwards did he "most eagerly take up the venerable writing of your spirit, and above all the apostle Paul" (VII,xxi,27), and come to recognize Paul's teaching of the gospel as the true spiritual interpretation of the Law. By seeing what Paul provided that Augustine's earlier and purely Platonic understanding of scripture could not, we can see what pushes Augustine toward a more "theological" position.

We have already studied the vision or visions of God that Augustine recounts in *Confessions* VII,x and VII,xvii. Since Augustine understands wisdom as the state of seeing God, he had, in a sense, already attained what he was seeking. But he tells us both in VII,x and in VII,xvii that he had not been able to *remain* in this state, or indeed to look at God at all, except in the way we are able to look at the sun. "When I first knew you, you took me up so that I could see that what I saw existed, but that I was not yet such as to see it; and you beat back the weakness of my vision, shining overpoweringly upon me, and I trembled with love and horror"

---

[47] On the date of the *Confessions*, see O'Donnell, ed. and comm., Augustine, *Confessions*, 1, p. xli: the date is between 397 and 401.

(VII,x,16). Again, at the beginning of VII,xvii, "I wondered that, though now I loved you and not a phantasm in your place, I could not remain to enjoy my God, but I was torn away to you by your beauty and then soon I was torn away from you by my own weight, and I fell back with a sigh to these things here [*ista*]; and this weight was carnal habit." And again, at the end of the same chapter, after he has "attained to *that which is* in the twinkling of an eye [*in ictu trepidantis aspectus*]" and seen the invisible things of God, "I was not able to fix my gaze, and when my weakness had been beaten back and I had returned to my habitual things, I brought nothing back with me but a memory that loved and desired the things which I had smelled, but which I was unable as yet to taste." In all of these places, Augustine traces his inability to fix his gaze on God to a *moral* weakness, a continued captivity to bodily passions; this is what the authority of Christ is to overcome, but it has not overcome it yet.

Augustine thinks, looking back, that at this time he had not yet "sought your [God's] way in Christ our savior" (VII,xx,26), as his salvation required him to do: up to this point he had only seen "*where* we must go," and had not seen "*how*, and the way that leads to the beatific fatherland [*ad beatificam patriam*], which we must not merely *perceive* but also *inhabit*" (ibid.). These are two crucially different things which Augustine had not yet clearly distinguished:

> It is one thing to see the country [*patria*] of peace from a peak in the forest, and to find no path to it, and to struggle in vain through the surrounding trackless wastes, where renegade soldiers watch and wait in ambush with their chief, the lion and dragon; it is another to hold to the way that leads there, guarded by the care of the celestial commander, where those who have deserted the celestial army will not attack, for they avoid it like death. (VII,xxi,27)[48]

Augustine had not found this distinction in Plotinus, who seems to identify the identify the fallen soul's vision of its fatherland with its return there: the "divine men," the true Platonic philosophers,

> by a better power and by the sharpness of their eyes, have seen the upper light as by sharp-sightedness, and have risen there as if above the clouds and mist here below, and have remained there, looking down on all things here and enjoying the true place which is their own, like a man arriving after much wandering at his well-ordered fatherland. (Plotinus *On Nous, Ideas, and Being*, V,9,1)

Thus Plotinus had led Augustine to hope that by struggling to overcome his "carnal habit" of thinking through the imagination and the senses, he would be able not only to *perceive* his intelligible place of origin in Nous, but also to *return* there. But Augustine was disappointed: though he might glimpse this country when the mists momentarily cleared, he remained planted on earth, subject to the conditions of an earthly body; even in the moment of his vision of God, "I found that I was far from you, in the

---

[48] For the image of a distant vision of the desired *patria*, cp. Hebrews 11: 13–16.

territory of unlikeness [*in regione dissimilitudinis*]" (VII,x,16).[49] What Augustine found in St. Paul was the distinction between the vision of the *patria* and the path that leads there, and directions for what he had to do to follow this path and to possess as a good what he had glimpsed from afar: "these things were brought home to me in marvelous ways when I read the least of your apostles" (VII,xxi,27).

Augustine describes the difference between the way of life of the Platonists, which does not lead to the *patria*, and the way of life of the Christians, which does, as "the difference between presumption and confession" (VII,xx,26). The Platonists, and Augustine when he assimilated Christianity to Platonism, *presume*, in that they hope to acquire the divine good through the exercise of their own power of knowledge. When Augustine had the Platonist method of searching for God, "I began to wish to appear wise . . . for I was puffed up by knowledge" (VII,xx,26): the allusion is to 1 Corinthians 8:1: "knowledge puffs up, but charity builds up." Augustine's claim is that we can undergo the moral transformation, the "charity," that we need in order to return to God, only if we first discard our pride in our knowledge, and, *confessing* that we are too weak to return to God by our own strength, seek God's grace to help us in returning. This is what Augustine read only in St. Paul and not in the Platonists:

I found that whatever I had read there [in the Platonists] that was true, was also said here [in Paul], together with praise of your grace, so that he who sees will not glory as if he had not received, not only *what* he sees, but also [the fact] *that* he sees; for what does he have that he has not received? And so that he should not merely be admonished in order to see you who are always the same, but also be cured in order to hold you; and so that even he who, from afar, cannot see you, may walk the way by which he might come to you and see you and hold you. (VII,xxi,27)

Confessing means acknowledging that whatever good we have, we have received from God, and of course the Platonists too grant that our power of knowledge comes from participation in Nous; beyond this, Augustine has already acknowledged God's special grace in establishing scriptural authority, which guides those who cannot see God until they come close enough to see him. But all this is consistent with assuming that, once we have acquired the power of seeing God, we will be able to do without further assistance. In turning from "presumption" to "confession," Augustine is acknowledging that he needs more help.

---

[49] The phrase *in regione dissimilitudinis* apparently translates Plotinus' *en tô(i) anomoiotêtos topô(i)* (Plotinus *What Are and Whence Come Evils?* I,8,13,17), for the soul submerged in matter and in vice. Plotinus is in turn citing Plato *Statesman* 273d–e1, describing the world without God's care as in danger of sinking *eis ton anomoiotêtos apeiron onta ponton*; Plotinus is following a manuscript of Plato which (like all manuscripts now extant, but unlike some manuscripts followed by other ancient Platonists) has the corrupt reading *topon* instead of the correct *ponton*.

Augustine claims that the Platonist "presumption" has not only moral but also doctrinal consequences, and that, in particular, it underlies both the Platonists' rejection of Christianity and Augustine's own (as he now sees it) excessively Platonizing first interpretation of Christian doctrine. In *Confessions* VII,ix, where Augustine first describes his reading of the books of the Platonists, he compares and contrasts these books with the Christian scriptures, citing a series of scriptural texts to show both "what I read there" on points where the Platonists teach the same doctrine as the Christians, "not indeed in these words, but entirely the same thing, argued by many and manifold reasons" (VII,ix,13), and "what I did not read there," those essential Christian teachings which the Platonists lacked. Since Augustine thinks the Platonists had the orthodox doctrine of the Trinity, what he "did not read there" was the Incarnation: he "read there" the doctrine of the eternal Word, as told in the first verses of John, but not that "the Word was made flesh and dwelt among us," nor that "to all who received him, believing in his name, he gave the power to become children of God" (John 1:14 and 1:12, cited *Confessions* VII,ix,13–14). But Augustine traces the Platonists' doctrinal rejection of the Incarnation (and their resulting inability to become "children of God") to their underlying presumption: "no one there [among the Platonists] listens to him who calls, 'come to me, you who are heavy-laden'; they disdain to learn from him, because he is meek and humble in heart" (VII,xxi,27, citing Matthew 11:25–30).[50] As Augustine interprets this passage of Matthew, it is precisely Christ's "humility" (meaning, ultimately, his voluntary descent into the flesh) that gives us a way to ascend to the *patria*; it is also his "humility" that leads the Platonists to reject this way, both because, doctrinally, they refuse to believe in such a humiliation of the eternal Word, and because, lacking humility themselves, they refuse to confess that they are "heavy-laden" and to seek help from Christ. In rejecting the possibility of the Incarnation, the Platonists are simply projecting their own lack of humility onto the eternal Word. Augustine thus explains both the persistent Platonist rejection of Christianity and his own past refusal (under Platonist influence) to follow the Christian path to the *patria*; and he explains and justifies his turning to Christianity once the obstacle of presumption was removed.

It is, on the face of it, strange for Augustine to say that when he read the books of the Platonists (thus at a time when, by his own account, he had already accepted the authority of Christ), he was rejecting the Christian path. But Augustine says that he had misunderstood the Catholic doctrine of Christ, or rather reinterpreted it in a way that was more compatible with Platonism, but eliminated the saving "humility" of Christ.

---

[50] Cited already in *Confessions* VII,ix,14: "lifted up as if on the cothurnus of a more elevated teaching, they [the Platonists] do not listen to him who says, 'learn from me, for I am meek and humble in heart, and you will find peace for your souls.'"

The Catholics believed that God's Word or Wisdom had become flesh in the person of Christ,

> but I thought otherwise; and I thought of my Christ only as of a man of exceeding wisdom, whom none could equal, especially because, marvelously [or miraculously] born of a virgin to be an example of despising temporal things by comparison with the acquisition of a divine immortality, he seemed by his care for us to have merited so much authority for his teaching. (VII,xix,25)

So despite accepting Christ as a teacher, "I did not humbly take the humble Jesus as my God" (VII,xviii,24), because he could not identify him with the divine Word. The scriptures tell us that Christ performed at different times all the actions of a human being, and so was mutable both in body and in mind: how then could he be identical with the immutable Word of God? Augustine could understand John's assertion that the Word had become flesh only by saying that divine providence had brought Christ forth as a mediator communicating the Word to humanity, "superior to others not by the person of truth, but by a great excellence of human nature, and a more perfect participation in wisdom" (VII,xix,25). Augustine's use here of the Platonist language of "participation" is deliberate. He means that, on his own earlier view, Christ was not Nous itself, but only a soul participating in Nous. Since Nous (as Plotinus understands it) exists purely in eternity, containing the intelligible standards of things, it cannot act within time to animate a body: Nous can cause motion in bodies only inasmuch as some soul comes to participate in Nous, and thus comes to direct the motion of its body according to an intelligible standard. By contrast, the Catholic doctrine that Augustine comes to accept is that the Word or Wisdom of God personally descended into the world of time, and became a human being, Jesus Christ, who does not merely *participate* in wisdom, but personally *is* Wisdom-itself. Augustine had said already in his first Christian work that "the most subtle reason would never have recalled souls blinded by the multiform darkness of error" to the intelligible world, "unless the highest God had, by a democratic clemency, sent down the authority of the divine intellect even to the very body of man, so that the souls, awakened not only by its precepts but also by its deeds, could return into themselves and perceive their fatherland even without the controversy of arguments" (*Contra Academicos* III,xix,42). Now, in the *Confessions*, Augustine is asking what we must understand by this "sending down" of "the authority of the divine intellect": and he is saying that, while some scriptural assertions can be legitimately allegorized to reconcile them with a Platonist understanding of God, the Incarnation cannot be handled in the same way: it is not a matter of expression, but a real intellectual contradiction between Christians and Platonists, and (Augustine thinks) it must be maintained to preserve the efficacy of the Christian path to salvation.

It is obscure precisely how Augustine thinks the Incarnation works in bringing about salvation. But Augustine's account in *Confessions* VII,xviii–xxi shows what some of the necessary conditions are supposed to be. Since we in our fallen condition are incapable of raising ourselves up to God, our salvation requires that God should act to raise us up to him: this requires (Augustine says) that God lower himself to us, since unless God comes down to our level, he will only be calling to us from above, where we cannot reach him. In the Incarnation, God's Word becomes visible, so that we can see his works; and he becomes a human being, subject like us to the conditions of a mortal body, so that we can *imitate* his works, while we are unable to imitate the eternal truths which we perceive in him through the intellect alone. By despising temporal things and accepting humiliation, he frees us from desires and fears that might keep us from following him, and prescribes by his example a discipline that is sufficient to turn us away from sin. But above all, by showing us that God himself is willing to abandon pride and suffer humiliation from love for us, he inspires us to abandon our pride and love God in return; and this brings about the moral transformation that we need to raise ourselves to God.

Your Word, the eternal truth, supereminent above the superior parts of your creation, lifts up to himself those who are subject to him: he has built for himself in the inferior parts a humble house [i.e. Christ's human body] out of our mud, by which he might lead those who are to be subject out of themselves and draw them up to him, curing the swelling [of pride] and nourishing love, so that they should not proceed further in confidence in themselves, but should rather be weakened, seeing before their feet the divinity weakened by participation in the garment of our skin, and, fatigued, should prostrate themselves before him, so that when he rises he should raise them with him. (*Confessions* VII,xviii,24)

But Christ's weakness will not have this effect on us unless we recognize him as God made flesh, since we cannot "know what his weakness was to teach" (ibid.) unless we recognize it as *God's* voluntary weakness.

The Incarnation, so understood, presupposes that God has a *will*, which is not reducible to God's knowledge or to the capacities of other things to receive God's influence. Thus in working out an understanding of the scriptures, Augustine is led to contradict a crucial aspect of Plotinus' understanding of the relation between God and the world. Nous, for Plotinus as for Aristotle, is directed to the contemplation of itself and its intelligible contents: it does not know what happens within the world of time, and has no will directed toward inferior things. For the Platonists, God rules in accordance with the natures of things: everything proceeds from him in order according to the capacity of the recipient, and there is therefore no need for him to choose what he should send where. But it is not at all in accord with the nature of the recipient that Nous itself should descend into a human body: this requires a will in God, and not a will naturally directed toward what is good and appropriate for the divine nature, but a

will capable of encompassing its own humiliation for the sake of the ele-
vation of fallen human beings.

Augustine thinks that the Platonists' rejection (or incomprehension) of
such a will in God, and of the Incarnation, arises from their presumption.
The Platonists, projecting their own presumption, cling to a conception
of God as remaining eternally satisfied in contemplating his own perfections. Hoping to imitate God in this exalted state, they reject him in his
humble state; vainly persisting in trying to raise themselves to God, they
reject his lowering of himself to them. For Augustine, it is this crucial
difference between Christians and Platonists that requires something like
theology, and not simply scripture on the one hand and allegorizing philosophy on the other: where Incarnation and, more fundamentally, will,
are central notions of this theology. We must begin, not simply by accepting an authority for sacred practice, but by believing the canonical
doctrines of Trinity and Incarnation, and then proceed as far as possible
toward understanding these truths; and while Platonist conceptions may
certainly be useful in reaching such an understanding, the final result will
be incompatible with Platonism as a whole.

This tells us all that we really need, for the purposes of our argument,
about the doctrinal content and the intellectual method of Augustinian
"wisdom." Still, Augustine has something more to say about how this
wisdom must be acquired, and (in particular) about how he himself had
to acquire it. To acquire wisdom it is necessary, but not sufficient, that
we have faith in the authority of Christ, that we apply the Platonist intellectual discipline to achieve an intellectual intuition of God, and that
we recognize a properly theological intellectual content in Christianity,
irreducible to pagan philosophy; but beyond all this, we must also *act* in
a particular way, performing outwardly visible actions as well as under-
going inward transformations, in order to make progress on the path to
the *patria*. As the *offer* of salvation involved a divine act of will (and self-
humiliation), so the *acceptance* of salvation involves a human act of will
(and self-humiliation, or rather acknowledgment of our objectively humble status). Augustine takes the path of action that God has prescribed to
involve, first, baptism, and then consequently an acceptance of the ritual
and moral discipline of the Catholic church: he assumes that this will
require him to abandon his aspirations to "honor, wealth and marriage"
(VI,vi,9), and, more concretely, his mistress and his profession as a teacher
of rhetoric. Only this discipline will bring about the moral improvement
we need so that we may "dwell with God" continuously, and not (like
Augustine in *Confessions* VII,xvii) be forced back down, after an instant
of vision, into the bodily phantasms habitually obstructing our sight.

Precisely because we need this change of life to overcome a moral deficiency, our attachments to "honor, wealth, and marriage" (or the like)
incline us to resist it. Here we should recall, from Section C, our twofold
condition of *ignorance* and *difficulty*, respectively "to approve false things

as true, so as to err unwilling, and to be unable to refrain from lustful works because of the resisting and tormenting pain of the carnal bond" (*De Libero Arbitrio* III,xviii,52). Here Augustine is concerned about the condition of "difficulty," which can obstruct us from following a path of action even after we have recognized it to be the right one. Augustine devotes *Confessions* VIII to analyzing this obstruction (in his own case), and to describing how it was overcome, through God's grace as well as through Augustine's own efforts.[51]

Augustine takes the data of the problem (as he experiences them) to be those described, both by the Greek philosophers in their accounts of *akrasia* or incontinence, and by St. Paul: "thus I understood, with myself as proof, what I had read, how 'the flesh lusts against the spirit, and the spirit against the flesh' " (*Confessions* VIII,v,11, citing Galatians 5:17). Augustine, who has recognized that he must renounce his attachments and accept Christian discipline, and yet delays doing so, is like an akratic late-sleeper: "there is no one who would wish to sleep forever, and waking is better in the sound judgment of all, but a man generally delays to shake off his sleep, when a heavy torpor is in his members, and he willingly takes the sleep which already displeases him, although the time for arising has come" (VIII,v,12). Augustine speaks of having within himself a "new will . . . to freely worship you [God] and to enjoy you" (VIII,v,10); and yet this will is frustrated, and Augustine tries to analyze what is preventing this will from being effective.[52]

Augustine notes, in *Confessions* VIII,viii–x, the paradox that the will that is frustrated here is simply a will *to will*: in more typical cases, our

[51] Augustine devotes *Confessions* VIII to a long description of this inner struggle, which I cannot do justice to here. Although the struggle culminates in Augustine's decision to be baptized, and although Book VIII is often described (in contrast to Book VII) as being concerned with Augustine's specifically Christian (rather than philosophical) conversion, it is striking that Augustine frames his choice as one between an active life (professing rhetoric, pursuing "honor, wealth, and [socially advantageous] marriage," and participating in the imperial patronage system) and a contemplative life, such as Augustine in fact pursued at Cassiciacum (withdrawing from the world to live in a small community holding dialogues about God and soul) until he was dragged back into political life in the service of the African church. This was a standard problem of Greek philosophy, and of Roman senators like Cicero or Seneca, considering philosophy as a retreat from a failed political career: here, as in so much else, Augustine seems to have taken Cicero as a personal model, though both Platonizing him and Christianizing him in a way Cicero would have found very surprising. For Augustine the choice of lives is intimately bound up with Christianity, since he thinks that the discipline of the Catholic church both forbids his current "active" life and will facilitate his pursuit of wisdom in the "contemplative" life; nonetheless, the problem Augustine is facing, and much of the language he uses in addressing it, is older than Christianity.

[52] Augustine's language is confusing here, since he uses "*voluntas*" sometimes for the faculty or power of will or free will, and sometimes for particular desires or volitions. Although texts of Augustine, including the texts of *Confessions* VII–VIII now under discussion, and the texts of the *De Libero Arbitrio* discussed above, did a great deal to form the notion of the faculty of will (in which it is important that a single power can underlie contrary acts), he does not observe a consistent terminology for the will.

will is frustrated because something else resists it, but in this case what resists is the same as what commands. "The mind [*animus*] commands the body, and it immediately obeys, [but] the mind commands itself, and is resisted" (VIII,ix,21); "it commands that it should will, and it would not command unless it willed, and [yet] it does not do what it commands" (ibid.). In resolving this *aporia*, Augustine is concerned to avoid the Manichean solution, namely that our will for the good is frustrated because of an evil nature, alien to the nature of our rational soul and impeding its freedom. To the contrary, Augustine insists that nothing can prevent us from willing what we will to will: the will obeys its own commands, or rather, it does not need to command or obey, because when it wills to will a thing, this is because it already wills the thing in question. But in cases of incontinence, "it does not fully will, and therefore it does not entirely command . . . it is not full when it commands, and this is why what it commands does not happen; for if it were full, it would not command it to be, since it would be already" (ibid.). Our difficulty, then, is not that our will lacks the power to bring us into the best condition, where we could contemplate God continuously; the difficulty is rather that, despite having seen the good, we do not fully will it, and so do not achieve it.

The explanation for this difficulty, in turn, is that the upward force of the perception of truth is counteracted by the downward force of habit. This downward force is not due to an alien nature, but is voluntary, in the sense that it results from previous acts of will: "from a perverse will, lust results, and when lust is served, habit results, and when habit is not resisted, necessity results; by the chain of these connected links a harsh servitude kept me confined" (VIII,v,10).[53] From the standpoint of the *Confessions* (against the more optimistic *De Libero Arbitrio*), it seems that we cannot free ourselves unaided from this condition of divided will and contrary impulses, even though we recognize the misery of this condition (and recognize that a better condition is possible), and even though we could free ourselves *if we fully willed to*. The point now is not simply that an act of will is needed to achieve wisdom, but that grace is needed to achieve this act of will.

But Augustine thinks that grace is available, complementing the "new will" that we acquire through perception of the good, but achieving what this partial and deficient "new will" cannot achieve by itself. Augustine gives, as a paradigm of the action of grace, the story of his own final conversion; and we may reasonably end our account of Augustine here.

---

[53] As Augustine suggests in the *De Libero Arbitrio* (discussed in Section C above), some of the previous volitions from which this condition results may be not our own but Adam's; they are still the act of a nature kindred to ours and formed like ours, not of the alien nature that the Manichees imagine. Augustine alludes to this in the present passage, at the end of *Confessions* VIII,x,22: "sin dwelt in me from the penalty of a freer sin, since I was a son of Adam." Adam's (first) sin was "freer" than our sins, because before his fall he did not have to labor under the condition of ignorance and difficulty that we are now born into.

As he tells it in *Confessions* VIII, he had been shamed by hearing how other less learned people had preceded him in accepting Christianity and renouncing their worldly honors: this state of shame, weakening his impulse to resist God's grace through pride in his own knowledge, brought his conflict to a crisis, and he went into a private garden to wrestle with himself until he could decide what to do. Still he could come to no result. "For I said within myself, 'let it happen now, let it happen now,' and with these words I was already moving toward a decision. Already I almost did it, but I did not do it; but neither did I fall back into the former things, but I remained close and I breathed again" (VIII,xi,25). Being unable to act, and in torment through his indecision, he was waiting for something to break the deadlock and push him where he could not push himself. In this state, lying under a tree in the garden and weeping, he heard a voice calling "take up and read, take up and read" (VIII,xii,29). Augustine "got up, interpreting that I was divinely commanded that I should take up the book [a volume of St. Paul's letters was lying on his table] and read whatever I should find at first look" (ibid.). He quickly found an appropriate passage, "and neither did I wish to read further, nor was there need: for immediately at the end of this sentence, as if a light of sureness had been poured into my heart, all the shadows of doubt dispersed" (ibid.). Wherever the mysterious voice may have come from, it would have had no effect if Augustine had not been prepared to accept it as a divine command. He was ready to accept a divine command as the basis for his decision because, in the struggle between "truth" and "habit" he had despaired of reaching a firm decision on his own authority; since the upward pull of the vision of the *patria* would not go away, he could attain peace of mind only by submitting to a divine command that would override the downward pull of habit. When the command came, he readily obeyed. In what seems to have been a remarkably businesslike manner, he told the people who had to be told of his conversion, quit his mistress and his job, wrote a letter to Ambrose asking to be prepared for baptism, and prepared himself for a Christian "philosophical life." Even before he was baptized, he had formed a community of friends, dedicated to a communal Christian life and to the pursuit of contemplation, striving to turn their faith into knowledge. From this early period begin the dialogues, and later treatises, in which Augustine works to bring his reader first to faith and then to an understanding of what has been believed. This is the outcome of Augustine's search for wisdom, in which both Christianity and Platonic philosophy were necessary means; and it is the genesis of Augustinianism as a systematic teaching of what claims to be wisdom.

Part Two
Descartes' metaphysics

5

The design of the *Meditations*

A. From the *Rules* to the *Meditations*

Having seen what Augustinianism was as a discipline for approaching wisdom, we can begin to see why Descartes found it fruitful for his philosophical project.

Descartes, like Augustine, is searching for wisdom. But the seventeenth-century expectation of wisdom will not be satisfied merely by knowing God and the soul: Descartes' goal is a discipline which is practical, yielding directions for action, in medicine and mechanics as well as in morals, and which is also a unified science, derived in strict sequence from directly intuited first principles. Descartes hopes to derive the practical branches of wisdom from a new scientific physics (and human physiology); but he can convert the fragments of empirical physics into a science only if he can discover the appropriate first principles. The Descartes of the *Rules* is looking for such principles, but has not yet found them. After 1628, after the conversation with Bérulle and the retreat to Holland, Descartes claims to have discovered in the rational intuitions of God and the soul, as produced by the Augustinian discipline of contemplation, adequate first principles for a universal science.[1] The thesis of the *Meditations* is precisely that these intuitions are "principles of philosophy," because God and the soul are "better known" than bodies: the *Meditations* argue first that we cannot know bodies unless we first know God and the soul (Meditation 1), then that we can know God and the soul independently of any knowledge of bodies (Meditations 2 and 3), and finally that we can derive a knowledge of bodies from this pure knowledge of God and the soul (Meditations 4–6). Augustine's metaphysics of God and the soul is a possible candidate to be Descartes' foundational discipline, because it does not depend on any doctrine of the physical world, and indeed results from a discipline of *aversio* from the senses. So Descartes can base his physics on this metaphysics without danger of circularity; this is important, not

---

I have presented some of the material of this chapter, in a briefer and more popular version, in "The Problem of the Third Meditation," *American Catholic Philosophical Quarterly*, 67 (Autumn 1993). That article, despite its title, is mostly not about the third Meditation, but about the overall design of the *Meditations*, and especially about the first Meditation, as setting the problem that the third Meditation was designed to solve.

[1] On Descartes' conceptions of his project before and after 1628, see above, Chapter 2, Sections B and C.

just because circles are bad in principle, but because Descartes cannot effectively challenge "our appetites and our teachers," the Aristotelian physics and the prejudices of the senses, if his starting-point is itself contaminated by Aristotle and the senses. Philosophically and sociologically, Augustine's metaphysics gives Descartes an Archimedean point: both its intellectual justifications and its prestige within society are independent of Aristotelianism, and can be used to subvert it.

Descartes found this metaphysics fruitful for the construction of science, fundamentally, because it understands God as Nous, as Truth, as a standard for the rightness or wrongness of our thoughts. The *Meditations* are designed to induce their readers to put this divine standard into practice as the standard by which they make their judgments: this will require a strict discipline, positively of intellectual contemplation, and negatively of separation from the senses. Descartes, like Augustine, finds that we have been immersed since infancy in a sea of error: we have habitually judged, not according to the standard of Nous, but according to the prejudices of our senses, and so have conceived the natures of things only according to the measure that the senses can represent them. Descartes needs a way to "withdraw the mind from the senses" (AT VII,12; AT VII,131), and he finds a model in Augustine's discipline of contemplation: the mind must first "remove its thought from its habit, withdrawing itself from the contrary crowds of phantasms" (*Confessions* VII,xvii,23), first turning inward to conceive its own spiritual nature without the aid of the senses, and then turning upward to contemplate God as the source and standard of truth to the mind, conceiving him without relation to bodies or to things perceived through the senses. The transformations that Descartes will bring about in the Augustinian metaphysics arise from his extending this discipline to contemplate, not just soul and God, but bodies themselves, without the use of the senses.

In the following chapters, we will see what Descartes found valuable in the Augustinian metaphysics by seeing how he actually used it in the *Meditations*. But the best way to grasp the essence of what Descartes found in Augustine is to go back to the Descartes of 1628, and see why the knowledge of God and the soul first appealed to him as a possible foundation for science. By seeing how Descartes' earlier candidates for a foundational discipline ran into difficulty, and how Augustinian metaphysics appeared to provide the solution, we can reconstruct the process by which Descartes designed the *Meditations*, and his new scientific system, around his central metaphysical idea.

From 1619 on, Descartes had the vision of a single universal science, derived from the "seeds of wisdom," which are intuitions of simple intelligible essences. But it is much less clear what these simple intelligible essences were to be. Pre-1628 texts, notably the fragmentary *Rules for the Direction of the Mind*, suggest some answers, but they also show both uncertainty and change in Descartes' thought on this question; no text prior to the conversation with Bérulle suggests that God and the soul are the first objects to be known.

On November 10, 1619, the night he was to have his vocational dreams, Descartes had "discovered the foundations of a marvelous science" (AT X,179 = Baillet I,51); the dream of a unified science merely confirms and interprets this discovery.[2] But the science Descartes had been working on (and numerous fragments of which survive in AT X) was a universal mathematics [*mathesis universalis*], in the sense in which that phrase was always taken in the early modern period, namely for a science of quantity in general, abstracting from the discrete quantity treated in arithmetic and the continuous quantity treated in geometry: and this universal mathematics was clearly Descartes' first candidate for his foundational discipline.[3] It is still the candidate in at least the earliest strata of the *Rules*. So in Rule 4 Descartes says that he is

not thinking of vulgar mathematics [sc. arithmetic and geometry, named just above], but expounding a certain other discipline, of which these are the husk rather than parts. For this discipline must contain the first rudiments of human reason, and extend itself to extracting truths about any subject whatever; and, to speak freely, I am persuaded that this is more powerful than any other knowledge handed down by men, as the source of all the others. (AT X,374)

Although the universal discipline is not "vulgar mathematics," Descartes does not distinguish it from true or universal mathematics. Indeed, in the remainder of the Rule he describes his efforts to recover the lost mathematics of the ancients, which he contrasts with the vulgar mathematics:[4] this true mathematics was a universal mathematics treating of measure in general, "not caring whether this measure is to be found in numbers or figures or stars or sounds or any other object" (p. 378). This true mathematics has been revived in the algebra of the moderns (p. 377), which

---

[2] On the dreams and their significance, see above, Chapter 2, Section B.

[3] So, in a letter to Beeckman of March 26, 1619, Descartes speaks enthusiastically of his work on "an entirely new science, by which in general all questions can be solved which can be proposed in any genus of quantity, continuous as well as discrete" (AT X,156–7, cited above, Chapter 2, Section B); Descartes says that this art can do more than the "common algebra" (p. 156) and that it is something of a different order from the art of Lully (p. 157). Many years later, when Descartes speaks in the *Discourse* of his original 1619 discovery of his method, he is still identifying this discovery with the universal mathematics: for he speaks of his method as combining the good points of philosophical logic, the geometrical analysis of the ancients, and the algebra of the moderns (AT VI,17–18, 20); and here, as in the old letter to Beeckman, Descartes sticks in a disparaging reference to the art of Lully (AT VI,17). In both places, Descartes' discovery does not differ from the common algebra in its basic goals, but only in that it is free from the cumbersome and constraining symbolism of early algebra (of which Descartes complains at AT VI,18), since it allows a simple standard representation of any type of quantities that may occur.

[4] Since the ancient philosophers "would not admit anyone ignorant of mathematics to the study of wisdom," they must have "recognized a mathematics very different from the vulgar one of our age" (AT X,375–6).

allows problems about discrete and continuous quantities to be represented in a single formalism; here as elsewhere, Descartes' new discipline is superior to algebra only in being free of the arbitrary rules and symbols that limit the range of problems algebra can solve. Thus in Rule 4 Descartes' foundational discipline, which contains all the rudiments of human reason, is simply universal mathematics: so it seems that the only simple intelligible essence, from which a science can be elaborated, is the essence of measure or quantity as such.[5]

But of course there are serious limits on what even a universal science of quantity can do, and it cannot have been long before Descartes recognized these limits. If universal mathematics contains all the simple principles our intellect can grasp, then we will be unable to think about anything except the modes of quantity, or anyway be unable to treat anything else scientifically (perhaps all objects of our thought are combinations of pure mathematical structures with raw sense data, and the only principles we have for drawing scientific conclusions about these objects

---

[5] Jean-Paul Weber, in *La constitution du texte des Regulae* (Paris: SEDES, 1964), followed by John Schuster, in "Descartes' *Mathesis Universalis* 1619–1628" (in Stephen Gaukroger, ed., *Descartes: Philosophy, Mathematics and Physics* (Brighton: Harvester, 1980), pp. 41–96), have argued for breaking Rule 4 into two parts, Rule 4A extending up to AT X,374 line 15, and Rule 4B from p. 374 line 16 to the end of the Rule: Rule 4B is supposed to be earlier and to be about universal mathematics, Rule 4A to be an independent later document about method. Schuster's argument seems to depend heavily on an implicit use of the principle of charity: "4B describes universal mathematics as a discipline of limited scope, applicable to properly mathematical fields only," while in 4A "the scope of method 'ought to extend to eliciting true results in every subject' " (Schuster, p. 46), and (implicit premiss) Descartes cannot have been so crazy as to think that all subjects capable of being treated scientifically belonged to mathematics. But it seems that Descartes did think this. Schuster says that the universal mathematics of 4B "bears only a modest propaedeutic relation to 'higher' studies" (ibid.), and it is true that Descartes speaks (not very modestly) of this mathematics as the indispensable preparation for philosophy, since this discipline is "the easiest of all and most necessary for educating and preparing the mind for grasping other greater sciences" (AT X,375–6), and he also resolves to follow proper order in his studies, beginning with the simplest things, and therefore to cultivate universal mathematics until he is ready to go on to higher sciences (pp. 378–9). But this does not imply that there are any principles of any science other than the principles contained in universal mathematics: on the contrary, universal mathematics deals with the simplest things and is therefore first in the logical order, whereas other sciences deal with more highly compounded things, and must therefore be treated later; Descartes' warning against proceeding too quickly to the higher disciplines presupposes that universal mathematics contains the principles of these higher disciplines (cf. p. 378), and more or less implies that there are no other uncompounded objects of study besides those of universal mathematics. The early Descartes is clearly under the spell of a quasi-Pythagorean enthusiasm for the universal explanatory powers of mathematics, and we should not gloss over this enthusiasm, as Descartes himself later did. I do not see sufficient reason to doubt that the discipline contrasted with vulgar mathematics as kernel to husk at AT X,374 lines 5–7 is the same as the true mathematics contrasted with vulgar mathematics at AT X,376 line 4. As Schuster admits, much the same things are said about both disciplines, and the fact that the term "universal mathematics" is not used in 4A or "method" in 4B does not seem to imply much. The text of the *Discourse*, AT VI,17–20, cited in a previous note, makes it very difficult to separate Descartes' method of November 1619 from his universal mathematics.

are the theorems of pure mathematics). But Descartes' ambition is not simply to reconstruct and extend arithmetic and geometry, but also to develop (at least) the other traditional branches of mathematics, astronomy and music and optics and mechanics; and while these sciences certainly depend on universal mathematics, universal mathematics by itself (or with sense data added) cannot solve the problems posed in these sciences, and Descartes must find some other principles if he is not to give up on understanding the physical world. Descartes makes this point explicit in Rule 8 (probably at least seven years after Rule 4),[6] giving as his example the problem of determining the anaclastic line, a boundary curve between two media that will focus parallel incoming light rays onto a single point. If "someone who studies only mathematics" (AT X,393) were to seek for the anaclastic line, then though he might reduce the problem to determining the "proportion that the angles of refraction observe toward the angles of incidence" (p. 394), he will not be able to determine this proportion: many different laws of refraction are mathematically conceivable, and it would be a gross violation of the rules of method for the mathematician to select one arbitrarily, because it seems the simplest or most plausible hypothesis. "He is compelled to stop here at the threshold" (ibid.) and admit his ignorance; and as the heading of the Rule suggests, "we are not to examine the other things that follow, but to abstain from a vain labor" (p. 392). Thus if we are not to resign ourselves to ignorance of the laws of nature, we must discover another source of knowledge beyond the principles of mathematics. Descartes suggests that in the case of the anaclastic line, and perhaps of physical problems in general, the fundamental intuition that we need is of "what a natural power is in general" (p. 395), from which we can build up to understand the behaviors of the specific powers in question, such as "illumination." But he makes no suggestion as to how we are to acquire this intuitive knowledge of natural powers, or what its content might be.

Descartes responds to this impasse, in what seem to be the latest portions of the *Rules* (the remainder of Rule 8, which is not directly connected with the earlier part, and Rule 12), by proposing a new foundational discipline, namely a study of the human cognitive faculties and their objects. Previously it was mathematics that was the indispensable preparation for all other studies; now anyone who loves the truth must first ask, "what is human knowledge, and how far does it extend?" (p. 397). The supreme problem is "to examine all truths for the knowledge of which human reason is sufficient" (p. 395), and to do this rightly we must break the problem down into the simple elements it presupposes, namely the cognitive faculties and the simple objects they can know: by examining these, rather than hurrying "rashly to dispute about the arcana of nature" (p. 398), we will discover "the true instruments of knowing and the whole of method" (ibid.). Since the only intellectual intuition we *obviously* have is the intu-

---

[6] See Schuster, p. 58.

ition of quantity, and this is not enough, Descartes' analytic procedure dictates that we take inventory of all our instruments of knowledge: thus the impossibility of passing directly from mathematics to physics leads Descartes to install psychology as the foundational discipline.

We must begin by understanding our own intellect – "nothing can be known before the intellect, since the knowledge of all other things depends on it, and not vice versa" (p. 395) – and then take stock of the sensory faculties, sensation and imagination and (Descartes sometimes adds) memory, not because these properly *know*, but because they may help or hinder the intellect in its task of knowing. Descartes tries in Rule 12 to lay out a psychology after this fashion: but, for good reasons, he is not satisfied with this attempt. To assess our faculties in proper scientific order, Descartes must demonstrate what they are and what they do, starting from the simple natures to which they are referred, and showing how the faculties arise: "I would have wished to set out in this place what the human mind is, what the body is and how it is informed by the mind, what are the faculties in the composite whole serving for the knowledge of things, and what each of them performs" (p. 411). So if his foundations are to be scientific, Descartes should be following an order like that of St. Thomas, who, treating of God's works in the First Part of the *Summa Theologiae*, examines first the purely spiritual and then the purely corporeal creation, and only then proceeds to man who has both a spiritual and a corporeal part, beginning with the nature of the soul in itself and in relation to the body, and proceeding to the powers that are in the soul or in the composite. Descartes should discuss these same topics, providing real demonstrations and correcting Thomas' errors; but he cannot. "This place" in Rule 12 "seemed to me too narrow to contain all the things that should be set down first [or premissed] before the truth of these things can be apparent to all" (p. 411): he is only giving a set of rules for applying our faculties, and has not established proper principles for a scientific account of the mind, the human body, and the composite.

Since the project of the *Rules* does not give him the basis for demonstrating the true theory of our faculties, Descartes instead sets forward a probable account of them, which will give some basis for advising the intellect in its use of the sensory faculties. So Descartes offers (pp. 412–15) a probable mechanistic account of sensation and the "instruments of knowing" consequent upon it. Sensation occurs when a sense organ is worked into some definite shape by contact with an external object, and communicates this shape to "a certain other part of the body, which is called the common sense" (p. 414), in the same way that my hand communicates motion to my pen, and shape to the letters it forms. When the shape reaches the common sense, it can be transferred to another part of the body, the *phantasia* or imagination, the receptacle of sensory images, which is also the "memory" insofar as it preserves the images it has received. All the actions we share with other animals, i.e. all those we perform without the aid of reason, result from this chain of mechanical actions: external objects act upon the exterior senses, which act upon the common sense, which acts upon the imagination, which can act upon the limbs and other mobile organs through the medium of the nerves. But the intellect is separate from this chain of bodily organs: it is a purely spiritual power, separate from the body but connected with it, so that it can apply itself to the common sense or the imagination. When it interacts with these, it is said to sense, remember, or imagine; by these acts it can play a part in governing the body. But it also has a proper act, pure intellection unmixed with sensation, which it performs without any assistance from the bodily organs. Through this act we apprehend the simple natures and their combinations, and so can come to scientific knowledge.

After Descartes has laid out this picture of our cognitive faculties, he gives some advice on how to use them. The senses and the imagination can only represent corporeal things; they are good at this, and the intellect should make every use of them in trying to conceive these corporeal things; but the imagination and the senses can only mislead and distract the intellect when it is trying to understand something incorporeal and so without any imaginable figure. Thus we are encouraged to purify ourselves from sensory distractions when engaged on tasks of intellect alone: "lest it be impeded by them, the senses should be kept at bay, and the imagination should be stripped, so far as possible, of every distinct impression" (p. 416).

But it is doubtful how useful this advice could be. Descartes has admitted that his account of the function of the faculties is only hypothetical, and he has said, with regret, "I always desire to write in such a way that I assert nothing on the things that are customarily drawn into controversy, unless I have set down first [or premissed] those reasons that led me to it, and by which I judge that others may also be persuaded" (pp. 411–12). But Descartes' theory of intellect and the sensory powers is certain to be drawn into controversy: it will be opposed by those who do not distinguish intellect from imagination as sharply as Descartes does, not just Epicureans and the like but also Aristotelians, who believe (as St. Thomas does) that our intellect never acts except by abstracting from some image. Descartes hopes that even a hypothetical account of the faculties will serve: "do not believe, if you prefer, that things are thus; but what will prevent you from following these suppositions nonetheless, if it appears that they do not take anything away from the truth of things, but only make everything much clearer?" (p. 412). But it will not appear this way to an Epicurean or Aristotelian. If such a philosopher reads Rule 12, bringing to it all his prejudices about the nature of the soul and its acts, he will certainly not discover "the foundations of a marvelous science." To come to such a science through Rule 12, he would have to accept unproved statements opposite to what his science tells him, and on that basis would have to follow the rule of thinking without sensory images – something that he believes impossible, and does not know how to do. It appears that the Cartesian science of nature is to be founded on a method which is founded on a doctrine of the operations of the soul which is founded on the Cartesian science of nature; there is no point of entry for a person schooled "by his appetites and his teachers" in a "science" based on immersion in the senses.[7]

It was, I suggest, these difficulties that led Descartes to conclude that psychology, like universal mathematics, could not meet his criteria for a universal foundational discipline. As the crisis of universal mathematics had led Descartes to try psychology, so now the crisis of psychology leads him to try Augustine-style metaphysics, or at least disposes him to try it on Bérulle's recommendation. The new foundational discipline is still, in a way, psychology, but it is a metaphysical rather than a physical psychology. In the *Meditations*, as in the science outlined in Rule 12, Descartes begins with an understanding of the nature of the human intellect, and proceeds to an understanding of a criterion for its right and wrong use. But in Rule 12, Descartes had wanted to begin by explaining "what the human mind is, what the body is and how it is informed by the mind, what are the faculties in the composite whole serving for the knowledge of things, and what each of them performs" (AT X,411), and then from this physiological and teleological account of the faculties to derive criteria for their right use; this produces the vicious circle. In the *Meditations*, following Augustine (and ultimately Plotinus), Descartes gives an understanding of the human soul independent of any evidence of the senses, and (*a fortiori*) from any systematic account of physical things; and he derives the criterion of the cognitive faculties, not from the mind's function in its bodily environment, but from its relation to God, where the understanding of God remains independent of the senses and of physical theory, and depends only on the primitive intuition of soul. If Descartes can give in this way a purely metaphysical account of the soul and its criterion, then he can without circularity apply this criterion to derive a physical science; if he can give a discipline for withdrawing the mind from the senses, and accustom it to judge according to a purely intellectual criterion, then he can break the circle of his science and his method to appeal to his Aristotelian and other philosophical opponents.[8]

---

[7] As Descartes would have known from Cicero, Epicurus (whom Descartes takes as the extreme representative of the prejudices of the senses; cf. the *Letter to Picot*, AT IX2,6) based his epistemology on his physics, as well as justifying the physics through the epistemology: according to Epicurus, "unless we have examined the nature of things, we will not be able to defend the judgments of the senses" (Cicero *De Finibus* I,xix,64). The Epicureans also argue (according to the same passage) that any non-Epicurean physical hypothesis that denies the reliability of sensations will have abolished any possible criterion of truth and so deprived itself of any foundation; the Epicurean complex of physics and epistemology thus renders itself immune to attack. The Epicurean position nicely exposes the difficulties Descartes faces in Rule 12.

[8] Perhaps in the final stages of his work on the *Rules* Descartes was already considering this plan of argument: for in a compressed, cryptic passage of Rule 12 he hints that there are arguments, of which most people are ignorant, to support the necessary inferences "I exist, therefore God exists" and "I understand, therefore I have a mind distinct from the body"

Descartes is doing something new with the old Plotinian and Augustin-ian metaphysics, but it is something this old metaphysics is peculiarly suited for doing. Plotinus and Augustine withdraw from the senses in their accounts of the soul, and of Nous or Truth, because they are trying to avoid Stoic or Manichean corporealist imaginations of soul and God. For Plotinus, soul is ontologically prior to body, and takes its essential nature not from its relationship to body, but from its relationship to Nous; that is, it thinks, and it strives to attain to Nous as far as possible, by perceiving the Ideas contained in Nous. Because Augustine wants only to understand the soul and God, the origin of moral evil and the discipline for avoiding it, he is free to ignore Platonic physics, accepting Plotinus' discipline of contemplation and his account of the soul's relation to Nous, without his picture of soul as animating the bodily world. When Augustine turns away from body and toward the soul which judges bodies, he discovers the "eye of the mind" striving to conform itself to the standard of immutable Truth, i.e. of Nous identified with the Christian God: God is related to the soul as the source of its rules of wisdom, and moral evil is a voluntary turning away from the light which the soul receives from God, and toward which it can turn itself again. For Descartes, this discipline of turning away from the senses, and toward God as the source of truth, offers the hope of guiding ourselves by a purely intellectual divine standard, not in our practical conduct, but in the judgment of truth and falsehood. For Descartes as for Augustine, the understanding of God as Nous gives the foundation for theodicy, for an explanation of the origin of evil and a discipline for avoiding it: but where Augustine takes God as a standard for practical rightness in our actions, the source of a morality or discipline for abstaining from sin, Descartes wants to take God as a standard for theoretical rightness in our judgments, the source of a *method* or discipline for abstaining from error. For Augustine, it is new intellectual knowledge of God and the soul that shows, against the Manichees, that it is within our power to avoid sin; for Descartes, this same knowledge shows that it is within our power to avoid error.

Descartes thinks that, once we have rightly perceived the soul and God, we will be able to use divine Truth as a standard, not just for contem-plating incorporeal divine Ideas, but also for thinking about the physical world. It is the same Nous which is the source both of subjective ration-ality in souls and of objective rationality in bodies: Augustine had com-pared Truth to a fire, diffusing the heat of wisdom to rational souls, and illuminating bodies more broadly with the light of number.[9] Because both

---

(AT X,421–2). But nowhere in the *Rules* does he say what those arguments are, let alone develop them into a comprehensive foundation for science avoiding the psychophysiology of Rule 12. When he did decide to ground his scientific project by arguing through God to a new criterion of our cognitive faculties, he abandoned the framework of the *Rules* and began writing in a different form.

[9] *De Libero Arbitrio* II,xi,32, cited and discussed in Chapter 4, Section B, above. As this simile suggests, Augustine thinks that God (as Nous or Truth) is directly related to rational

kinds of rationality proceed from the same source, the same patterns, and particularly mathematical patterns, are present for souls to know and for bodies to exemplify. God is the perfect standard of knowledge, not only because he knows most perfectly the things he knows, but also because he knows everything including bodies: God knows the things in himself by being them, and he knows the things outside himself by causing them, and by knowing himself as their cause; if our knowledge of God measured up to God's knowledge of himself, we would know not only the things in God, but also the order that proceeds from God to bodies.

Descartes' scheme of deriving a science of bodies from the knowledge of God is, in a way, quite un-Plotinian, but it is a very natural application for Descartes to make of Plotinus' ideas as he has read them in Augustine. Descartes wants to connect the intellect with bodies by some third term, because he wants to establish a criterion for the truth of our ideas about the physical world, that is, for their correspondence with bodies as they really are. For Plotinus, this is not what makes our ideas true. Truth, for Plotinus (and, it often seems, for Augustine), is defined by conformity with the intelligible archetypes of things in Nous: this is the sort of Truth that God has, and is, and it is the highest I can aspire to have. If I am thinking in accord with Nous, and the sensible images of the Idea do not correspond, the fault is theirs, not mine: my thought is still true, and it is physical "reality" that has not measured up to the standard. Naturally, this attitude does not lead Plotinus to any great scientific curiosity about physical objects, except as the environment our souls must rise above. But for Descartes, it is a physical science that will lead us to wisdom, if metaphysics can first lead us to this science; it is physical reality that imposes a standard on our thoughts about the world, that makes them true or false as they correspond or disagree, that sets the task for science. Descartes therefore takes Plotinus' doctrine – bodies can conform to the standard of reason insofar as Nous establishes its mastery over them – and uses it to answer his own concerns: reason can conform to the standard of physical reality, insofar as this physical reality is subject to the control of Nous.

The *Meditations* (or their first version, the lost metaphysics of 1629–30) result from Descartes' attempt to achieve the goals of the *Rules* with the help of the intellectual material newly come to his attention as a possible foundation for science. Descartes speaks as if his early work were merely a preparation for constructive studies in metaphysics and then in physics, and he even describes the *Meditations* as an application to questions of God and the soul of the "method that I had cultivated for resolving each and every difficulty in the sciences" (AT VII,3). But what Descartes had had (outside pure mathematics) was more a hope than a determinate method; it is a mistake to suppose that the *Meditations* merely add new

souls in one way, and directly related to bodies in another way; whereas for Plotinus Nous is related to bodies only indirectly, through souls that participate in Nous and so govern bodies rationally.

doctrine to results Descartes had already established, a still worse mistake to conclude (with Gilson) that Descartes imposed an alien form on Augustine's metaphysics by subjecting it to the constraints of "the mathematical method."[10] The procedure of the *Meditations* for turning away from the senses, toward the rational soul, and toward God, is derived from Augustine, so far as it is derived from anywhere: to the extent that it is not Augustinian, it comes from the necessity of *isolating* soul-and-God as the foundation of all knowledge. The most obvious novelty of the *Meditations*, beyond Augustine and beyond the *Rules*, is the radical doubt of the first Meditation; this doubt cannot be explained by a mechanical mixture of Augustine and the *Rules*, but it can be explained by Descartes' project of making the knowledge of God and the soul the foundation of all the sciences, and therefore of making this knowledge strictly prior to all other knowledge, especially sensory knowledge. Augustine must withdraw his mind from sensory images because the senses cannot picture a non-extended God; he must also recognize that the senses do not suffice for knowledge until they are judged by reason; but he does not have to doubt the main lines of what the senses suggest about the world of bodies. But since Descartes wants to remake not his actions but his judgments, including his judgments about bodies, he must eliminate all sensory prejudice, whether about God or about anything else: any prior acceptance of sensory imaginations would compromise the process of reconstructing the sciences. Since Descartes is trying not merely to understand God as the standard of truth, but to *isolate* God as the standard of truth, he must not only purge his idea of God of anything beyond the pure concept of Nous, but also eliminate from all his judgments anything that is not appropriately related to this divine standard.

In the remainder of this chapter I will try to show how Descartes conceives the function of the first Meditation, and how he constructs its detailed arguments to support the overall project of the *Meditations*. The first Meditation is designed to overcome the impasses of the *Rules*, and its argument is directed in an important way against the *Rules*. A careful reading of the first Meditation will show that Descartes is not concerned with any new sceptical crisis, to which the metaphysics of subsequent Meditations would be a response: on the contrary, the arguments of the first Meditation are specifically tailored to support the subsequent Meditations, by proving that only the metaphysics of soul and Nous can give the foundation for science; Descartes argues, in particular, that mathematics, or the study of the cognitive powers and their simple objects, cannot fulfill this function. After showing, in this chapter, how Descartes argues that Augustinian metaphysics is necessary as a foundation for science, I will in subsequent chapters examine Descartes' argument that this metaphysics is available and sufficient for establishing the sciences: in

---

[10] So Gilson, *Etudes sur le rôle de la pensée médiévale dans la formation du système cartésien*, p. 199–201, discussed in Chapter 1 above.

Chapter 6 I will examine the metaphysics of the second and third Meditations, in Chapter 7 the theodicy of the fourth Meditation, in Chapter 8 Descartes' attempt, in the two last Meditations and Part Two of the *Principles*, to derive the principles of physics from this metaphysics and theodicy. In each case I will argue that Descartes' text is the direct and almost necessary result of his project of establishing the sciences on the Augustinian metaphysics; and I will try my best to bring out the original appeal of this eccentric-looking project.

B. The uses of scepticism: withdrawing the mind from the senses

The first Meditation argues negatively that God and the soul are better known than bodies, since we cannot know bodies without first knowing God and the soul. Descartes sets out "the causes on account of which we are able to doubt about all things, especially material things: so long, that is, as we do not have other foundations for the sciences than those we have had hitherto";[11] and, implicitly, he isolates what these foundations must be if they are to overcome the reasons for doubting. Descartes does not invent these reasons for doubting for himself, but borrows them from the people most interested in constructing reasons for doubting, the sceptics: arguments from madness, dreams, and deceiving gods are commonplaces of ancient scepticism, and Descartes seems to have taken them from the most popular sourcebook, Cicero's *Academica*. Descartes anticipates, correctly, that his readers will charge him with reissuing well-known material:[12] he replies that

since nothing contributes more to attaining a sound knowledge of things than that we should first accustom ourselves to doubt all things, especially corporeal things, even though I had previously seen many books about this subject written by the

[11] From Descartes' description of the first *Meditation* in the *Synopsis* of the *Meditations*, AT VII,12.

[12] Descartes gets worried when the Second Objectors raise some very innocent cautions about the limits of the argument of the first two Meditations. He says, "I see what you are hinting at," namely that Descartes' readers, seeing how little he accomplishes in the first two Meditations, will conclude that the *Meditations* as a whole "are very meager, and unworthy of the public gaze" (AT VII,130); and so Descartes gives a preemptive defense of his rehearsing of the old sceptical arguments. Sure enough, Hobbes in the third Objections expresses regret "since Plato and other ancient philosophers have disputed concerning this same uncertainty of sensible things, and the difficulty of distinguishing waking from dreams is commonly observed, I would not want the excellent author of new speculations to publish these old things" (AT VII,171). Descartes replies that he was not using these arguments "in order to retail them as new" (ibid.), and again defends the utility of considering such arguments. I will discuss Descartes' defenses in the text. (In citing "Plato and other ancient philosophers," Hobbes is thinking, not only of the general Platonic theme of the unreliability of the senses, but also of the passage in the *Theaetetus* (157e–158e) where Plato uses the examples of dreamers and madmen to argue against the criterion of the senses. Perhaps, too, Hobbes accepts the New Academy's sceptical interpretation of Plato, as he would have found it in Cicero.)

Academics and sceptics, and though I could not reheat that old cabbage without distaste, yet I could not do otherwise than to devote a whole Meditation to it. (AT VII,130)

Descartes hopes to make better use of the old cabbage than Montaigne and other humanists were doing. These thinkers, disillusioned with scholasticism and despairing of any new philosophy, have resigned themselves to doing without science altogether, and so their attacks on scholastic claims of knowledge, while intense, are not very discriminating: since there is no knowledge they want to save, they have no interest in assessing how much each sceptical argument proves, and they simply follow rhetorical technique, amassing without discrimination all the arguments they can discover against knowledge.[13] The opening of the first Meditation brings out the contrast between Descartes and Montaigne or Charron: like them, he has "recognized how many false things I had accepted as true at the beginning of my life, and how doubtful are all the things I have since constructed upon them"; unlike these thinkers, Descartes "desires sometime to establish something firm and lasting in the sciences," and therefore decides that "once in my life I ought to overthrow all [my opinions] down to the bottom, and begin anew from the first foundations" (AT VII,17). So Descartes will use the sceptical arguments, not merely to overthrow old prejudices, but to assess precisely what constraints these arguments impose on knowledge. The first Meditation is titled "on what we can call into doubt," and uses the sceptical arguments to assess the extent of our power for doubting: if X (which we habitually accept without doubting) turns out to be doubtful, while Y remains immune to doubt, then Y will be a possible foundation for the sciences, and X will not. Again, a sceptical argument against our knowledge of X, even if it does not really prove "we cannot know X," may succeed in proving the conditional "we cannot know X if we do not know Y": this shows that Y is prior to X in the scientific order, and suggests that we should first establish Y, then seek to reestablish X on this new foundation.[14]

The Meditator's call for overthrowing his opinions "once in my life" [*semel in vita*] recalls Rule 8, where the seekers of truth are asked *semel in vita* to investigate the question "what is human knowledge, and how far does it extend?"[15] Descartes is now carrying out, by a new method, the

[13] For the contrast between Descartes and such humanists as Charron, see Chapter 2 above.
[14] For example, let X be "stones tend to fall toward the center of the earth" or "I have a body," and let Y be "I have a mind" or "I am the creature of a wise and powerful creator." Recall Descartes' statement in the *Synopsis* that the sole aim of the *Meditations* was to show that the reasons that prove "that there really is a world, that men have bodies, and the like, which no one of sound mind has ever seriously doubted," are "neither as firm nor as clear as those by which we come to a knowledge of our own mind and of God" (AT VII,16). Similarly, Descartes tells Mersenne that "the principal aim of my *Metaphysics* [i.e. the *Meditations*] is to show which are the things that can be perceived distinctly" (AT III,192).
[15] This quoted from AT X,397–8; but Descartes had said essentially the same thing on p.

investigation called for in Rules 8 and 12, and, in establishing claims of the form "we cannot know X unless we first know Y," he is carrying out the analytic project of tracing derivative objects of knowledge back to the primitive objects they presuppose. But Descartes now gives a new list of primitive intuitions as the foundations of his science: we still need an intuition of quantity, but the intuitions of the soul and God are deductively prior, and Descartes argues, in the first Meditation and after, that we need these intuitions in order to have scientific knowledge of anything else. Thus while some of the arguments of the first Meditation are consistent with the *Rules*, and show only the priority of mathematics (and perhaps psychology) over physics, others show, contrary to the *Rules*, that metaphysics is prior to all other sciences.[16] Descartes starts by presenting the easier arguments, turning on less radical reasons for doubt, that lead the Meditator to something like the position of Rule 12; he then turns to the more radical sceptical arguments, leading to the conclusion that only God is the source of truth, and that the Augustinian knowledge of God and the soul is the only possible foundation for science. I will discuss the first family of arguments in the present section, and the second in Section C.

So far I have been speaking of the function of the first Meditation in establishing the priority of some *cognitiones* over others. But it has an equally important function, not in establishing theses, but in instilling a certain discipline of thought. Descartes says in the Synopsis that the first Meditation has great utility in "freeing us from all prejudices, and clearing a most easy way for withdrawing the mind from the senses [*ad mentem a sensibus abducendam*]" (AT VII,12); in the second Replies he claims personal credit for this discovery, saying that "although many people have said before that the mind must be withdrawn from the senses to understand metaphysical things [*mentem a sensibus esse abducendam*], yet as far as I know no one up to now has shown how this can be done," but that

---

395, and then again on pp. 396–7; in each of the three parallel passages Descartes uses the catchphrase *semel in vita*.

[16] While Rule 2 says that arithmetic and geometry are "the easiest and clearest of all [disciplines], and have the kind of object we are seeking, since in them, apart from inadvertence, it scarcely seems human to be deceived" (AT X,365), and that "those who seek the straight path of truth ought not to occupy themselves with any object about which they cannot have a certainty equal to arithmetical and geometrical demonstrations" (p. 366), the *Meditations* promise a knowledge that is *more* certain than mathematics, and argue "that the certainty of geometrical demonstrations themselves depends on the knowledge of God" (AT VII,15). The sceptical arguments of the first Meditation lead first to the conclusion of Rule 2, that arithmetic and geometry, "which deal only with the simplest and most general things," are certain, while physics and other sciences of complex things are not (AT VII,20); Descartes then adduces further sceptical arguments to undermine the certainty of the mathematical sciences, and to show that they depend on knowledge of God and the soul. I go on below to discuss these stages of the argument of the first Meditation, and their relation to the position of the *Rules*.

he himself has found "a true way, and in my judgment the *only* way, to achieve this" (AT VII,131).[17] Descartes himself had been one of the "many" who had exhorted us to withdraw our minds from the senses, for he had said in Rule 12 that when the intellect "is concerned with things in which there is nothing corporeal or like the corporeal . . . the senses should be kept at bay, and the imagination should be stripped, so far as possible, of every distinct impression" (AT X,416). At the time of Rule 12, Descartes had not discovered how to achieve this separation from the senses: and so the psychology of Rule 12, although it is supposed to be foundational for physics and to give directions for using the senses, does not proceed from a standpoint independent of the senses and of physical theory. In the *Meditations*, Descartes thinks he has discovered a way to break the circle of Rule 12, and to give an account of the soul, and of the criteria of its cognitive faculties, that does not depend on any prior acceptance of sensory evidence. But it is not enough to give a verbal account of the soul without explicit reliance on the senses: Descartes must not merely speak but *think*, and induce his readers to think, these metaphysical things, without any coloring by the prejudices of the senses, or the senses will improperly influence the scientific system that results. The sceptical arguments against our knowledge of material things give Descartes the required discipline of contemplating the soul and God, not just "by the intellect" (as Augustine had shown how to do) but "by the intellect *alone*": for when, by repeated use of the sceptical arguments, we are habituated to doubt (or even to deny) all material things, we will still retain *cognitiones* of ourselves and of God, and these *cognitiones* will have been purified from all sensory contamination. If these *cognitiones* are certain in themselves,

---

[17] When Descartes speaks of his method *ad mentem a sensibus abducendam* (AT VII,12), or says that many have said before now *mentem a sensibus esse abducendam* to understand metaphysical things (AT VII,131), he is referring to Cicero's declaration at *Tusculan Disputations* I,xvi,38, *"magni autem est ingenii sevocare mentem a sensibus et cogitationem ab consuetudine abducere"*; as I have noted above (in a note to Chapter 4, Section A), Augustine alludes to this same passage of Cicero in describing his ascent to God at *Confessions* VII,xvii,23, although Descartes' use of the Cicero passage is apparently independent of Augustine's. When Descartes speaks at AT VII,131 of the "many" who have said this in the past, he surely intends his readers to recognize the reference to Cicero; but for the last several centuries, apparently no one has (Henri Gouhier, *La pensée métaphysique de Descartes* (Paris: Vrin, 1962), p. 52, correctly describes Descartes' phrase *abducere mentem a sensibus* as a *"consigne* [watchword] *de style platonicien,"* but does not notice the source in Cicero). As noted above (in the note to Chapter 4, Section A), both Augustine and Descartes are much more serious than Cicero had been (in this passage of the *Tusculans* and elsewhere) about the Platonist project of *abducere mentem a sensibus*. At AT VII,12 Descartes ascribes this effect to the *first* Meditation, while at AT VII,131 he ascribes it to the *second* Meditation; but the reference is in either case to the same process, the mind's discovery of its freedom to doubt all sensible things, which allows us (as Descartes says at AT VII,131 and again at AT VII,172) to purify our intellectual conceptions of the soul and of God. I will return in Chapter 6, Section A, to discuss how the second Meditation furthers the process of *abducere mentem a sensibus*.

and sufficient to give a criterion for the use of our faculties, then they will give the desired foundation for the sciences, and it will be possible to defeat at least some of the reasons for doubting material things.

The first Meditation describes a condition Descartes is seeking to overcome: defending himself to Hobbes, Descartes says that he could not omit the recitation of the sceptical arguments "any more than a writer on medicine could omit a description of a disease, if he were trying to teach a method of curing it" (AT VII,172). The disease Descartes is here intending to cure is not the sceptical view that all our customary judgments are uncertain: it is the objective uncertainty of our customary judgments, which philosophical scepticism merely recognizes.[18] If we are to cure this disease, and establish a rule of judgment that will not be liable to doubt, we must begin by describing the full extent of the doubtfulness infecting

[18] Thus Descartes tells Bourdin at AT VII,549–50 that the charge of "scepticism" or excessive doubt applies not to Descartes, but rather to everyone else, since it is other people who have not established any rule of certainty in their judgments. This passage of the seventh Replies is instructive for the sense in which Descartes sets out to "refute scepticism" in the *Meditations*. The *Letter to Picot*, in its survey of the history of philosophy, speaks dismissively of scepticism ("the error of those who inclined too much to the side of doubt was not followed for long," AT IX2,7); the *Principles* (which the *Letter to Picot* is introducing) are supposed to overcome, not serious philosophical scepticism, but Charronian humanist "scepticism" about the practical value of obvious theoretical truths. The *Meditations*, which do not approach the practical disciplines, do not help answer this kind of scepticism; but Descartes tells Bourdin that he has refuted scepticism in another sense. Bourdin (AT VII,530–1) had challenged the utility of trying to demonstrate truths about God and the soul with as much certainty as facts about numbers or about our own bodies. So Descartes replies that if Bourdin gives up the project of demonstrating the truths of natural theology, he will be unable to refute the sceptics; and Descartes warns Bourdin that "it is not to be thought that their [the sceptics'] sect is yet extinct"; indeed, it "flourishes today more than ever, and almost all the people who think that they have some more intelligence than others, finding nothing in the common philosophy [i.e. scholastic Aristotelianism] to satisfy them, and not seeing any other that is truer, defect to the sceptical philosophy" (pp. 548–9). (Compare the complaint of the *Letter to Picot* that "most of the best minds have conceived such a bad opinion of all philosophy, because of the faults they have noticed in the one that has been current until now, that they will be unable to apply themselves to searching for a better one," AT IX2,20.) In the seventh Replies, as in the *Letter to Picot*, Descartes distinguishes these moderns from the rigorous ancient sceptics, who are extinct; and Descartes thinks he must argue against them, not *quod aliquid scitur*, but that God and the soul are the proper starting-point of our knowledge. Thus in the seventh Replies Descartes says that "*omnes hodierni sceptici*" – as opposed to Descartes' caricature of the ancient sceptics – "do not doubt in practice whether they have a head, whether 2 and 3 are 5, and the like" (AT VII,549). Rather, lacking proof, they accept the *appearances* of these things. "And because it does not appear to them in the same way that God exists, or that the human mind is immortal, they do not think that these should be taken in practice as true, unless these should first be proved to them by reasons more certain than any of those on account of which they embrace all the appearances" (ibid.). The modern sceptics whom Descartes is opposing in the *Meditations* are thus the "libertines" or practical atheists, and Descartes presents his argument against them as a defense, not of the certainty of our knowledge, but of the greater certainty of our knowledge of God compared to the rest of our knowledge (cp. the Synopsis of the *Meditations*, AT VII,15–16, on the utility of the sixth-Meditation proof of the existence of bodies, discussed above, Chapter 2, Section C).

our habitual judgments, so that we can learn to withhold assent from all the doubtful judgments; and the only way to recognize the doubtfulness of our judgments is to discover reasons for doubting them. Descartes proposes to "attack immediately the very principles on which rested everything I had previously believed" (first Meditation, AT VII,18); everything else will then be shown up as doubtful, and will collapse of itself. By "principles" Descartes means, not exactly propositions from which we had deduced others, but criteria or rules we had used for passing judgment. Descartes will call our judgments into doubt by arguing that these criteria are insufficient to generate knowledge, and he will argue for this by showing how these criteria might lead us to assent to a false proposition: if one judgment that criterion C has led or could lead me to accept is false, then every judgment that relies entirely on criterion C is doubtful, and I do not have *scientia* of it, until I can establish it on some other foundation. The ancient Academics and Pyrrhonists gave arguments against the existence of a criterion of truth, and Descartes is happy to borrow their arguments in undermining all the *usual* criteria.

Descartes starts by attacking sensation. The Meditator, as Descartes initially finds him, is entirely dependent on the senses: "whatever I have hitherto accepted as most true I have received either from the senses or through the senses" (AT VII,18) – either he has judged for himself in according with his senses, or he has accepted the authority of his teachers as a criterion, and he relies on sensation to know what his teachers have said.[19] So if the reliability of sensation as a criterion can be undermined, there will be nothing left that the Meditator is inclined to assent to, and he will be freed to consider the genuine first principles of knowledge.

The initial argument against the senses is simply that we have caught them deceiving us in the past, "and it is but prudent never to trust fully in those who have deceived us even once" (AT VII,18). But this argument is not by itself sufficient to induce the universal doubt of the senses Descartes desires. The natural impulse of "healthy common sense" is to defend itself against threats to the status of its knowledge, and so to preserve as far as possible its habitual patterns of assent. The Meditator of the first Meditation is always shown following out this impulse of healthy common sense, and then being checked by new sceptical arguments, so that this Meditation (and much of its sequel) becomes a virtual dialogue between the philosopher and a naive representative of common sense; and in his unfinished dialogue the *Search after Truth*, which was to parallel the *Med-*

---

[19] In the *Conversation with Burman* (AT V,146), Descartes glosses the phrases "from the senses" [*a sensibus*] and "through the senses" [*per sensus*] as follows: "*a sensibus*, that is, by sight, by which I have perceived colors and shapes and all such things; but besides that I received the remaining things *per sensus*, that is, through hearing, for in this way did I receive and take in from parents and teachers [*praeceptoribus*] and other people those things which I know." Especially the mention of our teachers [*praeceptores*] makes inevitable the assimilation to the childish state of the *Discourse on Method* (AT VI,13), in which we are "governed by our appetites and our teachers [*précepteurs*]."

itations, Descartes actually incarnates the standpoint of healthy common sense in the "gentleman" [*honneste homme*] Poliandre, shown in conversation with Descartes' spokesman Eudoxe and the scholastic Epistemon.[20] We can distinguish two successive defenses of common sense, both of which Descartes will try to undermine: first, the errors of the senses are small, so the senses are reliable for the most part and on any large question; second, although we can imagine abnormal scenarios in which the senses would produce very large errors, I as a normal healthy person in a normal healthy environment am not deceived in this way, and the errors that would result from unhealthy situations do not undermine the status of my own healthy *cognitiones* as *scientia*.

The Meditator of the first Meditation is sitting by the fire, and he continues to believe that he *knows* he is sitting by the fire, even after the errors of the senses are called to his attention. The known errors of the senses have occurred when we were examining something small or distant, and so not well proportioned to our natural power of sensation. The framework provided by our grosser sensory perceptions (such as that of our own body before the fire) remains unshaken, and (the Meditator would suggest) we can use this framework to detect the circumstances where error is likely, by noting the proportions between ourselves and the object we are observing, or any other factor that could affect the accuracy of our perception: to guard against error, we can construct a system of rules for assuring the certainty of a sensory perception.[21] To undermine this defense, Descartes must show that the self-correction of the senses does not guarantee truth; to do this, he suggests the possibility of a deception of the senses too large to be detected or corrected, which could affect even the apparently "safe" part of our sensory perceptions.

The Meditator of the first Meditation, and Poliandre in the *Search after Truth*, while they cannot deny that such gross deceptions of the senses

---

[20] The *Search after Truth* announces itself from the beginning (AT X,495) as showing what an "*honneste homme*" can learn by his unaided natural reason, "without calling in the help of either religion or philosophy." Descartes' spokesman Eudoxe, in conversation with the unschooled *honneste homme* Poliandre, tries to bring Poliandre to awareness of what he can know by necessary inferences from the simple notions that are within him (pp. 496–7, 503; note "*honneste homme*" again on p. 503), and in particular to make him perceive truths about God and the soul more clearly than he perceives sensible things (p. 510). While Eudoxe must resolve Poliandre's "natural" impulses to resist his argument, Poliandre is much easier to bring to distinct knowledge than Epistemon, who has been spoiled by his scholastic education (and who is vainly begged to interrupt as little as possible, p. 504); Descartes hopes that his readers will identify themselves with Poliandre, and will find Cartesian education more accessible and promising than the scholastic education they have missed or rejected. Descartes is presumably influenced by Galileo's *Dialogue on the Two Chief World Systems* in presenting his philosophy, in the vernacular for a broad readership, in a dialogue between a spokesman for the true philosophy (Eudoxe = Salviati), a scholastic (Epistemon = Simplicio), and an eager but untrained gentleman (Poliandre =Sagredo).

[21] In this spirit, Cicero's character Lucullus tries to list sufficient conditions for the clarity and certainty of the senses, *Academica* II,vii,19.

sometimes occur, try to insulate their own healthy commonsense *cognitiones* from these abnormal cases of deception. The Meditator thinks he could not deny that "these hands and this whole body are mine . . . unless perchance I compared myself to I-know-not-what madmen, whose brains are so corrupted by the overpowering vapor of black bile that they constantly assert that they are kings, when they are very poor, or that they are clothed in purple, when they are naked, or that they are gourds, or that they are made of glass" (AT VII,18–19);[22] and he refuses to make this comparison, since "these people are mad, and I would seem no less mad myself, if I took from them any model for myself" (p. 19).

The Meditator's restriction of gross errors to madmen, and his refusal to see any likeness between ourselves and them, proceed from the healthy common sense Descartes is seeking to undermine. This is made especially clear by the parallel passage in the *Search after Truth*. Poliandre has said that sensible things are the most certain and knowable of all; Eudoxe undertakes to make him see God and the soul more clearly than he sees these sensible things, and begins by pointing out the known deceptions of the senses. But Poliandre replies that the senses deceive only in special circumstances, "when they are not acting freely according to the constitution of their nature" (AT X,510): these circumstances are easily recognized, and do not make us any less certain about the gross features of our present environment. Eudoxe considers out loud whether he might ask Poliandre "if you have never seen these melancholic men, who think that they are gourds, or that some part of their body is of enormous size; they will swear that they see and touch it as they imagine" (AT X,511). Eudoxe decides not to ask so pointed a question, for "it would give offence to a gentleman to tell him that he could have no more reason than they to be certain of what he believes, since he relies, like them, on what the senses and his imagination represent to him" (ibid.). Indeed, the Meditator of the first Meditation does take offence in just this way: "but these people are mad, and I would appear no less mad myself, if I took from them any model for myself." The voice of the "gentleman" or of healthy common sense protests against the assimilation of healthy to diseased constitutions, and asserts that a healthy constitution will suffice as a criterion of truth.[23]

---

[22] "Madmen" here are *insani*: the word has the connotation "sick," and the Meditator is conceiving these people as unhealthy specimens, their mental errors arising from a diseased constitution of the body. While Descartes does not himself believe in the theory of melancholy, or of the humors generally, he uses it both here and in the *Search after Truth* to express the popular conception of madness. Believing oneself to be a gourd – an earthenware vessel, not a vegetable – is a classic symptom of extreme melancholy; see Rufus of Ephesus, cited by Raymond Klibansky, Erwin Panofsky, and Fritz Saxl, *Saturn and Melancholy* (London: Nelson, 1964), pp. 50–1 (the symptom apparently arises from the "earthy dryness and coldness" of black bile). The words translated by "mad" in the phrase cited immediately below are *amens* and *demens*, "out of one's mind," indicating a mental rather than a physical condition.

[23] Descartes probably takes, as his model for "healthy" resistance to arguments from madness, dreams, and the like, Cicero's character Lucullus in *Academica* II,xvi,51–xvii,53.

The subsequent arguments are Descartes' means for overcoming this resistance, and showing that the healthy gentleman and the melancholic madman are in much the same condition with respect to *scientia*.

Both in the *Meditations* and in the *Search after Truth*, Descartes replies ironically to the naive insistence that we are something very different from the madmen:

> This is splendidly clear, to be sure: as if I were not a man, and in the habit of sleeping at night, and experiencing in dreams all the same things that these people do in waking, and sometimes things even less probable. Indeed, how often does my nightly rest persuade me of these familiar things, that I am here, wearing my clothes, sitting by the fire, when in fact I have taken off my clothes and am lying under the covers! (First Meditation, AT VII,19)

Again the natural man attempts to resist the conclusion that his sensory powers may be deceiving him in so radical a way: if I cannot maintain that such deception happens only to other people, at least I can be sure that it is not happening to me *at this moment*: "surely now I am looking at this paper with waking eyes, this head that I am turning is not asleep, I stretch and feel this hand consciously and deliberately; these things would not occur so distinctly to a sleeper" (ibid.). But again Descartes undermines this distinction with a sweeping sarcasm:

> As if I did not remember that I had at previous times been deluded by similar thoughts in my dreams; when I think more attentively about these things, I see that there can never be any certain signs by which waking could be distinguished from sleep – I see this so plainly that I am bewildered [*obstupescam*], and this very bewilderment [*stupor*] nearly convinces me that I *am* asleep. (Ibid.)

As we cannot say that gross deceptions of the senses happen only to madmen and not to us, so neither can we maintain that they happen only to us when asleep and not to us now: in fact, as Eudoxe suggests, the gentleman "can have no more reason than [the madmen] to be certain of what he believes, since he relies, like them, on what the senses and his imagination represent to him"; or, as the first Meditation put it, we in our current bewilderment show all the symptoms of being asleep.

Descartes has often been misinterpreted here. He is not concerned that we might, at this moment, be lying in bed asleep; he is concerned that, even though we are up and about, with regard to the status of our knowledge we might as well be asleep.[24] As Descartes poses the question in the

---

Lucullus is almost certainly Descartes' model for resistance to the theological argument for doubt: see Section C below.

[24] So, rightly, Margaret Wilson, *Descartes* (London: Routledge and Kegan Paul, 1978), pp. 22ff. As Descartes puts it in the *Discourse*, "considering that all the same thoughts that we have when awake can also come to us while we sleep, without any of them being true, I resolved to pretend that all things that had ever come into my mind were no truer than the illusions of my dreams" (AT VI,32). Note, for comparison, that while Plato at *Theaetetus* 158b–c asks how we can know whether we are presently waking or dreaming, at 158d–e he moves on to ask whether we have reason to think that our waking beliefs are

Search after Truth, "have you never heard in the comedies this expression of bewilderment [*étonnement*], 'am I awake or asleep'? How can you be certain that your life is not a continual dream, and that everything you think you are learning through your senses is false, now as well as when you are sleeping?" (AT X,511). The words I have translated as "bewilderment," *stupor* in Latin and *étonnement* in French, refer to a feeling of confusion and lack of control: this is a symptom that one is dreaming.[25] Characters in the comedies, when events confound their beliefs and expectations (as when they see someone they had believed dead), become bewildered, and begin to suspect that they are dreaming; and so does the Meditator, when the argument from dreaming confounds the beliefs he has acquired through the senses. But while characters in the comedies are going too far when they suspect that they are dreaming, the Meditator is just beginning to recognize his true condition. Indeed, at the end of the first Meditation he must struggle against the force of habit to maintain his separation from the senses: for

just as when a prisoner, who may have enjoyed an imaginary freedom in his dreams, begins afterwards to suspect that he is sleeping, he is afraid of being awakened, and conspires lazily with pleasant illusions: so I readily fall back into my old opinions, and am afraid to be awakened, lest afterwards, following upon my easy sleep, I must spend a toilsome waking, not in any light, but in the inextricable darkness of the difficulties that have now been raised. (AT VII,23)

Again in the second Meditation Descartes compares our habitual condition to sleep: when the Meditator has recognized that he himself must exist, but that "all these images, and generally whatever is ascribed to the nature of body, may be nothing but dreams," he must resist the temptation to fall back on the imagination to picture what he himself might be, since

having recognized these things, I would appear no less foolish to say "I will imagine, that I may learn more distinctly what I am," than if I said, "though I am now awake, and see something true, yet because I do not now see it evidently enough, I will purposely fall asleep, that my dreams may represent this to me more truly and evidently." (AT VII,28)

Descartes' point in these passages is that our habitual condition is, with regard to *scientia*, much the same as the condition of a dreamer, because it is characteristic of a dreamer that he "relies on what the senses and his imagination represent to him" (as the *Search after Truth* says of both the gentleman and the madman). Descartes does not deny that our sensory

any truer than our dreaming beliefs; it is the latter question that Aristotle discusses at *Metaphysics* IV,5 1010b3–11.

[25] Descartes intends the *étonnement* of the *Search after Truth* as equivalent to the *stupor* of the *Meditations*, and the French version of the *Meditations* translates *stupor* by *étonnement*. It is difficult to render these words in English: the most obvious word, "astonishment," seems too weak in modern English to bring out the sense. Cottingham, Stoothoff, and Murdoch use "daze."

faculties function differently when we are awake and when we are asleep: but the difference primarily affects our practical ability to respond to stimuli for our biological self-preservation, and does not change the status of sense and imagination as essentially non-rational faculties. When Descartes reassures us in the *Discourse* that "the reveries we imagine when asleep should not in any way make us doubt the truth of the thoughts we have when awake" (AT VI,39), his reason is, disconcertingly, that waking and dreaming are much the same: distinct intellectual perceptions are sound in either condition; and as for "the most ordinary error of our dreams, which consists in their representing various objects to us in the same way our external senses do," the truth is that sensory ideas deceive in much the same way whether we are asleep or awake, so that "whether we are awake or asleep, we must never let ourselves be persuaded except by the evidence of our reason: our reason, I say, and not our imagination or our senses" (ibid.).[26]

These considerations about dreaming and waking help to show the function of abnormal scenarios in Descartes' arguments against non-rational criteria of truth. When we recognize how closely dreams can mimic the apparent clarity of our waking perceptions, we also recognize that our waking perceptions are not genuinely clear, that they are dream-like. The abnormal scenarios point up the fact that our habitual criteria (such as the force with which a perception strikes our senses) are not sufficient for *scientia*. Descartes is not seriously worried that we might now be in such an abnormal scenario, but it is a useful exercise to proceed as if we were, in order to free ourselves from our habitual criteria of judgment, and to isolate a genuinely sufficient criterion of truth. Descartes wants us to recognize that, since our sensations arise from a bodily constitution which is not rational by its essence, they may yield falsehood as easily as truth; he wants ultimately to argue that we can have confidence in our judgments only when we derive these judgments from a source

---

[26] In the sixth Meditation, however, Descartes restores some cognitive value to sensation, and there he both gives some (rough-and-ready) rules for distinguishing waking from dreaming sensations (AT VII,89), and, more important, explains why and in what sense normal (healthy waking) sensations are superior to abnormal (diseased or dreaming) sensations (pp. 87–9). While sensation has no direct theoretical value (does not show us the natures of things), it has a practical value in guiding our use of the body so as to preserve ourselves as a mind–body union; and it has an indirect theoretical value in that we can make some inferences about what the bodies around us must be like in order for sensation to be practically valuable. For sensation to be practically valuable, there has to be some (intrinsically arbitrary) correlation between our sensations and the characteristics of the bodies around us. However, this correlation is not absolute, but only for the most part. So, just because normal sensations are more common than abnormal sensations (or, at least, more common than any particular *type* of abnormal sensation), it is normal sensations that allow us to make inferences about the characteristics of the bodies around us. Normal sensations are still not intrinsically *truer* than abnormal ones, and their numerical superiority could not be a proof that they present the true natures of things to us any more than the abnormal ones do. See discussion below, Chapter 8, Section C.

which is intrinsically rational, and supplies rationality to us – that is, from God understood as Nous.

But Descartes does not suppose that the argument from dreaming establishes this ultimate conclusion. Thus far he claims only to have found the procedure, desired but not yet found in Rule 12, for withdrawing the mind from the senses in conceiving incorporeal things, and for bracketing all physical theory in investigating our cognitive faculties and their objects. This may show that a non-physical science is prior to physics, but it has not yet specified this prior science as theology. Indeed, Descartes deliberately designs this stage of the argument to lead, not to his ultimate position, but to the position of the *Rules*, which he will undermine next. He represents the Meditator as concluding that, even if we are mistaken about the most basic of sensible things, still "at least [the most] simple and universal things are true, from which, as from true colors, are formed all these images of things, whether true or false, that we have in our thoughts" (AT VII,20): this is the same as the assertion of Rule 12 that "the simple natures are all known *per se*, and never contain any falsity" (AT X,420), deception arising only when these are wrongly combined. The Meditator infers, as Descartes had inferred in the *Rules*, that "arithmetic and geometry are far more certain than the other disciplines, because only these are concerned with an object so pure and simple that they presuppose nothing that experience would render uncertain, but consist entirely in rationally deducing consequences" (Rule 2, AT X,365): so now the Meditator suggests that

although physics, astronomy, medicine, and all other disciplines that depend on the consideration of composite things, are doubtful, yet arithmetic, geometry, and other disciplines of this kind, which treat only of the simplest and most general things, and do not care whether these things exist in nature or not, contain something certain and undoubted. (AT VII,20)

But this conclusion does not really follow from the claim that there is no falsity in simple intelligible natures: it all depends what these simple intelligible natures turn out to be. The Meditator tries, like Descartes in the *Rules*, to take inventory of these natures: "corporeal nature in general, and its extension, *seem* to be of this kind; also the figure of extended things, also quantity, or their size and number, also the place in which they exist, the time through which they endure, and the like" (AT VII,20). The problem is that there is nothing to back up this "seeming." The use of sceptical arguments against the senses will allow Descartes in the second Meditation to isolate a secure knowledge of the cognitive faculties, derived from introspection and independent of sensation or physical theory; but this knowledge, without the surrounding psychophysiology of Rule 12, is too weak to give a criterion of the faculties, or a list of the objects to which they should be applied. Descartes' subsequent argument aims to show that only a knowledge of God, and only a special kind of knowledge of God, can break the circle to give the appropriate criterion: only the Augustinian psychotheology, not psychophysiology and not mathematics, can give the foundations of the sciences.

C. The uses of scepticism: why only God is the source of truth

In order to establish that a knowledge of God is the only possible foundation for the sciences, and to direct the reader's mind toward the appropriate concept of God, Descartes goes beyond the *medical* arguments from disorders of the sensory powers, and gives *theological* arguments for doubt. The theological arguments are supposed to induce a deeper and more extensive doubt than the medical arguments: to achieve this result, Descartes begins by invoking a more extreme (and more bizarre) scenario of abnormal deception. But the extremism is only a means to an end. As before, the impulse of healthy common sense is to reject the suggestion that we are mad or dreaming or the plaything of a deceiving God: we can give plausible arguments against such extravagant suppositions, and so insulate our knowledge against threat. As before, Descartes allows the Meditator to produce these arguments, since the defensive arguments of common sense serve only to expose its weakness, and reveal the true causes that render our habitual judgments uncertain. Even if the *honneste homme* is neither a madman nor a dreamer, Descartes argues that "he could have no more reason than they to be certain of what he believes, since he relies, like them, on what the senses and his imagination represent to him" (AT X,511); in the same way, even if the psychologist and mathematician attempting to execute the program of the *Rules* is not deceived by a malicious divinity, Descartes wants to show that, unless he can base his science on a knowledge of God as the source of rationality, his judgments will be as uncertain as if he were so deceived.

Since Descartes wants to show that *all* our habitual judgments are uncertain, even our judgments about the things that seem to be simplest and most universal, and that we seem to perceive most clearly and distinctly, he begins by stating the possibility of divine deception in as radical a form as possible, invoking the "old opinion, implanted in my mind, that there is a God who can do all things, and by whom I have been created what I am" (AT VII,21). This is merely an opinion; but if it is true, then such a God could bring it about "that there is no earth at all, no heaven, no extended thing, no figure, no size, no place, and yet that all these things would *appear* to me to exist, just as they do right now" (ibid.). If God has created only me and my thoughts, and not a world of extended bodies, then everything I thought I had perceived through my senses is false; but Descartes wants to draw a yet stronger conclusion. Extended things and their figures, sizes, and places were all on the Meditator's list of the things that *seem* to be most simple and universal, and therefore still seem to be certain, whether we are dreaming or not. Heaven and earth are the objects of physics, but extension and its modes are the objects of the mathematical disciplines, and so these too fall under the scope of theological doubt. An omnipotent God could bring it about that "just as I judge that other people sometimes err about the things they think they know most perfectly, so I myself am deceived each time I add two and three together, or count the sides of a square, or do anything even easier that might be imagined" (ibid.). So it seems that Descartes is using the supposition of the deceiving God to induce a universal doubt, not only about the obscure perceptions of the senses, but also about the clear perceptions of the intellect.

But this is not quite right. Descartes never, anywhere, rejects or calls into question the general principle that everything we clearly and distinctly perceive is true: his point is that things we *think* we perceive clearly may in fact be perceived only obscurely, and may therefore be false: thus we cannot use the clarity of our perceptions as a criterion for reconstructing knowledge, unless we have a standard for discerning which perceptions are sufficiently clear. Thus at the beginning of the third Meditation, when the Meditator suggests that he may know "what is required in order for me to be certain about any matter," and proposes "as a general rule . . . that everything I perceive very clearly and distinctly is true" (AT VII,35), Descartes rejects the proposal without ever suggesting that something we clearly perceive might be false. He does not object to the "general rule" as a universal proposition, "whatever I perceive clearly is true"; he argues, instead, that this proposition cannot give a "general rule," in the sense of a practical procedure for deciding whether we can be certain about any given matter. The first reason Descartes gives is that we have previously accepted many beliefs about sensible things, "which, from a habit of believing, I thought I clearly perceived, but which in fact I did not perceive" (ibid.). But we might think that once we have undergone the discipline of doubting the senses, and recognized that sensory perceptions are unclear, we can now use the clarity of our perceptions as a rule for knowledge: when we turned away from the senses to consider elementary mathematical propositions, "did I not see at least these things clearly enough to affirm that they are true?" (AT VII,36). Descartes then recalls the scenario of the deceiving God to show that the rule of clarity does not yield a workable scientific method even now: *not* because God could deceive us even in the things we clearly perceive, but because God could deceive us "even about those things that *seemed* very manifest," or again, "even in the things I *think* I see most evidently with the eyes of the mind" (ibid.; my emphasis). Our elementary mathematical perceptions *appear* so clear that whenever we consider them, we are led spontaneously and invincibly to affirm their truth. But the fact that we are subjectively inclined to assent to the propositions of mathematics does not constitute objective evidence that these propositions are true, or even that we perceive them clearly. Descartes is not trying to make us reject our mathematical perceptions: this would be impossible and, since these perceptions are in fact clear, it would also be unprofitable. What he is trying to make us reject is the method of collecting the first principles of the sciences by a subjective psychological survey of the things that seem clear to us. The past errors of our senses show that the rule of clarity can mislead; the scenario of the deceiving God shows that it will not be safe, even when it avoids explicit reliance on sensation and on physical theory, so long as it is based merely on what *seems* to be clear. The scenario of the deceiving God is intended to point us in the direction of the true standard of clarity, by showing that we cannot have such a standard until we know who or what has created us: once Descartes has established a knowledge of God, he will have a new theoretical basis, independent of sensation, for deriving a criterion of clarity that he can use to build up the sciences.

Descartes wants to use the theological arguments of the first Meditation to discover what must be the case if science is possible. Minimally, we must not be the creatures of an omnipotent and malicious being; but Descartes wants conclusions more positive than this. We might imagine, crudely, three scenarios: our creator (whatever it may be, and whether or not it deserves the name "God") is either powerful and malicious, or powerful and beneficent, or not powerful enough to cause radical deception. The naive Meditator would prefer to dismiss the first scenario as unreasonably extreme, and then to suppose that his knowledge is secure without any more precise investigation into the nature of his creator. Descartes allows the Meditator to develop this thought, in order to show that it cannot succeed. Descartes' goal is to prove that we cannot have scientific knowledge unless we are in the second scenario, creatures of an omnipotent and beneficent God; and that this is still not sufficient unless God's power and beneficence are such that we can use the traditional Augustinian theodicy to infer the impossibility of some kinds of evils, and thus of some kinds of errors in judgment. In this way Descartes will isolate theodicy as the only possible foundation for science; more than this, as we will see, he will isolate the understanding of God as Nous as the only foundation for theodicy.

We can put the argument of the first Meditation in sharper focus by comparing it with Descartes' probable source for the deceiving God and other sceptical arguments, Cicero's dialogue *Academica*. Cicero's character Lucullus, the spokesman for the crypto-Stoic "Old Academy" of Antiochus of Ascalon, is defending against the sceptical New Academy the Stoic thesis that some impressions (*visa*, translating Greek *phantasiai*, literally "appearances" or "seemings") are so clear and so evident that the sage may assent to them without fear of deception. Lucullus thinks that his thesis depends on our having some *regula* or *iudicium* of truth and falsity, and that this is possible only if some of our impressions are, in Stoic terminology, *cataleptic*: an impression is cataleptic if it is "impressed and shaped by the thing it is from, with a character it could not have from anything other than the thing it is from" (*Academica* II,vi,18). The New Academics argue that an impression of any subjectively recognizable type can be derived from something other than the thing it purports to be of, and therefore that no impressions are cataleptic; in arguing that any subjectively recognizable class of impressions will include some false impressions along with the true ones, the New Academics invoke not only madness and dreams (II,xv,48), but also impressions produced by a deceiving god (II,xv,47). As Lucullus explains the deceiving-god argument, it depends on a sorites. The Stoics assert that the gods give us impressions through dreams and oracles (indeed, for the Stoics, *all* our impressions are produced by fate, and so by Zeus), and these impressions are often probable or truthlike, so that people are inclined to assent to them; thus a god has the power to give us at least a *probable* impression of something false.[27] But then the New Academics ask

why a god would be able to make these false impressions probable, but not be able to make them such that they closely approximate truth; and, if he can do this too, why he could not make them such that they are distinguished [from true impressions] but only with great difficulty; and if he can do this, why not such that there is no difference between them [and true impressions] at all? (*Academica* II,xv,47)

Lucullus objects to this argument at every possible step, but his basic point seems to be the implausibility of the conclusion about the gods, to which we have been led by degrees: "for who would concede to you either that a god can do all things, or that he would act in this way if he could?" (II,xvi,50).

Descartes' sympathies are neither with the New nor with the Old Academy. He does not believe that the sceptical arguments can defeat every possible criterion of truth, but he does believe that they defeat every criterion that the commonsense dogmatism of Antiochus and Lucullus could offer. Lucullus serves Descartes as a model for the naive Meditator who trusts in the claims of healthy common sense, and resists the arguments that challenge these claims. When the Meditator considers the implications of the scenario of the omnipotent deceiving god, two defensive responses occur to him: "perhaps God has not willed to deceive me in this way, for he is said to be supremely good"; but then again, "perhaps there would be some [*nonnulli*] who would prefer to deny any God this powerful, than to believe that all other things are uncertain" (AT VII,21).[28]

---

[27] The Stoics think that gods (and human sages) do in fact sometimes give us false *phantasiai*, although these *phantasiai* are not cataleptic and the gods or sages are not the cause of our assenting to them: see SVF II,994 for the sage implanting a false but persuasive impression in a fool, and SVF II,941 for the oracle, "in order that the drama of fate might be fulfilled," giving Laius the false *phantasia* that he could avoid his fate by exposing his infant son Oedipus, when in fact this was the only way his fated death could be accomplished. The oracle does this without actually lying, and if Laius had been a sage he would have known better; the god does not cause his assent.

[28] Of course, the God Descartes is considering is more powerful than anything Cicero had imagined, even if Lucullus mentions (perhaps as a *reductio ad absurdum*) the thesis that "a god can do all things." In Cicero, the theological scenarios of deception are no more

No Christian thinker, sceptical or dogmatic, would choose to make such a denial: *nonnulli* must refer back to pagan antiquity, and it seems to refer back in particular to Lucullus, and to the two escape routes he finds equally reassuring: "who would concede to you either that a god can do all things, or that he would act in this way if he could?" The Meditator of the first Meditation, like Lucullus, makes no serious attempt to prove that divine deception *must* be impossible; he is content to offer two plausible arguments, each suggesting a different way in which divine deception *might* be impossible. This may be enough if all we want is to refute a purported demonstration that there can be no criterion of truth; but it is not enough if we are trying to construct such a criterion for ourselves. Descartes wants to discover the true ground on which the sceptical arguments actually fail, not to suggest several different grounds on which they might possibly fail. Perhaps our creator is benevolent; perhaps he (or it) is impotent. Lucullus merely tosses out these suggestions; Descartes will explore their implications for knowledge. Descartes argues that healthy common sense is in no position to establish a science either on divine benevolence or on divine impotence; and he uses this argument to determine what kind of knowledge of God we would have to have for a criterion of truth to be possible.

radical than the medical scenarios: in either case, some unusual causal factor would produce *one single false impression* which could not be distinguished from true impressions. For Descartes, however, the scenario of the deceiving God sums up the earlier scenarios of madness and dreaming, and goes beyond them to suggest that *all* our habitual beliefs may *simultaneously* be false. As Descartes says, "there is an old opinion impressed upon my mind, that there is a God who can do all things, and by whom I have been made what I am." The effectiveness of the first Meditation does not require that the opinion of an omnipotent creator-God should be *true*, but it does require that this opinion should have been impressed on the Meditator's mind from childhood: this would be true for a meditator in the seventeenth century, but not for a meditator from pagan antiquity. We now habitually assume, or at least entertain the possibility, that God has created the world and brings about everything which happens within it; so we can also entertain the possibility that God has chosen *not* to create the world of extended beings, that consequently no such world exists, and that God produces in us all the impressions of a world without *any* corresponding reality. Cicero too had recognized the possibility that there might be no world at all, for he quotes Metrodorus of Chios:

> I deny that we know whether we know anything or nothing; [I deny] that we know even this very thing, that we do not know (or that we do know), or whether there is anything or nothing altogether [*nego scire nos sciamusne aliquid an nihil sciamus, ne id ipsum quidem, nescire (aut scire), scire nos, nec omnino sitne aliquid an nihil sit*]. (*Academica* II,xxiii,73)

But Cicero attaches no importance to this hyperbolic form of doubt (Augustine is more struck by it in the *Contra Academicos*), and Cicero does not connect it with the deceiving God. The concept of omnipotence allows Descartes to connect two Ciceronian hypotheses, the non-existence of the world and the deceiving God, in a way that would never have occurred to Cicero; and from these connected hypotheses Descartes derives a lesson he could not have derived from either hypothesis in isolation, namely that God is the first external object whose existence must be known, since if we do not know some facts about God (including his existence) we cannot know that anything at all exists outside ourselves.

Descartes considers divine benevolence first: "perhaps God has not willed to deceive me in this way, for he is said to be supremely good" (AT VII,21). Descartes himself believes that this is true, and he will ultimately use it as a foundation for science; but the Meditator of the first Meditation cannot. Descartes immediately raises an objection to using divine benevolence to justify our claims of knowledge: "if it were inconsistent with his goodness to have created me in such a way that I should always be deceived, then for the same reason it would also seem to be foreign to him to permit me to be deceived from time to time; but this last cannot be said" (ibid.). Descartes then dismisses the possibility of arguing from divine benevolence, and turns to Lucullus' other suggestion. This seems exceedingly quick: a philosophically sophisticated meditator might resist the dismissal of divine benevolence, and object that Descartes is disregarding the well-known distinction between God's *causing* an evil and his merely *permitting* it to happen: Augustine and the whole Christian tradition after him had elaborated a subtle theodicy to reconcile God's goodness with his permitting deception and other evils under certain conditions. Descartes, of course, is well aware of this distinction, but he does not allow the naive Meditator of the first Meditation to introduce it in responding to the sceptical challenge. This is not because Descartes has too little respect for the Augustinian theodicy, but because he has too much. Descartes does not intend to begin with the known existence of evil, then show how God's rumored goodness can be reconciled with what we know; on the contrary, he will begin with God's known goodness, and then examine what kinds of evil, in particular what kinds of deception, can and cannot occur. But for Descartes to argue in this direction, he needs a theodicy strong enough to prescribe sharp boundaries between the evils that can and cannot befall a soul created by a benevolent God: and we cannot have such a theodicy unless we first understand God and the soul and the relations between them. A theodicy introduced at the stage of the first Meditation could give no certainty, but at best a plausible conjecture that, though a benevolent God might allow us to be deceived on occasion, he would not deceive us always and in everything. Such an argument might serve, with Lucullus, to stave off universal doubt, but it could not yield a method for constructing science.

Descartes turns to Lucullus' second suggestion for avoiding theological scepticism: perhaps there is no god who has the power to produce in us impressions indistinguishable from the truth. Descartes explores this commonsense response to scepticism in order to prove that it is a dead end, that if, as Lucullus suggests, we do not proceed from a sufficiently powerful divine creator, then we have no knowledge at all. We modern Christians would not dare to say, with Lucullus, that God lacks some power; but we are implicitly agreeing with him when we base our habitual judgments on the natural processes of sensation: for we assume that bodies are naturally capable of causing in us sensory likenesses of themselves, and we disregard God's power to override any such natural causality. By arguing against Lucullus that God's power is a necessary condition of knowledge, Descartes is also trying to show that the perceptions we derive from merely natural powers are cognitively no better than the perceptions we might be given by a deceiving God.

Descartes might well refuse to consider the suggestion that there is no omnipotent God, either because it is an impious hypothesis, or because it cannot overcome scepticism as long as it remains a mere hypothesis. Instead,

> let us not contradict these people: let us grant that all this about God is fictitious, and let them suppose that instead I have come to be what I am through fate, or chance, or a connected series of things, or by any other means. Since being deceived and erring seems to be an imperfection, however much less powerful they make the author of my origin, it will be that much more likely that I am so imperfect as to be always deceived. (AT VII,21)

This reflection allows us to recognize the true scope of theological doubt in undermining any naturalistic foundation for knowledge. We ordinarily suppose that God has nothing to do with the question of knowledge. When we confront the possibility of an omnipotent deceiving God, we are forced to recognize that God is involved in knowledge, at least negatively, as a possible *obstacle* to knowledge. But we are still inclined to suppose that God has no *positive* function in supporting our knowledge under normal conditions: that if we can rule out implausible worst-case scenarios we will have all the knowledge of God we require for science. The current argument is supposed to bring out the deeper lesson of the deceiving-God argument, and to deprive us of our remaining confidence in our knowledge. The deeper lesson is that we do not automatically and of ourselves possess the power of forming conceptions in accordance with the natures of things. This power is, rather, a perfection that the soul will possess only if it receives it from an appropriate source. The God of popular belief, who creates the individual Meditator and the objects of his knowledge, might be an appropriate source of the perfection of knowledge: for he can give us knowledge even if no other source gives it, and he can deprive us of knowledge even if no other source withholds it. Descartes intends to go further and, refining the popular conception of God into the Plotinian and Augustinian conception of God as Nous, to show that *only* such a God can provide us with the perfection of knowledge.

When Descartes speaks of those who would deny that there is such a God, and who give other accounts of my origin, he is thinking of specific schools of ancient philosophy. The Epicureans deny that I have been created by an omnipotent God, and say that I have come to be "through chance"; the Stoics deny that I have been created by an omnipotent God, and say that I have come to be "through fate" or "through a connected series of things." In either case I would owe my existence and my nature, including my capacity to form beliefs, to the causality of merely natural powers. Descartes is making the point (which we have seen Plotinus arguing against the Epicureans, Stoics, and astrologers in III,1, *On Fate*; cf. Chapter 3, Section D, above) that these powers are insufficient to produce rationality in the desired sense. Nature may have produced me in such a way that I am determined to assent to particular impressions; I might even be determined to believe that I perceive those things clearly and distinctly. But, Descartes argues, there is no objective reason to expect that beliefs so formed would correspond to reality; and so my perceptions would fail to be *scientia*, even though they might happen to be true.[29] The power of conforming to the standard of truth is a specifically rational perfection, going beyond any physical quality, and cannot be derived from an irrational cause: I will not have the capacity for knowledge unless I derive it from some being which both possesses this rational perfection in itself, and also communicates it to me. If I and my beliefs are the result of a non-rational process, of fate or chance or a connected series of things, then I should expect to be systematically deceived, just as effectively as if I were the product of a deceiving god. As Descartes says, the deceiving-God argument gives a reason for doubt because "some god could have put such a nature in me that I should be deceived even about the things that seemed most manifest" (third Meditation, AT VII,36); but I might have this same defective nature whether it was produced by a god or not. The deceiving God or *genius malignus* symbolically stands in for whatever forces may be inclining us toward error, but it does not much matter for Descartes' argument whether these forces are a single personal agent or not: in reality, they are a multiplicity of impersonal forces, passions and habits, personal and social prejudices, inclining us to think we perceive clearly things that are in fact obscure, and so to assent to falsehoods.

Descartes expresses his attitude toward the deceiving God most clearly

---

[29] Objection: if I am a natural product, nature would have produced me in such a way that I am adapted to survive (whether because nature is providential, as the Stoics would say, or simply through natural selection); and if my perceptions are adapted to my survival, this guarantees that they must be true at least for the most part. Descartes rejects this line of thought, for two reasons. First, this kind of naturalism is not sufficient to guarantee any particular scientific knowledge-claim, let alone to justify an overall program of scientific investigation, because it gives no method for distinguishing which of our perceptions really come from nature and which come from habit or "second nature" (this is the difficulty of his Rule 12). Second, even if we can tell which of our impulses (including impulses to assent to some class of impressions) are from nature, and even if we know that all of these impulses are adapted to our biological preservation (premises that Descartes accepts in principle from the standpoint of the sixth Meditation, although not at earlier stages of his argument), this still does not guarantee that our biological nature will be strong enough to support theoretical knowledge of the essences of things, or long chains of connected reasoning (putting it in terms of natural selection, these are surely not the abilities that are selected for). Descartes' own conclusion in the sixth Meditation is that our natural impulses are (for the most part and in the long run) *practically* reliable, but cannot support theoretical knowledge, except indirectly, insofar as the intellect can draw theoretical conclusions from the fact that our natural impulses are practically reliable. Theoretical knowledge (intuitive and deductive) is guaranteed only by the intellect's direct relation to God, not by nature's governance of the mind–body composite. For detailed discussion, see Chapter 8, Section C, below.

in the seventh Replies, in answering Bourdin's exaggeration of the sceptical nature of Descartes' starting-point. Descartes rejects Bourdin's construal of the *Meditations* as a malicious distortion, "a mask badly put together out of fragments of my Meditations" (AT VII,454), and he tries to show that Bourdin is refuting this mask and not the real Descartes. Bourdin is always attacking "his one fiction, whose absurdity and staleness I will here declare by means of a parable" (p. 536). Descartes is like an architect who, intending to construct a permanent structure on unstable ground, must first "dig a trench, and remove from it all the sand, and anything else that is resting on or mixed in with the sand, so that he can then set the foundations in firm soil" (p. 537); Bourdin is a mere bricklayer who, envying the work of the architect which he cannot understand, seizes upon this initial act of digging the trench, and seeks to ridicule the architect's whole way of building by reducing it to this first unproductive act. Descartes makes it clear that the preliminary digging represents the methodological doubt of the first Meditation; and we can tell something about what he thought was the true purpose of that Meditation, and what he thought was Bourdin's distortion, from the speeches he attributes to the architect and the bricklayer. The architect explains his reason for beginning by digging by saying

that the surface of the earth on which we stand is not always sufficiently firm to support great structures; and that sand is especially unstable, because not only does it subside when pressed down by great weights, but also the waters that flow through it not infrequently carry it away with them, resulting in the unexpected collapse of the things it had supported; and finally, that when these collapses occur from time to time in the mines, the miners are in the habit of referring their causes to goblins [*Lemures*][30] or evil spirits [*malos genios*] who inhabit the places underground. (Pp. 537–8)

The bricklayer takes up this speech and, distorting its meaning, pretends that the architect takes his digging for the act of building, and that "the architect is so foolish that he is afraid that the earth on which he stands will divide under his feet, or that it will be overturned by goblins [*Lemuribus*]" (p. 538). The bricklayer then argues, as a *reductio ad absurdum* of the architect's sceptical starting-point, that, given the present danger of goblins, no foundation is secure enough, and that the architect must always continue to dig: the rock at the bottom of the trench must not be accepted as stable, nor, if it were, could any other material, which is all intrinsically unstable, be stably placed upon it.

Without exploring further the details of the parable, it is clear enough that the *Lemures* or *mali genii* are intended to represent the deceiving God

---

[30] I am not sure exactly what *Lemures* are (in antiquity, they were spirits of the dead conceived as abiding underground). "Goblins" is the suggestion of Cottingham, Stoothoff, and Murdoch, and it captures the tone which (I think) Descartes is taking: *Lemures* would not be beings anyone seriously believes in, but stories for frightening children, or a figure of speech like the printer's devil.

or *malignus genius* of the first Meditation. So the parallel shows that Descartes regards the *malignus genius* as a mythological representation of a real series of causes resulting in the unexpected collapse of our opinions, and that he is not motivated in the first Meditation by fear of some extraordinary demonic deception going beyond the catastrophes due to the intrinsic instability of our opinions. Descartes is not trying to make us reject (on arbitrarily supernatural grounds) the certainty of things we clearly perceive, but merely to make us reject constructions built on unstable assumptions, including those we wrongly thought were clearly perceived. But supernatural scenarios are peculiarly effective at getting us to reject unsafe constructions: as Descartes notes in the third Meditation, it was only the hypothesis of the deceiving God that led him to doubt that the apparently evident assertions of mathematics, considered as a totality, were true. The mythological representation, by gathering together the different sources of error and representing them as a single force, makes it psychologically much easier to concentrate on the danger and break our old habits of belief, so that, being aware of the full extent to which our beliefs have been infected with doubtfulness, we can search effectively for foundations not susceptible to any of the causes of doubt.

Although the image of the deceiving God is more vivid and compelling, the argument from "fate, chance, or a connected series of things" is deeper and more serious. The argument from the deceiving God describes one way in which the condition of error could be produced, which is not the way it is in fact produced. The condition of error is in fact produced when we pass judgment on the basis of the states of the sensitive faculties of the soul, which are determined by "fate, chance, or a connected series of things" – in other words, by external physical influences – and which may therefore fail to be in contact with the truth. These actual sources of our deception are like the water that washes out the sand from underneath the foundations of our dwellings; the deceiving God is the goblin who produces the same effect. No goblin actually does this; goblins are merely another means by which the same effect might possibly be brought about, and a mythological means of representing the actual occurrence. The deceiving God has the advantage of vividness: as we may walk more carefully in the mines if we have goblins impressed on our imagination, so we may proceed more carefully in our judgments if we keep constantly in mind the image of the deceiving God, or of "some malicious spirit, most powerful and clever, who has put all his labor into deceiving me" (AT VII,22).[31] The real worry, however, is not that we may be at the mercy

---

[31] There is no point in distinguishing between the deceiving God and the evil genius; Descartes himself casually refers to both as if they were the same thing. It is true that in the evil-genius passage at the end of the first Meditation Descartes is deliberately constructing a mental exercise to use for practice in doubting, while in his first mention of the deceiving God he is merely drawing on popular belief to illustrate one of the logical possibilities of deception; it is nonetheless the same scenario that he is considering in both passages. The imagined deceiver may loosely be called "God," for he falls under the childish and obscure

of an intelligent being who wishes to trip us up, but that we may be at the mercy of a blind natural process which cannot do otherwise than it does, and which cannot make the ground firm enough to support the weight of our constructions. If my creator is a being that possesses rationality in itself, but maliciously wills not to communicate this perfection to me, then I will lack rational perfection; but I will equally lack this perfection if my creator is a natural process with no rational perfection to communicate, and no will to bestow or begrudge it. The latter situation is the more serious threat: both because some sane people seriously believe that they are products of fate or chance, while no sane people seriously believe that they are products of an omnipotent deceiver; and also because it is to some extent true that our beliefs are determined by fate and chance, to the extent that we allow the senses to determine our judgments of the natures of things. The intellectual conclusion of the first Meditation (as opposed to its practical effect in helping us break old habits of assent) is that for our judgments to be scientific, they must be produced in us by an intrinsically rational cause, and produced in such a way that the rationality of the cause guarantees the rationality of the judgment it produces.

The explicit aim of the first Meditation was to "set out causes on account of which we are able to doubt about all things, especially material things: so long, that is, as we do not have other foundations for the sciences than those we have had hitherto" (AT VII,12). Implicitly, Descartes is also isolating what these foundations must be if they are to resolve the reasons given for doubting. We must know "the author of our origin," and be able to infer what kind of nature we would receive from such a cause, and under what circumstances such a nature would incline us to true or false judgment. Descartes will, in the fourth Meditation, present his adaptation of the theodicy of Augustine's *De Libero Arbitrio*, and use this to argue that we cannot be deceived in certain situations, and that if we use our freedom rightly we will never fall into error; in the first Meditation, as we have seen, Descartes is already isolating this strategy of argument as the only possible foundation for science. But the strategy of arguing from theodicy depends on a knowledge of the nature of our creator: a knowledge not just that God is non-deceptive or even benevolent, but also that he has whatever power is needed to produce a creature capable of knowledge.

We have said that our creator must be "intrinsically rational," or pos-

conception of God as an omnipotent creator; but Descartes often prefers to avoid the name "God," because the deceiver does not fall under the distinct conception of *what God really is*, which Descartes is trying to isolate. In different passages Descartes uses different locutions to avoid confusing the imagined deceiver with the true God: thus at AT VII,24 he is "*aliquis Deus, vel quocunque nomine illum vocem*"; on the next page, "*deceptor nescio quis, summe potens*"; and on the next page after that, "*deceptorem aliquem potissimum et, si fas est dicere, malignum*." This is obviously always the same being under consideration, whether it is called God or not.

sess "rational perfection," in order to communicate to us the perfection of knowledge: but it is not enough if my creator simply has scientific knowledge of things in the same way that I do. I do not have scientific knowledge *essentially* or from myself, because I do not by myself have the power to ensure conformity between my conceptions and the things: a malicious spirit, or a brute natural process, might bring it about that the things are otherwise, while everything appears to me the same. I can have the power of scientific knowledge if I receive it from God, if he is such as to produce in me thoughts that correspond to reality; but if God (like me) does not have knowledge essentially and from himself, then he too will be at the mercy of whatever causes him, and of whatever causes the objects of his knowledge, and there will be a regress to a further God. Descartes' implicit conclusion is that I can have scientific knowledge only if I can trace the origin of myself and my thoughts back to an *essentially* knowing being – that is, to a God who is not just potential *nous* like the human soul, but *nous* in actuality by his essence. Plotinus had concluded that the objects of God's knowledge (the Platonic forms) cannot be anything outside himself, since otherwise he would of himself be only potentially knowing them, and would need a further *nous* to give him knowledge in actuality. Because Descartes wants his science to grasp things outside God (including bodies), his God must also know things outside himself, and know them without being dependent on anything other than himself: the only solution is that God *creates* all the objects of his knowledge other than himself, that he knows them by knowing his will to create them, and that the objects are necessarily as he knows them because they are necessarily as he wills them to be.[32] Descartes needs an omnipotent God because he needs a God who is omniscient, and essentially omniscient: he is here thoroughly Plotinian and Augustinian, both in understanding our own imperfect knowledge through its relation to God's perfect knowledge, and in using God's perfect knowledge as the key to understanding God's nature.[33]

Interpreting the *Meditations* as an attempt to carry out the project of the *Rules*, we can see the first Meditation as an analytic investigation, showing what first principles are required if the problem of scientific knowledge is to be solved: science can be constructed only if we know ourselves as potential *nous* and our creator as essentially actual Nous and as the creator of all objects of knowledge other than himself. The second

---

[32] This is the standard scholastic account of God's knowledge of contingent truths, the so-called *scientia libera* (this account is often credited to Scotus, but is in fact older). For a discussion of Descartes and the scholastics on God's knowledge of creatures, and of the pressures leading these different philosophers to conclude that God knows things other than himself only by knowing his own will, see Chapter 8, Section A, below.

[33] This is not, of course, explicit in the first Meditation, but the first Meditation is written with a view to the third. I will develop these points further in discussing the third Meditation in Chapter 6, Sections B and C, and in discussing the creation of the eternal truths in Chapter 8, Section A.

and third Meditations undertake to construct (or rather to discover within ourselves) the knowledge of ourselves and of God; the fourth and subsequent Meditations take up the synthetic task of constructing science.

6

Isolating the soul and God

A. Isolating the rational soul

The second and third Meditations belong together as Descartes' attempt to prove the positive part of the *Meditations'* general thesis that God and the soul are the best known of all things, and are therefore the appropriate principles of philosophy. Descartes had argued in the first Meditation that we cannot know bodies without first knowing God and the soul; he now attempts to show that we can have some knowledge of God and the soul without making any assumptions about bodies. The second Meditation is actually entitled "of the nature of the human mind, that it is better known than the body,"[1] and the third Meditation makes the same claim about God.

In both the second and the third Meditations, Descartes is adapting the line of thought that Augustine uses, in *Confessions* VII and *De Libero Arbitrio* II and elsewhere, to bring us to knowledge, first of the soul, and then of God. Descartes' differences from Augustine arise from his attempt to show that the *cognitiones* of soul and God are the *first*, that is, both that these are independent of all other knowledge, and that no other *cognitiones* are similarly independent. Although the *Confessions* simply narrate an intellectual "vision" of God, in the *De Libero Arbitrio* Augustine tries to prove to Evodius that God exists, starting from Evodius' acknowledgment that he himself exists. Descartes too claims to prove existence (the third Meditation is entitled "of God, that he exists," and the second makes the same claim about soul); but Descartes is no more worried than Augustine about whether God and the soul really exist. As we have seen, in the *Letter to Picot* Descartes feels free to appeal to the *consensus gentium* in support of his principles, including the existence of the soul and of God: these principles "have been known for all time, and indeed accepted as true and indubitable by all men, excepting only the existence of God, which some have put in doubt, because they have attributed too much to sense perception, and because God cannot be seen or touched" (AT IX2,10), but Descartes is not much troubled by these doubters, for he goes on immediately to say that "all the truths that I put among my principles have

---

[1] On the title of the second Meditation, see above, Chapter 2, Section D: Descartes initially called it "of the human mind," then added "that it is better known than the body"; the word "nature" which appears in the printed title seems not to be Descartes'.

245

always been known to everyone" – what is not generally recognized is that these truths are the *principles* of other truths, and to show this will require a particular way of conceiving God and the soul.[2] Now, Augustine had been chiefly concerned not with God's existence but with God's nature: his reading of Plotinus had taught him to conceive God as an incorporeal Truth, and his proof of God's existence in *De Libero Arbitrio* specifically proves the existence of such a Truth. Descartes too is trying to prove the existence of a certain *kind* of God (and a certain kind of soul), and he uses the existence proofs to establish the *nature* of the things they prove. The second Meditation says that the soul, as conceived purely intellectually, is the first thing known to exist when everything else is doubtful; the third Meditation says that God, as conceived purely intellectually, is the first thing known to exist outside the soul. By meditating through the existence proofs, while maintaining our doubt of everything that has not been proved to exist, we come to recognize within ourselves intellectual concepts of soul and God, and to distinguish them both from concepts of bodies and from confused sensory representations of incorporeal things. These purely intellectual concepts can then be used to reestablish a science of bodies free of sensory prejudice.

I will devote the body of this chapter to the third Meditation, treating the second Meditation in the present section as a prologue to the third, and as a small-scale model of the greater task. The second Meditation carries out the promise of Rule 8 to show that "nothing can be known prior to the intellect, since the knowledge of all other things depends on it and not vice versa" (AT X,395); again, it carries out the injunction of Rule 12, that "if the intellect is considering those things in which there is nothing corporeal or like the corporeal . . . the senses should be kept at bay, and the imagination should be stripped, so far as possible, of every distinct impression" (AT X,416). By eliminating the prejudices of the senses at this fundamental level of the scientific project, we make it possible to evaluate the senses later from a position not biassed in their favor. But the second Meditation remains preparatory: the knowledge of soul alone, without any knowledge either of God or of bodies, is not sufficient to give a criterion for other knowledge. So, in the second Replies, where Descartes feels obliged to argue that the first two Meditations are not as "meager" as they look (AT VII,130), he defends the second Meditation not on the grounds of any positive result it may establish, but simply as an intellectual exercise:

since previously we have had no ideas of the things that pertain to the mind, except very confused ones mixed up with the ideas of sensible things – and this was the first and chief reason why none of the things that had been said about God and the soul could be understood clearly enough – I thought it would be well worth the effort if I could teach how to distinguish the properties or qualities of the mind from the qualities of the body. For although many people have said before that

[2] See discussion above, Chapter 2, Section B.

the mind should be withdrawn from the senses to understand metaphysical things, yet as far as I know no one up to now has shown how this can be done: but a true way, and in my judgment the *only* way, to achieve this is contained in my second Meditation. But it is of such a kind that it is not enough to have looked at it once: it must be exercised and repeated for a long time, in order that a whole lifetime's habit of confusing intellectual with corporeal things may be effaced by at least a few days' contrary habit of distinguishing them. And this seemed to me to be a very good reason why I should not treat anything else in this second Meditation. (AT VII,131)

The function of the second Meditation, then, will be to withdraw the mind from the senses by showing us how to conceive the soul through intellect alone; we are supposed to begin with a *partly* intellectual confused concept of soul, and the work of the second Meditation will be to refine this concept by eliminating its sensory elements. The thesis of the second Meditation will be that the resulting intellectual concept of soul is "better known" than our concepts of bodies, both in that it is more certain, and in that it gives a more distinct knowledge of what its object is.

When Descartes says that "many people have said before" *mentem a sensibus abducendam,* he expects his readers to recognize the allusion to Cicero's saying *"magni est ingenii sevocare mentem a sensibus et cogitationem ab consuetudine abducere"* (*Tusculan Disputations* I,xvi,38); as we saw in Chapter 4, Augustine had cited the same phrase (in a different abridgment from Descartes', *"abduxit cogitationem a consuetudine"*) to describe what he had achieved in "removing [his mind] from the contrary crowds of phantasms" and turning to perceive God as the mind's source of intellectual light (*Confessions* VII,xvii,23).[3] Descartes seems to be citing Cicero's phrase independently of Augustine, since he cites it in a different form. But both Augustine and Descartes are using this classical text in order to state their claims against the commonly accepted philosophical authorities: they are claiming to have actually achieved the goal that Cicero merely saw from a distance, and did not himself achieve. It is a bit strange that in the Synopsis of the *Meditations* Descartes claims to have accomplished this in the *first* Meditation (the exercise of doubting all things *viam facillimam sternat ad mentem a sensibus abducendam,* AT VII,12), whereas here he says that he has done it only in the second: but in both texts he is referring to the same process of thought, begun in the first Meditation and continued in the second, in which by withdrawing assent from all sensory ideas we are able to isolate and purify the intellectual ideas that can give the foundation for certain knowledge.

Since the first Meditation habituates us to doubt the existence of material things, it allows us to disentangle the intellectual concept of soul

---

[3] See notes above in Chapter 5, Section B (on Descartes' use of this Ciceronian phrase), and in Chapter 4, Section A (on Augustine's use of the same phrase). Descartes' use of the phrase is particularly appropriate here, since, in context, Cicero is talking about the difficulty of conceiving the human soul (when separated from the body) without imagining it in quasi-human form.

from other ideas that have been associated or confused with it. The Aristotelian and other established philosophical schools (representing, as Descartes sees it, the prejudices of ordinary life) conceive the human soul both as a thing that thinks, and also as the principle, whatever it may be, that gives life to the body: the former concept derives from the intellect, but the latter from sense and imagination, since it is only through the senses that we become aware of the body and vital phenomena. The first Meditation shows us how to withdraw our assent from the sensory concept of soul: if there is no *res extensa*, and all impressions which suggest it are deceptive, then we ourselves will have no body, and thus no organs of sensation; and we will have none of the faculties, such as the faculty of sensation, which belong to the soul only insofar as it operates through the body. But these are the only things the naive Meditator has ever noticed in himself; to the point that he wonders whether, if his body and his sensitive soul do not exist, he himself may not exist at all. Commonsense prejudice suggests that, by calling the sensory concepts of body and soul into doubt, we may have removed the whole content of our knowledge of ourselves. Descartes will attempt, in sifting through the Meditator's naive self-conception, to show that some parts of this conception do indeed survive when the senses are called into doubt; Descartes will isolate and develop the surviving core of our self-knowledge, and will argue that this knowledge is both sufficiently certain and sufficiently distinct to be the beginning of a scientific system.

The second Meditation begins by recalling the results of the first, and searching for whatever may remain certain in the worst-case scenario of the deceiving god. "There is I-know-not-what deceiver, most powerful and most clever, who always deliberately deceives me. Undoubtedly therefore I also exist, if he deceives me; and though he deceive me as much as he can, yet he can never bring it about that I am nothing, as long as I think myself to be something" (AT VII,25). This, after a few false starts, is the Archimedean point (p. 24), the one thing we now know to exist as we conceive it. But the Meditator finds this thought new and difficult, and (unlike Evodius in the *De Libero Arbitrio*) he puts up some initial resistance: "am not I, at least, something? But I have already denied that I have any senses or any body. And yet I pause; for what of it? Am I so bound to a body and to senses, that I cannot exist without them?" (pp. 24–5). Since I had never before thought of myself without also thinking of my body and my senses, I had supposed that I was logically dependent on them: but since I have now discovered that I can conceive of my body as not existing, but that I cannot conceive of myself as not existing, it must be at least *conceivable* that I am something other than my body, and other than the functions of the soul that operate through the body. The Meditator has thus acquired a concept of himself different from his sensible image of himself; he must always somehow have had it, but it had never before been separated from the senses and recognized as the purely intellectual *cognitio* it is.

Although the Meditator now knows *that* he is, he does not seem to know *what* he is: his old conception of his nature has been called into doubt, and he does not seem to have anything new to replace it. For Descartes to build a science on his new knowledge, he must clarify what we claim to know in saying "I know that I exist." Of course there is a meaning habitually associated with the word "I," but this meaning no longer serves. If, when I say "I exist," I surreptitiously import a concept of myself as body-and-soul, so that I mean, "my body exists and is animated by my soul," then this is not knowledge, and will be false in the worst-case scenario of malicious deception. "I may take something else in place of me" (p. 25), and so go wrong from the start. So the most urgent task is to clarify the concept of the soul that must be understood for "I" in the affirmation "I exist," and to distinguish it from other concepts it might be confused with.

"For this reason I will now meditate anew what I once believed myself to be, before I fell into these thoughts; from which I will then remove whatever can be weakened even the least bit by the reasons that have been offered, so that finally there will remain precisely what is certain and unshaken" (p. 25). "What I once believed myself to be" is not Descartes' autobiography: the Meditator is anyone who has come from being "governed by his appetites and his teachers" to seek a foundation for knowledge. So what Descartes presents as his former concept of himself is a digest, in the most general terms, of the picture of a human being suggested by the senses and the imagination, which (Descartes thinks) the Stoic, Epicurean, and Peripatetic philosophical anthropologies merely elaborate in different ways. What he gives will not be an adequate statement of any of these views, but this is not what interests him. Thus he suggests the definition of man as a rational animal as clarifying his understanding of himself, and then rejects it:

No, because afterwards I would have to ask what an animal is, and what rational, and thus I would slip from one question into many more difficult ones; nor do I yet have so much leisure, that I would expend it on subtleties of this kind. But here I will rather observe what previously used to occur spontaneously and naturally to my thought, whenever I considered what I was. (Pp. 25–6)

Traditional philosophical definitions merely codify the logical relations between terms, rather than exhibiting the clear ideas that ought to stand behind the terms we use. Descartes wants to discover a clear idea, and for this he turns to ordinary naive thought, which is the source of the philosophical abstractions: by sifting through all the things I habitually attribute to myself, I may discern what it is genuinely clear that I am.

Man is conceived, in the established philosophy, as body and soul. It seems most clear that I have a body, i.e. that "system of limbs" which is found in dead as well as living people (p. 26). Since there is evidently some difference between a living and a dead person, I suppose that I also have a soul, which dead people do not: this soul must somehow be responsible for the acts that distinguish a living from a dead body, which Descartes lists as four: "to be nourished, to move, to sense, and to think" (ibid.).[4] This list may be chosen with reference to Aristotle, who assigns these functions to different kinds of soul, but the point is not directed against him alone: these are four obvious conditions of a living body, which we do not know how to explain, and Aristotle is merely bowing to the obscurity and uncertainty of our sensory knowledge by ascribing them to something-he-knows-not-what, and giving this the title of the substantial form of a living body.

Although the Meditator recognizes that his concept of soul is obscure, he is inclined to believe that his concept of body is distinct:

> But I did not doubt at all about body, but judged that I distinctly knew its nature, which I might have explained thus, if I had tried to describe it as I conceived it in my mind: by body I understand all that to which it is suitable to be bounded by some figure, to be circumscribed in a place, and to fill a space in such a way that it excludes every other body from it; to be perceived by touch, sight, hearing, taste, or smell, and also to be moved in many ways, not by itself, but by something else that touches it. (Ibid.)

This is to say: body has been understood just as what appears to the senses, and what has the conditions necessary for coming into contact with the senses, especially vision and touch. Since we took the reports of the senses as the standard of clarity, we thought we perceived clearly what bodies were. We knew (or should have known) that we did not clearly perceive the soul, because this does not directly appear to the senses. Only body appears directly to the senses; and so we conceived soul only indirectly, by relating it to our perception of body: it is a power within the body, and if we thought about its nature at all, we imagined it on the model of sensible bodies, "as a thin I-know-not-what, like a wind, or a fire, or an ether, spread out among the grosser parts of me" (ibid.).

But how much of this do I in fact clearly perceive? Since my present knowledge does not exclude the possibility that there is a deceiving god and no extended reality, I cannot be clearly perceiving myself to be something that I would not be in this possible situation. Since there may be no bodies, I do not perceive that I have any of "all those things that I have already said belong to the nature of body" (pp. 26–7). Again, if I have no body, I cannot possess any of the functions commonly ascribed to the vegetative and sensitive souls: the functions of nutrition and self-motion are exercised through changes in the body, and if there is no body they do not occur. Nor can I have sensation, if this is understood as a function carried out in the body by the sensitive soul. But I do clearly perceive that I think, whether I have a body or not; and I can conceive of the activity of thinking, unlike any of the other traditional functions of

---

[4] "To move" is *incedere*, to initiate motion in some direction, rather than being pushed: the contrast is with the Meditator's description of bodies (cited below) as things that move only when pushed by other things.

soul, without reference to any bodily instrument. Thus the exercise of doubting all bodily things *refines* my naive concept of myself, until all that is left is the concept of a rational soul or *res cogitans*. So the Meditator, refusing to admit "anything but what is necessarily true," is led to conclude that he is "precisely a thing that thinks, that is, a mind, a spirit [*animus*], an intellect, or a reason – words whose meaning was previously unknown to me" (p. 27). Now, for the first time, the Meditator has a distinct concept that he can associate with the word "I" in claiming to know the truth of the sentence "I exist." This concept fits neatly into the blank that earlier philosophers had reserved for the name of "mind" or (potential) intellect or rational soul, but Descartes thinks these earlier philosophers did not succeed in eliciting in their readers' minds a distinct idea to fill in the meaning of the term.

Thus for Descartes, as for Augustine, the process of coming to understand incorporeal things is also a process of coming to *interpret*, coming to attach a meaning to words already in common use, such as "soul" or even "I": only by coming to understand the "higher" meanings of these words, as applied to intelligible things, can we genuinely know the truth of sentences previously accepted on authority, such as "the soul is distinct from the body" or even "I exist." Our language is primarily designed to describe bodies – "*anima* in good Latin signifies air or breath, and I think it was transferred from this to signifying the mind; this is why I said [in the second Meditation] that it is often taken for a corporeal thing" (AT III,362) – and our immersion in the ways of thought expressed and confirmed by the ordinary use of language makes it difficult for us to understand the meanings necessary for metaphysical knowledge. At the same time, I must somehow always have known the true meaning of the word "I," or I would not have been able to recognize that the sentence "I exist" is immune to doubt. So I do not have to look for an entirely new meaning of the words "I" or "soul" (and indeed this would be an impossible task), but merely to attend to the metaphysical meaning that I must have perceived indistinctly all along, and to distinguish it from the physical meanings also associated with the term.

The Meditator of the second Meditation is trying to obey the Delphic command "know yourself." Augustine has a useful discussion, in *De Trinitate* X, of how this can be done.

How will [the mind] seek to do what it is told, "know yourself," if it does not know what *know* is, or what *yourself* is? . . . When it is said to the mind, "know yourself," in the same moment when it understands what "yourself" means, it knows itself, for no other reason than that it is present to itself; but if it does not understand what is said, it certainly does not do it. So what it is commanded to do is what it does as soon as it understands the command. (*De Trinitate* X,ix,12)

Augustine thinks the only solution is that we have in fact known ourselves all along: what we are commanded is not to acquire some knowledge we do not yet possess, but rather to *think about* or attend to some knowledge we already have (X,v,7). The mind has (in the Aristotelian sense) *habitual* [*hexis*] knowledge of itself, and need only exercise this *hexis*; however, it has become difficult for us to exercise this *hexis*, because we have been so accustomed to loving and thinking about sensible things that the mind "cannot be in itself without their images": thus "it cannot separate [*se-cernere*] from itself the images of the things it senses, so as to see itself alone . . . when it tries to think of itself alone, it thinks [*putat*] that it *is* that without which it cannot think of itself" (X,viii,11). Augustine's point is not that the mind in this condition does not know itself – the mind *always* knows itself, because it is always immediately present to itself, and so better known to itself than anything else can be – the point is rather that the mind knows itself *confusedly*, having confused itself with bodies. So in trying to exercise (and in some sense to "recollect") our implicit knowledge of ourselves, we should try not to *add* anything to what we already know ourselves to be, but rather to *subtract* what we have illicitly added to our conception of ourselves (X,viii,11 and ix,13). As Augustine puts it, the task is not to catch sight of ourselves [*se cernere*] as if we were at a distance from ourselves, but rather to distinguish ourselves [*se discernere*] from bodies (X,ix,12), removing impurities from our confused self-knowledge so that a distinct self-knowledge remains.

This is the task of the second Meditation. And Augustine suggests a way to carry it out. Augustine describes the difference between the mind and bodies as the difference between what is known or certain and what is unknown or uncertain. To know the mind's true nature, we need only content ourselves with knowing what "not even those who thought that the mind was this or that body have doubted" about the mind (X,x,13), namely that it exists and lives and understands and wills and remembers and thinks and knows and judges: none of us could doubt that we do all these things, since all these activities are entailed by the act of doubting (X,x,14). By contrast, when the mind tries to answer the question what it itself is by identifying itself with something it knows under some other description, and judges, for instance, that it is air, then it is adding something uncertain. "When, for instance, the mind believes [*putat*] that it is air, it *believes* that air has understanding, but it *knows* that it itself has understanding . . . let it then set aside [*secernat*] what it believes, and hold to [*cernat*] what it knows" (X,x,13): it will then be left (Augustine says), not simply with a list of indubitable predicates of itself, but with a knowledge of its nature or substance (X,x,16). Augustine thinks that any further identification of the mind with anything *not* indubitably known is not merely superfluous and uncertain, but necessarily false: "[the mind] is certain of itself . . . but [the mind] is not entirely certain whether it is air or fire or some body or something belonging to a body. Therefore it is none of these things" (ibid.). The Delphic command is in fact telling it "to be certain that it is not any of those things of which it is uncertain, and to be certain that it is alone that alone which it is certain that it is" (ibid.). How, though, should the mind recognize that it is not certain that it is air? Perhaps simply by recognizing that this claim is contested among the philosophers; but also, Augustine thinks, the way we know air is not compatible with the kind of certainty required in the mind's knowledge of itself. The mind thinks bodily things by receiving in itself an *image* of them suitable for representing absent things, whereas the mind must know itself "by a real, not simulated, interior presence" (ibid.). If the mind were air, rather than fire, it would know air in this interior way, while knowing fire only from a distance, through an image; in fact, however, it knows all bodily things in the same external way, and its internal knowledge of itself (that it exists and lives and understands) shows that it is not one of these bodily things. So the mind should set aside everything it thinks through images, in order to know what it itself is.

Augustine's inference "the mind is certain of itself, the mind is not certain that it is X, therefore the mind is not X" is unsound, and Descartes avoids it in the second Meditation. Nonetheless, it seems to have given him his starting-point. The sceptical exercises of the first Meditation (which have no parallel in the Augustine text) give the Meditator a technique for "withdrawing the mind from the senses" once and for all, withdrawing assent from everything perceived through images, so that the mind can use its internal self-knowledge (as in Augustine, its knowledge of the activities entailed in its act of doubting) to answer the question what it itself is. Descartes, like Augustine, thinks that this kind of knowledge gives not only a list of predicates of the mind, but an answer to the what-is-it question, and an alternative to answering the what-is-it question by identifying the mind with some body or some attribute of a body. The Meditator of the second Meditation goes so far as to say "I am not that assembly of limbs which is called the human body; I am also not some thin air infused among these limbs, not a wind, not a fire, not a vapor, not a breath, not whatever I imagine [*fingo*] for myself, for I have supposed that all these things are nothing" (AT VII,27): but these declarations are parts of an exercise of thinking the world away, and not a series of truths that the Meditator clearly perceives. As Descartes was aware when he wrote the *Meditations*, I cannot know that I am not a body until I know what bodies are, and this does not become clear until the fifth Meditation. However, it seems that at an earlier period Descartes had believed that the second-Meditation argument establishes that the mind is not a body: for in the parallel passage of the *Discourse* he allows himself to infer "that I am a substance whose whole essence or nature is just to think, and which does not need any place or depend on any material thing in order to exist; so that this 'I,' that is, the soul by which I am what I am, is entirely distinct from the body, and indeed is easier to know than [the body], and would not cease to be everything that it is, even if the body did not exist" (AT VI,33).[5] Even in 1641, Descartes tells Arnauld that "if I had not

---

[5] Descartes more or less takes this back in the *Preface to the Reader* of the *Meditations*, where he is replying to criticisms of the hasty metaphysics of the *Discourse*; he says now that "I

been seeking a certainty greater than the ordinary" he would have "proved" the real distinctness of mind and body in the second Meditation simply by showing that we understand mind and body through independent concepts, since "no one who has perceived two substances through diverse concepts has ever failed to judge that these substances are really distinct. . . . for we ordinarily judge that everything is related in the same way in the order of truth as in the order of our perceptions" (AT VII,266): the more elaborate argument of the *Meditations*, Descartes says, was necessitated only by the first Meditation's hyperbolic doubt whether "things are in truth such as we perceive them" (ibid.).

In one sense, this is bluff: Descartes' readers, including the sympathetic Arnauld, were dissatisfied with his argument, for non-hyperbolic reasons. Nonetheless, the fact of the first Meditation helps to explain the difference between Descartes' argument for the real distinction and Augustine's. Here, as elsewhere, where Augustine simply reports some truth as perceived, or briefly cites some evidence without full argument, Descartes is concerned to answer objections, and to consider other possible explanations for the evidence. This is, typically, because Descartes is concerned with the possible gap between "the order of truth" and "the order of our perceptions," a gap which the first Meditation had been designed to open. Descartes, like Augustine, wishes to argue from the idea of a perfect God to a perfect God in reality, and from a knowledge of soul independent of knowledge of bodies to a soul distinct from bodies in reality. But whereas Augustine had thought that these inferences were straightforward (as we have seen, Augustine argues in *De Trinitate* X,x,16 that the mind cannot be (e.g.) air, because it does not *know* air in the interior way that it knows itself), Descartes' project of destroying and rebuilding our knowledge of bodies forces him to be more critical. Descartes wants to argue that our ideas of soul and God require that their objects have corresponding natures in reality, and he *also* wants to argue that most of our other ideas do *not* correspond to the natures of their objects: so he has to bring out the differences between our different ideas, to show the ways that ideas can fail to correspond to reality, and then to argue that none of these possibilities of failure can apply to the ideas of God and the soul.

The second Meditation does not argue that mind and body are really distinct, because we do not yet have a distinct knowledge of bodies. But Descartes does here, like Augustine, insist that our interior intellectual knowledge of ourselves as *res cogitantes* tells us what we are in reality: that

did not there wish to exclude these things [other attributes beyond thought that might belong to the nature of the soul] in the order of truth (which I was not considering there), but only in the order of my perceptions" (AT VII,8). The earlier form of Descartes' argument, which resembles Augustine's argument in *De Trinitate* X, is also close to Avicenna's so-called flying-man argument, given in the *De Anima* of the *Shifa'*, Book I, Chapter 1. I do not know any strong reason to believe that Descartes was aware of this Avicennian argument, even indirectly, but it is certainly possible (the passage is cited by Latin scholastic writers).

is, that it gives us *quidditative* knowledge of the mind, knowledge of what the mind is and not merely of some predicates it has. This needs argument.

All that the Meditator now knows about himself is that he has each of the modes of thinking involved in his activity of doubting: this is roughly, but not exactly, the list of activities that Aristotelian philosophy attributes to the *rational* soul. "What, therefore, am I? A thing that thinks. What is that? Surely a thing that doubts, understands, affirms, denies, wills, is unwilling, and also imagines and senses" (AT VII,28). Sensation and imagination, unlike the other activities on this list, are understood by the scholastics as acts not of the rational but of the sensitive soul, and as essentially involving bodily organs, so that, in doubting the existence of bodies, we would also be doubting these activities. But Descartes (like Augustine in *De Trinitate* X, following Stoic sources) takes these to be activities of the mind; or rather, he takes "sensation" to be ambiguous, referring on the one hand to a process occurring in the bodily organs (including the brain), and on the other hand to a mental activity which may or may not be *caused* by the physical process of sensation. The exercise of doubting all external things does not cast doubt on the reality of sensation in the second sense: even if there are no bodies to be sensed, even if I have no body, still "I am aware of bodily things *as if* through the senses. . . . I *seem* to see, to hear, to feel heat. . . . this [appearance] is what in me is properly called sensing, and taken precisely in this way, it is nothing other than [a kind of] thinking" (p. 29). In the usual psychologies, including the accounts of Rule 12 and of the sixth Meditation, this sensory appearance is said to arise when the mind turns its attention toward some bodily organ; nonetheless, we can initially isolate the concept of sensation in this sense without referring to anything outside the mind. And Descartes *must* proceed in this way to escape the impasse of the *Rules*: he cannot give a *Rules*-style physiological account of sensation and imagination until he has established the existence and nature of bodies, and he cannot establish the existence of bodies except by beginning with the sensory faculties and giving a criterion (independent of any account of bodies) for when they can give us knowledge. The second-Meditation account of mind, including sensation, is the first step on the path to a criterion of all the cognitive faculties.

For readers to accept Descartes' project for reconstructing science, we must be convinced that the mind's new knowledge of itself is distinct: for the mind is supposed to be the first and best known of all things, and this first *cognitio* is paradigmatic for all the knowledge to follow. To say that the mind's self-knowledge is distinct is to say that it is quidditative, i.e. that it tells us distinctly *what* the mind is, and not merely confusedly that it is something-we-know-not-what underlying some collection of accidents. The Meditator initially resists the claim that the mind's self-knowledge is quidditative or distinct, and so do many of Descartes' readers, notably Hobbes and Gassendi. So Gassendi complains that Descartes' arguments show "only a perception of the existence of the mind, but not of its nature," so that we conceive the mind "only confusedly and as an I-know-not-what" (AT VII,275). If so, the second Meditation has failed in its aim of showing that the mind is better known than the body: "whence also what was promised in the very title of the Meditation, that by it the human mind would be made better known than the body – I do not see how it has been done. For it was not your purpose to prove that the human mind exists, or that its existence is better known than the existence of body, since at least that it is or exists will not be controverted by anyone; doubtless, rather, you wished to make its *nature* better known than the nature of body, and this you have not done" (ibid.). The Meditator is supposed to have discovered what he is when he learns that he is "precisely a thing that thinks, that is, a mind, a spirit, an intellect, or a reason – words whose meaning was previously unknown to me" (p. 27); but Hobbes protests that these words cover an illegitimate attempt to convert a knowledge of our *act* of thinking into a knowledge of what *subject* underlies this act. To say *ego sum intelligens, ergo sum intellectus* or *ego sum cogitans, ergo sum cogitatio* – for this is the only sense Hobbes can make of Descartes' statement that he is a mind or intellect – is no better to say *sum ambulans, ergo sum ambulatio* (p. 172): it is to revert to the scholastic habit of creating an abstract noun out of some property of a thing, and promoting it to a separate immaterial substance (p. 177).[6] In fact, says Hobbes, the bare knowledge "I am thinking" yields, not only no *distinct* idea, but no idea at all, of the substance that thinks: for although we may form various propositions about something, we still do not have an *idea* of it until we have an *image* (p. 178). We will have an idea of the substance of the mind only when we can form a picture of the subject underlying the acts of thought, and this can only be understood to be a body (p. 173). So Hobbes thinks that Descartes, in jettisoning the knowledge of body and the images that might fill out the abstract concept of a thing that thinks, is abandoning all hope of gaining a distinct knowledge of what it is that does the thinking.

Descartes cannot have been very surprised by Hobbes' and Gassendi's reactions, since they are close to the Meditator's own initial reactions. That is, Descartes thinks that these reactions are the result of a natural tendency of the human mind, and so he makes his Meditator express and explore his doubts about whether the mind's new knowledge of itself is distinct or quidditative. Of course, Descartes thinks that in airing these doubts he can also dispel them, and he thinks that Hobbes and Gassendi have failed to understand the arguments of the second Meditation that were supposed to have anticipated their objections. But since the second

---

[6] This, for Hobbes, is the basic error that gives rise to the pseudo-discipline of metaphysics, and Descartes is slipping into it just as the scholastics had: compare *Leviathan*, chapter 46, "Of Darknesse from Vain Philosophy, and Fabulous Traditions" (in *Leviathan*, ed. C. B. Macpherson, London: Penguin, 1968, pp. 688–96).

Meditation "must be exercised and repeated for a long time, in order that a whole lifetime's habit of confusing intellectual with corporeal things may be effaced by at least a few days' contrary habit of distinguishing them" (AT VII,131, cited above), Descartes cannot be surprised that the lessons have not sunk in on all of his readers.

The Meditator, like Hobbes, is inclined to think that he does not truly know what a thing is until he has *pictured* it: "I am beginning to know somewhat better what I am; but it still seems, and I cannot help but think, that corporeal things, whose images are formed in thought, and which the senses themselves explore, are much more distinctly known than this I-know-not-what [part] of myself that does not fall under imagination" (p. 29). This inclination arises from a habit of immersion in the senses, leading us to accept sense perception as the standard for a distinct *cognitio*; it is also an expression of the tendency, which Descartes had deplored already in the *Rules*, to "despise obvious truths" such as our own existence as *res cogitantes*, and to suppose that no truth so obvious could have enough content to be the basis of a science.

Descartes' argument has two stages. First he argues that since any sensory knowledge we could have of ourselves would be *uncertain*, we must remain content with our intellectual self-knowledge, not trying to use the imagination to "fill out" its content; he then argues further that even if we *could* have sensory self-knowledge with certainty, it would still not be more *distinct* than what we know through intellect alone.

The first stage of the argument is almost too immediate to be called an argument; its main point is not so much to establish its conclusion as to introduce, for the first time in the *Meditations*, a clear explicit distinction between intellect and imagination as modes of thinking. The Meditator, having asked "what kind of thing" he is, and being dissatisfied with the answer, "a thinking thing," goes on to ask, "what else? I will imagine" (p. 27). Reexamining his earlier accounts of "what I once believed myself to be," a gross assemblage of limbs or some subtle body present inside them, the Meditator recognizes that, in the possible case that there is a deceiving god and no extended reality, there will be no body corresponding to what he imagines. Consequently, he does not *know* that he is anything he imagines himself to be. "To imagine is nothing other than to contemplate the figure or image of a corporeal thing; but I now know for certain that I exist, and that at the same time it could come to pass that all these images, and generally whatever has reference to the nature of body, would be nothing but dreams" (p. 28). Descartes, like Augustine in *De Trinitate* X, uses the verb *fingo* ("to shape, to depict, to make up") and its compounds as synonyms for "imagine": for both writers, the point is that in filling out our intellectual self-knowledge by the imagination we are filling it out with fictions, and that to attain distinct knowledge we must begin by subtracting those fictions. As Descartes puts it, to say "I will imagine, in order that I may learn more distinctly what I am" is no more reasonable than to say "I am now awake, and I see some truth, but because I do not yet see evidently enough, I will now deliberately fall asleep, that my dreams may represent this same thing to me more truly and evidently" (p. 28). Descartes compares sensation and imagination to dreams (which they may, of course, turn out to be) because, like dreams, these mental states have no necessary connection with the real existence or real nature of their objects. My intellectual knowledge of myself is like direct vision in that (far more than "vision" in the literal sense) it carries with it the certainty we would seek in direct contact with an object, that the link between thought and object cannot be broken. For this reason, only intellect can judge to what extent sensation or imagination happen to represent reality, just as only waking vision can determine whether (say) the treasure I have dreamed to be buried in my backyard is there in reality.

While the Meditator may now be resigned to knowing himself in the first instance by intellect alone (and setting aside the testimony of the sensory faculties until intellect can give a criterion for them), he still regards this situation as unfortunate. He does not see his intellectual self-knowledge as the beginning of the desired science, because he is not yet convinced that his intellectual self-knowledge is distinct: any knowledge (in particular, any self-knowledge) that he could have through the senses would be uncertain, but he is still inclined to think that if he *could* have such knowledge, it would tell him what he is more distinctly than does his current knowledge of himself as *res cogitans*. The point of the "wax passage" (AT VII,30–4) is to convince him that his intellectual self-knowledge is more distinct than any sensory acquaintance, and so (by anticipation) to resolve the objections of Hobbes and Gassendi.

The wax passage does not *extend* our knowledge of the mind, by telling us something new about ourselves beyond the fact that we think, in each of the modes of thinking that Descartes has listed. Gassendi would like Descartes to tell him something new: he wants a "quasi-chemical analysis" of the Meditator's "internal substance" (p. 277). Only such an analysis (Gassendi thinks) could give us a distinct knowledge that could make the mind better known than the body, of which we know so much through sensory observation and through the sciences of chemistry and anatomy (ibid.). Descartes, by contrast, thinks that he has already given a distinct knowledge of the mind: the only problem is to *show* that it is distinct. He cannot show this directly, by appealing to an absolute standard of distinctness, any more than he can show the certainty of his principles by appealing to an absolute standard of certainty: all he can do is to show that they are *more* certain or *more* distinct than anything else we can know. He does this by examining the rest of our knowledge, and showing that it is *less* certain and *less* distinct. Direct sensory contact, especially visual contact, is the commonly accepted paradigm both for certainty and for distinctness of knowledge; as the first Meditation had undermined our belief in the certainty of our senses, so the wax passage of the second Meditation will undermine or deconstruct the standard of distinctness that we take from the senses, and leave us with our intellectual self-knowledge as a new paradigm for science.

We ordinarily think that particular bodies are what we know most distinctly (AT VII,30). Descartes had discussed the *general* notion of body as a part of his pre-reflective concept of himself: its key properties were to occupy a definite place and to interact with the senses. A *particular* body that can be handled and perceived by all five senses will be the senses' best candidate for something of which they can say *what it is*. Descartes selects a piece of wax as his example.

A piece of real beeswax can be perceived by all five senses, and Descartes describes it in such a way as to make it vividly present to the imagination: but the purpose of all this description is to show that even what seems to be most distinctly given to the senses is not truly grasped by them. The wax is chosen because it is paradigmatically malleable, because the sensible qualities received in it can be erased while the wax itself which is their substratum remains. Descartes wants to examine our knowledge of some bodily substance present to our senses, and to analyze it to the extent that it is quidditative knowledge, that is, to the extent that we know what the substance is; he will attempt to isolate the quidditative knowledge, the knowledge of the substance, by stripping the sensible qualities away.

As the Meditator melts the wax before his fire, it loses its characteristic taste, smell, color, shape, consistency, and temperature, all the sensible qualities the Meditator had accepted as what "is required for a body to known most distinctly" (p. 30). And yet, even though the marks by which the senses had recognized the wax are gone, everyone agrees that the same wax remains. This physical stripping of the accidents from the wax helps us to perform a logical stripping: we recognize that the quidditative concept we have always had, our concept of what the wax *is*, has never been a sensory image of the wax. We must have conceived the wax in some other way, as something that can survive the passing of whatever particular qualities the senses perceive.

What, then, is the distinct conception of the wax? The Meditator tries out the same thought that Aristotle tries in *Metaphysics* VII,3: the wax is not its qualities but the substrate that underlies these qualities, "this body which appeared to me a little while ago distinguished by these forms, and now by different ones" (p. 30). While this is certainly a true description of the substance of the wax, it has no clear positive content (beyond dictating how we should *not* conceive the wax): it is not clearly distinguished from the I-know-not-what to which Gassendi reduces it (pp. 271–3). To isolate what is distinct in his conception, Descartes removes everything belonging not to the quidditative concept of the wax but to the concepts of its accidents, and examines what remains: "nothing other than something extended, flexible and changeable" (p. 31), which is the material substrate of bodies.

If some concept is to be more distinct than the concept of mind, it will be this concept of matter, which is the kernel of distinctness in our ordinary sensible concepts. But how is matter itself conceived? Not by the senses, since every sensible quality has been stripped from it: so distinctness will be found not in a *sensible* concept, but in something else that supports our sensible concepts. Is it a concept of the imagination? So Hobbes and Gassendi would say, and indeed it seems plausible to say that we regard an extended piece of matter as malleable because we *imagine* it being molded in different ways. If so, imagination will provide the simple concept of geometrical extension, and the many complex ideas that can be derived from it: this will be the basis of an imaginative science of geometry, which will have a strong claim to being what we most distinctly know, and thus will rival Descartes' science of pure intellect. It may, then, still be true that we know something most distinctly only when we can imagine it, and thus that the knowledge of the second Meditation is at least relatively obscure.

But Descartes denies this, because he denies that geometry is a science of imagination. While imagination may be an aid to the intellect in geometry, it cannot possibly constitute its standard of truth, since we know many things about geometrical extension that could not be known through imagination alone.[7] Imagination alone cannot conceive the nature of the matter that receives the various geometrical forms, Descartes says here, "for I comprehend that it is capable of innumerable changes of this kind, but I cannot run through innumerably many in imagination; therefore this comprehension is not accomplished by the faculty of imagination" (p. 31).

"It remains therefore that I should concede that I do not even perceive by imagination what this wax is, but by the mind alone" (ibid.): the quiddity of a corporeal thing is perceived, on the charitable assumption that it is perceived at all, neither by sensation nor by imagination but only by intellect. Thus the concepts of the sensory faculties are not, as they seemed to be, the most distinct: the mind's only competitors for being known best will be other things known through the intellect. Ordinarily we place the standard of distinctness in the senses, saying "I saw it with my own eyes" of the things we think we know most distinctly; but in fact (says Descartes) we did not see the wax with our eyes, or not what the wax *is*: all we see with our eyes, or perceive through our other senses, is a collection of sensible qualities, none of which is the substance of the wax. When we judge, rightly or wrongly, that we know what the wax itself is, we are going beyond the reports of the senses, bringing the mind to bear on a subject reserved to it: "and thus what I thought I saw with my eyes, I comprehend only by the faculty of judgment, which is in my mind" (p. 32).[8] If we do not distinguish the substance of the wax from its sensible

---

[7] Descartes will try to sort out more precisely the relations between intellect and imagination in the (fifth and) sixth Meditation (AT VII,72–3); here only the basic point is needed.

[8] As we will see in Chapter 7, Descartes does not really believe in a faculty of judgment, certainly not in one that could be said to "comprehend." But this does not really matter

qualities, our perception contains nothing "which it does not seem that any animal could possess"; but "when I distinguish the wax from the external forms, and consider it bare, as if its clothing were removed, then although there may still be error in my judgment, still this cannot be perceived without a human mind" (ibid.).

So we need compare our intellectual knowledge of the mind only with our knowledge of the other things we perceive by intellect, and not with what we perceive by the senses. But the knowledge that results from these other operations of the intellect is both more doubtful and less distinct than the mind's knowledge of itself. "Do I not know myself not only much more truly and much more certainly, but also much more distinctly and evidently?" (p. 33). I have quidditative knowledge of the wax only to the extent that I form a mental judgment that conforms to the nature of the wax; and by the very fact that this judgment belongs to my mind, it necessarily contributes to my knowledge of my mind itself, whether or not it corresponds to anything else. So any knowledge of the nature of other things implicitly includes a knowledge of the mind, while not every beginning in knowledge of myself extends beyond me. Quantitatively I know more properties of myself (I judge that the wax is as I see it, smell it, etc.) than I could hope to know of the wax (the wax may be as I see it, smell it, etc.), and the modes of thought are known at least as distinctly as the modes of extension.

Furthermore, if the perception of the wax seemed more distinct after it became known to me not only through sight and touch, but through many causes, how much more distinctly should I say that I myself am known, since no reasons can aid in the perception either of the wax or of any other body, without at the same time better proving the nature of my mind! (P. 33)

This is certainly one sense in which the mind can be said to be better known than the body, and in replying to Gassendi (p. 360) Descartes seems to suggest that this is the chief sense he intends.

But Descartes has also argued that the mind is best known in the stronger sense that knowledge of it is the condition of all distinct or scientific knowledge. If we find something lacking in this first *cognitio* (as if we complain that it does not reveal the mysterious "internal substance" of its object), then these are complaints which attach to all human knowledge and to which we must resign ourselves. If we would explore what our knowledge can yield, we cannot do better than to begin with the knowledge of our mind and its different ways of judging things, then to try to pass from this to a knowledge of how far these judgments correspond to reality. To do this Descartes follows Augustine by turning his attention from the idea of the rational soul to the idea of God as the standard of its rationality.

at this stage: the point is that the senses do not tell us what things are, and that the mind must do its best on the question.

B. Isolating God as Nous

B.1. The goals of the third Meditation

The third Meditation is the high point of the *Meditations* as a whole: the first and second Meditations are exercises in preparation for it, and the fourth through sixth draw out its consequences for science. The third Meditation is also the most distinctively Augustinian portion of Descartes' work, and represents the decisive Augustinian insight which Descartes had taken over (as I have claimed) in 1628. So I will devote the greatest attention to this Meditation: a close analysis of its details will reveal both the intimacy of Descartes' connection with Augustine, and the extent to which he transforms Augustine's thought in adapting it to his project of a new philosophy.

The third Meditation continues the line of thought of the second Meditation, and its project is closely analogous. The second Meditation argues that the soul is better known than bodies; the third Meditation argues that God is better known than bodies. The second Meditation achieves its end by showing that we have certain knowledge of the soul, even if we suspend judgment about the existence of bodies; the third Meditation argues that we also have certain knowledge of God, still without making any assumptions about bodies. In each case Descartes argues for the *existence* of the soul or of God, and so shows that the existence of the soul and God is better known than the *existence* of bodies; but in each case the arguments about existence are merely instrumental, and Descartes' real concern is with the *nature* of the soul and of God. By giving an argument for the existence of soul which proves *only* the existence of soul, and not the existence of anything bodily, Descartes teaches us to disentangle the concept of soul from all concepts of body; further, since the argument proves the existence only of a soul conceived intellectually, as a mind, and not of a soul conceived as the source of life to the body, Descartes also teaches us to disentangle the intellectual concept of soul from other concepts of soul; through these disentanglements I discover that I am "a mind, a spirit, an intellect, or a reason – words whose meaning was previously unknown to me" (AT VII,27). The project of the third Meditation is analogous: it is not just that Descartes gives a proof for the existence of God which does not (like most of the usual proofs) presuppose the existence of bodies; he is also giving a proof of the existence of God which cannot prove the existence of anything *except* God, and which can prove the existence of God only if God is conceived in a special, purely intellectual way, not as the mover or creator of the physical world, but as the standard of intellectual perfection to the soul. By meditating through this argument, while continuing to suspend belief in the existence of bodies, the reader discovers a distinct concept of God (or the *meaning* of the term "God"), independent of any concepts of bodies. Here as in the second Meditation, Descartes expects that his readers will have the greatest difficulty in recognizing and isolating the intellectual concept; once we have done this, we will readily see that the soul and God exist as we have conceived them to exist, and we will accept our *cognitiones* of soul and God as principles of philosophy.

The proof of God's existence that Descartes selects for the third Meditation is unmistakably Augustine's, and closely resembles a form of the argument that Augustine gives in *Confessions* VII. In this subsection I want to consider why the goals of the third Meditation led Descartes to select precisely this proof, and how these same goals lead him to modify Augustine's presentation of the argument; in the remainder of the section I will turn to a detailed analysis of the third Meditation itself, showing how and why Descartes argues as he does, both that we can know the existence of God, and that we cannot have equally immediate knowledge of the existence of anything else.

I have spoken of Descartes as "selecting" Augustine's proof. Descartes is well aware that there are other, and superficially less difficult, arguments that God exists. Descartes does not reject these other proofs (those collected by St. Thomas, and others like them) as illegitimate, but he gives reasons why he does not use them in the *Meditations*, and takes Augustine's proof as the only way to the special kind of knowledge of God he requires.[9] In the dedicatory letter of the *Meditations*, where Descartes explains his reasons for offering proofs of the existence of God and the real distinction of the mind from the body, he says that although everyone agrees that these two propositions are the province of natural reason, many people are of the opinion that they have never been proved, and for this reason refuse to believe that they are true (AT VII,1–3). At this point we might expect Descartes to say that, though the atheists are right that these truths have not been proved up to the present, they are wrong to conclude that they cannot be proved at all, and that he will offer in the *Meditations* the first genuine proofs of these important truths. Instead he says something much more modest:

I do not in any way agree with them, but think on the contrary that almost all the reasons which great men have brought to bear on these questions, when they are sufficiently understood, have demonstrative force; and I am persuaded that hardly any could be given which had not first been discovered by other people. (AT VII,3)

---

[9] Descartes does, of course, give two other proofs of the existence of God further on in the *Meditations*, first in the latter part of the third Meditation (AT VII,47–52) and then in the fifth Meditation (pp. 65–71), although neither of these is a "cosmological" argument like the majority of traditional proofs for God's existence. But Descartes does not present either of these arguments as independent of the main, Augustinian, argument of the third Meditation (through p. 47): they are both drawing out consequences of the purified intellectual concept of God that has been achieved through the Augustinian proof, and (as we will see) they are both chiefly designed to show that *only* this concept of God can give a knowledge of the actual existence either of God or of anything else outside the soul.

Descartes then cites the command of *nonnulli* [that is, Bérulle] that he apply his "method" to the questions of God and the soul; in obedience to this command, Descartes says that he will "once and for all carefully seek out the best of all [the proofs which have been given], and set them out so clearly and accurately that it will afterward be evident to everyone that they are demonstrations" (ibid.).

Of course, there is a catch in Descartes' remark that the traditional arguments are demonstrative "when they are sufficiently understood." Descartes, by selecting the best arguments and rearranging them according to the rules of method, is ensuring that the arguments proceed in order from what is first and most evidently known to what is posterior: this yields arguments which look rather different from Augustine's, and very different indeed from Thomas'. Descartes recognizes that the main argument of the third Meditation will seem strange and difficult, and he warns the reader in the Synopsis that "since, in order to withdraw my readers' minds from the senses as much as possible I chose not to use there any comparisons drawn from corporeal things, many obscurities may have remained" (AT VII,14). Descartes means, not that his argument is really obscure, but that it will seem obscure to readers who still find sensation the clearest form of perception; these readers would prefer the usual cosmological arguments, which begin with bodies or some bodily phenomenon perceived by the senses, and establish the existence of a God as a cause of these. Descartes avoids this type of argument, not just because he wants to show that the existence of God is more certain than the existence of body, but also and more fundamentally because he needs to give a distinct knowledge of what God is; and we cannot know what God is by knowing that he creates the physical world, any more than we can know what the soul is by knowing that it animates the body.

Descartes expands on this point in two parallel passages explaining why, if other people had already succeeded in proving God's existence, he should have had to construct the elaborate and unusual argument of the third Meditation.[10] He reaffirms the remark of the dedicatory letter, that all the classical proofs for God's existence are sound: "there is no effect coming from him from which one cannot prove his existence" (AT IV,112) as the cause of this effect. But Descartes thinks that

all these proofs, taken from his effects, reduce to a single one; and also that they are not complete, if the effects are not evident to us (this is why I considered my own existence rather than that of heaven and earth, of which I am not as certain), and if we do not add to them the idea we have of God. (Ibid.)

The first condition for a complete proof, that the effect it takes as a premiss must be evident, is obviously necessary, and is enough to explain why

---

[10] Descartes gives essentially the same answer both in the first Replies (AT VII,106–8) and in a letter to Mesland (AT IV,112). I will follow the letter to Mesland, which is simpler and clearer.

Descartes starts the proof from his own existence rather than the existence of bodies; but it is not enough to explain why Descartes does not (as Locke will do) simply begin from his own existence, and prove the existence of God as a first cause of himself.[11] Descartes insists here that it is also necessary, for two reasons, to include the idea of God in the effect being explained:

for, my soul being finite, I cannot know that the order of causes is not infinite, except inasmuch as I have within me this idea of the first cause; furthermore, even if one admits a first cause which conserves me, I cannot say that this is God unless I truly possess the idea of God. (Ibid.)

The goal is to prove, not merely that our chosen effect has some cause, and that this cause fills more or less the causal role usually ascribed to God, but that this cause is *God*: an argument showing merely that the world has a creator would not prove that this creator is not a deceiving demon, and would be of no use in establishing the sciences.[12] Descartes concludes that we must start from a quidditative concept of what God is, and only then argue that there is some cause which instantiates this concept. As Descartes says in the first Replies, "according to the rules of true logic, one should never ask of any thing *whether it is*, unless one has first understood *what it is*" (AT VII,107–8); this is a criticism of St. Thomas, who attempts to prove God's existence while maintaining that we cannot know God's essence in this life.[13] The embarrassment of the usual proofs in trying to exclude the possibility of an infinite regress is merely a symptom of the fact that we do not have a clear concept of what God is, or a proof that the first cause must conform to such a concept: we are con-

[11] So Locke, *Essay concerning Human Understanding*, Book IV, Chapter X. Descartes does, in the third Meditation's *second* proof of God's existence, prove God as the cause of the Meditator's own existence; but this proof, as Descartes presents it, depends crucially on the fact that the Meditator contains the idea of God: it would not work simply to begin with some-being-or-other and argue that the chain of causes of this being must ultimately lead up to God. As I will argue when I discuss this second proof in Section C below, much of Descartes' aim is negative, to show that this kind of proof *cannot* work without assuming the idea of God as part of the effect to be explained.

[12] One way to put the point: the *Letter to Picot* lists three principles of metaphysics, namely the existence of our "soul or thought," "that there is a God who is the author of everything which is in the world," and that this God, "being the source of all truth, did not make our understanding of a nature such that it could be deceived in the judgment it makes of the things of which it has a very clear and very distinct perception" (AT IX2,10). The third Meditation is entitled "of God, that he exists" (AT VII,34), and so seems to correspond to the second of these principles; but if it proves merely "that there is a God who is the author of everything which is in the world," without determining what this God is in himself, Descartes will be unable to derive the third principle from the second, and so will be unable to use his knowledge of God as a standard for deriving a knowledge of bodies. To prove that God is "the source of all truth" and so on, Descartes needs to know that the creator-God is *Nous*: the concept of God as Nous (properly elaborated) will be the quidditative concept of God that Descartes requires.

[13] For Descartes' intention here *contra* Thomas, see Descartes' comments on this passage in a letter to Mersenne, AT III,272–3.

ceiving the first cause so obscurely that we do not even know that it is not an infinite chain, and the fact that we cannot comprehend an infinite chain sheds no light on what the first cause really is.[14] To give a distinct knowledge of what God is, Descartes needs a proof that includes a distinct idea of God in its premises: and since the plan of all these proofs is to prove God as the cause of some given effect, this means that he needs to begin with the idea of God, or with some effect which includes the idea of God, and then show that the cause of this effect conforms to this idea of God.

This is precisely what Augustine does in *Confessions* VII,xvii,23, his detailed presentation of his ascent to the contemplation of God after reading the books of the Platonists. Augustine, like Descartes, is seeking to establish not just *some* sort of God, but a God answering to Plotinus' descriptions of Nous. Augustine's proofs, offered as a means of inducing an understanding of God, are derived from this strict conception of God, and attempt to demonstrate, not merely that the universe has a creator (this Augustine had always believed), but that there is an incorporeal source and standard of truth to the soul. Augustine is trying to understand God without images, and without relating him in any way to sensible objects, so that he can shed light on a problem (the origin of moral evil) which the senses cannot resolve. This makes his proofs of the existence of God (like the whole of the metaphysical structure they support) perfectly suited for Descartes' project of "withdrawing the mind from the senses" to metaphysical certainties, to gain an intellectual basis for a true science of sensible things.

Augustine describes how he ascended in contemplation from the sensible world to the "invisible things of God" (Romans 1:20) by seeking out the source of his judgments on sensible things, that is, the source of truth in his judgments or the standard by which he judged. He rises from bodies to the senses which perceive them, and thence to the common sense and the "reasoning power, to which what is received from the senses of the body is referred for judgment" (*Confessions* VII,xvii,23). He then ascends further, from his own mind to the immutable light of truth which he has discovered above the human mind:

This [reasoning power], discovering that this part of me too was mutable, raised itself up to its own understanding, and drew my thought away from its habit, withdrawing itself from the opposing crowds of images, in order that it might find what light was shed on it [i.e. by what illumination it was able to see] when it proclaimed without any doubt that the immutable was preferable to the mutable, and by which [light] it knew the immutable itself (for unless it had somehow known this, it could not have preferred it for certain to the mutable); and it attained to *that which is*, in the stroke of a trembling glance. Then indeed I caught sight of your invisible things, which are understood through the things which are made.

---

[14] For the point about infinity, see the first Replies, AT VII,106–7, and the letter to Mesland, AT IV,112–13.

Augustine here finds the immutable God he has been seeking by discovering that this God is the source of Augustine's own knowledge of the immutable; Augustine recognizes that he has some knowledge of the immutable because he recognizes that the immutable is superior to the mutable; and he recognizes that the immutable is superior to the mutable because he recognizes that, since his own mind is mutable, it cannot be the supremely perfect being he has been seeking. Although many details are left obscure in this extremely compressed account, it is clear that Augustine is beginning with his own concept of God as the immutable (or, more specifically, as something superior through its immutability to the mutable human mind), and then discovers that the cause of this concept of God is something which instantiates this concept of God. Descartes adopts this way of proving God's existence from Augustine because it does not rely on any physical theory or physical description of the effects God produces, because it concludes that God conforms to the intellect's conception of a perfect immutable being, and because it comes to know God precisely as a source of truth to the human mind, and as the perfect model which the human mind strives to imitate.

The whole of the third Meditation can be understood as an extended commentary on this passage of Augustine. But it is very much extended indeed: it spells out the argument in great detail, refutes possible alternative explanations for the origin of our cognition of God, and compares the argument from the idea to the reality of God with arguments for the reality of other things. So we will have to explain, not just why Descartes takes over Augustine's account of the knowledge of God, but also why, instead of repeating Augustine's straightforward description of an ascent from soul to Nous, Descartes gives us the complex argumentative structure of the third Meditation.

There is an obvious answer: Descartes is trying to give an absolutely conclusive argument for the existence of God, whereas Augustine is giving an autobiographical report of the process by which he came to a true understanding of God. Augustine came to this understanding by reading philosophical works, and meditating philosophically on their content, but what he is giving in the *Confessions* is something less, or anyway something other, than a philosophical argument for the conclusions he reaches. Descartes' argument for the existence of God may have been inspired by something he read in the *Confessions*, but he could not simply have taken it from there, as an argument: where Augustine simply affirms his perception of the divine reality as the source of his knowledge of the immutable, Descartes must *prove* that only God can be the source of the idea of God, by considering every alternative explanation an objector might devise, and eliminating each one as impossible.

Although this answer contains elements of truth, it oversimplifies the difference between the intentions of the *Confessions* and the *Meditations*, and it does not do enough to explain what objections Descartes does and does not consider. Descartes, like Augustine, deliberately avoids the form of a philosophical treatise, and substitutes the immediacy of a first-person narration. His intention, like Augustine's, is to help his readers to achieve an intuitive cognition of the reality of God, by retracing for them the steps by which he himself was led to this cognition. It is perfectly true that Descartes, unlike Augustine, is concerned to reply to possible difficulties that can be brought against the argument to God; but the reasons why he does this, and the particular kinds of difficulties he finds it necessary to answer, must be sought in the particular kind of intuitive cognition Descartes is trying to induce. The crucial point (as usual) is that while Augustine merely wants to induce an understanding of God as something *other* than the objects of sensation, Descartes' scientific project requires him to show how we can know God *better* (both more certainly and more distinctly) than we know sensible things. In the third Meditation, as in the second, he faces a double task: to show that his arguments yield indubitable knowledge of the existence of God or of the soul, and at the same time that these arguments do *not* yield a knowledge of bodies (or of our confused imaginative conceptions of soul and God), which remain susceptible to universal doubt. This ambition forces Descartes to add a great deal of elaboration to Augustine's argument.

For Augustine, the hard part seems to be the recognition that we do have some *cognitio* of the immutable; once we have recognized this, it seems to follow automatically that we came to know the immutable by *seeing* the immutable, and thus that an immutable being is the cause of our knowledge of the immutable, and thus that an immutable being exists. But if this argument proves the existence of an immutable object, it should equally prove the existence of a *red* object; and Descartes wants to show that the existence of God is more certain than the existence of something red. Worse: if the argument proves that the cause of our idea of an immutably perfect object is as we represent an immutably perfect object to be, it should equally prove that the cause of our idea of a red object is as we represent a red object to be; and Descartes' science is supposed to show that there are no such objects, or at least that no such objects are the causes of our sensations. We are ordinarily much more confident in assuming that our sensation of redness comes from something red than in assuming that our intellectual concept of God comes from God; Augustine makes the assumption about God, perhaps on the model of the assumption about redness; but Descartes is trying to show both that the assumption about God is genuinely certain, and that the assumption about redness is not.

What Augustine is implicitly asserting is that our idea of God as Nous is *cataleptic*; Descartes is asserting that this idea is cataleptic, and that sensory impressions are not. Recall that in the first Meditation Descartes had invoked the arguments of Cicero's *Academica*, which turn on the question of whether any of our impressions are cataleptic: that is, whether we can have an impression of X which is both causally derived from X, and "stamped" in accordance with the nature of X, in such a way that it could not be derived from anything other than X. Cicero's character Lucullus, the spokesman for a commonsense dogmatism, recounts and then tries to refute the sceptical arguments that none of our impressions are cataleptic (because for any true impression, a deceiving god or some similar agency might produce a false impression indistinguishable from it, etc.); Lucullus himself believes that many of our ordinary sensory impressions are cataleptic. Descartes uses the sceptical arguments in the first Meditation to show that we do not have any cataleptic sensory impressions; now, in the third Meditation, he argues that Augustine was right that we do have a cataleptic intellectual idea of God, i.e. that this idea is internally of such a character that it could only have been produced by such a God as it represents.

The third Meditation is structurally more complex than any of its parallels in Augustine, just because Descartes is trying to show simultaneously that the idea of God is cataleptic and that other ideas are not: as Descartes tells Clerselier, "I insisted on how little certainty we have about what we are persuaded of by the ideas we regard as coming from outside, to show that there is none of these ideas which makes anything known with as much certainty as the idea we have of God" (AT V,354). Descartes first recalls the positive results of the second Meditation, proposes the "general rule . . . that everything I perceive very clearly and distinctly is true" (AT VII,35), and then recalls from the first Meditation the reasons why this rule cannot yield certainty until we can derive some standard of clarity from a knowledge of God (pp. 34–6).[15] Although the second Meditation gives some knowledge of the mind, it does not (like the projected psychology of Rule 12) give a rich enough theory to determine when the mind is functioning well or badly. To do this we will need some knowledge of the nature of things outside the mind; and we will need to gain such knowledge by starting from our knowledge of the mind. The obvious way out of the circle is to discover some cataleptic idea, which can bridge the gap between knowledge of our thoughts and knowledge of the nature of things; this knowledge of the nature of things might then support a theory of the mind's operations, and thus a criterion of the truth or falsity of our other thoughts. If Augustine is right that we have a cataleptic idea of God, and if this is our *only* cataleptic idea, then a knowledge of soul and God (not of soul and body, as in Rule 12) will give the unique foundation for science: this is the gambit of the *Meditations*. So, in the third Meditation, Descartes analyzes the problem of science, examining what passages there might be from knowledge of what is in the mind to knowledge of what is outside it, that is, examining what grounds we can have for thinking that some of our ideas are produced in us by the things they purport to represent. Descartes will tease out the principles of our habitual confidence that (at least some) sensory impressions are of this character; he will expose the falsity of these principles, and isolate the only remaining

---

[15] On the first-Meditation arguments, see above, Chapter 5, Section C.

principle for recognizing ideas as cataleptic (namely, their degree of "objective reality"); he will then argue that the idea of God, and only the idea of God, is cataleptic by this standard. As we will see, it is precisely the Plotinian–Augustinian idea of God as Nous which this procedure isolates as the only possible basis for scientific knowledge of things outside us, whether of God or of anything else.

B.2. Judgments and the causes of ideas

At the foot of AT VII,36, Descartes has finished reviewing the sobering lessons of the first Meditation, and he concludes that "the first time the occasion occurs, I should examine whether there is a God and, if there is, whether he can be a deceiver; for if I am ignorant of this matter, it does not seem that I could ever be fully certain of any other." But rather than arguing directly that God exists and is not a deceiver, Descartes is determined to examine systematically the things we already know (our own thoughts), and to discover what passages might lead to the things we desire to know (the nature of things outside us, which might make our thoughts true or false); besides being in accord with the *esprit géometrique*, this procedure allows Descartes to rule out any passages other than the passage from the idea of God to God.[16] The examination of our thoughts requires, in the first place, that we divide our thoughts into their categories, to see "in which of them truth or falsity properly subsist" (AT VII,37), and then that we consider what criteria they give us for discerning this truth, "what reason might move me to judge that [certain of my thoughts] are similar to [external] things" (p. 38).

Descartes bases his analysis of thoughts on the distinction between ideas and judgments, his preferred way of formulating the Stoic distinction between impressions [*phantasiai*] and assents to impressions.[17] Ideas,

---

[16] As Descartes writes to Clerselier, "having the plan of drawing a proof of the existence of God from the *idea* or *thought* which we have of him, I thought I was obliged to begin by distinguishing all our thoughts into certain kinds, in order to note which of them could be deceptive; and, in showing that even chimeras have no falsity in themselves, to forestall the opinion of those who might reject my reasoning because they count the idea of God as chimerical. I also needed to distinguish between the ideas we are born with and the ideas which come from elsewhere or which we ourselves produce, to forestall the opinion of those who might say that the idea of God is made by us, or acquired from what we have heard said about him. Furthermore, I insisted on how little certainty we have about what we are persuaded of by the ideas we regard as coming from outside, to show that there is none of these ideas which makes anything known with as much certainty as the idea we have of God. Finally, I could not have said that 'another way occurs' [AT VII,40: the passage through the objective reality of ideas], if I had not previously rejected all the others, and in this way prepared my readers to conceive the better what I had to say" (AT V,354–5).

[17] I briefly discussed the Stoic theory of impressions, as it appears in Cicero's *Academica* (which would have been one of Descartes' main sources), in Chapter 5, Section C, above; I give a more detailed discussion of similarities and differences between the Cartesian, Stoic, and scholastic theories of judgment in Chapter 7, Section A, below. Let me stress

whether sensory or intellectual, are "like images of things" (p. 37), while other thoughts contain something more than a simple representation. The most important of these are judgments, containing some affirmation or denial; since only judgments can be in the strict sense true or false, it is only these "in which I must beware lest I be deceived" (ibid.). We might therefore expect Descartes to examine the causes of good and bad judgment, and to give conditions under which our judgments will be non-deceptive; and Descartes in fact does this in the fourth Meditation. In the third Meditation, however, he examines the classes of *ideas* rather than of judgments. This is reasonable, since his primary intention is not to give rules for forming judgments, but to extend the scope of *scientia* from the mind to other things; and, of things within the mind, it is our ideas which may give us a clue to the natures of things outside us. If we have some cataleptic idea, this idea will accurately reflect the thing which causes it, and so will give some knowledge of the natures of things. Only in this way can we derive a scientific criterion, without the circularity of Rule 12; we will fall into error if we do not use a first cataleptic idea to establish a criterion of truth, and instead assent to non-cataleptic ideas as if they were cataleptic.

Descartes says that "the principal and most common error which can be found in [my judgments] consists in my judging that ideas, which are in me, are similar or conformable to certain things which are placed outside me" (AT VII,37); and (Descartes implies) we most commonly make this judgment because we believe that our idea of X has been *caused* by a corresponding external X.[18] Descartes proceeds to examine the evidence

that Descartes had no particular interest in Stoicism (except to a limited degree in ethics), and would not have thought of his account of judgment as especially Stoic. But Descartes' project makes central the question about the conditions under which we should suspend our habitual judgments, and the *locus classicus* on this question is Cicero's *Academica*: the two parties there, the sceptical New Academy and the dogmatic "Old Academy," both accept the Stoic theory of judgments as assents to impressions, but disagree about whether any impressions are cataleptic and so deserve our assent. Descartes (like Augustine in the *Contra Academicos*) thinks that neither of the parties in Cicero is right, that sceptical weapons can defeat a sense-based dogmatism but are defeated by a purely intellectual criterion of truth. But neither Augustine nor Descartes seriously considers Stoicism (or Antiochus' "Old Academy") as a live option, or is concerned to argue against it: the preeminent representative of sense-based dogmatism is for Augustine Manicheism, for Descartes scholasticism. And they consider the theory of judgments as assents to impressions, and the notion of a cataleptic impression, not as Stoic property, but as a way of stating the disputed question about when we should assent. Descartes has good reasons for using this particular theory of judgment (rather than, say, the scholastic theory of judgment as combination), because he wants to stress both our freedom to suspend judgment with regard to obscure ideas (discussed below, Chapter 7, Section A) and the gap between our, non-cataleptic, sensory ideas and the world they purport to represent (discussed in the present section and in Chapter 8, Sections B and C).

[18] Again, it is part of the Stoic theory of impressions that, in assenting to an impression, I judge that something outside me is "similar" to the impression, and (typically) that this external thing is the *cause* of my impression, stamping its likeness on me: this is how cataleptic impressions are actually produced (e.g. *Academica* II,vi,18; II,xxiv,77; Sextus

for such belief. His language here may suggest that he thinks of external objects as implanting little images of themselves in the soul, but really this is the view Descartes ascribes to his philosophical opponents and to the prejudices of the senses, not one he himself accepts. After reviewing the kinds of evidence which (he thinks) we habitually accept in passing judgment on the natures of things, Descartes concludes that "it is not from a certain judgment, but only from some blind impulse, that I have hitherto believed that there existed things different from me, which impressed ideas or images of themselves upon me by the organs of the senses, or by any other arrangement" (AT VII,39–40). Although Descartes will propose a *kind* of causal reasoning to give us knowledge of the existence and nature of God, this will be based on a different kind of causality, the properly *rational* causality through which the soul is affected when it perceives some truth by the light of reason; Descartes thinks that we commonly accept a merely natural, subrational causality – the "fate, chance, or a connected series of things" of the first Meditation, which *impel* the soul without illuminating it – as a criterion of the truth of our ideas, and Descartes is determined to show that this is a false criterion which gives no knowledge of the natures of things.

Ordinarily it is our *sensory* ideas which we usually suppose to proceed from, and to correspond to, external things. When Descartes classifies the apparent genera of our ideas into those which seem to be innate, those which seem to be adventitious, and those which I seem to have made myself (AT VII,38),[19] all the examples of adventitious ideas are sensory impressions: "that I now hear a noise, see the sun, or feel a fire, I have previously judged to proceed from certain things placed outside me." Descartes says that he will examine this kind of idea, typified by the idea of

---

Empiricus *Against the Logicians* I,247–52), and when I assent (wrongly) to a non-cataleptic impression I am treating it as if it were cataleptic. Descartes does not say much about the different possible logical forms of ideas and of judgments (e.g. if I assent to an idea with a complex propositional form, am I judging that this idea was directly *caused* in me by the corresponding fact?): he is, of course, chiefly concerned to undermine our confidence that bodies outside us resemble our sensory ideas of them. Descartes is also not very explicit about what *kind* of "similarity" or "conformity" I might judge an idea to have with an extramental object: but he does not mean that the extramental thing would share properties with the idea as a mode of thought, but only with the objective content of the idea. As I argued in "The Greatest Stumbling Block: Descartes' Denial of Real Qualities" (in *Descartes and His Contemporaries: Meditations, Objections and Replies*, ed. Roger Ariew and Marjorie Grene (Chicago: University of Chicago Press, 1995)), Descartes is chiefly concerned with *structural* properties of ideas and their objects: my ideas of sensible qualities are *tanquam rerum*, and represent the qualities as present in bodies *tanquam res in rebus*, when in fact the qualities are merely privations or modes of bodies, so that the structure *in re* does not correspond to the structure of my ideas (see AT VII,43–4 on the sense in which the idea of cold might be materially false; I have some brief discussion below, Chapter 8, Sections B and C, but see "The Greatest Stumbling Block" for a full discussion).

[19] "Adventitious" means (as the French translation has it) "foreign and coming from outside" (AT IX1,29).

the sun, in order to determine "about these [ideas] which I consider as being taken from things existing outside me, what reason may move me to judge that they are similar to these things" (ibid.). Descartes' principal question here is not whether my ideas have *some* external cause (merely knowing this will not give us distinct knowledge or *scientia* of the cause) but whether the cause of the ideas, even supposing it is outside the mind, conforms to the ideas. Descartes offers two arguments to this conclusion, which he regards as making explicit our customary grounds for what we take to be *scientia*; by refuting these arguments he will expose the weakness of our ordinary criteria, and prepare us to see that only the idea of God will do.

The first reason for believing that my sensory ideas proceed from external objects which resemble them is that "I seem to be so taught by nature" (p. 38). Since this can only mean, as Descartes will comment in refuting this argument, "that I am borne by a certain spontaneous impulse to believe" that my idea of the sun proceeds from a real sun resembling it, this first argument leads naturally to the second:

I experience that these [impressions] do not depend upon my will, and therefore not upon *me*, for they are often observed despite me: as now I feel heat whether I will or no, and I therefore think that this sensation or idea of heat comes to me from something different from me, namely from the heat of the fire before which I sit. (Ibid.)

This second argument explicates the presuppositions of the first: when I reflect that nature seems to teach me that my idea of heat proceeds from something hot, I am observing the phenomenological character of my reception of the idea of heat, and noting that it is presented to me with such force or vividness that I "naturally" suppose it to come from something outside me. Descartes formulates this into the argument that since the force of the idea is independent of, and can override, my will, it must come from something outside me. I am inclined to believe that this cause of my idea resembles the idea, just because "there is nothing more plausible than to judge that this thing should impress its own likeness upon me, rather than something else" (ibid.).

"I will now see whether these reasons are firm enough" (ibid.). The argument from nature is not firm enough to prove what it is designed to prove, because "nature" in the sense of a spontaneous impulse merely impels me; it does not shed any light upon the object that I am considering. One may certainly speak of a "natural light of reason" which does, when it operates, illuminate the objects of our understanding, and so gives us a certainty about them based upon the truth of the matter. But "there is a great difference between these two things" (ibid.): what I am shown by the natural light is indubitable, and must always be taken as true, because it is the standard of truth for all the other cognitive faculties, and can never itself be called into question by any of them. But reason often discovers that the natural impulses (or, as the French translation qualifies them, those which *seem* to be natural – they may be simply habits which have become "second nature") have acted in error. These are known simply as psychological powers, and as such are not *necessarily* in any relation to the truth; their truth or falsity must be judged by a higher standard. Descartes had begun the first Meditation by noting how many false beliefs these spontaneous impulses had led him into; then, for the purpose of separating himself from them more effectively, he had represented them to himself as acting all together, under the form of the deceiving God or evil genius, and resolved to believe nothing which he had only upon this deceptive authority. Now, in the third Meditation, where Descartes systematically investigates the possible means for going from a perception of ideas to a perception of realities, he will not accept this substitution of psychological powers for the light of truth; his purpose is to reject all pathways to reality that depend on such a substitution, and isolate the perception of the intellectual light as the only way to a knowledge of reality.

The same considerations show why the second argument must be rejected. To observe that my impression of heat at a given moment does not proceed from my will does not enlighten me about the nature of heat: it does not give me a perception of a hot object in reality as the source of my idea, but merely reveals the obscurity of the causes of what takes place in my mind. There may well be some unknown power in me which produces my impressions; as Descartes adds, this seems to be the case in dreaming, and I do not yet know anything about my ordinary sensory impressions that distinguishes them from a dream. It is probable that these impressions do proceed from an external cause; but this argument has not given me any perception of it, any more than it gives me a perception of the causes of my dreams. The cause, even if external, need not resemble the idea it produces; it may, in the extreme case, be an evil genius. Descartes makes no mention here of the evil genius or deceiving God, a powerful image needed only for "bending the will in the opposite direction" (AT VII,22), and out of place in an analytic argument; but he does describe the kind of discrepancy which actually arises between ideas and their causes, and which is symbolized by the images of the first Meditation. My sensory idea of the sun, says Descartes, "is eminently to be reckoned among those I regard as adventitious, and through it [the sun] appears to me very small" (p. 39). If I yielded to the impulse to suppose that it came from something external which resembled it, I would have been convinced (like Epicurus; cf. AT IX2,6) that the sun was no bigger than it appears; which is contrary to everything that the reasonings of the astronomers have taught us. The sensory idea of the sun exemplifies those impressions which have in their favor only the vividness with which they strike the mind, and Epicurus, in accepting this theory of the sun, exemplifies those thinkers who accept this vividness as a criterion of truth. The idea which astronomical reasonings can give us of the sun has no such vividness in its favor, and does not proceed by as direct a causal route from the object it represents; but reason tells us that it is correct, or at least that it is more likely to be correct than the sensory idea, and it is rational justification, rather than the strength of our natural inclinations, which must guide our judgment of the correspondence of our ideas to reality.

Although Descartes alludes specifically to Epicurus when he mentions the sensory idea of the sun, he means to catch Stoics and scholastic Aristotelians also in the same condemnation. Recall Lucullus, the spokesman for dogmatism in Cicero's *Academica*: he thinks that many ordinary sensory impressions are cataleptic, and to refute the objection that dreaming impressions may be indistinguishable from waking sensations, he replies that the impressions of dreamers and madmen are *weaker* than real sensations.[20] For Lucullus, the *strength* of an impression (its vividness, or vividness plus stability) constitutes its clarity, and serves as a criterion for its truth.[21] This is just what Descartes is denying. The strength with which we are inclined, whether by Epicurean *eidôla*, Stoic alterations of the soul, or scholastic sensible species, is a product of the causality of nature – of "fate, chance, or a connected series of things" – and does not reveal the natures of things. At best, if the inclination is truly the result of a healthy nature, it can show us how to act to preserve our soul–body union; such practical direction cannot yield scientific knowledge, unless it is controlled by some intellectual perception. But while the causality of nature produces the force with which ideas strike the soul at any given time, it is not responsible for the objective content of these ideas: to the extent that these ideas do have objective content (and are not simply impulses of pursuit or avoidance), they must derive this content from a properly *rational* causality, the causality which acts on souls by showing them and not by pushing them. Descartes concludes that the clarity of our ideas must be sought in their objective content, not in their vividness or their independence of our will; and if any idea is cataleptic, it will be through an extreme of "objective reality" and not through an extreme of motive power.

B.3. Objective reality and the isolation of the idea of God

After rejecting the arguments from the vividness of our ideas, Descartes says that "another way occurs for inquiring whether some of those things whose ideas are in me exist outside me" (AT VII,40): namely, an analysis of the objective realities of our different ideas. As Descartes tells Clerselier, he had been aiming all along at this new criterion of our ideas; but, as Descartes makes clear in the same letter, his ultimate aim is not just to

[20] So Cicero puts it in his reply to Lucullus (II,xxvii,88); Lucullus had said that drunks "assent more weakly" to their hallucinations, and afterwards realize how "light" these impressions were in comparison with ordinary sober ones (II,xvii,52).
[21] Note the Stoic definition of opinion as "weak assent," which Cicero had cited at *Academica* I,xi,41, and also at *Tusculan Disputations* IV,vii,15.

single out ideas with content (as against the vivid but empty ideas of sensation), but to single out the idea of God from all other ideas.[22]

The degree of objective reality of an idea, or the "being of the thing represented, insofar as it is in the idea" as a pure essence (AT VII,161), is of course a measure of the truth of the idea, in one sense of the word "truth"; but Descartes is concerned with the truth of the judgment that the idea proceeds from an actually existing cause which resembles it, and this is something over and above the amount of reality contained in the essence. So it is not enough to say that the criterion for the truth of our ideas must be sought in their objective content; we must also discover what principle about the objective content of our ideas warrants the assertion that these ideas proceed from a cause which resembles them. By formulating the proper principle, and showing that it applies only to an intellectual idea of God, Descartes aims both to single out this special idea of God from non-cataleptic ideas whether of God or of other things, and to present the resulting knowledge as the foundation for all *scientia* of things existing outside the mind.

Descartes' assertion that the idea of God is cataleptic is (as we have seen) inspired by Augustine's sequence of thoughts at *Confessions* VII,xvii,23: since my mind has recognized that it is inferior to the immutable Truth (or Nous), it must somehow have known this Truth itself; the source of this illumination can only have been "that which is," the reality contained in the Truth itself. But Augustine does not consider the problem of passing from *cognitiones* to the existence of their objects. He seems to feel that, for ideas of pure intellect, the problem does not arise: all genuine intellectual knowledge is knowledge of some thing, and must derive from contemplation of that thing. The kind of intellectual knowledge that Augustine is concerned with is not knowledge of the actual existence of physical things: it is knowledge of God, or knowledge of the rules of wisdom ("the immutable is preferable to the mutable") or of number ("$7 + 3 = 10$"), or judgment on how bodies *ought* to be. For Augustine, the fact of our knowledge that $7 + 3 = 10$ implies the existence of eternal objects outside our minds, the numbers, or the rules of number, or the eternal truth in which these rules are true; we know the proposition by intellectually "seeing" the objects it concerns. In a certain sense Descartes agrees with these claims: he will say in the fifth Meditation that his geometrical knowledge requires that the triangle have "a certain determinate nature or essence or form, immutable and eternal, which was not made up by me, and does not depend on my mind" (AT VII,64); but even so, triangles "may not exist anywhere outside me" (ibid.). The ob-

---

[22] "I insisted on how little certainty we have about what we are persuaded of by the ideas we regard as coming from outside, to show that there is none of these ideas which makes anything known with as much certainty as the idea we have of God. Finally, I could not have said that 'another way occurs,' if I had not previously rejected all the others, and in this way prepared my readers to conceive the better what I had to say" (AT V,354–5, quoted in a previous note).

jects of intellectual knowledge must be real in the order of essences or eternal truths, but not necessarily in the order of existing things: Descartes, living after St. Thomas, takes this distinction for granted,[23] but Augustine has never heard of it. Augustine assumes that any "nature or essence or form, immutable and eternal," will be an eternal substance, indeed somehow consubstantial with God; both in the *De Musica* and in the *De Libero Arbitrio* he uses this argument to raise us through numbers to knowledge of God. Descartes cannot accept so easy a passage from essences or objective contents of ideas to actually existing things.[24]

Indeed, Descartes' plan is to make us as conscious as possible of the gap between essences (or idea-contents) and existence, in the case of *bodies*, so that he can argue that only a knowledge of God will allow us to cross this gap and to judge whether bodies actually exist as we conceive them. Descartes agrees with Augustine that no gap arises in our knowledge of *God*; and this is why God (who is the source both of idea-contents and of existing things) can allow us to cross the gap in the case of other things. But by raising the issue of whether an idea might not be derived from the thing it represents, Descartes can isolate the idea of God as the *only* idea whose objective content implies the actual existence of the thing it represents, and thus demonstrate that the knowledge of God is the only way to a science of other actually existing things.

Descartes therefore proposes, as a means of passing from ideas to externally existing things, the principle that each idea has some particular objective content, and that "this it must surely have from some cause in which there is at least as much formal [i.e. actual] reality as the idea contains of objective reality" (AT VII,41): this will equally be true whether I get my concept of a horse by looking at an actual horse, or by looking at a divine archetype which eminently contains all the perfections of horseness. Thus

if the objective reality of one of my ideas is so great that I am certain that it cannot be in me either formally or eminently, and therefore that I myself cannot be the cause of this idea, it will necessarily follow that it is not I alone who exist in the

---

[23] So when Hobbes raises some doubts about the fifth Meditation's talk about eternal essences or natures of non-existing things, Descartes replies simply, "*nota est omnibus essentiae ab existentia distinctio*" (AT VII,194). One consequence of admitting non-actualized essences is that (against what Augustine seems to assume) the *causes* of our intellectual perceptions must often be something other than their *objects*, since non-actualized essences can be *objects* of knowledge, but cannot be (efficient) *causes* of our knowledge, or of anything else.

[24] Caution: the objective realities of ideas (discussed in the third Meditation) are not exactly the same as the essences of things (discussed in the fifth Meditation). While in the fifth Meditation we can distinguish the essence of triangle from the essence of square (by recognizing predicates that must be affirmed of one and denied of the other), in the third Meditation we can only be sure that there must be something that contains at least as much reality as is represented in the idea of triangle, and something that contains at least as much reality as is represented in the idea of square: these might be one and the same thing.

world, but that some other thing, which is the cause of this idea, also exists. But if no such idea is found in me, I will have no argument at all to make me certain of the existence of anything distinct from me; for I have most diligently inspected them all, and thus far I have been able to find no other. (AT VII,42)

Descartes does not argue for the principle that each idea must be caused by something containing as much reality as the idea represents, since he regards this as a primary notion, "than which there can be nothing more evident or more true" (AT VII,135), and which therefore cannot be proved from anything better known.[25] But he thinks that we always implicitly presuppose this principle, and that we will not be tempted to reject it: "on this alone hangs every opinion we have ever had about the existence of things placed outside our mind: for whence have we come to suppose that they exist, but from this alone, that ideas of them come to our mind through the senses?" (p. 135).[26] If this reconstruction of our habitual reasoning is correct, then Descartes' principle is strictly *notior* than any truths about the physical world; and Descartes does not aim at any stricter demonstration of certainty. He devotes himself, rather, to arguing that his principle does not support the knowledge of actual existence we habitually take it to support, and does support a knowledge of the actual existence of God. Here I will not venture to provide *grounds* for Descartes' principle (and so rush in where Descartes fears to tread); but, by sketching the general theory of the causes of ideas which Descartes states on the authority of the "natural light," I will try to bring out why the idea of God as Nous enjoys the special status that it does on this theory.

Descartes speaks of effects as receiving reality from their causes: by this

---

[25] What look (vaguely) like arguments for the principle in the third Meditation are better described as attempts to restate the principle, and to show that the intuition it expresses is also presupposed in other more familiar formulae: see below on the relation of the common maxim *ex nihilo nihil fit* to Descartes' causal principle. But none of these other formulae are more basic, or more provable, than Descartes' causal principle, and we can only embarrass ourselves by trying to extract from the text an argument for Descartes' principle.

[26] So too at AT VII,165, in the fifth "axiom or common notion" of his geometrical presentation of his metaphysics, Descartes asserts that his causal principle is an axiom "which it is so necessary to admit, that on it alone the knowledge of all things, sensible as well as non-sensible, depends"; and he argues that we have implicitly applied this axiom in all our ordinary judgments of existence, e.g. in judging that the heaven exists, where we can only have been relying on our idea of the heaven, and judging that the objective reality of this idea must have a really existing cause, which we judged (rightly or wrongly) to be the heaven itself. Descartes is apparently claiming, not merely that his causal principle is the only justification *ex post facto* for our judgments of existence, but also that we must have been using this principle when we made our judgments. Even if I rely (mistakenly) on the *vividness* of my idea of the heaven in judging that this idea has been produced in me by an actual heaven, I am judging that the cause is something external that *resembles* the idea, and this can only mean that it resembles the *objective reality* of the idea: I know that the objective reality of my idea of the heaven must come from somewhere, and I make the "natural" assumption that it comes from an actually existing heaven.

he means not simply that their existence or actuality is due to their causes, but that they receive from their causes whatever perfections they have. This leads, in the first place, not to a principle about the sources of objective reality, but to a principle about the sources of formal (or garden-variety) reality: "it is clear by the natural light that there must be at least as much in the efficient and total cause as in the effect of this cause. For whence, I ask, could the effect receive its reality, if not from the cause? And how could the cause give it, if it did not also have it?" (AT VII,40). This principle is related to the common maxim *ex nihilo nihil fit*, not so much by being derived from it, as by being a more adequate expression of the intuition this maxim presupposes, namely that for a thing to acquire any reality it must *receive* it from some source (even God, for Descartes, receives his reality from God). If an effect receives its existence exclusively from its cause (as the phrase "efficient and total cause" implies), then the effect must derive its whole content or reality or perfection from this cause: any surplus in the effect would, absurdly, have to arise from nothing.[27] But the effect can certainly be *less* perfect than the cause, since it can fail to receive all the perfections of its cause, or else reflect them in a distorted way: there is no need to posit a source for imperfections as there is for perfections.

Descartes wants the principle about the sources of objective reality to be closely analogous to the principle about the sources of formal reality: "it is also a primary notion that every reality or perfection which is in ideas only objectively must be either formally or eminently in their causes" (p. 135), and this is supposed to be undeniable for the same reason that the principle about formal reality is undeniable. "For if we suppose that anything occurs in an idea which was not in its cause, it will follow that the idea has this from nothing" (p. 41); and this is absurd as before. Descartes is assuming that, whenever I have an idea with some positive content, I acquire this idea by "looking" at some actually existing thing, and this thing is the cause of my idea: since the effect receives its reality (including its objective reality or representative content) from its cause, any additional reality in the effect would have arisen from nothing. Here, as in the case of formal reality, there is no need to posit a special source for *imperfections*, since the idea can omit or distort some of the perfections of its cause: "it is clear to me by the natural light that ideas exist in me like images, which can easily fall short of the perfection of the things from which they are taken, but which cannot contain anything greater or more perfect" (p. 42). Indeed, some ideas may not receive any reality from a model, or from any positive cause at all, but may result merely from imperfection and ignorance: for if any of my ideas are "false," in that they

---

[27] Here I am paraphrasing Descartes' own discussion (in the second Replies, AT VII,135) of the relation between his causal principle and the common maxim *ex nihilo nihil fit*. Descartes stresses that the two statements express the same *notio*: it is not that one of the two statements is more basic, for either can be derived from the other.

fail to have any representative content, then "it is known to me by the natural light that these ideas proceed from nothing, that is, that they exist in me for no other cause than that my nature is lacking something and is not fully perfect" (p. 44). But any positive reality or perfection existing in the soul (in the characteristic way that things exist in the soul, i.e. objectively) must be derived from elsewhere, from some actual being whose perfection the soul receives or imitates according to the measure of its own nature.[28]

Descartes' thought here is very close to the Plotinian theory of the existence of things in the soul and above and below it. For Plotinus and Augustine, the form of this table, before it was received in the table, existed in a different way in the mind of the carpenter; and, to the extent that carpentry is a mathematical discipline, the carpenter himself has received this form by looking at the rules of number contained in Nous or Truth. When the soul sees some reality in Nous, reproduces it in itself, and transmits it to a body, perfection can be lost in the transmission, but cannot be gained; any positive reality represented in soul must be derived from some model. Descartes gives the example of someone who "has in his intellect the idea of some machine thought out with the greatest design" (in the first Replies, AT VII,103; presumably we know he has this in his intellect because he actually builds the machine):

Different kinds of causes might be given for this design: either it is some real machine of this kind which has been seen before, and in whose likeness this idea was formed; or it is a great knowledge of mechanics which was in that intellect; or perhaps a great subtlety of mind, through which he was able to make the discovery even without previous knowledge. But it should be noted that all the design which is in this idea only objectively must necessarily be in its cause, whatever kind of cause it turns out to be, either formally or eminently. (AT VII,103–4)

Descartes admits that the engineer might derive his art from someone else who had the same knowledge before him, and this person would possess the design objectively rather than formally;[29] but for Descartes, as for Plotinus, this just defers the real question of the origin of the art, and we must eventually get back to the original model: "although one idea may sometimes arise from another, no infinite regress occurs here: some first idea must be reached, whose cause will be like an archetype, formally containing all the reality which is in the idea only objectively" (AT VII,42).[30]

[28] The source of the perfection might, of course, be in the soul itself considered in its formal reality, as an actually existing substance which we can represent as we can any other.
[29] Descartes makes this possibility explicit in a note in the Synopsis of the third Meditation (AT VII,14), which refers back to the present passage of the first Replies.
[30] Contrast Aristotle, to whom it seems open to say: all human beings by nature possess the art of carpentry *in potentia*; this man, from being potentially a carpenter, was made actually a carpenter by his teacher, who was actually a carpenter; he in turn was made actually a carpenter by his teacher; and so back *ad infinitum*. There would thus be an infinite transmission of the form of the table (as contained in the art), just as there is an infinite

Descartes will not agree with Plotinus and Augustine that the mathematical arts have archetypes in God. But the basic Plotinian claim is that everything positive represented in soul derives from *some* actual model, not that this model is always in Nous. Plotinus admits, in particular, that mimetic arts do not have archetypes in Nous: the painter looks to his corporeal model, and not to anything divine (though the model itself might have a higher archetype). What we clearly cannot have derived from looking at bodies are our ideas of the standards by which we judge how bodies *ought* to be: if these standards are never perfectly satisfied by any actual body we have seen, then we must have derived them from looking at something more perfect than bodies. This is an argument that Augustine uses, in *Confessions* VII,xvii,23 and elsewhere, to establish the existence of something superior to body.[31] But Descartes is not trying in the third Meditation to prove the existence of something superior merely to bodies, since he has, from the beginning, had the knowledge of the rational soul. The causal principle of the third Meditation will establish some new claim of actual existence, beyond the existence of the rational soul, only "if the objective reality of one of my ideas is so great that I am certain that it cannot be in me either formally or eminently, and therefore that I myself cannot be the cause of this idea" (AT VII,42). The only idea that we clearly cannot have derived from looking at the mind is our idea of the standard by which we judge how the mind *ought* to be: if the mind does not perfectly satisfy this standard, then we must have derived it from looking at something more perfect than ourselves. The idea of Nous, as the standard by which we measure the rightness of our thought and the extent of our knowledge, is the only idea that remains to prove the existence of something outside the soul.

B.4. The proof of God's existence

After arguing (AT VII,42–5) that no ideas except the idea of God have enough objective reality to require the existence of something outside the mind, Descartes turns to argue (pp. 45–7) that the idea of God does represent something greater than the mind, and that what it represents must actually exist. But there are many different ideas of God, and different arguments tending to show that one or another of these ideas is instan-

---

transmission of the form of a human being. For the contrast between Plotinus and Aristotle on this point, see Chapter 3, Section C, above.

[31] "For seeking *whence* I approved the beauty of heavenly or earthly bodies, and *what was present* to me when I judged rightly about mutable things and said, 'this ought to be so, that ought not to be so' – thus seeking that *whence* I judged when I so judged, I discovered the immutable and true eternity of truth above my mutable mind" (*Confessions* VII,xvii,23): discussed above, Chapter 4, Section B. Augustine does, of course, immediately go on in *Confessions* VII,xvii,23 to give the more precise argument about the kind of immutable standard (namely Nous) that is required specifically for judging the *mind*: but he does not address the question of how these arguments are related, or of how much each can prove.

tiated. Descartes is much concerned, both by the way he brings us to the idea of God and by his subsequent argument, to isolate one particular idea of God, which is supposed to give quidditative knowledge of what God is. Since God cannot be defined, the verbal formulae Descartes uses to paraphrase "God" do not give much enlightenment about what Descartes thinks God is; but by seeing how Descartes intends the idea of God to function in our thought, and how he argues that God actually exists, we can see to what extent he is using the Plotinian–Augustinian conception of God as Nous, and the Plotinian–Augustinian proofs that a God so conceived actually exists.

Descartes' initial description of his idea of God looks formally like a definition: "by the name 'God' I understand a substance which is infinite, independent, supremely intelligent, supremely powerful, by whom I myself, and everything else that exists if anything else does exist, have been created" (AT VII,45).[32] But this is not a definition, since its terms do not specify independent conditions that a thing must satisfy in order to be God: each single attribute which applies to God, in the sense in which it applies to God, applies *only* to God; and all the different names given to God signify the same simple thing. As Descartes says later, "the unity, simplicity, or inseparability of all these things which are in God is one of the principal perfections I understand to be in him" (p. 50): so I can understand what God is only through a simple intuition, and the terms in the "definition" (all standing for the same reality) can only help me to *recognize* this intuition.[33] Rather than arguing separately that each perfection he attributes to God must formally exist outside his mind, and then arguing that these all coexist in the same thing, Descartes simply argues that his idea of God is instantiated, and he takes it to follow that God has all these perfections. Indeed, Descartes claims that this holds, not just for perfections like knowledge and power, but even for God's relational property of being the creator of anything else that exists: to Hobbes' complaint that he has not proved creation, Descartes replies that "this idea includes a power so immense that we understand it to be contradictory, if God exists, for anything else to exist besides him except what is created by him" (AT VII,188). We will see below how Descartes can make good the claim that his idea of an infinitely perfect being implies this relational property.

[32] Descartes had given a similar list earlier, when he had noted the idea of God as one of his many ideas, AT VII,40.

[33] In asserting the unity of the divine perfections, and therefore God's undefinability, Descartes is not saying anything radical, or even anything controversial. The scholastics unanimously agree that God is undefinable, and (except for the Scotists) they agree that the divine attributes are identical *in re* and at most rationally distinct, i.e. that our reason distinguishes them, and our language imposes different words for them, only because we compare God to different creatures or consider him in different relations to creatures. For one exposition of this standard scholastic doctrine, see Thomas, *Summa Theologiae*, Pars Prima, Q. 13 aa1–4. On Descartes' commitment to God's simplicity, and against "radical" readings of Descartes' claim, see also below, Chapter 8, Section A.

In the course of his argument, Descartes refers to God as an "infinite substance" (p. 45) or an "infinite and supremely perfect being" (p. 46): these expressions are useful as shorthand, but they are purely formal descriptions and do not afford a distinct knowledge of what God is, since they do not show what perfections God is conceived to possess.[34] In following Descartes' argument, we may start by using his neutral terminology of "infinite being"; but the course of the argument will help us to fill in the concept of God, and to see that Descartes' argument essentially depends on, and works to isolate, a concept of God as Nous.

Descartes' official task is to show that the idea of an infinite being could have arisen only from an actual infinite being. Descartes thinks this conclusion is already implied by his causal principle: he does not now try to construct additional positive arguments for God's existence, but simply refutes possible objections, possible alternative origins for the idea of God; by this means he hopes not just to clear away doubts but also to elucidate more distinctly the idea of God. The first and most obvious objection is that I might derive my idea of the infinite, not by contemplating something infinite, but by negating my concept of the finite; this explanation is suggested by the grammatical structure of *infinitum* as *non finitum*.[35] In this case, Descartes' causal principle could still be true, but his conclusion would not follow, since the idea of the infinite would not have a positive representative content, but would merely negate some features observed in finite things, and "project" the negations onto an imagined infinite being.

To answer this objection, Descartes has to establish that the idea of the infinite is neither a negation nor a confusion based on a negation, but distinctly represents some positive content.[36] Descartes says that infinity

[34] God is supposed to contain *all* intelligible perfections: "whatever I clearly and distinctly perceive, that is real and true, and bears with it some perfection, is entirely contained in this [idea]" (AT VII,46). But this does not help until we can spell out what these perfections are. Even then, these perfections may be in God not formally, but only eminently: since extension is a perfection, and God is not formally extended, he must be eminently extended, but this does not give us a distinct idea of what God is. I will argue below that the distinct content of the idea of God comes entirely from conceiving him as Nous, that is, as the infinitely perfect standard by which we measure the perfection of *knowledge* (and not, say, of extension).

[35] This is a natural objection to Augustine's claim that, in order to have judged that the immutable is superior to the mutable, I must have seen the immutable itself: why is it not enough to have seen the mutable and judged that its mutability is a defect?

[36] The cases Descartes must exclude are (i) that our idea of the infinite is like our idea of rest, which is not a "true idea" in itself, but is merely the negation of the positive idea of motion, and does not represent its object as something positive; and (ii) that the idea of the infinite is like the idea of cold, which does present its object to us as something positive, but which will be "materially false," will be misrepresenting a non-*res* as a *res*, if coldness is in fact just the negation of heat (see AT VII,46 for the comparison between infinity and coldness, AT VII,43–4 for the sense in which the idea of cold is "false"). In the second case, our positive idea of the infinite would be the result of a confusion, so that if we restricted ourselves to what we conceive *distinctly* in the infinite, we would find a mere negation like the idea of rest. (On representing non-*res* as *res*, and on the point Descartes

cannot be a negation, because "I manifestly understand that there is more reality in an infinite substance than in a finite one" (p. 45). This might mean only that, in order to arrive at the idea of an infinite substance, I have to add something positive to my idea of a finite substance, and cannot reach the infinite by adding a mere negation. Descartes in fact believes something much stronger, that I have a "prior . . . perception of the infinite than of the finite, i.e. of God than of myself" (ibid.): for I could not "understand that I doubt, that I desire, that is, that I lack something and am not entirely perfect, if there were in me no idea of a more perfect being, by comparison with which I might recognize my defects" (pp. 45–6).

Descartes is claiming that we judge a thing's degree of perfection by measuring it, at least implicitly, against something (not just quantitatively more perfect but) having the perfection *by its essence* and without any limiting imperfections. This is the crucial presupposition of Plotinus' and Augustine's arguments for God, and is originally the teaching of the *Phaedo*, arguing that the perception of the approximately equal depends on a recollection of the equal-itself:

When someone sees something, and thinks that this thing he is now seeing *wants* to be like some other thing, but falls short and cannot be what that other thing is, but is inferior – then, necessarily, the person who thinks this must somehow already have known the thing that he says this resembles but falls short of. (*Phaedo* 74d9–e4)

In order to recognize that I, or any other finite being, "want" or lack further perfections, I must first know the ideal standard that the finite being falls short of: as Descartes says against Gassendi, "it is not true that the infinite is understood by negating a *finis* or limitation, since on the contrary every limitation contains the negation of infinity" (AT VII,365). Descartes' point is most easily understood through the analogy with spatial limitation: I conceive of a limited space by adding the idea of limits to the idea of space as such, and space as such is infinite. I cannot reach the idea of infinite space by negating the idea of spatial limits, or by amplifying the idea of a small bounded region; on the contrary, the idea of bounds presupposes the idea of a space outside the bounds, and ultimately the idea of infinite space. Similarly, Descartes says, the idea of a being of limited perfection presupposes the idea of the perfections this being lacks, and ultimately the idea of infinite perfections. I cannot reach the idea of an infinite being by negating the idea of limits or amplifying the idea of a finite being, since I conceive of a finite being by adding the idea of limits to the idea of being as such, and being as such is infinite: "from this alone, that I conceive *being* or *that which is*, without thinking whether it is finite

is making about the idea of cold, see my "The Greatest Stumbling Block: Descartes' Denial of Real Qualities"; the topic is glanced on, though not properly discussed, in Chapter 8, Sections B and C, below.)

or infinite, it is infinite being that I conceive; in order to conceive a finite being, I must subtract something from this general notion of being, which must therefore precede it" (AT V,356).[37] So when I first conceive of myself, if I am aware of my defects, I presuppose a concept of an infinite standard of perfection; if I am not aware of my defects, this is because I have not yet distinguished a proper concept of myself from my prior concept of an infinite being.

The characterization of the concept of God as the concept of an infinite standard of perfection does not make it clear what God is: we have not yet distinguished Descartes' concept of God from Plato's concept of the triangle-itself, which is absolutely (infinitely, if you like) triangular, and the standard for judging the imperfect triangularity of other things. To reach a distinct concept of God, we must know *what* perfections to ascribe to him. It is true, but still insufficient, that an infinite being contains *every* perfection either formally or eminently: doubtless God is eminently triangular, but this does not tell me what he is formally, and does not give me a distinct knowledge of his essence. To understand distinctly what God is, I must understand at least some particular perfections;[38] and I must understand what these would be if they existed in an infinite degree, so as to be freed from any dependence on imperfections, and so as to imply all other perfections.[39]

---

[37] In several parallel texts (fifth Replies, AT VII,365 and 370–1, and the letter to Hyperaspistes, AT III,427), Descartes admits that the mind does have "the power of amplifying all created perfections, that is, of conceiving something greater or more ample than them" (AT VII,365); but he argues that we can have this power of amplification only because we already (at least implicitly) have an idea of an infinite being. So the human power of amplifying ideas is not an *alternative* to positing an actual infinite being as the source of our idea of an infinite being.

[38] Descartes seems to be saying, in the passage at AT VII,46 from which I have just quoted, that our idea of God is supremely distinct, even if we do not understand his attributes. But the objection Descartes is considering is that "there are innumerable other things in God which I cannot comprehend," not that he understands nothing at all of what is in God; and when he concludes that the idea of God is *maxime clara et distincta*, the only standard of "*maxime*" he can apply is that "the idea which I have of him is the most [*maxime*] true, and the most [*maxime*] clear and distinct, *of all those which are in me*" (p. 46; my emphasis), because it contains everything which I clearly conceive in other things. If I could distinctly conceive no perfections at all, my idea of an infinitely perfect being would still be at least as distinct as anything else I could conceive; but this would show only that I could conceive nothing at all distinctly. Thus in order to bring out a positively distinct idea, Descartes must teach us to understand at least some of God's perfections.

[39] In scholastic language, a perfection will be formally in God if and only if it is a *pure* perfection, i.e. a perfection that does not entail any imperfection; by contrast, a *mixed* perfection is an attribute that is good for a certain kind of imperfect being to have, but is possible (or is a perfection) only for that kind of imperfect being. (To use Aristotle's example from *Nicomachean Ethics* X,8, temperance is a perfection for the kind of being that is susceptible to base appetites, but it is not a perfection for a god, and cannot be attributed to gods at all.) Thus while extension is a perfection, and while there are other perfections that presuppose extension, these cannot be *pure* perfections, since extension entails divisibility, which is an imperfection (as Descartes points out, AT VII,138). This is why God is not a triangle, and why there is in a strict sense no "perfect" triangle: this

The details of Descartes' argument show that his conception of the infinite being corresponds, not to Plato's concept of any particular Form, but to the Plotinian–Augustinian concept of Nous. Descartes' proof in fact leads us through the same sequence of thoughts as do Plotinus' and Augustine's ascents to Nous or Truth; this fact is obscured by Descartes' use of the scholastic terminology of the "infinite being," but becomes apparent when we examine what is distinctly conceived within the idea of the infinite being. When I, the Meditator of the third Meditation, try to clarify my concept of an infinite being, I conceive this being as the standard by which *I myself* am judged to have a certain limited degree of *knowledge*; the result is that I conceive God as having infinite knowledge, and that this knowledge is the only perfection I distinctly conceive in God. This result could be deduced even if the text of the third Meditation did not make it explicit, since at this stage of the meditative process I am the only finite substance I distinctly conceive, and since I distinctly conceive myself only insofar as I am a thing that thinks. But in fact the third Meditation repeatedly reminds us that God is to be conceived, not just as a standard of perfection in general, but specifically as a standard of intellectual perfection to the soul.

We have already seen Descartes' argument that I could not "understand that I doubt, that I desire, that is, that I lack something and am not entirely perfect, if there were in me no idea of a more perfect being, by comparison with which I might recognize my defects," and his conclusion that I must have a "prior . . . perception of the infinite than of the finite, i.e. of God than of myself" (AT VII,45–6). I myself am the finite being I perceive, and I know I have a prior concept of an infinite being only because I recognize that I myself lack something; and I recognize this only by recognizing that I lack some knowledge.

It is easy enough to see that the deficiencies the Meditator perceives in himself reduce to lack of knowledge and lack of power, and that the attributes he assigns to God all follow from omniscience and omnipotence.[40] It is less obvious that the Meditator's deficiencies all reduce to lack of knowledge: he understands not only that he doubts, but also that he desires, and the phrase "I lack something" glosses both of these recognitions. Surely when I judge that I am imperfect from the fact that I desire, what I am lacking is the *power* to obtain the thing I desire. But the Med-

---

is already the line of thought that Plotinus uses in arguing that various kinds of things do not have forms in the intelligible world.

[40] God is understood to be infinite and supremely intelligent, also independent, supremely powerful, and the creator of anything else that may exist (AT VII,45; the same attributes, with eternity in place of independence, p. 40). My judgment that God is independent or eternal is clearly supposed to follow from my perception of his power to maintain himself in existence without the cooperation of any external cause; if I can also judge from my idea of God that he is the creator of anything else that exists, this is because "this idea includes a power so immense that we understand it to be contradictory, if God exists, for anything else to exist besides him, unless it is created by him" (p. 188).

itator recognizes his own impotence only by recognizing his ignorance. This conclusion is inevitable, since he has come to know himself in the second Meditation only as a thing that thinks. He can say "I understand that I desire" only because in the second Meditation he discovered the attribute of desire in his new concept of himself as thinking; and this was because "it is I myself who now doubts almost everything, who however knows something, who affirms that this one thing is true, who denies other things, *who desires to know more* and does not wish to be deceived" (AT VII,28; my emphasis). I derive all these attributes by reflecting on the intellectual perfections (i.e. the *cognitiones*) which I either know that I possess, or conceive that I might come to possess. I can properly affirm that I desire to know more things, since I distinctly conceive what the power of knowing more things would be, and I perceive that I *could* possess this power, and wish to possess it, but do not. I could not affirm in the same way that I desire to rule the empires of Mexico and China, even if I have some obscure idea of these countries, and imagine that I would be happier if I ruled them: for I do not know that there are such countries, or that power over them is something I might intelligibly possess. In such cases the recognition of a desire (as a subjective feeling) does not reveal any real imperfection in me, except the imperfection of my knowledge revealed by the very obscurity of my desires.

The proper consequence of all this is not that we are inferior to God only in our ignorance, but that our ignorance prevents us (in our present condition) from knowing any of the other ways in which we are inferior to God. But in one passage of the third Meditation Descartes comes close to drawing the stronger conclusion. He says, in considering the possibility that he might himself *potentially* possess the divine perfections:

I observe that my knowledge is already increasing little by little, and I do not see any further obstacle to its increasing more and more, to infinity; *nor do I see why, with my knowledge thus increased, I could not by its aid acquire all the other perfections of God.* (P. 47; my emphasis)

This is strange enough that Mersenne suggested that "acquire" might be a slip of the pen for "understand"; but Descartes told Mersenne that he meant what he said (AT III,329), and in reply to Burman's query he says not merely that the Meditator (in his ignorance) could not perceive what more beyond knowledge he was lacking, but that the Meditator's suspicions contained some truth. Burman had asked, "but what can knowledge contribute toward acquiring the other perfections of God?"; and Descartes replies, "much in every way; for through it we become wiser, more prudent, we know those perfections more clearly and thus we more easily acquire these things which are clearly known: with wisdom and prudence the means to gathering them should be available" (AT V,154).

These texts help us to specify the content of Descartes' idea of God. Descartes has claimed that we can prove that the objects of our ideas actually exist only by showing that the ideas must have been produced in us by the things they represent; he has claimed that we can know this only if the objective content of the idea is something greater than we ourselves are. The idea of God was isolated as the only idea which meets this standard: that is, as an idea of something containing and exceeding our own perfections. We recognize that we have such an idea only by recognizing that we have been implicitly using it as a standard to measure our perfections: and these perfections, so far as we know them, are intellectual perfections. We thus know God's nature, and will come to know his existence, only insofar as he is the absolute standard of intellectual perfection; any further knowledge of God must be derived by drawing out implications from this basic idea.

Descartes describes his idea of God, toward the end of the third Meditation, in terms which manifest its Plotinian and Augustinian ancestry, and which show how inseparably it is twinned with the idea of the rational soul. God has made me in his own image and likeness, Descartes says, and

I perceive this likeness, in which the idea of God is included, by the same faculty by which I perceive myself: that is, when I turn the mind's eye in on myself, I understand not only that I am something incomplete and dependent upon another, and something that aspires indefinitely to greater and better things; but at the same time I also understand that he upon whom I depend has all these greater things within himself not just indefinitely and potentially, but really infinitely, and is therefore God. (AT VII,51)

"By the same faculty" here amounts almost to "by the same act": Descartes claims that the concept of the soul we acquire by looking inward is intrinsically a conception of the soul *as related to God*. When we learn in the second Meditation that the soul thinks (knows, judges, doubts, desires to know more), we are already implicitly conceiving an ideal standard of thought, a being which possesses of itself the intellectual perfections we can only gradually acquire: just as, for Plotinus, conceiving the soul as rational means conceiving it as *nous dunamei*, and so conceiving it in relation to *nous* in the primary sense. The task of the third Meditation is to spell out the concept of God implicitly used already in the second, and to make it clear that the God so conceived actually exists.[41]

To say that Descartes conceives God as the standard of the soul's intellectual perfections is not to say that this God is merely omniscient, and need not possess the other divine attributes. This would be the case if he were merely a *soul* possessing all the knowledge souls can possess; but God is not here conceived on the model of the soul. To say with Plotinus

---

[41] Contrast St. Thomas, for whom the agent intellect is simply the highest faculty of the soul; the soul can be understood on its own, without involving a conception of God; God is to be known, not by beginning with the soul, but by beginning with the contingency of creaturely existence. For Descartes, as for Augustine, this relation between God, the soul, and the "truths" of things which are present in them is essential both for understanding God and for understanding the soul.

that God is *nous energeiâ(i)* is to say not just that he is omniscient, but that he is *essentially* omniscient; and since the fact that God knows X cannot be dependent on anything outside God, it follows that God must have knowledge by being himself the standard according to which knowledge is assessed, and not merely by being perfectly conformed to that standard. This is, for Plotinus and for Augustine and for Descartes, the primary way of knowing; souls have knowledge only in a weaker and derivative way, and we confuse our conceptions of God's knowledge if we imagine it along the model of psychic knowledge. From the principle that God knows everything, in the special way that God knows and not in the way that souls know, we are able to infer other divine attributes. Thus Plotinus concludes that Nous not only *knows* all the intelligibles, but also *is* them, or contains them all within itself; otherwise, Plotinus argues (following Aristotle), it would have to connect up with something outside itself in order to know the intelligibles, and so of itself it would be *nous* only potentially. Descartes cannot accept this conclusion, since his soul aspires to be and his God actually is *omniscient*, knowing intelligible bodies and not just separate intelligible Forms; so Descartes accepts the scholastic amendment that God can know X essentially *either* if X is identical with God, *or* if X depends essentially on God's will: in the latter case God knows X just by knowing his own will to produce it, and so he does not become dependent for his knowledge on anything outside himself. Since God essentially knows everything, everything is either identical with God or essentially dependent on God's will. Thus the conclusion that God is the creator of everything outside himself is not an added stipulation in the idea of God, but an implication of the idea of God's infinite intellectual perfection.[42]

[42] On the scholastic accounts of God's knowledge, and Descartes' adaptation of these accounts, see Chapter 8, Section A, below (for Descartes and the scholastics the object of God's knowledge must either be identical with God or depend essentially on God's will: there is no need to mention the Plotinian option that it might be *contained* in God, since God's simplicity implies that whatever is contained in God is identical with God). For further discussion of the relation between God as Nous and God as creator, see Section C below. It is important to Descartes' argument that the non-relational idea of God entails God's relational perfection of being the creator of everything else that exists. It would not be enough to include "creator of everything else that exists" by stipulation in the idea of God, since (as Hobbes points out, AT VII,187) I could have derived the idea "creator of everything else that exists" from many individual finite agents, and derived the ideas of God's non-relational perfections from an infinite being that is not a creator; Descartes can answer this only by arguing that the different perfections represented in the idea of God are mutually implying, and thus that the non-relational perfections imply the perfection of being the creator of everything else that exists. Descartes explicitly claims at AT VII,188 that infinite *power* entails being the creator of everything else that exists, but this also follows from *knowledge*. No *finite* knowledge, i.e. no knowledge of the kind souls can have, would imply creation; but because the absolute standard of knowledge is not just omniscience but *essential* omniscience, a being that has this kind of knowledge must be the creator of everything it knows other than itself, i.e. of everything that exists other than itself.

What I have said so far explicates Descartes' claim that his idea of God has a determinate positive content, and that this content entails the traditional divine attributes. This claim is a crucial step, but not the final step, in Descartes' proof of God's existence. Descartes has argued that the idea of God represents a real essence and thus a *possible* existence, and that it contains objectively at least as much reality as a finite mind potentially possesses, and more than a finite mind actually possesses. Descartes' causal principle allows him to infer that the idea of God proceeds from some cause which contains formally all the perfection that the idea of God contains objectively, that is, infinite perfection, and in particular infinite intellectual perfection. It seems that Descartes should now be able to infer that a God actually exists outside the Meditator's mind, and that this God has all the perfections Plotinus and Augustine attribute to Nous or Truth.

Descartes draws this inference, but not immediately. He first considers the objection that the idea of God might arise, not from a God existing outside the mind, but from something potentially present within the Meditator himself. From the way Descartes formulates this objection, and from the fact that he feels obliged to refute it, we can see more clearly and precisely how Descartes' argument restates and develops the Plotinian argument for a separate Nous-in-actuality.

The objection looks very strange:

Perhaps I am something greater than I myself understand, and all the perfections I attribute to God are somehow in me potentially, even though they do not yet reveal themselves and are not reduced to actuality. For I observe that my knowledge is already increasing little by little, and I do not see any further obstacle to its increasing more and more, to infinity; nor do I see why, with my knowledge thus increased, I could not by its aid acquire all the other perfections of God; nor, finally, do I see why the potentiality [or power] for these perfections, if this is now in me, should not be sufficient for producing an idea of these perfections. (AT VII,46–7)

The suggestion is: although it has been shown that God either does or can exist, *I myself* have the potentiality to become God, and so I may have derived my idea of God, not from observing an actual God, but from observing the potential God, myself. This starts to sound less bizarre when we translate it back from Descartes' language about God into Plotinus' language about Nous. "Perhaps it is ridiculous to ask whether there is a *nous* among beings; though probably some would doubt even this. We should ask, rather, if it is as we say, and if it is something separate, and if the [intelligible] beings and the nature of the forms are in it" (Plotinus V,9,3,5–8). Plotinus wants to show that Nous is other, prior and superior to the soul: "for it is not the case, as they think, that soul when it has been perfected generates Nous" (V,9,4,4–5). This is Plotinus' statement of the Stoic position that intellection does not exist separately from rational souls, which develop from irrationality by a natural process. In order to establish, against the Stoics, the separate existence of Nous, Plotinus takes up the Aristotelian argument that, although the soul may pass from potential to actual intellection, it can do so only through the agency of something already possessing actual intellection; this will be Nous in the strict sense, having actual intellection in its essence, and it will be separate and divine.

Descartes too adapts this same ultimately Aristotelian argument to show that the intellectual perfections attributed to God have not only a potential existence in the soul, but also an actual existence in something actually infinite. Descartes' conclusion is the same as Plotinus'. His strategy of argument is different, in that Plotinus uses the Aristotelian argument to give a direct proof of the existence of a separate Nous, while Descartes is merely removing an objection to his main argument. Plotinus argues that the soul cannot acquire intellectual perfections unless something else first has these perfections essentially; Descartes avoids this physical or metaphysical argument, and restricts himself to the logical argument that the soul cannot have an *idea* of its acquiring perfections unless it first has an *idea* of something else possessing them essentially; and he makes this argument, not to prove the main claim that God exists, but to refute the objection that the idea of God might be derived from the idea of the soul. Still, the substance of Descartes' argument remains much the same: for the idea of the soul could be the origin of the idea of God only if the soul, by reflecting on itself, could recognize itself as potentially divine. So the picture Descartes has to refute is much like the Stoic picture Plotinus is attacking, which holds that the soul is naturally capable of intellectual perfections, and that once it realizes this capacity it will satisfy the full content of the idea of Nous. Both Descartes and Plotinus have to argue that what *primarily* possesses intellectual perfections is something superior and prior to the soul which realizes its intellectual capacity. The crucial difference is that, while Plotinus and Augustine do not distinguish between proving that this superior Nous is real as an object of intellectual perception and proving that it exists in actuality, Descartes must be very careful to make this distinction; but Descartes' proof for the irreducibility of the *idea* of Nous remains very much like Plotinus' proof for the irreducibility of Nous itself.

The Meditator's suggestion that "all the perfections I attribute to God are somehow in me potentially, even though they do not yet reveal themselves and are not reduced to actuality" is a version of the suggestion in Plotinus that "soul when it has been perfected generates Nous." But Descartes proposes all this, not to explain the origin of God, but merely to explain the origin of our *idea* of God: "nor [do I see] why the potentiality for these perfections, if it is already in me, should not suffice to produce the idea of them." To show that the idea of the actually X could not be derived merely from contemplating something potentially X, Descartes invokes his own version of the Aristotelian and Plotinian principle that actuality is prior to potentiality.

Descartes first argues that not everything we conceive to be actual could have emerged from potentiality; then he argues that even if everything actual did emerge from potentiality, the *idea* of the actual still could not be derived from the *idea* of the potential, but would have to exist before it. To prove his first claim, Descartes argues that it is unintelligible for a being *essentially* possessing a perfection to have acquired its perfection from a state of having it only potentially. As he says,

> though it be true that my knowledge is gradually increasing, and that there are many things in me potentially which are not yet actual, still none of these things pertains to the idea of God, in which nothing at all is potential; indeed this very thing, to be "gradually increasing," is a most certain mark of imperfection. (AT VII,47)

Thus although beings can emerge from potentiality to actuality, the fact of having done so marks them as intrinsically potential, so that nothing produced in this way could be God. In Plotinian language, Descartes is saying that although a soul, as "potential Nous," might over time acquire the different truths which are eternally co-present in Nous, this could not transform it from being "potential Nous" to being "actual Nous" in the strict sense: it still will not possess these truths through its essence, but only through an accidental relation of participation in something else, and so it will still be in potency both to having them and to not having them. As a corollary, it will not have them infinitely, that is, in the greatest degree that they can be had: "even if my knowledge should always increase more and more, I understand nevertheless that it will never for this reason be actually infinite, because it will never happen to it that it is no longer capable of further increase; whereas I judge that God is actually infinite in such a way that nothing could be added to his perfection" (ibid.).

In a traditional Platonist context, this argument would have been directed against the Stoic claim that Nous is soul *pôs echon*, and used to prove that actual Nous exists separately from soul and cannot be derived from soul. Descartes cannot use the argument here to prove that actual Nous exists separately from soul, for he does not yet know that such a Nous exists at all: he uses it, instead, to show that the *idea* of Nous (and he does know that this idea exists) cannot be derived from the *idea* of soul. The bare claim that Nous is not derived from soul in reality does not automatically imply that the idea of Nous could not be derived from the idea of soul; but Descartes thinks his argument shows not merely that the transition from a potential to an essentially actual Nous does not occur, but also that it is unintelligible. If we cannot conceive the transformation of soul into Nous, then we cannot generate the idea of Nous by conceiving our soul transformed; by eliminating this story of the origin of the idea of Nous, Descartes answers the objection to his main argument that his idea of God could arise only from the God it represents.

Descartes also claims that even if the soul *could* transform itself into God, the idea of God could not be explained by this process. Once more Descartes is relying on a version of the principle of the priority of actuality to potency. The Platonists argued that, even if a soul can become Nous (as, in a weak sense, it can), it can do this only through the help of a preexisting Nous; they rely on the Aristotelian physical principle that the potentially X can become actually X only through an efficient cause which is already actually X. Descartes does not want to rely on this principle, and he is able to avoid it: he needs a principle about what thoughts presuppose other thoughts, not a principle about what beings presuppose other beings. He uses the principle we have seen from the *Phaedo*, that "when someone sees something, and thinks that this thing he is now seeing *wants* to be like some other thing, but falls short and cannot be what that other thing is, but is inferior − then, necessarily, the person who thinks this must somehow already have known the thing that he says this resembles but falls short of" (74d9–e4); but Descartes does not infer (as Plato does) that the ideal standard, which the intellect must already have known, must also already have existed in actuality. Descartes needs only the conclusion that the *idea* of the standard is prior to the *idea* of the imitation. He says, "I perceive that the objective being of an idea cannot be produced by potential being alone, which properly speaking is nothing, but only by actual or formal being" (AT VII,47). That is: I cannot derive an idea of X from perceiving something which is potentially X but actually only Y (here: I cannot derive an idea of Nous from perceiving myself, potentially Nous but actually just soul); the reason, surely, is that I cannot recognize Y as potentially X unless I already have the idea of X. Again, this serves to answer an objection to Descartes' main argument: once we reject the hypothesis that the idea of the perfection X arose from something having this perfection only potentially, we are back to admitting that the idea was derived from something which *actually* possessed at least as much perfection as the idea represents. Since the intellectual idea of God represents a being which has *all* perfections in the highest degree, the source of this idea must be the God it represents. Descartes thus confirms, for the case of Nous-itself but not for the case of other particular *noêta* or Forms, the conclusion which the *Phaedo* had assumed without sufficient argument to hold in every case, that the ideal standard essentially possessing each intelligible perfection must exist in actuality.

C. From God as Nous to God as creator

Descartes has given a proof for the existence of God, and so achieved the stated aim of the third Meditation. Furthermore, in the course of this proof, he has presented a purely intellectual conception of God, such as he thinks we need to conceive God distinctly, or to prove his existence with genuine certainty. So we might expect that Descartes would be satisfied with what he has done to induce a knowledge of God, and end the third Meditation here; he might now go on to write more Meditations applying his understanding of God and the soul to the foundations of a science of bodies. Instead Descartes spends another five AT pages (more than a quarter of the whole third Meditation), first giving another proof of God's existence, then adding some unargued reflections on the relations between God, the soul, and the idea of God. Why is the knowledge of God that results from the first proof not enough, and what does Descartes hope to gain with the rest of his Meditation?

Descartes gives an answer in the third Meditation itself; but this answer gives only a part of the truth. Although Descartes is satisfied that the *cognitio* of God as Nous is intrinsically the most distinct we can have, it is abstract and remote from the usual *cognitio* which conceives God as the creator of the world. And as Descartes had said in the Synopsis, "because, in order to draw the minds of the readers as much as possible away from the senses, I did not wish there [in the third Meditation] to make use of any comparisons drawn from corporeal things, it is possible that many obscurities have remained" (AT VII,14). And the Meditator finds himself troubled by these "obscurities" when he has finished meditating through the first proof of God's existence:

> Nor indeed is there anything in all this that is not plain to someone who attends diligently to the natural light. . . . But when I am less attentive and the images of sensible things blind the mind's eye, I do not so easily remember why the idea of a being more perfect than I must necessarily proceed from some being that really is more perfect. (P. 47)

So Descartes tries to build a bridge from his superior but esoteric *cognitio* of God as Nous to a more palpable *cognitio* of God as creator. He gives a new proof of the more usual causal type, establishing God as the cause of a substance (the Meditator himself, the only created substance now known to exist) and not of something as tenuous as an idea-content. Both here in the third Meditation and in the second Replies, Descartes seems to describe the second proof as a mere concession to human weakness.[43] But it is something more than this: the bridge between God-as-Nous and God-as-creator will be essential, both for defending the *priority* of the knowledge of God as Nous, and for supporting the argument of subsequent Meditations.

Descartes asks "whether I myself who have this idea [of a being more perfect than myself] could exist, if no such being existed" (p. 48); he proceeds to argue that, if some substance possesses the idea of a perfect being, the ultimate cause of the existence of this substance must be an actual perfect being. Descartes' goal is not just to demonstrate the existence of a creator God, but also to show how our knowledge of God as creator depends on our having the conception of God as a perfect being, by showing that the proof that God is my creator depends essentially on the premiss that I have the idea of God. By tracing Descartes' use of this

[43] From the second Replies: "for those whose natural light is so weak that they do not see that it is a primary notion 'that every perfection which is objectively in an idea must be really in some cause of it,' I have demonstrated the same thing yet more palpably, from the fact that the mind which has this idea cannot be from itself" (AT VII,136).

premiss, we can see both how he defends the priority of the knowledge of God as Nous to other knowledge of God, and how he exploits his concept of God's nature to derive knowledge of other things.

"From what would I exist?" if not from a perfect God: "from myself, or from my parents, or from any other things less perfect than God; for nothing more perfect than he, or even as perfect, can be thought or imagined" (AT VII,48). Descartes proceeds to eliminate these possibilities, arguing that as a substance containing the reality of God objectively, I must proceed from a cause superior to myself, which contains the reality of God formally and is therefore God. The chief burden is to show that I need a cause other than myself: once this is shown, the same reasons that imply that my cause cannot be me will also imply that it cannot be anything else inferior to God. Descartes takes it for granted that I do require some cause for my existence: for he takes it as obvious that my existence at one instant does not entail my existence at the next, and therefore that there must be some cause preserving me in existence; and he considers that such a preserving cause produces my existence at every instant, just as much as the cause that produced me at the first instant.[44] The only question is whether I myself might be this cause.

Once the question is posed in these terms, it looks easy enough to construct a proof for God's existence, without the premiss that there is a substance containing the idea of God. If everything that exists (and not just things that had a first instant in time) requires a cause for its existence, then I need merely argue backwards from any substance (such as myself) to its first cause. If an infinite regress is impossible here,[45] I will ultimately reach a first cause which is the cause of its own existence, and this self-caused cause will be God.

But Descartes deliberately rejects this simple scholastic argument: as he wants to show, the knowledge of God as creator that it purports to give is dependent on a knowledge of God as Nous. Although a straightforward causal ascent will reach a self-caused cause, I will not know that this cause is God, i.e. that it possesses infinite perfections. If I begin by assuming an effect with perfection X, all I can infer is that each of its causes contains perfection X formally or eminently, and that its *first* cause also has the power to maintain itself in existence. To conclude that the first cause possesses the divine perfections, I must somehow include a conception of these perfections in the premisses.

Descartes thinks he can show that the first cause is God by beginning with a substance (himself) which possesses the divine perfections objec-

---

[44] On the need of a cause for a thing's persisting in being, see the first Replies, AT VII,109.

[45] Since this is a series of *essential* causes, Descartes thinks that an infinite regress is impossible: "it is plain enough that no progression to infinity can be given here, especially since I am concerned here not just with the cause which once produced me, but indeed principally with that which preserves me at the present time" (AT VII,50). On essential causes as causes *secundum esse* rather than *secundum fieri*, and on the impossibility of an infinite regress of such causes, see the fifth Replies, AT VII,369–70.

tively represented in an idea. Descartes argues that *if* a substance X contains the idea of God, *then* X cannot be self-caused, unless it is God. Once this is granted, Descartes can prove that the first cause of my existence must be God. Each cause in the series of causes of my existence will have to contain all my perfections either formally or eminently, and thus will contain the divine perfections at least objectively. If an infinite regress is impossible, the series must ultimately reach a self-caused cause; since this is a self-caused substance containing the idea of God, it will have to be God.

Descartes observes that a substance possessing God's perfections objectively and potentially, but not possessing them actually, is intrinsically incomplete, and he infers that such a substance cannot be self-caused: it is because I have the idea of God, he says, that "I understand that I am something incomplete and [therefore] dependent on another" (AT VII,51). An incomplete being like the human soul cannot be the cause of its own existence, since if it could have produced itself it would have made itself complete: "if I were from myself, I would not doubt, nor desire, nor would I lack anything at all; for I would have given myself all the perfections of which there is any idea in me, and thus I would myself be God" (p. 48). The conclusion is narrowly drawn, and is supposed to depend essentially on the premiss that I am a substance containing the idea of God. Descartes is *not* saying that every self-caused substance must be infinitely perfect, and must therefore be God; he is claiming merely that a self-caused substance must be "complete," a perfected example of the kind of thing it is. Although a stone is less perfect than a human soul, it remains possible (for anything the present argument says) that a stone might be self-caused: since the stone does not have the idea of God, or contain objectively or potentially or in any other way perfections going beyond its nature, it is not incomplete in the way I am, and so (not knowing what it's missing) it may have made itself just as it is.[46] Since I, by contrast, am "something incomplete and dependent upon another, and something that aspires indefinitely to greater and better things" (p. 51), namely to further intellectual perfections, I am not a perfected example of the kind of thing I am, namely a *res cogitans*.

Descartes assures us that anything that could produce itself could (and

---

[46] When Descartes has established that I have some first self-caused cause, and then wishes to argue that this cause is God, he says that it must have "the power of possessing in actuality all the perfections of which it has an idea in itself" (p. 50) – not the perfections *I* can conceive, but the perfections *it* can conceive: the further conclusion that this being has all the perfections *I* can conceive depends on the premiss that it, being at least as perfect as I am, can conceive everything I can conceive. Thus the claim that X cannot be self-caused depends on the premiss that X is incomplete, as will be guaranteed if X has an idea of something greater than itself; the only way to show that a self-caused cause is God is to assume that something it causes contains the idea of God. In the end, of course, once I prove God's existence, I will be able to infer from God's omnipotence that the stone depends essentially on God, and so cannot create or conserve itself.

therefore would) also give itself all the perfections appropriate to its nature: for

> it is plain that it would have been much more difficult for me, i.e. a thinking thing or substance, to emerge from nothing, than to acquire the *cognitiones* of many things of which I am ignorant, since these *cognitiones* are merely accidents of this substance. (P. 48)

This way of putting the point is needlessly bizarre. We should not picture the mind struggling to emerge from a primordial swamp of nothingness: a substance "causes itself," not by emerging from nothing, but by sustaining itself in existence (without external help) from one moment to the next; for Descartes, this is as much as to say that one substance-stage creates a successor substance-stage. Descartes is saying that it is harder for me to create a new substance-stage than to produce a further accidental perfection in a substance-stage that is going to exist anyhow; to put the point the other way around, it requires less power to produce new knowledge than to produce a new *res cogitans*. Only a perfected *res cogitans* can produce a *res cogitans*; since I am not a perfected *res cogitans*, I cannot produce a *res cogitans*, and in particular I cannot produce myself.

Once again a Plotinian comparison is illuminating: it is not enough to refute the Stoic claim that "soul, when it has been perfected, generates [or begets] Nous" (V,9,4), and to argue that souls require a prior Nous to actualize their potential intellectual perfections; Plotinus also insists that souls, because they are incomplete and because they are powerless to maintain their own existence, must be generated and preserved by Nous. "We must posit that the first beings are in actuality and unwanting and perfect, and imperfect things are posterior and derive from these first beings, and then are perfected by the same things that begot them, like fathers perfecting what they begot imperfect: [the imperfect things] are matter in relation to what first made them, and then completes them and gives them form" (ibid.).[47] Since soul is only imperfectly and potentially Nous, and since the imperfect and potential members of any species are produced by the perfect and actual members, the soul must be produced by some perfect and actual Nous. Both Plotinus and Descartes believe that by reflecting on the concepts of soul and Nous, we will see that the

---

[47] Plotinus immediately adds that "if soul is passible, and there must be something impassible (otherwise all things would be destroyed by time), there must be something prior to soul"; without some first principle immune to change, and exerting a uniform action on other things, "nothing will remain the same" (ibid.). Plotinus is not saying, with Descartes, that things other than God need a continual divine conservation or re-creation to keep them from annihilation; he is making the traditional Platonist point that things in matter require the continued guidance of something outside of matter to keep them from relapsing into chaotic formless matter. But both for Plotinus and for Descartes the soul does not have the power to continue to exist as soul without the continuous influence of Nous; and this is what shows that souls are not merely perfected by Nous, but have also been "begotten" by it. (As we will see, Descartes takes the biological metaphor just as seriously as Plotinus does.)

concept "soul" is like the concept "kitten" and not like the concept "cat"; a soul will not be produced by a soul any more than a kitten is produced by a kitten. The biological analogy breaks down, because a kitten is produced by a cat which was previously a kitten, and so back *ad infinitum*; but both Plotinus and Descartes believe that, by looking for causes of *being* or *remaining* a soul and not merely of *becoming* a soul, they will avoid the possibility of infinite regress, and arrive at something that is essentially and eternally whatever the soul is potentially.

We can see that Descartes' first and second proofs of God's existence are constructed on the same model, and resemble each other closely. The second proof uses the ontological principle of the priority of actuality to potentiality, which the first proof had tried to avoid; but the first proof had had to assume similar principles, both the priority of formal to objective reality and the priority of the idea of the actual to the idea of the potential. Indeed, when the second proof traces back the causes of soul-as-bearer-of-the-idea-of-God, it follows the same causal chain as the first proof, which traces the causes of the idea of God itself; both arguments claim that we will eventually reach something that possesses the reality of God in actuality, and not just objectively or potentially.

Why, then, does Descartes add a second proof? I have already mentioned two reasons: first, our imagination is moved more strongly by a proof that establishes God as our creator than by a proof that makes him merely the source of an idea; second, Descartes wants to show how our knowledge of God as creator depends on our knowledge of God as Nous. But Descartes also wants to establish a truth about the soul, namely that it is the product of Nous. The third Meditation was methodologically necessary in order to resolve the doubts of the first Meditation: if I am the product of a powerful deceiver, or if I am the product of something too weak to produce rational perfection, then I cannot know that the beliefs I form will be true. To resolve these doubts and to give positive criteria for knowledge, it is not enough to know that God exists and is the source of truth: I must also know that I am the product of this God, and not the product of irrational or malicious powers. The second proof of God's existence, by arguing that God created me, that he recreates me at every instant, and that he is the source of all positive reality present in me at each instant, gives Descartes the foundation for arguing, in the fourth and subsequent Meditations, that at least some of my ideas and judgments come to me from God, and are therefore true.

If God both creates me, and is also the source of my idea of God, then "the only remaining question is how I have received this idea from God" (p. 51). Descartes answers, in terms of his earlier classification of the origins of ideas (p. 38), that the idea of God cannot be factitious or adventitious, but must be innate, "just as the idea of myself is innate in me" (p. 51). But Descartes is making a much deeper point than the classificatory scheme might suggest. To say that an idea is innate is to say that I have it "from my very nature" (p. 38), that is, from God's original constitution of me as a *res cogitans*. God does not first create me, and then, temporally or logically afterwards, give me the idea of God (if he did this, the idea would be adventitious); rather, my having the idea of God is a necessary concomitant of God's creating me as a *res cogitans*. Although Descartes does not explicitly argue for this conclusion, the argument is easy enough to supply. One of Descartes' initial examples of an innate idea was *"quid sit res"* in general (p. 38), and indeed every thing that thinks necessarily has the idea of *res*, since every act of thinking either is an idea or presupposes an idea, and since every idea represents its object as a *res*. For similar reasons, every thing that thinks necessarily has the idea of God, since (as Descartes has argued) the idea of the infinite is prior to the idea of the finite: since I have the idea of a *res*, I must also have the idea of a *res* without any limitations, and this is the idea of God.[48]

Since my idea of God is a necessary concomitant of my nature as God creates it, and since my idea of God is an evident sign that God has created me, Descartes says that "God, in creating me, implanted this idea in me, so that it would be like the mark of the craftsman stamped on his work" (p. 51). This means that the idea is cataleptic, but it also means something more. As Descartes immediately adds, "from the mere fact that God created me, it is very believable that I am somehow made in his image and likeness," and the idea of God is part of this likeness (ibid.). Descartes is following Augustine in locating the scriptural image of God in the likeness that we as rational souls bear to God as Nous. But Descartes goes to lengths that are quite surprising in a Christian philosopher. For Plotinus it was very natural to conclude that, since Nous generates soul, soul must be the image of Nous: "Nous begets soul, since it is a perfect Nous; for being perfect, it had to beget, and not be without offspring, when it is such a great power. And the offspring cannot be superior to the begetter even here below, but must be inferior and an image of the begetter, and likewise indeterminate, but determined and informed by what begot it" (*On the Three Principal Hypostases* V,1,7). Coming from Descartes, the same inference is much more surprising: surely his God is not a natural

---

[48] As Descartes puts it in a letter to Clerselier, "from this alone, that I conceive *being* or *that which is*, without thinking whether it is finite or infinite, it is infinite being that I conceive; in order to conceive a finite being, I must subtract something from this general notion of being, which must therefore precede it" (AT V,356). More specifically, if I have an idea of myself as a finite thinking or knowing being, I must first have a general notion of knowledge and of a knower; and if I simply think of a knowing being, without thinking of any limitations on it, I am already thinking of God as Nous. Descartes makes the point at the end of the third Meditation that whenever I think of myself as a finite being, in the same act I am aware of God as an infinite being, and of myself as bearing God's image and likeness: "when I turn the mind's eye in on myself, I understand not only that I am something incomplete and dependent upon another, and something that aspires indefinitely to greater and better things; but at the same time I also understand that he upon whom I depend has all these greater things within himself not just indefinitely and potentially, but really infinitely, and is therefore God" (AT VII,51). See discussion of these texts in Section B above.

begetter of the soul, but an artisan creating the world *ex nihilo* on whatever plan he chooses. So Gassendi insists (AT VII,306); but Descartes replies that Gassendi is wrong to "prefer to compare God's creation with the working of an artisan, rather than with a parent's generation"; in fact, "although these three ways of acting belong to different genera, it is a closer argument to divine from natural production than from artificial" (p. 373). Indeed, when Burman objects "could not God have created you without creating you in his image?" (AT V,156), Descartes calmly says "no: for it is a common and a true axiom that the effect is similar to the cause; but God is my cause and I am his effect, and therefore I am similar to him" (ibid.). Even stones "have God's image and likeness, but very remote and weak and confused; but I, who have more from God's creation, have his image more" (ibid.).

When Augustine draws this neo-Platonizing conclusion, he is usually preparing a moral exhortation: since you are made, not after the kind of the animals, but in the image of God, God has made you capable of following his law, and it is your calling as a rational being to do so. Descartes is preparing an analogous epistemological exhortation: since you are made in the image of God, God has made you capable of knowing the truth, and it is your calling as a rational being to do so. When we had "forgotten our father God, and whence we came, and what we are" (Plotinus V,1,1; pronouns changed), we did not know that we were capable of knowledge; this was the ultimate ground for doubt in the first Meditation, and at the beginning of the third. Now that we know what our creator is, and in whose image we were made, "it is sufficiently evident that he cannot be a deceiver; for it is manifest by the natural light that all fraud and deception depends upon some defect" (AT VII,52). The cause for doubt is thereby removed, and we may press on, with God as guarantee, to seek positive knowledge of the truth of things. This is the task of the subsequent Meditations, and of the *Principles of Philosophy*.

7

Theodicy and method

A. The doctrine of judgment

A.1. Interpreting the fourth Meditation

Already in the first Meditation Descartes had proposed to guarantee the truth of our judgments by inferring that a good God would not deceive his creatures. Descartes defers this plan of argument until he can prove that God is our creator, and show in what way he is good: until we know this we can only guess blindly what kinds of error God's goodness would or would not exclude. By the end of the third Meditation, however, Descartes has argued that we do proceed from a perfect creator, and that his perfection is such as to contradict his being a deceiver. By eliminating the scenarios of a powerless or malicious creator, which would make human knowledge impossible, Descartes is free to develop the remaining option, a good and perfect God, which makes knowledge at least a possibility. So in the fourth Meditation Descartes confronts the question he had raised in the first: what is it legitimate to infer from God's goodness, since we are *sometimes* deceived? Evidently we cannot exclude *every* type of error: since error exists and since God is non-deceiving, there must be some type of error that does not proceed from God, even though God permits it to happen. The task is to understand how this is possible, and to delimit the areas of thought where such errors can occur from those in which we cannot be deceived. If we can discover within ourselves thoughts that could be in error only if, *per impossibile*, God were deceiving us, then here, and here alone, we will have certain knowledge of the truth. Descartes thinks he has shown in the first Meditation that this is our only chance for establishing science; the fourth Meditation will try to make this one chance work, by studying the circumstances under which error is compatible with a beneficent creator. Descartes will use his understanding of God and error to derive a method for reconstructing knowledge, and in particular a knowledge of bodies. He will thus try to show in a *positive* sense that God and the soul are better known than bodies: having shown in previous Meditations that bodies *cannot* be known without God and the soul, and that God and the

---

I have presented a somewhat abridged version of the material of this chapter in "Descartes, Augustine, and the Status of Faith," in *Studies in Seventeenth-Century European Philosophy*, ed. M. A. Stewart (Oxford: Oxford University Press, forthcoming).

soul *can* be known without bodies, he will now show how bodies *can* be known if we begin from a knowledge of God and the soul.

At one level, the fourth Meditation is simply trying to reconcile various truths the Meditator has acquired: that God is omnipotent and that he is good, and yet that human beings whom he has created sometimes fall into error. These truths can be reconciled only by showing that there are some errors that God is not responsible for: although God *permits* these errors to happen, he does not himself produce the deception. Although it may seem an abstruse problem to distinguish those (impossible) errors that God would have to produce, from those (possible) errors that could arise through God's mere permission, Descartes in solving the problem is guided by a long tradition, and above all by Augustine. The problem of error is a special case of the problem of evil; and Augustine in the *De Libero Arbitrio* had treated the origin of evil in general in terms that could easily be restricted to describe the origin of any particular kind of evil, such as the cognitive evil of error. Augustine had formulated precisely the problem the Meditator faces at the beginning of the fourth Meditation: how to understand together the different propositions he is committed to believing, that "all things which are, are from one God, and yet that God is not the author of sins," although sins do exist: "for it disturbs the mind, if sins are from these souls which God created, and those souls are from God, how sins are not referred by a small step to God" (*De Libero Arbitrio* I,ii,4). After demonstrating that God does exist, and is as he has been believed to be, and after explaining the nature of sin, Augustine explains how these truths can coexist by developing a theory of divine and human action, which allows us to judge how far God is responsible for the created world, and to distinguish between the goodness the world must possess (even if it appears not to), and the goodness it may well be lacking.

The theodicy of the *De Libero Arbitrio* became the common property of the later Christian tradition. Descartes accepts it without qualification, and restates it in the fourth Meditation in terms that seem unusually faithful to Augustine's argument. But to interpret the fourth Meditation we must understand that Descartes is only *instrumentally* concerned with reconciling God and error. This is, of course, a real problem, and Descartes thinks that the *De Libero Arbitrio* gives a real solution. But Descartes' main concern is to determine what kinds of error are impossible, because inconsistent with God's power and goodness; and he thinks that the theory of the *De Libero Arbitrio* will allow him to do this. It is important for us to distinguish Augustine's insights on theodicy, which Descartes enjoys as common intellectual property, from the real work of the fourth Meditation, which is to fit the problem of error into the framework of theodicy, by fitting the theory of judgment into the general theory of action. So to understand the real accomplishment of the fourth Meditation, we have to step back a bit from the text. Descartes cannot simply let his Meditator say, "I have read a persuasive account of action in Augustine, so now I will try to locate error in terms of it": instead, Descartes allows his readers to discover each of Augustine's insights for themselves, each time with reference to the immediate problem of error and not to the problem of evil in general. But our goal is not the same as Descartes': we want to attain, not a realization of the truth as Descartes perceived it, but an understanding of Descartes' work. To do this we have to step back from the mind of the Meditator to understand Descartes' plan in making the Meditator go through his predetermined train of thoughts.

A.2. Ignorance and error

In the first substantive passage of the fourth Meditation, after reviewing the conclusions of the previous Meditations, Descartes again proposes the hope of passing from the knowledge of God to the certainty that we are not deceived in our judgments:

And now I seem to see a way by which, from this contemplation of the true God, "in whom," indeed, "all treasures of the sciences and of wisdom are hid [*in quo nempe sunt omnes thesauri scientiarum et sapientiae absconditi*]," one might arrive at a knowledge [*cognitio*] of other things. (AT VII,53)

The quotation is from St. Paul's letter to the Colossians (2:3), in the Latin of the Vulgate; but Descartes has transformed the genitive singular *scientiae* (knowledge) into the plural *scientiarum* (the sciences), and placed it before instead of after wisdom. Descartes is going to make good the pious sentiment we have always quoted from scripture, and show how we can actually achieve a true system of the sciences, and thus build up to wisdom, starting from the knowledge we have of God.[1]

The God Descartes has discovered is the "true" God, not just because he actually exists, but also because, unlike the false God of the first Meditation, he is the "source of truth" (AT VII,22). The third Meditation has shown not only that God exists, but also that he is not such as to deceive: "for in every fraud or deception some imperfection is found; and although the *power* to deceive seems to be some evidence of ingenuity or power, beyond a doubt the *will* to deceive bears witness of either malice or weakness, and therefore cannot occur in God" (AT VII,53). The question of the fourth Meditation will be how far we can proceed from this knowledge to the knowledge of other things.

Descartes starts by proposing a simple argument: "I observe that there is in me a certain faculty of judgment, which I have certainly received from God, as I have all the other things that are in me" (pp. 53–4). Since God does not will to deceive me, this must be, not a "faculty of erring" (p. 54), but a power that should, when used correctly, lead me to judge truly.

---

[1] On the relation between the sciences and wisdom, and for the "treasures of the sciences," compare Descartes' vocational dreams of 1619, and also the acount of wisdom in the *Letter to Picot*, discussed above, Chapter 2, Section B.

The problem is that this does not explain how I can ever err. Looking to God, from whom I receive everything I have, I will find no explanation: since God is supremely veracious, there can be no source in him of my errors. But obviously I do make mistakes. Whence do these derive, if not from God?

This is just the question of the *De Libero Arbitrio*: "tell me, I beg you, whether God is not the author of evil?" (I,i,1). Since he is not, or at least not the author of *moral* evil, the evil that occurs when someone does something wrong, and since people do in fact do things wrong, we must explain where this evil comes from. It comes from our will; but then, if the will in turn comes from God, it seems that God has given us something bad; if the will does not come from God, then something exists independently of God. Augustine asks about the source of our *acting* wrongly; Descartes restates the question for *judging* wrongly, and his answer follows Augustine's argument step by step.

Descartes starts by proposing a true but inadequate account of error; then he calls attention to the insufficiency of this first account, and uses this insufficiency to motivate his full and adequate account of error. First Descartes notes that he has the idea, not only of God, but also of something negative and opposite to God, "a certain negative idea of nothing" (AT VII,54). I myself am constituted as an "intermediate between God and nothing, or between the supreme being and non-being" (ibid.). Error then becomes possible, "not insofar as I am created by the supreme being," but "inasmuch as I participate somehow in nothing or in non-being" (ibid.). Thus Augustine had said that sin or the *motus aversionis* cannot come to us from God, "since it is a defective motion, and every defect is from nothing" (*De Libero Arbitrio* II,x,54); and, more fully, that

Corruptible natures would not be natures at all, if they were not from God; nor would they be corruptible if they were *of* him, for they would be what he himself is. Therefore that they are of any measure, any form, any order, is because it is God by whom they have been made; but that they are not immutable is because it is nothing out of which they have been made. (*De Natura Boni* x)

Descartes and Augustine conclude: the cause of my errors is found not in God, but in the fact that, being other than God, I have been created out of nothing, and continue to have some character of nothingness about me. I am not nothing, but I have been created from nothing purely by God's decision, and can as easily be returned to nothingness: so I have no prior claim on any perfections, before God decides what to give me. In creating me, he gives me some perfections I did not have before, but there are other perfections that he does not give me; the lack of these other perfections is not itself something that comes from God, but merely a remainder of the original nothingness or lack of all perfections out of which I was drawn.

This, at any rate, is the analysis of the origin of error that Descartes, following Augustine, suggests at AT VII,54. Descartes believes it, as does

Augustine; indeed, there is no other way they can account for creaturely imperfections. But as Descartes immediately says, "nevertheless this does not yet altogether satisfy." It would be satisfactory as an account of *ignorance*: as we do not have our existence from ourselves, so we do not have knowledge from ourselves, but only to the extent that God gives us a share of intellectual perfection. If he chooses not to give us some item of knowledge, we remain ignorant of it, and so continue to "participate somehow in nothing or in non-being." But this does not explain why we should be in *error* about the things we do not know: we do not know how many stars there are, and we must confess that the nature God gave us is insufficient for knowing such things: but this does not make us opine that there are precisely a million, or any other particular number that might be in error.

Error is thus something more than a mere negation, a "not-knowing" or ignorance: Descartes formulates the difference by saying that "error is not a pure negation, but a privation, or the lack of some *cognitio* that somehow ought to be in me" (AT VII, 54–5). "Negation" and "privation" are scholastic technical terms, and Descartes appends glosses (only after "privation" in the Latin, after both terms in the French) which explain their traditional meanings accurately enough: while privation is a lack of something that *ought* to be in me, negation is "the simple lack or absence of some perfection that is not owed me" (French translation, AT IX,43–4).[2] But Descartes' use of the term "privation," in his description of error, is rather different from his official explanation. What distinguishes error from mere ignorance is not that it is an ignorance of something we ought to know, but that it involves my *making a judgment* in ignorance, and thus (sometimes) making a judgment that disagrees with the truth of the matter: error arises, not simply when I lack some item of knowledge, but when I *do something* with what knowledge I have, by making some judgment.[3] To understand the point that Descartes is making by saying that error is a privation, it will help again to compare the fourth Meditation with the *De Libero Arbitrio*.

The *De Libero Arbitrio* argues that God is not responsible for the free acts of his rational creatures. These acts could not have occurred unless God had provided the means for them to occur, by creating the agents and endowing them with *liberum arbitrium*, the capacity for free action.

---

[2] As Aristotle puts it, "something which is capable of some power or positive state [*hexis*] is *deprived* when that power or state is not present in that in which, and at the time at which, it should naturally be present" (*Categories* 12a28–31); in contrast, we can speak of the *negation* of a state whenever it is not present in something, without reference to the nature of the thing it is not present in, or to whether this nature somehow *ought* to include this state.

[3] The best hope for fitting Descartes' description of error as a privation into the Aristotelian definition is to say: error is not simply the absence of truth, but the absence of truth from the kind of thing (namely, a judgment) which could and should be true. This works well for making it a privation in my judgment, but less well for making it a privation in *me*, the absence of some knowledge which should be in me.

But if creatures use their gifts for acting badly, this is not God's responsibility: all *God* has done is to give the gifts, and these gifts are good, despite the incidental capacity for abuse which is inseparable from them. "Will . . . which is an intermediate good" (*De Libero Arbitrio* II,xix,53), in that it is necessary for the happy life and yet capable of being abused, can and should attach itself to the eternal good, and so doing "achieves the great and primary goods of man" (ibid.). When it decides to follow itself rather than following God, "turning away from the incommutable and common good, and turning toward its own good or toward something external or toward something inferior" (ibid.), this turning away [*aversio*] is a sin, an evil we do, inescapably bearing with it the evils we suffer. Yet this moral evil, and the natural evils bound up with it, do not at any point involve any positively evil "nature" or substance: the will which chooses badly is itself a good, and so are the things it chooses – it is wrong to choose them only because they are *less* good than other possible objects of choice. The only thing here that is evil *per se* is the *aversio*, which is a movement or act of a created nature. It has the ontological status of a privation, a deviation from the divine standard of the "immutable and common good"; the only way that such an evil can occur in me is by my willing it, incidentally to my willing something that is not the chief good. As Augustine says, because the *motus aversionis* is a defect it cannot come from God; he immediately infers that it comes from us. "Since this defect is voluntary, it is placed within our power. For if you are afraid of it, you should not will it, and if you do not will it, it will not be. What therefore is safer than to be in that life where what you do not want cannot befall you?" (*De Libero Arbitrio* II,x,54). Thus evil can occur, in my acts although not in my nature; but its occurrence is within my power, and my will can determine itself to avoid it.

By saying that error is not a negation but a privation, Descartes means to argue that it cannot belong to our nature as we receive it from God, but is instead a deviation from the standard God intends us to conform to. For Descartes, as for Augustine, this explanation of error or of moral evil depends on understanding God as Nous, as the objective standard of truth and of right action. Before Augustine read the books of the Platonists, he could not understand the origin of moral evil: he could only ask "who planted in me the seed of bitterness?" (*Confessions* VII,iii,4), that he should will evil. But once he understands that God is related to the soul as the measure to the thing measured, he also understands that evil is not a substance in the soul, that the image of the "seed" is wrong. If God is Nous or Truth, then error will consist in deviation from him, like the deviation of a curve from a straightedge. The inference that God is not the author of error does not rest on any appeal to God's "human decency": it is simple nonsense to suggest that Truth causes us to deviate from Truth. Deviation is possible, not because of God, but because the soul is by its essence only *potential nous*. Descartes has followed Augustine in achieving an understanding of God as the standard for the soul; he

306

continues to follow Augustine in the fourth Meditation, in using this understanding of God to derive an analysis of error.

The metaphysical explanation of error furthers Descartes' purpose in the fourth Meditation, because it shows that error, "since it is voluntary, is placed within our power," and can be avoided by the proper discipline.[4] This had been the original goal of the fourth Meditation: to derive, from the knowledge that God cannot be the source of falsehood or imperfection, a rule for avoiding error, and making at least some of our judgments free from doubt. To derive a practicable rule for avoiding error, Descartes must draw out the consequences of the theory of error as privation: first he will give a precise account of how the soul acts in judging; then he will use this account to derive the conditions under which we can know that our act of judgment will not deviate from the divine standard, and therefore will not err.

A.3. Judgment, will, and intellect

In Descartes' Augustinian language, to say that error, or the judgments of which error can be predicated, proceed from us and are within our power, is to say that they depend on the faculty of *will*. There is, then, no autonomous faculty of judgment spontaneously producing judgments as the faculty of imagination spontaneously produces sensory images. If error could result from such a faculty, this would mean that God had implanted in us a positive source of the privation of error; and while we cannot understand the reasons for God's actions, we do perceive that this would contradict his nature as Nous.

Descartes' doctrine on this point is in sharp contrast with the humanist

---

[4] Objection: even if error, as a privation, cannot be produced in us by God, why must it be the result of our own will: why couldn't it be produced in us by some other creature? Augustine's answer in the *De Libero Arbitrio* is that a superior nature would be unwilling to damage a virtuous soul, and an inferior nature (by God's just order) would be unable; external things can damage a *vicious* soul, but something must have originally turned it to vice, and this can only be its own will. While Descartes does not give such a clear answer, he seems to believe the same thing: thus in the sixth Meditation he says that a sick person is as much God's creature as a healthy person, and that God would not deceive the sick person by allowing him to be *indefeasibly* deceived by his bodily conditions; thus Descartes agrees with Augustine that God would be acting unjustly, and authoring moral evil, if he allowed a soul to be damaged by something else independently of any bad act of its own will. But Descartes does not raise this argument in the fourth Meditation (unless it is implicit in the invocation of the image of God: since God has made me in his image, he guarantees me, and would not allow his image to be effaced by other things). Perhaps, in the argument of the fourth Meditation, the recognition that error is a privation is not supposed to *prove* that error is within my power, but only to prove that it cannot come from God, and thus to lead me to ask whether it might come from me: this train of thought leads me to recognize the dependence of error on will, and it is this recognition, not the thesis that error is a privation, that proves that error is not produced in me by some other creature. But it seems more likely that, already in the fourth Meditation, Descartes is assuming that God would be responsible for moral evil if he allowed me to be deceived by another creature independently of any bad act of my own will.

theory of judgment as we might find it in Montaigne or Charron. As we saw in Chapter 2, Sections A and B, Descartes' program of attaining wisdom through building up the sciences runs counter to the humanist program, which seeks wisdom in practical moral reflection, and counsels us to avoid the unprofitable labor of the sciences. We can now see, from the fourth Meditation, that Descartes bases his disagreement with the humanists on a differing analysis of judgment. The importance of Descartes' theory of judgment can be brought out most sharply by contrasting him with Montaigne.

As Montaigne tells us in his essay "Of Presumption,"

> It is commonly said that the fairest division of her favors nature has given us is that of sense; for there is no one who is not content with the share of it she has allotted him. Is that not reasonable? If anyone saw beyond, he would see beyond his sight. . . . I think my opinions are good and sound; but who does not think as much of his?[5]

That is: nature has endowed each of us with a certain degree of judgment and good sense, leading us to form opinions of greater or lesser accuracy and perceptiveness on the things we come to deal with. Nobody's judgment is perfect, and all will produce opinions deficient in some respect, but this is an inescapable limitation of human nature, and we are in no position to complain. We can try by a good education to *develop* our faculty of judgment, and Charron in the *Sagesse*, or Montaigne in "Of the Education of Children," give us a picture of how this is to be done; but the main value of this education is to "teach our judgment to recognize its own imperfection and natural weakness, which is no small lesson,"[6] rather than to develop any positive conclusions in the sciences.

Descartes is not ashamed to borrow Montaigne's maxim for the opening sentence of the *Discourse on Method*: good sense is the best-shared thing in the world, for precisely Montaigne's reason: who will complain of lacking it? But Descartes uses this observation to support a very different attitude toward our natural endowments: "it is not enough to have a good mind: the main thing is to apply it well" (AT VI,2). The key to right judgment is not quick wit, or anything we might call "intelligence"; it is the *use* we freely make of the generally equal talents we are given. So the "good sense" or "sparks of wisdom" belonging to our natural endowment are not tendencies to develop right opinions, but simply a certain store of clear perceptions that people can use in different ways, in forming different judgments. The imperfections of our judgments, which we recognize when we compare them with the judgments of others, are due not to limits or differences in our natural gifts, but to different choices in using our cognitive endowments. For this reason it is possible to develop a "method

---

[5] *Complete Essays of Montaigne*, tr. Donald Frame (Stanford: Stanford University Press, 1958), p. 499.
[6] Montaigne, p. 116.

of rightly conducting one's reason," which, by carefully and deliberately redirecting the ways we form our judgments on scientific questions, should lead us to a firmer and broader science than anything that human "intelligence," unguided by method, has been able to achieve.

This is very different from Montaigne's conclusion. Montaigne has no hope for such a science, and consequently no interest in one. Wisdom is to be attained by domesticating our judgment, not by trying to make it escape its limitations. Now, if Descartes held Montaigne's theory of the faculty of judgment, he would doubtless have to agree. But for Descartes there is no faculty of judgment, and thus no limits placed upon it. What Montaigne regards as *negations* or limits on judgment are for Descartes voluntary *privations*: they are not the result of human nature but of sin. Thus they can and must be overcome. Montaigne is right that there are limitations on good sense – that is, on what we can clearly perceive. These limitations constitute ignorance, not error. Montaigne is right that these cannot be overcome, and if error were such a limitation, it also would be inescapable. But if error is within our voluntary control, then Descartes is confident that we can construct an error-free scientific system, through which we will overcome not only error but also (to a limited degree) ignorance, and which will ultimately bring us to wisdom.

The "faculty of judgment," which the Meditator had originally claimed to perceive within himself (AT VII,53), consequently disappears. Since we judge freely or voluntarily, the only real faculty that might be called a faculty of judgment would be the faculty of *will* in its act of judging. Montaigne and other humanists had made our "good sense" a faculty of judgment, and had applied to right judgment and its privation, error, concepts appropriate only to knowledge and its negation, ignorance. Descartes, having cleared up this confusion, should proceed to discuss the will's activity in judging, so that he can determine how we should use the will to avoid error.

First, however, he must deal with the faculty of intellect or understanding, since this faculty determines our knowledge or ignorance of the things about which we judge. This is what we are given, and logically precedes our activity in response.

Descartes' theory of the intellect contrasts sharply with the scholastic theory. The scholastics describe judgment as an operation of the intellect: for Descartes to describe judgment as an act of the *will*, and to give directions for its right performance, he must first correct the scholastic conception of the intellect, and show that judgment does not arise from intellect alone.[7]

---

[7] Although scholastic writers always treat judgment as *formally* an act of the intellect, they may think that the will can be a (partial) *efficient* cause of judgment in some cases. But they never treat judgment as the kind of free acrion to which the theodicy of the *De Libero Arbitrio* could be applied: the will is not involved in *every* judgment, and it chiefly influences *habits* of judgment rather than individual acts (e.g. a bad use of the will can lead to the formation of a bad moral character, and thus to distortions of moral judgment). It is

On the scholastic account, the intellect has three kinds of operations, "simple apprehension," judgment, and reasoning from premises to conclusions. The first operation merely apprehends a concept or "forms the quiddity" of some thing, without asserting or denying any predicate of the thing conceived; simple apprehension therefore cannot be called true or false, except in an improper sense. Truth and falsehood properly reside only in the second operation of judgment or (as it is frequently called) "the intellect composing and dividing," i.e. conjoining or disjoining a subject and a predicate: the judgment is true if the things conjoined by the intellect are conjoined in reality (or if things disjoined by the intellect are disjoined in reality), false if the things conjoined by the intellect are disjoined in reality (or if things disjoined are conjoined).[8] Descartes' theory of judgment is quite different, and his theory of the intellect must also be different. The distinction between judgment and simple apprehension corresponds to Descartes' distinction between judgment and knowledge or intellection [*cognitio, intellectus*]; but intellection is the *only* act of the faculty of intellect, and judgment belongs not to the intellect but to the will.

typical that while St. Thomas says very little about the will in his general account of judgment, he gives it a larger role in theological discussions of *fides* and *credere*, where he is constrained by Augustine's authority, and where the nature of the case does seem to require some role for the will. Augustine says in *De Praedestinatione Sanctorum* ii,5 that *credere* is *cogitare cum assensione*, following a Stoic or Ciceronian picture of judgment as assent to impressions, and in v,10 he draws the explicit conclusion that *credere vel non credere . . . est in arbitrio voluntatis humanae*, so that *fides . . . in voluntate est*; Thomas cites the latter formula (*Summa Theologiae*, Secunda Secundae, Q. 4 a2 obj1), but he thinks it is imprecise. Thomas says rather that *credere* is "an act of the intellect inasmuch as it is moved by the will to assent" (Q. 4 a2; as the parallels Q. 4 a1 and Q. 2 a9 show, Thomas is asserting this only of belief in divine revelation, not of belief in general): *credere* is thus formally an act of the intellect, but, to be completed, requires both a virtue of intellect (and this is *fides*) and also a virtue of the will. ("Not only does the will need to be prompt to obey, but also the intellect needs to be well disposed to follow the command of the will, just as the concupiscible [appetite] needs to be well disposed to follow the command of reason [as a requirement for acts of temperance]. So there needs to be a habit of virtue not only in the will which commands, but also in the intellect which assents," Q. 4 a2 ad3.) For further discussion, see Thomas *De Veritate* Q. 14 aa1–4, esp. a1. I thank Jim Ross for drawing my attention to these texts.

[8] One foundational text for the scholastic theory of the intellect was from *De Anima* III,6: "there is no falsehood in thinking [*noêsis*] about indivisibles; where there is truth and falsehood, there must already be some composition of the things thought [*noêmata*] as one . . . . For falsehood is always in composition: even if we call the white not-white, we have compounded not-white to white." St. Thomas distinguishes the properties of the first two acts of the intellect in what seems to be the *locus classicus* on this subject, *De Veritate* Q. 1 a3. The list of all three acts, and the standardization of the terminology, take some time: for an account of this process, see Benoît Garceau, *Judicium: vocabulaire, sources, doctrine de saint Thomas d'Aquin* (Paris: Vrin, 1968). The theory of the three acts of intellect became the standard framework for logical discussions: John of St. Thomas, for example, explicitly cites this theory as the justification for his order of topics (*Cursus Philosophicus Thomisticus* (Turin: Marietti, 1930), 1, p. 5); but the same order, with the same implicit justification, is followed even by the Port-Royal *Logique, ou l'art de penser* (generally ascribed to Arnauld, and reprinted in his *Oeuvres* (Paris, 1775–81), vol. 41), with the addition of a fourth book on method.

The intellect is essentially a *facultas cognoscendi* (AT VII,56), and since "by the intellect alone I merely perceive ideas about which I can pass judgment," no "error properly so-called is found in it thus precisely regarded" (ibid.), since error in the proper sense occurs only in judgment.

From the scholastic point of view, it might seem that Descartes is simply redefining the faculty of intellect to restrict it to its first act of simple apprehension alone, so that he can apply the doctrine of the freedom of the will to judgment. But this is not quite right. The basis of the distinction Descartes draws between intellect and will is that intellect is passive or receptive, and will is active. For Descartes, following the Stoic and Augustinian against the Aristotelian analysis, judgment is distinguished from apprehension, not because it involves composition but because it involves an act of *assent*: the difference is not in the form of the object (simple or complex), but in the attitude we take toward the object. Intellection, by contrast with judgment, is purely receptive: the intellect is the faculty for the perception of ideas, and not, as Thomas says, for their formation. This reception is knowledge; so knowledge is simply the passive perception of an idea-content, where this is a real being deriving ultimately from God.

Because the scientific system is a body of knowledge, it must consist of ideas, and not of judgments. Thus the scholastic "third act" of reasoning to conclusions, the cement of science, is for Descartes a kind of simple apprehension, the intuitive perception that the premisses imply the conclusion.[9]

It is important here to understand Descartes' terminology for the different kinds of knowledge; only thus will what he says about the relation of judgment to knowledge have its proper force. The intellect is a *facultas cognoscendi*, and all of its operations are described by the derived noun *"cognitio."* *Cognitio* is knowledge, and *cognoscere* to know, in the most general sense, covering any understanding of a thing that we can gain in any way. Knowledge in the stricter sense of scientific knowledge, the knowledge Descartes wants to develop as a firm and indubitable foundation for wisdom, is a special kind of cognition, for which Descartes reserves the traditional word *"scientia."* But although Descartes is willing to use Aristotelian terminology to describe the highest kind of knowledge, he does not share the Aristotelian syllogistic conception of science. For Aristotle, science is *demonstrative* knowledge: it is to be achieved by a series of syllogisms, beginning with intuitive first principles about the genus in question, and proceeding through a chain of causes as the middle terms. Descartes certainly does not deny that scientific knowledge is built up out of evident first principles; but he is uninterested in any formal criteria (structure of propositions and of demonstrations, etc.) to distin-

---

[9] Deduction as it is described in Rule 3 is not a separate act, but simply the intellect's relation to the things it knows by a chain of intuitions rather than a single intuition: each inferential step must still be grasped by intuition (AT X,369).

guish science from other cognitions. What is interesting about science is that it is science; that is, that it is something we know for certain, and on which other knowledge can be based. Science is one species of *cognitio*, of knowledge in general, and this is its differentia. It is not something that must be expressed in a different form. In particular, it is quite foreign to Descartes to distinguish *scientia* as propositional knowledge from *cognitio* as acquaintance with objects; he is perfectly happy to describe both sorts of knowledge in each of these ways; the difference is simply one of certainty. So in Rule 2, urging us to concentrate on what we can know for certain, he begins, "every *scientia* is a certain and evident *cognitio*" (AT X,362); and so, in the second Replies, "I do not deny that 'an atheist can clearly know [*cognoscere*] that the three angles of a triangle are equal to two right angles'; I simply affirm that his *cognitio* is not true *scientia*, since no *cognitio* that can be rendered doubtful seems worthy to be called *scientia*" (AT VII,141).

Given this description of the passive faculty of intellect, we can go on with Descartes to discuss the active faculty of will, which is responsible for judgment.

Already in the third Meditation Descartes had offered a tentative classification of his thoughts. His hesitation is for the benefit of the reader; by suggesting in rough outline here what will become a technical apparatus later, Descartes can painlessly introduce the terminological and conceptual distinctions that will bear the weight of the fourth Meditation. In the third Meditation, the basic division of thoughts is between ideas on the one hand, and acts of will including judgments on the other:

Some of [my thoughts] are as-it-were images of things, to which alone the name "idea" properly applies: as when I think of a man, or a chimaera, or heaven, or an angel, or God. But others have other forms besides this: as when I will, when I fear, when I affirm, when I deny, I still always apprehend some thing as the subject of my thought, but I also embrace in my thought something more than the likeness of that thing; and of these some are called volitions or affections, while others are called judgments. (AT VII,37)

To say in these latter cases that we apprehend, i.e. that we grasp or embrace, something other than the thing of which we perceive a likeness, is not to say what we are doing in such thoughts. Only ideas will be analyzed in any depth in the third Meditation; the other thoughts are distinguished from them as containing something more, but we are not told what. The fourth Meditation fills in this blank.

Embracing something other than an idea is always an act of will, as Descartes has suggested by grouping judgments together with volitions and affections. In each of these cases the will is *assenting* to something, or refusing to assent: in the case of judgments it may affirm or deny, or it may refuse to do either. In any case something is "put forward to us by the intellect" (p. 57), and we are free to dispose of it as we will: if we are to say that there is any additional content in these acts, it is the content we ourselves contribute by the act of affirming or denying.

What is put forward by the intellect – perhaps better, to avoid any suggestion of activity, what we *receive* through the intellect – must be an idea. Somehow judgment must be an assent to an idea. It is not immediately obvious how, and Descartes, uninterested in formal logic, neglects to work out the details. But his paradigmatic example is clear enough: "the foremost and most frequent error that can be found in them [judgments] consists in my judging that ideas that are in me are similar or conformed to certain things placed outside me" (p. 37). Perhaps this is the only example, "for certainly if I only consider these ideas as so many modes of my thought, and do not refer them to anything else, they can hardly give me any material for error" (ibid.). Presumably Descartes would say that in any judgment, I have a complex idea of the proposition I am considering, an idea of what it would be for the proposition to be true, and that I judge that this idea is "conformed" to actuality (or to these actual objects?) – he would have to say *something* like this, and he does not seem to care just what. But Descartes is above all concerned with *simple* ideas, the ideas of yellow, of body, and of God, and with the judgments that affirm that these ideas come from and resemble something in the world outside my representations.

A.4. Judgment, will, and nature

The theory of the act of judgment as assent to an idea is originally Stoic: Cartesian ideas are Stoic *phantasiai* or impressions, although of course they do not have to be *sensory* impressions. Descartes is probably taking the theory of judgment as assent chiefly from Cicero, although it is also implicit in Augustine's account of belief in the *De Utilitate Credendi*. But Descartes is inserting this theory of judgment into a very un-Stoic metaphysics, which gives him a very un-Stoic view of which impressions should, and of which impressions necessarily do, elicit our assent. Descartes also locates the theory of judgment within the specifically Augustinian version of theodicy, and so he adopts the Augustinian description of the will.

Although the Stoics say that assent is "up to us," they do not describe it as an act of will: they analyze volition [*hormê*] as a species of assent, not assent as a species of volition. Descartes, like Augustine in the *De Libero Arbitrio*, traces all our free activity to the faculty of will. Each assent is a special act of the will, and all willing is free: the *voluntas sive arbitrii libertas* "consists just in this, that we can either do or not do the same thing (that is, affirm it or deny it, pursue it or flee it); or rather just in this, that we are so disposed to what is proposed to us by the intellect for affirming or denying, or for pursuing or fleeing, that we feel ourselves to be determined to it by no external force" (AT VII,57). For Descartes, as

313

for Augustine and the Stoics, "I do not have to be drawn both ways, in order to be free" (ibid.). Some impressions, for the Stoics, are so clear that, although I am not *constrained*, my nature is such that I will inevitably assent to them;[10] and Descartes (following Augustine) agrees that "neither divine grace nor natural knowledge ever diminishes liberty, but rather increases and strengthens it" (AT VII,58), although both grace and knowledge can produce situations in which I will always assent. Such a situation arose in the second Meditation, when the Meditator recognized the force of the inference "I think, therefore I exist": as the Meditator now says in retrospect, "I could not not judge what I so clearly understood to be true; not that I was compelled to it by any external force, but because from a great light in the intellect there followed a great propensity in the will, and I believed the more spontaneously and freely as I was less indifferent to it" (pp. 58–9).

However, these situations arise only where the "light in the intellect" is so clear that for the mind not to assent would be contrary to its nature. Wherever the *cognitio* or "light" is less clear than this, I am equally free to assent or withhold assent: I have liberty of indifference, and not merely of spontaneity. (Not assenting to P does not require denying P: I can suspend judgment, and this is the right action if I do not clearly perceive whether P is true or false.) Descartes' crucial disagreement with the Stoics is about the "nature" of the mind, and, therefore, about what impressions are genuinely so clear that my nature inevitably leads me to assent to them.

Descartes had concluded in the third Meditation that the mind is made in the image of God, that is, of Nous: the mind's nature (for Descartes as for Augustine and Plotinus) is exhausted by its being potential *nous* and by its relation to actual *nous*. This nature only requires it to assent to those purely intellectual *cognitiones* whose objective content is such that not assenting to them would contradict rationality. Since the nature of the mind has no essential relation to bodies or sensation, it never requires assent to sensory impressions, however probable these seem: this was the lesson of the third Meditation's investigation of the "teachings of nature," as distinguished from the natural light of reason.[11] The Stoics regard sensory

---

[10] Thus Cicero, reflecting Antiochus: "as a scale in a balance is necessarily depressed by the weights that are placed on it, so the mind necessarily yields to things that are clear: for as no animal can not seek after that which appears adapted to its nature (what the Greeks call *oikeion*), so it [the mind] cannot not approve a clear thing brought before it" (*Academica* II,xii,38). Strictly speaking, the Stoic view is not that we inevitably assent to any cataleptic impression, but that we inevitably assent to a cataleptic impression unless some obstruction is present that prevents us from recognizing it as cataleptic (cf. Sextus Empiricus *Against the Logicians* I,253–7), whereas Descartes apparently thinks that we *always* assent to a clear and distinct idea, as long as we are attending to it.

[11] Objection: couldn't my nature as a mind–body composite, as opposed to the nature of my mind alone, require me to assent to some things? Answer: no, since assent is an act of the mind alone, and not of the mind–body composite. As Descartes says in the sixth Meditation, my "nature," in the sense in which that belongs to me as a mind–body composite, "teaches [me] to flee those things which produce a sense of pain, and to pursue those

impressions (when formed under favorable conditions) as clear, and Descartes can agree that they are "vivid and express and even in their own way . . . distinct" (AT VII,75), but they are not *so* clear that I cannot doubt them when I attend to the content of my perceptions. Through the exercise of doubting them, I recognize that it was not a necessity of my nature, but only a habit of my will, that had led me to assent to them.

The point of the fourth Meditation is not simply to prove that "everything that I perceive very clearly and distinctly is true" (AT VII,35), but to provide a standard for "very clear," for how clear a perception must be to be included within the scientific system. A perception is not clear enough to be included if I have the liberty of indifference not to assent to it; and

this indifference extends, not just to those things about which the intellect knows nothing at all, but generally to all those which it does not know sufficiently clearly at the time when the will is deliberating about them: for however much probable conjectures draw me in one direction, the bare knowledge that they are just conjectures, and not certain and indubitable reasons, suffices to push my assent in the opposite direction. (AT VII,59)

This lesson has already been taught by the *practice* of earlier Meditations; the fourth Meditation, by explaining the roles of the will and the intellect in judgment, gives a theoretical justification for withholding assent from everything except the clear perceptions of the intellect.

For Descartes, as for Augustine in the *De Libero Arbitrio*, the free will is the ultimate explanation of errors. This does not mean that the will is an evil, or that God should not have given it: as Augustine had said, the will is a great good, because it is impossible to live rightly without it, even though, because it can be used wrongly, it cannot be *supremely* good. Descartes, like Augustine, argues that our errors can arise without God's having given us any privation, or anything that is not good. The will, in particular, is perfect after its kind, and Descartes denies that God could have made it any better than he did: since the will "consists in just one thing, and as it were in an indivisible, it does not seem that its nature can bear that something be taken away from it" (AT VII,60). Thus if God is to give me any freedom, he must give me an unlimited freedom, indeed as much freedom as he himself possesses: God's will is much more effective than mine, because it is joined to infinitely greater knowledge and power, but "considered formally and precisely in itself" (p. 57) as will or freedom, it seems to be no greater than mine.

Since God has given me an infinite free will, and since (just because I

which produce a sense of pleasure, and the like; but it does not seem that it also teaches us, on the basis of these perceptions of the senses, to conclude anything about things outside us without a previous examination by the intellect: for it seems to pertain to the mind alone, and not to the composite, to know the truth about these things" (AT VII,82–3). For further discussion of the teachings of nature and their relation to theoretical judgments, see Chapter 8, Section C, below.

am a creature) I do not have his infinite knowledge, I am capable of erring. Lacking clear knowledge of many things, I have used my will to affirm or deny them arbitrarily. If, as often happens, my judgment does not agree with the truth as God sees it, I will be in error; even if my judgment does agree with the truth, this is merely a happy accident, and I am still abusing the gift of free will. This abuse of free will is the final explanation of my errors. Error arises, not from a limited faculty as such (this alone could not yield the privation of error), nor from a defective faculty (God has not given me anything defective), but from the conjunction of the finite faculty of understanding with the infinite faculty of will. The juxtaposition of these faculties does not of itself produce error; but it gives me occasion to err, since my will extends beyond the bounds of my understanding and is capable of passing judgment on things I understand only obscurely. It is the will itself that uses and abuses itself, and no further cause can be assigned for its activity. The defective disposition of my will cannot be explained (as Montaigne and Charron, with Stoic sources, explain it) through a deficiency in judgment, since wrong judgment proceeds from the will. This reflection is supposed to show, not only how we fall into error, but also how we can escape from it.

We may not find it obvious that we still have the full freedom to escape our ingrained habit of error. Although Descartes follows Augustine in making the will the ultimate cause of its own activity, he also follows Augustine in admitting a non-causal "explanation" of the will's propensity to error, by noting the *conditions* (the occasion, not the cause) in which I am tempted to abuse my freedom. For Descartes, as for Augustine, we are all born into such a condition: it is this that explains the universality of error, and the difficulty of extricating ourselves once we have become enmeshed in it.

Descartes does not detail in the fourth Meditation this process of sliding "naturally" into error, but he had certainly reflected on it in composing the *Meditations*, in describing the state of intellectual confusion that we are all in until we undertake a rational reconstruction of our beliefs: the *Meditations* implicitly repeat the *Discourse*'s description of the formation of our judgments in childhood, "governed by our appetites and our teachers" (AT VI,13). To include this description explicitly in the fourth Meditation, Descartes would merely have to spell it out in terms of the theory of judgment as assent to ideas; and indeed he goes on to do this in the sixth Replies, where he analyzes how he (and everyone else) came to hold certain beliefs which are contrary to those he has now discovered to be true, and which still prevent his critics from promptly recognizing the truth of the Meditations.

Since these opinions are very different from those I had previously held about the same things, I then began to consider from what causes I had previously believed otherwise; and I noticed that the principal cause was that I had first, from infancy on, passed various judgments about physical things, inasmuch as they contributed to the preservation of the life I was beginning; and that I afterwards retained those same opinions which I had then preconceived about these things. And since the mind at that age used the organs of the body less correctly, and being more firmly attached to them did not think without them, it perceived things only confusedly . . . And since I had never then freed myself from these prejudices in the rest of my life, there was nothing at all that I knew distinctly enough . . . (AT VII,441)

In the context of the Replies, Descartes is making a point about the particular kind of error we will be inclined to fall into: it is Aristotelianism. I will return to Descartes' analysis of this error in Chapter 8, Section C; here it is enough to note Descartes' diagnosis of childhood as a condition predisposing us to error, arising from the way the mind is bound up with the body in infancy, the "appetites" of the *Discourse*. These lead to a general childishness of judgment, a serious systemic condition that cannot be cured simply by growing up. While Descartes does not describe precisely the logical form of the judgments we are tempted to make, the temptation arises because ideas are presented to us confusedly: so when a natural impulse rightly tells me to assent to some idea (e.g. that this fire is painfully hot for me), I accidentally assent also to other ideas that I have not clearly distinguished from it (that pain or heat is objectively inherent in the fire), and in this way I begin a pattern of erroneous assent.

The theory of a universal childish condition inclining us toward false judgments, like the broader theory of judgment itself, is shared in a general way between Augustine (and Plotinus) and the Stoics. But Augustine's teaching has an anti-naturalist emphasis that the Stoics lack; Descartes follows Augustine, as he must in order to shake off the "natural" influences on his thought and begin anew. For the Stoics, as in the Cicero passage that had sparked Descartes' meditations in the second part of the *Discourse*,[12] nature always teaches us aright; the distorting influence comes from society. For Descartes, as for Augustine, our own spontaneous, "natural" impulses lead us astray: the root of error is in substituting our own impulses for the truth as it proceeds from God, not in substituting social conventions for our natural impulses. All society can do is to amplify and systematize what our appetites are telling us already.

For Augustine, of course, this condition of susceptibility to error is not a feature of human nature as God made it, but a penalty for sins (our own or our ancestors'):

For there are indeed two penalties for every sinful soul, ignorance and difficulty. From ignorance error disgraces it, from difficulty torment afflicts it. But to approve false things as true, so as to err unwilling, and to be unable to abstain from lustful works because of the resisting and tormenting pain of the fleshly bond, is not the nature of man as established [by God], but the penalty of man as condemned. (*De Libero Arbitrio* III,xviii,52)

---

[12] See above, Chapter 2, Section B.

This is what comes to be technically known as original sin; it is not an actual sin, but the double condition Augustine describes, the legacy of the sin of Adam, which makes actual sin likely and almost inevitable.[13] We are born ignorant, so that confusion is possible, and subject to the bodily passions or to "difficulty," so that it is a temptation. This produces both the error in judgment which is Descartes' special concern, and moral evil in general. Since Descartes is avoiding theology, he does not say that this childish state is a punishment; but he adopts Augustine's view of the results, and uses it to describe the disease he is intending to cure.[14]

A.5. Deliverance from error

In our present condition of ignorance and difficulty, we will need help in establishing true knowledge. Two kinds of help are available: "neither divine grace nor natural knowledge ever diminishes liberty, but rather increases and strengthens it" (AT VII,58). Descartes' concern in his scientific project is with the latter kind of help: is the natural light sufficient, first to deliver us from error, and then to bring us to scientific knowledge?

Descartes' intention in the fourth Meditation is to use his theodicy to derive a method, in the sense of a discipline of judgment. My errors arise because, "since my will extends more broadly than my intellect, I do not contain it within the same limits, but extend it even to those things which I do not understand" (ibid.); so the discipline of avoiding error will be to restrain my will to the limits of what I perceive through the intellect. But this formula is not enough: Descartes wants to show both that we are *capable* of exercising this discipline, and that, if we do the best we are capable of, God will preserve us from error. To fulfill the fourth Medi-

---

[13] See above, Chapter 4, Section C; as noted there, "original sin" does not mean Adam's sin, but, rather, the condition of (culpable, non-excusing) ignorance and difficulty into which we are born, which as a matter of (alleged) historical fact has been imposed on humanity as the result of Adam's sin.

[14] It would be possible to suggest that Descartes is not simply *applying* Augustine's doctrine of original sin, but *transforming* it, secularizing it, replacing it in his account of error by its structural equivalent, the childish condition. It is hard to refute this definitively, given Descartes' refusal to discuss the theological question, but there is no reason to believe it. What Descartes says about childhood, Augustine also says; what Augustine says about sin and ingratitude to God, Descartes also says; the only difference we can observe in their accounts of this condition is that Augustine adds the historical account of its origin in the sin of Adam, on which Descartes is silent. But there is no reason to doubt that Descartes, if he had addressed the question of the historical origin of error, and been willing to refer to revelation, would have given Adam the central role in the story. Indeed, he could hardly have done otherwise. For Adam, unlike us, was never a child, and so would never have gone through the process of gradual acquisition of beliefs described in Part Two of the *Discourse*; it is only after Adam has deliberately sinned and substituted a false belief for a true one that he will be subject to the general condition of error, and only after children are born following the expulsion from the Garden that the rest of humanity can be born into childish prejudices. This exercise in Biblical Cartesianism was to be worked out, in all seriousness, by Malebranche.

tation's original promise of "a way, from the contemplation of the true God . . . to a knowledge of other things," we must know how much theodicy proves. Just how bad is our present condition? How bad would be consistent with God's goodness in creating us? Descartes follows Augustine in describing what we can and cannot infer from God's goodness, and in concluding that we are capable of turning from our errors and using our will according to the divine standard.

There are limits to what we can infer from God's goodness. We do in fact abuse our will, and consequently are deceived; in Augustine's starker terms, we are in sin and misery. The Meditator recognizes that God could have created him in such a way that he would have been a more perfect individual than he now is. Since free will is a great good, and needed for living rightly, God could not have improved me by taking away my freedom, even though this would preserve me from sin. But, the Meditator objects, God could have left my freedom and supplied me with other goods in such a way that I would never abuse this freedom.

God could easily have brought it about that, even while I remain free and of finite knowledge, I would never err: either if he had implanted in my understanding a clear and distinct perception of all things about which I would ever deliberate; or if he had merely impressed on my memory, so firmly that I could never forget it, [the rule] that I should never judge about any thing that I did not clearly and distinctly understand. (AT VII,61)

There is no necessary reason why God should not have done this. Descartes follows Augustine here: certainly a creature could be constituted so that it would never sin, and thus it would be better than what we are now. But this does not give a ground for complaint against God, since in fact God has created some creatures in such a way that he foreknew they would not sin. We cannot complain that God has made both more and less perfect creatures; we could only make the essentially first-person complaint that *we* are not the most perfect creatures in that world, and this implies nothing against God. As Augustine puts it,

It is not true reason, but envious weakness, when you think that something ought to have been made better, to wish that nothing else inferior should be made, as if, having observed the heaven you wished that the earth had not been made; this would be quite wrong. For you would rightly pass censure if you saw that the earth had been made and the heaven had been left out, since you would say that it [the earth] ought to have been made as you are capable of thinking the heaven. Therefore, since you see that that has been made in whose kind you wished to remake the earth, but that this is called not earth but heaven, I believe that, since you have not been cheated of the better thing in order that there should also be something inferior to be made and that the earth should exist, you ought not to be envious in any way. (*De Libero Arbitrio* III,v,13)

"Heaven" here corresponds to the angels, who are not liable to sin (perhaps for one of the two possible reasons Descartes cites); "earth" is human souls, who are liable to sin. Augustine is saying that God produced natures liable to sin, namely us, and that the world is better for including us; he is *not* saying that God produced sin, or that the world is better for including sin. On the contrary, sin is an evil and a deviation from the divine standard, and it would contradict God's nature to have produced it. God allows sin, not because it contributes to the world's goodness, but because he cannot eliminate it without eliminating natures that are liable to sin (us), and we contribute to the world's goodness.

Descartes speaks much more briefly than Augustine, but he makes all the same points, at least by allusion. He can speak more briefly because he does not feel he has to establish all the distinctions and conclusions Augustine had drawn: he seems to assume that the reader already knows the *De Libero Arbitrio*, or some similar treatment of theodicy, and needs only to be shown the application of this familiar material to the problem of error. So Descartes quickly disposes of the Meditator's objection:

> I easily understand that, considered as an individual totality, I would have been more perfect than I now am, if I had been made in such a way by God. But I cannot therefore deny that it is somehow a greater perfection in the entirety of things that some of its parts are not immune from error, and others are, than if they were all completely alike. And I have no right to complain that God wanted me to play a role in the world that is not the foremost and most perfect of all. (AT VII,61)

Descartes here quietly assumes the existence of angels (how many readers has this escaped?); and he, like Augustine, assumes that it is better for the world to contain both natures liable to error and natures immune to error. But Descartes, like Augustine, takes it as self-evident that error itself is an evil and damages the perfection of the world; it proceeds, not from God, but from the free creature. Descartes tacitly follows Augustine's thesis that God has given me an inferior "role" or cosmic function to play, so that I will not seriously damage the cosmos if I sin; the "foremost and most perfect" roles in sustaining the cosmos go to reliable angels. But I am not cast as a sinner: I perform my role best if I resist the temptations to which I am liable, and avoid actual sin.

God could have made me immune to error by "impressing on my memory, so firmly that I could never forget it, [the rule] that I should never judge about any thing that I did not clearly and distinctly understand" (AT VII,61). In fact God did not make me so that I *would* not err, but he made me so that I *need* not err: although I do not automatically remember the rule of how I ought to judge, I can deliberately apply my will to keeping this resolution in mind. For Descartes, as for the Augustine of the *De Libero Arbitrio*, this is possible even in our condition of "difficulty": "although I discover in myself an infirmity, so that I cannot always cling with concentration to one and the same *cognitio*, nonetheless, by attentive and frequently repeated meditation, I can bring it about that I remember it as often as practice demands, and thus that I should acquire a habit of not erring" (p. 62); and in this, Descartes immediately adds, "the chief and greatest perfection of man consists." Thus the discipline of meditation, beginning with the suspension of all judgment in the first Meditation, and continuing in the second and third Meditations by gradually extending the range of purified distinct ideas we can assent to, and reinforced by constant repetition, acquires a cosmic significance: it is the means by which we learn to fulfill the role God gave us, and, overcoming our disabilities, to assimilate ourselves as far as possible to the angels.

For Descartes, as for Augustine, theodicy depends on noetic. The fourth Meditation begins from the conclusions of the third, that God is Nous, that God is my creator, and that I am created in the image of God. Because this God creates me in his image, my nature does not require me to assent to anything except the *noêta*, the intelligible contents of ideas which I as potential *nous* receive from God as essentially actual *nous*. If I were created by a deceiving demon, or if I were produced by an irrational nature and in the image of that irrational nature, then my nature would impose irrational constraints on my judgment: that is, it would lead me irresistibly to assent to some range of impressions, without this constraint's being justified by the objective content of the impressions. Since I am created by God, and therefore (Descartes says) created in his image, I am not constrained in this way: even if God then hands me over to a demon, or (more likely) to an irrational nature, I still retain God's image, and the demon or nature cannot constrain me to irrationality.

It may seem strange that, while the third Meditation had located the *imago dei* in my objectively infinite *idea* of God, the fourth Meditation asserts that my *will* or freedom is formally infinite, and that "it is chiefly this by reason of which I understand that I bear a certain image and likeness of God" (AT VII,57). And this "infinite" will, which seems to exhibit itself chiefly in my errors, may seem even less divine when Descartes admits that it gives me no real freedom not to assent to the clear ideas I receive from God. But the freedom that reflects the *imago dei* is not liberty of indifference: it is specifically freedom from *irrational* constraint. The right use of this freedom is negative. Because I am, by my essence, potential *nous*, nothing compels me to deviate from the divine standard. In fact, I do yield (like the newly incarnate souls of *Timaeus* 43–4) to the impulses of irrational nature, and assent to impressions that are not objectively clear; but the image of God is not effaced, and I am still capable of *not* assenting to irrational impulses, and restricting my assent to the things that my intellectual nature irresistibly determines me to assent to. If I doubt everything I am capable of doubting, I exclude everything in my judgments that comes from deviation or privation, and retain only what comes from God; and God, by his essence as Nous, is necessarily the source of true intellectual contents. "Whenever I restrain my will in bearing judgment, so that it extends itself only to the things that are clearly and distinctly exhibited to it by the intellect, it plainly cannot happen that I should err: for every clear and distinct perception is doubtless *something*, and therefore it cannot be from nothing, but necessarily has God for author – God, I say, that supremely perfect being, for whom it is contradictory to be a deceiver – and therefore it is doubtless true" (AT VII,62).

B. Consequences for reason and for faith

Descartes' system of the sciences depends, in its content, on Augustine's intuitions of the soul and God; it depends, in its method, on Augustine's theodicy. But what becomes of the other side of Augustinian wisdom: the function of faith in addition to reason, the need of grace to guide us on the road to the fatherland, the specific intellectual content of Christianity over and above what philosophy can grasp?[15] Descartes justifies his candidate for wisdom by the theodicy of the fourth Meditation, but the contents of this wisdom are the clear ideas of the understanding, and faith seems to have no function in the resulting system. This is what leads Gilson and Gouhier to reject all talk of an "*augustinisme de Descartes.*" Gilson claims that, though Descartes "integrates into his teaching a whole series of Augustinian theses," he is adopting the form of these theses without their Augustinian meaning, since "it is not St. Augustine's spirit that animates him"; this follows (for Gilson) because Descartes is opposed to Augustine on "the most essential point of Augustinianism, the relations of reason with faith," and thus on "his idea of philosophy itself."[16]

It should be clear that Gilson's conclusion distorts Descartes' relationship to Augustine. Gilson is arbitrarily circumscribing the "essence" of Augustinianism: there is no reason to give Augustine's attitude toward faith any special priority over his discipline for contemplating God and the soul, his conception of God's relations to souls and bodies, or his explanation of the origin of evil; and there is no reason to suppose that Descartes is altering (much less trivializing or subverting) the meaning of Augustine's theses on these matters when he applies them to the construction of his scientific system. But Gilson raises a legitimate question: in adapting the Augustinian metaphysics for the construction of a scientific system, does Descartes frustrate Augustine's intention of confirming the Christian faith? If Descartes' philosophical achievement consists in working out latent consequences of Augustine's metaphysics, why does the resulting system contain no specifically Christian content, no interweaving of faith and reason?

There is no question about the fact that Descartes tries to keep revealed theology out of his philosophy. While he everywhere shows the highest respect for Christian theology, he everywhere makes it clear that it is none

[15] For these three distinct aspects of the specifically Christian side of Augustinian wisdom, see above, Chapter 4, Section D.
[16] The Gilson quotes are from René Descartes, *Discours de la méthode: texte et commentaire par Etienne Gilson*, p. 298; discussed above, Chapter 1.

of his business.[17] Indeed, according to the autobiographical account of the *Discourse*, he would seem to have set theology aside early from his search for truth in the sciences:

I revered our Theology, and aspired as much as anyone else to get to heaven;[18] but having learned, as a very certain thing, that the road there is no less open to the most ignorant than to the most learned, and that the revealed truths that lead there are above our understanding, I did not dare to submit them to the weakness of my reasonings, and I thought that to undertake to examine them, and succeed, one would need to have some extraordinary assistance from heaven, and to be more than human. (AT VI,8)

In the context of the *Discourse* this is only one part of a series of rejections of all the disciplines Descartes had learned in school, none of which lead to the promised wisdom; but revealed theology somehow always retains its immunity to method. Whenever, as in the *Letter to Picot*, Descartes describes the means of acquiring human wisdom, he is careful to note that divine wisdom is acquired only by grace, and stands outside of his universal science.[19]

To understand what attitude Descartes is taking toward faith and reason, and why, we must go back to the fourth Meditation and explore its consequences. The fourth Meditation's analysis of error is supposed to support the practicability and reliability of a certain method or discipline of judgment: Descartes claims to have been following this discipline implicitly from the beginning of the *Meditations*, and he proposes to practice it explicitly, beginning in the fifth Meditation, in reconstructing science. We may begin by describing the science that Descartes builds according to this method, and then show what status faith has in relation to this science. We will be able to show that on the question of faith, as elsewhere, apparently anti-Augustinian aspects of Descartes' work are byproducts of his attempt to build a philosophy consistently on Augustinian principles. There are several distinct points here. First, we can show that Augustine's principles, as applied to method in the fourth Meditation, lead to an exclusion of the truths of faith from the scientific system: this will make it clear that Descartes has not abandoned his Augustinian principles for some alien motivation in practicing this separation. Second, we can show that the application of these principles does not exclude the possibility of faith in revealed religion *outside the bounds* of the scientific system; and, third, that this non-philosophical faith is in fact *required* by the internal

---

[17] Thus Descartes tells Mersenne: "As for your question of theology, although it surpasses the capacity of my mind, yet it does not seem to me to be outside my profession, since it does not touch on what depends on revelation, [which is] what I call properly theology; it is, rather, metaphysical, and should be examined by human reason" (AT I,143–4).

[18] This formula refers back to Descartes' earlier description of the utility of the different sciences: "theology teaches us how to get to heaven" (AT VI,6).

[19] In the *Letter to Picot*, in discussing the ways in which we make progress toward wisdom, Descartes adds, "I am not including divine revelation, because it does not guide us by degrees, but raises us in a single step to an infallible belief" (AT IX2,5).

necessities of the philosophical program. Descartes is not the agent of a sort of suicide of Augustinianism, in which its principles would lead to a destruction of its original goal. The place of revealed religion, far from being destroyed by the work of reason, will be confirmed by it; it will simply be *distinguished* from the philosophical project, and in a way that is not foreign to Augustine himself.

The fundamental characteristic of Descartes' science is that it is composed of clear ideas. At the end of the fourth Meditation, the Meditator assures himself that he will attain the truth, "if I only attend sufficiently to all the things I understand perfectly, and segregate them from the rest, which I apprehend more confusedly and obscurely" (AT VII,62); and he begins in the fifth Meditation to reconstruct science according to this maxim. He wants to see whether he can achieve certainty about the things he began to doubt in the first Meditation. But before reexamining whether bodies actually exist, he begins by purifying or separating out his clear ideas concerning body: "before I inquire whether some such things exist outside me, I ought to consider the ideas of them, insofar as they are in my thought, and see which of them are distinct, and which confused" (p. 63). Setting aside here the fifth Meditation's function in supporting Descartes' physics, we may take it simply as a specimen of method, showing the relation of science to the clear ideas of the intellect.

The Meditator discovers that he clearly perceives "that quantity which the philosophers commonly call 'continuous', or the extension of that quantity (or rather of the *res quanta*) in length, breadth and depth" (p. 63); he also perceives the modes of extension, such as the shape and motion of its parts. When he turns his attention to these things, he can perceive "innumerable particulars about figure, number, motion, and the like" (ibid.); the longer he contemplates these things, the more truths he is led to assent to by the clarity of the things themselves. The spontaneity and certainty of this assent is strong enough that the Platonic theory of recollection is a plausible explanation.[20] But however the perception comes about, it is a clear perception, and so must be true, and true *about something*: as Descartes puts it, "it is manifest that everything that is true is *something*" (p. 63). The contents of these perceptions are real essences, which the mind does not create but rather discovers in the things it considers: this is why these perceptions are a *science*, which progresses in

---

[20] Descartes' reference to the *Meno* (perhaps mediated through Cicero *Tusculan Disputations* I,xxiv,57) is unmistakable: the Meditator perceives "innumerable particulars about figure, number, motion, and the like, whose truth is so manifest and so accordant with my nature that, when I notice them for the first time, I seem not so much to be learning something new as to be remembering things I had known before; or attending for the first time to things that had long been in me, though I had never before turned my mind's gaze upon them" (AT VII,63–4). The last clause ("or attending . . .") gives the true account: but the Platonic account is supposed to be tempting. On Descartes' application to bodies of the language of Platonic intelligibles, see further Chapter 8, Section B, below.

discovering reality as more and more things become clear through contemplation.

Science is composed of clear ideas; in particular, it is composed of ideas. Since *scientia* is a kind of *cognitio*, it consists in passive intellectual perception, and not in judgment: judgment merely supervenes on the attainment of scientific knowledge. Geometry is the model of science, and Descartes aims to introduce a "geometric spirit" into philosophy.[21] He promises, like the geometers, to build up from sure foundations, to extract all the consequences, to restrain himself from jumping ahead to problems he cannot yet solve; he is enabled to do this by the clarity of some of his ideas, the objective assurance that what he clearly perceives is true, and his ability, through an effort of will, to restrict himself to assenting to what he clearly perceives. The Meditator can apply the geometric spirit because God gives him clear ideas with real positive content: to apply the geometric spirit is just to adhere to this content, and the resulting science consists in the perception of this content, expanding as we perceive more and more of the series of interrelated real essences.

It is obvious enough that faith cannot be part of such a scientific system. Faith, whether in revealed religion or in anything else, is an act of the will, and no act of the will can be part of the system, which consists entirely of passive intellectual perceptions. Faith must be an act of the will, rather than of the understanding, because faith is a species of judgment, of the mind's assent to something that claims to be true, and (as we have seen) all judgments are acts of the will. But faith is more *obviously* an act of will than some other kinds of judgment; for when the will assents to ideas that are clearly perceived to be true, the active function of the will (though genuinely active and spontaneous) follows automatically on the passive function of the understanding. It would barely be worth Descartes' while to distinguish the operations of the will and the intellect, if these were the only cases; but the distinction is of crucial importance in the case of things we perceive only obscurely, and so Descartes is careful to mark it in general. Faith is an act of will in the stronger sense: it is not consequent on knowledge, does not depend on an idea that is intrinsically clear and therefore certain; faith is an assent to something that is obscure in itself, so that not all who perceive it assent. Thus even in the *Rules for the Direction of the Mind*, before he has worked out his mature psychology of will and intellect (what is to be directed is the *"ingenium"*), Descartes singles out faith as an act of the will: although the *ingenium* should refuse to assent to things it has not clearly intuited or deduced, this "does not at all prevent us from believing that the things that are divinely revealed are more certain than all knowledge [*cognitio*], for whatever faith in them is about things that are obscure, is not an action of the *ingenium*, but of the will" (AT X,370). Descartes has not yet made the subtle point that

---

[21] See above, Chapter 2, Section B, for a discussion of the "geometric spirit" in Descartes.

the will is involved even in assenting to clear perceptions; but he already finds it obvious that faith is an act of the will, going beyond what we perceive, and that this somehow excludes faith from the scope of the method.

But if faith is an act whereby the will assents to something that remains obscure to the understanding, and if (as Descartes continually repeats) we should never assent to anything unclear, then it seems that we should never *believe* anything, as opposed to knowing it with certainty; so Descartes should recommend against faith in anything, whether in divine revelation or in anything else we do not clearly and distinctly perceive to be true. Perhaps Descartes can escape this consequence by saying, as he does in the fourth Meditation, that divine grace, like natural knowledge, can irresistibly incline us to assent to the ideas we are considering. But in that case the faith induced in us by grace should be on a par with our assent to distinct *cognitiones*, and would equally deserve to be included in the scientific system: the fact that, as an act of judgment, it is not formally identical with an act of understanding, should not exclude it from scientific practice any more than it excludes any other judgment. So when we see that Descartes does not, in fact, involve revealed doctrines in his scientific research or writing, we could only explain this by supposing that he has some personal prejudice against including them – perhaps arising from a desire to avoid theological controversy, if not from some secret disbelief.

Descartes can deal with all these difficulties: he does deal with them in the second Replies, under the heading "Fifthly" (AT VII,147). The objection has been put:

Fifthly, if the will never strays or sins when it follows a clear and distinct *cognitio* of its mind, and exposes itself to danger when it pursues a conception of the intellect that is far from clear and distinct, then see what follows from this: namely, that a Turk, or anyone else, not only does not sin in not embracing the Christian religion, but also sins if he does embrace it, since he does not clearly or distinctly know its truth. Indeed, if this rule of yours is true, the will will hardly be permitted to embrace anything, since we know hardly anything with that clarity and distinctness that you require for a certainty vulnerable to no doubt. See therefore that when you desire to protect the truth, you do not prove too much, and overturn rather than build up. (Pp. 126–7)

Descartes replies that it is obvious that the will exposes itself to danger by following an unclear perception. This is not controversial either among philosophers or among theologians: everyone agrees that we run less risk of error the more clearly we understand something before assenting to it, and that "they sin who pass a judgment without knowing its cause" (p. 147).

It is obvious that pursuing something obscure is dangerous, and the Second Objectors could not have brought any positive reasons against this claim. But they are plainly worried about its consequences: these seem to be at least irreligious, and possibly suicidal, if the will is forbidden to make those probable judgments it needs for the preservation of life. Descartes tries to reassure the Objectors by showing what does and does not follow from his rule about what the will should embrace.

Since Descartes is not saying anything beyond what all philosophers and theologians have said, he does not think he is in any more trouble than they are; so he comes to the common defense, using what he apparently takes to be the standard line of reply. There is no force to the objection about embracing the faith: "for although faith is said to be *about* things that are obscure, yet that on account of which we embrace it is not obscure, but brighter than any natural light" (ibid.). For, says Descartes, we require clarity only in the *ratio formalis* that moves the will to assent, and not in the "matter or the thing itself to which we assent"; and in the case of someone moved by grace to assent to the truth of Christianity, the *ratio formalis* on account of which he assents "consists in a certain internal light, such that when we are supernaturally illumined with it by God, we are confident that the things that are put forward for us to believe have been revealed by him, and that it surely cannot be that he would lie, which is more certain than any natural light, and often even more evident on account of the light of grace" (p. 148).

The "cause" (p. 147) or justification that can provide a clear *ratio formalis* for a judgment can thus be of either of two types: "one is from the natural light, the other from divine grace" (p. 148). I may rightly assent to something that is obscure in itself, if my confidence in it comes from grace. I do not find any reason for assent in examining the proposition itself, but I do in perceiving it in a certain relationship to God (whatever exactly this is supposed to feel like when it happens). This seems to be no different in principle from my assent to a proposition I might read in the newspaper ("NIXON RESIGNS"), which does not seem evident merely from considering the ideas of Nixon and of resignation, but which I come to believe through considering the relationships between the newspaper, myself (would they lie to me?), and the proposition (could they be mistaken?) – with the difference, of course, that the newspaper story is less certain than the natural light of reason, while divine revelation is more so.

Descartes gives an example, even in the case of the natural light, where we can have a clear *ratio* for assenting to something that is itself obscure; but the discrepancy between the clarities of the *ratio* and the subject matter is inessential in the case of the natural light, and becomes important only in the case of faith. When I judge by the natural light that "*obscurity should be removed from our concepts*," the subject matter of the judgment is "obscurity itself" (p. 147). This may not be quite as trivial as it sounds (delicate questions of logic are involved), but here too the *ratio* for assenting to the proposition arises from a clear perception of the relations between the different terms of the judgment, although this is not a perception of the *subject* of the judgment: it can become one through a rearrangement of the sentence. But when we are led by grace to certainty in matters of faith, no such rearrangement is possible, because the certainty is not derived from anything within the objects of the judgment: it is derived from a particular grace of God shown to the individual who is to assent, and since this varies from one individual to another (and from one time to another), the *ratio formalis* moving the will cannot be reduced to any feature of the things judged, without reference to the person judging and to God.

Choosing our words carefully, we may say that the certainty coming from divine grace is a *subjective* certainty, while the certainty coming from the natural light is an *objective* certainty. There is, of course, no anti-realism here: the *truth* of propositions accepted by faith is objective, that is, the propositions are true when and because they correspond to their object. What is *not* objective, i.e. not derived from a corresponding property of the object, in propositions maintained by faith, is the *certainty* of the judgment. We may say that whenever a person has no doubt about something that he affirms, he has a subjective certainty of its truth. Descartes thinks that if this person is *right* not to doubt, then his subjective certainty must have come to him from God (otherwise it is self-manufactured). But God could have given it in either of two ways: in the case of the natural light, the subjective certainty is given *mediately* via the clarity God gives to the objects of our perception, so that the certainty of the subjective act, like its truth, comes from something corresponding in the object; whereas in the case of grace, God creates the subjective certainty *immediately* in the soul, by an extraordinary causality bypassing the causality of created natures.

It should now be clear why the truths of faith, even when their certainty (like that of our clear perceptions) comes to us by a divine illumination, cannot be incorporated into the scientific system. The scientific system is composed of ideas that we clearly and distinctly perceive, and that we therefore know with certainty to be true. The truths of faith are not of this kind: they concern things that we perceive only obscurely, and we therefore do not *know* them to be true, although we may *believe* them, and, through God's grace, we may even achieve a justified subjective certainty about them. If, out of a misplaced enthusiasm, we tried to mix them in with our clear ideas, we would not be contributing to scientific progress, since we make progress only by acquiring more and more clear perceptions, and since no clear perception can be supported on a foundation that is itself obscure. Indeed, our enthusiasm for the faith may quickly lead us into philosophical and theological error, if it tempts us to assume that obscure ideas are clear. If God inspires me to believe that he consists in a trinity of persons comprising a single essence, and if I convince myself that I clearly understand this to be true, and try to build up a science out of it, I will have to invent some general notion of a divine person, and show that the properties of divine persons in general clearly imply that there must be three of them; but since I do not in fact clearly perceive this, I will be inventing obscure propositions, and as soon as I go beyond the revealed doctrine these are just as likely to be false as to be true.

Besides damaging my philosophy, this may also lead me into a heretical theology – and so may get me into trouble, either with the Inquisition or with God at the last judgment. As the *Discourse* reminds us, the road to heaven is as open to the most ignorant as to the most learned, and we can only be more likely to miss it if we pretend to understand things that are beyond our capacity.

This explains, for Descartes, why the truths of faith and the truths of reason must be kept in separate compartments: it is a natural consequence of his doctrine of knowledge as the evident perception of clear ideas. To believe something, even something that turns out to be true, because I falsely think that I perceive it clearly, is to be opinionated: this is what Descartes has been combatting from the beginning, and is the opposite of the right use of the will needed for philosophy. Indeed, if the Turk of the second Objections,

led by some false reasoning, embraces [the revealed doctrines of Christianity] although they are obscure to him, he will not therefore be a believer [*fidelis*]; rather, he will be sinning in not using his reason rightly. Nor do I think that any orthodox theologian has ever felt otherwise about these matters. (P. 148)

An opinion based on the false judgment that one has understood something does not deserve to be called belief or faith; it cannot be a legitimate basis for acceptance of revealed religion.

Descartes claims that there is another, legitimate, basis for revealed religion: it is *faith*, that is, trust that some proposition (or body of propositions, such as those contained in the Bible), although we do not clearly perceive it to be true, nonetheless comes to us (by some route) from God, and is therefore true. Sometimes we must make a decision, or choose an authority to trust, under conditions of uncertainty, but sometimes a particular circumstance may produce a subjective certainty that our choice is justified. In those cases where God brings about this subjective certainty through grace, we cannot be going wrong in our assent.[22] As we have seen, this answer is possible and consistent with Descartes' theory of judgment. But we may still ask whether this answer is *necessary*. Would it not have been more plausible to say that we should assent only to what we clearly

[22] Faith in a proposition may be practically justified even in cases where it is not accompanied by a subjective certainty derived from grace. But the case where there is such a subjective certainty (not just a decision to act on the assumption that the proposition is true) is the most important for the present discussion, since it is hardest to see why *this* kind of proposition should not be incorporated into the scientific system. Perhaps it is best to say that the certainty derived from grace, that is, the help God gives us in choosing among things we do not clearly perceive, comes in degrees: short of perfect subjective certainty, God could make something look plausible to us, either by acting directly on our minds, or by doing something externally that makes one option look plausible. Thus God might (as Augustine says) make one sacred book widely accepted throughout the world, so that, if we are going to take some sacred book as our guide, this one will look more plausible than its competitors. This kind of divine action should count as grace, though it is not the intense and subjective kind that Descartes is most interested in.

perceive, and make no mention of a special category for faith? The theory of faith has the look of an extraneous addition to Descartes' philosophical system, dictated merely by the fact that Descartes was living in a Christian country, or was himself a Christian, and not by any strictly intellectual necessity.

In fact, this is not the case. Descartes' doctrine of judgment, indeed his whole philosophical project, necessitate the doctrine of faith he gives in the second Replies. To see this, we need look no further than the next paragraph of his reply:

Besides, I wish you to recall here that I have very carefully distinguished, with regard to the things the will is permitted to embrace, between the practice [usus] of life and the contemplation of truth. For as far as the practice of life is concerned, I am so far from thinking that we should assent to nothing except things clearly perceived, that on the contrary I do not think that we should always wait even for *likely* things [verisimilia], but that sometimes we must choose one out of many things entirely unknown, and hold it no less firmly after it is chosen (so long as we can give no reasons for the opposite choice), than if it had been chosen on account of very clear reasons, as I have explained on p. 26 of the *Discourse on Method*.[23] But where we are concerned only with the contemplation of truth, who has ever denied that we should hold back our assent from things that are obscure and not distinctly enough perceived? But that I have dealt with this alone in my *Meditations*, the thing itself bears witness, and I have also declared it in express words at the end of the first Meditation, in saying that I could not give way too much here to distrust, since I was concerning myself not with doing things, but only with knowing them. (P. 149)

Descartes is quite right to refer the Objectors back to Part Three of the *Discourse*, and to the statement of the project of the *Meditations*, for this distinction between practical and speculative concerns. As Descartes recognizes in these places, the difference between speculative and practical standards of evidence is essential to beginning the project of the reconstruction of belief: it is a practical necessity that we accept a great many things that we realize that we do not *know* to be true, if we are to survive long enough for any certainty to emerge from our doubt.

Now, it is clear that this constitutes Descartes' appropriate reply to the last part of the Objection – "if this rule of yours is true, the will will hardly be permitted to embrace anything, since we know hardly anything with that clarity and distinctness that you require for a certainty vulnerable to no doubt" (p. 126) – and that this clarification is supposed to show that Descartes' method does not have suicidal implications. It is not quite so clear what follows for religion: does assent to divinely revealed truths belong to "the contemplation of truth" or to "the practice of life"? Is the practical justification of assent under conditions of uncertainty also sup-

---

[23] Descartes' reference is to his discussion of the second maxim of his provisional morals in the third part of the *Discourse*, AT VI,24–5, and particularly to p. 25, lines 7ff.

posed to justify religious faith, or will faith be justified on a "speculative" basis, as a step toward contemplation of the truth?

We have seen that Descartes does not regard faith in divine revelation as a step toward scientific knowledge, because it is not a *cognitio*, nor immediately connected with one; and it seems plausible to identify *cognitio* with the "contemplation of truth." So we might conjecture that Descartes is thinking of religious faith as part of the "practice of life," and that the justification of acting without clear knowledge (or even verisimilitude) would be equally a justification of faith. Fortunately, Descartes confirms this conjecture in a passage of the fourth Replies: this passage will help us clear up the remaining questions about the status of faith in the second Replies, and in the philosophical project generally.

Descartes says, in replying to Arnauld:

> That in the fourth Meditation I discussed only "the error that is committed in the judgment of true and false, not that which occurs in the pursuit of good and evil," and that I always excepted "the things that pertain to faith and to the conduct of life" when I asserted that "we ought not to assent to anything except what we clearly know," is shown by the context of my whole writing; and I also expressly explained this in the reply to the second Objections, in number 5; and I also gave notice beforehand in the Synopsis. (Pp. 247–8)

Descartes explains that he is restating all this now "in order to declare how much I yield to this most eminent man's [Arnauld's] judgment, and how acceptable to me are his counsels" (ibid.) – rather than to criticize Arnauld for repeating a point that had already been established. For Arnauld had first urged Descartes to declare that in the fourth Meditation he was concerning himself only with truth and falsehood, not with good and evil (p. 215, here cited by Descartes), and then immediately gone on to the second point that Descartes takes up, namely,

> that when [Descartes] asserts that we ought not to assent to anything except what we clearly and distinctly know, he is dealing only with the things that aim at learning, and belong to understanding [*ad disciplinas spectant & sub intelligentiam cadunt*], and not with the things that pertain to faith and to the conduct of life [*ad fidem pertinent, & ad vitam agendam*], so that he is condemning the rashness of the opinionated, not the persuasion of those who prudently believe. (P. 216)

Descartes agrees, and points out that he had already said this in the passage we have considered from the second Replies. Arnauld's "things that aim at learning and belong to understanding" are, in Descartes, the things the will is permitted to embrace for the "contemplation of truth"; Arnauld's "things that pertain to faith and to the conduct of life" are what the will is permitted to embrace for the "practice of life." Descartes confirms this correspondence in accepting Arnauld's comments; and this helps us to interpret the passage from the second Replies. For it is clear that for both Arnauld and Descartes, the things that pertain to faith, though they may not be strictly *identical* with the things that pertain to the practice or conduct of life, at least fall under the same category with them, and are immune to methodological doubt for the same reason.

Arnauld says that Descartes is condemning "the rashness of the opinionated, not the persuasion of those who prudently believe." So those who believe can do so *prudently*: that is, their belief is justified by its place in the conduct of life, rather than by any quality the believer might perceive in the ideas to which he assents.[24] Faith or confidence in divine revelation is prudent for the same reason that the faith or confidence that one's food is not poisoned is prudent. We do not *know*, we do not certainly and evidently perceive, that our food is not poisoned – we certainly cannot prove this during the six-day course of Meditations, since we do not even prove the existence of body until the last day – and yet it is prudent to eat between Meditations, and this presupposes a confidence *for practical purposes* that food procured in a normal manner will not kill us. And this is indeed Descartes' practice, as he explains it in Part Three of the *Discourse*, in giving his provisional code of morals. We do not need to consider here the justification of the whole scheme of the provisional morals; we need only note how religious faith fits into the scheme, and thus how it is justified by its place in the conduct of life. In Part Three of the *Discourse*, the truths of the faith are "set apart" from the process of the destruction of "all the rest of my opinions" (AT VI,28), along with the maxims of the provisional morals.[25] And indeed, remaining in the faith is already included in the first maxim of the code, where "keeping constantly the religion in which, by the grace of God, I have been instructed since childhood" (p. 23) was a condition for the choice of the best opinions to be guided by in all spheres of outward activity until the reconstruction of knowledge was complete. Descartes gives no special reason for this, beyond the general necessity of choosing rules for life that will enable him to live as happily as he can, until he can replace these opinions with certain knowledge. But it is clear enough that the confidence in revealed truths is analogous to confidence in the other sorts of truth we need for living as happily as possible; just as belief in the nutritive value of food is necessary for my physical health, so belief in the saving value of grace is necessary for my spiritual health, for my general well-being in this world and the next. This would have been Descartes' belief prior to his philosophical reflection; he does not *know* that this is so, but he is not yet in a position to be ruled by knowledge alone; and *starting from this belief*, his conclusion

---

[24] Again, this is not anti-realism: what one assents to is either true or false, but the truth or falsity of an obscure idea is not a quality of the idea which is immediately available to the perceiving subject. Note that Descartes and Arnauld are not concerned with the prudential value of *pretending* to believe what in fact one knows or believes to be false, but only with the prudential value of actually believing.

[25] From the perspective of the *Meditations*, of course, the truths of faith are not opinions at all, and should be set apart from "all my opinions," not from "all the *rest* of my opinions." Descartes does not lack the concept of this distinction in the *Discourse*; he merely lacks the terminology.

will be to retain it, along with his belief in food, during the meditative process.

This gives, in outline, Descartes' justification for the necessity of faith as an act of will, in the interim before knowledge can replace it. It is clear that some kind of faith will have to be preserved during the process of reconstruction; it may not be logically necessary that this should include a religious as well as a medical component, but this is surely more plausible than the contrary possibility. Descartes is not justifying *opinion*, in the narrower sense in which Arnauld intends that term; opinion would be an attempt to pass judgment on things one does not know, insofar as they "belong to understanding," that is, for the speculative purpose of advancing knowledge, which can only be hindered by such accretions. In this sense the "rashness of the opinionated" is rightly condemned by the fourth Meditation, while the persuasion of believers remains immune to the censure.

At this conclusion, it might be said in defense of Gilson: perhaps I have correctly described Descartes' doctrine of faith, as it follows from his philosophical methodology, and perhaps this doctrine of faith accounts for the attitude Descartes actually takes toward faith in his philosophical or scientific practice. But this is unsatisfactory as a way of making Descartes an Augustinian: surely this grudging acceptance of the necessity of faith as an interim measure is far beneath the religious aspirations of the philosophers and theologians of the age of faith, and especially of Augustine and his followers.

This is an understandable way of looking at Descartes, but it is a distortion. In fact, Descartes' doctrine of faith is indistinguishable from Augustine's. We find in both authors virtually identical descriptions of knowledge and faith, and prescriptions for our attitude toward them. We incline to read them differently, because prejudices about the men and their times suggest that Descartes concedes a place to faith grudgingly, while Augustine does so with all his heart. But by brushing aside these prejudices and analyzing the relevant texts, we have seen that their doctrines of faith are the same; and naturally so, since Descartes' doctrine of faith is a consequence of his adoption of the Augustinian doctrine of the free exercise of will in judgment.[26]

Let us recall, from Chapter 4, Section D, how Augustine came to his acceptance of a necessary place for religious faith, bringing out the main points of his position to show how close to it Descartes remains. When Augustine was a Manichee, he refused to allow a place for faith in religious

---

[26] Note that, although the Stoics believe in something like the free exercise of will in judgment (though without the Augustinian and Cartesian notion of the faculty of will), they are not committed to this consequence, because they think that cataleptic impressions are quite common, and are sufficient both for living our daily lives and for attaining wisdom. For Augustine and especially Descartes, clear perceptions are much rarer (and not available through the senses), and not sufficient as a practical guide: so we must supplement them through faith.

questions, and hoped to achieve a rationally grounded *knowledge* of God, the world, and the soul through the Manichean *gnosis*, without having to commit himself to anything he had not rationally determined to be true. After his conversation with Faustus, he came to see that the Manichees did not offer any genuine knowledge, but demanded an implicit faith all the more "blind" for being unrecognized. On coming into contact with Ambrose and the other Catholics at Milan, and deciding that orthodox Christianity was not (as he had earlier supposed) contrary to reason, he also reevaluated its demand for faith in things yet unknown, which earlier he had ridiculed:

Already preferring the Catholic doctrine, I thought that it did more modestly and less deceptively to bid that what was not demonstrated should be believed (whether it had been demonstrated, but not to some person, or whether it had not been demonstrated at all), than with a rash promise of knowledge [*scientia*] to laugh at credulity [as did the Manichees], and then afterwards to command that so many most fabulous and absurd things, which could not be demonstrated, should be believed. [Then I considered] . . . that I believed innumerable things that I had not seen, nor had I been present when they happened, like so many things in the history of nations, so many things about places and cities that I had not seen, so many things that I believed from friends and doctors and other people; if these things were not believed, we would get nothing at all done in this life. Finally I considered how unshakenly firm I held by faith what parents I was born of, which I could not have known except by believing what I heard. In this way you [God] persuaded me that not those who believed your books, which you have established with so much authority in almost all nations, but those who did not believe them, should be censured; nor should I listen if they said, "how do you know that those books have been delivered to the human race by the spirit of the one true and most truthful God?" (*Confessions* VI,v,7)

Thus for Augustine (as for Descartes) some truths are to be accepted on faith, because it is practically necessary, if we are to be able to do anything at all, to believe things that we do not yet know, and perhaps can never know, or never in this life. For Augustine (as for Descartes) faith extends, on the same principle, to many everyday things, things that "no one has ever seriously doubted" (quoting from the Synopsis of the *Meditations*); by reflecting on our faith in these things, we can see that faith in the Bible is more plausible than its contrary. But for Augustine (as for Descartes) the search for truth does not stop here: we are not to be *satisfied* with the degree of certainty we have been forced to accept, but are to press on toward knowledge. Faith is a halfway house toward knowledge, given where "we are too weak to find the truth by pure reason" (*Confessions* VI,v,8), guiding and protecting us until we can discover by reason the truths that we have all along believed by faith. Augustine is everywhere insistent that we must attain to "understanding," to "proof," or to "knowledge," so that faith will no longer be needed; his disagreement with those who would have knowledge immediately is a disagreement only about the *means* to knowledge.

This and nothing else is Augustine's justification for religious faith – however much the "age of faith" may have been glorified by the nostalgia of later times. This is the tradition Descartes inherits, and he preserves it faithfully. Descartes' philosophical project depends on the Augustinian theory of knowledge and judgment, and so he accepts the necessity of faith for the same reason that Augustine does. It is true that Descartes does not "blend" faith and reason, but we have seen the justification for this in his scientific project, and it is not an essential difference from Augustine. For Augustine, faith stands in the same relation to knowledge as chicory does to coffee: it is a more readily available but less attractive substitute. He sometimes "blends" them in the same work, but we do the same with coffee and chicory, if we have some amount of coffee but not enough to go around. This does not mean that faith and reason lose their separate origins and their separate natures for Augustine, any more than they do for Descartes. For Augustine's purpose in his writing – deepening the religious knowledge of believers – it is convenient to blend them, to discuss them together; but this is not binding on Descartes when he uses the same principles for different purposes, and he is not in any way betraying Augustine when he confines his discussion of pragmatic and religious faith mainly to the third part of the *Discourse*.

It is clear that by the time Descartes wrote the *Meditations*, he was not a stranger to the Augustinian distinction between knowledge, belief, and opinion. It is something he presupposes, not something he needs to be told. In this light it is easy to understand Descartes' reaction when Arnauld proposes the considerations that we have already seen about faith and the conduct of life. Arnauld attaches to his comments a long quote from Augustine's anti-Manichean treatise *De Utilitate Credendi*, which systematizes the conclusions described in our chapter from the *Confessions*, distinguishing belief, knowledge, and opinion, and condemning opinion while justifying belief as a step on the road to knowledge:

There are three things which, though very close together, are most worthy of distinction in the minds of men: to understand, to believe, and to opine.

He *understands*, who comprehends something by certain reason. He *believes*, who, moved by some weighty authority, judges something to be true even though he does not comprehend it by certain reason. He *opines*, who thinks that he knows what he does not know.

To *opine* is for two reasons very shameful: if someone has persuaded himself that he already knows something, he cannot learn when it becomes possible to learn it; and also, in itself rashness is not a sign of a well-ordered soul.

What we understand, therefore, we owe to *reason*; what we believe, to *authority*; what we opine, to *error*. These things have been said that we may understand that we, in holding by faith even to the things that we have not yet comprehended, are innocent of the rashness of the opinionated.

For those who say that we should believe nothing except what we know are afraid of this word "opinion," which is said to be most shameful and wretched. But if someone diligently considers how much difference there is between thinking that one knows and understanding that one does not know, he may believe, moved by some authority, and so surely avoid the sins both of error and of inhumanity and pride. (AT VII,216–17)[27]

Arnauld proposes this passage, the intellectual core of the *De Utilitate Credendi* (the same treatise Gilson had chosen to illustrate the Augustinian spirit Descartes is supposed to contradict!), to show why Descartes is condemning only the rashness of the opinionated, and not the persuasion of believers; he urges Descartes to accept this clarification of his meaning. Descartes accepts it almost without comment. He knows it already, and feels that he has also *said* it already: whether or not he already knew the particular quote Arnauld supplies, he certainly knows the idea it contains, which he could easily have found in *Confessions* VI,v, or in any of its numerous parallels in other texts of Augustine.

Descartes seems to feel that what Arnauld wished to clarify was already clear enough; but he prints and endorses Arnauld's statements, and in addition makes the corrections Arnauld had suggested in the text of the *Meditations*, to guard against misinterpretation. Descartes accepts the clarifications, not because he himself had not understood that his teaching was in conformity with Augustinian orthodoxy, but because his readers might not. Only a naive reader unversed in Augustine and in the Christian philosophical tradition risks being led astray by the *Meditations*; for such a reader, the second and fourth Objections and Replies give a useful handle for grasping Descartes' attitudes toward faith and reason, and help to explain how a scientific use of Augustine's metaphysics can fit together with Augustinian religious intentions.

[27] Although Arnauld introduces this passage with the phrase "as blessed Augustine wisely advises, in *De Utilitate Credendi*, chapter 15," and although it is printed in roman type to distinguish it from the surrounding text of Arnauld (which is in italics), it is not precisely a quote, nor is it from *De Utilitate Credendi* xv. It is from *De Utilitate Credendi* xi,25, and it is a series of passages stitched together, with the intervening elaborations deleted. In the edition in the *Corpus Scriptorum Ecclesiasticorum Latinorum*, ed. Zycha (Vienna: Tempsky, 1891), the first paragraph is from p. 31, lines 23–5; the third from p. 32, lines 13–16; the fourth from p. 32, lines 22–4; and the fifth from p. 33, lines 20–6. The second paragraph is apparently not a verbal extract from Augustine, although it gives an accurate summary of how Augustine is distinguishing the terms in question. Arnauld is thus treating the texts of Augustine in a rather familiar manner; but he is not in any way modifying or distorting Augustine's thought, merely selecting the texts so as to make the point in a small compass while remaining as close as possible to Augustine's original words. (Arnauld is not to be blamed for the wrong chapter reference, which was supplied by Mersenne (AT III,359). Perhaps Mersenne was also responsible for printing the whole text, including a paragraph of Arnauld summarizing Augustine, as if it were a continuous quotation from Augustine.)

8

From God to bodies

A. The creation of the eternal truths

Descartes has argued that we can establish a science of bodies only if we first secure an independent knowledge of the soul, and establish a criterion of its cognitive faculties; and he has argued that we can establish such a criterion only through knowing God as Nous. This knowledge of soul and God may be a necessary condition for science; but is it also sufficient? Descartes, like Plotinus and Augustine, conceives God as the source of knowledge to the soul; like Plotinus and Augustine, he uses this conception to lead us up to God; but unlike Plotinus and Augustine, he is equally interested in leading us back down. The fourth Meditation already is looking for "a way . . . from the contemplation of the true God . . . to the knowledge of other things" (AT VII,53), without specifying which "other things" these are; the fifth and sixth Meditations turn specifically to derive knowledge of the essence and existence of *bodies*, and Part Two of the *Principles* claims to derive the "principles of material things" from the metaphysical principles of Part One. In the present chapter, without discussing Descartes' physics in detail, I will describe Descartes' strategy for arguing from metaphysics to physics, to the extent that this affects the meaning of his metaphysics and of his philosophical project as a whole.

Descartes conceives God as the "source of truth" (AT VII,22), and this is what makes it possible to argue from God as cause to the laws of nature as his effects. The crucial link between Descartes' metaphysics and his physics is the creation of the eternal truths. Since the meaning and motivations of this doctrine have been deeply obscure, I will devote the present section to its interpretation, before proceeding in subsequent sections to study its applications to the foundations of physics.

Descartes first speaks of a creation of the eternal truths in his letters to Mersenne dated April 15, May 6, and May 27 of 1630, where he intimates that it is a crucial metaphysical principle of his physics; but he does not explain *how* it will be used in physics, and when, in the last two Meditations and in Part Two of the *Principles*, he does try to derive the principles of physics from his metaphysics, he does not explicitly cite this doctrine. Some scholars have concluded that the creation of the eternal truths was somehow an esoteric doctrine, which Descartes was unwilling to discuss in his published works, but which served some covert function in his scientific project, at least in 1630 if not in 1640; and ingenious conjectures have been made as to what this function was. But Descartes does not write as if he were concealing anything: indeed, in the letter of April 15, 1630, Descartes asks Mersenne not to "be afraid to affirm and declare everywhere" his doctrine (AT I,145). Nor did Descartes abandon or lose interest in this doctrine between 1630 and 1640: for he is ready to state it in the fifth Replies over a fairly minor provocation from Gassendi, and to defend it on challenge in the sixth Replies, although still without stating its function in his philosophy. But if we begin from our analysis of Descartes' metaphysics, both of its Augustinian content and of its intended scientific function, we will be in a position to understand why Descartes must maintain a creation of the eternal truths, and we can see how this doctrine functions in the transition from metaphysics to physics, not only in 1630 but also in 1640 and 1644, without being stated in so many words in the *Meditations* or the *Principles*.

It will help to begin with a schematic contrast between Descartes and Plotinus. Descartes diverges from Plotinus, not only in the aim of his scientific project (to know corporeal as well as incorporeal things), but also in the conception of God this project presupposes. For Descartes, as for Plotinus, God is the standard against which the soul's knowledge is measured; God must therefore be omniscient, and *essentially* omniscient. "Omniscient" here means that God knows everything that can be known (since "*A* knows *B*" logically presupposes "God knows *B*"); but Descartes and Plotinus disagree on the range of things that can be known. For Plotinus, as for any Platonist, what is changing or enmattered is unknowable: the realm of the knowable or intelligible is the realm of separate eternal substances, and these are what God knows. Descartes cannot accept such a restriction of the scope of God's knowledge, not only because his religion insists that God knows everything that exists, but also because his scientific project requires that God knows material things: the whole project presupposes that it is a perfection for the soul to know material things, and therefore that God possesses this perfection in his essence, and is able to communicate it to the soul.

Because Descartes rejects Plotinus' restriction of the scope of God's knowledge, he must also reject Plotinus' conception of the relation between God and the objects of his knowledge. Plotinus argues, following Aristotle, that if God *essentially* knows *X*, *X* cannot be something external to God: for otherwise God would have to "make contact" with *X*, and so his success in knowing would depend on things external to his own essence. Since Plotinus thinks that God knows only the Forms (since only these are knowable), he is able to argue without manifest absurdity that "the *noêta* are not outside Nous," and that God knows them just by *being* them: if God also knew material and changing things, this solution would clearly be impossible. Because Descartes insists that God knows material things, he must reject Plotinus' solution to the problem of God's knowledge: Descartes, like the Christian tradition generally, must try to reconcile the claim that what God knows he knows *essentially*, with the claim that God knows everything that exists, or has existed or will exist or can exist, including many things outside God himself. Descartes, like Duns Scotus and most later scholastics, adopts what is probably the only possible solution: God knows things outside himself because he knows his own *will*, and because he knows the necessary truth (entailed by God's essence) that whatever God wills is as he wills it to be. So God does not have to "look at" or "make contact with" things outside him, and his success in knowing does not depend on anything outside his own essence: he "looks" only at himself (and from eternity, before there is anything but God to look at), and his ability to know his creatures depends only on his power to produce them as he wills. In Scotus' terms, God has *scientia naturalis* only of his own essence, and of things necessarily resulting from his essence; everything else he knows by *scientia libera*, "voluntary" knowledge resulting from his own free choice.[1]

Descartes shares with the scholastics both the problem of God's knowledge and its solution. But the problem, and its solution, have a much more important place in Cartesian than in scholastic philosophy: God's essential omniscience is, for the scholastics, just one particular corollary of God's perfection, but for Descartes it is fundamental both to the way he originally formulates his conception of God, and to the function he wants God to fulfill in his philosophy. Descartes wants to use God's knowledge of X as a source for his own scientific knowledge of X: so if God knows X by *scientia libera*, by knowing his will to produce X, then we too should seek to know X, following God's own knowledge, by knowing God's will to produce X. Things other than God are intelligible only because God (who is Reason-itself) wills to produce them in an intelligible fashion: if, instead, the world were governed by a non-rational pseudo-God (be it an irrational nature or a malicious demon), no science of the world would be possible. So God serves as a bond between the human intellect and what is intelligible in bodies, or in anything else. God is the "source of truth," and truths proceed from him in two directions, both to bodies (where they are received as essences and as laws of natural motion) and to the human intellect (where they are received as the *ideas* of these natural things): those ideas which we receive from God will correspond to the nature of bodies, because the ideas and the bodily nature have a common origin.

All this is one way of stating the doctrine of the creation of the eternal truths; it is close to the way Descartes states the doctrine on its first appearance, in the letter to Mersenne of April 15, 1630:

I beg you, do not be afraid to affirm and declare everywhere that it is God who has established these laws in nature, as a king establishes laws in his kingdom. And there is none of them in particular which we cannot understand if our mind

---

[1] An excellent source for Scotist and other scholastic accounts of God's knowledge of contingent things is Luis de Molina, *On Divine Foreknowledge: Part IV of the Concordia*, translated with introduction and notes by Alfred J. Freddoso (Ithaca: Cornell University Press, 1988).

is brought to consider it, and they are all inborn in our minds, as a king would impress his laws in the heart of all his subjects, if he had so much power. (AT I,145)

So far this seems traditional and innocent enough: Descartes is merely spelling out the thought contained in Augustine's image of God (or Truth) as a fire, radiating the "heat" of wisdom to rational souls (the things placed next to God), and at the same time radiating the "light" of number to bodies (the things placed furthest from God).[2] Indeed (as we will see) Descartes attributes his doctrine of the creation of the eternal truths to Augustine; he also feels that it follows immediately from the Christian conception of God, and that any attempt to deny or subvert the creation of the eternal truths is an implicit surrender to paganism. What is remarkable, and needs explaining, is that although Descartes takes his doctrine to be a straightforward consequence of Christian and Augustinian commitments shared by the whole tradition, he also understands it to include extreme voluntarist theses (e.g. "God could have willed that four and four are not eight") that struck his contemporaries as bizarre and paradoxical. But if we pursue the implications of Descartes' conception of God's relation to the objects of knowledge, bearing in mind the requirements of the scientific project, we can see how Descartes was led to a radicalization of Augustine's conception of God as the source of truth; we can then see why Descartes formulates this radicalization by asserting that the eternal truths are created by God, and we can see why this formulation brings him into conflict with the scholastics and with almost all other philosophers.[3]

---

[2] Similarly, in *Le monde*, when Descartes describes the eternal mathematical truths that he will use in deriving the laws of motion, he cites Augustine's favorite passage from the Wisdom of Solomon, with Augustine's interpretation: he is speaking of "those truths according to which God himself has taught us that he has disposed all things in number, weight, and measure, and the knowledge of which is so natural to our souls that we are cannot but judge them infallible when we conceive them distinctly" (AT XI,47). These truths, then, are the numerical rules or forms which proceed from the divine wisdom, and which are received both as intuitions in the human mind and as governing principles in the world of body.

[3] Note, however, that while *most* scholastics (including the Thomists and Scotists, and Suárez) would strongly oppose Descartes' thesis that the eternal truths are created and depend on God's will, Thomas Bradwardine agrees with Descartes' thesis, and apparently pushes it to more paradoxical lengths than Descartes will do. Bradwardine argues that God's free will is the immediate and total cause, not only of all substances and accidents, but of all truths, including future, past, and modal truths: anything that is possible, is possible because God now wills it to be possible; anything that is impossible, is impossible because God now wills it to be impossible; anything that happened in the past, happened in the past because God now wills it to have happened in the past; and so on. Fortunately, God's will is immutable; but were it not for his continuously sustaining will, not only would the world cease to exist, but it would cease to *have* existed, and indeed it would become logically impossible for it ever to have existed (summarizing from Bradwardine, *De Causa Dei contra Pelagium et de Virtute Causarum* (London, 1618; repr. Frankfurt am Main: Minerva, 1964), Book I, especially chapters 13–14). I know no reason to think that Descartes was influenced by Bradwardine, directly or indirectly: both Bradwardine and Des-

First we must understand what Descartes means by an "eternal truth." In the letter where Descartes first mentions the eternal truths, he tells Mersenne that he will "touch in my Physics on several metaphysical questions, and particularly this: that the mathematical truths which you [Mersenne, in letters to Descartes dated March 14 and April 4, now lost] call eternal, have been established by God, and depend entirely on him, just as much as all other creatures" (AT I,145). In this letter Descartes does not spell out what truths these are: he assumes Mersenne knows what they are, since it was Mersenne who had mentioned them in the first place. But from other passages we can see better what range of truths Descartes means: often, as here, he seems to be thinking especially of truths of pure mathematics, but other truths are also included. Thus when the Sixth Objectors ask "how it can be that the truths of metaphysics or geometry, such as you have mentioned, should be immutable and eternal, yet not independent of God?" (AT VII,417), Descartes replies that nothing at all can exist without depending on God, and he explains that he means "not only nothing subsistent, but also no order, no law, and no reason [*ratio*] of truth or goodness" (AT VII,435). Descartes is using "order," "law," and "*ratio*" here as loosely equivalent expressions to indicate a whole range of entities, including the truths of metaphysics and geometry, which are *real* in that our conception of them has a positive intellectual content, and which serve as rules or standards by which we can judge other things, but which are themselves neither substances nor attributes of substances. Descartes is asserting that all such things have been created by God, and remain dependent on him; the creation of the truths of metaphysics and geometry is an instance, and must be understood in light of the general principle.

The concept of an eternal truth is closely linked, for Descartes, with the concept of *essence*. Thus Descartes says in reply to Gassendi that he "does not think that the essences of things, and those mathematical truths which can be known of them, are independent of God" (AT VII,380). Here the eternal truths are the propositions that necessarily follow from the essences, but Descartes' terminology is not consistent, and he *identifies* eternal truths with essences in writing to Mersenne: "it is certain that [God] is the author of the essence as well as the existence of creatures; but this essence is nothing other than these eternal truths" (AT I,152).

cartes seem to be starting chiefly from Augustine, and radicalizing Augustine's conclusions, in different ways, for their different contemporary reasons. Gouhier, and more recently Jean-Luc Marion, have taken Descartes' doctrine of the creation of the eternal truths as a radical break with the traditional Augustinian (and scholastic) conception of God, dictated by a new Cartesian insistence on God's radical simplicity. I have shown how far Descartes' project depends on taking up the Augustinian concept of God as Nous (i.e. as a being essentially omniscient, and known to us because he is essentially omniscient, as a standard for judging our own intellectual perfections). I will argue in this section that Descartes' undeniable radicalization of Augustinian voluntarism is best understood as his working out the consequences of this Augustinian conception of God, dictated by the role the knowledge of God must play in supporting the scientific system.

So when Descartes says that God created the eternal truths of geometry, he means either that God created the essences of the various modes of extension (e.g. the essence of circle), or, equivalently, that he established the propositions which predicate the essential attributes of these things (e.g. that a circle has all its radii equal [Descartes' example, AT I,152]). Descartes first claims that it is God who creates these essences; then, since the truth or falsity of the propositions depends on the essences, Descartes infers that God makes the propositions true or false. If there is some eternally true proposition that, like the law of contradiction, is so universal and contentless that it is not about any particular essence, then Descartes does not claim that God establishes this proposition: there is nothing for God to create and no action he needs to take to make this proposition true.[4]

Descartes thinks that philosophers generally, and especially the scho-

---

[4] Thus Descartes *is not claiming* that God created what a modern mathematician might recognize as eternal truths of mathematics, namely the principles of formal logic and the mathematical theorems that follow from them. It would indeed be bizarre to suggest that God has created the law of contradiction, and that God could equally well have chosen the contrary of this law. Descartes gives some plausibility to this interpretation when, at *Principles* I:49, he cites the law of contradiction in a list of eternal truths (without saying that these truths are created), and when, in a letter to Mesland, he says that God was free to bring it about that contradictories should be true together. But the context of the latter assertion shows Descartes' meaning: he is saying that we should not be deterred by our difficulties in conceiving "how it was free and indifferent for God to make it not true that the three angles of a triangle are equal to two right angles, or generally that contradictories cannot be together" (AT IV,118). It is of the essence of triangles, as God has created this essence, that the sum of their angles is equal to two right angles; if God made a triangle with three right angles, he would be making two things which are currently contradictory (triangle and three-right-angles) to be true simultaneously of the same subject. But he would do this by making the essence of triangle otherwise than it now is. The point is not that God has the power to falsify the law of contradiction, but that he has the power to determine the essences of things, and thus to determine whether a given proposition contains a contradiction or not.

Descartes knows that the essence of triangle must come from God, because he possesses a clear and positive conception of it, and, as he asserts at the end of the fourth Meditation, "every clear and distinct perception is doubtless *something* [*aliquid*, French *quelque chose de réel, et de positif*], and therefore it cannot be from nothing, but must necessarily have God as its author" (AT VII,62). The law of contradiction, when applied to triangles, has a positive content and implies certain positive propositions, but it derives this content entirely from the content of the idea of triangle; considered in itself as a logical formula, the law of contradiction has no positive content, and involves no apprehension of an essence; this law is not *aliquid*, and it makes no sense to ask whether it was created by God or is independent of him. As Descartes tells Clerselier, "One may say that 'it is impossible for the same thing to be and not be at the same time' is a principle which can generally serve, not properly to make anything's existence known, but only to bring it about that, when one knows it, one may confirm its truth by a reasoning of this type: 'it is impossible that what is, is not; but I know that such a thing is; so I know that it is impossible that it is not.' This is of very little importance, and renders us none the wiser" (AT IV,444). Descartes wants to trace back to God, not empty and general truths of this kind, but the positive content of our apprehensions of the simple natures, which are the basis for all scientific knowledge.

lastics, recognize essences or eternal truths as one distinctive realm of being, not "existing" in the full sense (not "subsisting," as Descartes says at AT VII,435), but also not nothing. Descartes asserts that these beings, like finite subsisting beings, are created by God; by contrast, Descartes interprets the scholastics as thinking that the essences have their peculiar kind of reality independent of any act of God's will. This was a common way of interpreting the scholastics: Descartes shares it, notably, with Gassendi. Indeed, when Gassendi reads the fifth Meditation, and finds Descartes speaking of the "essences" of geometrical figures, he supposes that Descartes is just saying "what they repeat in the Schools, that the natures or essences of things are eternal [further down, "eternal and independent of God"], and give rise to propositions that are always true"; Gassendi criticizes this (as he thinks) scholastic and Cartesian assertion, and says against it "that it seems hard to posit any immutable and eternal nature apart from thrice-great God" (AT VII,319). It is in reply to this challenge of Gassendi's that Descartes first states in public his doctrine of the creation of the eternal truths: distinguishing his own position from what he and Gassendi take to be the scholastic position, Descartes says that although the essences are eternal and immutable beings *other* than God, they are not *independent* of God, but are eternal and immutable because God has willed them so (AT VII,380). Here Descartes and Gassendi are both assuming the basic axiom of all Christian philosophy, that every real being other than God has been created by an act of God's will. Gassendi uses this axiom to conclude that essences are nothing real, and therefore that "a rose is a flower" is not true except when some rose actually exists (AT VII,319); Descartes turns the argument around to conclude that, since there obviously are eternal intelligible truths, these must be dependent on God's will. This mode of argument is not simply a strategic reply to Gassendi, but expresses the core of Descartes' thought about the intelligibles: as Descartes had said to Mersenne already in 1630, "I do not conceive [the eternal truths] as emanating from God like rays from the sun, but I know that God is the author of all things, and that these truths are something, and therefore that he is their author" (AT I,152).[5]

Descartes knows that the scholastics too (like all Christian philosophers) are committed to the metaphysical axiom that everything other than God

[5] Jean-Luc Marion (*Sur la théologie blanche de Descartes* (Paris: Presses Universitaires de France, 1981), pp. 140–59) takes this passage to show that Descartes is rejecting a (Plotinian and Augustinian) emanationist theory of the eternal truths, in favor of a creationist theory. But Descartes is doing nothing of the kind: he is simply saying that his doctrine that the eternal truths proceed from God does not depend on any particular materialistic image of what their procession might look like. There is nothing wrong with the emanationist image, except that it is an image. It is all wrong to speak of a Plotinian emanationist *doctrine*: emanation has never been more than one handy material image among others, necessarily inadequate to describe an essentially immaterial process. Descartes is not insisting on any radical voluntarism here: he is simply insisting that the intelligible truths depend on God; this proposition then has voluntarist corollaries, which Descartes will draw on when he needs them.

is created by God, but he thinks their philosophical practice implicitly contradicts this metaphysical commitment. The scholastics simply assume that the objects the scientist encounters have certain determinate essences, and that these essences entail eternal necessary truths about the objects in question: these essences and necessary truths are brute facts, which the scientist tries to infer *a posteriori* from the behavior of the objects in question, with no attempt to derive the essences *a priori* from God as their cause. On this view, it seems that the essences of things are brute facts, not only for the human scientist, but also for God, who passively observes what essences or *possibilia* there are, and then decides which of them to actualize at what time (as Gassendi says, if the essences are what is most real in things, then God in adding existence is no more than a tailor putting a new suit on a man, AT VII,319). Descartes thinks that a scientist who regards essences as brute facts, and who supposes (implicitly or explicitly) that God too confronts the essences as brute facts, is operating with a pagan mythological conception of a limited God, however much he may profess the Christian doctrine of creation. As Descartes says to Mersenne in the first letter on the creation of the eternal truths, "to say that these truths are independent of him, is in effect to speak of God as of a Jupiter or Saturn, and to subject him to Styx and the Fates" (AT I,145). Descartes proposes to construct his philosophy by taking seriously the Christian philosophical concept of God: where the scholastics start with physical things, elaborating the necessary truths of physics on their own terms and letting God and metaphysics suffer the consequences, Descartes will start with God and derive the truths of physics from him.[6] This is Descartes' point in telling Mersenne about the eternal truths: he has already said that the study of God and the soul is the chief aim of human reason, that he has made this the beginning of his studies, and that this study has led him to discover the foundations of physics (AT I,144); he now says that his treatise on physics will touch on several metaphysical

---

[6] Of course Descartes does not make his conclusions contingent on Christian revelation: he thinks we can have this knowledge of God by the natural light of reason. All the same, it is something he thinks all Christian philosophers should be committed to (recall his use of the phrase "Christian philosopher" in the dedicatory letter of the *Meditations*, AT VII,3). Descartes seems to think of a more limited conception of God's power as typically pagan: this is surely the point of protesting the reduction of God to "a Jupiter or Saturn." In a subsequent letter to Mersenne, Descartes says that "if people understood the meaning of their words, they could not say without blasphemy" that any truth exists prior to God's knowledge of it (AT I,149); people feel free to speak this way because "most people do not consider God as an infinite and incomprehensible being, the sole author on whom all things depend; they stop at the syllables of his name, and think it is knowing him enough if one knows that 'God' ['*Dieu*' – Descartes is writing in French] means the same as what is called '*Deus*' in Latin, and that it is what people worship. Those who have no higher thoughts than this can easily become atheists . . ." (AT I,150). While all of this may be said simply in defense of natural religion, Descartes does seem to think that Christian philosophers, who have been working unawares with a "blasphemous" and pagan conception of a limited God, can be appealed to on Christian grounds to throw over this conception and to replace it with one more in accord with Christianity.

questions, and especially on the creation of the eternal truths (p. 145). Descartes is claiming that the creation of the eternal truths is a fruitful metaphysical doctrine, contained in the doctrine of God as creator but usually denied or suppressed, and that if we take it seriously and work out its consequences it will lead us to the true foundations of physics.

Descartes' emphasis here is on the claim that God is the source of everything real, not just as the bestower of existence on essences, but also and especially as the source of the intelligible content of things. Although the doctrine of the creation of the eternal truths has radically voluntarist implications, and might easily seem irrationalist as well, Descartes treats the voluntarism ("God *could* have done otherwise") as a mere corollary of the main doctrine, and he sees no irrationalist implications at all. On the contrary, he takes the doctrine as a charter for rationalist science, against the scholastic positing of a radical plurality of essences discoverable only *a posteriori*. As soon as Descartes states his claim that "it is God who has established these laws in nature," he infers that "there is none of them in particular that we cannot understand if our mind is brought to consider it, and they are all inborn in our minds, as a king would impress his laws in the heart of all his subjects, if he had so much power" (AT I,145, cited above). If the essences were brute facts independent of God, Descartes' scientific project would not get off the ground. Of course, God might communicate to us a knowledge of the intelligible essences even if these essences were independent of God; but then how would God himself first acquire this knowledge? Descartes' scientific project depends on connecting the potential *nous* in us with the *noêta* in the world through a being that is essentially actual *nous*: we might give some other being the name "God," but unless *by its own essence* it knows all intelligible reality, it is not the *nous* we have been seeking as the criterion for science. And Descartes claims that if God is essentially omniscient, every intelligible object X must either be identical with God or proceed causally from God. If X is identical with God, then God knows it by *being* it; if X proceeds causally from God, then God knows it by *willing* it and *making* it;[7] in the first case

---

[7] "In God willing and knowing are the same, so that from the very fact that he wills something, he also knows it, and only for this reason is such a thing true" (AT I,149); "you ask me what God has done to produce [the eternal truths]. I say that from the very fact that he eternally willed and understood them to be, he created them; or rather (if you apply the word 'created' only to the existence of things), he ordained them and made them. For in God it is one and the same thing to will, to understand, and to create, without any of these preceding the others even rationally" (AT I,152–3; similar language at VII,432). Descartes reaches this conclusion, not from any radical commitment to God's simplicity, but because he has good reasons for denying that God can understand something before he wills it, and because (obviously) God cannot will something before he understands it. On Descartes' allegedly radical doctrine of God's simplicity, see further discussion below. Descartes' account of God's knowledge stays close to the Scotist and generally scholastic account of how God knows creatures; but Descartes is asserting that essences and eternal truths are themselves creatures, and thus are known by God in the way that God knows creatures, not in the way that God knows himself. Of course, this applies only to God's

God knows X by his essence (in scholastic terms by *scientia naturalis*), and in the latter case he knows it by his will (by *scientia libera*), but in neither case does he depend on something outside himself in order to acquire this knowledge.[8] If, however, X were independent of God, then, on Descartes' analysis of knowledge, God could know X only by participating in some prior *nous* that would essentially contain knowledge of X: and then it is this prior *nous* that is the God of the third Meditation.

Given the Christian philosophical assumptions that God is "the author of all things" and that he is essentially omniscient, are there any alternatives to Descartes' solution? Clearly it is not an option to say that the essences of things are "eternal and independent of God," and Descartes and Gassendi are mistaken in supposing that the scholastics said this;[9] nor could the essences of creatures be identical with God himself.[10] But the scholastics are also unwilling to say that the eternal truths depend on God's will, and that God could equally well have ordained the contraries of the eternal truths he has in fact ordained: if this were admitted, then before God began to create, he would have no standards of value to guide him in creating, and the resulting creation would not be objectively good.[11]

---

knowledge of the essences of *creatures* (and of propositions following from these essences), not to God's knowledge of his *own* essence and (therefore) existence, which do not depend on God's will. Descartes can state the doctrine of the creation of the eternal truths by saying that "the existence of God is the first and most eternal of all the truths there can be, and the single one from which all the others proceed" (AT I,150); this first eternal truth is not itself created.

[8] Note that, while it follows from God's essence that he knows everything that exists, nonetheless, if God knows X by *scientia libera*, it does not follow from his essence that he knows X: for in such a case "X exists" is not necessary, and therefore "God knows X" is also not necessary. But the conditional "if X exists, then God knows X" is necessary and follows from God's essence.

[9] When Gassendi alleges that the scholastics say that "the natures or essences of things" are "eternal and independent of God" (AT VII,319), he is in fact repeating a scholastic slander with a movable target: Suárez notes (*Disputationes Metaphysicae*, Disputation 31, section 2) that though the Thomists falsely accuse Scotus of saying this, Scotus had accused Henry of Ghent of saying it. In fact, this is probably not true even of Henry (who makes a similar accusation against Giles of Rome!). But scholastic nominalists, taking up the accusation, had turned it against the realists, and particularly the Thomists; and Gassendi turns it indiscriminately against all the scholastics.

[10] As Aristotle argues against Plato in *Metaphysics* VII–VIII, and as all scholastics accept, the essence of a thing cannot be a substance separate from, or prior to, the thing itself.

[11] This is ultimately the argument of *Timaeus* 29a that, because the demiurge is good and wishes to produce a beautiful world, he must produce it in the image of some model; and, furthermore, that this must be an eternal model if its image is going to be beautiful. The demiurge must look to the forms to have an objective standard of beauty; if he did not know the forms, he could not expect to produce a beautiful world. The forms themselves cannot be produced by the demiurge, or (if they are to be beautiful) he would need some anterior model for them. Of course, the forms might (as Plotinus thinks) be identical with the demiurge himself. Augustine repeats this Platonic argument in *De Genesi ad Litteram* V, which I will discuss below. Descartes simply accepts the conclusion that there is no objective standard of goodness or beauty guiding God's choice of how to create the world (sixth Replies, AT VII,431–2 and 435–6).

So the scholastics are caught in a dilemma. They are forced to say that the essence of a creature, before that creature actually exists, is not itself a real being: it is, as Suárez says, "nothing at all," and so it is not a being independent of God.[12] But then the scholastics must explain why such propositions as "a rose is a flower" are eternally true, if sometimes there is neither an actual rose nor a real essence of rosehood. The standard answer is that "a rose is a flower" can be eternally true *in God's knowledge*, because rosehood and flowerhood have an eternal *esse cognitum*, a being as objects of God's knowledge: this "being" is not something real in the rose or the flower, but an extrinsic denomination from God's knowledge, consisting simply in the fact that God knows roses and flowers. Since the eternal *esse cognitum* of rosehood is not something real, God does not have to create this "being" by an act of his will: he produces it by an act of his intellect, by thinking and knowing roses.

This gives the scholastics a reasonable way of describing the status of the eternal truths, without admitting that they are products of God's free choice. But then, to explain how the *esse cognitum* of rosehood arises, they must explain how God knows roses: he cannot get his knowledge from a rose or from rosehood when no real rose or rosehood yet exists (and when we are trying to explain how rosehood first gets the quasi-existence it has); indeed, if God is *essentially* omniscient, he cannot receive his knowledge from roses or rosehood even when these do already exist. The scholastics are unwilling to accept Descartes' solution, that God knows the essence of rosehood in the same way that he knows the actual existence of a rose, through *scientia libera*, God's knowledge of his own will: he must somehow know it through *scientia naturalis*. But the scope of *scientia naturalis* is strictly limited: everything God knows, he knows by contemplating himself, and if he does not know something by contemplating his will, he must know it by contemplating his essence. So we are led back to Plotinus' solution: God has eternal knowledge of roses because he contains in his essence an Idea of rose, a real eternal being that is the exemplar for all sensible roses.

This is, in fact, the standard scholastic solution, expounded by St. Thomas in the *Summa Theologiae*, Pars Prima, QQ. 14–15: God contemplates his own essence, and in knowing his essence he also recognizes the different ways that his essence can be imitated, or the different ways that his perfections can be shared (to some finite degree) by another being. When God knows his essence as imitable in a certain way, he knows himself as the exemplar or Idea of a certain kind of creature, since "the particular nature of each thing consists in its participating in the divine perfection

---

[12] Suárez, *Disputationes Metaphysicae*, Disputation 31, section 2, paragraph 1. As Suárez says, "this principle is not only true, but also certain according to the faith"; he denies that it has ever "entered into the mind of any Catholic doctor that the essence of a creature, of itself and apart from any free action of God, is a true *res*, having a true *esse reale* distinct from the *esse* of God" (paragraph 3).

in some way"; by knowing himself as the Idea of a rose, he also knows rosehood, not by looking at roses but by looking at himself.[13] By this account God would produce the *esse cognitum* of rosehood, or the eternal truths about roses, not by any act of his will, but by his knowledge of his own essence through *scientia naturalis*. Sixty years after Descartes' death, Leibniz is still commending this solution as the way to grant Descartes' point that the necessary truths of things are not independent of God, while avoiding the anarchic consequences of a creation of the eternal truths: contingent truths depend on God's will, but "necessary truths depend only on his intellect, and are its internal object."[14]

This solution would be acceptable for Plotinus, who can admit a real plurality of forms or truths in Nous, but Descartes rightly rejects it as inconsistent both with the Christian commitment to God's simplicity and with Descartes' own scientific project.[15] Descartes agrees with Leibniz that the eternal truths proceed from an act of God's intellect, but he insists that this act of God's intellect is dependent on, or rather identical with, an act of God's will: "it is in God one and the same thing to will, to understand, and to create, without one of these preceding another even *ratione*" (AT I,153). Descartes' point here has usually been missed: he has been misunderstood as proclaiming a new and radical doctrine of God's simplicity, which would deny even *rational* distinctions in God. But in fact Descartes holds the traditional position (with St. Thomas and many others) that there are *rational* distinctions in God, but no *real* distinctions or real multiplicity (except the distinction of persons in the Trinity, which Descartes refuses to discuss).[16] When Descartes infers that God's act of understanding does not precede his act of willing even *ratione*, this is not because there is no distinction or priority in God: Descartes would grant that God's essence precedes *ratione* any act of God's will, and that God's knowledge of his own essence precedes *ratione* his knowing and willing things other than himself. Descartes' point here is that God's act of understanding things other than himself cannot precede his act of willing

[13] The quote is from *Summa Theologiae*, Pars Prima, Q. 14 a6; Thomas spells out the doctrine of ideas in Q. 15 a2, though some obscurities remain. For a thorough discussion of the options available to the scholastic doctrine of divine ideas, see Suárez, *Disputationes Metaphysicae*, Disputation 25, especially section 1 (as Suárez notes, there are texts of Thomas supporting all three of the different possible views Suárez considers!).

[14] "We must not imagine (like some people) that the eternal truths, being dependent on God, are arbitrary and dependent on his *will*, as Descartes . . . seems to have held" (Leibniz, *Philosophische Schriften*, ed. C. J. Gerhardt (Berlin: Weidmann, 1885), 6, p. 614). The subsequent quotation is also taken from this same page.

[15] Plotinus is, like Thomas and Descartes, committed to saying that the first principle is simple; but for him the first principle is not Nous, but a One prior to Nous.

[16] As noted above, Chapter 6, Section B, the third Meditation clearly maintains a plurality of perfections in God, really identical but rationally distinct: this is the standard scholastic realist position. Only the Scotists believe that the divine attributes are more than rationally (formally, though not really) distinct. The nominalists, notably Holkot, hold the radical position, falsely attributed to Descartes, that there are not even rational distinctions in God.

and creating things other than himself, since prior to this there would be nothing for God to understand except his own essence. Since God's essence is simple, there is precisely one thing that God knows prior to creation: his *scientia naturalis* cannot give him knowledge of a plurality of intelligible contents (such as the many truths of geometry), and he cannot produce a plurality of essences in *esse cognitum* prior to his willing and creating. Since Thomas shares Descartes' commitment to God's simplicity, he cannot avoid Descartes' conclusion. Thomas tries to solve the problem by saying that God knows himself in one way as the paradigm of roses, in another way as the paradigm of lions, and so on. But since the divine ideas are not a real multiplicity, but are all really identical with the divine essence, and distinguished only by reason comparing the divine essence with the different creatures that can imitate it,[17] God cannot recognize a plurality of truths by looking at himself, unless he also looks at creatures for comparison: so Thomas has no explanation of how God can know a plurality of things by *scientia naturalis*. The only honest way to explain a plurality of content in God's knowledge, prior to any act of will, is to posit some real complexity in God himself: not merely a complexity in God's intellect, but a complexity in God's essence, giving rise to the complexity in the intellect. Leibniz, unlike Thomas or Descartes, is willing to pay this price (God has an infinite number of perfections, and by distinctly contemplating each of these, and their possible combinations, he knows all possible creatures); but for Descartes this is no better, either religiously or scientifically, than subjecting God to Styx and the Fates. We would merely be saying that Styx and the Fates belong to the structure of God's essence. This complex essence (and it must be *very* complex, if all possible creatures are derived from combinations of its components) would be simply a brute fact; and the Meditator, in reflecting on soul and ascending to Nous, could not attain knowledge of it.

Descartes is concerned to reject the radical plurality of essences which the Aristotelians (and Leibniz) are ready to admit: his physics will be based on something much more like the Augustinian "rules of number" proceeding from God to bodies. Descartes, like Augustine, takes it for granted that the truths proceeding from God will be eternal and immutable, and that they will be mathematical in content: he does not feel that he is putting these Augustinian rationalist assumptions in any danger by asserting that essences are created. Indeed, Descartes is unaware that he is going against Augustine. When Descartes explains to Mesland that God's understanding does not precede God's willing and creating, he also adds that Augustine had believed the same: "this is what these words of St. Augustine, 'because you see them, they are,' etc., express very well; because in God to see and to will are one and the same thing" (AT IV,119). The quotation is from the very last chapter of the *Confessions* (XIII,xxxviii,53), and must be one of the texts of Augustine for which

---

[17] So Thomas, *Summa Theologiae*, Pars Prima, Q. 15 a2.

Descartes had thanked Mesland earlier in the same letter; but Descartes is bending the text in his own direction. Augustine is contrasting human and divine cognition:

We see these things that you have made, because they are; but they are, because you see them. And we see [by looking] outside ourselves that they are, but inside ourselves that they are good; but you see that they have been made [by looking] in the same place [sc. inside yourself] that you see that they *ought* to be made.

So God knows that a thing has been made by looking within himself, in the same way that he knows that it *ought* to be made; and it is reasonable to suppose that God knows that it has been (or will be) made precisely through knowing that it ought to be made, i.e. through willing to make it. But this is only the way that God knows the existence of *things that are made*, and for Augustine the eternal truths are not made: so with regard to these Augustine is not saying that "in God to see and to will are one and the same thing." And although God may know the actual existence of creatures by seeing their goodness, he sees their essence and their goodness as uncreated paradigms within his own essence. So Augustine expounds John 1:3: "the Wisdom of God, through which all things were made, knew them before they were made," knowing them through the "divine, immutable, and eternal *rationes*" which exist in the divine Word: for "if he knew them, where if not in himself, since with him was the Word through which all things were made? For if he knew them outside himself, who taught him?" (*De Genesi ad Litteram* V,xiii,29).[18] So also in the *De Libero Arbitrio*, the rules of number exist originally in the divine wisdom, and thence proceed to creatures: although these rules proceed to creatures according to God's will, the rules themselves are not established at God's command, but exist in God and are coeternal with him. Augustine can make these assertions because, following Plotinus, he is willing to admit a real multiplicity in the divine Nous, identified with the second person of the Trinity; so he is not forced to conclude that the multiplicity of essences proceeds purely from the will of God, and he prefers to keep the paradigms of things in God, to give God objective standards of goodness in the work of creation.[19]

---

[18] This last remark of Augustine's recalls Plotinus' argument in *On Nous, Ideas, and Being* that Nous does not think the beings "as if they were elsewhere" than in itself. Augustine's question "who taught him" is not just rhetorical (as at Isaiah 40:13–14, here echoed): it is an encapsulation of Plotinus' argument that if Nous did not possess the intelligibles within itself, it could come to know them only through participation in a further agent Nous, leading to an infinite regress.

[19] Still, there is an idea in Augustine which is suggestive of Descartes' position. Augustine deals with the verse of Ecclesiasticus (1:4) that "the first of all created things is wisdom" by distinguishing a *created* wisdom alongside the *uncreated* wisdom which is the second person of the Trinity; in the *De Genesi ad Litteram* (V,iv,10; and earlier, IV,xx,37ff.) Augustine identifies this created wisdom with the "day" of the second creation narrative in Genesis. Augustine cites Genesis 2:4–5 as saying that "when day was made, God made heaven and earth and every green thing of the field before it appeared above the earth,

Descartes' voluntarism does not prevent him from drawing Augustinian conclusions about the things that proceed from God. The objective contents of our intellectual apprehensions proceed from God, and because they proceed from God, they are *true*: that is, they have reality as essences or as possibilities which God may actualize in subsistent things. Again, because these truths proceed from God, they are *eternal* and immutable: not, as Leibniz thinks, because they are independent of God's will, but because they are dependent on God's will, and because God's will is such as to produce an immutable effect. When Gassendi objects "that it seems hard to set up any immutable and eternal nature apart from thrice-great God" (AT VII,319), Descartes agrees that the objection would be fair, not only against an immutable existing thing, but also against an immutable essence, "if I were setting up something so immutable that its immutability did not depend on God" (p. 380); but he explains that this is not the sense in which his essences are immutable. Here Descartes finds a positive use for the same pagan fables he had so deplored in the April 15, 1630, letter to Mersenne: there may be a legitimate point in representing God as Jupiter or Saturn, and subjecting him to Styx and the Fates, if we mean merely that God always obeys the same eternal and universal laws; we need only modify the fables to show that these laws proceed from God himself, and that he is not bound to them by anything outside himself. By 1641, Descartes seems to have found poets who put things this way:

As the poets pretend that although the fates were established by Jupiter, yet after they were established he bound himself to observe them, so I do not think that the essences of things, or the mathematical truths which can be known of them, are independent of God, but I think nonetheless, that because God so willed, because he so disposed, they are immutable and eternal. (AT VII,380)

This does not mean that it is subject to God's arbitrary choice whether to establish mutable or immutable truths; Descartes means rather that because these truths are the immediate objects and effects of God's will, receiving their being from him at every moment, and because God is

---

and all the grass of the field before it sprang forth"; this must refer to a creation of these realities prior to their current mode of existence as visible bodies, but it cannot refer to their preexistence in God's wisdom, since this would be *before* day was made; rather it refers to an intermediate stage in which, *when* day was made, God created things in their *rationes seminales* (the Stoic and Platonist *logoi spermatikoi*). God creates these *rationes* at the beginning of time, and the *rationes* contain the numerical laws that govern the development of the different species of creatures in the course of time (cf. *De Genesi ad Litteram* IV,xxxiii,51). The *rationes seminales* are neither transcendent paradigms nor sensible particulars; they function as a kind of immanent essence existing within the sensible particulars, and *this* essence is created by God. And this is what is important for Descartes in making the transition from metaphysics to physics. It does not much matter whether God could have willed that 2 and 2 should equal 5; what matters is that the movements of bodies should be determined by numerical laws implanted by God at their creation, and not by essences or natures independent of God and endowed with their own autonomous dispositions.

immutable in his actions as well as his being, what he establishes as true at *any* moment he will establish as true at *every* moment. This conception of the immutability of God's actions is thoroughly traditional, and we can verify that it is Descartes' intention by recalling the dialogue Descartes imagines in the April 15, 1630, letter to Mersenne: if someone objects, "if God had established these truths, he would be able to change them as a king does his laws," we must answer, "yes, if his will can change"; if he again objects, "but I understand them as eternal and immutable," we reply, "and I judge the same of God" (AT I,145–6). If, when we describe the essences of things as products of God's free legislation, we appeal to a confused idea of God which merely magnifies our idea of a powerful human being, then these essences will appear to us not as eternal truths but as legal fictions to be altered at convenience; but if we begin from the distinct idea of God as Nous or *fons veritatis*, we will understand that what proceeds from him is genuinely and eternally true.

Descartes, with Augustine, assumes that what proceeds from God to bodies are the "rules of number," the truths which the human intellect (illumined by God) knows most distinctly in bodies, and which apply to all bodies without exception. Accepting as a principle of physics nothing except what proceeds from God to bodies (and is also received in the human mind), Descartes sets out to reconstruct an understanding of bodies without the plurality of essences and motive powers which the Aristotelians posit in the different species of natural bodies, and which they cannot trace back to intelligible first principles. The Aristotelians posit these natures, not out of sheer caprice, but because the senses seem to indicate different visible and tactile (etc.) qualities, and different characteristic motions, in the various species of natural bodies, and so seem to demand a plurality of principles in nature from which these qualities and motions could proceed. But Descartes' criterion allows him to admit as principles of natural science only what proceeds from Nous, not what the senses suggest. His task, therefore, is to proceed synthetically from these intelligible principles, and to show that they are sufficient to yield the phenomena which had led the Aristotelians to posit additional principles. In the sixth Meditation and in Part Two of the *Principles* Descartes outlines how the mathematical essence of bodies (described in the fifth Meditation) could give rise to our sensations and to regular patterns of motion in bodies; he tries in these places to derive from his metaphysical principles the criteria for the practical and speculative uses of the sensory faculties, and the fundamental laws of motion. Descartes' ambition, which he could only very partially fulfill in his lifetime, was to derive from these principles all the phenomena of nature that Aristotelian physics could describe. Without pursuing the details of Descartes' physics, I will describe his derivation of the essence of body (Section B), the criterion of the sensory faculties (Section C), and the laws of motion (Section D): these are the fundamental principles of Descartes' physics, derived from the metaphysical principle that God is the source of truth.

352

B. The essence of body

The way down from the contemplation of God to the knowledge of other things begins at the end of the fourth Meditation.[20] "Every clear and distinct perception," i.e. the objective content of every such perception, "is doubtless *something*, and therefore cannot be from nothing, but necessarily has God as its author – God, I say, that supremely perfect being, for whom it is contradictory to be a deceiver – and therefore it is doubtless true" (AT VII,62). Here the creation of the eternal truths (presented without calling attention to its voluntarism)[21] serves as the charter for the task of reconstructing science: "I will attain [truth] indeed, if I simply attend sufficiently to all those things which I perfectly understand, and segregate them from the others which I apprehend more confusedly and obscurely" (ibid.).

In the fifth Meditation, Descartes begins to apply this method to reconstructing the judgments about body which had been called into doubt in the first Meditation. Since he must first distinguish between what he perceives clearly and what only obscurely, he begins, "before I inquire whether such things [bodies] exist outside me" (p. 63), by "considering the *ideas* of them, insofar as they are in my thought, and seeing which of them are distinct and which obscure" (ibid.). Descartes takes this to be equivalent to saying that, before he inquires into the actual existence of bodies, he must first determine their essence: as the titles indicate, the fifth Meditation is (in part) "on the essence of material things," while only the sixth considers "the *existence* of material things." If, from the complex of our usual conceptions of bodies, we can separate out the *distinct* ideas, i.e. those ideas which, "beyond being clear, are so separated and distinguished from all other ideas that they contain nothing at all within themselves other than what is clear" (*Principles* I:45), then we will know that bodies, insofar as they are represented by these ideas, "have their own true and immutable natures," and thus, "even if perhaps they do not exist anywhere outside me, still cannot be said to be nothing" (AT VII,64). By

---

[20] I have discussed much of the material of this section and the following, from a different point of view, in "The Greatest Stumbling Block: Descartes' Denial of Real Qualities." On the controversial issues between Descartes and the scholastics discussed in the present section, especially about the ontological status of sensible qualities, the apparent content of our sensory ideas, and the ontological composition of bodies, I would like to direct readers to the fuller treatment I give there. Besides going further, textually and philosophically, into Descartes' thought on these issues, I am also able there to give a fuller and fairer treatment of the scholastic point of view, and to note relevant differences between different scholastic thinkers. However, the details of Descartes' argument with the scholastics – as opposed to his broad program for reconstructing physics on an understanding of body as extension – have little to do with his use of Augustinian metaphysics, and I have felt no obligation to discuss them all here.

[21] Compare, from the third letter to Mersenne on the creation of the eternal truths, "I know that God is the author of all things, and that these truths are something, and therefore that he is their author" (AT I,152); and see discussion in the preceding section.

attending to the intelligible essences of bodies, and noting the propositions that these essences imply, we can make scientific judgments about what bodies *would* be if they exist, but not about their actual existence.

Alongside the discussion of the essence of bodies, Descartes also inserts into the fifth Meditation an argument that God's essence entails God's existence: he does this, in large part, to underline the contrast between our knowledge of God and our knowledge of material things. Since the essences of material things, unlike the essence of God, do not imply actual existence, the method of the fifth Meditation is not sufficient to prove that any of the possible kinds of bodies actually exist.[22] The fifth Meditation uses *nous* as a criterion, and concludes that the objects of our intellectual ideas are real as essences, and *possibly* existent; the sixth Meditation must invoke a different criterion, namely the senses and (more generally) the teachings of nature, to prove that bodies actually exist, and to give rules for deciding which geometrical patterns are actualized when. But the senses and the teachings of nature are criteria *only* for actual existence, not for essence: they help us to decide which intelligible essences are actualized, but they do not also give us reason to believe that there are additional essences or natures in bodies beyond the (geometric) essences we perceive by pure intellect. We will examine in the next section why and how Descartes uses sensation as a criterion for existence. Here we note that in *not* accepting sensation or other irrational powers as criteria for essences, Descartes is following the implications of the doctrine of the creation of the eternal truths, as he expresses it in the letters to Mersenne: since the only essences in things are those that proceed from God, and since the truths about these essences are "all inborn in our minds" (AT I,145), we can understand the world through our innate intellectual ideas,

---

[22] In accepting the distinction between essence and existence for things other than God (i.e. in accepting that the essence of such things does not entail their existence, so that we can understand what they are, and make true essential predications about them, even when they do not actually exist), Descartes is simply following what had become common sense, thanks to centuries of scholastic philosophizing; by contrast, Plato and Plotinus assume that if we can know (truths about) equality, then equality must exist, if not in sensible things than as a separate form, but in any case as an actually existent thing, not a mere non-actualized essence (see above, Chapter 6, Section B, for a contrast between Descartes and Augustine on this point). The Meditator, who is not especially well educated, regards the essence–existence distinction as a commonplace, and Descartes thinks that the danger from commonsense thought is not that the essence–existence distinction will be ignored, but that it will be improperly extended to the case of God: "for since I have been accustomed to distinguish existence from essence in all other things, I easily persuade myself that [existence] can be separated from *God's* essence too, and that God can thus be conceived as not existing" (AT VII,66). The scholastics, like Descartes, think that there is no essence–existence distinction in God; and St. Thomas agrees that from a quidditative concept of God (a distinct knowledge of *what God is*) it can be inferred that he actually exists. The dispute comes down to Descartes' assertion, and Thomas' denial, that a finite mind can have a quidditative concept of God. The procedure of thought of the third Meditation is designed to lead to such a quidditative concept, and is presupposed in order for the fifth-Meditation proof of the existence of God to succeed.

without having to posit principles in things whose nature we do not clearly know (as the *Letter to Picot* says all earlier philosophers have done, AT IX2,7–8).

The fifth and sixth Meditations progressively reverse two stages of the doubts about bodies that the first Meditation had raised. The initial arguments of the first Meditation are devoted to discrediting the evidence of the senses; their conclusion is that of all the commonly accepted sciences, only "arithmetic, geometry, and others of this kind, which treat only of the simplest and most general things [Descartes lists 'corporeal nature in general, its extension,' and its various modes], and which do not care whether or not these things exist in nature, contain something certain and undoubted" (AT VII,20). Descartes goes on to reject even these sciences of pure essences, until he has acquired a knowledge of God: not because he does not clearly perceive the objects of arithmetic and geometry, but because, without the knowledge of God, he has no criterion for deciding which perceptions are clear, and is still habitually inclined to suppose that sensory perceptions are the clearest. But now, having established a knowledge of God, Descartes is in a position to reevaluate the grounds for doubt and to reestablish the sciences. The fifth Meditation, proceeding from the idea of God as the source of truth, offers a direct and unqualified reestablishment of the sciences of pure essences; by contrast, the sixth Meditation, arguing from God as the source of the order of nature, can only partially restore the evidence of the senses and the sciences of actual existence, and concedes that at least some of the first Meditation's doubts are permanently valid. In this section I will deal only with the fifth Meditation and the knowledge of the essence of bodies, deferring to the next section the more complicated argument of the sixth Meditation.

Although the fifth Meditation is officially devoted to determining the essence of material things, Descartes never actually says in this Meditation what the essence of body is, either in general or for some particular species of body. Presumably he avoids an explicit statement of his doctrine of the essence of body in order not to antagonize the Aristotelians prematurely (cf. AT III,298). But Descartes is implicitly establishing his doctrine of the essence of body, by enumerating the distinct components of our conceptions of bodies, and leaving us to infer that these and only these constitute the essence of material things. But which concepts of bodies are distinct? In the fifth Meditation Descartes does not really argue for an answer to this question; he simply collects what he sees as the positive results of the investigations of earlier Meditations.

In the second and third Meditations, in isolating the ideas of soul and God as the only path to knowledge, Descartes also reevaluates which perceptions are clear and distinct. Thus, in the wax passage of the second Meditation, Descartes argues that the sensory perceptions of the sensible qualities of bodies are less distinct than the intellectual perceptions of their geometrical properties, and that even these are less distinct than the mind's intellectual perception of its own thought. Again, in the third Meditation, Descartes argues that the objective content of our ideas is our only ground for judging that the ideas come from something external that resembles them; he then assesses the objective contents of our different ideas, to show that none except the idea of God is so great that it could not have originated within the mind itself. Most important, Descartes assesses our ideas of bodies. "If I inspect [these ideas] more thoroughly, and examine each of them as yesterday I examined the idea of wax, I notice that there are very few things which I perceive clearly and distinctly in them, namely magnitude or extension in length, breadth, and depth," also figure, position, motion, substance, duration, and number (AT VII,43). Sensible qualities, on the other hand, "I think only very confusedly and obscurely, so that I do not even know whether they are true or false, that is, whether the ideas which I have of them are ideas of things or of non-things" (ibid.). For if some sensible quality which is represented in an idea turns out to be a non-thing, such as a negation, then the idea will have no objective reality, and will indeed be "materially false" or deceptive, inasmuch as it represents a negation as if it were a positive reality. But "for example, the ideas which I have of heat and cold are so little clear and distinct that I cannot learn from them whether cold is only the privation of heat, or whether heat is the privation of cold, or both of them are real qualities, or neither" (pp. 43–4): if these ideas of sensible qualities do represent something real, then we cannot distinguish this something from nothing merely by considering our ideas.[23]

Thus of all our ideas of body, only the ideas of extension and its geometrical modifications have a discernible positive content. These are the ideas that the Meditator of the fifth Meditation recognizes as distinct: "I distinctly imagine that quantity which the philosophers commonly call 'continuous,' or the extension of that quantity (or rather of the quantified thing) in length, breadth, and depth," and the magnitude and figure and position of its parts, and motion and its duration (p. 63). The objective reality of these ideas is not enough to allow us to argue from the ideas to the actual existence of their objects; as the third Meditation argues, we

---

[23] Descartes is relying here on the scholastic realist doctrine that negations and privations (and "relations of reason") are not real beings or *res* but only *entia rationis*; likewise, a mode (such as a figure, which is a mode of extension or continuous quantity) is not a true *res* but only a *way* that some *res* is. Descartes thinks that sensible qualities of bodies such as heat and cold are in fact not *res* but (at best) modes of extension: our sensory ideas are therefore materially false, because they represent these modes of extension confusedly, as if they were simple positive *res* superadded to extension, rather than representing them *as* particular ways of being extended. While sensory ideas represent their objects, misleadingly, *as if* they were *res*, they represent them so indistinctly that we cannot tell by examining our ideas whether the objects are *res* or modes or *entia rationis*. See my "The Greatest Stumbling Block" for a detailed discussion of the issue of whether heat and other sensible qualities are "real qualities" (that is, qualities which are *res* rather than modes or *entia rationis*), and of the sense in which our ideas of heat and cold represent these qualities "as if" they were *res*.

need the idea of God for this. But once we have established the actual existence of God, and are descending from God to creatures, the objective content of our geometrical ideas is enough to establish the reality of their objects as essences. Since we distinctly conceive continuous quantity and its modes, and understand geometrical theorems that are entailed by the essences of these things, we know that "even if perchance they should not exist anywhere outside me, they still cannot be said to be nothing, but have their own true and immutable natures" (p. 64). Here Descartes is not saying merely that, since we gain our geometrical ideas by contemplating *something*, the reality they represent must exist in something at least *eminently* (this is obvious, since every reality exists at least eminently in God); Descartes' claim is that, since these perceptions come to us from a veracious God, there must be something of which the theorems of geometry are *formally* true.

In Chapter 6 we saw an analogy between Descartes' argument for the existence of God and the *Phaedo*'s argument for the existence of an equal-itself. Plato argues that, before we can judge that a sensible thing conforms imperfectly to some intelligible standard, we must first have known this intelligible standard (e.g. the equal) in itself; since we knew it, it must exist, and since it does not exist within sensible things, it must exist outside them. Descartes cannot accept this argument in general, since he accepts the essence–existence distinction in creatures, and so recognizes that something can be an object of knowledge without actually existing; but Descartes reconstructs the argument, with additional premises, for the special case of our intellectual knowledge of God. Here Descartes is returning to the general case. When I clearly conceive a triangle, this triangle may not "exist, or ever have existed, anywhere outside my thought," but still there is "a certain determinate nature or essence or form of it, immutable and eternal, which was not produced by me, and which does not depend on my mind" (p. 64). This "nature or essence or form" is neither a Platonic eternal being apart from Nous, nor a Plotinian eternal being existing within Nous, but a non-subsistent essence or eternal truth proceeding from Nous to creatures. But once it is understood that we are arguing only for real essences and not for actually existent things, Descartes feels free to draw on the argument of the *Phaedo*. Descartes argues, like Plato, against the suggestion that we might have drawn our ideas of geometrical forms from the senses: his argument that "I can think of innumerable other figures about which there can be no suspicion that they ever struck me through the senses" (ibid.) is a version of the Platonic argument, avoiding the controversial assumption that we have never seen a perfect triangle, and substituting the safer assumption that we have never seen a perfect chiliagon. Here Descartes may merely be arguing in parallel with Plato, but surely he deliberately alludes to Plato when he says of the "innumerable particular things" he perceives about the geometrical essences, that "their truth is so open and concordant with my nature that, when I first uncover them, I seem not so much to learn something new,

357

as to be reminded of things which I already knew beforehand" (pp. 63–4) – "or," as Descartes immediately corrects himself, "to turn for the first time to things which had long been in me, although I had not turned my mind's vision on them before" (p. 64). Descartes does not believe in the theory of recollection any more than the mature Augustine did; he believes in separate recollectable Forms even less than Augustine did; but, like Augustine, he uses the terms of the *Phaedo* to describe the purely intellectual knowledge he claims to have discovered. But for Descartes, this knowledge is not knowledge of an intelligible world existing separately from bodies, but of the possibly existent bodies themselves: the intelligible world is the only real world there is, and physical extension must be intelligible extension.

The fifth Meditation does not explicitly say that *only* geometrical truths can be distinctly conceived in material things, or that they constitute the whole essence of bodies, but Descartes thinks he is entitled to this conclusion, and he draws it explicitly at *Principles of Philosophy* II:4, entitled "that the nature of body consists not in weight, hardness, color, or the like, but in extension alone." Descartes' evidence here is not simply his inability to discover distinct ideas of sensible qualities, but his positive ability to form a distinct conception of an extension existing by itself without any superadded qualities. Since "all the things that I clearly and distinctly understand can be made by God such as I understand them" (AT VII,78), God can make extension exist without any sensible qualities or anything else attached to it, and since extension can be separated from these other things (even if only by God's absolute power), it must be really distinct from them. Indeed, there is no need to call on God's absolute power: in *Principles* II:4, taking the case of hardness, Descartes shows how bodies could be constructed in such a way that we would never feel this quality in them, although the bodies would remain equally bodies; "and by the same reason it can be shown, that weight, and color, and all other qualities of this kind, which are sensed in the corporeal matter, can also be removed from it, while it remains whole: whence it follows that its nature depends on none of them." The reasoning recalls the argument of the wax passage that our ideas of the sensible qualities of a body do not distinctly represent that body, since the qualities can perish while the body remains; Descartes had concluded there that extension alone belongs to the distinct *concepts* of bodies, and he concludes here that extension alone belongs to their essence in reality.[24]

---

[24] Objection: while I can conceive a body without any *specific* sensible quality (without yellowness, or without sweetness), Descartes seems to be illegitimately inferring that I can conceive a body (and that God can create a body) without *any* sensible qualities; if this inference were legitimate, it would also show, absurdly, that God could create a body without any shape. In fact, given the assumptions Descartes shares with his scholastic opponents, his argument is valid. Since body can exist without each sensible quality, each sensible quality is either a *res* really distinct from body or else a mode of body. Since body cannot exist without extension, body is either really identical with extension or else a mode

In *Principles* II:4, Descartes presents his doctrine of body in such a way as to bring out its contrast with the scholastic account. He identifies "[the nature] of body considered in general" with "the nature of matter," and he says that this "consists . . . only in its being a thing extended in length, breadth, and depth." For the scholastics, by contrast, the substance of bodies is composite, containing not only matter but also a substantial form superadded to matter. Furthermore, for most scholastics, the prime matter of bodies is not intrinsically quantified: an accident of continuous quantity must be added to give the matter (and thus also the substantial composite) some determinate extension, and then a further series of real qualities must be added to the quantified substance to make it the kind of body we perceive with our senses.[25] When Descartes says that the nature of body consists only in its being a thing extended in three dimensions, he is stripping away any real qualities and any substantial forms to leave only the quantified matter. Descartes claims that if God creates the quantified matter by itself (as we know that he can), he has thereby created body; perhaps God has also created some substantial forms or real qualities which we do

of extension; but, since body is a substance, it is not a mode. Thus the essence of body is really identical with extension, and does not include any sensible quality; and God can create this essence without attaching any other *res* to it. This holds just as much for shapes as for colors. It does not follow that God can make a body without shape: bodies are nothing but extension, but they may have any shape, and must have *some* shape, because shape is simply a mode of extension (it is the way that the extension is terminated), not a superadded *res*. There would be a sophism here if Descartes were concluding that bodies (because they are merely extension) are uncolored, but Descartes does not conclude this, nor does he believe it: again, see "The Greatest Stumbling Block" for discussion.

[25] This is the usual doctrine of the scholastic realist schools; it is rejected by Ockham, in *Summa Logicae* I,44, "Of Quantity, against the Moderns," which gives perhaps the clearest brief statement of the view Ockham is opposing. (Ockham's own view is that qualities inhere directly in substances and that quantities, whether continuous or discrete, are nothing beyond the substances or qualities which they quantify; there is no unquantified matter.) "Substantial" form and "real" quality are scholastic technical terms, and Descartes is generally careful about using them correctly: a substantial form is a form that is a substance really distinct from the matter it is united to (there are also accidental forms, i.e. forms which are accidents); a real quality is a quality which is a *res* really distinct from its subject (there are also qualities which are not *res*, but modes only modally distinct from their immediate subjects). Descartes believes in forms and qualities, but not in substantial forms or real qualities. Despite Gilson's protests (*Etudes sur le rôle de la pensée médiévale dans la formation du système cartésien*, pp. 162–3), Descartes is correctly following scholastic usage in saying that a substantial form is a form that is a substance: for a typical account, see Suárez, *Disputationes Metaphysicae*, Disputation 15, section 1, which includes the definition of substantial form cited above, Chapter 2, Section C. (Gilson is also mistaken in saying that the scholastics did not believe that substantial forms could exist apart from matter.) Suárez notes that, although heat and figure are both in the category of quality, heat is a *res* and figure is only a mode (Disputation 39, section 1, paragraph 17; in "The Greatest Stumbling Block" I incorrectly gave the reference as section 2). When Descartes denies that heat is a real quality, he is saying against the scholastics that heat, like figure, is only a mode of extension; he is not denying that bodies are really hot, any more than he denies that bodies are really figured. I give a full discussion of these issues in "The Greatest Stumbling Block."

not clearly understand, but if so these are not constituents of body but things superadded to an already complete bodily nature.[26]

Descartes is also making another anti-scholastic claim. When he says that "the nature of matter" consists in "its being a thing extended in length, breadth, and depth," he is denying that there is an indeterminate prime matter to which quantity must be added. When we eliminate real qualities and substantial forms, we are stripping down to what we can clearly conceive; but if we then try (like Aristotle in *Metaphysics* VII,3) to strip away quantity too and reach an unquantified matter, then we are eliminating what we clearly conceive, and are left with an obscure idea of something-we-know-not-what. Thus philosophers who "distinguish the substance from the extension or quantity either understand nothing by the name 'substance,' or else they have only a confused idea of an [unquantified and therefore] incorporeal substance, which they falsely attribute to the corporeal" (*Principles* II:9). If we could clearly conceive matter without quantity, then we would know that God could create matter without quantity, and so we would know that quantity is an accident really (or at least modally) distinct from the matter it quantifies; but since in fact we understand matter as already involving quantity, Descartes concludes that "quantity is not really different from extended substance, but only in our concepts" (II:8).[27]

This conclusion allows Descartes to restate his claim: the true substance

---

[26] The scholastics agree that real qualities are not part of the essence of body, but are superadded to an already constituted bodily nature. But the scholastics think that substantial form, as well as matter, belongs to the essence of body, and that quantified matter by itself does not constitute a body; Descartes is claiming that quantified matter just *is* body, and that any form superadded to quantified matter is superadded to an already constituted body. Descartes states his thesis precisely in a letter to Regius: "by the name 'substantial form,' when we deny it, is understood a certain substance adjoined to matter, and *composing with the matter a merely corporeal whole*" (AT III,502; my emphasis); the human mind is a substance adjoined to matter and composing a whole with matter, but this whole is not merely corporeal.

[27] What Descartes says in full is "quantity is not really different from extended substance, but only in our concepts, in the same way that number differs from the thing numbered" (*Principles* II:8): he is thus referring to scholastic debates about both of the kinds of quantity, discrete quantity or number and continuous quantity or extension. The debate about number is not directly relevant to Descartes' argument here, but it was generally agreed that it was harder to maintain a real distinction between discrete quantity and what it quantifies than between continuous quantity and what it quantifies: so, since Descartes wants to deny the real distinction even for continuous quantity, it is to his dialectical advantage to refer to the problem about discrete quantity. Descartes was already aware of the scholastic debates, and takes what is essentially his mature position on the crucial issues, as early as Rule 14, AT X,442–7, some of which parallels *Principles* II. See also *Le monde*'s criticisms of the scholastic doctrine of an obscure prime matter: Descartes says that the difficulty arises only from the fact that "they want to distinguish [prime matter] from its own quantity and its external extension, that is to say from its property of occupying space" (AT XI,35); Descartes, by contrast, "supposes that the quantity of the matter I have described does not differ from its substance any more than number does from the things numbered," and he "conceives its extension, or its property of occupying space, not as an accident, but as its true form and essence" (p. 36).

of bodies is *nothing other than quantity*. Descartes does not say that the scholastics did not have the true idea of the substance of bodies; he says that they had this idea (namely, the idea of continuous quantity), but that they wrongly dismissed it as representing a mere accident, and went off on a vain search for some more mysterious substance.[28] Continuous quantity, for the scholastic realists, is a very peculiar accident, with many of the features of substance: it is attributed to itself (the whiteness present throughout a body is not white, but the two-foot-longness present throughout the body is two feet long); it is individuated through itself (whereas, at least for St. Thomas, other accidents are individuated through substance, substance through signate matter, and signate matter through quantity); and it is the proximate substratum of other accidents (this whiteness is in one foot-length, and that whiteness is in the other foot-length). Indeed, when in the Eucharist the accidents of bread and wine exist without inhering in a substance, the quantity subsists by itself and is the *ultimate* substratum of the other accidents.[29] In one striking passage, after Thomas has explained how God can preserve accidents without their substances, he adds that

this can be said especially of dimensive quantities: indeed, the Platonists posited that these subsisted by themselves [sc. as separate mathematicals, intermediate between physical things and Forms], since they are separated in the intellect. But it is clear that God can do more in actual operation than the intellect can in apprehension [and therefore, since the intellect can understand quantity apart from a substrate, *a fortiori* God can create quantity apart from a substrate]. (*Summa Contra Gentiles* IV,65)

Thus Thomas grants that God *could* have created the subsisting mathematical extension of the Platonists in the physical world; and he actually does so, but only on rare occasions, in the Eucharistic bread and wine. But the Eucharistic bread and wine nourish us and affect our senses in just the way that ordinary bodies do: there is no way to tell the difference without divine revelation. For all we know, God has made the entire world out of subsisting mathematical extension; and Descartes proposes that he has in fact done so.[30]

---

[28] "They leave the true idea of this corporeal substance to extension, which, however, they call an accident: and thus they plainly proclaim in their words something other than what they comprehend in their mind" (*Principles* II:9).

[29] There is a comprehensive account of the scholastic realist doctrine of continuous quantity in Suárez, *Disputationes Metaphysicae*, Disputation 40: Suárez comments on the "peculiar condition of quantity, which is not only the form by which something else is *quantum*, but is also itself denominated *quanta*, since it is not only the *ratio* on account of which other things become extended and divisible, but is also extended and divisible in itself; nor could it extend something else unless at the same time it were coextended with it, and had its own parts corresponding to the parts of its object" (section 1, paragraph 6).

[30] Descartes' Benedictine follower Robert Desgabets makes the point explicit: "saint Thomas parlant de la quantité ou étendue de l'hostie consacrée, dit expressément que c'est un accident séparé de la substance et qui subsiste en cet état par miracle, mais il attribue à cet admirable sacrement tout ce qui fait la propre nature de la substance corporelle parmi

It is thus easy for Descartes to dispose of any obscure prime matter really distinct from quantity. It will be more difficult to dispose of obscure substantial forms and real qualities superadded to quantity. It may be a sound precept of method never to posit anything we do not clearly understand; but the goal of the method is to understand the causes of the things that affect the human composite, including the different activities of the different kinds of body, and the different ways they affect our senses; and it will be hard to explain this diversity if the nature of physical things is just mathematical extension.

In the next section I will discuss what kind of explanation Descartes thinks we owe to the sensible characteristics of things. Here I will merely note the restrictions that Descartes has placed on himself by identifying body with extension.

By refusing to posit anything in bodies beyond extension, Descartes has eliminated all the characteristics that are usually taken to distinguish one kind of body from another. Most obviously, if body is just extension, a vacuum is impossible, and so the diversity of phenomena cannot arise from the pattern of empty and occupied regions of space. Descartes cannot admit an extension in length, breadth, and depth which is not the extension of any body: since three-dimensional extension is what constitutes the nature of a body, the supposedly empty space is already itself a body.

For as from this [premiss] alone, that body is extended in length, breadth, and depth, we rightly conclude that it is a substance, since it is entirely contradictory that there should be an extension of *nothing*, so also we should draw the same conclusion about the space which is supposed to be empty: namely, since there is extension in it, there must necessarily also be substance in it. (*Principles* II:16)

Descartes had listed a prejudice in favor of the void as one of two reasons for resisting the truth that the essence of body is extension (II:5), but he must be thinking of a prejudice among the unlearned, or among Epicureans, since the Aristotelian and scholastic position agrees with Descartes' own: indeed, Descartes' argument against the void echoes a scholastic commonplace.[31] Eliminating the void may put Descartes at a disadvantage

les nouveaux théologiens [i.e. the Cartesians], car il [Thomas] enseigne que la substance, qui est distinguée de la quantité, n'est pas le sujet nécessaire des accidents. C'est cette quantité qui est elle-même le sujet de tous les accidents que nous y [in the Eucharist] voions. C'est elle, toute séparée qu'elle est de la substance, qui nous nourrit, qui se convertit en notre propre substance, et dont nous sommes en partie composés après la communion et la digestion. C'est elle qui se mêle parmi la matière du monde et qui en compose une partie, sans que Dieu rétablisse la matière du pain qu'il a détruite, ny qu'il en crée de nouvelle; enfin c'est cette quantité dont le monde entier pourroit être composé et paroître tel qu'il est, sans que nous ayons aucun moïen de le distinguer du monde substantiel que Dieu a créé" (from a manuscript cited by Jean-Robert Armogathe, *Theologia Cartesiana* (The Hague: Nijhoff, 1977), p. 111).

31 For scholastic arguments about the void, see Pierre Duhem, *Medieval Cosmology*, tr. Roger Ariew (Chicago: University of Chicago Press, 1985), chapter 9. The argument Duhem

in comparison with such neo-Epicureans as Gassendi in explaining the origin of phenomena, but it does not distinguish him from Aristotle or most other traditional philosophers.

But Descartes must also accept another consequence, which puts stricter constraints on the project of explaining the phenomena. The other reason for resisting the identification of body with extension is that "many people think that many bodies can be rarefied and condensed in such a way that when they are rarefied they have more extension than when they are condensed" (II:5); this opinion has led "certain subtle thinkers" (ibid.) to distinguish between a body's substance, its quantity, and its extension.[32] Condensation and rarefaction seem evident to the senses, and they give a plausible foundation for the variations of bodies: the earliest pre-Socratics took them as the basic explanation for all physical phenomena. But if extension is the whole nature of body, then a body cannot acquire a greater or lesser extension while remaining substantially the same and preserving the same quantity of matter. Quantity of matter will be measured precisely by quantity of extension, and the "density" of a body (the ratio of its mass to its volume) will be constant for all time and through all bodies: "it is plainly contradictory that anything should be increased by a new quantity or a new extension, unless there is simultaneously added to it a new extended substance, that is, a new body" (II:7). The different qualities our senses perceive in bodies cannot be explained through density or rarity, since "there cannot be more matter, or more corporeal substance, in a vessel, when it is full of lead, or gold, or any other body however heavy and hard, than when it contains only air, and is judged to be empty: since the quantity of the parts of matter does not depend on their weight or hardness, but on extension alone, which in the same vessel is always equal" (II:19).

Descartes' conclusion here is strikingly Parmenidean. What we can genuinely *think*, says Parmenides, must be entirely being, with no admixture of non-being; "nor is it divided, since it all exists alike; nor is it more here and less there, which would prevent it from holding together, but it is all

---

quotes from Roger Bacon on p. 389 makes a point much like Descartes': there cannot be an extension of nothing, because this would be an accident that was not an accident of any substance. After the condemnation of 1277, the scholastics all admit that God can (at least miraculously, as in the Eucharistic species) create an accident without a substance, and so they generally admit that God can create a vacuum. But this does not touch Descartes, since for Descartes extension is not an *accident* of body, but is really identical with the *substance* of body.

[32] Descartes is apparently referring to the position, defended notably by Suárez (Disputation 40, section 4), that the essence of continuous quantity is not the *actual* extension or size of the parts of a substance, but their *aptitudinal* extension, i.e. their *tendency* to occupy a determinate amount of space, and to resist being compressed further or becoming coextended with each other; thus a substance can be rarefied or condensed while keeping the same quantity. Other scholastics identify continuous quantity with actual extension, and others simply with the divisibility of the substance into distinct parts.

full of being. So it is all continuous: for what is draws near to what is" (Fr. 8, lines 22–5).[33] Parmenides thus rejects his predecessors' account of physical phenomena through condensation and rarefaction: for it depends on the absurd supposition that a given extension might not be full of being, but have also some quantity of non-being mixed in with it. Since Parmenides believes that "there is a furthest limit," the world is "perfected, like the bulk of a ball well-rounded on every side, equally balanced in every direction from the centre" (lines 42–4); since all there can intelligibly be of extended being (and thus, for Parmenides, of any being) is this uniformly solid sphere, there is no intelligible foundation for change, or for any variety in phenomena.

Indeed, Descartes' world threatens to be even more featureless than Parmenides', since Descartes rejects the thesis of a "furthest limit," which Plato and Aristotle had accepted from Parmenides. As Melissus had argued that the world must be unlimited, "for the limit would limit it against the void" (Aristotle *On Generation and Corruption* I,8), so Descartes argues that

this world, or the totality of corporeal substance, has no limits to its extension. For wherever we pretend that these limits are, we will not merely always *imagine* that there are spaces indefinitely extended beyond them: we will also always perceive that they are *truly imaginable*, that is, that they are real; and therefore also that an indefinitely extended corporeal substance is contained in them, since, as has been copiously demonstrated, the idea of that extension which we conceive in any space is entirely identical with the idea of corporeal substance. (*Principles* II:21)

Descartes must thus reject the scholastic claim that extension outside the sphere of the fixed stars is merely imaginary, unlike the extension within the world of bodies: any extension which is genuinely intelligible is real, and this intelligible extension is the whole nature of body.

For the same reason, Descartes must reject the usual post-Parmenidean solution of positing different primitive matters, all equally "full" and unmixed with void, which could be combined with each other in different proportions and arrangements to produce the phenomenal varieties of bodies. "The matter of the heaven and the earth is one and the same" (*Principles* II:22), against Aristotle, who distinguishes celestial matter, capable by nature of circular motion around the center of the universe, from the matter of sublunar things, capable by nature of the contrary rectilinear motions toward or away from the center of the universe. But the universe does not have a center; and even if it did, its matter is simply extension throughout, and it is no more "naturally" moved in one direction than in another. Nor can Descartes admit that this single matter is differentiated either by substantial forms or by real accidental forms (like Aristotle's basic qualities of heat, cold, wetness, and dryness) into the different "el-

---

[33] I cite Parmenides in the translation given in G. S. Kirk, J. E. Raven, and M. Schofield, *The Presocratic Philosophers* (Cambridge: Cambridge University Press, 1983), pp. 250–3.

ements" (like earth, water, air, and fire) whose combination yields the phenomenal bodies. Any difference between celestial and sublunar bodies, and any variety of sublunar "elements," must proceed merely from the different figures and motions of the parts of extension in the different regions.

Indeed, it is not enough to reduce the properties of bodies to their different *figures*, since a body has a figure only when it has a boundary, that is, when some property demarcates it from the surrounding bodies, and this happens only through motion: "for a division into parts which exists in thought alone alters nothing; but all variation of matter, or the diversity of all its forms, depends on motion" (*Principles* II:23). If there were no motion, the world would be the uniform plenum of Parmenides and Melissus, and there would be no variety in phenomena. Now, the Eleatics had supposed that, because the world is a plenum, there could be no motion, since there would be no room for anything to move into; later Greek philosophy had saved the possibility of motion by supposing that the parts of a plenum could displace each other in a simultaneous circular motion, and Descartes accepts this solution. But the variety of phenomena depends on motion for Descartes in a much stricter sense than it had for any previous philosopher. For Empedocles or Aristotle, since the elements are intrinsically different, their different mixtures and orderings can produce perceptibly different kinds of bodies. But for Descartes, since there is no plurality of elements, sensible phenomena must arise through the reciprocal displacement of *indiscernible* parts of a plenum. So the motion of the parts of body is not simply the means of *generating* sensible qualities: the qualities must be *constituted* at every moment by this motion, since if it ceased they would instantly vanish into an Eleatic One.

Our knowledge of the essence of bodies cannot take us any further than this: it cannot determine which of the possible patterns of motion in bodies is presently actualized, nor (if the present pattern of motion is known) can it predict what future motions will succeed it. Somehow we must use the senses to detect which of the intellectually possible patterns is presently actualized; but surely the senses by themselves do not give us knowledge of the interchange of indiscernible parts of a plenum. The intellect must somehow use the senses as its instruments to gather this knowledge. So it becomes a very important task for the intellect to formulate criteria for using the senses in this way: the sixth Meditation takes up this task far enough to give grounds for the judgment that a bodily world actually exists, and for other fundamental and uncontroversial judgments; and, at the same time, it implicitly gives rules for making the controversial scientific judgments that Descartes plans to reveal when his readers have got used to the conclusions of the *Meditations*. Another very important task for the intellect is to give laws of motion, that is, laws (going beyond what can be known from the geometric essence of body) determining what present motions will produce what future motions in bodies. This task is far more important for Descartes than for any previous philosopher, since for

Descartes any phenomenal characteristic of a body is preserved or altered only inasmuch as some pattern of motion is preserved or altered; and, since there is nothing in bodies except motion which could preserve or alter a motion, this depends entirely on the laws of motion. In the *Principles of Philosophy*, Descartes will try both to formulate laws of motion, and to give rules for discovering what patterns of motion lie behind the sensible qualities of bodies. He will then have used the metaphysics of the *Meditations* to solve the problems he could not solve in the *Rules*: both to give criteria for the intellectual and sensitive faculties, and to solve physical problems (like the problem of the anaclastic line, and the more basic problems about natural powers) which could not be solved by mathematics alone; and he will be on the road to the scientific practical wisdom promised in the *Letter to Picot*.

C. The teachings of nature

The sixth Meditation has the task of reconstructing a criterion for using the sensory faculties. Before beginning to meditate, we had used a free-and-easy criterion, judging that each of our ideas of sensation comes to us from a real quality in bodies resembling our idea. The first Meditation had raised doubts about this judgment, and the third Meditation had teased out and rejected the grounds on which it was based. We had supposed that our ideas of sensation come from external things which resemble them because we seemed to be taught so by nature, because the presence of these ideas is independent of our will, and because it seemed reasonable that any cause of our ideas would generate its own likeness rather than something else. Descartes rejects these arguments: only an intuition with a clear cognitive content, and not the blind impulses of nature, can reveal the natures of things outside us. Descartes turns to the argument from objective realities of ideas; but sensory ideas do not have enough objective reality to imply an actual external object as their cause, or even a potentially existent essence as their content. We can use our clear intellectual ideas to acquire a knowledge of God, and then to build up the sciences of essences; the fifth Meditation takes this project as far as it can go. In the sixth Meditation, in examining the actual existence of bodies, Descartes must reopen the question of what we can infer from the reports of our sensitive faculties.

The sixth Meditation therefore takes up the failed project of the *Rules for the Direction of the Mind*. In Rule 12, Descartes had hoped to derive a criterion for the scientific use of both intellectual and sensitive faculties by explaining the nature of the human being as a composite of mind and body, and showing the powers and functions of each cognitive faculty within the composite. If we use our faculties as our nature directs, surely we will not fall into error. But it is not clear what genuinely does follow from our nature, and what is merely an ingrained habit of assent; and we cannot presuppose an account of nature in deriving a criterion for constructing a science of nature. Descartes' only option is to begin from the intellect, and to construct a criterion of the cognitive faculties on this basis alone. The ascent to God as Nous is designed to lead us to a purely intelligible standard, independent of any physical hypotheses, by which the different faculties can be judged. In the fourth Meditation Descartes uses this standard to give rules for using the intellect; in the sixth he turns back to the sensitive faculties.

Descartes has in the sixth Meditation what he did not have in the *Rules*, an intellectual knowledge of himself and God. God is essentially the agent intellect; and human beings, insofar as they are God's immediate production, are made in the image of God, and are therefore potential intellects. Since the Meditator distinctly conceives himself as a thing that thinks (passively in intellection, actively in volition and judgment), he knows that the content of this conception is a real essence, which he himself actually instantiates. This is sufficient (says Descartes) to establish that the Meditator's essence consists only in being a mind, and that he is really distinct from all bodies. For "since I know that all things which I clearly and distinctly understand can be made by God as I understand them, then if I can understand one thing clearly and distinctly without another, this is sufficient for me to be certain that one is diverse from the other, because it can be posited separately at least by God" (AT VII,78); this implies that they are "diverse" in the sense of "really distinct," since the mark of a real distinction is that either of two beings should be able (by some natural or supernatural power) to subsist without the other. Nonetheless, the Meditator, whose essence is simply to think or to be a mind, finds that he possesses, beyond his essence, various passions, sensations, and imaginations, which he seems to derive from "a body which is very closely conjoined to me" (ibid.), and from its interactions with other bodies. Descartes does not immediately assume that these passions and sensations and imaginations really do arise from the union of the mind with a body; his task is, first to argue for this claim, and then to explain how these nonintellectual thoughts arise and how they are directed toward the perfection of the mind–body composite. If Descartes can do this, he will be in a position to reevaluate the argument from the teachings of nature. "There is no doubt that everything which I am taught by nature has some truth" (p. 80), since the things I am taught by nature, like the things I perceive by the natural light of reason, proceed ultimately from God; as in the fourth Meditation, the problem is to discover which things genuinely belong to our nature as we receive it from God, and which are the result of our own actions. By understanding himself as an essentially intellectual soul which comes to be united to a body, the Meditator can discover what his true nature is, and can thereby discern what it is genuinely teaching him.

Descartes distinguishes between a broad and a narrow sense of "nature." In the broad sense, "I understand by nature in general nothing other than God himself, or the coordination of creatures which is instituted by God; and by *my* nature in particular I understand nothing other than the complex of all those things which are bestowed on me by God" (ibid.). "Nature" in this sense would cover "every order, every law, and every *ratio* of truth or goodness" (AT VII,435) which is present in creatures, since all such things proceed from God. So *my* nature would include the full measure of law which governs my mind and my body: it would include both "many things which pertain to the mind alone, as that I perceive that what is done cannot be undone, and all the other things that are known by the natural light" (p. 82), and "many things which apply to the body alone, as that it tends downwards, and the like" (ibid.). But when Descartes speaks of being taught something by nature (or by *his* nature) he is concerned not with a "nature" so broad as to occur in all created beings, but with one narrowly specified realm of being: "nature" in this narrow sense signifies "those things which are bestowed on me by God inasmuch as I am a *composite* of mind and body" (ibid.; my stress).

This narrow use of "nature" recalls a theme from ancient philosophy. For the Stoics, nature is an active principle working upon matter, which is not yet soul but which becomes soul when properly disposed. But Plotinus, responding to the Stoics, describes nature as something *posterior* to soul, which emerges when the soul comes into contact with a body. Each soul is intrinsically rational, and remains exclusively an intellect as long as it subsists by itself; but when it descends into a corruptible body, and takes on the functions of governing this body and preserving it from harm, it generates nature as an image of soul performing these operations in the body. Descartes, of course, does not believe in the preexistence of the human soul; nor does he believe that there are immanent active powers which perform the organic functions; but he is close to Plotinus when he describes nature as supervening on the rational soul in the presence of the body, and he draws thoroughly Platonist conclusions in assessing what nature teaches.

After he has made clear what nature is, Descartes examines what it does and does not teach us. "This nature does indeed teach [us] to flee those things which induce a sense of pain, and pursue those which induce a sense of pleasure, and the like" (p. 82). Indeed, this is *all* that nature does, since "it does not appear that it teaches us, in addition, that we should conclude anything about things placed outside us from these perceptions of the senses, without a previous examination of the intellect; for to know the truth about these things seems to pertain to the mind alone, and not to the composite" (pp. 82–3). That is: the proper function of *nature*, as distinguished from intellect, is to give practical guidance for action, and not to perceive the truth of things. The operations of the intellect tend toward the perfection of the intellect, which is knowledge of reality; but the operations of nature tend toward the perfection (in the first instance, the preservation) of the human mind–body composite.

For this reason, when Descartes assesses the modes of thought that we derive from nature, he gives first place to the *passions* (pleasure, pain, and the bodily appetites), and only secondarily draws conclusions for the five external senses. It is obvious that the proper usage of the passions is practical rather than theoretical; but we might mistakenly think that the *senses* had also a theoretical value, that is, that they gave us knowledge of the truth of things. By giving a justification of the teachings of nature which applies primarily to the passions, and only secondarily to sensations, Descartes is putting the senses in their proper place, as practical rather than theoretical guides.

The Meditator of the sixth Meditation is not seeking practical advice: he is seeking knowledge about the world of bodies. But he gains this knowledge only by drawing theoretical inferences from the fact that the teachings of nature are practically reliable: this is true even for the most fundamental conclusions, as "that there really is a world, that men have bodies, and the like, which no one of sound mind has ever seriously doubted" (AT VII,16). The Meditator knows that his confused sensory impressions of bodies proceed from *some* active power in *some* substance; he also knows that his own essence involves only the powers of intellect and will, and so he infers that he himself does not contain the power that generates these impressions. But this is as far as his intuitions of essences can take him. But he has "a great inclination to believe" (AT VII,80) that his sensory impressions of bodies proceed from bodies and not (say) from God; and he thinks he can be sure that, although we may interpret our sensations in different ways, our fundamental inclination to relate them to bodies is not a human artifact, but is given by our nature, and therefore by God. Since God is not a deceiver and has not given us an inclination toward non-existent things, we may conclude that bodies exist. But the structure of this judgment is very different from the structure of the judgment that the angles of a triangle are equal to two right angles, or that God exists, as Descartes explains these judgments in the fifth Meditation. We were irresistibly inclined to believe these judgments, simply because our intellects perceive that they are true. Here, however, we have two distinct inclinations to believe that bodies exist: first, a natural and scientifically worthless inclination, without any clear perception; then, subsequently, an intellectual perception deducing that bodies exist, from the very fact of this natural inclination. Only this intellectual perception allows us to make the *scientific* judgment that bodies exist.

Further judgments follow by a refinement of the argument which proved that bodies exist. What nature inclines me to believe, it inclines me to believe in order that I might act to preserve myself from harm as a composite of mind and body. Thus all these inclinations presuppose a more basic inclination to believe that I have a body, and that this can be affected to the benefit or harm of my composite nature. The union of my mind to this body is the source of my passions and other sensory impressions. Descartes repeats the Plotinian and Augustinian formula of a "total mixture" of mind and body: just because the mind is indivisible and unextended, it can be immediately united to all the parts of the extended body (sixth Meditation, AT VII,85–6; *Passions of the Soul*, AT XI,351); echoing Augustine, Descartes says that the mind is "coextended with the body, whole in the whole, and whole in each of its parts" (AT VII,442).[34] Although I am essentially a mind, and thus entirely diverse from my body, I am "very tightly conjoined and as it were intermixed with it, in such a way that I form some one thing with it" (AT VII,81). This conjunction or intermixture explains my confused but forceful sensory impressions, such as the sensation of pain: if I were merely present in the body as a sailor in a ship, then "when the body is injured . . . I would not feel pain, but would perceive this injury by pure intellect, as a sailor would perceive by sight if anything were broken in the ship; and when it needs food or drink, I would understand this expressly, and would not have confused sensations of hunger and thirst" (ibid.). Instead, God has endowed the composite of mind and body with a "nature" connecting the two components; when the body is in an appropriate condition, this nature impresses the mind with sufficient force to incline it to act so as to preserve its union with the body. Although the impressions thus produced are inferior in content to the conclusions of pure intellect, they are appropriate to the task of guiding the practical operations of the mind within the composite: our intellects are too limited to give us knowledge of everything that might affect the conduct of our lives, and so God has given us sensation as a substitute, and implanted in us a strong natural inclination to be guided by it in our actions. Most obviously, pleasure and pain are given as an index of the well-being of the composite, and the appetites are given as guides to its needs; but the senses of sight, hearing, smell, taste, and touch are also directed to the practical end of allowing us to judge how the bodies that surround us may affect our well-being, and how we may best respond to them to satisfy the needs of the composite.

Using this theory of our nature and its function, Descartes takes up again the project of Rule 12. Although the primary function of the senses is practical, we can also, just by reflecting on their practical function, use them to make theoretical judgments about bodies: not merely "that there really is a world, that men have bodies, and the like, which no one of sound mind has ever seriously doubted" (AT VII,16), but also judgments on controverted questions of physics. Descartes offers this theoretical reflection on the senses, not only to show us how to use the senses correctly, but also to explain how they have led us into error in the past. Following Descartes' own order in the sixth Meditation, I will discuss this negative theoretical reflection on the senses before discussing their positive use in reconstructing physics.

---

[34] Augustine had said that the soul in its body "*et in toto tota est, et in qualibet ejus parte tota est*" (*De Trinitate* VI,vi,8). Descartes says at AT VII,442, "nor do I understand the mind to be coextended with the body in any other way, *totam in toto, et totam in qualibet ejus parte.*" This is therefore a quote: not necessarily a quote directly from Augustine, but at least a quote of an Augustinian tag that had become standardized in this word-for-word form (it is quoted in this way by St. Thomas, and doubtless by many other writers).

The senses lead us into error because we misunderstand their proper function; and we misunderstand the function of the senses because we misunderstand what our own nature consists in. We misunderstand the senses when we take them as having not only a practical but also a direct theoretical value:

I have habitually perverted the order of nature, since although the perceptions of the senses are properly given by nature just for signifying to the mind what things may be beneficial or harmful to the composite of which it is a part, I use them as certain rules for immediately discerning what the essence of the bodies placed outside us might be: about which, however, they signify nothing, except very obscurely and confusedly. (AT VII,83)

We fell into this perverse habit in infancy, and have been immersed in it since. Descartes' theory of human nature thus allows him to take up from a theoretical perspective the complaint of the *Discourse on Method* about the childish condition in which we formed our habits of judgment, making it "almost impossible that our judgments should be as pure or as solid as they would have been if we had had the full use of our reason from the point of our birth, and had never been guided except by it" (AT VI,12). As we have already seen, the idea of a childish immersion in error is a commonplace, which Descartes found in Cicero, but to which he gave a specifically Platonist or Augustinian interpretation.[35] We are born in a condition of ignorance, and subject to the sensations and passions we receive from the motions communicated through our body. In this condition we do not know our own nature, and so we do not know what our faculties are for: in Plotinus' phrase, the souls "have forgotten their father God, and whence they come, and what they are." Although the senses are only messengers to an incorporeal intellect, we are inclined to regard them as our most authoritative faculty. Hampered by ignorance, and swayed by the passions, we freely but predictably fall, and accept the senses as representing the nature of reality.

This fall is supposed to explain, not just casual errors, but bad philosophy. Plotinus had tried to show that Epicureanism and Stoicism were the natural results of our fall, and of our resulting reliance on the senses; Augustine tries to show the same for Manicheism, modifying Plotinus' account of Stoicism as little as possible to get the desired result; and Descartes does the same thing again for scholasticism. When we accept the senses as revealing reality, we identify the real with the sensible. For Plotinus and Augustine, this meant identifying the real with *body*. For Descartes, however, body is not sensible but intelligible: when we identify the real with the sensible we give up, not only the mind and God, but also body as properly conceived, and retain only bodies confusedly imagined

---

[35] See above, Chapter 2, Section B, for discussion of the *Discourse* passage and of the Ciceronian text (*Tusculan Disputations* III,i,2) on which it is based; and Chapter 7, Section A, for Descartes and Augustine on our childish condition of ignorance and difficulty, and the errors it gives rise to.

as the bearers of sensible qualities. While Plotinus and Augustine criticize the Stoics or Manichees chiefly for misunderstanding soul and God as bodies, Descartes is attacking, as much as anything, the scholastic misunderstanding of bodies themselves.

Descartes gives his clearest account of the origins of scholastic errors in the sixth Replies: after recounting the process of thought which led him to the novel conclusions of the *Meditations*, and especially to the denial of real sensible qualities, he offers some reflections on "the reasons why I had previously believed otherwise" (AT VII,441). This is not autobiography, but a reconstruction of how the prejudices of childhood might lead to the customary view of body, and to its elaboration into scholastic doctrine. The main reason for our past errors is that

> from infancy I had passed various judgments about physical things, insofar as they contributed to the preservation of the life I was beginning, and that I had afterwards retained those same opinions which I had then preconceived about these things. And since the mind at that age used the corporeal organs less correctly, and, being more firmly attached to them, thought nothing without them, it considered things only confusedly. (Ibid.)

As a result of this confusion, the mind fails to distinguish those conceptions which apply to mind from those which apply to bodies:

> Although it was conscious of its own nature, and had in itself an idea of thought as well as of extension, still, because it understood nothing without also imagining something at the same time, it took them to be one and the same, and it applied to the body all the notions it had of intellectual things. And since in the rest of my life I never freed myself from these prejudices, there was nothing at all that I knew distinctly enough, and nothing that I did not suppose to be corporeal; even if, of those things which I supposed to be corporeal, I often fashioned such ideas or concepts as apply to minds rather than to bodies. (Ibid.)

Note that Descartes is making two distinct criticisms of the "fallen" philosophy. On the one hand, it supposes that everything is corporeal (a description originally meant for Stoicism, and fitting the scholastics rather badly); on the other hand, it falsifies the nature of bodies themselves, by attributing to them properties that in fact can only belong to minds. The second kind of criticism may seem less Plotinian than the first; but when Plotinus criticizes the Stoic doctrine that God and souls and natures and qualities and active powers are subtle bodies (*pneumata*) totally intermixed with the grosser bodies they affect, he says that the Stoics falsify the nature of bodies by attributing to them total mixture, when in fact total mixture can only be of an incorporeal with a body, or of two incorporeals. In an important and striking passage, Descartes takes up this criticism of the Stoics, and adapts it for use against the scholastics:

> When I conceived of heaviness (for example) as a certain real quality which was present within the gross bodies, even if, inasmuch as I applied it to the bodies in which it was present, I called it a *quality*, yet because I added that it was *real*, I

was really thinking that it was a *substance*: in the same way as a suit of clothes, considered in itself, is a substance, even if it is a quality when applied to the clothed person; and the mind too, even if it is really a substance, can nonetheless be called a quality of the body to which it is attached. And although I imagined the heaviness to be dispersed throughout the whole of the body which is heavy, yet I did not attribute to it that extension which constitutes the nature of body, for the true extension of body is such as to exclude all penetrability of its parts; but I thought that the same amount of heaviness which is in a piece of wood of ten feet was in a lump of gold or some other metal of one foot – indeed, I judged that it could all be contracted into a mathematical point. And even while it remained coextended with the heavy body, I saw that it was able to exert its whole force in each of its parts, because if that body were suspended from a rope by any of its parts, it would still pull the rope with its whole heaviness, in just the same way as if that heaviness were only in the part which touched the rope, and were not dispersed throughout the other parts. And indeed I now understand the mind to be coextended with the body in no other way, both whole in the whole, and whole in each of its parts. But it is especially apparent that that idea of heaviness was taken from the idea which I had of the mind, from the fact that I thought that heaviness drew bodies down toward the center of the earth, as if it contained in itself some knowledge of this goal. And yet I also attributed some things to heaviness which could not be understood of a mind in the same way, such as, that it was divisible, measurable, and so on. (Pp. 441–2)

Heaviness is a "real" quality for the scholastics, i.e. it is a real being present in and really distinct from the body it qualifies;[36] it is supposed to be coextended with the body and divisible along with it; it also has some properties that other qualities may not, namely teleological activity and (as Descartes ingeniously argues) *sumpatheia* of its parts dispersed through the parts of the body. It is thus very much like a Stoic *pneuma*. Of course, the scholastics do not *say* that heaviness is a body, but Descartes thinks that in making it extended they are attributing to it a property that can belong only to bodies; at the same time, they attribute to it other properties, such as total mixture, that can belong only to incorporeals (since "the true extension of body is such as to exclude all penetrability of its parts"). Descartes thus explains the origin of the scholastic conceptions of real qualities and substantial forms in much the same way that Plotinus explains the origin of the Stoic conceptions of qualities and souls (and so on): the Stoic or scholastic philosophers have been able to rise above their senses enough to catch a glimpse of a something incorporeal, but not enough to fix their gaze upon it; so they fill out their conception of what they have seen with sensory images appropriate only to corporeal things. Thus the Stoic and scholastic conceptions of quality are exposed as the result of a confusion of corporeal with incorporeal things, which cannot really apply to either; it is almost irrelevant whether the opponent *says* that qualities (and so on) are corporeal or incorporeal.

---

[36] On the meaning of "real" quality, and generally on the scholastic doctrine of qualities and their connections with substances and quantities, see the brief discussion in the preceding section, and the fuller discussion in "The Greatest Stumbling Block."

But there is a crucial difference between Plotinus' criticism of the Stoics and Descartes' of the scholastics. For Plotinus, there are several degrees of incorporeals present to bodies, some (like qualities) closer to bodies and more divided, others (like souls) more unified and separable; the Stoics misrepresent all these realities as *pneumata*, and the task of the Platonist philosopher is to lead each of them back to its proper position in the hierarchy of incorporeals. Descartes takes a radically different attitude toward the nicely distinguished degrees of reality above bodies and below the rational soul: while Plotinus wants to restore each of them to its proper place, Descartes wants to abolish them *in toto*. (Had Descartes been aware of Plotinus' doctrine of quality, he would have treated it in much the same way that he treats the scholastic doctrine.) Descartes, like Plotinus, thinks that his opponents' conceptions of qualities (and so on) result from confusing a true idea of body with a true idea of something incorporeal; but for Descartes, the only true idea of an incorporeal (inferior to God) is the idea of *mind*: certainly the ideas of body, mind, and God are the only clear simple ideas that have been uncovered in the process of meditation. Indeed, immediately after the passage just cited, Descartes says that "after I had sufficiently considered these things, and accurately distinguished the idea of the mind from the ideas of body and corporeal motion," he was able to grasp that "all the other ideas that I had previously had of real qualities or substantial forms had been conflated and fashioned by me" out of these primitive ideas of mind and body (AT VII,442–3).

Descartes concludes, not merely that any real qualities truly existing in nature would be incorporeal, but that they would be *minds* or rational souls. The result is that Descartes' challenge to scholastic physics is much more radical than Plotinus' challenge to the Stoics. Plotinus says to the Stoics: "you say that all bodies have certain qualities intermixed with them; so no doubt they do; but if so, then these qualities must be incorporeal." Descartes says instead to the scholastics: "you say that all bodies have real qualities and forms intermixed with their matter; but if so, then these qualities and forms must be minds; since it is absurd to attribute minds to all the bodies in the universe, we must deny that these bodies have such forms or qualities, and affirm instead that they are nothing but matter."

Descartes does not conclude that there are *no* real qualities or substantial forms: the mind is "the true substantial form of man" (AT III,505), but it is "the *only* substantial form, while the other [forms that have been taken to be substances] consist in the configuration and motion of the parts" (AT III,503). Descartes also allows (in the long passage quoted above) that "the mind too, even if it is really a substance, can nonetheless be called a quality of the body to which it is attached," but once again all *other* qualities of body consist in figure and motion, and are not really distinct from the matter. Descartes can accept the formula that there are no substantial forms, but only in a restricted sense: "by the name 'substantial form,' when we deny it, is understood a certain substance adjoined to matter, and composing with it some merely corporeal whole, and which is a true substance (or thing subsisting by itself) not less but rather more than matter, since it is said to be *act*, while matter is only *potency*" (AT III,502). Such a "substance or substantial form, diverse from matter, in merely corporeal things" (ibid.), Descartes entirely denies. The human mind is an immaterial substance adjoined to matter, but the whole it composes with matter is not "merely corporeal"; since matter constitutes the whole essence of body, the mind is not a *constituent* of the human body, but something superadded to it. The scholastic error is not to believe that there are substantial forms, but to believe that there are forms (substantial or accidental) superior to matter but inferior to mind, and that they enter into the constitution of bodies. The scholastics fall into this error by confusing the ideas of mind and body; when, through the meditative process, we have learned to sort out the distinct ideas of body and of mind, we can recognize that our old beliefs arose from confusing them, and through this recognition our old beliefs will lose their attraction.[37]

The scholastic belief in real forms, at least in real accidental forms of the sensible qualities, comes from overestimating the value of the senses, i.e. from accepting them as theoretically valid representations of the nature of bodies. But Descartes agrees that there is *some* legitimate theoretical use of the senses. The practical validity of the senses must have *some* basis in bodies: reality cannot be a Parmenidean One. Apart from the metaphysical difficulty of supposing that a single uniform cause could give rise to effects as diverse as the variety of sense impressions we receive, the senses could not be providing useful practical guidance for preserving the mind–body union, if the bodies which cause our different sensations were themselves all alike. If sensation is truly to guide us in choosing what to pursue and what to flee, then

I rightly conclude, from the fact that I sense very diverse colors, sounds, smells, tastes, heat, hardness, and the like, that there are, in the bodies from which these varied perceptions of the senses come, variations *corresponding* to these, even if perhaps not *similar* to them; and from the fact that some of these perceptions are pleasing to me, and others displeasing, it is plainly certain that my body, or rather all of me insofar as I am composed of mind and body, can receive various advantages and disadvantages from the surrounding bodies. (Sixth Meditation, AT VII,81)

Although we cannot give our senses a *direct* theoretical use in representing corporeal reality, as we could if the variations in bodies were *similar* to

[37] The credit is Gilson's, in the chapters "De la critique des formes substantielles au doute méthodique" and "Anthropologie thomiste et anthropologie cartésienne" of his *Etudes sur le rôle de la pensée médiévale dans la formation du système cartésien*, for having pointed out the importance of this letter to Regius, and of the passage from the sixth Replies, for understanding Descartes' attitude toward hylomorphism. Gilson's work has made it unnecessary to refute further the suggestion that Descartes does not really believe what he is telling Regius.

the variations in the ideas they produce, we can give them an *indirect* theoretical use, by reflecting on their practical function in guiding our reactions to the surrounding bodies, and observing what this practical function presupposes about the bodies themselves. What it presupposes is that there are variations in the bodies *corresponding* to the varieties of our sensory ideas, in something like the set-theoretic sense of "correspondence." Some bodies produce in me the sensation of pleasure, while others produce the sensation of pain; nature teaches me to pursue the former and flee the latter. Since what nature teaches is for my preservation, there must be some intrinsic difference in the bodies themselves, which explains why the pleasure-inducing bodies tend to preserve the mind–body composite, and the pain-inducing bodies tend to destroy it. This difference in the bodies will be sufficient to explain why nature gives me a sensation of pleasure in the presence of the first kind of body, and a sensation of pain in the presence of the second: there is no need for the intrinsic attribute of the pleasure-inducing bodies to be anything like pleasure.

Descartes' scholastic opponents would accept this analysis in the case of pleasure and other passions; but Descartes, taking the passions as a model, extends the analysis to all the ideas of sensation. Take any two distinguishable sensory ideas, say the ideas of orange and black, which are aroused in us on different occasions; if this distinction is to serve in guiding our actions toward the preservation of our composite nature, there must be some intrinsic difference between the situations in which we perceive orange and the situations in which we perceive black. Perhaps this difference is not intrinsic to the orange-inducing or black-inducing *bodies*, but only to the *configurations* in which we perceive orange or black: it may depend not only on the internal structure of the body we perceive as black or orange, but also on the surrounding bodies (light sources and medium), and on the internal state of our own bodies. But however this may be, we know by reflection on the practical reliability of our nature that there must be at least as many varieties of geometrical configurations in the bodies around us as there are varieties of our sensory ideas, and that these geometrical configurations are mapped onto our ideas in a lawlike fashion, so that geometrically indiscernible configurations produce sensibly indiscernible ideas. There is no need for the varieties of bodies to resemble our ideas. Our nature inclines us to flee when we perceive a certain pattern of orange and black, and recognize it as a tiger; this inclination could not help to preserve us if the geometrical configuration constitutive of tigers did not involve two different kinds of surface region, one of which might produce the sensation of black and one the sensation of orange; but our preservation does not depend on knowing what structures in the fur are responsible for these sensations. In establishing our nature, God instituted laws connecting certain configurations in our environment with the vivid presence of certain sensory ideas to our mind: these connections had to be lawlike and universal in order to serve their function, but God had to choose arbitrarily which type of configuration would be universally linked

376

with orange and which with black. God did not implant the knowledge of these arbitrary connections either in our intellect or in our sensory faculties; it will be the task of the intellect, passing judgment on the sensory faculties, to construct a system of physical and psychological science sufficient to find them out.

This is much like the task laid out in Rule 12; but now Descartes can presuppose an account of the mind, the body, and their relations in the composite, established from first principles without the need of any physical hypothesis. The very end of the *Meditations* gives a rapid sketch of how the intellect should use the senses to discover truths about bodies. Descartes uses his understanding of mind and body, first, to explain why the senses do not give us complete information about the configuration of bodies; second, to explain why the senses on some occasions fall into "error" (that is, why the normal correlations between our ideas and the configurations of external bodies sometimes fail); and third, to indicate (in very crude and general terms) how we can correct the "errors" of the senses, and so use the senses to build up a science of nature.

The Meditator recognizes that the mind is indivisible and the body divisible. The mind is present to the whole of its body, whole in the whole and whole in each of the parts; but it is specially united to one particular part of the body, namely "the brain, or perhaps only one small part of it, namely that in which the common sense is said to be" (AT VII,86), in such a way that the configuration of this particular part of the body immediately determines what idea is presented to the mind, as, conversely, the mind's volition immediately determines the configuration of this part of the body. Thus "however many times this [part of the body] is disposed in the same way, it exhibits the same thing to the mind, even while the other parts of the body may be disposed in diverse ways" (ibid.). Descartes goes on to describe how motion is communicated to this region from the distant parts of the human body, through nerves stretched out like cords between the extremities and the brain. When the part of the cord which reaches the brain receives the type of motion that it would naturally receive from an impulse in the extremity, nature presents to the mind the idea of pain or of some other appropriate sensation in this extremity.

This is essentially the same account of sensation that was proposed hypothetically in Rule 12. But now that the mechanical nature of body and the incorporeality of the intellect have been established unhypothetically, Descartes can readdress the question of Rule 12 about the capacity of the sensory faculties. He can explain why the senses do not give a complete report of the physical world, or even of bodies close to us: although sensation is not *about* the brain, it is only the conditions of (some special organ in) the brain which are naturally linked with sensations, so that information is lost between the external objects of sensation and what the senses perceive. It is therefore up to the intellect, making proper use of the senses, to reconstruct the inner structure of the external causes of sensation. Descartes can also explain what principles the intellect must use to detect and correct the errors of the senses. For "if, in the cord *ABCD*, its furthest part *D* is moved, the first part *A* will be moved in just the same way as if one of the intermediate parts *B* or *C* were pulled, while the furthest part *D* remained unmoved" (AT VII,86–7). Thus

> since the nerves must pass through the shin, the thigh, the loins, the back, and the neck in order to arrive at the brain from the foot, it can happen that, even if the part of the nerves which is in the foot is not touched, but only some one of the intermediate parts, exactly the same motion will occur in the brain as occurs when the foot is harmed, from which it necessarily follows that the mind will feel the same pain. And we must think the same about every other sense. (P. 87)

Since information is lost through the mechanical transmission of motion, nature can assign only one sensation to a motion in the brain which might follow either from a motion in the foot or from other motions in the intermediate regions of the nerves; since nature is given for our preservation, it assigns that sensation which is "most and most frequently conducive to the preservation of a healthy man" (ibid.), that is, the sensation which would be appropriate if the motion in the brain were caused by the condition which would most frequently produce it, as here a motion at the extremity of the nervous cord. On the relatively rare occasions when the motion is produced by some other condition of the body, a sensation will result which is *not* the most conducive to our preservation, and which will be, in that sense, an error.

This consideration is supposed to help us "not only to recognize all the errors to which my nature is liable, but also to correct or avoid them with ease" (p. 89). Descartes' advice is unsurprising: we should examine each thing by as many different senses as possible, and then compare the data with the known results of memory and understanding. But there is a new justification for this advice, "since I know that all the senses indicate truth much more often than falsehood *about those things which concern the advantage of the body*" (ibid.; my emphasis). The voice of "healthy common sense" in the first Meditation had also assumed that the senses would tell the truth for the most part, making small errors or errors about small or distant objects, or temporary errors in abnormal circumstances, so that the agreement of the different senses (at one time and over time) would be a safe criterion of truth. "Healthy common sense" goes wrong, because it supposes that the agreement of the senses will reveal the truth, not only about the advantage of our body, but also about the nature of external things; the Meditator of the sixth Meditation recognizes that irrational natural powers cannot reveal the nature of things, but he also recognizes the genuine function of our nature. Waking has no direct *cognitive* superiority over sleeping, or normal over abnormally functioning sense organs; but the condition that our senses are in for most of the time is *practically* superior, and so we can use it to learn the truth at least about what will preserve the mind–body union.

The Meditator thus finally resolves the doubts raised by the sceptical hypotheses of the first Meditation. Perhaps (it was said) I am dreaming, and none of the things which appear to me are as they seem to be; perhaps I am the creature of a deceiving God or evil demon, so that I *think* I perceive most clearly things which in fact are obscure and false; perhaps I am the product of fate, chance, or a connected series of events, so that the occurrence of ideas in me is unrelated to the truth of the things they purport to represent. The fundamental doubt raised by these hypotheses lingers even after the hypotheses are refuted (as the second and third hypotheses are refuted in the third Meditation): even after I know where *I* come from, the worry remains that (at least some of) my *thoughts* may be determined by an irrational "nature," and may thus be incapable of attaining the truth.

Nature is indeed less than rational, and it has some influence on our thoughts. But, as Descartes argues in the fourth Meditation, our assent to clear ideas is not determined by any irrational influence of nature, and comes directly from God through the natural light: once we have the knowledge of God as Nous and as our creator, there is no ground for doubt about the ideas we perceive so clearly that we cannot withhold assent. But in the sixth Meditation Descartes is concerned with the ideas of sensation, which have no discernible objective content, and are not given to us for theoretical use: the will can and should exercise its freedom from irrational influences by refusing to judge that there are things really resembling these ideas. So the doubts of the first Meditation seem to remain in force for these ideas.

The doubts are resolved by reflecting on the practical uses of the senses. Here the will should not withhold its assent: we have no other guide to put in place of nature. But now we know that this nature is not an autonomous reality, a system of fated laws or random processes, which might be represented by an evil demon: it is what the mind–body composite receives from God. It therefore inclines us toward truth essentially and for the most part; it inclines us toward error only by accident, either when the will wrongly puts it to a theoretical use, or when some mechanical interference frustrates the practical intention of nature. The origin of error in theoretical matters lies in the soul and not in its God; in practical matters it is mechanical and not demonic. In making the initial separation from the senses, Descartes puts forward the hypothesis that nature is anti-rational and governed by a counter-God; now, returning from the intellect to the senses, he discovers that it is the last production of God, and that its errors proceed only from the inevitable limitations of divisible matter. So the sixth Meditation ratifies theoretically at least some of the practical maxims (e.g. eating between meditations) which the Meditator had accepted provisionally during the meditative process. Once we have isolated the genuine voice of nature, we can have no better rule than to act as it teaches; and on most occasions it will truly have picked out the best course of action. If we are deceived, it will not be systematically; since the faculties are generally reliable, we can use them to correct one another, and follow the most consistent reports of our faculties without fear of being led further astray. By checking the senses against each other, and against the results of intellect and memory, we can find the truth about matters of practical concern, so far as human finitude allows; by reflecting on the theoretical presuppositions of this practical ability, we can work toward deciphering the true configurations of bodies.

D. The laws of motion

For Descartes to reach the knowledge of bodies by the downward way, and so to deliver on his promise of a scientific wisdom, he needs not only to give directions for decoding the patterns of motion underlying sensible phenomena, but also to set out intellectually grounded laws of motion, or rules according to which one pattern of motion succeeds another.[38] Indeed, he needs to do this even in order to decode sensible qualities: for the only way to discover the structure of the sensibly qualified body is to determine how it produces some effect on our sense organs, and it produces its effect on our sense organs only according to the laws of motion. Once Descartes has the laws of motion, he can proceed to show, first, how matter moving by these laws gives rise to the structures of the physical universe, and then also how these physical structures (i.e. these patterns of motion) explain what we perceive through the senses. The *Principles of Philosophy* carries out this plan, in an incomplete and provisional way: after establishing the laws of motion in Part Two, Descartes uses these principles in Parts Three and Four to "describe this earth, and this whole visible world, on the likeness of a machine, considering in it nothing beyond shapes and motions" (IV:188); then at the end of Part Four, since "our senses display many other things to us, namely colors, smells, sounds, and the like" (ibid.), Descartes borrows ahead, from his unfinished work on animal and human physiology (what would have been the fifth and sixth parts of the *Principles*), enough material at least to suggest how these motions in the bodies that surround us, and in our own bodies, can produce our sensations through the mind–body union.

The discovery of the laws of motion is thus a crucial test for Descartes' philosophy, deciding whether he can move beyond metaphysical principles, and beyond the knowledge of mathematical essences, to a science of actually existing bodies. It is not obvious that the principles Descartes has established are sufficient for the task. The difficulty here is very much like the difficulty Descartes had confronted in Rule 8 of the *Rules for the Direction of the Mind*, in the problem of finding the anaclastic line, the

---

[38] This section overlaps with my article "Descartes and Some Predecessors on the Divine Conservation of Motion," *Synthese*, 83 (May 1990). I make many of the same points there as here; but I give a fuller discussion there especially of the Aristotelian and Platonist prehistory of the doctrine of the conservation of motion.

curve through which parallel incoming light rays would be refracted to focus on a single point. The mathematician may reduce this to the problem of determining the relation between the angle of incidence and the angle of refraction; but the mathematician cannot solve this more basic problem, since many different laws of refraction are, from a purely mathematical standpoint, equally intelligible. To solve the problem, we must know "how a ray penetrates a transparent whole," which depends on understanding "the nature of illumination," which must ultimately rest on a simple intuition of "what a natural power is in general" – an intuition which must be drawn from something other than mathematics. Likewise, in Part Two of the *Principles*, Descartes must investigate the laws which relate the motions of bodies at one instant to the motions of bodies at the next, perhaps after some critical event such as a collision or a change of medium; thus in order to determine which of the many mathematically intelligible laws of motion is true, he must search outside of mathematics for some knowledge of the power which causes motion. Descartes takes up this challenge in the second half of Part Two of the *Principles*, where, as he says, "having considered the *nature* of motion, we must now consider its *cause*" (II:36).

This cause of motion, for the *Principles*, is just God, or God and the laws that proceed from him. The new knowledge that Descartes has in the *Principles*, that he did not have in the *Rules*, is precisely the intuition of God as Nous, and this must be used to solve the problem of the laws of motion. Descartes' strategy in *Principles* Part Two will be to argue *a priori* from Nous to the bodies it governs, and thus to derive laws of their motion. For Descartes, as for Augustine, the God who is the source of truth to the mind is equally the source of numerical order in bodies; to the extent that we know bodies as subject to God, we will know them as subject to mathematical laws. Indeed, after saying that God is the "universal and primary [cause of motion], which is the general cause of all the motions which there are in the world" (II:36), Descartes goes on to say that it is these very "rules or laws of nature" which are the "secondary and particular causes of the various motions which we notice in the individual bodies" (II:37). It is important to note the ontological status of these laws. Like "every order, every law, and every *ratio* of truth or goodness" (sixth Replies, cited above), they are dependent on God, and proceed from his free creation; even though they are neither substances nor things inhering in substances, and so not subsistent things at all, they possess enough reality that they can be causes of motion to individual bodies. Now, in discussing the "creation of the eternal truths," we noted the connection between the concept of an eternal truth and the concept of an *essence*. But the realm of eternal truths, of orders, laws, and *rationes* of truth or goodness, is broader than the realm of essences. Purely mathematical truths or laws about bodies will follow from the geometrical essence of body; but the fundamental laws of the motion of bodies are underdetermined by geometry, and so cannot be included in the essences of the bodies. These rules or laws of nature are not essences of the things in which they operate, but rather *substitute* for such essences. The scholastic physics, as Descartes understands it, derives the characteristic motions of the different species of bodies from active powers which are supposed to reside within the bodies, and to follow from the essences of the particular species of body. Descartes, by contrast, wishes to derive the motions of bodies not from arbitrary and irreducible essences within the things themselves, but rather from God as the source of intelligible order. Descartes is willing to say that bodies have their characteristic patterns of motion because they are governed by nature; but "nature" here must mean "nothing other than God himself, or the coordination of creatures which is instituted by God" (this is the "general" sense of "nature" from the sixth Meditation, cited above). God has not entrusted bodies with active powers whereby they could direct their own motions; rather, he reserves the direction of natural motions for himself, or for the laws which proceed from him. These laws allow Descartes to reduce body to extension without reducing physics to geometry; over and above the geometrical principles, they give him metaphysical principles from which a science of nature might proceed.

The controversial point is not Descartes' claim that God is the primary cause of all motion (all Christian philosophers would agree, though they might not find this a promising beginning for physics), but rather his further claim that even the *secondary* causes of motion are not subsistent created things, but only laws or *rationes* proceeding toward creatures from God. It seems that Descartes is in effect making God the *sole* cause of motion, that he is, like the Ashʿarite theologians of Islam, denying all efficacy to created things.[39]

This may not be too far wrong as a way of stating Descartes' conclusion. But Descartes is relying, not on a metaphysical argument that creatures *qua* creatures cannot necessitate, but on a physical argument that bodies *qua* bodies contain no active powers. It is instructive to compare Descartes' position with the traditional Platonist physics. Descartes knew and cared little about this physics; his Platonism is entirely mediated through Augustine. But what Descartes took from Augustine was the discipline Plotinus had used to produce an understanding of the Platonic principles of physical things, and thus a recognition that these principles are distinct and incorporeal. Augustine is interested, not in justifying Platonist physics, but only in understanding himself and God; and so he effectively discards all levels of the Platonic system of principles, except Nous and the rational soul. Descartes takes over from Augustine the discipline for conceiving the mind and God; but his attitude toward other incorporeal

---

[39] Some of Descartes' followers, most notably Malebranche, will take up the doctrine that God is the only genuine cause. In the fifteenth Elucidation to the *Search after Truth* Malebranche explicitly cites, as sharing his doctrine, the Muslim theologians attacked by Averroes, i.e. the Ashʿarites (*Oeuvres*, 1, p. 973).

principles is not benign neglect but active hostility. Descartes' doctrine that God is (with the necessary qualifications) the sole cause of motion in bodies follows directly from his elimination of the rest of the Platonic system of principles.

For the Platonists, as for Descartes, bodies are essentially inactive, and cannot cause motion in themselves or in other things.[40] The causes of motion in bodies must be incorporeal: they are either principles immanent in bodies (natures, qualities, powers, or material forms), or else souls, or else Nous as the primary cause of motion. But Descartes denies what he sees as the confused supposition that there are incorporeal principles subsisting in or constitutive of merely corporeal things: any incorporeal principle must subsist by itself, and the only incorporeal substances of which we have any idea are God as Nous, and rational souls like our own. It follows, not that the laws proceeding from God are the only particular causes of motion, but that these are the only particular causes which operate within merely corporeal things (causes which "are themselves corporeal," as Descartes puts it in an unfortunate but intelligible expression, *Principles* II:40); for "we are not yet inquiring whether and in what way human or angelic minds have a power to move bodies" (*Principles* II:40). Descartes defers this question to a treatise *On Man*, which he was never to finish; but it seems clear that he thought that finite minds did have powers to move bodies, and that the motions they produce in the bodies immediately united to them need not obey the same laws that *God* follows when he himself moves bodies.[41]

Since God, understood as Nous, is the cause of all purely physical motions, Descartes can argue *a priori* from the nature of the mover to the laws which govern the motions. Descartes is thus reversing the *a posteriori* procedure of the Platonic and Aristotelian tradition. Aristotle had argued in *Metaphysics* XII, from the eternally constant motion of the heavenly bodies, that they must be moved by some eternally constant mover, a mover which would not be itself subject to any variation or transition from potentiality into actuality (since otherwise its effect would be a variable motion), but must be, by its essence, entirely in actuality. The proper activity of this unmoved mover, according to Aristotle, is intellection [*noê-sis*]; and since it is essentially in actuality, it must be Nous in the strict

---

[40] Marsilio Ficino makes this point at the very beginning of the argument of his *Theologia Platonica de Immortalitate Animorum*: "since body, according to Plato, consists of matter and quantity; and to matter belong only being extended and being affected; and extension and affection are passions; and quantity is either nothing other than the extension of matter, or, if it is something else, is still something such that it is always subject to division and to all the passions consequent on matter, and does not bestow anything different on matter; it follows that body, inasmuch as it is body, does not act, but is only subject to passion" (this is the first sentence of Book I, chapter 2; cited from the edition Paris, 1559; repr. Hildesheim: Olms, 1975, p. 2).

[41] On finite minds as causes of motion, see Daniel Garber, *Descartes' Metaphysical Physics* (Chicago: University of Chicago Press: 1992), esp. pp. 276–7, as well as Garber's earlier papers there cited.

sense, the agent Nous which is identical with its intelligible object [*noêton*]. The Platonic tradition after Aristotle preserves the thesis that Nous is the primary mover of the heavens, and ultimately of all physical things; it also preserves Aristotle's argument that Nous, because it is invariable in itself, must produce a *constant* motion, and indeed that it is responsible for all constancy in the otherwise chaotic motions of bodies. But for the Platonists there are also many other sources of motion: Nous, rational and irrational souls, and the natures and qualities in bodies all cause motion in different ways. In the heavens, these causes all operate in harmony, and the motion they produce is rational and eternally constant, just because celestial soul and celestial nature are in accordance with Nous;[42] but in the sublunar realm, the many inferior movers will often operate contrary to Nous and to each other, and so produce inconstant and irrational motions. For this reason, the Platonic and Aristotelian tradition concludes that there is no hope of a precise mathematical science of sublunar motions. Descartes, however, has eliminated all the inferior powers which might resist the divine impulse toward rational motion: there are no "natures" or qualities or irrational souls immanent in bodies, and finite minds are sources of motion only in a small class of exceptional instances. Descartes can therefore reverse the argument of *Metaphysics* XII, and argue *a priori* from Nous as the mover to the constancy of all the motions that proceed from Nous, that is, of *all* natural motions, whether in heaven or earth.

In *Principles* II:36, where he introduces the doctrine of God as the universal cause of motion, Descartes says that "we understand this perfection to be in God, not only that he is immutable in himself, but also that he operates in the most constant and immutable manner [*modus*]." That God is immutable follows immediately from the fundamental understanding of God as the intelligible standard by which variations in the mind and other things are judged: God so conceived will be immutable not only in himself but also in his operations, whereas even those beings

---

[42] For details, see my "Descartes and Some Predecessors on the Divine Conservation of Motion." Let me repeat from that article a nice summary statement of the Platonist doctrine of Nous, soul, and nature as causes of the celestial motions, from Simplicius' commentary on the *De Caelo*: "if someone asks which local motion of the heaven comes from nature and which from soul, we say that soul, through the mediation of nature, makes the heaven move in a circle, and that it is one and the same motion. But it has from nature the connatural and unforced disposition, according to its very form, for being moved; while from soul it has the actuality of the motion toward which it was disposed by nature [i.e. circular rather than linear motion]. So, too, it has from Nous its turning always and in the same way and according to the same [direction] and about the same [center] and in the same [place] [this is an expansion of *Timaeus* 34a]. For by these things, under the leadership of Nous, the psychic motion which is impressed through nature in bodies is constituted, and stabilized in the likeness of the activity of Nous. Whence also that divine man, having asked why the heaven moves in a circle, says that it is because it imitates Nous [the reference is to the opening sentences of Plotinus II,2, *On the Motion of the Heaven,* which in turn are explicating *Timaeus* 34a]" (*In De Caelo Commentaria,* ed. I. L. Heiberg, in *Commentaria in Aristotelem Graeca* (Berlin: Reimer, 1882–1909), 7 (1894), p. 382).

created in God's own likeness (like the human mind), although they may be immutable in their substance, are variable in their operations and can be more or less in accord with the divine standard. "From this same immutability of God, certain rules or laws of nature can be known, which are the secondary and particular causes of the various motions which we notice in particular bodies" (beginning of II:37). Here Descartes relies on his claim that the laws or truths which God establishes are eternal and immutable, because proceeding from God's immutable will. Thus at the end of *Principles* II:36, Descartes says that it follows from God's immutability that

it is most in accordance with reason that we should think from this alone, that God moved the parts of matter in various ways when he first created them, and now preserves the whole of this matter in entirely the same manner [*modus*] and the same *ratio* in which he first created it, that he also preserves in it the same amount of motion.

It is not obvious from this passage what Descartes means by *modus* and *ratio*; but in a parallel passage in II:42, he says that God preserves the totality of motion "by preserving [the world] by the same action and with the same laws with which he created it." This action and these laws must be the same as the *modus* and the *ratio* of II:36: all these words refer to the laws which proceed from God toward bodies, and which immediately direct those bodies' motion. Because we conceive God as Nous, we conceive him as immutable in the strictest sense: we are explicating this, or noting the consequences, when we say that his action or the laws proceeding from his action are constant. Because this action or these laws are the immediate causes of natural motions in bodies, we infer that the natural motions are constant.

Descartes' thesis, unlike Aristotle's, is universal, applying indifferently to celestial or sublunar motions. It is easy to see why Aristotle limits himself to celestial motions, harder to see how Descartes means to account for sublunar phenomena. Aristotle, on the upward way, may either observe or argue *a posteriori* that there is a single primary motion, the eternally uniform circular motion of the heavens (or at least of the outermost heaven); he then argues from this motion to Nous as its mover, without implying that Nous is also the mover of sublunar things. On the downward way, Aristotle finds it reasonable that Nous should produce a single motion in the heavens, a motion which is constant because its mover is unmoved, and that the heavens themselves should produce motions in sublunar things, motions which are variable because their movers are moved. Sublunar motions are not constant and cannot be constant, because they are not circular: sublunar bodies move along straight lines between the heavens and the center, and their motions thus reach a natural limit, beyond which they cannot continue without change. The circular motions of the heavens are intelligible and mathematizable because they are a direct imitation of Nous; sublunar motions are only imperfectly intelligible to the extent that, under the influence of the heavenly bodies, they follow a roughly cyclical pattern of ascent, descent, alteration, transmutation, and combination. There would thus be little or no hope of a mathematical physics of sublunar things.

Descartes wishes to argue that the constancy of motion which proceeds from Nous occurs not only where it is empirically observed, in the heavens, but also here on earth; he wishes to construct, on this basis, a mathematical physics of sublunar things, or rather a general mathematical physics which will apply equally to the celestial and to the sublunar case. Against the Aristotelian and Platonic tradition, Descartes refuses to admit either that there are fundamentally different principles governing two different kinds of bodies, or that the same principles apply perfectly in one case and only approximately in the other: the whole physical world is composed of a single intelligible nature, and all its operations must arise from a single law of motion, applied in highly complex configurations of matter. By deriving this first law of motion and working out its consequences, Descartes hopes ultimately to explain the apparent complexity and inconstancy of terrestrial motions, and thus to reveal "even this continual mutation of creatures" as an "argument for the immutability of God" (II:42).[43]

For Aristotle, the only motion that is constant by nature is the circular motion of the heavenly bodies; since we see that sublunar bodies have characteristic (or "natural") motions of rising and falling, motions which cannot continue indefinitely, Aristotle infers that these motions are naturally transient, exhausting themselves when the body reaches its natural place. For Descartes, this is a fundamental error, born of a naive trust in our senses, and contrary to the true laws of nature as they proceed from God:

because we dwell here about the earth, whose constitution is such that all the motions which come to be near it are quickly stopped, and often for causes which lie hidden from our senses, therefore from the beginning of our lives we have often judged that those motions which were thus stopped by causes unknown to us ceased of their own accord. And we are now inclined to judge about all motions what we seem to have observed in many motions, namely that of their own nature they cease, or tend toward rest. Which is in truth most opposed to the laws of nature: for rest is the contrary of motion, and nothing can be borne of its own nature toward its contrary or toward its own destruction. (II:37)

For Descartes, to say that a motion does something "of its own nature" is to say that this follows from the divine action by which the motion is constituted: since that divine action is constant, all motion (and indeed everything else which God produces) tends of its own nature to remain constant, and not to change or cease.

---

[43] "*Argumentum*" here means something like material evidence, or a demonstration in the sense of a display of power, not evidence or demonstration in the logical sense: Descartes is not involved in a vicious circle.

But it is of course impossible for all motions to remain constant in a plenum of bodies moving in different directions: since no body can continue its motion indefinitely in the same direction without colliding with some other body, its motion must change or stop in the collision, if it has not changed direction before. For Aristotle, this is sufficient reason to conclude that *linear* motion cannot be constant by nature, and that the primary constant motion proceeding directly from God must be a *circular* motion. Descartes must reject this conclusion, both because it would restrict the primary motion to only one portion of the physical universe, and also because Descartes' purely intelligible principles of natural things could not give rise to a primitive circular motion: since the geometrical essence of body is uniform everywhere, with no specially marked center or direction, and since God's nature as Nous does not favor any particular center or direction, the primitive motion proceeding from God to bodies cannot be an Aristotelian natural motion "around the center," any more than it could be "toward the center" or "away from the center." Descartes concludes, against the Aristotelian and Platonic tradition, that the primary motion is a *linear* motion, and that a body tends of its own nature to persist in uniform *linear* motion; since bodies do not *actually* persist in uniform linear motion, either in the heavens or on earth, Descartes has the task of explaining how the uniform divine impulse to motion, applied in complex situations of matter, produces as its byproducts the deviations from uniform linearity that we always observe.[44]

We must distinguish the law of the constancy of motion, which Descartes insists must *always* be observed, from the specific tendency of *linear* motion to persist in the same direction, which can be overridden in collisions. But Descartes thinks that the primacy and persistence of linear motion are an immediate consequence of the "immutability and simplicity of the operation by which God preserves motion in matter":

for he does not preserve it except precisely as it is at that moment of time at which he conserves it, with no regard to what it may have been shortly before. And although no motion takes place in an instant, it is still plain that everything which is moved, in the individual instants which can be designated while it is being moved, is determined to continue its motion in some direction, according to a straight line, and not according to any curved line. (*Principles* II:39)

Here Descartes does not elaborate his *a priori* argument, instead confirming his claim *a posteriori*, from observations of centrifugal force in con-

---

[44] Descartes in fact agrees with the Platonists and Aristotelians that, since the world is a plenum, the *actual* motions of bodies must be at least roughly circular; and Descartes explains the observed motions of the heavenly bodies (and other phenomena as well) by appeal to the circular motions of "vortices." But the circular motion is not "natural" or primitive, and must be explained by the deflection of motions from their "natural" linear path; indeed, many of Descartes' detailed physical explanations depend essentially on the tension between the actual (constrained) circular motion of bodies and their continuing tendencies to linear motion.

strained circular motions. But in a parallel passage of *Le monde*, Descartes is more explicit in arguing for God's preservation of specifically rectilinear motion. A body is determined at any instant toward rectilinear motion, Descartes says, because this motion is *simple*:

Of all motions it is only the straight which is entirely simple, and whose whole nature is comprehended in an instant. For, to conceive it, it suffices to think that a body is in the act of moving in a certain direction, which occurs in each of the instants which can be determined while it is moving; whereas to conceive a circular motion, or whatever other motion it may be, it is necessary to consider at least two of its instants, or rather two of its parts, and the relation between them. (AT XI,44–5)

To some extent, Descartes' statement reflects a truth of geometry: it takes fewer parameters to specify a rectilinear motion than to specify (say) a circular motion, so that God, like a human geometer, can "produce" or continue a rectilinear motion without referring to as much information about the history of the motion as he would need to continue a circular motion. But there is no purely geometrical reason why the position and (in modern terms) the first derivative of the position of a body should be said to be contained in an instant, while the second derivative should not. Descartes' point is that, for a body to continue in motion, God must supply it at each instant with an inclination to move, and this inclination will give (as we would say) the first derivative of the position. At each instant, God preserves what he has put in the body at that instant, which is just this inclination to move, not to move linearly or circularly or in any other determinate way; preserving this inclination in its simplicity, without variation, God produces a uniform linear motion. Any curving to the left or right would be extraneous to the nature of the inclination, and would require God to add something new, contradicting the simplicity of God's operation. Thus Descartes concludes that

according to this rule, one must say that God alone is the author of all the motions which exist in the world, inasmuch as they exist and inasmuch as they are straight, but that it is the various dispositions of matter which render them irregular and curved; just as the theologians teach us that God is also the author of all our actions, inasmuch as they exist and inasmuch as they have some goodness, but that it is the various dispositions of our wills which can render them vicious. (AT XI,46–7)

So the dispositions of matter are responsible for deviations from linearity in motion, as our wills are responsible for the sins and errors in our actions and judgments; the deviations from linearity, like the sins and errors, are not properly beings, and so need not and cannot proceed from God. The parallel seems very close with Augustine's explanation of the soul's deviation from Truth, or with the Platonist account of the deviation of sublunar motions from the circular motion in imitation of Nous. But for Descartes the deviation of bodily motions from linearity cannot be perfectly analogous to the mind's deviation from truth, since the mind has the liberty to *resist* the causality of Nous, and Cartesian bodies do not. Indeed, if any bodies *could* resist the causality of Nous, then Descartes would have to conclude, with the Platonists, that there are no precise laws of these bodies' motion, or that the bodies can violate their laws as easily as we violate the moral law.

Descartes therefore tries to explain how the dispositions of matter can produce variations of motion, without positing any source of natural motion other than God, and without admitting any violation of the law of constancy of motion. So long as the linear motion of a body is unobstructed, God will preserve its motion by continuing its motion further along the same line; but if two bodies collide, their motions cannot continue along the same lines, but must change in some way. God continues, as always, to preserve the motion that he creates, but because of the situation of the bodies, some of the motion must be transferred from one body to another:

> since all things are full of bodies, and nonetheless the motion of each individual body tends in a straight line, it is clear that God from the beginning, in creating the world, not only moved the various parts of matter in various ways, but also at the same time brought it about that some of them would push others and transfer their motions to them: so that now, by preserving [the world] by the same action and under the same laws with which he first created it, he preserves motion, not always attached to the same parts of matter, but passing from some to others as they encounter one another. (*Principles* II:42)

What God produces, primarily, is just the continuing motion; if we consider precisely the *transfer* of motion, this will arise from the bodies themselves rather than from God. As Descartes had said in *Le monde*, from the mere fact that God conserves matter in the same manner in which he created it, "it follows of necessity that there must be many changes in its parts; and since it seems to me that these cannot be properly attributed to God's action, because this action is unchanging, I attribute them to nature" (AT XI,37). This "nature," as Descartes takes pains to make clear, is not "some goddess, or any other kind of imaginary power" (ibid.), nor indeed is it any autonomous agent, but simply the name under which we collect the consequences of God's action in matter. When God conserves the variously moving and colliding bodies, he conserves them "in the same manner" in which he created them, but not "in the same state"; "that is to say that, while God always acts in the same way, and consequently always produces *substantially* the same effect, there occur as it were *per accidens* many diversities in this effect" (AT XI,37-8). Certainly it is a traditional enough idea that of himself God produces a single uniform effect, and that the diversity arises from the side of creatures, receiving God's causality according to their different capacities; what is new is Descartes' insistence that bodies have neither powers to obey or resist God's causality, nor different natures to receive it in different ways, but that all the diversity must arise from a single law of motion, combined with itself in complicated ways, but not interacting with any other nature or power.

Descartes' universal mathematics was designed to study such complex consequences of simple natures. Once metaphysical principles have given a precise universal law of motion, supplying the need that Descartes recognizes in Rule 8, then mathematics should be able to derive the consequences for different physical situations. So Descartes tries to give a mathematically precise formulation of the universally valid law of conservation of motion. Since God always preserves the same total quantity of motion in matter, sometimes allowing this motion to be redirected or transferred from one portion of matter to another, there should be a numerical measure for the total quantity which must be conserved. With naive optimism, Descartes thinks that there is no difficulty in computing this quantity: for motion, he says,

has a certain and determinate quantity, which we easily understand might always be the same in the whole universe, though it may change in its individual parts. Thus we should reckon that when one part of matter is moved twice as quickly as another, and this other part is twice as large as the first, there is the same amount of motion in the smaller as in the larger; and that, however much the motion of one part comes to be slower, the motion of another part equal to it will come to be that much faster. (*Principles* II:36)

From this conserved quantity, and from the tendency of bodies to continue in uniform linear motion when the conditions of matter permit, Descartes tries to deduce rules by which he can determine "how individual bodies increase or diminish their motions, or turn in other directions, because of encounters with other bodies" (II:45). Proceeding from the simpler to the more complex, he starts by deriving a series of rules which would apply perfectly "if only two bodies encountered one another, and if they were perfectly solid, and separated [*divisa*] from all the rest in such a way that their motion would be neither hindered nor advanced by any surrounding bodies" (ibid.).[45] Since in fact "no bodies in the world can be separated in this way from all the rest, and usually none of those around us are entirely solid" (II:53), we must make complex deductions from these rules to describe the motions of actual bodies, just as we must make complex deductions from the principles of geometry to describe the shapes of actual bodies at rest. But Descartes is confident that it can be done, and the *Principles* represents a few first steps, and a sketch of many further steps, toward deriving the particular phenomena of nature from the fundamental laws of motion.

Because all natural phenomena are constituted by motion, and because all motion proceeds from God, the knowledge of God as Nous opens the

---

[45] Bodies might be "separated" in this way from all other bodies without entailing a vacuum, as long as they are immersed in an ambient matter which does not resist their motions. Although, as Descartes goes on to say, this is actually impossible, it is not *conceptually* impossible, as a vacuum would be for Descartes.

way to a scientific physics, beyond what "someone who studies only mathematics" (Rule 8, AT X,393) can know about bodies. This allows Descartes to answer the challenge of Rule 8, without positing anything in bodies beyond extension and its modes, and without abandoning the intellectualism of the *Rules*, or the *Meditations'* insistence that God is the only criterion of truth. It is hard to exaggerate the radicalism this implies in Descartes' approach to physics. He was not content to remain in contemplating God, and has descended again from God to bodies, but he has descended to bodies without ever abandoning the God's-eye view. As we have said, Descartes takes God's *essential omniscience* as the key, both to God's nature, and to the possibility of our own knowledge of things other than God: the way that God, as agent intellect, knows the intelligible objects, is the model for our own knowledge of these same intelligibles. Of course, this does not mean that we can know them just as God knows them, by knowing ourselves and what proceeds from us; rather, we will know them by knowing God, and then knowing what proceeds from God, following the order of God's own knowledge. In a sense, this is a traditionally Platonist stance: for Plotinus too, Nous knows the intelligibles by containing them within itself, and we know the intelligibles by contemplating them as they exist in Nous. But for Descartes, the objects that Nous knows include actually existing bodies, and the laws that govern them and the motions and configurations that result from these laws: God knows these things, not because they exist within him, but because they are entirely determined by him. For Plotinus, by contrast, bodies are not *entirely* determined by Nous: Nous contains the intelligible standards that bodies *should* conform to, but actual bodies, and especially sublunar bodies, conform to these standards only imperfectly, since their matter is a source of indeterminacy and resistance to order. For Plotinus, therefore, actually existing bodies are not known by Nous, nor can they be known scientifically by us, nor would they be worth knowing. But Descartes has eliminated anything in bodies that could resist the causality of Nous, indeed he has eliminated any natures in bodies that could receive the causality of Nous in different characteristic ways; since bodies are entirely determined by Nous, they are perfectly known by Nous, and in principle we too can have perfectly precise scientific knowledge of them. Descartes no longer holds the impossible dream of achieving universal science through pure mathematics alone; but his mature vision of science is remarkably similar to that earlier project, and nearly as audacious.

Put another way: the inquiry of the *Meditations*, culminating in the deduction of the laws of motion in *Principles* Part II, is Descartes' mature way of carrying out the investigation promised in Rule 12, examining both our cognitive faculties and the nature of the simple objects which are to be known, and asking whether and how the faculties are adequate to comprehend these objects. For the mature Descartes, we can do this only if we have the knowledge of Nous, as the connecting link between the intellect in us and the intelligible objects outside us. If our soul were not

391

made in the image of God, but were enslaved to the irrational causality of nature, then we could not have scientific knowledge. Again, if the world of bodies were governed by an irrational nature, or if it contained a material principle that resisted the governance of Nous, or even if it were governed according to a radical plurality of "natures" or "eternal truths" independent of God, then we could not have scientific knowledge of this world of bodies. But by withdrawing from the senses, and understanding ourselves as potential reason, we catch a glimpse of the nature of Reason itself, and we can understand that this Reason actually exists and that we are made in its image. And by understanding the nature of this Reason, its essential omniscience and (in Descartes' terms) its "infinity," we see that its nature implies that everything else is entirely determined by it; that all truths and essences proceed from it and are eternally stable because they proceed from it; and that motion too proceeds from it and is eternally stable because it proceeds from it, that "even this continual mutation of creatures is an argument for the immutability of God" (*Principles* II:42). And that is why a science of bodies is possible.

9

Conclusion

Having explained, as far as in me lies, Descartes' presentation of Augustinian metaphysics and his derivation of the foundations of his physics, I would like to add some reflections on the questions that were my initial point of departure.

Part of my purpose was to answer Gilson's denial of an "*augustinisme de Descartes.*" It has become clear that there is such an Augustinianism, although it is Augustinianism of a peculiarly seventeenth-century variety: it is an attempt to develop from Augustinian principles a complete philosophy to replace that of Aristotle. Descartes applies Augustine's theodicy to construct rules of scientific method; he applies Augustine's concept of God as the source of mathematical regularity to derive the principles of a mechanical physics. But there remains a sense of mystery here, a feeling which perhaps underlay the negative judgments of Gilson and other scholars discussed in Chapter 1, and which no amount of historical work will dissipate entirely. To put the question baldly: how did it happen that an ancient Christian saint produced a metaphysics that could later serve this modern scientific function? I will try to address this lingering sense of mystery in what follows.

What Descartes took from Augustine was not, fundamentally, a set of metaphysical theses, but a *discipline* for approaching wisdom (the focus of our study of Augustine in Part One), and therefore also the series of intellectual intuitions produced by this discipline. Augustine was searching for wisdom even before he became a Christian; his Christian conversion was a decision to accept the practical guidance of Christian authority while he continued his search for the vision and enjoyment of God. Although faith in scriptural authority could provide a beginning, it would have to be developed into understanding in order to become wisdom. In trying to develop his faith into understanding, while Augustine follows some Christian precedents (notably Ambrose's allegorization of scripture), he makes central use of the discipline for contemplating the soul and God that Plotinus had developed in defense of Platonism. Surprisingly, the core of what Descartes will take from Augustine is this discipline that Augustine had himself taken from Plotinus; this makes it all the more mysterious how a discipline of such provenance could be useful for Descartes' scientific project.

The Platonic school-philosophy that Plotinus practiced contradicts Cartesian mechanist science on a wide range of topics. Had Descartes read

DESCARTES' METAPHYSICS

Plotinus for himself, he would have been disgusted with the defender of cosmic animation, and bewildered at the man who had on four occasions seen a God beyond being. Fortunately, Descartes did not read Plotinus: he read Augustine, or writers under Augustine's influence, and in such writers he would find the Plotinian discipline of contemplation presented in a Christianized and de-Platonized form. Augustine and Augustinians, as Christians attempting to satisfy a Christian expectation of wisdom, use the Plotinian discipline of contemplation to know themselves and their God; but they have no interest in defending the Platonist hierarchy of principles, and they leave the vitalist physics behind.

How then did Plotinus, working within the Platonist school-philosophy, develop an intellectual discipline that could be preserved, and applied to new problems, even by those who did not accept the Platonist system, and entirely rejected its physics? To put it negatively, Plotinus developed a way of conceiving soul and God that did not depend on the senses, and could therefore be preserved apart from any particular doctrine about the sensible world. Plotinus did this because he had to, if he was to argue effectively against Stoics and Stoicizing Platonists. It was, of course, a general Platonist expectation that we should be able to intuit soul and Nous and other intelligible principles of sensible things; but only the challenge of Stoic corporealism (as a claim, not only to truth, but to the interpretation of Plato's principles) forced the Platonists to recognize that they had not yet given an adequate path to knowledge of soul and Nous, and that they needed to provide some further discipline for grasping the essence of these principles, and so for recognizing them as incorporeal. Without granting that Platonism as a systematic philosophy was right, or even relatively in the right in its quarrel with Stoic corporealism, we can recognize that Plotinus made a positive contribution to knowledge in restating the claims of Platonism against the Stoics: for he was forced to *purify* the concepts of soul and Nous from the images or pictures that might support a corporealist interpretation of these principles. Thus when Plotinus argues that the soul is not a body or divided about the bodies, and that individual souls are not parts of the world-soul, he asks the soul to consider itself as essentially a thinking thing, and only accidentally the source of vital activities present within an organic body. Again, when he argues that the demiurgic Nous is prior to soul, he leads us to understand this Nous, not as a magnified rational soul animating the world, but as Reason itself, the standard according to which rational souls are rational. Plotinus remains committed to a vitalist physics, but his clarifications of the concepts of soul and Nous have a value separable from this vitalism.

Plotinus' discipline of contemplation could be useful for Augustine, and indirectly for Descartes, because both Augustine and Descartes, in their quite different intellectual situations, are trying to escape the constraints of some ideology that they see as bound to the senses, and believe that they can attain wisdom only through an intellectual intuition purified of sensory traces. Augustine wishes to know the true meanings of the divine

394

things described in scripture, and to overcome the Manichees' corporealist way of imagining God; Descartes wishes to grasp the intelligible first principles from which a scientific wisdom could be deduced, and to replace the sense-based principles of scholastic philosophy. The requirements imposed by the different situations of Plotinus, Augustine, and Descartes are close enough that the same discipline of contemplation, and the same intuitions of soul and Nous, can satisfy all of them.

Augustine, and then Descartes, progressively detach this Plotinian discipline of contemplation from the Platonist cosmology: we can see this most clearly in the fate of the world-soul. Plotinus had wanted to argue that our soul is related to the world-soul, not as a part subordinated to a whole, but as equal and even in a sense identical beings. To serve this argument, Plotinus gives us an understanding of soul from within. Augustine takes over this procedure, but once he has come to understand his own soul, and seen that it is not subordinated to a world-soul, he no longer cares whether there is a world-soul or not. In early writings Augustine occasionally asserts that there is a world-soul, but in later writings he retracts the assertion and professes agnosticism; what is noteworthy is how easily Augustine makes this shift, and how little difference it makes in his thought. Augustine's Christian commitment gives him a conception of divine freedom, which is his most important *addition* to Plotinus' philosophy; this facilitates the equally important *subtraction* of the world-soul, since God is free either to rationalize the world by means of a soul, or to impose a rational order himself without mediation. Most of Augustine's readers never notice that he believed at one time in a world-soul; certainly it is easy to discard the world-soul altogether in pursuing Augustinian lines of thought, and it was almost as easy for Descartes to discard all vital and non-rational functions of the soul, in appropriating the Plotinian and Augustinian metaphysics for the foundations of his physics.

We need, however, a more positive formulation of what Descartes could find useful in the Plotinian concepts of soul and Nous, beyond saying simply that these concepts do not depend on sensation. It helps to recall the expectations of knowledge that Plotinus' ascent to soul and Nous was designed to satisfy. All Platonists (before and after Plotinus) hope to achieve an intuitive knowledge of the intelligible principles of sensible things, where these principles are supposed to include soul and Nous as well as Platonic forms. Since first principles cannot be grasped either by sensation or by demonstration, we must begin with their effects among what immediately appears to us, that is, among sensible things, then somehow reason back to their intelligible causes: this process of reasoning back to first principles is traditionally called "analysis." The Platonists expect that, once such a process of analysis has brought us to awareness of the first principles, we will be able to grasp the principles directly, and not merely by inference from their effects. In learning what the principles must be like (and how they must be unlike the sensibles) for the appearances to be as they are, we will learn to distinguish the principles from

the sensible things that we had previously confused them with; and in removing this confusion we will remove the obstacles that prevented us from
intuiting the principles all along.[1]

The fact that the Platonists believed they could reason in this way, and
believed they *were* reasoning in this way, does not imply that they *did*
reason in this way. Being human, they tended to prove only as much as
the demands of a particular intellectual situation, and especially the challenges of their philosophical rivals, forced them to prove; and they tended
to believe that they had acquired more knowledge than they had actually
acquired, or could possibly have acquired by their methods. If Descartes
had read (say) the *Timaeus*, he would have protested, rightly, that Plato's
descriptions of the principles involve imaginative conceptions that are appropriate only to bodies, and not justified by reasoning to what the principles of bodies must be like (thus soul is described as extended, forms as
eternal but conspecific with sensible things). But the Platonists' ideal of
reasoning back to the principles, and of purifying the principles from assimilation to sensible things, helped them to criticize, and to try to im-
prove, arbitrary or inappropriate representations of intelligible things.
Plotinus' method of ascent, through the soul's reflection on its own rationality and so on its relation to Nous, is an attempt to realize the Platonists' shared ideal of analysis, provoked by his need to purify the
concepts of soul and Nous in his arguments against Stoics and Stoicizing
Platonists. If further purifications were necessary, if Plotinus' arguments
needed to be reexamined more critically to see what they did and did not
establish about the principles, this is only what we would expect.

Suppose Descartes is right that all human minds contain the pure intellectual concepts of soul and God, concepts that are usually not distinctly
present to our consciousness, but are implicitly involved in our ordinary
acts of judgment. We should then be able to become more directly aware
of these concepts by reflecting on what our ordinary judgments presuppose; and we should be able to distinguish the intellectual concepts of soul
and God (and any other purely intellectual concepts we have) more and
more clearly from the sense-based concepts with which we confuse them
in everyday life; and once we have isolated the purely intellectual concepts,
we should be able to use them to acquire a knowledge of soul and God
as they are in themselves, prior to their relations with sensible things. If

---

[1] Maybe the best reflective statement on this is in Augustine *De Trinitate* X, talking about
the mind's seeking knowledge of itself. Since nothing is more in the mind than the mind
itself is, the mind must always have known itself, but because of its love for sensible things,
the mind has never been present to itself without the accompaniment of sensible images:
"the disgrace of error comes upon it when it cannot separate [*secernere*] from itself the
images of the things it senses, so as to see itself alone: for they are marvelously stuck
together by the glue of love" (X,viii,11); "so let it not try to catch sight of itself [*se cernere*]
as if it were absent, but take care to distinguish itself [*se discernere*], since it is present; let
it not discover itself [*se cognoscat*] as if it did not yet know itself, but distinguish itself [*se
dinoscat*] from what it knows to be other than itself" (X,ix,12). These texts were partially
cited and discussed above, Chapter 6, Section A.

we are capable of acquiring knowledge in this way, there is no reason to think we should be able to do it quickly and perfectly. It is likely to be a difficult process of conceptual clarification, detachment from prejudice, and reflection on the presuppositions of our reasoning; we may think at several stages that we have reached the desired clarity and certainty, discovering only later that we are still caught in confusions, and that there is more work to be done. There is no reason to think that this process could be completed within the lifetime of any one individual. On the contrary, we would expect the history of metaphysics to make progress, slowly and unevenly, like the history of any other science: individuals at all stages, overestimating the power of their particular research programs, will make premature and grandiose claims of knowledge, but the science as a whole progresses through emulation, criticism, and refinement.

The history of Platonist metaphysics is a history of this kind; and Descartes is part of this history. If we distinguish narrow and broad senses of Platonism, we can say that Augustine and Descartes are Platonists in the broad sense. Platonism in the narrow sense was a specific school of philosophy, one of the four schools with an endowed chair at Athens, with definite and stubbornly defended answers on all the main questions of logic, ethics, physics, and metaphysics; this school became extinct in the sixth or seventh century AD, although it was revived to some extent by various figures of the Byzantine and Italian renaissances. The full doctrine of this school is incompatible with the revealed religions as normally understood, and even more clearly incompatible with any variety of modern science. But there is also a broader history of Platonism, the history of the uses and transformations of Platonism in the narrower sense; and these uses and transformations have brought Platonism into many different relations with the revealed religions, and with developments in the empirical sciences. Augustine and Descartes are Platonists in the broad sense because, desiring intellectual intuitions for their different purposes, they see in the Platonist discipline of analysis and its successive refinements the means to achieving their goal.

Descartes is an unlikely-looking Platonist. Those who have called him a Platonist in the past have intended an unhistorical assimilation between Descartes and Plato himself; they have not been looking at Plotinus or at Augustine's transformation of Plotinus, and so they have missed the really deep sense in which Descartes does belong to the history of Platonism. Descartes' ideal of mathematical physics seems poles apart from Plotinian Platonism. But it is precisely his goal of scientific construction that leads him to Augustine's version of Plotinus. When Descartes argues, against the humanists, that wisdom must consist in knowledge derived from rationally intuited principles, he is repeating the polemics of Socrates and Plato against the sophists, or of Augustine against the Academics; when he argues, against the scholastics, that these principles must be kept free from sensory contamination, he is repeating the polemics of Plotinus against the Stoics and of Augustine against the Manichees. The Platonist discipline of analysis, and more specifically the Plotinian and Augustinian discipline of ascent through soul to Nous, give Descartes the principles he needs to begin the synthetic construction of his science. Descartes' doctrine of body is radically un-Platonist in its denial of sensitive souls and other active powers, but it is strikingly similar to the Platonist doctrine of intelligible matter as intelligible extension. Unlike Plotinus or Augustine, Descartes is not satisfied with ascending to soul and Nous; he is serious about the goal of returning to construct a science of body. Descartes therefore promotes bodies to the intelligible realm, where they might become the objects of a science. Descartes agrees with the Platonists that the sensible is merely apparent, and that only the intelligible is really real; but Descartes makes bodies non-sensible and intelligible and real, leaving only the sensible qualities of bodies in the realm of the merely apparent. Descartes' science of body, for better or for worse, is the development of a Platonist ideal: he sets the tone when he begins his Meditation on the essence of body with an allusion to the Platonic doctrine of recollection.

The question of Descartes and Platonism, or of Descartes and Augustine, is bound up with larger questions about the history of philosophy: in asking how much remains constant, and how much changes, between the metaphysics of Plotinus or Augustine and the metaphysics of the *Meditations*, we are also asking about the degree of continuity between ancient and modern philosophy as such. I will not try here to sum up the results, for these larger questions, of hundreds of pages of study of Descartes. But I would like to add some reflections on views of the history of philosophy that see an essential break between Descartes and his predecessors.

Gilson had said that "even when the two philosophies [of Descartes and Augustine] employ the same concepts and arrange them in the same order, they do not mean the same things."[2] For Gilson, it is especially Descartes' (alleged) divergence from Augustine's doctrine of faith and reason that prevents him from sharing Augustine's true meaning; but beyond this, Gilson and many others think that there is something essentially *modern* underlying Descartes' whole project of thought, and that this modern orientation excludes any real community of intention between Cartesian and pre-modern metaphysics. Different writers characterize this element of modernity in different although not unrelated ways. Descartes may be modern because he rejects all merely plausible opinion and insists on reconstructing knowledge from the beginning; because he wants to construct a complete world view in accord with, and on the model of, the new mathematical physics; or because he studies the natures of things only as far as they are clearly present to our consciousness, and does not explore the ontological structure of our surroundings. All of these are said to be new with Descartes, and they are said to determine a new kind of philosophical project, which begins with the knowing subject as the thing most

---

[2] Gilson, "The Future of Augustinian Metaphysics," pp. 92–3; quoted above, Chapter 1.

accessible to itself, and then essays the problematic transition from subjectivity to objectivity. Gilson and Heidegger intend this description of
Descartes' project as a censure; Husserl and Brunschvicg and Gueroult
intend it as praise. But they all think that Descartes, by undertaking this
project, breaks with the naive realism of the past, and (as Gueroult puts
it) "ushers in the era of modern idealism."[3]

I can find no truth in any of this. Naturally, it is easy to regard Descartes' philosophy as a break from past traditions, if we avoid studying
and understanding those traditions;[4] but we have now come to recognize
some of the real ancient sources of Descartes' philosophical project. Descartes, like Plotinus and Augustine, wants to turn the mind's eye from
contemplating bodies to contemplating the mind itself, and then to contemplating God as Nous; but this is not a retreat from objectivity to
subjectivity, since God and the soul are at least as objective as bodies.
Descartes shares with Plotinus and Augustine the belief that God and the
rational soul and mathematical essences are perfectly clear in themselves,
and that, once we detach ourselves from our senses, we will recognize that
we know these intelligible things better than we know the sensibles, so
that the things that are most real (and most worthy of philosophical contemplation) will also be the things most clearly present to our minds. Of
course, Descartes pursues in a more radical way the consequences of the
thesis that God and the soul are better known than bodies; this is because,
as we have seen, Descartes is serious about the goal of returning, from
the ascent to soul and God, to construct a science of body. So Descartes
takes care to establish that the metaphysics is independent of any physics,
by showing that the metaphysical knowledge can be achieved even while
we suspend judgment about physical things; he also takes care to argue
that no knowledge of physical things can be established except through a
knowledge of God and the soul, and he isolates the intellectual idea of
God as the only way to knowledge of things outside the soul, by arguing
that this idea is cataleptic while ideas of physical things (as actually existing outside the soul) are not. We have seen why Descartes wanted to do
all this, and how he accomplished it; none of it involves any incommen-
surability between Descartes' "modern" metaphysical project and the
"pre-modern" projects of his predecessors. Descartes' scientific project
leads him to repeat critically the Plotinian and Augustinian method of
ascent or analysis, refining the concepts of soul and God to ensure their
independence of physical theory. But such a refinement is an inherent
possibility of the method of analysis; we cannot say that Descartes has

---

3 Gueroult, vol. 1, p. 3; quoted above, Chapter 1.

4 In the words of Gilson, "Nous ne nous dissimulons aucunement à quel point notre ar-
gumentation manque de force probante, étant donnée l'incuriosité générale où l'on est de
la pensée médiévale. Jamais la philosophie de Descartes ne s'insérera dans une tradition,
pour ceux qui suppriment cette tradition en l'ignorant" (*Etudes*, p. 293).

gone past refining the concepts to alter their fundamental meaning, or that his metaphysical method is itself something new. It is just this method and these concepts for which Descartes went back to Augustine.

Husserl says in his *Cartesian Meditations* that "Descartes had the serious will to free himself radically from prejudice; but we know from recent inquiries, in particular the fine and profound researches of M. Gilson and M. Koyré, how much scholasticism lies hidden, as unclarified prejudice, in Descartes' *Meditations*."[5] Husserl therefore consigns Descartes to the dustbin of history, along with his medieval precursors. But this is not the lesson Husserl ought to have drawn. There is nothing peculiarly Cartesian, or peculiarly modern, about the ambition to attain a knowledge free from prejudice; there is nothing irrational about drawing on the researches of earlier thinkers, repeating their reasoning critically, perhaps enabled by developments in other fields of knowledge to eliminate old errors or add new refinements. This is how science progresses. If Descartes drew on pre-modern thinkers, the lesson is not that Descartes was not really a modern; the lesson is that we have no reason to posit a separation between pre-modern and modern metaphysics.

The conclusions we have reached are to some extent anti-historicist, if historicism requires that a philosopher's thought be understood purely through its contemporary context and not through the thought of much older texts. Descartes' philosophical project was shaped by the intellectual culture of the seventeenth century, but one crucial feature of that culture was the hope of developing a new philosophy by recapturing and developing the thoughts in old texts; and, in pursuing that hope, Descartes does indeed take up thoughts from Augustine, just as much as he does from more contemporary writers. Our conclusions are also anti-historicist if historicism dictates that a metaphysics has meaning only in the context of a whole scientific system or world view, and therefore that two philosophies with radically different pictures of the natural world cannot share any metaphysical content. I have stressed throughout that physics is part of philosophy, and that it is crucial for understanding Descartes' philosophical project, and indeed also Plotinus'; but in studying historically the relations between physics and metaphysics, one thing we learn is that Plotinus' work, especially as taken up by Augustine, helped to make the Platonist metaphysics of soul and Nous independent of physical premises, and so allowed it to survive when the Platonist physics perished. These conclusions help to undermine the historicist reasons for positing a *coupure épistémologique* between Descartes' metaphysical thought and that of his predecessors. By the same token, they help to undermine the historicist reasons for positing such a break between Descartes' metaphysical thought and our own. So it is natural to ask whether Cartesian metaphysics remains open to us, and whether it remained open to philosophers between

---

[5] Edmund Husserl, *Cartesian Meditations*, tr. Dorion Cairns (The Hague: Nijhoff, 1960), pp. 23–4.

Descartes' day and ours, in the same way that Augustinian metaphysics was open to Descartes.

I think the answer is neither simply yes nor simply no. What chiefly discredited Cartesianism in the later seventeenth century was, of course, the swift and thorough destruction of Cartesian physics, and then the successes in physics of the alternative Newtonian model. Cartesian *philosophy* as a whole is certainly not a live option; and the failure of (say) Descartes' theory of light is a more serious embarrassment for Cartesian metaphysics than the failure of Augustine's theory of light is for Augustinian metaphysics, since Augustine had never pretended that his theory of light was a deduction from his metaphysics. Still, anyone since 1700 who has looked back to Descartes as a model has been looking, not for an alternative to modern science, but for something much narrower, a metaphysics or perhaps a theory of knowledge; and while any would-be neo-Cartesians must acknowledge that Descartes' physics went wrong, they are free to locate the error, not in Descartes' metaphysics, but in the deduction from the metaphysics of the foundations of physics, or in the detailed working out of the physics itself.

I think the more serious obstacle separating Cartesian metaphysics from more recent philosophy arises not from the development of physics, but from developments internal to metaphysics itself. The argument of the *Meditations* depends crucially on isolating the clear simple ideas of soul, God, and body. But many of Descartes' readers claim to be unable to discover these ideas within themselves: thus Hobbes denies having the idea of God, and Berkeley denies having the abstract idea of body as extended matter. Other readers, even if they admit that we have such ideas, doubt whether the ideas contain within them any objective warrant (such as Descartes claims to discover especially in the idea of God) sufficient to justify their application to reality. Descartes' usual response to such critics is to tell them to meditate harder, and to question whether they have been meditating in good faith. Descartes may, of course, be right in this; but he does not offer any objective procedure for resolving this kind of metaphysical dispute. This kind of metaphysical irresolvability played a crucial role in discrediting, not only Descartes' metaphysics, but a whole Cartesian *style* of metaphysics, and in generating scepticism about the possibility of metaphysics as such. It is from this crisis, if anywhere, that what Gueroult calls "modern idealism" arose. For one of the many modern responses to this crisis has been Kant's project of a "transcendental deduction of the pure concepts of the understanding." Kant knows that many dogmatic metaphysicians, including Descartes, claim to have metaphysical knowledge (going beyond the kind of knowledge attained through sense experience) through some number of pure concepts of the understanding, which either come to us from the objects through a direct intellectual contact, or are implanted in us by a veracious God, and therefore correspond to objects. But no two metaphysicians agree on the list of pure concepts of the understanding, and the suspicion arises that at least some of the claimed knowledge is spurious, that the allegedly pure concepts are merely products of the imagination, disguising their lack of justification by claiming an extrasensory origin. Now, it is a very Cartesian problem how, beginning from an immersion in the senses and the imagination, we can "withdraw the mind from the senses" to reach a criterion that we can use to pass judgment on the sensory faculties without prejudice in their favor; and Descartes knows that earlier philosophers, despite having said that we must withdraw the mind from the senses in contemplating metaphysical things, have not actually accomplished this, and that their metaphysics is therefore tainted by arbitrary imaginations. But Descartes does not offer anything like Kant's solution. Kant derives a list of pure concepts of the understanding from the different logical forms of our acts of judgment (as universal or particular judgments, affirmative or negative judgments, and so on). Then, since these concepts arise from the mind's own activity of judgment, and are not "stamped" on the mind (whether through the senses or through a direct intellectual intuition) by corresponding objects, Kant explains how we can nonetheless know that these concepts apply to external objects, by arguing that we can represent an object only by combining many sensory intuitions according to some logical form (and not by being passively "stamped" by the object), and that the logical form built into our representation of a given object allows us to judge that the object falls under the corresponding pure concept of the understanding.

I am not advocating Kant's solution. But my point is that Kant offers a hope of an objective procedure for deciding what the pure concepts of the understanding are, and when they can give knowledge of objects; and that his solution depends on analyzing the logical form of our concepts and judgments. Descartes is barred from giving any such solution by his contempt for logic. Notoriously, Descartes recommends learning "logic" or the art of reasoning by studying mathematics, and staying away from the logic of the schools (AT IX2,13–14); he analyzes judgments (following, ultimately, the Stoic analysis) as assents to ideas, but he does not ask what logical form an idea must have if we are to assent to it, and he never tries to explain the origin even of the types of judgment distinguished in Aristotle's *De Interpretatione*, let alone the much richer variety distinguished by scholastic logicians. (To illustrate the problem: although I have an idea of horse, I cannot assent to "horse" in the way that I can assent to "every horse is either male or female"; Descartes suggests, following Stoic precedent, that assenting to an idea is judging that the idea has been produced in me by a cause resembling the idea, but surely not all judgments are of this form.) Rather than analyzing the logical form of our ideas and judgments, Descartes hopes, through the meditative process and especially through the practice of suspending judgment, to bring us to focus on the purely intellectual ideas and to isolate them from all the other ideas they might be confused with; and Descartes expects that, if we carry out this discipline in good faith, we will spontaneously perceive the special features of these ideas that justify our judgments that (to begin with) the soul and God exist. At least some of these special features of our purely intellectual ideas are *logical* features: thus it is a logical (modal) feature of the idea of God that it includes not merely possible but actual existence, and it is a logical feature of the idea of the infinite that it is not a privation of the finite but vice versa. Descartes believes that our ordinary ideas presuppose the existence of ideas having these special logical features; but rather than *arguing* for this conclusion by a systematic analysis of our ideas and judgments, he simply leaves us to discover the special ideas through meditation. Again, in showing that the idea of God is cataleptic, Descartes relies on the rule that the first efficient cause of an idea must contain formally or eminently all the reality that the idea contains objectively; he does not argue for this rule, but assumes that we will simply come to perceive it. Since Descartes thinks this rule is a first principle, he could not directly demonstrate it; but he does think that this rule gives the only possible basis for knowing the existence of external objects, and therefore that the existence of God, as following immediately from this rule, is better known than the existence of anything else outside the mind. But Descartes does not *argue* in any serious way that this rule is presupposed in our ordinary judgments of existence; and this is the kind of argument he needs to make to resolve the disputes about the third-Meditation proof of God's existence.

These, broadly speaking, logical questions, about the logical structure of our ideas and judgments, about which ideas are part of our basic stock and which we construct by logical operations out of them, and about which judgments are basic and which we derive by inferences from them, became central to post-Cartesian metaphysics.[6] This was partly in response to the disputes of Cartesian-style metaphysics, partly in response to radical empiricist challenges (like Hobbes' and later Hume's) to all metaphysical concepts. But although Descartes had, inadvertently, helped to make these questions central to metaphysics (and only in this sense is he the founder of "modern idealism"), he has too little interest in logic, and too much faith in spiritual discipline, to try to resolve them by standards that later metaphysicians would accept. I do not mean to suggest

---

[6] Thus John Stuart Mill, *System of Logic*, Introduction, section 4, actually *identifies* metaphysics, as practiced in his own time, with "that portion of mental philosophy which attempts to determine what part of the furniture of the mind belongs to it originally [i.e. is known by intuition], and what part is constructed out of materials furnished to it from without [i.e. is known by inference]" (in *Collected Works* (Toronto: University of Toronto Press, 1963–91), 7 (1973), p. 8). Mill's description of metaphysics should be set alongside Kant's project of determining the range of our *a priori* concepts and the conditions under which they can be legitimately applied to objects; these two conceptions of the discipline differ, but they bear a family resemblance to each other and to other eighteenth- and nineteenth-century conceptions of the task of metaphysics. I am trying here to indicate some of the central concerns that metaphysicians of different schools might share, whether they construed the issues in more psychological or more purely logical terms; they all contrast with Descartes.

that these questions could not be addressed in a Cartesian spirit, starting from suggestions in Descartes himself. They could be, and to some extent they were, in the subsequent history of philosophy. This later history of Cartesianism is far beyond the scope of the present study. But it seemed only fair to end on a positive note. One moral of the study of Descartes and Augustine is the lasting vitality of the old Platonist and Augustinian metaphysics, which was able not merely to survive and to adapt in vastly different scientific and religious contexts, but to be reawakened by change and to become the source of new intellectual possibilities. I do not believe that this long history is over.

Works cited

[Albinus] Alcinoos, *Enseignement des doctrines de Platon*, ed. John Whittaker, tr. Pierre Louis (Paris: Belles Lettres, 1990)

Alfaric, Prosper, *L'évolution intellectuelle de saint Augustin* (Paris: Nourry, 1918)

Apuleius, *De Philosophia Libri*, in *Opera*, vol. 3, ed. Paul Thomas (Leipzig: Teubner, 1938)

Armogathe, Jean-Robert, *Theologia Cartesiana* (The Hague: Nijhoff, 1977)

Arnauld, Antoine, *Logique, ou l'art de penser*, in *Oeuvres*, vol. 41
Oeuvres, 49 vols. in 45 (Paris, 1775–81)

Augustine, Saint, *On Free Choice of the Will*, tr. Anna H. Benjamin and L. H. Hackstaff (Indianapolis: Bobbs-Merrill, 1964)

Augustinus, *Confessiones*, ed. Martin Skutella, rev. H. Juergens and W. Schaub (Stuttgart: Teubner, 1981)
De Libero Arbitrio, in *Corpus Christianorum, Series Latina*, vol. 29 (Turnholt: Brepols, 1970)

Baillet, Adrien, *La vie de Monsieur Descartes*, 2 vols. (Paris, 1691; repr. New York: Garland, 1987)

Bradwardine, Thomas, *De Causa Dei contra Pelagium et de Virtute Causarum* (London, 1618; repr. Frankfurt am Main: Minerva, 1964)

Brown, Peter, *Augustine of Hippo* (Berkeley and Los Angeles: University of California Press, 1967)

Charron, Pierre, *De la sagesse* (Paris: Fayard, 1986)

Courcelle, Pierre, *Les lettres grecques en Occident* (Paris: De Boccard, 1943)
Recherches sur les Confessions de saint Augustin (Paris: De Boccard, 1950)

Denzinger, Henricus, *Enchiridion Symbolorum, Definitionum et Declarationum de Rebus Fidei et Morum* (Freiburg: Herder, 1937)

Descartes, René, *Discours de la méthode: texte et commentaire par Etienne Gilson* (Paris: Vrin, 1925)
Discourse on Method and Meditations on First Philosophy, tr. Donald Cress (Indianapolis: Hackett, 1980; 3rd ed., 1993)
Oeuvres de Descartes, ed. Charles Adam and Paul Tannery, nouvelle présentation, 11 vols. in 13 (Paris: Vrin, 1974–83)
The Philosophical Writings of Descartes, tr. John Cottingham, Robert Stoothoff, Dugald Murdoch, and Anthony Kenny, 3 vols. (Cambridge: Cambridge University Press, 1984–91)
Principles of Philosophy, tr. Valentine Rodger Miller and Reese P. Miller (Dordrecht: Reidel, 1983)

Dillon, John, *The Middle Platonists* (London: Duckworth 1977)

Duhem, Pierre, *Medieval Cosmology*, tr. Roger Ariew (Chicago: University of Chicago Press, 1985)

Ficino, Marsilio, *Theologia Platonica de Immortalitate Animorum* (Paris, 1559; repr. Hildesheim: Olms, 1975)

Frege, Gottlob, *Philosophical and Mathematical Correspondence* (Chicago: University of Chicago Press, 1980)

Garber, Daniel, *Descartes' Metaphysical Physics* (Chicago: University of Chicago Press, 1992)

Garceau, Benoît, *Judicium: vocabulaire, sources, doctrine de saint Thomas d'Aquin* (Paris: Vrin, 1968)

Gassendi, Pierre, *Dissertations en forme de paradoxes contre les aristotéliciens*, ed. Bernard Rochot (Paris: Vrin, 1959)

Gilson, Etienne, *Etudes sur le rôle de la pensée médiévale dans la formation du système cartésien* (Paris: Vrin, 1930)

"The Future of Augustinian Metaphysics," in *A Gilson Reader: Selected Writings of Etienne Gilson* (New York: Image Books, 1957), pp. 82–104

La liberté chez Descartes et la théologie (Paris: Alcan, 1913)

Glucker, John, *Antiochus and the Late Academy* (Göttingen: Vandenhoeck und Ruprecht, 1978)

Gouhier, Henri, *Cartésianisme et augustinisme au XVIIe siècle* (Paris: Vrin, 1978)

La pensée métaphysique de Descartes (Paris: Vrin, 1962)

La pensée religieuse de Descartes, 2nd ed. (Paris: Vrin, 1972)

Gueroult, Martial, *Descartes' Philosophy Interpreted According to the Order of Reasons*, tr. Roger Ariew, 2 vols. (Minneapolis: University of Minnesota Press, 1984)

Hadot, Pierre, "Etre, vie et pensée chez Plotin et avant Plotin," in *Les sources de Plotin* (Vandoeuvres-Geneva: Fondation Hardt, 1960), pp. 107–141

Henry, Paul, *Plotin et l'Occident* (Louvain: Spicilegium Sacrum Lovaniense, 1934)

Hobbes, Thomas, *Leviathan*, ed. C. B. Macpherson (London: Penguin, 1968)

Husserl, Edmund, *Cartesian Meditations*, tr. Dorion Cairns (The Hague: Nijhoff, 1960)

Jansenius, Cornelius, *Augustinus*, 3 vols. in 1 (Louvain, 1640; repr. Frankfurt am Main: Minerva, 1964)

John of St. Thomas, *Cursus Philosophicus Thomisticus* (Turin: Marietti, 1930)

Kirk, G. S., J. E. Raven, and M. Schofield, *The Presocratic Philosophers* (Cambridge: Cambridge University Press, 1983)

Klibansky, Raymond, Erwin Panofsky, and Fritz Saxl, *Saturn and Melancholy* (London: Nelson, 1964)

Leibniz, Gottfried Wilhelm von, *Philosophische Schriften*, ed. C. J. Gerhardt (Berlin: Weidmann, 1885)

Malebranche, Nicolas, *De la recherche de la vérité*, in *Oeuvres*, ed. Geneviève Rodis-Lewis (Paris: Gallimard, 1979), vol. 1

Marion, Jean-Luc, *Sur la théologie blanche de Descartes* (Paris: Presses Universitaires de France, 1981)

Menn, Stephen, "Aristotle and Plato on God as Nous and as the Good," *Review of Metaphysics*, 45 (1992), pp. 543–573

"Descartes and Some Predecessors on the Divine Conservation of Motion," *Synthese*, 83 (May 1990), pp. 215–238

"Descartes, Augustine, and the Status of Faith," in *Studies in Seventeenth-Century European Philosophy*, ed. M. A. Stewart (Oxford: Oxford University Press, forthcoming)

"The Greatest Stumbling Block: Descartes' Denial of Real Qualities," in *Des-*

cartes and His Contemporaries: Meditations, Objections and Replies, ed. Roger Ariew and Marjorie Grene (Chicago: University of Chicago Press, 1995), pp. 182–207

"The Intellectual Setting of Seventeenth Century Philosophy," in *The Cambridge History of Seventeenth Century Philosophy* (Cambridge: Cambridge University Press, forthcoming)

"Physics as a Virtue," *Proceedings of the Boston Area Colloquium in Ancient Philosophy*, vol. 11, pp. 1–34

Plato on God as Nous (Carbondale: Southern Illinois University Press for the *Journal of the History of Philosophy* Monograph Series, 1995)

"Plotinus on Identity of Knowledge with Its Object," manuscript

"The Problem of the Third Meditation," *American Catholic Philosophical Quarterly*, 67 (Autumn 1993), pp. 537–559

"The Stoic Theory of Categories," manuscript

Mill, John Stuart, *A System of Logic*, in *Collected Works* (Toronto: University of Toronto Press, 1963–91), vol. 7 (1973)

Molina, Luis de, *On Divine Foreknowledge: Part IV of the Concordia*, tr. with introduction and notes by Alfred J. Freddoso (Ithaca, NY: Cornell University Press, 1988)

Montaigne, Michel de, *Complete Essays of Montaigne*, tr. Donald Frame (Stanford, CA: Stanford University Press, 1958)

O'Connell, Robert J., *The Origin of the Soul in St. Augustine's Later Works* (New York: Fordham University Press, 1987)

St. Augustine's Confessions: The Odyssey of Soul (Cambridge: Belknap Press of Harvard University Press, 1969)

St. Augustine's Early Theory of Man (Cambridge: Belknap Press of Harvard University Press, 1968)

O'Donnell, James J., ed. and comm., Augustine, *Confessions*, 3 vols. (Oxford: Oxford University Press, 1992)

Patrizi, Francesco, *Nova de Universis Philosophia* (Ferrara, 1591); repr. with Croatian translation as *Nova sveopća filozofija* (Zagreb: Liber, 1979)

Plotinus, *Enneads*, ed. and tr. A. H. Armstrong, 7 vols. (Cambridge, MA, and London: Loeb Classical Library, 1967–88)

Schuster, John, "Descartes' *Mathesis Universalis* 1619–1628," in Stephen Gaukroger, ed., *Descartes: Philosophy, Mathematics and Physics* (Brighton: Harvester, 1980), pp. 41–96

Simplicius, *In De Caelo Commentaria*, ed. I. L. Heiberg, in *Commentaria in Aristotelem Graeca* (Berlin: Reimer, 1882–1909), vol. 7 (1894)

Suárez, Francisco, *Disputationes Metaphysicae*, in *Opera Omnia* (Paris: Vives, 1856–78), vols. 25–6 (these vols. 1866; both repr. Hildesheim: Olms, 1965)

Theiler, Willy, *Porphyrios und Augustin* (Halle: Niemeyer, 1933)

van Steenberghen, Fernand, *Thomas Aquinas and Radical Aristotelianism* (Washington: Catholic University of America Press, 1980)

von Arnim, Hans, *Stoicorum Veterum Fragmenta* (Leipzig: Teubner, 1903–5)

Weber, Jean-Paul, *La constitution du texte des Regulae* (Paris: SEDES, 1964)

Wilson, Margaret, *Descartes* (London: Routledge and Kegan Paul, 1978)

Wolfson, Harry Austryn, *Religious Philosophy: A Group of Essays* (Cambridge: Harvard University Press, 1961)

Index